D1568563

University Textbook Series

November, 1992

Especially Designed for Collateral Reading

HARRY W. JONES
Directing Editor
Professor of Law, Columbia University

ADMINISTRATIVE LAW AND PROCESS, Second Edition (1992)
Richard J. Pierce, Jr., Professor of Law, Columbia University.
Sidney A. Shapiro, Professor of Law, University of Kansas.
Paul R. Verkuil, President and Professor of Law, College of William and Mary.

ADMIRALTY, Second Edition (1975)
Grant Gilmore, Professor of Law, Yale University.
Charles L. Black, Jr., Professor of Law, Yale University.

AGENCY (1975)
W. Edward Sell, Dean of the School of Law, University of Pittsburgh.

ANTITRUST LAW, PRINCIPLES OF (1993)
Stephen F. Ross, Professor of Law, University of Illinois.

BANKRUPTCY, THE ELEMENTS OF (1992)
Douglas G. Baird, Professor of Law, University of Chicago.

BUSINESS ORGANIZATION AND FINANCE, Fourth Edition (1990)
William A. Klein, Professor of Law, University of California, Los Angeles.
John C. Coffee, Jr., Professor of Law, Columbia University.

CIVIL PROCEDURE, BASIC, Second Edition (1979)
Milton D. Green, Professor of Law Emeritus, University of California, Hastings
College of the Law.

COMMERCIAL TRANSACTIONS, INTRODUCTION TO (1977)
Hon. Robert Braucher, Associate Justice, Supreme Judicial Court of Massachusetts.
Robert A. Riegert, Professor of Law, Cumberland School of Law.

**CONFLICT OF LAWS, COMMENTARY ON THE, Third Edition (1986) with 1991
Supplement**
Russell J. Weintraub, Professor of Law, University of Texas.

CONSTITUTIONAL LAW, AMERICAN, Second Edition (A TREATISE ON) (1988)
Laurence H. Tribe, Professor of Law, Harvard University.

CONTRACT LAW, THE CAPABILITY PROBLEM IN (1978)
Richard Danzig.

CONTRACTS, CONCEPTS AND CASE ANALYSIS IN THE LAW OF (1990)
Marvin A. Chirelstein, Professor of Law, Columbia University.

CORPORATE TAXATION, FEDERAL, Second Edition (1990)
Howard E. Abrams, Professor of Law, Emory University.
Richard L. Doernberg, Professor of Law, Emory University.

CORPORATIONS, Second Edition (1971)
Norman D. Lattin, Professor of Law, University of California, Hastings College of
the Law.

CORPORATIONS IN PERSPECTIVE (1976)
Alfred F. Conard, Professor of Law, University of Michigan.

[i]

CRIMINAL LAW, Third Edition (1982)
Rollin M. Perkins, Professor of Law, University of California, Hastings College of the Law.
Ronald N. Boyce, Professor of Law, University of Utah College of Law.

CRIMINAL PROCEDURE, Third Edition (1993)
Charles H. Whitebread, II, Professor of Law, University of Southern California.
Christopher Slobogin, Professor of Law, University of Florida.

ESTATES IN LAND & FUTURE INTERESTS, PREFACE TO, Second Edition (1984)
Thomas F. Bergin, Professor of Law, University of Virginia.
Paul G. Haskell, Professor of Law, University of North Carolina.

EVIDENCE: COMMON SENSE AND COMMON LAW (1947)
John M. Maguire, Professor of Law, Harvard University.

JURISPRUDENCE: MEN AND IDEAS OF THE LAW (1953)
The late Edwin W. Patterson, Cardozo Professor of Jurisprudence, Columbia University.

LABOR RELATIONS The Basic Processes, Law and Practice (1988)
Julius G. Getman, Professor of Law, University of Texas.
Bertrand E. Pogrebin, Member, New York State Bar.

LEGAL CAPITAL, Third Edition (1990)
Bayless Manning.

LEGAL RESEARCH ILLUSTRATED, Fifth Edition with 1990 Assignments Supplement
J. Myron Jacobstein, Professor of Law, Emeritus, Stanford University.
Roy M. Mersky, Professor of Law, Director of Research, University of Texas.

LEGAL RESEARCH, FUNDAMENTALS OF, Fifth Edition with 1990 Assignments Supplement
J. Myron Jacobstein, Professor of Law, Emeritus, Stanford University.
Roy M. Mersky, Professor of Law, Director of Research, University of Texas.

PROCEDURE, THE STRUCTURE OF (1979)
Robert M. Cover, Professor of Law, Yale University.
Owen M. Fiss, Professor of Law, Yale University.

PROPERTY, PRINCIPLES OF THE LAW OF, Third Edition (1989)
John E. Cribbet, Dean, Chancellor, Professor of Law Emeritus, University of Illinois.
Corwin W. Johnson, Professor of Law Emeritus, University of Texas.

TAX, FEDERAL INCOME, Second Edition (1992)
Douglas A. Kahn, Professor of Law, University of Michigan.

TAXATION OF S CORPORATIONS, FEDERAL INCOME (1992)
John K. McNulty, Professor of Law, University of California, Berkeley

TAXATION, FEDERAL INCOME, Sixth Edition (1991)
Marvin A. Chirelstein, Professor of Law, Columbia University.

TAXATION, PARTNERSHIP INCOME (1991)
Alan Gunn, Professor of Law, University of Notre Dame.

TORTS, Second Edition (1980)
Clarence Morris, Professor of Law, University of Pennsylvania.
C. Robert Morris, Professor of Law, University of Minnesota.

WILLS AND TRUSTS, THE PLANNING AND DRAFTING OF, Third Edition (1991)
Thomas L. Shaffer, Professor of Law, University of Notre Dame.
Carol Ann Mooney, Associate Professor of Law, University of Notre Dame.

WILLS, TRUSTS AND ADMINISTRATION, PREFACE TO (1987)
Paul G. Haskell, Professor of Law, University of North Carolina.

PRINCIPLES

OF

ANTITRUST LAW

By

STEPHEN F. ROSS
Professor of Law, University of Illinois

Westbury, New York
THE FOUNDATION PRESS, INC.
1993

COPYRIGHT © 1993 By THE FOUNDATION PRESS, INC.

615 Merrick Ave.

Westbury, N.Y. 11590

Library of Congress Cataloging-in-Publication Data

Ross, Stephen F., 1955–
    Principles of antitrust law / by Stephen F. Ross.
       p.   cm. — (University textbook series)
    Includes index.
    ISBN 1–56662–003–1
    1. Antitrust law—United States—Cases. I. Title. II. Series.
KF1648.R67 1993
343.73'0721—dc20
[347.303721]

92–40855

Ross Antitrust Law UTS

In Honor and Loving Memory
Albert E. Ross
1920–1991

*

PREFACE

Why You Should Read This Book, and
Who Deserves the Real Credit

This treatise is intended for both academic and professional audiences. First and foremost, it is for *students*. The treatise discusses every principal case in seven of the leading antitrust casebooks in the country.[1] Thus, in addition to black letter law and analysis of current doctrine and trends in the law, the student can review precise holdings and fact summaries about each case likely to be discussed in class. In analyzing these cases, I have also tried to make some appropriate comments that will hopefully contribute to the legal literature, so the book is for *antitrust scholars* as well. In particular, I believe this is the first comprehensive work that tries to systematically incorporate the "neo-populist" view—that antitrust should primarily focus on preventing consumers from having their wealth taken by misconduct of sellers.

Many attorneys who did not take an antitrust course in law school find the area bewildering, and the multi-volume treatises that discuss almost every scenario or contain an encyclopedic recitation of the case law can be somewhat intimidating. Thus, the treatise is intended to provide *general practitioners or associates* with a good introduction to the area, as a launching pad into a more detailed inquiry that other texts provide. Finally, notwithstanding the efforts of recent federal antitrust enforcement officials, there remains a large number of law firm *partners and career government attorneys who specialize in antitrust* who are always looking for a new angle or insight into how they approach the law; hopefully, the analysis herein will prove helpful to them as well.

A quick glance at any chapter reveals that I have not been reticent to offer my own commentary on cases and trends in the law, and I alone am responsible for these conclusions. Professors and attorneys with whom I have discussed many of these ideas are too numerous to name, and a number of colleagues and distinguished practitioners read sections of a draft manuscript and offered particularly trenchant comments. Special thanks are due to Herb Hovenkamp of the University of Iowa (Chapter 1); Harvey Goldschmid of Columbia University (Chap-

1. William Anderson & C. Paul Rogers, Antitrust Law: Policy and Practice (1985); Philip Areeda & Louis Kaplow, Antitrust Analysis (4th ed. 1988); Milton Handler, Harlan Blake, Robert Pitofsky & Harvey Goldschmid, Trade Regulation (3d ed. 1990); Eleanor Fox & Lawrence Sullivan, Antitrust (1989); Richard Posner & Frank Easterbrook, Antitrust (2d ed. 1981); Louis Schwartz, John Flynn & Harry First, Antitrust (6th ed. 1983); E. Thomas Sullivan & Herbert Hovenkamp, Antitrust Law, Policy and Procedure (2d ed. 1989).

ter 2); Tom Kauper of the University of Michigan (Chapter 6); and Peter Maggs of the University of Illinois and Irving Scher of the New York offices of Weil, Gotschal & Manges (Chapter 7).[2]

Although the University of Illinois has a rich tradition in treatise authorship, my senior colleagues did not fully warn me of the difficulties in bringing a task like this to fruition. I received outstanding research assistance from J. Pieter van Es, who left me in the top of the ninth inning to study for the bar, and Julie Hill, who provided top-notch relief work. An author could not be more fortunate than to have a secretary like Pat Estergard for thorough and conscientious work.[3]

Speaking of fortune, I would be surprised if more than a handful of legal academics are lucky enough to have a spouse whose editing skills were recognized and honed as an editor-in-chief of a leading law review,[4] and perhaps fewer with one with sufficient love and patience to apply her still-sharpened editor's pencil to an entire treatise manuscript. My debt to Kit Kinports for these matters professional, as well as those personal, far exceeds the nation's deficit.

Champaign, Illinois
July, 1992

---

2. In addition, I would be remiss in not acknowledging the past and continuing contribution made by several people to my general understanding of antitrust law, starting with my professors at the University of California's Boalt Hall School of Law, Larry Sullivan and Tom Jorde; Barry Grossman and the talented cadre of dedicated public servants in the appellate section of the Department of Justice's Antitrust Division; continuing with my colleague on the Senate Judiciary Committee staff, Eddie Correia (now of Northeastern University); and John Lopatka (formerly of the University of Illinois and now of the University of South Carolina) and my present economics colleagues at the University of Illinois, Larry DeBrock, Shane Greenstein, and Tom Ulen.

3. Accord, Mack Player, Elaine Shoben & Risa Lieberwitz, Employment Discrimination xxv (1990); Elaine Shoben & Wm. Murray Tabb, Remedies xxiii (1989). I am also grateful, for some key pinch-hitting, to Bonnie Anderson, Carol Haley, and Linda Payne.

4. See 128 U.Pa.L.Rev. viii (1979).

SUMMARY OF CONTENTS

SUMMARY OF CONTENTS

TABLE OF CONTENTS

TABLE OF CONTENTS

*

PRINCIPLES

OF

ANTITRUST LAW

*

CHAPTER 1: THE GOALS
OF ANTITRUST

Many attorneys and law students who have an opinion about antitrust believe that it is, or at least has become, merely another application of law and economics. Those who find it attractive do so in part because they find applied economic analysis stimulating; those who loath the subject usually despair of grasping the graphs and curves they envision as necessary to understand antitrust concepts. To be sure, a basic understanding of rudimentary economics is necessary to understand the controversies surrounding the future direction of antitrust doctrine. But scholars, judges and public officials do not differ about the proper direction of antitrust policy in this country because some are right and some are wrong about economic theory, or even (for the most part) because they subscribe to competing economic theories. Their differences are primarily political, rather than economic. This makes sense: fundamentally, *antitrust is not about economics, but about power*. Antitrust policy is concerned with the extent to which private individuals should be able to acquire and maintain economic power, and the extent to which society, through the courts, should do anything about it.

(1) Political economy.

Judicial opinions in antitrust cases sound recurring themes about the proper goals of antitrust and about the application of those goals in constructing sound antitrust doctrine. These themes, which will be discussed below, emanate from different sources; though complimentary at times, they are often contradictory. Ultimately, however, one's personal conclusion concerning the ideal antitrust doctrine will not be based on one's abstract view of the goals of antitrust; rather, it will depend on one's assumptions about markets and government—in short, what 19th century philosophers used to call "political economy."

One major assumption that leads to disputes about antitrust doctrine concerns the nature of the role antitrust laws should play in society. Antitrust traditionalists argue that the economy should be controlled, whenever possible, by the free market, and that by preventing private parties from restraining the market, the antitrust laws enhance the marketplace and keep it free from administrative regulation. In contrast, advocates of the so-called "Chicago school," who favor a limited role for antitrust law,

1

believe that the antitrust laws are themselves intrusions into the free marketplace and constitute government regulation.

A second value heavily implicated in antitrust doctrine concerns the proper role of the courts in our society. The Chicago school favors an antitrust policy strictly limited to a single goal of economic efficiency—in part because any attempt to accommodate multiple goals will require courts to balance one goal against another. The balancing process, they believe, is fundamentally inconsistent with the proper role of a non-elected judiciary in a democracy. As one of their leading spokespersons, Judge Robert Bork, has written, the history of antitrust "should constitute a warning about the weakness of the adjudicative process and the danger of relying on courts to evolve major social policy."[1] In contrast, others believe that courts can and do balance competing interests in every field of law and properly should do so in antitrust. Congress, these more traditional observers note, is always free to correct an imbalance if it so desires.

The true economic effect of many business practices is impossible to determine. The best experts can only assert probabilities or tendencies, not certainties. Whether courts should prohibit conduct as violative of the antitrust laws thus necessarily turns on a third value judgment, about the degree of certainty that should be required before an individual is prohibited from freely pursuing private goals. Daniel Oliver, who chaired the Federal Trade Commission under President Reagan, argued that the government has the same heavy burden of establishing a clear public interest before it interferes with economic rights as it must bear before it interferes with political rights.[2] This certainly does not reflect current law. For example, every court in the land would invalidate a law that purported to prohibit "public expression where the effect may be to harm national security." In contrast, § 7 of the Clayton Act prohibits mergers where "the effect *may be* to *substantially lessen competition*."[3] The disparate treatment of political and economic rights stems from the widely held beliefs that government should be able to regulate business affairs more closely, and that the right to maximize profits does not deserve the kind of judicial protection reserved for those rights expressed or implied in the Bill of Rights.

Finally, views about the soundness of particular antitrust doctrines will turn on individual opinions—since the truth cannot be empirically verified—about two factual issues. First, how well

1. The Antitrust Paradox 16 (1978).

2. "FTC Chairman Says Agency Must Establish Public Interest Before Limiting Freedoms," 51 BNA Antitrust & Trade Reg. Rep. 428 (1986).

3. 15 U.S.C. § 18.

do markets correct abuses by themselves? And second, how well can courts understand markets and correctly prohibit undesirable conduct while permitting legitimate business behavior? Those with greater faith in the market and less faith in the judiciary will favor a far more restrictive antitrust doctrine than those with the opposite view.[4]

(2) Alternative goals for antitrust.

These political values and assumptions underlie judicial opinions that reflect still different fissures. In the 100 years since passage of the Sherman Act, four clear alternative themes have emerged about the goals of the antitrust laws. These themes appear, disappear, and reappear across time and the various areas of antitrust policy.

(2a) Allocative efficiency.

The now ascendant view is that antitrust laws should promote allocative economic efficiency. With only a few limitations, business conduct that ultimately results in an efficient allocation of society's resources should be permitted and encouraged under this view, and antitrust law should only proscribe conduct that ultimately harms allocative efficiency. In other words, the goal of antitrust is to promote a market system that maximizes societal wealth by deploying our resources where they are most highly valued.[5]

There is broad agreement that society is harmed when a single firm acquires monopoly power by inefficient means, or when rivals conspire to raise price or reduce output. Basic economics teaches that increasing the price of a product means that fewer consumers will purchase the product. Thus, when firms with economic power raise prices to obtain monopoly profits, an inefficient quantity of the product is produced for society. Monopoly pricing thus defeats the ultimate economic goal of those seeking to promote allocative efficiency—maximizing the amount of desired goods produced by society within our limited available resources. Economists and their fellow travelers often refer to this goal as "maximizing consumer welfare."

It is important to note that maximizing "consumer welfare" does not always maximize the welfare of the majority of consumers. When we seek to maximize societal wealth, we do so in terms of dollars and markets, not people. Suppose, for example, that

---

4. For an excellent discussion of this theme, see William Page, Ideological Conflict and the Origins of Antitrust Policy, 66 Tulane L. Rev. 1 (1991).

5. See, e.g., Bork, supra note 1; Richard Posner, Antitrust Law: An Economic Perspective (1976).

Sony has an electronics plant, and at the same cost can produce each month either 100 huge multi-purpose "entertainment centers" or 400 Trinitron television sets. If the wealthy are willing to pay $3000 for each entertainment center ($300,000 revenue), and the rest of us are willing to pay no more than $500 for the television set ($200,000 revenue), economists will say that societal wealth is maximized by having Sony build the centers, even though the majority of us would rather have the television sets. Thus, the term "consumer welfare" can be misleading.

It should also be noted that "allocative efficiency" does not always mean "competition." Congress has determined, for example, that awarding inventors an exclusive monopoly on their inventions for 17 years will encourage inventions. In such cases, competition may be eliminated in the short run, but the long-term result is a more efficient allocation of resources to innovative products and processes.

Finally, the Chicago school's use of microeconomic theory to explain allocative efficiency has focused primarily on short-term efficiencies. Thus, it strongly encourages business conduct that is likely to immediately lower the cost of production. For example, Professors Ronald Coase and Oliver Williamson suggested that businesses contract with others or integrate economic activity within one firm, depending on which practice is the most efficient way of producing, distributing, and marketing goods and services. To illustrate, some steel companies might enter long-term contracts for coal supplies; others will find that the transaction costs and uncertainties involved in relying on strangers are sufficiently high that it would be better to own their own coal mines. Thus, the implications of the "theory of the firm" is that antitrust law should not be skeptical of mergers, joint ventures, or contract agreements among firms, and should be wary of interfering with these ways of efficiently doing business.[6]

Recent economics scholarship, pushed prominently by Professor Michael Porter, has instead argued that competition policy should advance consumer welfare by focusing on long-term, dynamic efficiencies.[7] That is, society is better off with firms that are constantly bringing new and improved goods to market. Under this approach, industries should be organized to maximize the likelihood of continuing technological innovation, even at the cost of higher production expenses in the short run. Porter would have been less concerned in the early 1980s with the price of

6. See generally Ronald Coase, The Nature of the Firm (reprinted in Readings in Price Theory 386–405 (George Stigler and Ken Boulding, eds. 1952)); Oliver Williamson, Markets and Hierarchies: Analysis and Antitrust Implications (1975).

7. Competitive Advantage of Nations (1990).

phonographs, and more interested in ensuring a competitive environment that would lead to development of compact disc players. There is a strong antitrust tradition focusing on innovation as an antitrust goal. In a landmark opinion, Judge Learned Hand wrote that

> "[m]any people believe that possession of unchallenged economic power deadens initiative, discourages thrift and depresses energy; that immunity from competition is a narcotic, and rivalry is a stimulant, to industrial progress; that the spur of constant stress is necessary to counteract an inevitable disposition to let well enough alone." [8]

The principal effect that a dynamic approach to efficiency has on antitrust doctrine is to be more skeptical of mergers, joint ventures, or other conduct justified to permit immediate cost savings, where the deal simultaneously reduces the number of independent firms in a market that might participate in the "race to innovation."

(2b) Wealth transfers.

More recent scholarship has developed a rival theory: that antitrust is primarily intended to protect consumers from exploitation by monopolists and carteleers. Senator Sherman, for example, argued that his bill would block tactics that tended to "artificially advance the cost to the consumer." [9] In technical terms, this view argues that antitrust policy should seek to maximize not overall societal wealth, but rather should prevent consumers from exploitation by monopolists or conspirators whose higher prices take money from consumers' wallets.[10]

To illustrate, suppose that Sony exercises monopoly power by increasing the price of Trinitrons by 20%, and as a result only 80% of those who would have bought the television at the prior price are still interested in making the purchase. Before Sony's price hike, buyers enjoyed what economists call "consumer surplus," which is the difference between the maximum price consumers would pay and the lower actual price paid. Although those interested solely in allocative efficiency would be concerned about the fact that fewer sets are being produced, those interested in wealth transfers would be concerned about the 80% of Sony brand loyalists who were paying more for the television than necessary to cover the costs of production (including a normal

---

8. United States v. Aluminum Co. of America, 148 F.2d 416, 427 (2d Cir. 1945).

9. 19 Cong. Rec. 6041 (1888).

10. See, e.g., Robert Lande, Wealth Transfers as the Original and Primary Concern of Antitrust: The Efficiency Interpretation Challenged, 34 Hastings L.J. 65 (1982).

profit). Because the number of Americans who buy televisions is greater than the number who own stock in Sony, this view of antitrust law has a distinct majoritarian, or "populist" flavor.

(2c) "Jeffersonian" protection of small, independent businesses.

A decidedly non-economic theme recurring in many judicial opinions holds that the antitrust laws should protect and preserve the independence of smaller, locally controlled businesses. This theme echoes a policy articulated by Thomas Jefferson in debates with Alexander Hamilton when the country was founded. Jefferson believed in the importance of preserving a nation of independent farmers and entrepreneurs, rather than employees. He thought that independent entrepreneurs would make better citizens, who would be more committed to a democracy; their continued existence was therefore desirable, even if Hamilton's plans to industrialize the economy would do more to increase overall societal wealth. Similarly, Justices Louis Brandeis and William O. Douglas condemned the industrial giants of the turn of the century for transforming entrepreneurs into corporate employees whose lack of participation in management would weaken their ability to participate as citizens of the republic.[11] Along the same lines, those who enacted the antitrust laws strove to preserve an equality of economic opportunity for all. This was a lively concern in 1890, for those old enough to be in power had seen a half century where the average citizen's ability to function as an entrepreneur had diminished markedly. Although large, vertically integrated, capital-intensive corporations that focused on long-term profits may have been the natural outgrowth of economic changes following the Civil War, many viewed them as illegitimate, unnatural, and sinister.[12]

Jefferson, Sherman, and Brandeis obviously did not seriously consider the modern insights of economics. The theory of econo-

---

11. Standard Oil of California v. United States, 337 U.S. 293, 318–19 (1949) (Douglas, J., dissenting) (quoting Brandeis, Other People's Money 110 (1933)). See also Justice Rufus Peckham's opinion in United States v. Trans–Missouri Freight Ass'n, 166 U.S. 290, 324 (1897):

... it is not for the real prosperity of any country that such changes should occur which result in transferring an independent business man, the head of his establishment, small though it might be, into a mere servant or agent of a corporation for selling the commodities which he once manufactured or dealt in, having no voice in shaping the business policy for the company and bound to obey orders issued by others.

12. Note that this goal seeks to preserve small businesses as an end in itself, because these firms benefit society. It is not necessarily consistent with the interests of the owners of small firms, who may profit from a merger policy that permits them to sell their assets at a premium to large industrial concerns.

mies of scale, for example, teaches that many products can be produced most efficiently at large plants.[13] To the extent that Sherman recognized that powerful monopoly trusts might have lower costs, he nevertheless preferred a competitive market of small firms with slightly higher costs because he was convinced that the trusts would never pass the lower costs or to consumers. As the Supreme Court recognized in the *Brown Shoe* case, however, a policy that insists on locally owned manufacturing firms might result in higher costs to consumers.[14] In this sense, the goal of protecting entrepreneurs conflicts with both the economic goals of antitrust discussed above. It also raises some difficult questions of statutory interpretation, for the 51st Congress' knowledge of economics probably led it to believe that prohibitions on restraints of trade and monopolization would help both consumers *and* small businesses. How the members of Congress would have reacted had they become enlightened about modern microeconomic theory is anyone's guess. Nevertheless, the Jeffersonian ideal retains some of its political vitality even today: witness the continuing political support for family farms and the opposition to a banking system such as England's, which is dominated by a few large nationwide concerns.

The Jeffersonian concern for preservation of small firms is also based on a fear that the accumulation of economic size and power necessarily results in political power. Historically, there is much truth to this fear. When the powerful Bank of the United States was abolished by Jacksonian Democrats, the Bank's president was able to send the country into a deep recession. Moreover, much of the clamor for the Sherman Act was due to the states' inability to regulate powerful banking and railroad interests that pulled the strings in the statehouses. Today, however, we should question whether this is a continuing source of concern. The growth of lobbying and political action committees suggests that alliances of small, locally owned firms may wield far greater political power than major industrial concerns. For instance, would a weak-kneed member of Congress from outside the Detroit area be more likely to kow-tow to some General Motors executive or to a delegation sent by the GM Dealers' Association from the member's own district?

13. By contrast, Brandeis strongly believed in the superior economic efficiency of smaller firms. See Note, Mr. Justice Brandeis, Competition and Smallness: A Dilemma Re-examined, 66 Yale L.J. 69, 74–75 (1956). Such a belief is really necessary for a true Jeffersonian; if "natural" economic growth leads to larger firms and corporations, then the only way to preserve small firms is by direct government intervention. But government action would subvert the Jeffersonian ideal of entrepreneurs independent of either monopolists or the government.

14. Brown Shoe Co. v. United States, 370 U.S. 294, 344 (1962).

(2d) "Madisonian" dispersion of economic power.

Another non-economic goal of antitrust policy is to disperse economic power. James Madison felt that political liberty could be preserved by separating power among the three branches of the federal government and between the federal government and the states. Under his scheme, no one could become so politically powerful as to wield abusive discretionary power against the citizenry. Similarly, a small farmer has no choice but to follow the market in making basic economic decisions; heads of powerful industrial conglomerates, on the other hand, have the power to exercise discretion in ways that can cause others economic injury. The goal of dispersing economic power responds to the populace's natural inclination to view economic hardship (such as the inability to acquire a scarce good) with greater tolerance when it results from the impersonal hand of the marketplace than from the discretionary choice of some powerful individual.

(2e) Analysis and synthesis.

Many business practices offend each of these antitrust goals. Consider, for example, a price-fixing cartel. The higher price charged by cartel members misallocates goods and transfers money from consumers to the cartel. Cartel members will be anxious to take steps to bar others from entering the market, thus offending the goal of equal opportunity; and a cartel is definitely not the type of "independent" firm Jefferson had in mind. Finally, discretionary power exercised by a cartel is inconsistent with the Madisonian goal of dispersed power.

Other practices, however, bring these goals into conflict. Although those generally satisfied with the development of antitrust law in the post-World War II period endorsed the multiple objectives of competition policy, those who advocate allocative efficiency as the sole goal of antitrust have focused their attack principally on what I have called the Jeffersonian model.[15] Efficient

---

15. Neither Robert Bork nor Richard Posner respond to the wealth transfer argument at length. Posner wrote in the mid-1970's that protection of small businesses is "the only competing goal suggested with any frequency or conviction." Antitrust Law: An Economic Perspective 4 (1976). Bork listed five possible alternative definitions of "competition," none of which discuss the protection of consumers from wealth transfers. The Antitrust Paradox 58–61 (1978). See also I Philip Areeda & Donald Turner, Antitrust Law 8 (1978) (listing three alternative policies, none of which discuss preserving wealth for consumers).

Posner argued that the wealth-transfer argument is "appealing" but "undermined" because monopoly profits may not be pocketed by rich stockholders but may be dissipated through inefficient spending to gain monopoly power (examples that come to mind—mine, not Posner's—include advertising, bribes or campaign contributions for government favors, or paying a premium to buy out one's competitor). Posner, supra, at 18. But see F.M. Scherer, Book Review, 86 Yale L.J. 974, 967–81

practices by one or more leading firms might drive out small businesses; survival of small firms in a dynamic economy might be enhanced by anti-consumer agreements. Chicago school advocates have demonstrated, with great force, that in these situations a law intended to foster competition must choose efficient practices and oppose restraints of trade; Congress should use tax preferences, subsidies, or other more direct means to aid smaller firms.

In the last decade, new scholarship has emerged to assert consumer well-being, as opposed to overall economic efficiency (or "consumer welfare," as economists misleadingly call it), as the prime goal for antitrust. Professor Robert Lande's landmark article [16] documented the legislative history of the Sherman Act that demonstrates Congress' overriding concern with protecting consumers from wealth transfers. Speeches about outlawing arrangements that raise prices to consumers were cited by both Bork and Lande. Bork appears correct in suggesting that a consumer protection intent is often inconsistent with the Jeffersonian goal of protecting of small business. But Lande is more correct in arguing that the focus on consumers was intended as an end in itself, not merely a means of maximizing societal economic wealth through allocative efficiency. The legislative debates recognized that some of the undesirable trust arrangements Congress clearly sought to outlaw might be cost-saving and thus efficient, but remained undesirable because their benefits would not be passed on to the consumer.[17] This history suggests that today's efficiency

(1977) (challenging empirical validity of this assumption because "observation of real-world industries reveals that monopoly profits exist in abundance"). Regardless of where the monopoly profit ends up, however, consumers are still being exploited, and wealth is being transferred from their pockets to someone else.

Bork seems to use phrases such as "protection of consumers," "consumer welfare," and "economic efficiency" interchangeably. For example, he criticizes the antitrust goal of supporting "fragmented" industries as incoherent. This goal, Bork writes, "has no assignable meaning unless we read it as a description of that number of units which in the particular industry best serves *consumers.*" But, he continues, "that is to convert it to a consumer welfare test." Bork, supra, at 60 (emphasis added). This is incorrect. As this chapter demonstrates, allocative efficiency (or "consumer welfare" in economic jargon) and protection of consum-

ers are not always identical. See note 19 below.

16. Lande, supra note 10.

17. Id. at 91 & n.104. Lande quotes Senator John Sherman, who pointed out during the legislative debates that "[i]t is sometimes said of these combinations that they reduce prices to the consumer by better methods of production, but all experience shows that this saving of cost goes to the pockets of the producer." 21 Cong. Rec. 2460 (1890).

As Eleanor Fox and Lawrence Sullivan observe, to the trust's supporters, they "signified wealth, cooperation, and progressive development. To its detractors, the trust was a monolithic, impersonal, centrally administered organization that represented greed, inhumanity, and economic stratification." Cases and Materials and Antitrust 30 (1989). The very passage of the Sherman Act suggests which argument prevailed.

concern with output was not the historical concern of Congress: prices and consumers were.

Professor Herbert Hovenkamp has supplied an important theoretical underpinning for this "neo-populist" approach to antitrust. Hovenkamp traced the intellectual history of the efficiency approach to economics and public policy, showing its focus on overall societal wealth, regardless of how it is distributed among the people. In contrast, a democratic form of government, where each citizen gets one vote and votes may not lawfully be sold, presupposes that society's laws will not maximize societal wealth but will maximize wealth for the majority.[18] The conclusion one draws from Hovenkamp's insights is that, if forced to choose between an antitrust law that permits various arrangements that raise prices but allocate resources more efficiently, or a law that makes products cheaper for more Americans (even if in strictly economic terms the result is inefficient), Congress would again vote for a law designed primarily to protect the millions of Americans who are consumers—thus confirming Lande's historical analysis.[19] Moreover, a judicial interpretation of federal antitrust law contrary to the interests of the consumer majority simply invites a panoply of less coherent state and federal laws to redress similar or more specific problems.[20]

18. Legislation, Well–Being, and Public Choice, 57 U. Chi. L. Rev. 63, 74–94 (1990).

19. An extreme example of this distinction was the heated internal debate within the FTC in *Allied Corp.*, 101 F.T.C. 721 (1983), where a 3–1 majority refused to approve a merger between two firms that produced industrial acids. The merger involved firms in a highly concentrated industry (only a few firms produced almost all the output) and, as discussed in detail in Chapter 6, the law of mergers is based on the notion that prices will increase if too few competitors remain in the market. In the opinion of the Commission's Bureau of Economics and Chairman James Miller III, the merger should not have been be challenged because the demand for the product was so great that even a 10% increase in price would not reduce the number of purchases. Because the sole effect of the price increase caused by the merger would be to transfer money from consumers to producers, these efficiencianados would have upheld the merger. See "Cost–Benefit Analysis, Miller Style," FTC: Watch, Jan. 14, 1983, at 1–5.

To provide a grossly simplified model, suppose an industry has three firms with large efficient plants. As a result, their costs of production are $3. But, as is discussed in later chapters, because there are only three firms, oligopoly pricing occurs and they all price the product at $7. In contrast, suppose the same industry can be organized with 15 firms operating smaller, less efficient plants. Suppose their costs of production are $5. But, because there are so many firms, each will vigorously compete on price and the price will therefore be $5. The efficient number of firms for this industry is three; the number of firms that best serves consumers is 15.

20. See Robert Taylor, The State of Antitrust—1992, 61 Antitrust L.J. ___ (forthcoming). Examples might include state laws defining unfair competition to outlaw practices exonerated by federal judges, as well as federal laws protecting certain types of businesses from exploitation by larger firms.

The various goals of antitrust are frequently complementary. When there are disputes, they are often based more on underlying assumptions than value choices. For example, the Madisonian desire to disperse power might lead to the condemnation of a series of mergers that centralized control of an industry in New York; the Chicago school would not think to question these mergers if sufficient firms remained in the market to keep prices at competitive levels. But there is only a conflict between these goals if one assumes, as many Chicago school adherents do, that mergers are usually efficient. If mergers do not result in a more efficient use of resources by the newly combined corporation,[21] society can achieve the Madisonian goal at no expense to consumers or economic efficiency.

Throughout the book, we will explore in detail how specific antitrust doctrines do and should serve these various goals. Because the antitrust laws were passed by a Congress elected by voters who are, first and foremost, consumers, interpreting the law so as to minimize prices and maximize quality[22] for American consumers would appear to be most faithful to the purposes of the antitrust laws.[23]

21. See David Ravenscraft & F.M. Scherer, Mergers, Sell–Offs, and Economic Efficiency (1987) (most mergers are not efficient).

22. Here too, Michael Porter's insights into dynamic efficiency come into play. Because consumers are better off over time if a market structure is conducive to technological innovation, both in terms of new and better products and improved means of production, a "neo-populist" applying Porter's insights would be less concerned with keeping current prices down.

23. Judge Bork has offered some forceful arguments for confining antitrust to a single goal. A one-dimensional focus, he argues, would be clearer, would force Congress (rather than the courts) to make the broad policy decisions involved in weighing conflicting goals, and would avoid arbitrary or anti-consumer rules. Bork, supra note 1, at 80–89. Of course, such an approach argues equally for a single goal of maximizing consumer well-being and for allocative efficiency.

CHAPTER 2: THE DEVELOPMENT OF THE LAW OF CONTRACTS IN RESTRAINT OF TRADE

The evolution of the common law governing contracts in restraint of trade is not particularly unique in legal history. In this area, as in others, judges have transformed the common law to reflect changes in the economic conditions and mores of society. Like the federal antitrust laws, the common law today reflects the varying goals of antitrust doctrine discussed in the previous Chapter.

(1) Early common law.

One of the earliest concerns of the common law dealing with contracts that restrain trade was to ban "forestalling, regrating, and engrossing" [1]—all primitive forms of arbitrage. An arbitrageur buys goods from one party for the sole purpose of reselling them later, at a higher price, to another party; it usually happens where, for some reason, the ultimate buyer is unable to purchase the desired good directly from the original source. For example, a growing town in England might have placed a higher value on grain than a neighboring town with a static population, yet traditional patterns of business might continue to send the same amount of grain to both towns. A forestaller would bid against the traditional buyer in the smaller town, obtain the grain, and resell it where it could command a higher price in the larger town.

Forestalling did not harm allocative efficiency. Indeed, it was a highly effective means of reallocating scarce goods to their most highly valued uses—the very definition of efficiency. Rather, forestalling was objectionable, and thus prohibited as a restraint of trade, because the bidding process necessarily resulted in higher grain prices in many parts of the country. Thus, a populist concern with *low* prices, rather than an economist's concern with free market prices, underlay the early laws criminalizing these restraints of trade. Indeed, when the English economy changed in the early 19th century and consumers realized the benefits of a nationwide market for goods, Parliament repealed the forestalling laws. [2]

1. For a thorough discussion, see William Letwin, The English Common Law Concerning Monopolies, 21 U. Chi. L. Rev. 355 (1954).

2. There is a more cynical explanation for the history of the forestalling laws. In early times, politically powerful guilds and merchants controlled lo-

Other early cases show a recognition of the economic harm caused by monopolization. One of the landmark English cases concerning monopolies was the *Case of Monopolies*,[3] which held that a patent monopoly in playing cards granted by Queen Elizabeth to one of her courtiers was void as against the common law. Despite the court's relatively sophisticated understanding of the economic dangers of monopoly,[4] its principal objection to the playing card monopoly was that it was granted by the Queen rather than by Parliament. Indeed, shortly thereafter, Parliament passed the Statute of Monopolies, providing that with few exceptions (such as "true inventors"), only Parliament could grant patent monopolies, and shortly after that Parliament actually did grant a monopoly over the very playing card market at issue in the *Case of Monopolies*. This time, however, a local guild rather than some crown favorite was the recipient.[5] This episode foreshadows the Madisonian concern with concentrated political power. It was permissible, under this view, for the public to suffer the injuries of higher prices and lower quality resulting from a conscious decision of their elected representatives, but not from a royal favor to a court crony.

Early common law judges shared with their modern successors the view that the principal evil of monopoly power is higher prices and reduced output. But while the Chicago school focuses on the misallocation of resources resulting from the reduced output, and the populists focus on the higher prices to consumers, the principal focus of the English common law was the reduced employment opportunities that accompany a loss of competition. Thus, the early rule of *Dyer's Case*[6] suggested that the common law would prohibit any restrictive covenant in a contract providing that employees would not compete with their employers or

cal markets, and enterprising entrepreneurs who bought agricultural goods on the highways disrupted this pattern of control. The well-connected turned to Parliament for relief. Later, when the guilds weakened, the pressure to interfere with the free market weakened and the laws were repealed. Id. at 370.

3. Darcy v. Allen, 11 Coke 84, 77 Eng. Rep. 1260 (K.B. 1602).

4. [T]here are three inseparable incidents to every monopoly against the commonwealth, 1. That the price of the same commodity will be raised, for he who has the sole selling of any commodity, may and will make the price as he pleases.... [2.] after the monopoly is granted, the commodity is not so good and merchantable as it was before: for the patentee having the sole trade, regards only his private benefit, and not the commonwealth. 3. It tends to the impoverishment of divers artificers and others, who before, by the labour of their hands in their art or trade, had maintained themselves and their families, who will now of necessity be constrained to live in idleness and beggary....

Id. at 86b, 77 Eng. Rep. at 1263.

5. Letwin, supra note 1, at 367.

6. Y.B. 2 Hen. 5, vol. 5, pl. 26 (1415).

that one who sold a business would not compete against the buyer.[7]

(2) Modern antecedents.

The law governing restraints of trade had become substantially modified by the time of the leading English case in this area, *Mitchel v. Reynolds*.[8] That case involved the sale of a bakery; the sale agreement contained a non-competition covenant whereby the seller promised not to engage in the baking business within the local parish for five years. Distinguishing permanent restraints on employment and restraints covering all of England, the court found that the non-competition covenant was reasonable, and thus permissible under the common law. According to *Mitchel*, a restrictive covenant would pass muster under the common law if it was: (1) given in return for consideration; (2) voluntary; (3) reasonable in scope; and (4) ancillary to the main purpose of the contract between the parties.

The rationale for allowing reasonable non-competition covenants has changed over time. *Mitchel* itself, antedating the primacy of consumer interests in competition policy, justified its use of a rule of reason analysis on the ground that non-competition agreements "may be useful and beneficial, as to prevent a town being overstocked with any particular trade; or in case an old man ... is likely to be a loser by continuing his trade."[9] These rationales would not pass muster today. As made clear below in Chapter 4, the case law governing agreements among competitors would not allow a cartel of competitors to justify price fixing or other restraints on competition by arguing that the market was "overstocked" with sellers or that an elderly entrepreneur needed protection from economic harm. Moreover, Reynolds' interest in litigating the case showed that at least *he* believed that the market for bakers in the local parish was not "overstocked." *Mitchel*'s analysis is consistent, however, with the early 18th century focus on the interests of the parties to the restraint, rather than the public.

Today the common law retains this traditional concern for fairness to the restricted covenantor, a concern that is not motivated by allocational or consumer-oriented interests. The Restatement (Second) of Contracts adopts *Mitchel*'s holding that any restrictions broader than necessary to protect the legitimate inter-

---

7. At the time of *Dyer's Case*, a tradesman who promised not to work in his hometown effectively deprived himself of any income from his trade; the guilds were so strong that the option of plying one's trade in another locale was not feasible. Harlan Blake, Employment Agreements Not to Compete, 73 Harv. L. Rev. 625, 633–34 (1960).

8. 24 Eng. Rep. 347 (K.B. 1711).

9. Id. at 350.

ests of the covenantee violate the common law.[10]   The English court asked why a tradesman in London should care if his covenantor works in Newcastle.[11]   This rhetorical question reflects a concern that is not based on preserving competition.   In such a case, the societal harm is not likely to be a competitive one, unless the covenantor's work is highly specialized.   Presumably, many other tradesmen are available in Newcastle.   Nor do the consumers in the market most directly affected by the restrictive covenant care whether or not the covenantor can work elsewhere; the loss of competition will be felt by them in either event.   Rather, the traditional concerns with overbroad agreements reflect notions of fairness,[12] and macroeconomic policies of minimizing aid to the unemployed, and lost contributions to both the tax rolls and the gross national product on the part of the covenantor.

The common law subsequent to *Mitchel*, however, has taken on a more consumer-oriented tone.   In an 1831 case, an English court held that courts analyzing the reasonableness of a contract should not only consider fairness to the parties, but should also inquire whether the covenant's scope is "so large as to interfere with the interests of the public."[13]   The Restatement (Second) also requires courts to weigh the "injury to the public,"[14] thus suggesting that in determining whether a restraint is reasonable, courts focus both on traditional fairness notions and on more modern concerns about protecting allocative efficiency and consumer interests.   In recently explaining *Mitchel*, Justice John Paul Stevens revised its rationale to fit modern concerns.   Conceding that the restraint at issue there caused some harm to the public, he reasoned that "the long-run benefit of enhancing the marketability of the business itself—and thereby providing incentives to develop such an enterprise—outweighed the temporary and limited loss of competition."[15]   In other words, to encourage sellers to build up "good will" in their businesses, they may exact valuable

---

10. See Restatement (Second) of Contracts § 187 (1981).

11. *Mitchel*, 24 Eng. Rep. at 350.

12. This concern for fairness to the parties explains why restrictive covenants in contracts between employers and employees are scrutinized more closely than covenants ancillary to the sale of a business.   The comment to the Restatement notes that the former restraints are often the product of unequal bargaining power and may be unfair to the employee.   See Restatement (Second) of Contracts § 188, comment g (1981).   Again, neither consumer nor allocational issues are implicated in this distinction.

13. Horner v. Graves, 131 Eng. Rep. 284, 287 (C.P. 1831).

14. Restatement (Second) of Contracts § 188(1)(b) (1981).

15. National Soc'y of Prof. Engineers v. United States, 435 U.S. 679, 690 (1978).

Enhancing the marketability of a business also lowers the average return necessary to attract people into the business in the first place, by reducing the risk that they will be stuck with assets they cannot sell.   (Thanks to my colleague Peter Maggs for this observation.)

consideration for the sale of good will, and buyers may provide such consideration knowing that the good will just purchased will not be swiftly eroded by competition from their predecessors.[16] Similarly, restrictions on employees' opportunities to compete with their employers may encourage owners to share confidential information with employees, or to give employees unsupervised contact with key customers. Although Justice Stevens' historical exegesis may depart from historic accuracy concerning the legitimacy of using restraints as an incentive for developing good will,[17] and provide an ill-considered opening for all sorts of competition-lessening agreements,[18] it demonstrates the updating of the common law to fit within contemporary debates about competition policy.

(3) Modern focus of American law.

American courts adopted *Mitchel* and applied it with a consumer/efficiency focus. In *Oregon Steam Navigation Co. v. Winsor*,[19] for example, the United States Supreme Court sustained a restrictive covenant ancillary to a California company's sale of a steamship to an Oregon firm. The buyer, which sought the ship for commerce on the Columbia River, promised not to use the ship in California waters for ten years, and then resold the ship to a second buyer for use in Puget Sound (in Washington State) with a covenant barring use in either California or Oregon waters. The Court sustained the agreement as promoting "the general interests of commerce on the Pacific Coast."[20] The covenant did not, the Court emphasized, deprive the public of the "industry" of the restricted firm.[21] Presumably, at the time of the sales, the ship was more valuable in northern waters than in California. Absent contrary evidence, we assume that the California firm might have

---

16. Suppose, for example, the parish really does not need additional bakers, but Reynolds now wishes to cease his trade and profit from the good will he has developed. In that case, the covenant protects Mitchel and causes no harm to the public, for one baker is simply substituted for the other. See William Howard Taft, The Anti–Trust Act and the Supreme Court 8 (1914).

17. For example, Judge Robert Bork's study of the common law concluded that a restraint met the *Mitchel* requirement that the restraint by ancillary to the main purpose of a lawful contract only if it were "subordinate or collateral to another transaction *and necessary to make that transaction effective.*" Ancillary Restraints and the Sherman Act, 15 A.B.A. Section on An-

titrust Law Proceedings 211, 211 (1959) (emphasis added). According to Bork, the reason that non-competition covenants were protected were to make "salable properties of a type that might otherwise be impossible to transfer." Id. at 217. Nothing in Bork's study suggests that restraints may be justified solely in order to increase the value of good will in order to provide incentives for entrepreneurs to develop their businesses.

18. See the discussion of good will below in subsection (3).

19. 87 U.S. 64 (1873).

20. Id. at 69.

21. Id. at 68–69.

been reluctant to make the sale if the buyer planned to compete in California. Allowing the buyer to make a legally enforceable promise not to compete facilitated the sale and provided Columbia River traffic with one more needed ship.

The different foci of *Mitchel* and *Winsor* also explain the early English law concerning combinations in restraint of trade. Because the common law's competition policy originally focused on the individual's right to trade, a host of English cases defended competition-reducing agreements among rivals as voluntary schemes unlikely to cause public injury.[22] As American courts began to appreciate the economic benefits of competition to consumers, they began to condemn such agreements.[23]

Today, the prime issue litigated in restrictive covenant cases is whether the restraint is reasonable in scope. Courts determine the scope of any non-competition restraint by focusing on: (1) the type of activity prohibited, (2) the geographical area encompassed, and (3) the length of time the covenant is in effect.[24] According to the Restatement, when "the restraint is too broad to be justified by the promisee's need, a court may hold it to be unreasonable without the necessity of weighing the countervailing interests of the promisor and the public."[25] As one commentator politely noted, the concept of reasonableness does not have "a single, clearly defined meaning but is a concept of some complexity."[26] In truth, the determination of reasonableness often turns on whether the restraint is broader—in terms of activity, geographic area, and time period—than necessary for the "legitimate" protection of the covenantee. In the case of a covenant ancillary to the sale of a business, this analysis depends on the notion of good will, at best an incoherent concept.

As a matter of accounting, good will is a tautological concept—it represents the amount of purchase price in excess of tangible assets. As a matter of business practice, good will may be characterized as "the customer contact which the owner of the

22. Mogul Steamship Co. v. McGregor, 21 A.B.D. 544 (1888), aff'd, 23 Q.B.D. 598 (1889), aff'd, 1892 A.C. 25 (rebates to exclusive customers); Hearn v. Griffin, 2 Chitty 407 (1815) (price fixing and market allocation agreements between two coach services); Wickens v. Evans, 148 Eng. Rep. 1201 (1829) (price fixing and market allocation agreements between three manufacturers of trunks and boxes).

23. See Herbert Hovenkamp, The Sherman Act and the Classical Theory of Competition, 74 Iowa L. Rev. 1019 (1989).

24. Restatement (2d) of Contracts, § 188, comment d.

25. Id. To be more precise, this generalization more accurately summarizes the state of the common law applicable to non-competition covenants ancillary to the sale of a business. Many states, motivated by concerns about employee exploitation, take a harsher view of non-competition covenants in that context.

26. Annot., 45 A.L.R.2d 77, 129 (1956).

business was able to develop." [27]   It is clear that where a business is sporadic and intensely personal—such as the practice of a doctor or lawyer—a broad covenant is necessary to ensure that the value of the good will is not nullified should the seller reenter the market.[28]   At the other extreme, for a business like the typical retail establishment that customers patronize regularly at short intervals, the location of the business may be much more significant than the owner's personal reputation and the seller's effort to reenter the market after a brief hiatus is unlikely to lead to any greater loss for the buyer than would be caused by any other new entrant of similar skill and industry.[29]

Providing a coherent definition of the term "good will" requires resolution of the fundamental policy questions surrounding restrictions intended to protect the buyer from the seller's reentry not because of the customer relations the latter has developed over the years, but due instead to the seller's superior skill and business acumen. Language in some cases suggests that the seller ought to be able to profit from this skill by selling an ongoing business at a premium.[30] Yet this same logic would allow a skilled entrepreneur to sell a promise not to compete even if it were not ancillary to the sale of a business. These types of agreements are uniformly held to be unlawful.[31] Thus, maximizing the reward a seller can receive from the fruits of its demonstrated business acumen does not appear to be a sound basis for upholding the reasonableness of a covenant. Rather, the scope of the covenant should be tailored to give the buyer the benefit of purchasing an established business, but no more. In this way, society benefits from an efficient transfer of assets, but is not deprived of the superior skill of an entrepreneur who, upon re-entering the market, is in no better position than any new entrant of similar skill and industry.

We will revisit this aspect of the common law of contracts later, when we consider the appropriate rule governing agreements among competitors under § 1 of the Sherman Act. The important point for antitrust purposes is that the inquiry into the reasonableness of a restrictive covenant ends once the court deter-

---

27. Id. at 101.

28. Id. at 156.

29. Id. at 164.

30. See National Soc'y of Prof. Engineers v. United States, discussed above at note 15; Plunkett v. Reeves Apothecary, Inc., 351 So. 2d 867, 868 (La. App. 1977) (rationale for enforcing non-competition covenants is to allow "the ven-

dor who, by his skill and diligent attention to business, accumulates good will, an opportunity to obtain a price for it").

31. See Monopolies, Combinations and Restraints of Trade, 36 Am. Jur. 473 § 50; Monopolies, Restraints of Trade & Unfair Trade Practices, 54 Am. Jur. 2d § 515.

mines that the covenant is broader than necessary to protect the promisee's legitimate interest.

(4) Application of the Sherman Act to non-competition covenants.

The foregoing analysis should apply to litigation involving non-competition covenants that arises under § 1 of the Sherman Act as well as under the common law. Federal courts have been reluctant to apply the Sherman Act to these complaints, however, because of concerns that individually the challenged covenants "have only a small impact on commerce and ... have traditionally been handled in state courts." [32] Given the opportunity in *Newburger, Loeb & Co. v. Gross* [33] to venture into the area, the Second Circuit declined to "pass on the general applicability of the federal antitrust laws to post-employment restraints." Nevertheless, the court did opine that "employee agreements not to compete are proper subjects for scrutiny under section 1 of the Sherman Act," citing academic commentary suggesting that widespread use of overbroad restrictions causes significant competitive harm. [34]

Newburger, Loeb set forth a sensible approach for evaluating non-competition covenants under the Sherman Act. First, restraints that protect no legitimate interest of the covenantee are per se invalid. The court applies a rule of reason analysis only if the restrictive clause is not "overbroad *per se.*" If the restraint survives per se condemnation, the court considers whether the resulting harm to competition outweighs the justification for the covenant, an inquiry similar to that undertaken by the common law. [35]

(5) Effect of overbreadth.

Assuming that a restraint is overbroad, is the non-competition covenant null and void? The modern trend among the courts is to enforce an overbroad covenant to the extent that it is reasonable, but no further. Thus, in *Karpinski v. Ingrasci,* [36] the plaintiff had developed a practice in oral surgery in Ithaca, New York, and established an office there for use by his employee, Dr. Ingrasci. The New York Court of Appeals found that a non-competition covenant permanently barring the defendant from practicing dentistry or oral surgery within five rural counties was overbroad, but

---

32. Bradford v. New York Times Co., 501 F.2d 51, 60 (2d Cir. 1974).

33. 563 F.2d 1057, 1082 (2d Cir. 1977), cert. denied, 434 U.S. 1035 (1978).

34. Id. (citing Harvey Goldschmid, Antitrust's Neglected Stepchild: A Proposal for Dealing with Restrictive Covenants under Federal Law, 73 Colum. L. Rev. 1193, 1206–07 (1973)).

35. Id.

36. 28 N.Y.2d 45, 320 N.Y.S.2d 1, 268 N.E.2d 751 (1971).

that a restraint limited to oral surgery alone would be reasonable. Accordingly, the court enforced the restriction as modified.[37] This approach has been criticized because it provides an incentive for employers and sellers of existing businesses to insist on overbroad covenants in hopes that the fear of litigation will deter competition by risk-averse or unsophisticated covenantors.[38] A rule more sensitive to competitive concerns might disallow, rather than modify, overbroad restrictions drafted by a covenantee who enjoys superior bargaining power and sophistication.

(6) Summary.

The current common law rules governing contracts in restraint of trade recognize that such restraints can have positive effects in facilitating the sale of a business, the investment in goodwill as a marketable asset, and the training of skilled employees. At the same time, the law remains wary of promises not to compete because of the risk that these promises will unfairly hinder the covenantor in pursuing her profession and will deny the public the benefits of competition. In balancing these interests, the courts employ a rule of reason methodology, looking first to see if the restraint is broader than necessary to achieve the positive effects described above, and next to determine whether the activity, area, and time covered by the restraint are reasonable. By requiring courts to consider the restraint's impact on the public at large, this approach serves the law's interest in both promoting economic efficiency and protecting consumers from the higher prices and lower quality that can occur with limited competition. By protecting covenantees from oppressive restrictions, the law acts to preserve an individual's economic opportunities and limits abuses by those in a position to wield economic power.

37. Some courts will modify contracts only by use of the "blue pencil," rewriting the contract only by deleting grammatically severable parts. See, e.g., Wood v. May, 73 Wash.2d 307, 438 P.2d 587 (1968). These courts would not, for example, modify a contract that barred a defendant from competing for an unreasonably lengthy period of time even if a shorter-term restriction would have been permissible.

38. See, e.g., Welcome Wagon Int'l, Inc. v. Pender, 255 N.C. 244, 120 S.E.2d 739, 748 (1961) (Bobbitt, J., dissenting) (citing Mason v. Provident Clothing Supply Co., 1913 A.C. 724, 745).

CHAPTER 3: MARKET STRUCTURE AND MONOPOLY POWER

Section A: Introduction to Monopolization

(1) The problem—and Congress' solution.

Different markets have different structures, covering the spectrum between perfect competition and perfect monopoly. An understanding of basic economic principles concerning the importance of a competitive market structure is necessary to appreciate the antitrust law's concern with monopoly power.

At one extreme is the atomistic market with vigorous competition. The owner of a small family farm is an archetypical example. Each firm in the market accounts for only a small fraction of total sales. No farmer has the ability to affect the market price by individual action. The market price remains the same, whether the farmer increases production or stops growing crops altogether. The result for society is a market where price equals cost.[1]

At the other extreme is the market with one seller who faces no competition—the perfect monopoly. A familiar example would be a company that holds an exclusive government license to provide cable television services in an area where over-the-air reception is poor. The firm offers a unique product and faces no competition from rivals. Its pricing power is limited only by consumers' income and willingness to pay for the product. Unlike the farmer, the cable monopolist has the discretion to sell to fewer homes at higher prices, or to more homes at lower prices, in whatever manner will maximize its profits. Compared to a competitive market, the results of monopoly are higher prices and lower output. As noted in Chapter 1, monopoly power also leads to an inefficient allocation of resources (too few consumers obtain cable services and there is insufficient pressure on the company to innovate), a transfer of wealth from consumers to the cable company, and an accumulation of economic power that is subject to abuse.

---

1. For purposes of this chapter, "cost" includes what economists term a "normal" profit. In the case of the small family farm, for example, a normal profit would include a reasonable salary for the farmer's labor and a return on capital investments approximating the return on a typical investment in that economy.

Congress' principal response to the negative consequences of monopoly markets was to enact § 2 of the Sherman Act.[2] Section 2 provides that "[e]very person who shall monopolize ... any part of the trade or commerce among the several States, or with foreign nations, shall be deemed guilty of a felony." [3]. There are two important elements of § 2. First, the defendant must be a monopolist—that is the firm must have monopoly power over some defined market. But § 2 does not criminalize the mere status of being a monopolist. Thus, the second element is that the defendant must have "monopol*ized*," or acted in some way that warrants condemnation.

Intent is not an essential element in § 2 cases. The criminal law distinguishes between so-called "general intent" crimes and "specific intent" crimes. To prove the former, the prosecution must merely show that the defendant's acts were conscious and deliberate—any further purpose of motive is irrelevant. For example, the crime of assault with a deadly weapon merely requires a conscious attack on the victim with a specified weapon. In contrast, specific intent crimes require proof that the defendant acted for the purpose of achieving some illegal end. Thus, the crime of assault with intent to kill requires the prosecution to show not only the deliberate act of assault but also the defendant's purpose to kill the victim. Monopolization is a general intent crime. A § 2 case does not require proof that the defendant desired or planned to achieve a monopoly.[4] Rather, is sufficient that the challenged acts are condemned under the antitrust laws and, as is almost always true in cases involving business conduct, were performed by the defendant consciously and not accidently.

(2) The early cases.

Early decisions made it clear that monopolists violate § 2 when they acquire or maintain power by blatantly illegal or anticompetitive acts. The first major § 2 case was *Standard Oil Co. of New Jersey v. United States.*[5] In that case, the Supreme Court recognized that Congress did not prohibit "monopoly in the concrete," i.e., the mere operation of a monopoly business.[6] Instead, Congress had reached a "consensus that the freedom of the individual right to contract *when not unduly or improperly exercised* was the most effective means for the prevention of monopo-

---

2. 15 U.S.C. § 2.

3. Section 2 also condemns attempting and conspiring to monopolize. These are considered below in sections G and H, respectively.

4. United States v. Aluminum Co. of America, 148 F.2d 416, 431–32 (2d Cir. 1945) (it would make "nonsense" of § 2 to require a showing of specific intent).

5. 221 U.S. 1 (1911).

6. Id. at 55.

ly." [7] In explaining why Standard Oil was not a mere "monopoly in the concrete," the Court noted that the company's acquisition of a dominant position in the oil industry was not the result of "normal methods of industrial development." Rather, "new means of combination" (presumably growth through merger, acquisition, and trust devices) gave rise to a "prima facie presumption of intent and purpose" to maintain dominancy of the oil industry by illegal means.[8] When combined with evidence that Standard Oil obtained discriminatory preferences (i.e., lower rates than smaller customers) from railroads, engaged in unfair practices against competing pipelines, conducted industrial espionage, and periodically engaged in predatory pricing,[9] the presumption became "conclusive." [10]

Similarly, in *United States v. American Tobacco Co.,*[11] the Court found a § 2 violation where the defendant had acquired monopoly power in the tobacco industry by blatantly illegal conduct. The company was formed by the merger of several rivals to end a price war. It further eliminated competition by giving other rivals a choice between joining the combination or being put out of business by price wars; dividing the world market with foreign concerns; acquiring the raw elements necessary to enter the market in order to prevent new entry by others; buying up plants and then closing them to reduce production; and obtaining unreasonably long covenants not to compete from former rivals whose companies had been acquired by the tobacco trust.

In contrast, in *United States v. United States Steel Corp.*[12] the Court found that the defendant did not monopolize the steel industry. U.S. Steel had been formed by the merger of 180 separate firms in 1901, giving it 80–95% of the market. By the time the case was decided almost two decades later, however, its market share had declined to 50%. The essence of the government's case was that U.S. Steel had been formed illegally, that it was still a monopoly, and that it continued to exercise price leadership (today we would say that it led a fairly tight oligopoly).

In a narrow 4–3 vote,[13] the Court ruled against the government, finding no violation of the antitrust laws because the

---

7. Id. at 62 (emphasis added).

8. Id. at 75. Thus, although intent is not an element of monopolization, it can be used as evidence to distinguish unlawful dominance from "normal methods of industrial development."

9. But see John McGee, Predatory Pricing Revisited, 23 J.L. & Econ. 289 (1980).

10. 221 U.S. at 75.

11. 221 U.S. 106 (1911).

12. 251 U.S. 417 (1920).

13. Justices James McReynolds and Louis Brandeis recused themselves from the case. McReynolds had been Attorney General during the government's litigation against U.S. Steel. In 1912, Brandeis had testified before a House Committee that was investigating U.S. Steel. Although neither the House nor

defendant was not currently a monopolist and was not currently conspiring with others. Rejecting the government's arguments concerning the allegedly illegal formation of U.S. Steel, the court did not expressly hold that the suit was barred either by estoppel or laches,[14] but it did observe that the Justice Department had waited until 1911 to file suit, after the defendant had spent millions of dollars during the ten-year period following its allegedly illegal combination in 1901.[15] Moreover, the Court noted, U.S. Steel had engaged in none of the "brutalities or tyrannies" found in earlier cases.[16] Focusing its attention on U.S. Steel's current status, the Court reasoned that evidence of the defendant's efforts to conspire with rivals to fix prices was actually proof that it did not possess monopoly power itself. Moreover, the Court emphasized that U.S. Steel's growth seemed a natural reflection of increasing economies of scale and scope in the mass production of steel.[17] Finally, the Court rejected the government's arguments about U.S. Steel's price leadership, rhetorically asking whether judges should "declare the law to be that size is an offense, even though it minds its own business, because what it does is imitated?"[18]

Today, the Court's analysis in *U.S. Steel* appears outmoded. Both the majority and the dissenting opinions focused on whether U.S. Steel's size was the result of "natural" growth. The majority, relying on trends in the industry, concluded that it was. The dissent argued to the contrary, observing that U.S. Steel had paid a considerable premium to acquire its dominant share of the market.[19] The Court's focus on natural growth is understandable given the generally accepted view, at the time the Sherman Act was passed, that eliminating the trusts would allow all to compete fairly. At that time, it appeared that any trust would necessarily have been formed unnaturally and with malice towards rivals and consumers, and therefore that all the goals of antitrust could be harmonized simply by breaking up all trusts.[20] Today, however, it

the Senate took action, Brandeis had warned the committee about the dangers of U.S. Steel. Phillipa Strum, Brandeis, Justice for the People 153 (1984). Moreover, in his widely read article, "Other People's Money," Harper's Weekly, Nov. 22, 1913, Brandeis had harshly criticized U.S. Steel.

14. Relying on either doctrine would have been problematic because neither has traditionally been applied against the sovereign. Dan Dobbs, Handbook on the Law of Remedies § 13.4, at 991–92 (1973).

15. 251 U.S. at 452–53. The majority suggested that U.S. Steel's critics "underestimated the influence of the tendency and movement to [what economists call vertical integration], [i.e.,] the appreciation of the necessity or value of the continuity of manufacture from the ore to the finished product." Id. at 442.

16. Id. at 440–41.

17. Id. at 442.

18. Id. at 451.

19. Id. at 458–61.

20. See Chapter 1.

is evident that the goals of antitrust actually conflict with one another in many situations. *U.S. Steel*, for example, reflects the tension that necessarily occurs when economies of scale naturally lead to the growth of large firms that have a distinct advantage over smaller rivals, thus enabling them to reduce competition and exploit consumers through non-malicious conduct like price leadership. A court today, with the benefit of the study of oligopoly pricing, would not be so quick to exonerate a firm that uses dubious tactics to achieve a size such that it sets its own price and is then imitated by others.

Another significant § 2 case in the early years following passage of the Sherman Act involved the government's efforts to break up American Can's monopoly of the can industry. The defendant had acquired a dominant share of the market through merger. Many smaller firms sold out for fear that they would be unable to compete against such a large rival, especially one that was receiving discriminatory discounts from a major tin supplier. American Can also obtained 15–year non-competition covenants from former rivals, and closed many of the plants it had acquired. In addition, it purchased a number of patents for use in manufacturing, and paid a premium to machine manufacturers in return for exclusive contracts (promises that the manufacturers would not sell their machines to any rival can company). New entries were nonetheless attracted into the industry when American Can's prices increased. The district judge in *United States v. American Can Co.*[21] found that, due to the defendant's reduction in its prices following new entry, the overall price of cans had not increased since the creation of the monopoly, and that American Can's size allowed it to produce a can of higher quality with more reliable delivery. Because the defendant had done nothing wrong for many years and now faced a competitive threat from a number of actual or potential rivals, the court refused the government's request for a divestiture decree. Rather, the judge retained jurisdiction over the case, while disclaiming an interest in regulating the industry, and invited the government to return to court if American Can abused its monopoly position.[22]

By the time the trial judge ruled in 1916, he had witnessed the dissolution of a number of trusts by the Roosevelt and Taft administrations. Nevertheless, he concluded that trust-busting had not helped the public. Although he gave lip service to Congress' purpose to "prevent the concentration in a few hands of control over great industries,"[23] he seems to have been as uncritically accepting of the concept that American Can enjoyed signifi-

---

21. 230 Fed. 859 (D. Md. 1916).   **23.** Id. at 901, 902.

22. Id. at 904.

cant economies of scale as Brandeis had been of the theory that small firms can always compete with larger concerns absent restraints of trade.[24] To be sure, American Can may have been more efficient than small, family-owned, single-plant operations; whether consumers would have been harmed or helped by an order dividing the defendant's multiple-plan combination into several competing multi-plant companies is, however, another question.

(3) The *Alcoa* case.

The first modern case to seriously consider the question whether less blatant conduct warrants condemnation as "monopolization" was decided by the Second Circuit in 1945. In that case, *United States v. Aluminum Co. of America (Alcoa)*,[25] the defendant had controlled approximately 90% of the sales of virgin aluminum ingot in this country for many years. It had achieved its dominance prior to 1912 by a host of anticompetitive acts, including the acquisition of the exclusive license for an important patent, the purchase of covenants from electric power companies that prevented them from selling power to rivals, and the exclusion of foreign companies from the United States by agreeing not to sell in certain foreign countries. In a prior suit, the government had entered into a consent decree that did not break up the aluminum monopoly but merely ordered Alcoa to cease and desist its blatant misbehavior. Thus, to win on a renewed effort to break Alcoa up into competing aluminum companies, the government had to prove that the defendant's conduct subsequent to the 1912 consent decree constituted illegal monopolization.[26]

Writing for the court, Judge Learned Hand found that Alcoa had, indeed, engaged in conduct violative of § 2. His opinion, however, is riddled with internal inconsistencies. In fact, various parts of the opinion articulate three conflicting definitions of monopolization. At one point Hand suggested that deliberately conducting business as a monopolist is sufficient—no additional improper conduct is necessary. "A monopoly is always an 'unreasonable restraint of trade,'" he wrote. In support, he explained that price-fixing cartels are per se illegal (we shall explore this

---

24. See Chapter 1 for a discussion of Brandeis' views.

25. 148 F.2d 416 (2d Cir. 1945). The case reached the Second Circuit in an unusual manner. The government had lost in the trial court and had exercised its right under a special statute to file a direct appeal to the Supreme Court. The Court, however, could not muster six justices who were not disqualified from hearing the case for one reason or another, and the appeal was therefore referred to the three senior judges on the Second Circuit. Id. at 421.

26. For a discussion of the remedial aspects of *Alcoa*, from the original 1912 consent decree through the 1950's, see subsection (6) below.

assertion in Chapter 4), and that the economic effect of a monopoly is identical to that of a perfectly operating cartel.[27]

Elsewhere in the opinion, however, Hand recognized that this "no-fault" construction is really at odds with the language of the Sherman Act. Drawing the distinction between being a monopolist and monopolizing, Hand suggested that a defendant that had a monopoly "thrust upon it" would not be guilty of violating § 2. He noted, for example, that "changes in taste or in cost [could] drive out all but one purveyor."[28]

Perhaps cognizant of the relevant legislative history,[29] however, Judge Hand suggested a third approach, declaring that a defendant would not be guilty of violating § 2 if it acquired monopoly power because of "superior skill, foresight and industry."[30] This approach is inconsistent with Hand's second theory because a firm that enjoys "superior skill, foresight and industry" obviously did not have its monopoly power "thrust upon it." Hand's application of this standard is also difficult to understand. Alcoa was guilty of monopolizing, he concluded, because, with "a persistent determination to maintain the control" of the aluminum market, Alcoa "effectively anticipated and forestalled all competition" by "doubling and redoubling its capacity before others entered the field" in order that it could "always anticipate increases in the demand for ingot and be prepared to supply them." Thus, Alcoa could not fall within the "exception" to § 2 for monopolists "who do not seek, but cannot avoid, the control of a market."[31] His holding seems, then, to apply his second test for monopolizing—whether a monopolist saw power "thrust upon it"—rather than his third test—whether growth was due to superior skill and industry.[32]

The Supreme Court subsequently confirmed *Alcoa*'s third view—that a firm acts lawfully if it actively develops a superior product or uses its "business acumen" to obtain monopoly power— as the governing standard for monopolization. In *United States v.*

27. 148 F.2d at 427–28.

28. Id. at 429–30.

29. During the debates on the Sherman Act, the Senate engaged in a lengthy discussion concerning the meaning of the word "monopoly." Senator Hoar emphasized that the word was "a technical term known to the common law."

But in response to a question from Senator Kenna, Hoar also said that the term required "something like the use of means which made it impossible for other persons to engage in competition"; it therefore did not include "a man who merely by superior skill and intelligence ... got the whole business because nobody could do it as well as he could." 21 Cong. Rec. 3152 (1890).

30. 148 F.2d at 430.

31. Id. at 430–31.

32. See subsection (4) below for a discussion of why Judge Hand concluded that continued expansion does not constitute superior skill and industry.

Grinnell Corp.,[33] the Court held that the offense of monopolization under § 2 involves "the willful acquisition or maintenance of [monopoly] power as distinguished from growth or development as a consequence of a superior product, business acumen, or historical accident."[34] Other than indicating what conduct is protected, however, *Grinnell* does not further explain what behavior can be characterized as "willful." The defendant in that case had engaged in conduct that was clearly unlawful under the early precedents: Grinnell acquired monopoly power by acquiring competitors and engaging in agreements to divide markets.

Significantly, then, *Grinnell* interprets § 2 to prohibit a firm from improperly gaining or retaining monopoly power. It does not prohibit a monopolist from exercising power where such exercise does not affect the firm's ability to maintain power. Thus, for example, simply charging high prices would not violate § 2, because such a straightforward exploitation of consumers does not entrench the monopolist's position—indeed, it may have the opposite effect, by attracting new entry. The approach taken under the Sherman Act contrasts somewhat with the approach taken in Europe. Article 86 of the Treaty of Rome, which prohibits "abuse of a dominant position," defines such abuse to include "unfair selling prices."[35]

(4) *Alcoa's* progeny.

Grinnell's standard remains highly imprecise, and while Judge Hand seemed to put the no-fault view of monopoly to rest in the *Alcoa* opinion itself, his successors on the Second Circuit expressly rejected his second view—that a monopoly is legal only if it was "thrust upon" the defendant—in *Berkey Photo, Inc. v. Eastman Kodak Co.*[36] In that case, the court confirmed that *Grinnell*'s requirement of "willful" maintenance effectively abandoned Hand's second view. A "willfulness" test is necessarily based on "considerations of fairness and the need to preserve proper economic incentives," the court explained. Therefore, a firm that actively seeks to gain or maintain power by "purely competitive means" does not violate § 2, even though it cannot be said that monopoly power has been "thrust upon" that firm.[37]

In rejecting Hand's second view, *Berkey* helped to explain the concept of "willful" conduct. The decision established that the plaintiff in a § 2 case must prove both that the defendant's

33. 384 U.S. 563 (1966).

34. Id. at 570–71.

35. Treaty Establishing the European Economic Community, art. 86, 298 U.N.T.S. 11, 48.

36. 603 F.2d 263 (2d Cir.), cert. denied, 444 U.S. 1093 (1979).

37. Id. at 274.

conduct was anticompetitive (a term open to different definitions, depending on one's view of the goals of antitrust) and also that condemning the defendant's conduct will not unduly deter desirable business behavior. The court then applied this standard in rejecting the plaintiff's claim that Kodak, a monopolist of cameras and film products, had illegally refused to disclose new innovations to its rivals prior to releasing them on the market. The refusal, the plaintiff claimed, deprived Kodak's rivals of the opportunity to manufacture similar products. The court reasoned that § 2 clearly does not require monopolists to make pre-disclosures of its inventions in all contexts.[38] Although Berkey forcefully argued that Kodak had special obligations to disclose, lest Kodak's film monopoly be used to gain an advantage in the camera market, the court held that it could not discern workable guidelines for imposing liability for non-disclosure, and it was inappropriate to allow courts and juries to engage in retrospective review of a monopolist's strategic decisions. Such a doctrine, the court concluded, would chill aggressive competitive behavior.[39]

Like *Alcoa*, *Berkey Photo* contains some broad, inconsistent language.[40] Unlike *Alcoa*, though, *Berkey Photo* provides a satisfactory paradigm for judicial decisionmaking. Explicitly recognizing that § 2 allows courts to create a "common law against monopolizing," [41] the court's dual concerns with fairness to monopolists who have competed on the merits, and with preserving economic incentives, provide content to the term "willful" behavior that is missing in *Grinnell*. The standard articulated in *Berkey Photo* also reflects a reasonable accommodation of conflicting antitrust goals. To be sure, the court's approach does not serve the purely non-economic concerns with maintaining small firms and dispersing power: these concerns call for a no-fault monopoly standard. If we are to distinguish between "monopoly in the concrete" and unlawful monopolization, however, preserving incentives for monopolists to produce new and better products serves allocative efficiency and also improves the lot of most consumers.

---

38. "Because, as we have already indicated, a monopolist is permitted, and indeed encouraged, by § 2 to compete aggressively on the merits, any success that it may achieve through 'the process of invention and innovation' is clearly tolerated by the antitrust laws." Id. at 281 (citing United States v. United Shoe Machinery Corp., 110 F.Supp. 295, 344 (D. Mass. 1953), aff'd per curiam, 347 U.S. 521 (1954)).

39. Id. at 282.

40. For example, the Second Circuit suggested that a firm with lawfully acquired monopoly power "may not wield the resulting power to tighten its hold on the market." Id. at 275. But, the court also said, a firm that uses its size or ability to develop related products in order to prevail over rivals does not abuse monopoly power. Id. at 276.

41. Id. at 272 (citing III Phillip Areeda & Donald Turner, Antitrust Law 40 (1978)).

Berkey's goal of preserving the incentive for monopolists to innovate is particularly important when a court believes the innovation will truly benefit consumers. In *California Computer Products, Inc. v. IBM Corp.*,[42] for example, IBM redesigned its mainframe computers so that disk drives and memory units were included in one physical unit rather than sold separately as "peripheral" products. This design had a significant exclusionary effect on firms such as Cal Comp that had previously competed with IBM in selling this peripheral equipment to users of IBM mainframes. The court found that IBM's integrated system provided significant cost savings and was more efficient for buyers to use. Thus, the court held that IBM "had the right to redesign its products to make them more attractive to buyers—whether by reason of lower manufacturing cost and price or improved performance." [43]

Berkey left unanswered another recurring issue in § 2 cases: whether a monopoly that continuously expands its production to meet the demand for its product is unlawfully monopolizing or merely using superior skill and foresight. In *Alcoa*, Judge Hand held that such conduct was unlawful, specifically rejecting the defendant's position that expansion was illegal only if motivated *solely* by a desire to bar competition.[44] More recently, in *E.I. du Pont de Nemours & Co. (TiO₂)*,[45] the Federal Trade Commission permitted du Pont to exploit a temporary cost advantage over its rivals by expanding capacity, thereby increasing its own market share from 30% to 55%. Although the FTC attempted to distinguish *Alcoa*,[46] the thrust of the two decisions is flatly inconsistent. The Commission expressly distinguished du Pont's conduct from that of a hypothetical monopolist who "was attempting solely to preserve its market power ... to deter new entry or expansion by existing competitors." [47] In the FTC's opinion, the antitrust laws should not, be used to "block hard, aggressive competition that is solidly based on efficiencies and growth opportunities, even if monopoly is a possible result." [48]

42. 613 F.2d 727 (9th Cir. 1979).

43. Id. at 744. This case is also discussed in section D(7).

44. *Alcoa*, 148 F.2d at 431.

45. 96 F.T.C. 653 (1980).

46. The Commission held that du Pont's 55% market share did not constitute monopoly power and hence the case was more akin to an attempted monopolization case than to *Alcoa*. Id. at 731–32.

47. Id. at 749.

48. Id. at 751.

In *du Pont (TiO₂)*, the FTC staff claimed that the defendant had engaged in classic monopolistic behavior, sacrificing short-term profits in order to invest in capacity expansion that would only be profitable if it could realize super-competitive profits in the future. Investment in a new, unique product, however, would surely be lawful even if it were profitable only if the investor were to realize super-competitive profits in the future. The key question is whether the investment in question— here, expansion of capacity—is sufficiently similar to a new or improved

Whether the acquisition of monopoly power through expansion constitutes "superior skill and efficiency" ultimately depends on one's view of the goals of antitrust. Judge Hand read § 2 as expressing a congressional desire, "because of its indirect social or moral effect, to prefer a system of small producers, each dependent for his success upon his own skill and character, to one in which the great mass of those engaged must accept the direction of a few." [49] Under this "Jeffersonian" view, simple expansion is different from the actual creation of a new product, process, or service. It can be more readily assumed that an increase in demand will induce someone other than the monopolist to enter the market to fill the demand; thus, society can reap the economic benefits of increased capacity as well as the social benefits of diffused economic power. This view is consistent with the statement of Senator Hoar, one of the authors of the Sherman Act, that monopolization includes "the use of means which make it impossible for other persons to engage in fair competition;" [50] small firms are less likely, purely because of their size rather than any inefficiency in their operations, to continuously expand to meet anticipated demand.

On the other hand, the FTC's *du Pont (TiO₂)* decision reflects the ascendant concern with economic efficiency. It also reflects the efficiencianados' faith in the marketplace to yield efficient results. According to this view, a monopolist will be the first to expand output only when the monopolist is the firm able to expand most efficiently. To prohibit such expansion will, from this perspective, inevitably result in less efficiency. Therefore, the argument goes, monopolists should be encouraged to expand because they expend fewer societal resources than others. Any subsequent reduction in output owing to monopoly power is highly speculative, and we have no way of predicting whether the loss society suffers from such a reduction would outweigh the gains it realizes from the monopolist's efficiency. The FTC appears to read "superior skill, foresight and industry" to mean "not predominantly motivated by inefficiency." From an efficiency perspective, this appears sensible, especially when combined with the bias against government intervention in the marketplace characteristic of many advocates of this school of thought.

Somewhat different concerns arise when a monopolist's expansion is due to asset acquisition, rather than internal growth. [51]

product that we want to avoid any interference with the defendant because of the cost-saving potential of capacity expansion.

49. *Alcoa*, 148 F.2d at 427.

50. 21 Cong. Rec. 3152 (1890).

51. In the merger context, the Supreme Court has clearly indicated its preference for internal growth over expansion through acquisition. United States v. Philadelphia National Bank, 374 U.S. 321, 370 (1963).

The antitrust laws should treat asset acquisition and internal expansion identically where they occur before the defendant obtains monopoly power. For example, in *SCM Corp. v. Xerox Corp.*,[52] the Second Circuit accepted the plaintiff's argument that Xerox could reasonably have foreseen that its acquisition of key photocopying patents would give it monopoly power.[53] Nevertheless, Xerox contributed substantially to the research and development of this technology, and the court properly reasoned that "to impose antitrust liability upon Xerox would severely trample upon the incentives provided by our patent laws and thus undermine the entire patent system."[54] On the other hand, the court made it clear that a firm with pre-existing monopoly power violates § 2 when it "acquires a patent covering a substantial share of the same market." Similarly, liability would attach for any asset acquisition that allows the firm to maintain or expand its monopoly power. In so holding, *SCM v. Xerox* recognized that a monopolist might be the most efficient purchaser of an asset (in the sense that it might be able to put the asset to its highest valued use), but that those efficiency advantages are outweighed by the societal costs attendant the maintenance or expansion of monopoly power.[55]

(5) Using the FTC Act in monopolization cases.

The neo-populist concern for consumers views the permissibility of expanding to meet demand in a different light. Although the FTC wrote in *du Pont (TiO$_2$)* that "the essence of the competitive process is to induce firms to become more efficient *and to pass the benefits of the efficiency along to consumers*,"[56] Senator Sherman recognized that many of the trusts he sought to condemn might have lower costs but were nonetheless undesirable because the cost savings were not likely to be passed on to consumers.[57] It will generally require a very significant cost reduction before a monopolist's price will fall below that charged by a firm with higher costs that faces vigorous competition. The monopolist's ability to use its superior financial resources to take advantage of expanding markets before its rivals can act therefore will not usually redound to the benefit of the majority of Americans—i.e., to consumers. As a result, neo-populists argue that firms should not be encouraged to preempt sales by other firms by undergoing an

52. 645 F.2d 1195 (2d Cir. 1981), cert. denied, 455 U.S. 1016 (1982).

53. This argument seems highly questionable. After all, IBM had notified Xerox that it was not interested in marketing photocopying machines because they were bad business risks. Id. at 1209.

54. Id.

55. Id. at 1205.

56. 96 F.T.C. at 750–51 (emphasis added).

57. 21 Cong. Rec. 2460 (1890).

expansion likely to result in monopoly power, unless the cost-saving efficiencies of the expansion are sufficiently large that consumers will benefit in the form of lower prices.

One foreseeable criticism of this neo-populist approach is its administrability. Faced with potential treble-damage liability, firms with market shares approaching monopoly levels will shy away from even the most innovative or efficient expansions for fear that years later some jury will decide that their costs savings were insufficient to benefit consumers. This argument is not without force, and suggests that the higher, more clear-cut standard of *du Pont (TiO₂)* should apply to cases brought under § 2 of the Sherman Act. Unlike Sherman Act cases, however, suits to enforce the Federal Trade Commission Act can only be brought by the government and can only lead to prospective equitable relief, and not to penalties or money damages. The likelihood of an adverse *in terrorem* effect is thus significantly reduced, and consumers would benefit if the Federal Trade Commission forbade monopoly-creating expansions that do not lead to significant cost savings to consumers as an "unfair method of competition" in violation of § 5 of the FTC Act.[58]

The FTC Act might also be profitably employed to attack long-term monopolies that appear to be impervious to erosion by new entry.[59] In litigation under § 2 of the Sherman Act where the defendant has not engaged in blatantly illegal conduct, the government bears the burden of proving a negative: that the defendant's acquisition or maintenance of monopoly power was *not* due to superior skill, foresight and industry. Judge Charles Wyzanski, a noted antitrust jurist who presided over the trial in *Grinnell*, wrote that evidence showing that the defendant has maintained market dominance for some time should create a rebuttable presumption that the defendant is guilty of unlawful monopolization. The defendant would then have the burden of proving that its dominance was achieved due to superior skill or efficiency, or other legitimate causes. Shifting the burden is appropriate, Wyzanski reasoned, because his experience convinced him that durable monopolies were inevitably the result of unlawful acts; thus, the government should not have the expensive and time-consuming burden of proving such acts in every case.[60]

Whether or not Judge Wyzanski's empirical observation is accurate, the question remains whether society must tolerate long-

---

58. 15 U.S.C. § 45.

59. With the growth of global competition, this problem may be of lesser significance today than it was in earlier times.

60. United States v. United Shoe Machinery Corp., 110 F.Supp. 295, 341–43 (D. Mass. 1953) aff'd per curiam, 347 U.S. 521 (1954).

term monopoly power in order to induce firms to achieve superior skill. As with the specific problem of expansion, the fear of criminal penalties or treble damages would have a chilling effect on vigorous competition if Wyzanski's suggestion were adopted. Thus, another approach to the problem of long-term monopolies would be to construe § 5 of the FTC Act to empower the Commission to divest such monopolies where it concludes that a more competitive structure would benefit consumers by leading to lower prices for products of similar quality while retaining incentives for continued innovation.[61]

(6) Remedies for monopolization.

The *Alcoa* litigation provides an excellent case study of the remedial issues involved in monopolization cases. The original 1912 consent decree, ordering Alcoa to cease the improper behavior that allowed it to acquire monopoly power, completely failed to provide consumers with the benefits of competition in the aluminum industry. This failing illustrates why the remedy of divestiture (requiring a monopolist to sell off most of its assets to separate firms that will proceed to compete in the market) is desirable in § 2 cases. Divestiture allows the court to restructure an industry and then withdraw from the scene as the new firms compete with each other.[62]

On the other hand, divestiture has its limits. A firm may need to achieve a minimum size and obtain competent management as well as an assured source of supply in order to compete effectively in the market. For example, consider the remedy fashioned after the Second Circuit's 1945 decision that Alcoa had again monopolized in violation of § 2. Relief was deferred until after World War II. During the war, the government built large aluminum facilities, which it then sold off to two separate firms, Reynolds and Kaiser.[63] By 1948, Alcoa's market share had dropped to approximately 50%.[64] The district court ordered Alcoa to divest itself of its Alcan Canadian subsidiary, but allowed the

---

61. See Chapter 1 for a discussion of the argument, made forcefully by Professor Michael Porter, that a competitive structure is more likely to result in continued innovation.

62. Because divestiture is so drastic and thus fervently opposed by defendants, the courts have not been particularly aggressive in effectively using the remedy. Few successful monopolization cases resulted in meaningful divestiture remedies, and a 1968 study showed little difference between the concentration levels in the United States and England, see Richard Posner and Frank Easterbrook, Antitrust 424 (1980), even though the England had no procedure to require a monopolist's divestiture until 1965 and, even then, such a remedy requires approval of both houses of Parliament. See Valentine Korah, Competition Law of Britain and the Common Market 32–33 (1975).

63. United States v. Aluminum Co. of America, 91 F.Supp. 333, 354–55 (S.D.N.Y. 1950).

64. Id. at 364.

firm to keep both of its U.S aluminum plants. The judge was particularly concerned that Alcoa's East St. Louis plant might not be able to obtain necessary supplies if it were not integrated into Alcoa's operation. Between the court's order and the fortuity of the government's war efforts, Alcoa now faced three new competitors—Kaiser, Reynolds, and Alcan.[65]

Even this sort of industrial restructuring may not be sufficient. For example, in *United States v. American Tobacco Co.*,[66] the court overseeing the dissolution of the tobacco trust[67] approved a divestiture plan resulting in four separate companies. The court rejected objections that the plan should require further disintegration of the trust, even though the court recognized that the common stock ownership (shareholders in the original American Tobacco corporation would receive stock in the new companies as well) might cause the new firms to yield to the "natural temptation to co-operate which such common stockholding may be calculated to induce," notwithstanding an injunction against such cooperation. The basis for the court's decision to allow only four companies was that this sort of oligopoly would not itself be considered "repugnant to the anti-trust statute."[68] Future events demonstrated the need for injunctive relief to go beyond simply ensuring that the new industrial market structure was not itself illegal—in 1946 the Supreme Court found three of the four companies guilty of conspiring to monopolize.[69]

The judiciary's experience with restructuring these industries teaches several lessons about monopolization remedies. The trial court's solicitude for the economies of scale inherent in the industry demonstrates that, in fashioning a remedy, judges must again wrestle with the trade-off between a more efficient monopolist and a less efficient group of competitors. (Because of the new entry, the *Alcoa* judge was arguably spared from resolving this dilemma.) Moreover, because of the time required to litigate major monopolization cases, marketplace forces may overtake the courts in remedying the problem.

Because divestiture remains the most effective remedy for monopolization, however, it is imperative that the courts be able to employ it in § 2 cases. In *California v. American Stores Co.*,[70] the Supreme Court rejected the Ninth Circuit's view that the Clayton Act permits courts to order divestiture only in cases

---

65. Id. at 417–19.

66. 191 Fed. 371 (S.D.N.Y. 1911).

67. See 221 U.S. 106 (1911), discussed above in subsection (2), which found that the trust violated § 2 of the Sherman Act.

68. 191 Fed. at 376–77.

69. American Tobacco Co. v. United States, 328 U.S. 781 (1946). The case is discussed in section H(2).

70. 495 U.S. 271 (1990).

brought by the federal government, and not in those brought by other plaintiffs. Instead, the Court read § 16 of the Clayton Act, which authorizes the courts to issue "injunctive relief ... against threatened loss or damage by a violation of the antitrust laws" in cases brought by private plaintiffs, to extend to all types of equitable relief usually available in the courts, including divestiture.[71]

Section B: Identifying Monopoly Power

A firm cannot be guilty of monopolization in violation of § 2 unless it has monopoly power. Without monopoly power, a firm has no ability to unilaterally raise prices or reduce output or quality. (Efforts by firms to act in concert with others to accomplish these results are considered in subsequent chapters.) Without power, the firm cannot misallocate resources, transfer wealth from consumers to producers, deny equal economic opportunity to others, or centralize and abuse discretionary power. Identifying those firms that possess monopoly power, however, can be a difficult task.

In economic terms, a firm with monopoly power can choose to gradually raise prices while gradually lowering output or to lower prices and increase output. The demand curve for the monopolist's product (the graphic depiction of the effect of price changes on sales) is said to be "inelastic." At the opposite extreme, the small farmer who attempts to charge more than the market price will not be able to sell a single kernel of corn, and the farmer will be able to sell all of his crop whether it is offered at the market price or at some discount. The demand curve for the farmer's corn is "highly elastic."

For many firms, however, even rough estimates of the demand curves for their products are difficult, if not impossible, to establish reliably. Hence, antitrust law has developed three principal proxies to identify firms with market power: profits, conduct, and market structure.

(1) Profits as evidence of power.

A firm with persistent excess profits probably has market power. Without such power, the firm would be unable to maintain those profits because others would enter the industry to

---

71. Although *American Stores* involved a challenge to a merger, its rationale applies equally to monopolization litigation because § 16 of the Clayton Act is the general remedial provision for suits brought by private plaintiffs under any of the antitrust laws.

compete with the firm lowering prices (and profit margins) in order to attract consumers.

Basing a finding of power on profits, however, must be done carefully. Profits must be maintained at a high level for some time; a short-term increase in profits may merely signify business success, and the market will indeed respond with new entries. In innovative markets, firms may continue to earn high profits by continually introducing new products or processes that give them a competitive advantage. The profit levels must also be in excess of those found generally in the economy. If American industries are generally enjoying high profits, a firm that is keeping up with others does not necessarily have economic power.

Conversely, as Judge Hand observed in *Alcoa*, the absence of profits does not exclude the possibility of market power.[1] A monopolist's balance sheet could show normal, or even subnormal, profit levels for a number of reasons. First, accounting practices may underestimate profit levels. To measure profits, one must first determine revenues and costs; both of those figures must then be apportioned when a firm manufactures multiple products. Apportionments of items like administrative overhead according to generally accepted accounting principles may not necessarily reflect economic reality.

Second, a monopolist may be operating inefficiently and passing on higher costs to consumers. Consumers thus suffer, even though the monopolist's profit level may not appear unreasonable. As Judge Hand explained "possession of unchallenged economic power deadens initiative, discourages thrift and depresses energy; ... immunity from competition is a narcotic, and rivalry is a stimulant, to industrial progress."[2]

Third, when the ownership of a monopoly has changed, the prior owners may have sold at an inflated price that reflects the opportunity to exploit consumers. Thus, the new owner may charge monopoly prices, but may not show high profits while it pays off the debt incurred when purchasing the company.[3]

(2) Monopoly conduct as evidence of power.

The second proxy used to identify the existence of monopoly power is conduct. A court may find that a defendant possesses monopoly power if the defendant acts consistently with the way a

1. United States v. Aluminum Co. of America, 148 F.2d. 416, 427 (2d Cir. 1945).

2. Id.

3. Judge Hand offered another policy reason to reject low profits as a defense in § 2 cases: constant judicial and executive monitoring of a firm would be necessary to ensure that over the years the firm's profitability did not rise to a level sufficient to justify a monopolization charge. Id.

monopolist would be expected to act, and inconsistently with the way a firm facing vigorous competition would probably act.

The conduct in question need not necessarily be illegal to show power, just as legal conduct does not necessarily establish lack of power. For example, du Pont raised prices in the TiO_2 case, in order to finance what the FTC found was an efficient expansion of capacity to meet growing demands.[4] Although the FTC held that du Pont's conduct was lawful, du Pont's ability to raise prices in order to finance new projects demonstrated that du Pont did have monopoly power. No matter how worthy the project, a firm facing vigorous competition that tried to raise its price to finance the project would lose all its business to rivals. Conversely, in *U.S. Steel*, the Supreme Court found that the defendant was not a monopolist because it expended a great deal of effort trying to organize a price-fixing cartel of steel producers.[5] Such conduct, as we shall see in Chapter 4, was clearly illegal under § 1 of the Sherman Act; nevertheless, the Court reasoned, a firm that had monopoly power could control prices by itself and need not waste time setting up a cartel.

(3) Market structure as evidence of power.

The third and most common means of identifying monopoly power is the structural approach: a relevant market is defined, and the existence of monopoly power "ordinarily may be inferred from the predominant share of the market."[6] To appreciate the structural approach, imagine a scenario where a firm wishes to increase profits by reducing industry-wide output by 10%. A 10% reduction unilaterally executed by a firm with 90% of the market would require the firm to cut its own production by only 1/9th. To expand capacity to bring industry-wide production back to normal levels, the firm's smaller competitors would have to double their own combined output (from 10 to 20%), a difficult and unlikely prospect. In contrast, a firm with only 30% of the market would have to suffer a 1/3 cutback in production in order to unilaterally reduce overall output by 10%; its rivals, who currently had 70% of the market, could return output to normal levels merely by increasing their own combined sales by 1/7.[7]

4. E.I. du Pont de Nemours & Co. (TiO₂), 96 F.T.C. 653, 747 (1980).

5. United States v. United States Steel Corp., 251 U.S. 417, 444–45 (1920).

6. United States v. Grinnell, 384 U.S. 563, 571 (1966).

7. This model assumes, of course, that the market has been defined with some precision, which often may not be the case. A firm with a small share of "the market" may be able to exercise power if its products are sufficiently different from those of the other firms in "the market." A firm with a large share of "the market" may not be able to successfully reduce output and raise prices because consumers will shift to other goods. Thus, the three-tiered approach suggested by Judge Hand in *Al-*

In the *Alcoa* case, for example, Judge Hand suggested a three-tiered approach: a firm with a 30% market share does not have monopoly power; a firm with a 60% share may have such power; and a firm with a 90% share does have monopoly power.[8] *Broadway Delivery Corp. v. United Parcel Service of America, Inc.* suggests that firms with over 70% of the market have monopoly power; absent "strong evidence" to the contrary (presumably evidence of excess profits, conduct evincing monopoly power, or direct economic evidence of power), firms with less than 50% of the market do not have such power.[9]

When the defendant's market share is below 50%, courts are divided as to whether the plaintiff is foreclosed as a matter of law from proving monopolization, or, if not, how much evidence is necessary to overcome a presumption that the defendant lacks monopoly power.[10] Some courts have suggested that the so-called "rebuttable" presumption that a firm with less than half the market does not possess monopoly power is really conclusive. An illustrative case is *Dimmitt Agri Industries, Inc. v. CPC International, Inc.*[11] Noting that no case had found monopolization when the defendant's market share fell below 50%,[12] the Fifth Circuit rejected the plaintiff's effort to meet *Broadway Delivery's* requirement of "strong evidence," although the court acknowledged that "Dimmitt can, with some justice, claim to have presented one of the clearest . . . cases supportive of a monopolizing intent that has been presented to a court." [13]

The defendant in *Dimmitt Agri* was the leading manufacturer of cornstarch and corn syrup (and also the successor corporation to Corn Products, which in 1916 had been found guilty by Judge Hand of monopolizing the manufacture of starch and glucose [14]). The industry was highly concentrated, with five firms accounting for 71% of the market, and demand for the product was inelastic.[15] Dimmitt persuaded a jury that its new technology allowed it to produce products at lower cost than the established firms, that

coa, infra, should not be invoked unthinkingly, especially in cases raising difficult market definition questions. See Eleanor Fox & Lawrence Sullivan, Cases and Materials on Antitrust 123 (1989).

   8. *Alcoa*, 148 F.2d at 424.

   9. 651 F.2d 122, 129 (2d Cir.), cert. denied, 454 U.S. 968 (1981).

   10. See Phillip Areeda & Herbert Hovenkamp, Antitrust Law 519–23 (Supp. 1991).

   11. 679 F.2d 516 (5th Cir. 1982), cert. denied, 460 U.S. 1082 (1983).

   12. Id. at 528 & n.11.

   13. Id. at 524.

   14. United States v. Corn Products Refining Co., 234 Fed. 964 (S.D.N.Y. 1916), appeal dism'd, 249 U.S. 621 (1919). The market definition aspects of *Corn Products* are discussed below in section C(1).

   15. Probably because corn products are used as inputs and represent only a small percentage of the total cost of the finished product, buyers will not significantly reduce their purchases in the face of significant price increases.

demand equalled or exceeded existing industry capacity, and that it had been excluded from the market due to the defendants' anticompetitive conduct. The plaintiff also provided evidence that CPC was the price leader, with the other firms following CPC's lead in setting prices at predatory levels to exclude the plaintiff.[16] Most significantly, Dimmitt produced a number of incriminating memoranda discovered in CPC's files. A confidential CPC strategic report endorsed a policy of using prices to ensure "long-term strength of position as a clear priority over short-term profitability." Another memorandum indicated that in order to stabilize corn syrup prices, "we must realize we can go into a negative profit situation for an extended period of time.... I am sure that all competition will announce new market policies within a few hours after our announcement." The same document stressed the need for unprofitable price reductions so that "our competitors and customers fully understand that we are determined to be the price leader."[17]

Nevertheless, the court of appeals reversed the jury's verdict, finding as a matter of law that CPC's market share was too low to sustain a finding of monopolization. The evidence showed, the court explained, that the "industry is only an oligopoly, with CPC as its price leader." Therefore, CPC's power "is dependent upon joint action by at least some of its rivals."[18] Because the jury had found that CPC had not conspired to monopolize, the verdict for actual monopolization could not stand.

The court's analysis seems flawed as a matter of antitrust doctrine. In fact, the court's restatement of the legal precedents points in the opposite direction of its holding. The opinion's doctrinal section begins with the settled black letter law from *Cellophane*, defining monopoly power as "the power to control price or exclude competition."[19] It goes on to conclude that market shares in CPC's range are "insufficient—*at least absent other compelling structural evidence*—as a matter of law to support monopolization."[20] Dimmitt, however, met both of these standards. Its evidence showed that CPC had established itself as a price leader, which meant that it had the power to control price. To be sure, CPC's power depended on the willingness of others to follow its lead, but the same would be true for a dominant firm

---

16. The court remanded the case to the district court for reconsideration of the question whether CPC's prices were below cost to such an extent that § 2's ban on predatory pricing was violated. For discussion of this issue, see section D of this chapter.

17. 679 F.2d at 522–23.

18. Id. at 531.

19. Id. at 525. (citing United States v. E.I. du Pont de Nemours & Co., 351 U.S. 377, 391 (1956) ("*Cellophane*")). The case is discussed below in section C(2).

20. Id. at 529 (emphasis added).

with 75% of the market. Although it is less *likely* that oligopolists will follow the leader than "pygmies" in a market with a giant, Dimmitt's evidence showed that CPC did, in fact, exercise price leadership. Persuasive evidence that the defendant operated in an oligopolistic market, with no effective substitute products, inelastic demand, barriers to entry, and a clear pattern of price leadership would seem to be "compelling structural evidence" sufficient to overcome the general presumption that firms with low market shares cannot possess monopoly power. Structural evidence is, in the end, merely a proxy to determine whether the defendant really had monopoly, price-raising power. Dimmitt met that burden through more direct evidence.

There are three logical explanations for what really happened in the corn syrup marketplace. One is that CPC management misjudged the market, and that although they tried hard to monopolize, they really could not hope to do so. Another is that CPC did hope to eliminate the plaintiff and become the price leader, but only through lawful, aggressive price competition. (CPC executives testified to this effect, but apparently the jury did not find them credible.) Finally, CPC's strategic planners may have been more familiar with their own marketplace than the Fifth Circuit, and thus may have understood that CPC could exercise power over price in spite of its 25% market share, by establishing itself as the price leader. The third explanation seems most plausible; at least, the jury thought so.

The best defense for the Fifth Circuit's position in *Dimmitt Agri*—that a 25% market share is insufficient as a matter of law to establish a monopolization claim—is an unstated concern that a blanket rule is necessary to prevent wasteful discovery and litigation costs as many plaintiffs pursue claims that will ultimately prove (unlike Dimmitt's claim) to be meritless. This approach to antitrust doctrine, however, uses the proverbial axe when a scalpel would be more appropriate. It bars meritorious cases such as Dimmitt's and is not *necessary* to screen out insubstantial cases.

Alternatively, the substantive antitrust law should continue to focus, as *Cellophane* requires, on whether the defendant has the power to control prices. Ordinarily, defendants with market shares well below 50% will not have such power; thus, undisputed evidence of low market share should entitle a defendant to summary judgment, absent evidence presented by the plaintiff to create a disputed factual issue by showing why and how the defendant does have price-controlling power. The trial judge can stay voluminous or burdensome discovery of documents intended to elicit evidence concerning the defendant's intent for a reasonable period of time, limiting the plaintiff's discovery to evidence supporting a plausible theory as to how the defendant exercises price-controlling or competition-excluding power, and allowing the defendant the opportunity to demonstrate that, as a matter of law, no reasonable person could conclude that it has monopoly power. If the plaintiff finds evidence sufficient to warrant a trial, either because of doubts about the defendant's proposed market definition, or because conduct evidence (such as a pattern of price leadership by a leading oligopolist) creates a factual dispute as to whether the defendant can control price, then the plaintiff should be able to proceed with reasonable discovery of evidence concerning the defendant's intent.   This approach allows plaintiffs to prevail in cases like *Dimmitt Agri*, while providing a way to screen out most meritless monopolization claims.[21]

This alternative appears consistent with the Supreme Court's recent opinion in *Eastman Kodak Co. v. Image Technical Services, Inc.*[22] In that case, Image Tech, a firm that serviced and maintained photocopiers, challenged Kodak's policy of selling replacement parts for Kodak photocopying machines only to buyers of Kodak equipment who either used Kodak's own service or repaired their own machines.   Kodak's policy effectively excluded Image Tech and other independents from dealing with these customers, and the complaint alleged, *inter alia*, that this practice constituted an attempt to monopolize the market for repairing Kodak machines in violation of § 2.   Kodak argued that because the plaintiffs conceded that it lacked market power in the sale of equipment, it was entitled to summary judgment: as a matter of economic theory, a firm without power in the equipment market could not exploit consumers by charging too much or providing inferior quality for service.   The Supreme Court rejected this argument and remanded for trial.

Like Dimmitt, Image Tech presented evidence that suggested that, for some consumers, Kodak possessed the power to "control price or exclude competition."   This included direct evidence that Kodak's service was more costly and of a lower quality than service provided by some independents.[23]   Responding to Kodak's argument that competition among equipment sellers precluded exploitation of consumers in servicing, Image Tech argued that certain aspects of the market allowed Kodak nonetheless to exercise monopoly power.   Consumers would not necessarily desert

---

21. Special thanks to my proceduralist colleague Tom Mengler for his insights concerning this issue.

22. 112 S.Ct. 2072 (1992). The case concerned allegations that Kodak unlawfully tied the sale of replacement parts to its photocopying machines to the provision of repair and maintenance services on the machines, in violation of § 1, and attempted to monopolize in violation of § 2. The first claim is discussed below in several subsections of Chapter 5, section H.

23. Id. at 2081.

Kodak for other equipment makers because of exploitation in servicing, because it is quite costly and complex to gain information about the "lifecycle pricing" of a photocopying machine, and, once a Kodak machine has been purchased, the cost of switching to another machine was too high to prevent exploitation.[24] Departing from the approach taken by the Fifth Circuit in *Dimmitt Agri*, the Supreme Court rejected any blanket rules limiting proof of monopoly power. "In determining the existence of market power, and specifically 'the responsiveness of the sales of one product to price changes of the other,'" the Court noted, its approach has been to "examine[ ] closely the economic reality of the market at issue."[25] The majority in *Kodak* insisted on a fuller development of the record, notwithstanding complaints by the dissent that allowing plaintiffs such as Image Tech to go forward to trial on claims that defendants like Kodak have monopoly power "threatens to release a torrent of litigation and a flood of commercial intimidation that will do much more harm than good to enforcement of the antitrust laws and to genuine competition."[26]

Similarly, *Kodak* applied hornbook monopolization law in rejecting the defendant's argument that, despite evidence that it had the power to control prices in its own replacement parts and servicing Kodak machines, it should nonetheless be entitled to summary judgment on the § 2 claim because, as a matter of law, a single brand of a product or service can never be a relevant market.[27] Properly taking the evidence in the light most favorable to the plaintiff, the Court noted that Kodak parts and service are not interchangeable with other manufacturer's parts and service. By emphasizing instead the need for a "factual inquiry into the 'commercial realities' faced by consumers,"[28] the Court rejected the creation of prophylactic rules that sacrifice legitimate

24. Id. at 2085–87.

25. Id. at 2082 (quoting *Cellophane*, 351 U.S. at 400) (citations omitted).

26. Id. at 2094 (Scalia, J., dissenting).

Dimmitt Agri is arguably distinguishable from *Kodak*. *Dimmitt Agri* involved allegations of predatory pricing, and *Kodak* reaffirmed the court's desire to avoid deterring legitimate price cutting by creating rules that would "'chill the very conduct the antitrust laws are designed to protect.'" 112 S.Ct. at 2088 (quoting Matsushita Electric Industrial Co. v. Zenith Radio Corp., 475 U.S. 574, 594 (1986)). Kodak's conduct, in contrast to price cutting, was "simply not one that appears always or almost always to enhance competition, and therefore to warrant a legal presumption in its favor." Id.

Although this discussion could justify a blanket rule immunizing defendants in predatory pricing cases where initial market analysis indicates a lack of market power, the general skepticism toward unthinking adoption of economic theory displayed in *Kodak* suggests that, instead, courts should simply exercise great care in demanding that plaintiffs in predatory pricing cases present, as the Fifth Circuit purported to demand in *Dimmitt Agri*, *compelling* structural evidence that the defendant exercised power over price.

27. 112 S.Ct. at 2090.

28. Id. (quoting *Grinnell*, 384 U.S. at 572).

§ 2 claimants because of fears by antitrust minimalists that litigation may deter some lawful conduct.

———

The *Alcoa* case typifies the structural approach to identifying monopoly power. There, the court found that Alcoa wielded monopoly power because for some time it had manufactured 90% of the virgin aluminum ingot sold in the United States. Alcoa denied that it had power; it alleged that it faced competition from both importers and sellers of recycled aluminum. In other words, while the court determined that the relevant market was virgin aluminum ingot sold in this country, the defendant essentially argued that the relevant market was virgin and recycled aluminum sold anywhere in the world. How the market is defined, then, becomes the critical question in many antitrust cases.

Section C: Market Definition

(1) The general problem.

Market definition is the process of identifying those sellers who are in a position to keep their prices down, expand their output, and maintain the quality of their products so as to prevent the defendant from successfully raising its price, lowering its output, or reducing the quality of its product. Although we usually think of markets in terms of products (a market for "beer," or for "all beverages") or geographic areas (a local, regional, or national market), the key inquiry is the search for potential rivals who can ensure that competition is maintained.

Three types of firms can pose the type of competitive threat that prevents monopolistic behavior. One category includes firms whose products compete with those sold by the defendant. Were the defendant to attempt to exercise economic power (by raising price, for example), consumers would switch to the products sold by these rival sellers. A second category consists of those who sell in other geographic locations. If consumers are willing to patronize these establishments instead of the defendant's, the relevant market must be defined so as to include them. A third category includes sellers who are not currently competing with the defendant, but who are potential competitors. Were the defendant to attempt to exploit consumers, these sellers would either move into the geographic area where the defendant's customers shop, switch their current manufacturing facilities to begin to produce goods that will substitute with the defendant's, or quickly commence production of substitute goods from new facilities.[1]

(2) The *Cellophane* test and its critics.

Perfect market definition is virtually impossible. No firm has such a complete monopoly that it can raise prices without losing *any* consumers to a substitute product, and few firms face competition from rival brands or products that are so substitutable that *all* consumers will switch. The key question for antitrust doctrine is the degree to which products must be substitutable in order to be considered part of the same market. In *United States v. E.I. du Pont de Nemours & Co. (Cellophane)*,[2] the Supreme Court introduced the economic concept of cross-elasticity of demand to answer this question. This concept simply measures the degree to which consumers will switch from one product to another in the event that the price or quality of one of the items changes, while the other remains the same. A high elasticity of demand occurs where a small increase in the price of Product A will cause a large shift of patronage to Product B. The government alleged that du Pont was a monopolist, because it controlled 75% of the market for cellophane. The defendant countered that the relevant market was not cellophane but flexible wrapping material (including Saran Wrap, wax paper, and a host of other products). If the defendant's market definition were upheld, the § 2 case would have been defeated because du Pont only had 17% of the broader market. In *Cellophane*, the Supreme Court ruled for du Pont, holding that cellophane and other flexible wrapping material were in the same market because there was a high degree of cross-elasticity between these products.[3]

In measuring cross-elasticity of demand, an initial question concerns *which* consumers are the focus of the inquiry. In *Cellophane*, the record indicated that although for many consumers there was a high cross-elasticity between cellophane and other flexible wrapping material at current prices, tobacco companies had a marked preference for cellophane.[4] Does this make cellophane a relevant product market by itself? The Court held that it did not. On the other hand, in *United States v. Grinnell Corp.*,[5]

1. The need to focus on sellers, and not products, is illustrated by the Supreme Court's decision in United States v. Grinnell Corp., 384 U.S. 563 (1966). In that case, the Court included sellers of various different types of burglar and fire alarms within the market of accredited central station services. The Court found that to compete effectively, sellers must offer all or nearly all of these services. Id. at 571–75. Thus, even though an automatic sprinkler system clearly does not compete with a burglar alarm, *firms* that sell one do compete with firms that sell the other.

2.   351 U.S. 377 (1956).

3.   Id. at 394–95, 400.

4.   Id. at 399 (75–80% of cigarettes are wrapped in cellophane).

5.   384 U.S. 563 (1966).

the Court found that accredited central station alarm services[6] were a separate market because many customers strongly preferred them to potential substitutes (such as security guards or audible alarm systems).

These two cases are easily reconciled by understanding the concept of arbitrage. Where arbitrage exists, those with a marked preference for one product cannot be exploited by a defendant who also seeks the patronage of more price-sensitive customers, because the latter group of fickle customers could buy the product at a low price and resell (arbitrage) it to those willing to pay more. To illustrate, if du Pont tried to exploit the tobacco companies' particular need for cellophane by charging them a higher price than that charged to butchers (who were fairly price-sensitive), butchers could simply order a large amount of cellophane, in excess of the amount they needed to wrap meat, and then resell it at a profit to tobacco companies.[7] In contrast, *Grinnell* properly recognized that those with a special need for accredited alarm services constituted a separate market; services, unlike many goods, cannot be arbitraged because the purchaser of a service cannot easily "resell" the service to a third party. Thus, Grinnell could successfully engage in price discrimination, charging those with a particular need for their services a higher price than that charged other customers.

The *Cellophane* model is a fairly good one for a court that wishes to determine whether a merger or a new agreement will *increase* the market power of the defendant(s). Indeed, the Justice Department essentially adopted this methodology in its 1984 Merger Guidelines. The Justice Department guidelines suggest that the sellers of Product A and Product B belong in the same market if a one-year increase of 5% in the price of Product A would induce so many consumers to shift to Product B that the manufacturers of Product A would find it unprofitable to continue the price increase.[8] The problem with *Cellophane*, however, is that it fails to account for the distinct possibility that an alleged monopolist's current prices *already* reflect monopoly power.

6. A central station alarm service installs hazard-detecting devices on the protected premises, which automatically transmit an electric signal to a central station, staffed 24 hours per day. Upon receipt of a signal, the central station dispatches guards to the premises or notifies police or fire authorities. Accredited services are those approved by insurance underwriters. Id. at 566–67.

7. Alternatively, a third party could buy cellophane from the butchers and resell it to the tobacco companies.

8. 1984 Department of Justice Merger Guidelines, 4 Trade Reg. Rep. (CCH) ¶ 13,103, at 20,551 (June 14, 1984). This essential framework has been maintained in joint guidelines published by the Justice Department and the FTC in 1992. See Merger Guidelines—1992, 4 Trade Reg. Rep. (CCH) § 13,104.

Thus, decades before *Cellophane*, in *United States v. Corn Products Refining*,[9] Judge Learned Hand recognized that, because of consumer income and preferences, every monopolist faces some price level at which it will lose so many customers that further increases become unprofitable. The issue in *Corn Products* was whether "refined grits" competed with "brewers grits." Noting that there was no difference in the quality of the two products that would lead purchasers to prefer one over the other, Judge Hand nevertheless found that the relevant market included only "refined grits" (where the defendant had a large market share) because refined grits were less expensive to produce than brewers grits. Of course, the price advantage enjoyed by a monopolist of refined grits would allow it to raise prices only up to the level where any further increase would lead consumers to switch to brewers grits. At that price level, the cross-elasticity of demand between the two products would be high. As Judge Hand concluded, "[s]uch a monopoly is therefore only a limited one, but within the limits [of the cost of production] it may be a true one."[10]

If cross-elasticity is to be used in defining markets in § 2 cases, one must not ask, as *Cellophane* implicitly did, whether the products are reasonably interchangeable at *current* prices. Rather, one must ask whether the products would be reasonably interchangeable if both were priced at competitive levels. Determining a product's "competitive" price is very difficult. Moreover, this focus on price and cost ignores the argument, suggested by Judge Hand's description of monopoly as a "narcotic" in *Alcoa*, that rivalry is an incentive to innovation and quality for all firms, including those whose products may compete in some ways with qualitatively distinct goods.[11] Thus, *Cellophane* may not be a particularly helpful contribution to the problem of market definition.[12]

(3) Alternatives to *Cellophane*.

Rather than focusing on the relative current prices of two products, Professor Donald Turner suggested that market definition analysis should examine the relation between costs and

9. 234 Fed. 964 (S.D.N.Y. 1916).

10. Id. at 975. The same analysis applies to geographic market definition, which is discussed below. In *Alcoa*, for example, Judge Hand recognized that imported aluminum could compete with Alcoa's product, but that tariffs and oceanic transportation made imports more costly than domestic aluminum.

Again, the monopoly power was limited, but, within those limits, Alcoa did exercise power. 148 F.2d at 426.

11. 148 F.2d at 427.

12. The recent decision in *Kodak* suggests that the Supreme Court may now recognize this. See subsection (6) below.

prices.[13]   In cases like *Corn Products*, where the defendant has lower costs than putative rivals that offer similar products at similar prices, the high-cost competitors should not be placed in the same market.   (It is important to keep in mind that the possession of monopoly power, especially if attributable to lower costs, does not mean that a firm is guilty of monopolization in violation of § 2.)

Where the defendant has both higher prices and higher costs than its competitors, however, those rivals might be included in the same market.   If consumers think of an expensive, high-quality product as a substitute for an inexpensive item of inferior quality, none of the sellers of either product will be able to exploit the situation, and they should all be included in the market. Thus, *Cellophane* properly rejected the government's argument that markets should be limited to "substantially fungible" goods sold at the same price, and instead ruled that markets should include any goods that are reasonably interchangeable "for the purposes for which they are produced—price, use, and qualities considered." [14]

Turner's analysis suggests that the Court's opinion in *Grinnell*, while reaching the right result, was too simplistic.   Consumers preferred central station service alarms (the market that the defendant allegedly monopolized) because of their superior quality, but may have been willing to purchase in-house alarm systems of lower quality if their prices were low enough.   The Court observed, for example, that users of Grinnell's services received substantial discounts on insurance premiums.   If the inferior products were so much cheaper than Grinnell's that buyers would realistically consider buying the cheaper product and paying higher insurance premiums, then Grinnell competed with the firms offering the lesser products.   On the other hand, the Court also noted that many buyers could not risk the serious interruption of business resulting from a loss that could be avoided by use of Grinnell's products.   Even more important, many businesses could not obtain insurance without accredited central station alarms, and thus would not consider purchasing substitutes of inferior quality.[15]   This evidence suggests that those substitutes were properly excluded from the market and thus that the Court's focus on consumer preferences for superior quality products was not too narrow.[16]

13. Antitrust Policy and the Cellophane Case, 70 Harv. L. Rev. 281 (1956).

14. 351 U.S. at 404.

15. 384 U.S. at 575.

16. Where higher prices do not reflect higher costs, but solely a strong consumer preference for a certain product, the market should be drawn narrowly. Thus, world championship box-

(4) Geographic market definition.

The process for defining the relevant geographic market is similar to product market definition. Although we normally think of the market in terms of area, the real focus is on *sellers*, not cities, regions, or countries. This distinction often creates confusion. Justice Abe Fortas' dissent in *Grinnell*, for example, noted that consumers purchase alarm services only from local companies, and therefore challenged the majority's finding that the relevant market for alarm services was national.[17] The majority responded that "the business of providing such a service is operated on a national level."[18] The majority was correct if it meant that the only way to compete effectively in any local market was to develop on a national scale. In that event, the only sellers who could limit Grinnell's efforts to exploit consumers would be other national companies, even if each individual consumer could only turn to those who offered the services locally. There was some indication, however, that nationwide service was not necessary to compete. For example, the majority did not adequately respond to Fortas' point that Grinnell had lost money in 20 cities where it was the only accredited central station service but faced competition from local firms.[19] If by contrast, the facts showed that Grinnell was able to achieve monopoly profits in places where it faced little competition of any kind, then the dissent's point was well taken.

Special problems arise when considering whether a market should include foreign as well as domestic manufacturers. If foreign firms are permitted to import their goods freely and the supply of such goods is seemingly unlimited, a world market should be defined; in such cases, a defendant would need a huge share of worldwide sales to have monopoly power.[20] If, on the other hand, tariffs or quotas are imposed, imports should have limited weight in defining the market. As *Alcoa* noted, a tariff gives the dominant domestic firm substantial power—it can raise

---

ing is considered to comprise a market separate from other major professional boxing. See International Boxing Club v. United States, 358 U.S. 242 (1959).

17. 384 U.S. at 587–88.

18. Id. at 575.

19. Id. at 592.

20. The market should be deemed worldwide, even in the absence of imports, where U.S. firms sell both here and abroad at a price set by international demand. In order for this situation to occur, (1) transportation costs or trade barriers must be insignificant, permitting imports in response to price changes; (2) price discrimination between U.S. and foreign buyers must be infeasible due to arbitrage; and (3) U.S. firms must be willing and able to sell their entire output at the world price, rather than competing among themselves by lowering the price to U.S. buyers. (My thanks to economist Paul Godek for stimulating my thoughts on this issue.)

its prices up to the amount of the tariff.[21]   Quotas are even more pernicious, for they limit the ability of foreign producers to increase output in response to price increases by domestic manufacturers.

Moreover, our trade legislation may seriously interfere with the ability of foreign firms to constrain the exercise of monopoly power by an American firm.   These laws subject foreign firms to special customs duties to be imposed to offset "dumping," which can occur when a foreign firm's export prices to the United States are below its prices at home.[22]   Where, as is often the case, European or Japanese consumers are more concerned with quality and less conscious of price, or where markets in foreign countries are less competitive for other reasons, the price level will likely be higher overseas than it is in the United States.   Thus, a foreign firm could pose a competitive threat to an American firm without exposing its products to anti-dumping duties only by lowering its prices at home as well as in the United States.   These laws therefore give American firms substantial protection from foreign competition.

Even without trade limitations, there are reasons to be cautious before defining world markets.   Many factors, including domestic and international politics and loyalty to long-time customers, may prevent a foreign manufacturer from suddenly shifting a significant portion of its production capacity to defeat an effort by a dominant U.S. firm to exploit American consumers. The Department of Justice 1984 Merger Guidelines took an appropriately realistic perspective, including within a given market only that foreign capacity "likely to be used in the [United States] market in response to [a 5%] increase in price that continues for one year."[23]

---

21.   148 F.2d at 426.

22.   The statutory provisions governing dumping are found at 19 U.S.C. §§ 1673–1677j. For a good brief description of the operation of these laws, see Gary Horlick, The United States Antidumping System, in Antidumping Law and Practice: A Comparative Study 99–166 (J. Jackson & E. Vermulst eds. 1989).

Dumping can also be shown by evidence that the foreign firm's export prices are below its total cost of production.   In order to take advantage of a temporary opportunity caused by an American monopolist's price hike, a foreign firm will often need to price below its total costs.

To impose anti-dumping duties, the government must also find that the dumping is causing "material injury," to U.S. industry.   Proving such injury, however, is not all that difficult.   See id. at 157–59 (describing criteria).   In any event, the threat of duties may deter foreign firms from competing at a lower price in the U.S. than they charge at home.

Thanks to my colleague Bill Davey for help on this issue.

23.   4 Trade Reg. Rep. (CCH) ¶ 13,103 § 2.11 (June 14, 1984).   This approach was inexplicably deleted from the 1992 guidelines.

Professor William Landes and Judge Richard Posner have argued that the

Another reason to limit market definition to the United States is Professor Michael Porter's finding about the importance of vigorous *domestic* rivalry to the dynamics of the market and to innovation.[24]   Porter argues that an industry characterized by vigorous domestic rivalry will be more dynamic and innovative than one where "national champions" face competition only from foreign firms.   Pride and "bragging rights" propel firms to out-compete domestic rivals, while a foreign firm's success is often attributed to unfair advantages.   Vigorous local competition forces firms to be internationally competitive in order to sustain growth because the domestic markets will become satiated more quickly.   Domestic rivalry also forces firms to continue to innovate when a monopolist might be content to sit back and exploit some national advantage (lower labor costs, easy access to valuable natural resources, etc.).   Finally, new ideas diffuse more quickly within one nation than globally.   Indeed, Porter concludes that the advantages of domestic rivalry are so significant that they clearly outweigh short-run economies of scale.

(5) Supply considerations.

Just as a high cross-elasticity of demand between two products prevents the seller of one from exercising economic power, a high cross-elasticity of supply also precludes a finding of monopoly. Cross-elasticity of supply is high when any effort on the part of the defendant to exploit consumers would be checked by the prompt entry of new suppliers, lured by the opportunity to undercut the defendant's prices.   In such cases, the defendant cannot control prices or exclude competitors—the *sine qua non* of monopoly power under *Cellophane*.[25]

full capacity of foreign firms should be included in a market whenever those firms sell any goods within the United States.   Market Power in Antitrust Cases, 94 Harv. L. Rev. 937, 964–68 (1981).   Professor Louis Kaplow has responded by demonstrating that the Landes–Posner approach would grossly understate a dominant American firm's power where products are differentiated (i.e., where a foreign firm sells a particularly high quality or low cost product appealing to only a small segment of U.S. consumers). The Accuracy of Traditional Market Power Analysis and a Direct Adjustment Alternative, 95 Harv. L. Rev. 1817, 1836–37 (1982). Moreover, the Landes–Posner model makes the unrealistic assumption that a foreign firm will sacrifice long-standing business arrangements in its home country to momentarily profit by shifting its entire output to the United States.   As with many antitrust debates, the answer to this academic dispute ultimately comes down to the allocation of the burden of proof.   Those fearful of private monopolies will insist on some concrete assurance that foreign firms really do constrain the behavior of by a dominant American company; those professing greater faith in free markets will insist, as do Landes and Posner, on concrete reasons why a foreign importer cannot easily increase its output in the United States.

24. See The Competitive Advantage of Nations 117–22 (1990).

25. 351 U.S. at 391 (1956).

The Tenth Circuit's decision in *Telex Corp. v. IBM*[26] is illustrative of a case involving high cross-elasticity of supply. IBM and a few other large companies manufacture "central processing units." These firms compete with a number of smaller companies in the sale of "peripheral products," such as disk drives and printers, that are connected to the main computer unit. The trial judge found that IBM had monopolized the market for those peripheral products that were compatible with IBM central processing units.[27] The trial court correctly determined that buyers of these IBM computers would obviously not respond to IBM's efforts to exploit subsequent sales of peripheral products by switching, for example, to a printer compatible only with an RCA computer. However, the court of appeals reversed, finding the trial court's market definition too narrow. Given the negligible cost of developing connections that would enable peripheral products to be used with different brands of central processing units, the court held that the market should include firms that sold peripherals compatible with any brand of central units. However, market definition analysis must keep its focus on *firms*, not products or areas. If, as IBM's critics allege, IBM possessed the unique ability to package peripherals and systems so that manufacturers of the former products could not meaningfully compete, then IBM should be considered to possess monopoly power.[28]

Similar facts were at issue in *Transamerica Computer Co. v. IBM*,[29] but led to a different result. In that case, the court held that the output of potential entrants should not be included in the market absent evidence that these potential rivals had actually entered the market at some point in the past or were in a position to do so with ease. The conflict between the two cases reflects a recurring debate in market definition analysis, to which we shall return when discussing market definition for merger purposes.[30] Those who tend to be skeptical about the marketplace and who fear that those with economic power will exploit consumers demand that doubts about the degree to which a potential entrant can constrain the defendant be resolved against the defendant.[31]

26. 510 F.2d 894 (10th Cir.), cert. dismissed, 423 U.S. 802 (1975).

27. 367 F. Supp. 258, 291 (N.D. Okl. 1973).

28. See Lawrence Sullivan, Monopolization: Corporate Strategy, the IBM Cases, and the Transformation of the Law, 60 Texas L. Rev. 587, 607 (1982) (IBM's ability to charge monopoly prices for its central processing units and low prices for its peripherals insulated the firm from meaningful competition from peripheral manufacturers).

29. 481 F. Supp. 965 (N.D. Cal. 1979), aff'd, 698 F.2d 1377 (9th Cir. 1983).

30. See Chapter 6, section A(12) below.

31. "The world is not a frictionless plane; there are many constraints limiting such mobility. These must be considered and burdens of proof assigned correspondingly." Sullivan, supra note 28, at 609 (citing Robert Harris & Thomas Jorde, Antitrust Market Defini-

Those who tend to be skeptical about antitrust intervention and more sanguine about the self-correcting qualities of the marketplace tend to insist that the plaintiff carry the burden of proving that a plausible entrant does *not* constrain the defendant. Because predictions in these matters are hazardous, assigning the burden usually determines the outcome.

(6) *Cellophane* and the limits of the structural approach.

The "*Cellophane* fallacy" (high cross-elasticity of demand at current prices shows that the defendant does not have monopoly power, when in reality it may show that a monopolist is already charging the full monopoly price) reflects a major weakness in the structural approach to determining the existence of monopoly power. The Court and the parties in that case became so caught up in the fight about whether the relevant market was cellophane or flexible wrapping material that they overlooked the big picture: did du Pont have the ability to cause the kind of social harms the antitrust laws are designed to condemn? The Court forgot that market structure is simply one of several proxies used to ascertain whether a defendant enjoys monopoly power. Unfortunately, some later cases have continued in *Cellophane's* path, making "market definition" a legal element in monopolization suits and mechanically focusing on the defendant's precise share of a single market to determine the existence of power.[32] The Court recently, however, has signalled that it may be returning to square one and using the structural approach only as one of several available tools in determining the existence of economic power.

In *Cellophane*, there was ample evidence that du Pont had such power. First, its return on investments for a ten-year period showed profits of 31% before taxes, which certainly appear to be above normal levels.[33] Second, internal documents suggested that du Pont recognized that it had the discretion to raise prices in order to increase profits.[34] Third, du Pont engaged in extensive efforts to conspire with others to limit cellophane competition in the United States and to obtain a governmental tariff on imported cellophane.[35] This conduct is entirely consistent with the way a firm would act if it had a monopoly in cellophane, and entirely inconsistent with the way it would act if it faced vigorous competition from other forms of flexible wrapping material.

tion: An Integrated Approach, 72 Calif. L. Rev. 1 (1984)).

32. Id. at 612.

33. 351 U.S. at 420 (Warren, C.J., dissenting).

34. Id. at 423.

35. Id. at 418–19.

In a landmark opinion, the Supreme Court recently recognized the "*Cellophane* fallacy" and signalled a new emphasis on "market realities" over economic theory. In *Eastman Kodak Co. v. Image Technical Services, Inc.*,[36] the Court reversed a grant of summary judgment for a defendant whom the district court determined lacked market power. Kodak argued that the relevant market was not servicing Kodak-brand machines, but servicing of all photocopying machines, and it clearly did not have monopoly power in that broader market. Tracking du Pont's successful argument in *Cellophane*, Kodak claimed that, if it attempted to exploit consumers who had purchased Kodak products by providing inadequate or unduly expensive service, any increased profits would be offset by losses it would suffer in equipment sales as other consumers shifted to rival brands; thus, the market had to be broadened and Kodak exonerated from § 2 liability. The Court rejected this argument, in light of Image Tech's evidence (which, because of the case's procedural posture, it accepted) that Kodak's servicing of photocopying equipment was of higher price and lower quality than servicing by independent firms.[37]

Unlike the majority in *Cellophane*, who ignored significant direct evidence of du Pont's power, Justice Harry Blackmun's majority opinion held that Kodak bore "a substantial burden in showing that ... despite evidence of increased prices and excluded competition, an inference of market power is unreasonable." [38] Officially debunking the *Cellophane* fallacy, the Court wrote:

> The sales of even a monopolist are reduced when it sells goods at a monopoly price, but the higher price more than compensates for the loss in sales. Kodak's claim that charging more for service and parts would be a "short-run game" is based on the false dichotomy that there are only two prices that can be charged—a competitive price or a ruinous one. But there could easily be a middle, optimum price at which the increased revenues from the higher-prices sales of service and parts would more than compensate for the lower revenues from lost equipment sales.[39]

Perhaps *Kodak* is an extreme case, since its procedural posture required the Court to credit even more damaging evidence that, contrary to Kodak's theoretical claims, Kodak's service prices had increased but Kodak equipment sales had not dropped.[40] Moreover, the Court found that the plaintiffs had proffered a "forceful reason" why Kodak could exercise monopoly power over

36. 112 S.Ct. 2072 (1992).

37. Id. at 2081.

38. Id. at 2083.

39. Id. at 2084 (citations omitted).

40. Id. at 2083.

Kodak-brand servicing.[41] Finally, although only briefly touched
on by the majority opinion, the Court's finding that the seller of a
branded, differentiated product can monopolize the "aftermarket"
in parts and services for its own products may be particularly
appropriate in cases like *Kodak* where the broader interbrand
market is highly concentrated (Kodak, Xerox and IBM controlled
almost the entire interbrand equipment market), and thus the
defendant's rivals cannot be relied upon to exploit the defendant's
efforts to eliminate intrabrand competition.[42] But the message
seems broader: once the plaintiff shows direct evidence of the
power to raise price or exclude competition, courts should be very
skeptical of defendant's efforts to explain why the evidence should
be disregarded.

Absent such clear evidence, though, the *Cellophane* saga still
suggests that there is no easy formula for market definition. It is
all too easy for antitrust lawyers and economists to get lost in the
morass of demand curves and price elasticities. The important
focus should remain where we began: identifying those who constrain the defendant from maintaining prices above cost, and who
provide the defendant with the stimulant to innovation and, in the
words of Judge Hand, the constant stress "necessary to counteract
an inevitable disposition to let well enough alone."[43]

Section D: Predation

(1) Introduction.

Predation is best defined as a generic term to describe a firm's
sacrifice of short-term profits in the expectation that these losses

41. As noted in section B(3), consumers have difficulty in fully anticipating
repair costs in making a decision to
purchase a photocopier, and thus find
themselves "locked in" to Kodak once
the significant cost of the equipment
purchase has been made.

42. Id. at 2086, n.2. Thus, Justice
Antonin Scalia's dissent demonstrates a
fundamental error when it jumped from
the undisputed fact that Kodak lacked
market power in the equipment market
to the conclusion that Kodak was "a
manufacturer functioning in a *competitive* equipment market." Id. at 2096
(emphasis added). The dissent concludes with another example of this
naive dichotomy between monopoly and
vigorous competition:

 if the interbrand market is vibrant, it
 is simply not necessary to enlist § 2's
 machinery to policy a seller's intrabrand restraints. In such circumstances, the interbrand market functions as an infinitely more efficient

and more precise corrective to such
behavior, rewarding the seller whose
intrabrand restraints enhances consumer welfare while punishing the
seller whose control of the aftermar-
kets is viewed unfavorably by interbrand consumers. Because this case
comes to us on the assumption that
Kodak is without such interbrand
power, I believe we are compelled to
[uphold the grant of summary judg-
ment].

Id. at 2101. Scalia accurately describes
the probable effect of any effort by Kodak to exploit its consumers if there
were, say, ten different sellers of photocopying equipment. Consumers may
rightly question whether they wish to
rely on competition from IBM and Xerox as an "infinitely more efficient"
way to ensure that Kodak provides
parts and services at the lowest price
and highest quality.

43. *Alcoa*, 148 F.2d at 427.

will be recouped in the future through the realization of monopoly profits. As we shall see, administrative and policy considerations have led the courts to hold that § 2 prohibits only some predatory conduct. While "predation" is sometimes used in a narrower sense to refer to that conduct which courts have previously condemned as illegal, this treatise will use the term (as well as the term "generic predation") in the broader sense in order to evaluate the wisdom of the substantive doctrine in this area.

Identifying cases of predatory conduct raises difficult problems. Just as identical pricing by rival firms may indicate perfect competition or a perfect cartel, an entrenched firm that cuts prices or introduces a new product in response to actual or threatened competition could be responding in a predictable way to competition, or could be engaging in predatory behavior. Not only can predatory conduct look just like competitive conduct, but the intent—to gain or maintain one's market share at the expense of one's rivals—can underlie both predatory and competitive behavior. Accordingly, the key element in a predation case is evidence that the defendant's conduct is predicated on the removal or silencing of competition and the resulting recoupment of monopoly profits at a later date.

Rules concerning predation must necessarily be imprecise. On the one hand, narrow defense-oriented rules will inevitably permit some sophisticated firms to engage in predatory behavior and thereby harm competition. On the other hand, broader plaintiff-oriented rules will inevitably chill some go-for-the-jugular firms from competing aggressively in the market.

Proponents of narrow rules, such as Professors Areeda & Turner and Judge Bork,[1] often argue that because predation is rare or non-existent, their rules will encompass most cases of predation and will therefore avoid the chilling effect of broader rules at little cost.[2] They tell the following story. First, a firm needs a large market share to successfully engage in predatory pricing. Without a large market share, a firm seeking to lower its prices to levels that will drive out the competition will have to

---

1. See III Phillip Areeda & Donald Turner, Antitrust Law ¶¶ 712–715 (1978); Robert Bork, Antitrust Paradox 154 (1978).

2. Language in Matsushita Electric Industrial Co. v. Zenith Radio Corp., 475 U.S. 574 (1986), supports this view. In that case, the Court wrote that "predatory pricing schemes are rarely tried, and even more rarely successful." Id. at 589. The Court concluded that because cutting prices in order to increase business "often is the very essence of competition," erroneously inferring predation where none exists will "chill the very conduct the antitrust laws are designed to protect." Id. at 594.

dramatically expand its output. For the same reasons that the courts consider a market share of 50% the usual prerequisite for monopolization (see the *Broadway Delivery* discussion above in section B(3)), it is unlikely that a small firm would attempt such a strategy. Even a dominant firm that significantly lowered its price to drive out its rivals would suffer much more than the rivals during the initial sacrificial period, because it will be losing money on a greater volume of sales and will have to expand productive capacity that it does not intend to use in the long run. Thus, to make predation worthwhile, the long-term monopoly profits must be very significant to justify the sacrifice. In order to obtain these profits, however, the dominant firm must not only drive its existing rivals out of business, but prevent new firms from entering once its prices rise to monopoly levels. Absent significant barriers to new entry, this strategy is not very likely to succeed. Businesspeople are generally smart enough to realize this, and therefore unlikely to engage in predatory behavior in the first place.

Those who advocate a broader role for antitrust rules prohibiting predatory activity tell a different story, focusing principally on a firm's ability to create a credible threat of predatory activity. A firm can enjoy monopoly profits not only by driving rivals out of business, but also by intimidating them from engaging in vigorous competition. Making this threat is far less costly to the defendant than actually driving all rivals out of business. A firm with a reputation for selectively and extensively cutting prices to harm particularly pesky rivals can therefore maintain high prices even where traditional entry barriers (technology, huge capital costs, government licensing) are absent.[3] Indeed, one of the concerns underlying the passage of the Clayton Act in 1914 was Congress' fear that national firms could engage in widespread monopolization through selective price cutting that targeted regional or local firms for either extinction or merger on favorable terms.[4] Moreover, a predatory price might deceive potential entrants into falsely thinking that the incumbent firm really has lower costs, thus prompting them to focus their competitive efforts elsewhere and leaving the incumbent with monopoly profits.[5]

3. For an excellent summary of this view, see Janusz Ordover & Daniel Wall, Proving Predation after *Monfort* and *Matsushita*: What the "New Learning" Has to Offer, Antitrust, p. 5 (Summer 1987).

4. See E. Thomas Sullivan and Herbert Hovenkamp, Antitrust Law, Policy and Procedure 618 (2d ed. 1989). See also William Stevens, Unfair Competition, 29 Pol. Sci. Q. 282, 284–86 (1914), frequently cited in congressional debates. Section 2 of the Clayton Act, containing the original congressional prohibition on price discrimination, is discussed in Chapter 7, section B.

5. See Strategy, Predation, and Antitrust Analysis 19–22 (Steven Salop ed., 1981).

(2) Price/cost rules: general concepts.

The Supreme Court has never adopted a rule of liability for predatory violations of § 2 of the Sherman Act,[6] despite the clear split among the circuit courts. For the past several decades, the dispute about predatory pricing rules has focused on cost-based rules of liability—rules that determine liability based on the relationship between the defendant's price and its costs. In order to measure this relationship, lower courts and academics have divided a firm's costs into two categories. *Fixed costs* are incurred regardless of the level of output; they include plant and durable equipment, the payment of debt, and a return on invested capital. *Variable costs*, by contrast, fluctuate with output; they include the cost of labor, utilities, minor equipment (delivery trucks, for example), and the raw materials necessary to manufacture each product.[7] Together, fixed and variable costs comprise a firm's *total cost*.

The ongoing debate among lower courts and academics concerns the standards for liability in three circumstances: 1) when a firm's prices are set below average variable cost (or "AVC": i.e., the variable cost of producing a single unit of output); 2) when a firm's prices are above AVC but below average total cost (or "ATC": i.e., the total cost of producing a single unit of output); 3) when a firm's prices exceed ATC. Professors Phillip Areeda and Donald Turner have proposed a bright-line rule that would allow pricing above AVC and condemn prices below AVC.[8] On the other hand, in *William Inglis & Sons Baking Co. v. ITT Continental Baking Co.*,[9] the Ninth Circuit set forth an alternative approach that involved shifting the burden of proof depending on the precise relationship between cost and price. Other courts of appeals have weighed in, as we discuss below, adopting various aspects of these two approaches.

6. In Utah Pie Co. v. Continental Baking Co., 386 U.S. 685 (1967), the Court did decide an important case concerning predatory price discrimination in violation of the Robinson–Patman Act. (As discussed in detail in Chapter 7, section B, that statute prohibits, *inter alia*, a firm from price cutting in selected geographic areas where the effect may be to substantially lessen competition.) Language in the opinion suggests that pricing below a cost level that includes an allocation for overhead might justify a finding of predatory pricing. More recently, however, *Matsushita* made clear that, while predatory pricing "means pricing below some appropriate measure of cost," the Court had not determined for purposes of § 2 what that appropriate measure was. 475 U.S. at 585 n.8.

7. Economists actually focus on the abstract concept of marginal cost when analyzing predation: the cost of providing the additional increment of output at issue in the case. Recognizing that the computation of marginal cost is impossible, Areeda & Turner proposed average variable cost as a sufficiently close proxy. Areeda & Turner, supra note 1, at 173–76.

8. Id. at 153–54.

9. 668 F.2d 1014 (9th Cir. 1981), cert. denied, 459 U.S. 825 (1982).

In *Inglis*, the plaintiff alleged that Continental had cut the price of its private label bread below AVC, precipitating a price war that left Inglis bankrupt. Continental responded that it was merely competing vigorously against others (including the dominant firm, Campbell–Taggart, which had a 45% market share), that its low prices were legitimate in light of the excess capacity in the industry (demand was down because large stores like Safeway were baking their own bread), and that if certain costs were properly defined as fixed, their prices were actually above AVC.[10] The jury found for the plaintiff, the trial judge granted Continental's motion for judgment n.o.v., and the Ninth Circuit reversed and remanded for a new trial.

The court of appeals held that the process of defining costs as fixed or variable depends on the circumstances of the case, and thus a new trial was required to allow the jury to resolve the issue.[11] Areeda and Turner had proposed a rigid categorization of costs in the interest of administrative convenience and predictability.[12] The facts of *Inglis* illustrate the sensibility of the court's rejection of such an approach. Expenses such as truck rentals and wages for workers and drivers are normally considered variable costs. The court held, though, that Continental ought to be allowed to try to persuade the jury that increased bread production merely filled excess oven time and truck space already available, and thus, at least at the time of the alleged predatory behavior, these expenses were really fixed. Thus, *Inglis* held that costs are considered variable only if they increase as a result of the increased output that can be attributed to the defendant's allegedly predatory pricing.[13]

As to liability, the Ninth Circuit correctly held that the inquiry in any predatory pricing case should focus on whether the defendant engaged in generic predation. In the court's terms, "a plaintiff must prove that the anticipated benefits of a defendant's price depended on its tendency to discipline or eliminate competition and thereby enhance the firm's long-term ability to reap the benefits of monopoly power." Using general economic theory as a guidepost, rather than a legal standard, the court thus held that

> if the defendant's prices were below average total cost but above average variable cost, the plaintiff bears the burden of showing defendant's pricing was predatory. If, however, the plaintiff proves that the defendant's prices were below average variable cost, the plaintiff has established a prima facie case of predatory pricing and the burden shifts to the defen-

---

10. Id. at 1037 n. 37.

11. Id. at 1036–37 & n.36.

12. See Areeda & Turner, supra note 1, at 172–74.

13. 668 F.2d at 1037.

dant to prove that the prices were justified without regard to any anticipated destructive effect they might have on competitors.[14]

(3) Price/cost rules: below-cost pricing.

By imposing a stringent burden on defendants whose prices fall below AVC,[15] the Ninth Circuit comes quite close to the Areeda & Turner approach in accepting the notion that sub-variable cost pricing should not be permitted under § 2. Almost all other courts seem to agree.[16] A firm that cannot obtain a price at least equal to AVC is better off not making the sale than selling at a price that does not even cover the "out of pocket" expenses of producing the product. Thus, in most cases, the only rational motivation for a firm to price below AVC would be the expectation of future monopoly profits.

Moreover, a firm with strong financial backing that sets prices below AVC will probably eliminate from the market a firm that is equally efficient, or even slightly more efficient, with less staying power. This scenario offends our desire to promote equality of economic opportunity. It also results in an inefficient allocation of resources: just as efficiencianados dislike monopoly pricing because it allocates too few of society's resources to the monopolized product, below-cost pricing is disfavored because it devotes in too many of society's resources to the product.

Most of the controversy surrounding cost-based rules of liability concern prices in the intermediate range—those that are higher than AVC but lower than ATC. As *Inglis* noted, pricing in this range "may be a legitimate means of minimizing losses, particularly when the firm is 'temporarily' experiencing 'excess capacity' in its productive facilities."[17] A firm that is not engaged in

---

14. Id. at 1035–36.

15. *Inglis* suggests two cases where prices below AVC would not be illegal: where this pricing occurs because of innocent miscalculations that unexpectedly lead to losses rather than profits, id. at 1034; and where start-up costs are so significant, and the price war is seen as so temporary, that it makes sense to suffer losses even below the cost of making new products rather than shutting down entirely. Id. at 1035 n.32 (citing Paul Joskow & Alvin Klevorick, A Framework for Analyzing Predatory Pricing Cases, 89 Yale L.J. 213, 251 n. 77 (1979)). The FTC's opinion in the companion case to *Inglis* suggests two additional cases: where products are so obsolete and perishable that

any sale is better than no sale; and where the price is set at an introductory level to induce consumers to try the product. International Tel. & Tel. Corp. (Continental Baking), 104 F.T.C. 280, 404 (1984).

16. Keep in mind that this section concerns only the conduct element of § 2. § 2 cases alleging monopolization, a plaintiff that shows that the defendant engaged in impermissible conduct must still prove the existence of monopoly power. Section G, below, considers what additional evidence a plaintiff must present to prevail in a § 2 case alleging attempted monopolization.

17. 668 F.2d at 1035.

predatory behavior might also price below average total cost in order to respond to a rival's price cut or to promote a new product. Pricing for these reasons is not predatory because a competitive firm that is not seeking future monopoly profits would set prices in this intermediate range under similar circumstances.[18] Over the long term, however, pricing at this level is not economically rational because the firm will not recover a return on its investment, unless the firm anticipates future monopoly profits. Thus, economic theory indicates that a firm pricing in the intermediate range between AVC and ATC might be engaged in legitimate competitive behavior, or it might be engaged in predation. The Second Circuit has adopted the Areeda & Turner approach and refuses to condemn any intermediate range pricing as predatory, while the Ninth Circuit allows the plaintiff, in such cases, to demand through discovery a non-predatory justification from the defendant for prices in this intermediate range, and will impose liability if a persuasive explanation is not forthcoming.

Rather than seeking an explanation for the defendant's decision to price in the intermediate range, in *Northeastern Telephone Co. v. American Telephone & Telegraph Co.*[19] the Second Circuit refused to condemn the defendant's sales of switchboard equipment and specialized telephones at prices below ATC but above AVC. Historically, AT&T had not allowed its subscribers to connect its lines to non-AT&T equipment. Attracted by a Federal Communications Commission order ending AT&T's policy, new firms such as the plaintiff entered the telephone equipment market. In response to this competition, AT&T offered new equipment at what the plaintiff argued were predatory prices. Without inquiring into how AT&T could profitably sell at below-cost prices, the court held that legal rules should be "mindful both of the limits of the judicial process and the realities of the marketplace."[20] The Areeda & Turner bright-line rule was not only simple, but was also sound policy, the court held, in light of several factors. First, the court noted that only prices below marginal cost will harm equally efficient rivals more than the defendant itself. Second, a less determinate rule (such as that subsequently adopted by the Ninth Circuit in *Inglis*) would undoubtedly chill vigorous price competition—the very behavior the antitrust laws seek to promote. Third, the court expressed agreement with those who believe that predatory pricing is rare. Thus, because "the costs of a misjudgment are high and the prevalence

18. Transamerica Computer Corp. v. International Business Machines Corp., 481 F.Supp. 965, 996 (N.D. Cal. 1979), aff'd, 698 F.2d 1377 (9th Cir.), cert. denied, 464 U.S. 955 (1983).

19. 651 F.2d 76 (2d Cir. 1981), cert. denied, 455 U.S. 943 (1982).

20. Id. at 88.

of the conduct the law seeks to deter is low," the Second Circuit concluded that prices in the intermediate range should not be condemned under § 2.[21]

Although the validity of the latter two arguments cannot be tested empirically, *Northeastern Telephone* appears to err in arguing that prices in the intermediate range cannot result in the exclusion of equally efficient rivals. Because firms that cannot recover their total costs cannot stay in business in the long run, unjustified pricing below ATC could give a wealthier firm the means to eliminate rivals that were more efficient but did not enjoy an equal cash flow. Moreover, business today is becoming increasingly dynamic; a cash-weak firm might not be able to push ahead in the competitive race because, if forced to price below ATC, it could not generate the funds necessary for innovation or research and development. Because innovation often leads to vigorous competition and unstable market shares, dampening the dynamic process might suit the dominant firm. In contrast, an antitrust doctrine that tolerates unjustified intermediate range pricing by a leading firm does not promote the efficient allocation of resources, the interest of consumers, or a dynamic economy.

The Ninth Circuit's rejection of a bright-line rule is an effort to resolve the quandary noted at the beginning of this section— that low pricing in an industry may be indicative of vigorous rivalry or predation. As discussed in detail in the next chapter, in *Interstate Circuit Inc. v. United States* [22] the Supreme Court resolved a similar quandary involving identical pricing by all firms in an industry (in might indicate perfect competition or perfect collusion) by holding that an unlawful conspiracy could be inferred from evidence that is inconsistent with what would be expected to occur in a competitive marketplace and consistent with what would likely result from a cartel. Following *Interstate Circuit, Inglis* held that pricing below ATC, in the absence of an apparent non-predatory explanation, is inconsistent with what is likely to occur in a competitive marketplace and consistent with predation, and thus properly judged to be a violation of § 2.[23]

However, where excess capacity exists (and was not deliberately created as part of a predatory scheme), pricing in this

---

21. Id. at 87–88.

22. 306 U.S. 208 (1939). This case is discussed in chapter 4, section F(2).

23. *Inglis*, 668 F.2d at 1034 (citations omitted):

Our approach ... is to focus on what a rational firm would have expected its prices to accomplish. [A] price should be considered predatory if its anticipated benefits depended on its tendency to eliminate competition. If the justification for a price reduction did not depend upon this anticipated effect, then it does not support a [§ 2] claim ... even if it had the actual effect of taking sales from competitors.

intermediate range should be considered non-predatory because it can be designed to minimize losses and make some contribution to overhead. The Federal Trade Commission's own review of the Northern California baking market led the Commission to conclude that excess capacity, rather than an intent to monopolize, explained Continental's pricing strategy.[24] After retrial, the Ninth Circuit likewise granted judgment for the defendant because of the lack of anticompetitive intent.[25] A middle ground may be preferred to the polar approaches of *Northeastern Telephone*, which precluded any inquiry into pricing below ATC, and *Inglis*, which insisted on the need to "eschew dogmatic adherence to a particular, rigid test and to fashion broad and flexible objective standards concerned with accurately evaluating the purposes of business behavior."[26] As the FTC subsequently found, Continental's low market share and the lack of entry barriers in the California baking market (especially the ability of major buyers to bake their own bread), suggested that it was highly unlikely that Continental could have acquired monopoly power in the relevant market.[27] Where the plaintiffs predation theory is that implausible, antitrust law ought to permit the trial judge to forego the burden of litigating over endless cost data.

Pacific Engineering & Production Co. v. Kerr–McGee Corp.[28] illustrates another case where excess capacity seems to have justified pricing in the intermediate range. The parties in that case were two of the four firms that had supplied a particular chemical to space and defense contracting firms. In the early 1960s, however, sharp changes in government procurement policies severely reduced the demand for the product and caused the two other firms to leave the market. The plaintiff brought the suit after the defendant's prices had remained substantially below average total cost for a four-year period. In spite of some evidence that the defendant intended to eliminate the plaintiff as a competitor and had published plans to raise prices in the event of the plaintiff's demise, the Tenth Circuit reversed the trial court's judgment for the plaintiff.

The court of appeals found that demand for the chemical had been reduced to such an extent that either party could have produced enough to meet almost the entire demand.[29] The trial

24. International Tel. & Tel. Corp. (Continental Baking), 104 F.T.C. 280 (1984).

25. William Inglis & Sons Baking Co. v. Continental Baking Co., 942 F.2d 1332 (9th Cir. 1991) ("*Inglis II*"), rehearing granted in part on other grounds, 970 F.2d 639 (9th Cir.1992).

26. *Inglis*, 668 F.2d at 1031 n.18.

27. 104 F.T.C. at 412–15.

28. 551 F.2d 790 (10th Cir. 1977).

29. Id. at 796.

court concluded that a rational, non-predatory duopolist would have employed price leadership to engage in profitable oligopoly pricing with its rival, and condemned Kerr–McGee for not doing so here.[30] The court of appeals correctly reversed, holding that the Sherman Act did not require oligopoly pricing. *Pacific Engineering* appears to have involved a "natural monopoly" market, one where a single firm can efficiently meet the entire demand. As discussed more fully below,[31] firms operating in such markets are allowed to engage in "fair" rivalry to be the one remaining at the end of a price war, and pricing that makes some contribution to overhead (i.e., pricing above AVC) seems preferable to requiring a firm either to go out of business or to collude (tacitly or explicitly) with its rival.

(4) Price/cost rules: above-cost pricing.

Finally, a majority of courts and commentators favor a rule that always permits a firm to price at or above its own average total costs.[32] The Ninth Circuit's decision in *Transamerica Computer Co. v. IBM Corp.*[33] appears alone in permitting a plaintiff to show by "clear and convincing evidence" that prices above ATC are predatory. In that case, IBM faced emerging competition from rivals producing "peripheral" computer products that could be plugged in to IBM's computers. The defendant responded by introducing several products that were priced substantially below their antecedent models. Although the plaintiff claimed that the prices were predatory, the district court found they exceeded ATC and thus "should be conclusively presumed legal."[34] The court of appeals disagreed.

Barry Wright Corp. v. ITT Grinnell Corp.[35] is one of the leading cases rejecting *Transamerica*'s approach. In that case, Grinnell received a special discounted price when it purchased specialized equipment used in nuclear power plants from its co-defendant, Pacific Scientific. The parties agreed that Pacific had lawfully obtained a monopoly in the manufacture of this equipment; Barry Wright (Pacific's rival) argued that the discount to

---

30. Oligopoly pricing occurs when one of a few firms in an industry leads the way through price increases and the other firm(s) follow. Any discounts by the "followers" are immediately matched, so that there is no incentive to gain market share by lowering price. For a fuller discussion of oligopoly pricing and price leadership, see Chapter 4, section F.

31. See the discussion of the *Union Leader* case in section F(5) of this chapter.

32. For a discussion of much of the academic commentary, see Joseph Brodley & George Hay, Predatory Pricing: Competing Economic Theories and the Evolution of Legal Standards, 66 Cornell L. Rev. 738 (1981).

33. 698 F.2d 1377 (9th Cir.), cert. denied, 464 U.S. 955 (1983).

34. 481 F. Supp. 965, 991 (N.D. Cal. 1979).

35. 724 F.2d 227 (1st Cir. 1983).

Grinnell reflected an unlawful maintenance of power through predatory pricing. In light of the district court's finding that the price covered all the costs of production, the First Circuit concluded that the conduct was lawful. Where the defendant is pricing at or above its own ATC, the only rivals who cannot stay in the market are those who are less efficient (i.e., whose costs are higher). As the court noted, regulating the "proper" price above the level of the defendant's ATC would lead to severe administrative difficulties. Moreover, any rule that exposed a defendant to liability for pricing above ATC to liability would deter desirable discounting by established firms.[36]

In adopting the contrary approach, the Ninth Circuit is theoretically correct that above-cost pricing can be predatory, in the generic sense of the word. A dominant firm may, for example, engage in what economists call "limit pricing." A limit price is one that, while above the competitive level, is set below the monopoly level lower in order to preclude competition from new entrants. A firm that engages in limit pricing thus sacrifices short-term profits (the maximum monopoly price) in order to maintain its long-term monopoly position. Although consumers might benefit in the short run from slightly lowered prices, they might be better off without limit pricing in the long run if monopoly pricing would attract significant new investment by new competitors, thereby resulting in a competitive market. (This is particularly true when a monopolist generally prices at a monopoly level but when faced with the prospect of new entry selectively lowers its price to a level that, although above ATC, deters the new entry.)

Despite *Transamerica*'s theoretical validity, its explanation why there was insufficient evidence of predation by IBM provided no real guidance as to the type of proof necessary to satisfy its standard of clear and convincing proof. However, the court implicitly suggested two situations where above-cost pricing might be illegal when it noted that Transamerica had failed to prove either that IBM's prices had risen after competition had left the market or that IBM had engaged in limit pricing. As is discussed below,[37] the first type of evidence really incorporates a non-cost based test, and condemning limit pricing is quite problematic.

As explained by both the trial judge and the dissenting court of appeals judge in *Transamerica*, limit pricing, unlike pricing below ATC, is always consistent with competition.[38] Consider

36. Id. at 232–34.

37. See subsection (4).

38. Dissenting in *Transamerica*, Judge Lucas endorsed the trial court's opinion, which claimed that it "would be all but impossible to distinguish be-

Telex Corp. v. International Business Machines Corp.,[39] a case that appeared to involve limit pricing. IBM's previous models of peripheral equipment required purchasers to lease two devices at a price of $2,875 per month; when rivals like Telex began to offer similar devices at a lower cost, IBM issued a new model that operated with only one device priced at $1,500 per month. Telex sued, and the court of appeals exonerated IBM, finding that the defendant anticipated a 20% profit on the new device. (One can imagine what the monopoly profit must have been on the old device!) There was considerable evidence that IBM's purpose was exclusionary—at one point, in fact, it had directly targeted Telex through a coordinated program known internally as "SMASH." Nevertheless, the inherent trade-offs involved when antitrust courts condemn practices that are efficient in the short-run but exclusionary in the long-run militate against imposing liability in cases of limit pricing, unlike cases where pricing is below ATC.[40] The likelihood that a monopolist can continue to exclude rivals while enjoying a 20% profit is significantly less than the likelihood of exclusion if the monopolist is pricing below average total costs. The benefits to consumers of allowing monopolists freer reign in responding to new entry, even if they are motivated by a desire to exclude new entrants entirely, are particularly strong in the area of product innovation. Whether the antitrust laws are focused solely on allocative efficiency, more broadly on dynamic economic efficiency, or even more broadly on protecting consumers from exploitation, there are still reasons to prefer the lower price-in-hand over the possibly more deconcentrated market-in-the-bush.[41] Finally, given *Transamerica*'s agreement with Areeda and Turner that prices above ATC will rarely be predatory,[42] the

tween above cost limit pricing conduct and a monopolist's procompetitive reaction to lower priced competitors." 698 F.2d at 1390 (citing 481 F.Supp. at 991).

39. 510 F.2d 894 (10th Cir.), cert. dismissed, 423 U.S. 802 (1975).

40. Professor Lawrence Sullivan has correctly criticized the language in *Telex*, 510 F.2d at 928, that justified IBM's strategy of deliberately targeting specific rivals because their smaller rivals used similar tactics. See The Transformation of Monopolization Law, 60 Tex. L. Rev. 587, 618–19 (1982). As Sullivan notes, a firm without market power might permissibly engage in behavior that would be illegal if attempted by a monopolist. This criticism does not mean, however, that *Telex* was wrong in refusing to condemn limit pricing.

41. Even those concerned solely with the non-economic goal of preserving small businesses should be less troubled by limit pricing because of the reduced (albeit not zero) likelihood that a limit price set significantly above the defendant's cost would actually limit entry by small firms. Moreover, it is particularly difficult to justify an approach geared solely to these non-economic goals where they directly conflict with the goals of maximizing societal wealth and benefiting consumers (who are, from a populist perspective, of greater concern than small entrepreneurs).

42. 698 F.2d at 1386–88.

Ninth Circuit's opinion fails to justify adoption of such a fuzzy rule.

Transamerica provides an appropriate closure for this discussion on cost-based tests. Cost-based tests generally, and one calling for precise quantification like the Areeda & Turner test particularly, derive their benefits from their relative ease of administration (compared to more uncertain, gestalt approaches) and from their conformance to economic theory. Applying such tests to the price that a huge multi-product firm like IBM charges for individual computer products requires the courts to make incredibly difficult evaluations of variable costs, and thus calls into question the theoretical validity of the assumption that a price above some designated measure of cost is never the result of a deliberate sacrifice of short-term revenues in the hope of recouping long-term profits. Whether cost-based tests, like democracy, are the worst approaches except for all the alternatives remains for discussion in the remainder of this chapter.

(5) Use of evidence of intent.

One approach that courts might take to distinguish between predation and legitimate competitive behavior, in lieu of Areeda & Turner's bright-line rule, would be to consider evidence of the defendant's intent. Credible evidence of the defendant's subjective motives is arguably the best evidence of predation. If the courts could reliably ascertain that a defendant's low prices were truly set with the intent of excluding competition and recouping losses by realizing future monopoly profits, they could sensibly conclude that the defendant knows its business better than the judge or jury, and could therefore condemn such behavior regardless of some after-the-fact accounting of prices and costs.

A growing number of courts, however, have gone in the opposite direction. Not only is subjective intent evidence insufficient to prove predation, but such evidence has been held to be inherently unreliable.[43] In *A.A. Poultry Farms, Inc. v. Rose Acre Farms, Inc.*,[44] for example, the defendant's president told one of the plaintiff's executives that A.A. Poultry's "days are numbered" because "we are going to run you out of the egg business." Moreover, the defendant's treasurer testified that production costs had no influence on its prices. (In competitive markets, costs certainly have a keen influence on prices.) Nonetheless, the court

---

43. See, e.g., Directory Sales Management Corp. v. Ohio Bell Tel. Co., 833 F.2d 606 (6th Cir. 1987); Henry v. Chloride, Inc., 809 F.2d 1334 (8th Cir. 1987); Barry Wright Corp. v. ITT Grinnell Corp., 724 F.2d 227 (1st Cir. 1983); MCI Communications Corp. v. AT & T, 708 F.2d 1081 (7th Cir.), cert. denied, 464 U.S. 891 (1983); Northeastern Telephone Co. v. AT & T, 651 F.2d 76 (2d Cir. 1981), cert. denied, 455 U.S. 943 (1982).

44. 881 F.2d 1396 (7th Cir. 1989), cert. denied, 110 S.Ct. 1326 (1990).

rejected this evidence of predatory intent on the grounds that documents expressing a desire to eliminate a rival may merely reflect "macho" talk from low-ranking individuals or vigorous competitive instincts.[45]   Similarly, in *Inglis*, the Ninth Circuit refused to rely on evidence that a consultant had suggested that the defendant direct its employees to target the plaintiff for enhanced competitive efforts and to maintain prices to hasten Inglis' exit.[46] Citing Judge Posner's treatise, the court noted that sales executives tend to brag about their competitive prowess in ways that will mislead jurors, and that the availability of intent evidence often depends more on the fortuity of the discovery process or the defendant's lack of sophistication than on the guilt or innocence of the alleged predator.[47]

In *McGahee v. Northern Propane Gas Co.*,[48] by contrast, the Eleventh Circuit held that intent evidence was relevant and could be the basis for liability where prices are set below ATC. In that case, after investigating McGahee's financial position, Northern Propane instituted a new policy of providing gas customers with rent-free tanks. Although Northern could not cover its full costs with its rent-free policy, the policy was aimed at exploiting McGahee's financial inability to follow suit. Displaying skepticism about the ability of modern economic theory to accurately determine the existence of predation,[49] and noting that Congress was not familiar with economic theory when it enacted the Sherman Act, the court held that Congress intended that "objective, circumstantial evidence of prices and costs and direct and circumstantial evidence of subjective intent would both be important" in ascertaining the existence of predation.[50]

McGahee's reliance on intent evidence, it is important to emphasize, came in the context of a case where prices were set below ATC—conduct that many believe to be presumptively anticompetitive (i.e., wrongful absent some legitimate explanation from the defendant). The Eleventh Circuit's decision is thus is far different from a holding that intent unaccompanied by some misconduct (such as unjustified pricing below ATC) should serve as

45. Id. at 1402.

46. 668 F.2d at 1039, 1055.

47. Id. at 1028 n.6. See Richard Posner, Antitrust Law—An Economic Perspective 189–90 (1976). On remand, the trial judge excluded this piece of intent evidence entirely, because there was no showing that Continental had relied on or adopted the consultant's memo; on further appeal, the Ninth Circuit suggested that even if it had been admitted, the memo would have been insufficient to show anticompetitive intent. *Inglis II*, 942 F.2d at 1337 n.7.

48. 858 F.2d 1487 (11th Cir. 1988), cert. denied, 490 U.S. 1084 (1989).

49. See id. at 1493 n.9: "As a social science built on assumptions and statistics, economics is subject to the disparagement attributed by Mark Twain in his *Autobiography* to B. Disraeli: 'There are thee kinds of lie: lies, damned lies, and statistics.' "

50. Id. at 1500.

the sole basis for a finding of predation. To take an extreme example, we obviously would not condemn a monopolist that produced a better and cheaper product even if undisputed evidence showed that the only reason the monopolist did so was to eliminate rivals.[51]

The majority view rejects even the *McGahee* approach and refuses to impose liability for pricing above AVC even where the plaintiff produces evidence of anticompetitive intent. Based on their view that predatory pricing is exceedingly unlikely, most courts have reasoned that the principal effects of any rule imposing liability for pricing above AVC will be to chill highly desirable, pro-competitive price cutting, to give less efficient firms an "umbrella" permitting them to remain in business without meeting the rigors of competition, and to increase the number of meritless antitrust actions filed by those injured as the result of legitimate competition.[52] One who is less sanguine about the rarity of predation might wonder, however, why jurors are less capable of understanding arguments about loose, excessively "macho" talk in this context than in many other areas where subjective intent plays a critical role, or why trial judges cannot exclude evidence that really is, in context, unduly prejudicial.[53]

(6) Alternatives to cost–based rules.

The process of discovering the cost data required to apply cost-based rules in predatory pricing cases imposes an enormous bur-

51. Professor Lawrence Sullivan concludes that the "most disappointing aspect" of the IBM cases was that the courts "became so entangled in attempts to use objective standards to predict the effect of particular market strategies that [they] ignored the abundant evidence available on intent." Sullivan, supra note 40, at 635 (criticizing cases including California Computer Products, Inc. v. IBM, 613 F.2d 727 (9th Cir. 1979); Telex Corp. v. IBM, 510 F.2d 894 (10th Cir.), cert. dismissed, 423 U.S. 802 (1975); Transamerica Computer Co. v. IBM, 481 F.Supp. 965 (N.D. Cal. 1979), aff'd, 698 F.2d 1377 (9th Cir.), cert. denied, 464 U.S. 955 (1983)). A fair reading of these decisions suggests, however, that the real basis for the judgments in favor of IBM was the judges' view that IBM was providing real benefits to consumers, rather than a refusal to consider intent evidence. Indeed, Sullivan's review of the cases, id. at 636, reveals a profound disagreement with the judges about IBM's *conduct*, both descriptively and normative-

ly. Sullivan describes IBM's design strategies as "repackaging existing peripherals with no improvements or minor improvements and then introducing these 'fighting peripherals' at sharply reduced lease rates." On the other hand, the courts emphasized that, with one competitively insignificant exception, IBM's new products provided real benefits to consumers. See subsection (7) below. Sullivan also condemns IBM limit pricing that was specifically designed to cause the most harm to fledgling rivals who had fewer resources at their disposal. But his analysis fails to provide a basis for distinguishing between undesirable limit pricing and the response of a fat, lazy monopolist that is reluctantly forced by the competition into taking steps to maintain its market share.

52. See, e.g., *Northeastern Telephone*, 651 F.2d at 87–88.

53. See Fed. R. Evid. 403.

den on litigants. Even Areeda & Turner's approach has the advantages of creating a "bright-line" rule, after all, only after costs are ascertained. Indeed, many question both the accuracy of the accounting data supporting cost determinations,[54] as well as the policy judgment that the search for data is worth the effort. One alternative approach, advocated by economists William Baumol and Oliver Williamson, is premised on the observation that the real harm to consumers comes not from predatory pricing itself, but rather from the higher prices that are imposed in the future once rivals are driven from the market. Thus, Baumol and Williamson would permit firms to set prices at any level, but would prohibit them from reversing any decision to reduce prices or expand output for two years unless cost-justified.[55] They reason that predators will be deterred from misconduct given the long period of time they will have to wait in order to recoup future profits. Areeda has criticized this approach because, he argues, it will deter desirable price cuts and will involve courts in the difficult process of evaluating whether price increases are in fact cost-justified.[56] No appellate court to date has accepted the Baumol/Williamson approach as an alternative to considering cost data.[57]

Recently, in *A.A. Poultry Farms, Inc. v. Rose Acre Farms, Inc.*,[58] Judge Frank Easterbrook argued that both intent evidence and cost tests are unreliable and therefore endorsed another approach advocated initially by Professors Paul Joskow and Alvin Klevorick.[59] Under this approach, the courts would dismiss, at an

---

54. Whenever a firm's variable resources (e.g., labor, wear & tear on machines) are used to produce more than one product, accountants must allocate the cost of those resources to each product. Not only is this process necessarily an arbitrary one, but it often is particularly unrelated to the economic inquiry involved in predation cases because accounting rules are designed to paint a standard picture of the firm for investors and lenders, not industrial organization economists. Allocation issues also arise concerning accounting judgments about spreading expenses over several years. For instance, a decision to spread the costs of a major advertising campaign over several years might mean that current prices exceed variable costs, whereas including the entire expenditure in the current year would bring prices below AVC. The Second Circuit, which adheres to the Areeda & Turner test, leaves these questions about the propriety of ac-

counting practices to the jury. Kelco Disposal, Inc. v. Browning–Ferris Indus., 845 F.2d 404 (2d Cir. 1988), aff'd, 492 U.S. 257 (1989).

55. Williamson, Predatory Pricing: A Strategic and Welfare Analysis, 87 Yale L.J. 284 (1977); Baumol, Quasi–Permanence of Price Reductions: A policy for Prevention of Predatory Pricing, 89 Yale L.J. 1 (1979). Williamson focuses on output, Baumol on price.

56. Phillip Areeda & Herbert Hovenkamp, Antitrust Law 647–54 (1991 Supp.).

57. *Transamerica* adopts half of the approach, by allowing evidence of subsequent price increases to prove that the prior price level was predatory even though it exceeded total costs. 698 F.2d at 1388.

58. 881 F.2d 1396 (7th Cir. 1989), cert. denied, 494 U.S. 1019 (1990).

59. See supra note 15.

early stage of the litigation process, any case where the plaintiff could not establish that the market structure would permit recoupment of profits—for example, a case where low barriers to entry would prevent a predator from raising prices once its current rivals were driven out of the market. Dismissing lawsuits where recoupment is not feasible, Easterbrook reasoned, would not harm consumers and would avoid meritless lawsuits.[60]

From the consumer's perspective, Easterbrook is correct that the prime concern with predation is the back-end increase in price once the predator eliminates competition. If such future price increases are not possible, consumers get the benefit of low prices today and competitive prices tomorrow. Albeit in dicta, the Supreme Court seems to have endorsed this view. In *Cargill, Inc. v. Monfort of Colorado, Inc.*,[61] the Court instructed judges evaluating entry barriers in the context of predatory pricing claims to focus on whether barriers existed after the front-end efforts to exclude rivals had succeeded. The Court reasoned that recoupment will be thwarted and the predatory threat becomes illusory if the alleged predator's efforts to recoup lost revenues will itself attract new entry.[62] Nevertheless, there are several problems with *Rose Acre*'s approach.

First, *Rose Acre*'s emphasis on recoupment does not further the Jeffersonian interests in preserving small businesses and giving them an equal opportunity to compete. Avarice or an overly optimistic assessment of the possibility of recoupment may motivate dominant predators to drive others out of business through inefficient and unfair business practices. Therefore, those committed to maintaining rivalry as an end in itself will probably prefer cost-and intent-based tests, even though predatory pricing litigation consumes significant resources.

Second, *Rose Acre*'s approach will not work if the courts adopt the methods for determining the feasibility of recoupment that were in vogue in the late 1970s, when Joskow and Klevorick wrote their famous article. Rather, the Courts should make use of recent insights into strategic behavior, which show new and evolving ways in which dominant firms can create barriers to entry to facilitate recoupment, even if traditionally recognized entry barriers are non-existent. If *Rose Acre* is applied with care and sophistication, then, consumers will benefit. If used by busy district judges to summarily dismiss predation claims even though the defendant has engaged in inefficient and anticompetitive con-

---

60. 881 F.2d at 1401.

61. 479 U.S. 104 (1986). The case is discussed in detail in Chapter 6, section D.

62. Id. at 119 n. 15.

duct, the consumer goals of the antitrust laws will unfortunately be weakened.

Third, *Rose Acre*'s implicit assumption that evidence about market structure (i.e., market definition and ease of entry) is more ascertainable and more reliable than cost or intent evidence is not always valid. For example, in *McGahee* the district court granted summary judgment for the defendant, finding no significant barriers to entry in the propane gas industry because of the absence of any trade secrets, patents, or licensing. The Ninth Circuit came to the contrary conclusion in *Oahu Gas Service, Inc. v. Pacific Resources, Inc.*,[63] upholding a jury's finding that the propane market had high barriers to entry because a new entrant would have to make a large initial investment in capital outlays, excess capacity already existed in the market, and customers would incur high costs in switching from one supplier to another. Therefore, where cost or intent evidence *is* clear and reliable, our prior discussion about the difficulty of accurately ascertaining market structure suggests some reason to exercise caution in using a purely structural approach to cut off a plaintiff's proof.

Finally, *Rose Acre* does not instruct the courts as to the proper procedure to follow where the plaintiff passes this hurdle and proves that the market structure does not preclude recoupment of profits. Presumably, the courts that may be persuaded to adopt *Rose Acre*'s approach will revert to their prior use of costs and other evidence to determine liability in such cases.

(7) Predatory innovation.

A firm can engage in predatory behavior not only by lowering prices but also by designing its products so as to exclude competition. In *Transamerica Computer Co. v. International Business Machines Corp.*,[64] for example, the district court rejected a predatory innovation claim, effectively requiring plaintiffs to prove that the defendant's design had no redeeming virtue for consumers. The Court's language initially appears to invite an open-ended inquiry into the reasonableness of the innovation. The judge wrote that a monopolist's choice of design violates the Sherman Act only if it is "unreasonably restrictive of competition." *Transamerica* rejected the suggestion that the defendant should prevail whenever there was a valid engineering dispute about an innovation's superiority vis-a-vis prior technology.[65] *Transamerica* also

---

63. 829 F.2d 1471 (9th Cir. 1987), withdrawn and replaced, 838 F.2d 360 (9th Cir.), cert. denied, 488 U.S. 870 (1988).

64. 481 F. Supp. 965 (N.D. Cal. 1979), aff'd, 698 F.2d 1377 (9th Cir.), cert. denied, 464 U.S. 955 (1983).

65. Id. at 1003 (discussing ILC Peripherals Leasing Corp. v. International

rejected an intent-based approach, reasoning that "usually many results are intended, and if only one, even if the predominating, intent is illegal, and thus punished, legitimate incentives will be imperiled." [66]

Despite the court's use of a broad, vague test that might chill desirable innovation because of its uncertain scope, the application of the test to the facts in *Transamerica* demonstrates that it is much narrower than the typical open-ended rule of reasonableness. One design change at issue in *Transamerica* involved a significant alteration in the way that data tapes interfaced with IBM's central processing units. This innovation gave IBM a considerable advantage in the sale of its own tape drives and made it much more difficult for rival sellers of tape drives to compete. After describing the desirable aspects of the new system, the court concluded that it "was adopted by IBM because it was a product improvement, and even if its effect was to injure competitors, the antitrust laws do not contemplate relief in such situations." Similarly, IBM had strategically selected one innovative tape drive design over an alternative system because the former would be more difficult for rivals to copy. The court noted that, in addition to being a superior design, this particular innovation had only a negligible competitive effect, but the court's analysis of the first design change suggests that IBM would have not been liable even if the exclusionary effect had been greater.[67]

The court found only one innovation to be unreasonably anticompetitive, but even there refused to impose antitrust liability because Transamerica had suffered no injury. Two of IBM's computers were designed to include a "byte multiplexor" that permitted the attachment of devices for reading data from tapes. The original design plans called for a system that could read 50,000 characters per second (50KB/sec) or less. Because several of IBM's rivals sold tape drives that operated at 30KB/sec, IBM engineers redesigned the byte multiplexor so that it could only read 29KB/sec or less. The court concluded that in so doing "IBM degraded system performance, making its product less attractive to users"; the "only purpose served and the only effect of the degradation was the preclusion of competition." [68] Thus, as ap-

Business Machines Corp., 458 F.Supp. 423, 439 (N.D. Cal. 1978)).

66. Id.

67. Id. at 1003–04.

68. Id. at 1007.

The Ninth Circuit affirmed the district court's decision. The appeals court endorsed the district court's legal conclusion that IBM's design changes

(with the exception of the byte multiplexor) resulted in real product improvement and thus were not "unreasonably restrictive of competition" and concluded that the trial judge's determination that Transamerica suffered no injury concerning the multiplexor was not clearly erroneous. 698 F.2d at 1382–83.

California Computer Products, Inc. v. International Business Machines Corp.,

plied in *Transamerica*, predatory innovation is really unlawful only if it is without any real value to consumers.

Predatory innovation is another example of business behavior that simultaneously provides efficiencies and increases market power. There is a strong tradition, dating back to Senator Sherman's comments about efficient trusts,[69] that calls for careful analysis of this kind of ambiguous business behavior. Buyers might never benefit from certain efficiencies, such as changes in production methods, unless the threat of competition forces the manufacturer to pass the cost savings on in the form of lower prices. Nevertheless, there are strong reasons to treat innovations (such as computer redesigns) that actually benefit consumers differently from other changes in production methods. Unlike lowered production costs, improved products will definitely benefit consumers—in terms of higher product quality—while the reduced competition from the exclusionary effects of innovation is always somewhat speculative. Unlike predatory pricing, technological innovation will likely benefit consumers not only in the short run but in the long run as well, by providing an impetus for firms to continue to build upon new discoveries and development. Thus, *Transamerica* appears to draw the correct line, condemning only those innovations that do not in fact make the product more attractive to consumers.[70]

(8) The special case of regulated industries.

United States v. American Telephone & Telegraph Co.[71] raised questions of predatory pricing in the specialized context of a regulated industry. AT&T faced competition in providing intercity private telephone lines, but FCC regulations afforded AT&T a monopoly in leased lines ("WATS" lines). The government's evi-

613 F.2d 727 (9th Cir. 1979), also exonerated IBM from antitrust liability for an innovation that physically incorporated into the IBM central unit a device IBM had previously sold in competition with rivals.

69. See Chapter 1.

70. As is true in cases involving other types of "protected conduct," like petitioning the government (see Chapter 8, section B), it should be permissible to use evidence of predatory intent in the area of product design to prove a § 2 violation where there is affirmative misconduct in other areas. Suppose, for example, that a defendant is accused of attempted monopolization for charging prices below total costs but above variable costs. Where the defen-

dant offers a plausible but not compelling explanation for its behavior, evidence that the defendant's intent is clearly predatory might affect the result. Likewise, evidence that design changes were specifically chosen to exclude competition should be highly relevant to prove that the defendant's pricing strategies were similarly motivated. Similarly, if economic analysis did not provide clear answers to questions of market definition, evidence that the defendant deliberately targeted certain firms and not others in redesigning its products would help identify those firms that should be included in the relevant market.

71. 524 F. Supp. 1336 (D.D.C. 1981).

dence showed that AT&T set its intercity rates based on what it perceived to be the costs its rivals would incur in constructing private intercity lines.[72] Citing Areeda & Turner, AT&T moved to dismiss following the government's case-in-chief on the ground that the government's proof was legally insufficient because there was no evidence that it had set prices below cost. District Judge Harold Greene denied AT&T's motion, ruling that the government could proceed with a predation theory based solely on evidence of AT&T's predatory intent because the evidence showed that AT&T's pricing strategy was wholly unrelated to the cost of the services.[73]

The court's reasoning in rejecting AT&T's argument makes this a specialized case. The court noted that cost-based tests are all premised on the notion that the alleged predator is pricing below cost today to achieve monopoly profits tomorrow. In contrast, the government's evidence showed that AT&T was sacrificing profits from one service and simultaneously recouping monopoly profits in another service. It would appear that this scenario can occur only where the government regulates entry into the market and opts for a form of rate regulation that limits the licensed firms' overall rate of return—which precisely describes the situation in AT&T. If AT&T's rivals had been able to compete in all lines of business, AT&T would not have been able to immediately recoup its losses from the markets where predation was occurring. Likewise, if the FCC had regulated rates on a service-by-service basis, AT&T would not have been able to justify setting prices for some services at monopoly levels. Only the combination of these two factors allowed AT&T to stay within the FCC's target for overall profitability and use predatory pricing to keep rivals out of targeted markets.[74]

———

Enormously complex issues arise in determining whether a firm has violated § 2 of the Sherman Act by engaging in predatory behavior in order to obtain or maintain a monopoly. Resolution of these issues often depends upon one's view of economics, of the goals of antitrust, of the efficacy of antitrust intervention, and

72. Id. at 1364–67.

73. The parties subsequently entered into a consent decree divesting local telephone companies from AT&T's long distance business. 552 F.Supp. 131 (D.D.C. 1982), aff'd mem. sub nom. Maryland v. United States, 460 U.S. 1001 (1983).

74. Vertically integrated regulated firms also engage in generic predation when they establish a "price squeeze"— an overall pricing scheme of high wholesale and low retail rates such that their retail rivals (usually municipalities) cannot compete. This type of behavior is more akin to a vertically integrated firm's refusal to deal, and is discussed below in section E(3).

of the abilities of judges and juries in finding facts and applying the law. Generally, though, only those on the ideological extreme would disagree with the proposition that antitrust cases ought to be resolved as simply and easily as they can. Thus, many of the predation tests discussed above may be appropriate: dismissing cases when monopolization is implausible, but not when it is merely unlikely; relying on intent evidence not to punish bad motives alone, but to amplify ambiguous economic data; using facts if they are helpful to resolve the present case, rather than worrying about how similar evidence might conceivably be mis-used in future cases.

Defenders of those accused of predation always have a seduc-tive argument: the lower prices are benefitting consumers now, at least in the short run. Plaintiffs must bear the heavy burden of demonstrating that the long-term harm to the competitive process is worth the sacrifice of those short-term benefits. But the politi-cal economy of a free enterprise system is characterized more by long-term, rather than short-term, concerns. In the short term, for example, we would all benefit by the abolition of patent protection for expensive drugs and other innovations; only in the long run do patents benefit consumers by encouraging greater investment in research. Our own counselling of patience to con-sumers in Eastern Europe—just wait, higher prices now will result in more goods and services once the market incentives begin to work—is precisely the same argument made by plaintiffs in preda-tion cases.

Section E: Refusals to Deal

Unlike some areas of antitrust, the law governing a monopo-list's refusal to deal is relatively straightforward. In general, a refusal to deal constitutes illegal monopolization in violation of § 2 under two circumstances. First, monopolist may not refuse to do business with a firm because that firm also does business with the monopolist's actual or potential rival. Second, a refusal to deal that is part of a monopolist's efforts to vertically integrate violates § 2 where either its purpose or effect is to monopolize. Specifically, although § 2 monopolization claims generally do not require proof of specific intent to eliminate competition, a refusal to deal motivated by that intent is considered unlawful. In evaluating the effect of refusals to deal, courts have prohibited such practices when they increase barriers to entry, enhance the monopolist's ability to price discriminate, or enable the monopolist to evade governmental rate regulation.

(1) Conditioning sales on withholding patronage from rivals.

The first type of illegal refusal to deal is exemplified by *Lorain Journal Co. v. United States.*[1] The defendant in that case, a monopoly newspaper, refused to publish advertisements placed by any business that also advertised with its new rival, a nearby radio station. The Court held that this practice violated § 2. A key factor in the Court's decision was the defendant's control of what the Court called an "indispensible medium" for advertisers, and the use of that medium to exclude rivals.[2] The Lorain Journal's refusal to do business with paying customers because they also patronized rival firms was properly described as "predatory" by the trial court; the defendant was sacrificing short-term revenues in hopes of recouping the loss by realizing monopoly profits once the rival radio station was eliminated.

(2) Vertical integration.

The second type of impermissible refusal to deal arises in the context of vertical integration—when a firm acquires another company or expands internally in order to take over a function occurring earlier or later in the chain of distribution. Integration by acquisition is governed by § 7 of the Clayton Act;[3] a monopolist that integrates through acquisition or internal expansion is subject to liability under § 2 of the Sherman Act. As noted above, § 2 prohibits vertical integrations that have the purpose or effect of increasing monopoly power.

Eastman Kodak Co. v. Southern Photo Materials Co.[4] was an acquisition case that seemingly turned on the defendant's purpose—in particular, the defendant's intent to monopolize a "downstream" distribution function. Kodak, a leading manufacturer of photo supplies, refused to deal with a wholesale supplier of photographic equipment. Standing alone, the refusal to deal with a single supplier would probably not enable Kodak to illegally acquire or maintain monopoly power. However, the plaintiff's evidence showed that this was just one episode in a series of efforts designed by Kodak to monopolize. Kodak had elsewhere bought up and dismantled companies (illegal, you will recall under *American Tobacco*[5]) and had acquired a rival manufacturer and then refused to sell to the manufacturer's customers. This evidence sufficed to support the jury's finding that Kodak's refusal to deal

---

1. 342 U.S. 143 (1951).
2. Id. at 152.
3. See Chapter 6, section C.
4. 273 U.S. 359 (1927).

5. United States v. American Tobacco Co., 221 U.S. 106 (1911). See section A(2) above.

with the plaintiff was part of a plan to monopolize the wholesale market as well, and thus violated § 2.[6]

Paschall v. Kansas City Star Co.,[7] by contrast, was a vertical integration case that focused on the effects of the defendant newspaper's refusal to deal. In the newspaper industry, a non-integrated newspaper purchases ink and paper from independent suppliers, prints its issues, and then sells them at wholesale prices to independent delivery companies. When the newspaper vertically integrates into distribution, it usually refuses to deal with the independent firms it previously patronized. Thus, when the Kansas City Star vertically integrated by taking over the distribution of its newspapers, it refused to deal with independent delivery firms. This refusal was challenged and upheld in *Paschall.*

The Eighth Circuit's decision in that case set outs the proper framework for evaluating the effect of a refusal to deal following a monopolist's vertical integration.[8] The court identified the three principal ways in which integration can harm competition: (1) by increasing barriers to entry; (2) by facilitating the monopolist's ability to price discriminate; and (3) by allowing it to evade rate regulation.

With respect to barriers to entry, the Court noted that the defendant planned to deliver newspapers through agents whose delivery contracts specifically allowed them to deliver other newspapers as well. Thus, the integration did not increase entry barriers. In contrast, suppose the defendant had expressly prohibited its agents from delivering other newspapers. In such a case, any firm that attempted to compete with the Star would have had to build its own independent delivery system. Assuming this would be costly, competing with the Star would be more difficult. Because the integration would thus have had the effect of allowing the Star to maintain its monopoly power, it would have violated § 2.

With respect to price discrimination, the Eighth Circuit found that the purpose of the Star's integration was to charge uniform prices.[9] Because the prior system of distribution consisted of independent delivery persons operating in exclusive territories, consumers had only one possible source for their newspaper even

---

6. 273 U.S. at 375. Moreover, because of Kodak's dominant share in the film market, its few rivals could not find sufficient wholesale outlets to effectively compete if wholesale suppliers were all controlled by Kodak.

7. 727 F.2d 692 (8th Cir.) (en banc), cert. denied, 469 U.S. 872 (1984).

8. Caveat lector: I drafted the brief for the Justice Department as *amicus curiae* in *Paschall*, advocating substantially the same analysis as that adopted by the court of appeals en banc.

9. For a discussion of why the Star would want to obtain uniform prices, see the discussion of the *Albrecht* case in Chapter 5, section D(2).

prior to the monopolist's integration. Thus, price discrimination was equally possible regardless of the identity of the seller.[10]

In contrast, suppose that the sole American manufacturer of bright orange polyester apparel partially integrated into the retail market by reserving for itself sales in Illinois. Prior to the integration, Fighting Illini fans would have been able to purchase clothing in their school colors from competing retailers. Because of the special demand for such clothing in Illinois, the integrated manufacturer could refuse to sell to other retailers in the state and could thus charge a higher price to Illinois consumers. A non-integrated monopolist, however, could not raise its wholesale price for sales in Illinois. Retailers in Illinois could preempt those efforts by making arbitrage purchases from out-of-state retailers. In this situation, the orange polyester monopolist's ability to price discriminate, and hence its economic power, would significantly increase. Therefore, this conduct would violate § 2.

Otter Tail Power Co. v. United States[11] illustrates the third way in which refusals to deal accompanying vertical integration can harm competition. In that case, the defendant utility company generated power, transmitted it over long-distance power lines, and then distributed it locally to individual homes. Several other entities, including some federal government agencies, generated electric power, and a host of cities operated municipally-owned power companies to distribute electricity directly to individual homes and businesses. Otter Tail, however, had a monopoly on long-distance transmission. When potential rivals sought to compete in the local distribution market, the defendant refused to transmit power over its lines.

Ordinarily, this conduct would not increase a firm's economic power because it could extract the full monopoly profit as part of its long-distance transmission service fee. Otter Tail, however, was a regulated public utility; the federal government limited its ability to charge the monopoly price for transmission. By integrating into retail, Otter Tail therefore increased its chances of gaining some monopoly profit by obtaining monopoly power in local distribution as well.[12]

---

10. The Eight Circuit erroneously found that the Star's forward integration into the delivery business somehow eliminated "potential competition" in the delivery market. 727 F.2d at 704. The court reasoned that previously two rivals had existed in the market—the authorized retailer and the Star, a potential entrant. But the nature of the market was such that the only way the Star would ever enter the market would be by becoming *the* dealer, not by competing with its former distributor.

11. 410 U.S. 366 (1973).

12. Although Otter Tail's local distribution monopoly, like its transmission monopoly, is subject to rate regulation, the scheme increases Otter Tail's monopoly power in several ways. First, the possession of monopoly power

Where these three concerns are absent, refusals to deal are usually upheld. Thus, it is not illegal for a non-monopolist to refuse to deal with those who patronize its rivals. Because buyers have other options in these situations, the courts have held that these refusals to deal do not seriously threaten competition.[13] Likewise, other courts have permitted even a monopolist to replace one exclusive distributor with another one, reasoning that the identity of a local retail monopolist is irrelevant to competition.[14]

One of the reasons judges are wary of refusal to deal claims is that the remedy is so elusive. Unless the court flatly prohibits the defendant from making any effort to integrate, some independent arbiter will inevitably have to regulate prices because otherwise the defendant will be able to achieve the same effect as a refusal to sell by charging an exorbitant price for its product.

(3) Leveraging by means of a "price squeeze".

The cases discussed above demonstrate how a monopolist can blatantly eliminate competition in a downstream market by refusing to provide an essential good or service that its downstream rivals need to compete (photo supplies to the wholesale supplier in *Kodak*, newspapers to news distributors in *Paschall*, electric power to municipally-owned local electric companies in *Otter Tail*). Another less direct way that vertically integrated firms have been accused of leveraging power from one market into another is through a "price squeeze." In *United States v. Aluminum Co. of America*,[15] for example, Alcoa produced aluminum ingot, which it sold to aluminum fabricators, and also fabricated finished products such as rolled aluminum sheets and aluminum cable that Alcoa sold to industrial buyers in competition with non-integrated fabricators. The government charged that Alcoa set the price of ingot so high, and the price of its finished products so low, that

in two separate markets allows Otter Tail to manipulate its cost accounting procedures to obtain approval for higher rates from both federal regulators of its transmission monopoly and state regulators of its distribution. Second, the elimination of rival distribution enterprises deprives the state regulators of "yardstick competition"—the ability to determine whether Otter Tail is adequately serving its customers by comparing Otter Tail's service with that of another company.

The problems are even starker when a regulated firm integrates into a non-regulated field. Then, the firm can easily increase monopoly profits by charging high prices for goods or services that compliment the monopolized service. Suppose a regulated electric company was able to obtain a monopoly for household light bulbs. It could file low tariffs for its electricity that would easily pass regulatory muster, and then enormous prices for the light bulbs.

13. See, e.g., FTC v. Raymond Bros.-Clark Co., 263 U.S. 565 (1924); Andrew Jergens Co. v. Woodbury, Inc., 271 Fed. 43 (3d Cir.1920).

14. See, e.g., A.H. Cox & Co. v. Star Machinery Co., 653 F.2d 1302 (9th Cir. 1981).

15. 148 F.2d 416 (2d Cir. 1945).

independent fabricators could not compete in the sale of rolled sheets or cable.

If Alcoa's squeeze involved pricing its finished products below cost, the conduct could be analyzed as predatory pricing (discussed above in section D). What is distinct about a price squeeze claim is that (for purposes of this claim, at least) the plaintiff concedes that the defendant is pricing above cost, but alleges that the *relationship* between the defendant's wholesale price (i.e., the price of "raw" ingot) and retail price (i.e., the price for fabricated aluminum products) excludes competition. In *Alcoa*, the Second Circuit found that the defendant had violated § 2 by unlawfully squeezing rival aluminum sheet fabricators, because Alcoa could have charged less for its ingot and still returned a profit. But Alcoa was exonerated concerning the cable fabricators; the real "squeeze" they faced was not between Alcoa's high price for ingot and its low price for cable, but between Alcoa's price for ingot and the low price for cable charged by rival copper fabricators.[16]

Although the court found Alcoa guilty of unlawfully maintaining its monopoly in ingot,[17] Judge Learned Hand held that Alcoa's price squeeze did not contribute to that finding.[18] This analysis seems correct: it is difficult to see how Alcoa's price squeeze either contributed to its maintenance of monopoly power or enhanced its ability to exploit consumers. The squeeze was unlikely to increase entry barriers. Even if Alcoa succeeded in excluding rival fabricators of rolled sheet, there were probably enough other potential buyers of ingot (cable fabricators are just one example) to provide customers for another firm seeking to enter the ingot market.

The price squeeze was probably an effort to price discriminate—to charge a monopoly price for rolled sheets but to compete in the cable market with copper cable producers.[19] Because there were no ready substitutes for rolled aluminum sheets, Alcoa could obtain a monopoly profit from buyers of this product by charging either a high price for ingot or a high price for sheets. If Alcoa wished to compete against copper cable sellers, though, it had to sell its ingot to aluminum cable makers at competitive prices. But if Alcoa sold ingot to rival aluminum cable fabricators at a lower price, arbitrage would occur—these firms would resell some of their cheap ingot to rolled sheet fabricators. Therefore, Alcoa decided to keep its ingot prices high for everyone, allowing it to obtain monopoly profits from the sheet fabricators, foregoing sales

---

16. Id. at 437–48.

17. See section A(3) above.

18. 148 F.2d at 438.

19. See Eleanor Fox & Lawrence Sullivan, Antitrust 246 n.19 (1990).

to non-integrated aluminum cable firms, and selling directly in the aluminum cable market.[20]

Nevertheless, Judge Hand held that Alcoa unlawfully *exercised* its monopoly power via the price squeeze. This conclusion seems wrong. The court expressly noted that the squeeze was not part of an attempt to monopolize the rolled sheet market.[21] If the squeeze did not maintain Alcoa's power in the ingot market or contribute to an effort to extend that power into the rolled sheet market, then it simply reflected Alcoa's exercise of monopoly power. Condemning the mere exercise of power is inconsistent with the basic law of monopolization subsequently set forth by the Supreme Court: the Court has made it clear that a monopolist violates § 2 only by improperly obtaining or maintaining power,[22] not by simply exploiting its power to obtain monopoly profits.[23]

The Sherman Act has only limited application to the "mere" exercise of power because there are only two realistic remedies in a case like *Alcoa*, where the defendant was able to exploit its aluminum monopoly without fear of competition from any substitutes for rolled aluminum sheets: the court can regulate the price of ingot, or it can prevent Alcoa from fabricating any aluminum products. The difficulties of price regulation suggest, though, that divestiture is the only realistic remedy; and even that remedy ought not be employed when the efficiencies of vertical integration are so significant that it will lead to lower prices. The difficulties that arise in making these economic judgments suggest that price squeeze cases are best left to the Federal Trade Commission to adjudicate under § 5 of the FTC Act, rather than to private plaintiffs trying treble damage cases before generalist judges.[24]

---

20. Why, then, would the government claim that Alcoa set its aluminum sheet prices at "low" levels? The most plausible answer would appear to be that Alcoa enjoyed economies of scope because it was cheaper for Alcoa to produce ingot and fabricate rolled sheets at the same plant then for rival fabricators to purchase ingot from Alcoa and fabricate rolled sheets separately. Thus, Alcoa's "low" price was really its monopoly price, but it was sufficiently low to make it impossible for rival fabricators to pay Alcoa a monopoly profit on ingot and still compete in making the sheets.

21. 148 F.2d at 438. Perhaps *Alcoa* creates analytical difficulties because Judge Hand disagreed with this conclusion, but had a duty to affirm the district court's holding to this effect because it was not clearly erroneous.

22. United States v. Grinnell Corp., 384 U.S. 563, 570–71 (1966).

23. This interpretation of § 2 of the Sherman Act contrasts with the European interpretation of Article 86 of the Treaty of Rome, which prohibits "abuses of dominant position" and has been construed to limit exploitive conduct— such as excessive prices—even though such conduct does not increase or maintain the defendant's economic power. See Eleanor Fox, Monopolization and Dominance in the United States and the European Community: Efficiency, Opportunity and Fairness, 61 Notre Dame L. Rev. 981, 990–94 (1986).

24. See section A(5) above.

(4) Price squeezes in regulated industries.

The remedial difficulties of price regulation referred to above may be obviated in price squeeze cases where the defendant is in a regulated industry. But such cases raise other issues concerning competition policy and the role of the antitrust laws. A recent example is *Town of Concord v. Boston Edison Co.*[25] Edison is an integrated power company that generates, transmits, and distributes electric power in Massachusetts. As such, Edison not only generates and transmits the power that it distributes to homes and businesses, but it also sells some of the power it generates to rivals and uses its power lines to transmit electricity purchased by other distributors from still other generators. The rates Edison charges for selling wholesale power or for transmitting power are regulated by the Federal Energy Regulatory Commission (FERC). The rates Edison charges for distributing power to homes and businesses are set by the Massachusetts Department of Public Utilities. The plaintiff, the town of Concord, operates a municipally-owned distribution system that buys wholesale power from Edison. Over a three-year period, Edison successfully persuaded FERC to authorize increases in the wholesale rates it charged customers like Concord; it did not, however, seek an increase in its own retail rates during that period. Thus, Concord claimed that it was the victim of a price squeeze: the wholesale price was going up, while Edison was maintaining a low retail price. As a result, Concord's retail price became non-competitive with Edison's (Edison and Concord competed for the patronage of new firms that had a choice between locating their plants in Concord or within the areas serviced by Edison).

The First Circuit held that price squeezes do not constitute § 2 violations in the regulated industry context.[26] Although Judge Stephen Breyer's opinion carefully tried to distinguish Judge Hand's decision in *Alcoa*, the analysis is highly critical of Hand's approach. *Town of Concord* conceded that a price squeeze that allows a monopolist to extend its power into a second market (recall that Judge Hand had held that Alcoa's squeeze did *not* do

---

25. 915 F.2d 17 (1st Cir. 1990).

26. Id. at 28. Although the court limited its holding by saying that price squeezes would not "normally" be exclusionary, its analysis effectively bars successful prosecution of § 2 claims of municipally-owned electric companies against integrated sources of wholesale power.

In a classic case of judicial activism, the court set forth its broad critique of price squeeze claims in Part II of its opinion, and then explained, in Part III, why its discussion was really dicta because Edison did not possess monopoly power. The court found that the plaintiff did not have to rely on Edison to buy wholesale power (there were several other sources in New England), and that FERC regulations forced Edison to set a reasonable price for transmitting any electricity that Concord might buy from other sources. Id. at 29–31.

this) has two important anticompetitive effects: it raises entry barriers by forcing new firms to compete with the monopolist in two markets rather than one; and it deprives the market of non-price competition and pressures for innovation.   Nevertheless, *Town of Concord* gave three reasons suggesting caution before courts aggressively condemn price squeezes: the monopolist might be more efficient and innovative than its rivals; consumers will benefit if the victim of the price squeeze is itself a monopolist;[27] and, most important, a court cannot effectively determine, without engaging in rate-setting price regulation, whether a given set of wholesale and retail prices constitutes an unlawful price squeeze. *Alcoa* ignored these issues.

After raising these concerns about price squeeze claims in non-regulated markets, Judge Breyer proceeded to persuasively set out additional arguments that clinched the case against antitrust intervention in regulatory price squeeze cases. First, the court noted that the plaintiff, which enjoyed a legal monopoly in retail distribution within its municipal limits, was unlikely to be driven into bankruptcy given its stable customer base, even if it was put at some competitive disadvantage vis-a-vis customers who were free to choose their plant locations.[28] Second, imposition of antitrust liability for price squeezes will encourage utilities seeking wholesale rate increases to ask for retail rate increases as well; although Concord's balance sheet might be more favorable, consumers in the 39 Massachusetts cities where Edison distributed the electricity itself would clearly be harmed. Third, Judge Breyer showed that judicial second-guessing of rates set by government agencies would be an administrative nightmare and would discourage innovative types of rate proceedings. Finally, he observed that FERC is required to consider price squeeze claims and can condemn unreasonable squeezes.[29]

27. Judge Breyer added an appendix that demonstrated why "serial monopolies" are more harmful than single monopolies. Id. at 32. In short, Breyer's argument is that the second monopolist pays the monopoly price to the first monopolist and then adds its own monopoly rate hike; the integrated monopolist sells more by taking a single monopoly profit. For a more extensive discussion of this problem, see Chapter 5, section D.

28. It is probably true that the price squeeze did have the effect of transferring wealth from consumers in Concord to businesses located elsewhere in Massachusetts, but allocating the burden of paying for electric power within Massachusetts was the responsibility of the state regulators, and they were free to insist that Edison maintain higher prices for business customers.

29. Id. at 26–28 (citing FPC v. Conway Corp., 426 U.S. 271 (1976)).

Town of Concord also listed a fifth, less persuasive argument. Judge Breyer argued that, because regulators try to set prices that reflect costs, the only firms that will really be victimized by a price squeeze are those inefficient firms whose costs are higher than the defendant's. Frequently, however, local utilities face a price squeeze because of the nature of the regulatory process. Under federal law, wholesale rates go into effect shortly after filing, unless FERC

(5) Arbitrary refusals to deal.

Another reason for judicial restraint in refusal to deal cases that is not mentioned in *Town of Concord* is the American reluctance to force an independent entrepreneur to do business with someone against her will.[30] This reluctance is not based on efficiency concerns, but rather on non-economic notions of individual autonomy, freedom of traders, and avoidance of discretionary governmental power. For example, in *Official Airline Guides, Inc. v. FTC,*[31] the Second Circuit overturned a Commission order that required the respondent to include in its published list of airline flights the schedules of the commuter airlines along with those of the major airlines. The respondent's monopoly in the publication of airline flights (since superseded by computerized airline reservations systems) meant that its discriminatory treatment of commuter airlines imposed a significant economic disadvantage on these airlines and reduced the amount of information available to consumers, thus creating inefficiencies and diminishing competition in the airline market. Nevertheless, the court emphasized that the refusal to deal (or, more precisely, the refusal to deal on equal terms) had neither the purpose nor the effect of maintaining the *respondent's* monopoly. The court noted that the Commission's rationale would allow the government for example, to prevent a monopoly newspaper from refusing to publish advertisements placed by a firm whose officers held political views abhorrent to the newspaper, if the firm needed such advertising to stay in business. *Official Airline Guides* demonstrates why allocative efficiency should not be the exclusive goal of antitrust, and how non-economic concerns can sometimes be marshalled by defendants to limit, rather than expand, the reach of the antitrust laws.

takes extraordinary action. By contrast, many states require full regulatory approval before retail rates increases can be implemented. Integrated utilities can take advantage of this process by aggressively seeking wholesale rate hikes while taking a more restrained approach to their monopoly power at the retail level, all while squeezing rivals. See e.g., City of Mishawaka v. American Electric Power Co., 616 F.2d 976 (7th Cir. 1980), cert. denied, 449 U.S. 1096 (1981); John Lopatka, The Electric Utility Price Squeeze as an Antitrust Cause of Action, 31 U.C.L.A. L. Rev. 563 (1984). Thus, price squeeze victims are not necessarily less efficient. Nonetheless, because injury in such cases is a peculiar result of the administrative process, the remedy should be increased vigilance by FERC, not the cumbersome overlay of antitrust litigation.

30. In contrast, French law requires merchants to do business with others absent justification. See Milton Handler, Harlan Blake, Robert Pitofsky & Harve Goldschmid, Cases and Materials on Trade Regulation 632 (2d ed. 1987).

31. 630 F.2d 920 (2d Cir. 1980), cert. denied, 450 U.S. 917 (1981).

Section F: Exclusionary Conduct

We have previously canvassed the cases holding that a monopolist violates § 2 when it acquires or maintains monopoly power by means that are either restraints of trade under § 1 or that the authors of the Sherman Act clearly intended to prohibit. These cases also made clear that the acquisition or maintenance of monopoly power by creating obvious efficiencies would not violate § 2.[1] Difficult issues remain, however, in cases when the defendant's conduct is not blatantly anticompetitive but rather tends to exclude competitors without any obvious major efficiencies. These cases involve five types of monopoly conduct: (1) leveraging power from one market into another; (2) increasing barriers to entry; (3) raising rivals' costs; (4) depriving competitors of access to essential facilities; and (5) winning control of natural monopoly markets. In evaluating these cases, the courts rely on two principal factors: whether any modest inefficiencies are outweighed by the benefits of a competitive market; and whether the defendant's conduct represents a predatory sacrifice of short-term profit for long-term monopoly profits.

(1) Leveraging power from one market into another.

In *United States v. Griffith*,[2] the Supreme Court held that so-called "leveraging" of monopoly power from one market to another was unlawful conduct under § 2. The defendant, which owned the only movie theater in a number of small towns, packaged licenses for these theaters with licenses for its theaters in other, competitive markets. Thus, movie distributors who wished to show their movies in the "closed" towns were also required to give the defendant exclusive rights to show the movies in its theaters in the "open" or competitive markets. The Court quickly rejected the district court's effort to distinguish *Griffith* from a prior decision on the ground that the record in the earlier case included evidence of an avowed monopolistic purpose.[3] The Court correctly adopted Judge Hand's *Alcoa* reasoning that specific intent is not an element of § 2; otherwise, sophisticated firms might monopolize with impunity.[4]

Although the leveraging concept is subject to considerable academic debate, the Court correctly condemned it as a form of predation.[5] If the defendant was truly extracting the full monopoly price in the closed towns, it would not be able to force movie

---

1. See section A above.
2. 334 U.S. 100 (1948).
3. Id. at 104 (discussing United States v. Crescent Amusement Co., 323 U.S. 173 (1944)).

4. Id. at 105 (citing United States v. Aluminum Co. of America, 148 F.2d 416, 432 (2d Cir. 1945)).

5. For a fuller discussion of predation, see section D above.

distributors to make the additional concession of allowing the
defendant's theaters to show their movies in the open towns. By
definition, any additional concession above the full monopoly price
would lead the distributor to decide that the sale wasn't worth it.
Thus, Griffith was sacrificing some short-term profits in hopes of
achieving greater long-run profitability by reducing competition in
the open towns.

The language in the opinion condemning leverage is subject to
varying interpretations. In an oft-quoted phrase, Justice Douglas
stated that "the use of monopoly power, however lawfully acquired, to foreclose competition, to gain a competitive advantage,
or to destroy a competitor, is unlawful." On the other hand, the
Court condemned Griffith's use of its monopoly power as a "trade
weapon." [6] The latter phrasing suggests that the Court simply
meant to condemn conduct that is predatory in the sense used in
this treatise—the sacrifice of short-term gains in hopes of achieving longer-term monopoly profits. Yet a broad interpretation of
the Court's language prohibiting "the use of monopoly power" to
"gain a competitive advantage" would suggest that using monopoly profits to expand operations would be unlawful, a notion that
the FTC rejected in *du Pont (TiO$_2$)*[7] and is unlikely to be followed
today.

Requiring Griffith (if it so chose) to use the profits earned in
its closed towns to bid openly against its rivals in the open towns,
rather than foreclosing competition through packaged licenses,
would have a beneficial impact on the competitive process. Rivals
would at least have the option of matching Griffith's bid by
relying on their own sources of funds, greater efficiencies, or non-
price competition. Certainly those interested in protecting equality of economic opportunity can justifiably argue that *Griffith*
incorporates their concerns with no significant harm to resource
allocation. Likewise, those concerned about protecting consumers
and those who think the antitrust laws should constrain discretionary power properly object to a monopolist's arbitrary decision
to forego full exploitation of theatres (and indirectly consumers) in
"closed towns" in order to increase the exploitation of theatres
and consumers in "open towns." [8] Moreover, the populist's willingness to pay a small price in cost efficiencies for competitive
markets (see the discussion of *Alcoa* in section B) applies here as
well. Whatever efficiencies resulted from Griffith's offering of

---

6.   334 U.S. at 107.

7.   See E.I. du Pont de Nemours &
Co., 96 F.T.C. 653 (1980), discussed in
section A(4) above.

8.   See also United States v. Philadelphia National Bank, 374 U.S. 321,

370–71 (1963) (defendant cannot justify
reducing competition in Philadelphia
market in order to enhance competition
for large business accounts between
Philadelphia and New York banks).

package deals instead of requiring separate bids for licenses in each of its theaters (query why closed towns were invariably matched up with open ones?) were unlikely to have been passed on to consumers, and were probably outweighed by the loss of competition in the open towns.

The well-known break-up of the telephone industry in *United States v. American Telephone & Telegraph*[9] is another instance where the defendant's use of monopoly power in one market to "leverage" power in another is really best seen as a form of predation. AT&T, a fully integrated provider of telecommunications services, used its monopoly in local service to require long distance competitors to lease expensive and unnecessary connecting equipment, and thus maintained its monopoly position in long distance service.[10] Similarly, AT&T's local monopolies were required to buy equipment from its wholly owned equipment subsidiary, Western Electric, even though rival products were superior.[11] Because AT&T's conduct was demonstrably inefficient, it should have reduced the company's short-run profitability. However, the long-run benefit of maintaining a monopoly made such leveraging economically sensible.

(2) Increasing entry barriers.

Just as *Paschall* condemned a monopolist's refusal to deal that had the effect of permitting the monopolist to maintain its power by increasing entry barriers,[12] *United States v. United Shoe Machinery Corp.*[13] found that the defendant had engaged in a host of business practices that each made it harder for rivals to enter the market, and thus had illegally monopolized in violation of § 2. Specifically, Judge Charles Wyzanski, in a landmark opinion affirmed by the Supreme Court, found that United Shoe unlawfully maintained its decades-long monopoly of the shoe machine market by (1) adopting a policy of only leasing, and not selling, its machines; (2) including the cost of servicing and repairing machines in the lease price; and (3) price discriminating by setting prices that gave it a higher rate of return on machines that faced no competition and a lower rate of return on machines for which substitutes existed.

First, the lease-only policy prevented potential rivals from purchasing the defendant's machines in order to alter or improve

---

9. See 524 F.Supp. 1336 (D.D.C. 1981) (order denying defendant's motion to dismiss following government's case-in-chief); 552 F.Supp. 131 (D.D.C. 1982) (acceptance, with modifications, of consent decree), aff'd mem. sub nom. Maryland v. United States, 460 U.S. 1001 (1983).

10. 524 F. Supp. at 1352–57.

11. Id. at 1371–72.

12. See section E(2) above.

13. 110 F. Supp. 295 (D. Mass. 1953), aff'd per curiam, 347 U.S. 521 (1954).

them, and likewise precluded larger buyers from purchasing and then reselling the machines. In either instance, an after-market in used machines would have grown to compete with United Shoe, which would have facilitated product innovations by rivals. Moreover, firms purchasing and seeking to improve United Shoe machines would have been alternative purchasers of shoe machinery inventions, many of which went to United Shoe in the early years of the industry.[14]

Second, including the cost of servicing the machines in the lease price raised concerns similar to those that arise with tying arrangements.[15] One problem with this coupling is that it prevented the development of an independent market for the servicing of shoe machines. In addition, although United Shoe's customers may have been satisfied with this policy in the short run, the lack of an independent servicing market also helped United Shoe maintain its monopoly in the shoe machine market. Any potential entrant would also have had to develop its own servicing network in order to compete with United Shoe. Because creating such a network is costly, the coupling policy increased the barriers to entering the shoe machine market.

Finally, Judge Wyzanski criticized United Shoe's discriminatory pricing policy. He declined, however, to specifically condemn such pricing; rather, by creating a market in second-hand machines, Wyzanski hoped to end discriminatory pricing by creating competition for the higher-priced machines—i.e., those that for which no substitutes were readily available. This approach was well-founded: indeed, it is difficult to see how discriminatory pricing maintained, rather than simply reflected, United Shoe's market dominance. A firm that enjoys monopoly power in most markets but faces competition in a few might, if prohibited from

---

14. For a defense of United Shoe's lease-only policy, see, e.g., John Wiley, Eric Rasmusen & J. Mark Ramseyer, The Leasing Monopolist, 37 U.C.L.A. L. Rev. 693 (1990). The authors do not address the dynamic inefficiencies (such as reduced innovation) inherent in United Shoe's maintenance of monopoly power. Their analysis also appears to assume a positive answer to a question posed by Richard Posner and Frank Easterbrook, Antitrust 640 (2d ed. 1981): "won't shoe manufacturers realize that by entering into 10-year leases with United they may be reducing the competitive alternatives open to them in the future, and demand that United compensate them for this reduction?" See 37 U.C.L.A. L. Rev. at 707 (because buyers would expect that United Shoe's monopoly pricing would encourage later entry into the market, their agreed upon lease payments would not exceed the amount that United Shoe could have obtained by entering into a short-term lease at a monopoly rate for the early years of the lease followed by a short-term lease at the competitive rate in the later years after new firms had entered). Wiley et al. appear to assume that the hundreds of small firms were at no disadvantage, compared to United Shoe, in terms of their ability to anticipate future competitive prices and market entry, and cared enough to bargain aggressively with United Shoe over an item that contributed only 2% to the cost of shoes.

15. See Chapter 5, section G.

price discriminating, prefer to maintain high prices in the monopoly markets and simply withdraw from the competitive ones—benefiting no one. On the other hand, by fostering competition in the heretofore monopolized markets, the court provided the best remedy for this type of price discrimination.[16]

Curiously, while finding that these three practices supported a finding of unlawful monopolization, Judge Wyzanski wrote that United Shoe's power "does not rest on predatory practices."[17] This language is subject to two interpretations, neither of which was articulated. First, Wyzanski may have conflated what this text has called "generic" predation (any sacrifice of short-term gain for longer-term monopoly profits) with specific types of predatory activities that courts have condemned as illegal (below-cost pricing, or conduct done with a specific intent to exclude competition). Under this interpretation, he may have believed that United Shoe's leasing and service practices were not analogous to previously condemned predatory conduct, but were nonetheless inefficient and sacrificed short-term revenues for long-term monopoly profits (i.e., United Shoe might have profited in the short run from selling some of its equipment, or agreeing to shorter leases, but chose not to offer customers these options in order to maintain barriers to entry). Alternatively, the court may have determined that United Shoe's practices were not even generically predatory, but rather were both efficient and exclusionary—that is, that the defendant's conduct resulted in cost-savings for itself, but that the long-run effect was to exclude competition in shoe machines. Under this interpretation, Wyzanski may have implicitly felt that the defendant's monopoly power meant that much of the cost savings resulting from these efficiencies would not be passed on to shoe manufacturers (the lessors of the machines), and that consumers would therefore be better off with slightly less efficient competition. This is the trade-off preferred by populists, but rejected by the Chicago school. The former group would favor this approach because the shoe manufacturing industry was highly competitive and millions of consumers would have received the small benefits of competition in the shoe machine market. The latter group would oppose this approach because prohibiting United Shoe's efficient practices would devote too many of society's resources to shoe machines.

One's view of the wisdom of Judge Wyzanski's decision is also affected by one's paradigmatic view of the efficacy of government intervention. Populists would predict that creating competition in

---

16. For a fuller discussion of this problem in the context of the Robinson–Patman Act's prohibitions on price discrimination, see Chapter 7, sections A and B.

17. 110 F. Supp. at 345.

the secondary market for shoe machines and a new separate servicing market would ultimately benefit consumers, even if shoe manufacturers were not happy in the short run. Skeptics of government intervention, on the other hand, would fear that these predicted long-run benefits may not materialize; accordingly, they would be more reluctant to interfere with long-standing business practices that seemed to benefit buyers.

If a monopolist violates § 2 by maintaining monopoly power through practices that increase entry barriers, the definition of what constitutes barriers to entry becomes critical to coherent antitrust analysis. The federal government's policy, as reflected in its 1992 Merger Guidelines, borrows from Professor Joe Bain in considering barriers to exist whenever a firm is able to earn monopoly profits without attracting entry.[18] Under this theory, there were significant entry barriers in the shoe machinery business.

In *Echlin Manufacturing Co.*, in contrast, the Reagan-era Federal Trade Commission borrowed from Professor George Stigler in limiting barriers to "additional long-run costs that must be incurred by an entrant relative to the long-run costs faced by incumbent firms."[19] Thus, if potential rivals could effectively compete in the shoe machinery market by making the same kind of investment in both machinery and service personnel that United Shoe had made over the years, the FTC would have found no exclusionary potential.

Commentators have two persuasive theoretical criticisms of *Echlin*'s analysis.[20] First, it ignores the greater risk that a firm faces when investing in a new industry. For example, Ford will have an easier time raising $100 million for a new plant than Delorean. A second, related point is that *Echlin* fails to distinguish among markets based on whether the risky investment a new entrant must make consists of "sunk" costs. A firm that can enter a market by purchasing used trucks worth $1 million and

---

18. Merger Guidelines—1992, 4 Trade Reg. Rep. (CCH) ¶ 13,104, § 3 (Apr. 7, 1992). See generally Joe Bain, Barriers to New Competition (1956).

19. 105 F.T.C. 410, 485 (1985) (citing George Stigler, The Organization of Industry 67 (1968)).

Echlin was a merger case that the FTC dismissed because of the absence of barriers to entry. The merging parties competed in the sale of carburetor kits, which are packages of components used by auto mechanics to repair carburetors that do not need to be completely re-

placed. The Commission refused to characterize as entry barriers the cost involved in designing a new brand of kits, building an inventory, and introducing the new line; economies of scale; and the threat of retaliatory pricing by other incumbents. Id. at 488–91. (The FTC also found, as a factual matter, that these three alleged entry barriers probably did not actually exist.)

20. See, e.g., E. Thomas Sullivan & Herbert Hovenkamp, Antitrust Law, Policy and Procedure 560–62 (2d ed. 1989).

knows that it can sell the trucks for almost the same amount if the business fails is more likely to enter than a company that must spend $1 million on television advertising to counter the brand loyalty of established firms, knowing that none of its investment can be recovered in the event of failure. Commissioner Patricia Bailey, dissenting in *Echlin*, offered a more jurisprudential critique; she condemned the majority for "embrac[ing] the current 'Chicago School' economic 'State Religion' approach to barriers to entry, a view which simply is *not* generally accepted in the legal and economic communities." [21] Especially in light of the FTC's restatement of policy in the new merger guidelines, it is unclear whether *Echlin* still represents FTC policy.[22]

(3) Generic predation and raising rivals' costs.

A monopolist that sacrifices its short-term interests in order to maintain its long-term monopoly position engages in wilful monopolization in violation of § 2. Determining when specific conduct constitutes a sacrifice of short-term interests, though, can sometimes be difficult. This is particularly true for a strategy recently identified by economists as "raising rivals' costs." [23] This strategy is simply a subset of generic predation: a monopolist sacrifices its own short-term profits in order to impose higher costs on rivals, in order to weaken their ability to effectively compete. If a plaintiff can establish that the defendant obtained or maintained a monopoly by adopting this strategy, the plaintiff should prevail on a monopolization claim.

Aspen Skiing Co. v. Aspen Highlands Skiing Corp.[24] involved relatively easy questions about the constraints § 2 places on a monopolist's conduct, and is also instructive about the type of evidence courts can use in analyzing whether the monopolist's acquisition or maintenance of power was wilful. In that case, the operator of one of Aspen's ski slopes sued its sole and dominant rival, which operated the area's other three slopes, for cancelling a cooperative arrangement that allowed skiers to purchase tickets that could be used on any of the four slopes. The Court found that the conduct was inefficient and predatory, and therefore violated § 2.

---

21. 105 F.T.C. at 495 (italics in original). Bailey questioned the Commission's assertion that Stigler's approach was "widely accepted," responding: "Alas, that may be so, depending however on the circles in which one travels." Id. at 495 n.13.

22. A veteran FTC litigator has suggested that, notwithstanding *Echlin*, the Commission has never really limit-ed its inquiry to consideration of Stiglerian barriers. Interview: Steven Newborn, Antitrust (summer 1992), at 22.

23. See generally Thomas Krattenmaker & Steven Salop, Anticompetitive Exclusion: Raising Rivals' Costs to Achieve Power Over Price, 96 Yale L.J. 209 (1986).

24. 472 U.S. 585 (1985).

In so holding, Justice John Paul Stevens relied on three key facts: the defendant participated in cooperative arrangements in other ski areas where it did not possess monopoly power; its prior participation at Aspen appeared to be profitable; and it offered no plausible justification for cancelling the arrangement at Aspen. *Aspen* is thus important for teaching that the efficiency or inefficiency of a monopolist's conduct (i.e. whether the behavior represents a sacrifice of short-term profit for long-term monopoly position) can be demonstrated by (1) evidence describing how markets function elsewhere and (2) the defendant's inability to explain its conduct.

Some academics have suggested that a defendant should not be prejudiced by its inability to offer a justification for its acts, because there may be reasons why the market's invisible hand guided the defendant to engage in the challenged conduct, even if not explicable by the defendant. Indeed, Professor John Wiley suggested (two years after the Court's judgment) that the conduct challenged in *Aspen* was efficient because it permitted the defendant to promote the area more aggressively to skiers who might otherwise patronize other ski resorts, without fearing that some of these newly attracted skiers would spend their money on the plaintiff's slope.[25] Since this argument was not raised by the defendant, the record, of course, does not indicate whether the defendant's promotional expenses actually increased, whether three-fourths of the return on the promotional investment would have been a sufficient return, and—most important—whether the promotional campaign actually increased competition among ski areas by lowering price or raising the quality of the product. The slim likelihood that these suppositions were true argues against allowing such unarticulated justifications to deter courts from imposing antitrust liability in cases like *Aspen*. More importantly, almost all these *post hoc* justifications involved allegedly efficient business strategies that can only be achieved if the firm implementing the practice is consciously pursuing them.[26] Aspen Skiing's willingness to reduce short-term patronage as part of a long-term promotional campaign is not even plausible unless it had some idea of the trade-offs involved. If Aspen Skiing knew what it was doing, it was free to tell the jury about it.

Why would the defendant ski company have engaged in inefficient conduct? Even though its refusal to offer a multi-mountain ticket may have hurt consumers, and may even have discouraged some skiers from coming to Aspen, the defendant determined that

---

25. "After Chicago": An Exaggerated Demise? 1986 Duke L.J. 1003, 1005.

26. Louis Kaplow, Extension of Monopoly Power Through Leverage, 85 Colum. L. Rev. 515, 543–45 (1985).

it would rather have a bigger share of a smaller pie. This, of course, represents the sacrifice of short-term revenues for long-term monopoly profits, or predation.

Aspen Skiing's willingness to hurt itself a little in order to hurt Aspen Highlands a lot is a classic example of "raising rivals' costs." Professor Oliver Williamson provides an even clearer illustration: suppose that the dominant firm in an industry relies on heavy automation and thus is capital intensive, while most of its rivals are labor-intensive. Because it has relatively few workers, the dominant firm can give its workers a considerable wage increase, far above that necessary to attract workers or forestall organized industrial action, without expending a significant amount of resources. The union is then likely to demand and obtain comparable wage increases from the rival companies, who will face major increases in cost because they employ a relatively large number of workers.[27]

One significant post-*Aspen* decision that addressed the "raising rivals' costs" theory is *Ball Memorial Hospital, Inc. v. Mutual Hospital Insurance, Inc.*[28] The plaintiff hospitals challenged Blue Cross/Blue Shield's creation of a new health insurance package (a "Preferred Provider Organization" or "PPO") that fully reimbursed their insureds only if they used "preferred" hospitals, and then demanded major discounts from any Indiana hospital that wanted to be included on the "preferred" list. The hospitals argued that, as non-profit entities that enjoyed monopoly power but operated on a break-even basis, they would recoup the revenues lost as a result of the discount given to the Blues by raising fees to other insurance companies. Thus, they concluded that the Blues' scheme unlawfully imposed of higher costs on their rivals in violation of § 2.

Judge Frank Easterbrook's opinion for the Seventh Circuit correctly rejected the hospitals' argument. The court upheld the district court's findings that the Blues lacked market power and that "the discounts given on patients covered by the [Blues'] PPO are justified by reductions in cost."[29] If the Blues lacked market power, they could not have acquired or maintained monopoly power, a prerequisite to any § 2 case.[30] Unfortunately, Judge Easterbrook went on in dicta to opine that the evidence of cost

---

27. See Oliver Williamson, Wage Rates as a Barrier to Entry: the *Pennington* Case in Perspective, 82 Q.J. Econ. 85 (1968).

28. 603 F. Supp. 1077 (S.D. Ind. 1985), aff'd, 784 F.2d 1325 (7th Cir. 1986).

29. 784 F.2d at 1340.

30. The plaintiffs' complaint did not allege that the Blues' PPO scheme constituted an unlawful attempt to monopolize under § 2, and the court did not address that issue. For a discussion of attempted monopolization, see section G.

justification was unnecessary, and that courts should not function as "little versions of the Office of Price Administration and assess the 'cost justification' for prices charged." [31] The better argument would have been that the plaintiffs simply failed to prove a central tenet of the raising rivals' cost argument—that the defendant had hurt itself a little in order to hurt its rivals a lot. *Any* competitive edge gained by a defendant will force rivals to expend more resources in order to catch up. There was no indication in *Ball Memorial*, however, that the Blues' new insurance offering raised rival insurance companies' costs by hurting the Blues in the short run. Thus, no generic predation was shown, and the § 2 claim was properly rejected.

The reach of *Aspen* was also tested in *Olympia Equipment Leasing Co. v. Western Union Telegraph Co.*[32] Western Union enjoyed a monopoly in providing "telex" services (message, not voice, communications sent directly from one subscriber to another). It had historically packaged its telex services with leases on telex terminals, thus giving it a monopoly in the equipment market as well. Following FCC orders to "unbundle" its service and equipment sales, and apparently hoping to sell its equipment inventory to raise capital for other investments, Western Union initially encouraged firms like Olympia to enter the equipment market and sell terminals to Western Union customers. Later, however, Western Union decided that its inventory was not being liquidated quickly enough and stopped helping Olympia; specifically, it refused to refer customers to Olympia as it had previously done, and refused to provide its customer list to the plaintiff.

Olympia claimed that *Aspen* required Western Union to cooperate with it by providing vendor lists, arguing that just as Aspen Highlands (the plaintiff in *Aspen*) could not survive without the cooperation with its rival, so Olympia could not survive without Western Union's help. The Seventh Circuit correctly rejected this argument, distinguishing *Aspen* on two key grounds. First, unlike Aspen Skiing's unjustified refusal to cooperate with its rival, Western Union had a pro-competitive justification—its desire to sell its own supply as quickly as possible. As Judge Richard Posner observed, a "monopolist cannot be faulted for wanting to sell *more* output unless he is engaged in some predatory or exclusionary scheme.... There is no such scheme here; Western Union's long-run design is to get out of the telex terminal market." [33] Second, Aspen Skiing's refusal to cooperate with its rival in Aspen stood in stark contrast to its own decision to cooperate with rivals in other ski areas, suggesting that cooperation was an

31. Id.

32. 797 F.2d 370 (7th Cir. 1986).

33. Id. at 378 (emphasis in original).

efficient marketing tool. In *Olympia Leasing*, by contrast, the court correctly pointed to the absence of "evidence that suppliers of telecommunications equipment customarily provide their customers with lists." [34]

Olympia Leasing thus exemplifies what *Aspen* really stands for: the proposition that § 2 prohibits only generically predatory behavior—conduct that in the short-run is inefficient but is designed to enhance the monopolist's long-term power. Unfortunately, Judge Posner does not read *Aspen* that way:

> If [*Aspen*] stands for any principle that goes beyond its unusual facts it is that a monopolist may be guilty of monopolization if it refuses to cooperate with a competitor in circumstances where some cooperation is indispensible to effective competition.[35]

Concededly, *Aspen*'s facts are "unusual". What makes them unusual, however, are not the peculiarities of the ski industry but the plaintiff's persuasive evidence (based on the defendant's prior conduct in the Aspen market and its conduct in other markets) that the defendant's refusal to deal was inefficient. In that sense, *Aspen* reaches more broadly than Judge Posner would apply it. On the other hand, where a monopolist refuses to deal with a competitor based on legitimate business justifications, and where the result is efficient, it is not at all clear that § 2 has been violated, even if "cooperation is indispensible to effective competition." In such a case, the court should evaluate the efficiency/monopoly trade-offs as Judge Wyzanski did in *United Shoe*.

(4) Essential facilities.

In *Aspen*, the Supreme Court expressly declined to consider another exclusionary behavior claim asserted by the plaintiff: that the defendant unlawfully refused to give the plaintiff access to its "essential facility." [36] The elements of an "essential facility" claim were set out by the District of Columbia Circuit in *Hecht v. Pro–Football, Inc.*,[37] an opinion holding that the Washington Redskins unlawfully secured exclusive rights to play professional football at RFK Stadium. In order to make out such a claim, the court held, the plaintiff must prove that (1) access to the facility in question is essential to the plaintiff's competitive survival; (2) the facility cannot practically be duplicated; [38] and (3) the plaintiff can use the facility without interfering with the defendant's use.

34. Id. at 377.

35. Id. at 379.

36. 472 U.S. at 611 n.44.

37. 570 F.2d 982 (D.C. Cir. 1977), cert. denied, 436 U.S. 956 (1978).

38. The briefest reflection reveals that these first two elements are really

As described in *Hecht,* the essential facility doctrine is simply another subset of generic predation. If the plaintiff's team could have used RFK Stadium without interfering with the defendant's use (by scheduling all of the plaintiff's games on weekends when the Redskins were playing on the road), then why would the Redskins have wanted to pay any additional rent to induce the D.C. Stadium Authority to deny the plaintiff access? Only a defendant willing to pay more in the short run in hopes of acquiring long-term profits would pay a premium for exclusivity. This conduct is generic predation, and such a defendant is guilty of unlawful monopolization.

The Supreme Court wisely refused to apply this doctrine in *Aspen.* *Hecht,* and several other cases correctly applying the doctrine,[39] involved the defendant's use of monopoly power to deprive the plaintiff of access to a *third party's* essential facility. Where, as in *Aspen,* the plaintiff seeks access to the defendant's *own* facilities, the courts are normally reluctant to rule in favor of the plaintiff for fear of stifling the defendant's incentives to innovate.[40] Nevertheless, populists may persuasively argue that appropriate relief should be granted in cases where the judge finds with some confidence that the additional competition resulting from mandating access would increase output.[41] In any event, there was no need for the Court to resolve the knotty trade-offs involved in such an argument in *Aspen.*

(5) Natural monopoly markets.

Special rules come into play when firms acquire monopoly power in markets that, in the words of Judge Hand's opinion in *Alcoa,* are "so limited that it is impossible to produce at all and meet the cost of production except by a plant large enough to supply the whole demand."[42] Economists call these markets "natural monopolies." The fundamental premise of antitrust—

one and the same: if the facility could be duplicated, it would not be essential to the plaintiff's survival.

39. See also United States Football League v. National Football League, 644 F.Supp. 1040 (S.D.N.Y. 1986), aff'd on other grounds, 842 F.2d 1335 (2d Cir. 1988).

40. Cf. Berkey Photo, Inc. v. Eastman Kodak Co., 603 F.2d 263 (2d Cir. 1979), cert. denied, 444 U.S. 1093 (1980). A vertically integrated defendant's refusal to deal at one level with a competitor at another level may constitute monopolization, and may also involve denial of access to "essential facilities."

See, e.g., MCI Communications Corp. v. AT&T, 708 F.2d 1081 (7th Cir.), cert. denied, 464 U.S. 891 (1983) (AT&T's rival for long-distance services successfully challenged AT&T's refusal to grant it access to local telephone services). Such cases are better analyzed as a problem of vertical integration. See section E(2).

41. See generally James Ratner, Should There Be an Essential Facilities Doctrine?, 21 U.C. Davis L. Rev. 327 (1988).

42. 148 F.2d at 430.

that the economy should feature competition among several firms—simply cannot work in such markets. The fundamental remedy for monopolization—dissolution of the monopolist's assets among new competing firms—is also not available because, by definition, competition can not succeed in natural monopoly markets.

Nevertheless, the antitrust laws still have some role to play in these markets. The goals of providing consumers with the best products and of equalizing economic opportunity suggest that competition policy should favor rules that allow firms to vigorously compete for the opportunity to become the natural monopolist, and to subject the incumbent monopolist to periodic challenges by those who would dethrone them. As the First Circuit noted in *Union Leader Corp. v. Newspapers of New England, Inc.*, the leading opinion in this area, "we will not say that the public does not have an interest in competition even though that competition be an elimination bout." [43]   Thus, the court devised antitrust's version of the Marquis of Queensbury rules.[44] Under these rules, active but fair competition is permissible, even if done with the intent and effect of acquiring monopoly power. What has been broadly referred to in this chapter as predation—the sacrifice of short-term profits in anticipation of long-term monopoly power—is also permissible. *Union Leader* did not address whether classic predatory pricing—pricing below average variable cost—is lawful. If the goal is to promote a fair fight and encourage equally efficient challengers to take on the incumbent, however, such pricing should be unlawful.

What is the antitrust equivalent of a punch below the belt? *Union Leader* condemned soliciting of customers *not* to deal with rivals, and providing secret rebates to community leaders who were publicly advocating switching patronage to the defendant.[45] The court suggested (although finding that this did not occur in *Union Leader*) that banding together with other natural monopolists to fend off challenges would be illegal.[46] Each of these unfair tactics harm consumers and discourage equally efficient firms from fighting it out. Imposing treble damage penalties on those who fight unfairly is the best, and the most, the antitrust laws can do in these circumstances.

43. 284 F.2d 582, 584 n.4 (1st Cir. 1960), cert. denied, 365 U.S. 833 (1961).

44. For those not well-versed in sports trivia, the marquis was the British nobleman who devised the basic rules governing the modern sport of boxing.

45. Id. at 584–86.

46. Id. at 588.

Section G: Attempts to Monopolize

(1) Policy implications and basic concepts.

Section 2 of the Sherman Act condemns not only the acquisition or maintenance of monopoly power but also attempts to monopolize. The offense of attempted monopolization fills in a gap that would otherwise exist in antitrust law. Anticompetitive conduct by two or more firms acting in concert is illegal under § 1 as a conspiracy in restraint of trade. Anticompetitive conduct by a single firm with monopoly power is illegal monopolization under § 2. Attempted monopolization can thus cover anticompetitive conduct by a single firm that does not have monopoly power.

Those skeptical about the market's ability to prevent such behavior and sanguine about the courts' ability to detect and remedy violations favor broad definition of attempted monopolization. Free marketeers, on the other hand, favor narrow coverage, for they are skeptical that non-monopolistic conduct by a single firm can harm efficiency, and even more skeptical that courts can correctly distinguish when behavior by a single firm is anticompetitive and when it represents vigorous competition.[1]

The "hornbook" elements of attempted monopolization were established by the Supreme Court in *Swift & Co. v. United States*.[2] First, unlike monopolization, attempted monopolization is a specific intent offense: the plaintiff must prove that the defendant intended that its conduct, if successful, would give it monopoly power in a properly defined market. Second, even though the challenged conduct has not yet succeeded in achieving monopoly power, there must be a dangerous probability that it would do so if not stopped by the court.[3] Later cases have added another element implicit in *Swift*: the defendant's behavior must be anti-

---

1. In recent years, several factors have eased the practical necessity to use the antitrust laws as a means of reaching non-monopolistic conduct by a single firm. Traditionally, plaintiffs and antitrust activists favored expanding the scope of attempted monopolization in order to allow treble damages awards for injuries resulting from anticompetitive non-monopolistic conduct by a single firm. Expanded use of the treble damages remedy in civil suits filed under the Racketeer Influenced and Corrupt Organizations Act (RICO), 18 U.S.C. §§ 1961–1968 (1988), has allowed plaintiffs to attack many of these practices without needing to resolve tricky antitrust issues. Moreover, as federal judges become less hospitable to antitrust claims, plaintiffs' lawyers are finding that the opportunities for punitive damages in state tort suits make that route an attractive one as well. See, e.g., Browning–Ferris Industries of Vermont, Inc. v. Kelco Disposal, Inc., 492 U.S. 257 (1989) (affirming judgment of $153,438 in treble damages and $212,500 in attorneys' fees on claim of attempted monopolization in violation of § 2 of the Sherman Act, and $6,066,082 in compensatory and punitive damages on state tort claim of tortious interference with contractual relations).

2. 196 U.S. 375 (1905).

3. Id. at 396.

competitive.[4]

Swift read the element of specific intent into § 2 based on the sensible notion that Congress, in adopting an antitrust statute incorporating many common law concepts, also intended to adopt the common law rules concerning attempt offenses. Common law judges were concerned that they not punish innocent acts. Because conduct leading up to, but not actually constituting, unlawful activity may or may not be sufficiently dangerous to justify condemnation, an intent requirement was thought necessary to ensure that the defendant posed a sufficient danger to society to justify punishment. Similarly, an intent requirement lessened the likelihood that ambiguous acts would lead to the conviction of an innocent person. Of course, courts will infer a specific intent where the acts constituting the attempt are not ambiguous, and clearly have no plausible non-criminal purpose.

Walker Process Equipment, Inc. v. Food Machinery & Chemical Corp.[5] demonstrates the necessity of the second element—proof of a dangerous probability that the defendant will achieve unlawful monopolization. In that case, Food Machinery sued Walker Process for infringing its patent on a highly specialized piece of sewage treatment equipment. Walker Process denied the infringement and counterclaimed that the patent was invalid. After discovery, Food Machinery moved to dismiss its complaint because the patent had expired, but Walker amended its counterclaim to allege a § 2 violation, alleging that Food Machinery had knowingly misrepresented key facts to the Patent Office. The Court agreed that patent fraud could form the basis of an attempt offense,[6] but remanded for a factual hearing on the question whether the acquisition of the patent would, in fact, have given Food Machinery monopoly power. The Court noted that operators of sewage treatment systems might find that alternative products were perfectly satisfactory substitutes for the product made by the parties, in which case the patent would not have conferred monop-

---

4. Because the defendants in *Swift* controlled 60% of the nation's meat-packing industry, and conspired to refrain from bidding against each other, to jointly manipulate the cattle market, to fix prices, to establish uniform credit terms, and to obtain illegal rebates from railroads, id. at 394, Justice Oliver Wendell Holmes, Jr., can be excused for failing to elaborate on this point.

5. 382 U.S. 172 (1965).

6. To avoid chilling the legitimate exploitation of inventions under the patent laws, the court held that bad faith (in this case; knowing misrepresentation) was an essential element in establishing an antitrust violation in cases involving patent fraud. Id. at 174. The presumption that a patentee's infringement action is brought in good faith can only be overcome by "clear and convincing evidence." Handgards, Inc. v. Ethicon, Inc., 601 F.2d 986, 996 (9th Cir. 1979), cert. denied, 444 U.S. 1025 (1980).

oly power.[7]

Given that patent fraud is unambiguously harmful to society, why should we require plaintiffs to offer additional evidence to establish attempted monopolization? The dangerous probability of success requirement is based on the view that § 2 condemns social misconduct only where it has the potential to harm competition, and not simply because the conduct is intrinsically evil. Absent this competitive harm, other laws (patent fraud is a separate offense under the patent laws) provide appropriate protection against the wrongdoing.

The final element of attempted monopolization requires a showing that the defendant engaged in misconduct. Because the mere attainment of monopoly power is not illegal under § 2,[8] the mere attempt to attain such power likewise cannot be prohibited. Rather, the defendant must have engaged in conduct that, if successful, could be characterized as the "wilful" acquisition of monopoly power. A defendant who invents a superior product may attempt to secure a monopoly through its innovation, but such conduct obviously would not constitute illegal attempted monopolization.

The nature of the defendant's conduct was the key issue in *Photovest Corp. v. Fotomat Corp.*[9] Fotomat sought to quickly develop a new retail outlet for film processing and sales by operating small drive-through kiosks in shopping center parking lots. Initially, Fotomat licensed franchisees like the plaintiff; in return for an initial franchise fee and a promise of royalties, Fotomat agreed not to build Fotomat stores within two miles of Photovest stores and to sell materials to Photovest at cost. Once Fotomat realized that its profits from company-owned kiosks were higher than its return on franchised outlets, it began opening up its own kiosks near the plaintiff's stores and breached its contract to provide materials at cost. Fotomat argued that it was simply competing aggressively for retail business.

The Seventh Circuit affirmed the trial court's judgment in favor of the plaintiff. After determining that drive-through kiosks constituted a relevant product market and that Fotomat dominated that market, the court examined the defendant's conduct. Rejecting Fotomat's claim that it was vigorously competing, the court found that opening and maintaining unprofitable Fotomat

7. In a later chapter, we discuss other cases, primarily concerned with tying arrangements, where courts have presumed market power based on a patent. This line of cases, beginning with United States v. Loew's, Inc., 371 U.S. 38 (1962), has apparently ignored *Walker Process.* See Chapter 5, section G(3c–1).

8. See section A(2) and (3) above.

9. 606 F.2d 704 (7th Cir. 1979), cert. denied, 445 U.S. 917 (1980).

kiosks near existing Photovest stores and forcing Photovest to use a high-cost, low-quality supplier constituted predatory misconduct.[10] Such misconduct formed the basis for the finding of attempted monopolization. Fotomat's willingness to continue to operate unprofitable stores demonstrated a specific intent to monopolize.[11]

(2) The "elemental" approach.

The Supreme Court has not decided whether a plaintiff must establish each of these three elements separately in order to prevail on an attempt claim, and the lower courts are divided on that question. At one relatively isolated extreme, the district court in *Mt. Lebanon Motors, Inc. v. Chrysler Corp.*[12] held that clear proof of specific intent is sufficient to establish a § 2 violation. At the other extreme, the majority of the circuits require that each element be separately proved.

In *Mt. Lebanon*, Chrysler was accused of violating § 2 by driving an independent Chrysler dealer out of business. The court directed a verdict for the defendant on the monopolization charge because competition from other auto dealers prevented Chrysler from exercising monopoly power, but allowed the jury to consider the attempt claim.[13] The court explained that specific intent to monopolize was legally sufficient to sustain the attempt count,[14] and concluded that the jury was entitled to find that Chrysler's actions were not motivated by "honest business judgment," but rather "by personal animosity against plaintiff's president ... because of his prominent part in promoting opposition by privately-financed dealers to the operation of [Chrysler-owned dealerships]."[15]

---

10. Id. at 711–14. For a discussion of predation, see section D.

11. 606 F.2d at 714–20. The court also rejected Fotomat's argument that no monopolization occurred because Photovest always followed Fotomat's suggested list prices. The court reasoned that the fear of competition from Photovest may have constrained Fotomat's recommended prices, and noted that franchisees were not required to follow Fotomat's price recommendations. Although this analysis seems persuasive in the context of this case, a different result might obtain if the defendant could show that the nature of the industry was such that its monopolization would have no effect on price. Cf. United States v. Citizens & South-

ern National Bank, 422 U.S. 86 (1975) (allowing defendant to make otherwise anticompetitive acquisition of affiliated banks that had, prior to the acquisition, acted as if they were part of same company as defendant).

12. 283 F. Supp. 453 (W.D. Pa. 1968), aff'd an other grounds, 417 F.2d 622 (3d Cir. 1969).

13. The jury found that Chrysler had unlawfully attempted to monopolize, but that the plaintiff had not suffered any damage from that violation. 417 F.2d at 623.

14. 283 F. Supp. at 461.

15. Id. at 456.

The attempt charge should not have gone to the jury in this case. Even if the evidence showed that Chrysler intended to take control of its own retail operations by driving the plaintiff out of business, and carried out that plan through unlawful means (predatory pricing was alleged), the evidence was clear that Chrysler could not monopolize because of the competition it faced from Ford and General Motors. Therefore, Chrysler's conduct might injure the plaintiff, but it would not harm consumers or the competitive process as a whole. These kinds of cases are best governed by the legal doctrines concerning unfair competition, which focus more on society's concepts of fairness toward competitors than on competition.[16]

Even the Jeffersonian goal of equality of economic opportunity should not be extended to cover cases, like *Mt. Lebanon*, which simply involve an unfair business practice directed by one firm against another. Just as the economic goals of antitrust focus on the effect of the defendant's conduct on consumers or the economy as a whole, the Jeffersonian concern is also aimed at the "big picture." Thus, Jeffersonians condemn practices that have the effect of denying economic opportunities to entrepreneurs because of their size or lack of power. In *Mt. Lebanon*, however, there was no evidence that Chrysler had sufficient market power that its conduct could harm consumers or the economy, or that its behavior was part of a pattern of predatory activity that could have a widespread impact on the economic opportunities of car dealers generally.

16. For example, in Northwest Power Products, Inc. v. Omark Industries, Inc., 576 F.2d 83 (5th Cir. 1978), cert. denied, 439 U.S. 1116 (1979), the plaintiff challenged its termination as one of Omark's Dallas–Fort Worth distributors of masonry-related tools. The plaintiff alleged that its termination was due to a conspiracy between Omark and Northwest's former sales manager, who left Northwest along with several other top employees to form a new firm, which then received the new Omark distributorship. At the time, Omark was the nation's second largest producer of these type of tools, with 25% of the market, and Northwest was the second largest distributor in Dallas, with 18–20% of the market. There was no evidence that the unfair conduct threatened competition in any relevant market. In rejecting the antitrust claim, the court explained:

> [T]he purposes of antitrust and unfair competition generally conflict. The thrust of antitrust law is to prevent restraints on competition. Unfair competition is still competition and the purpose of the law of unfair competition is to impose restraints on that competition.

Id. at 89. Although the *Omark* court joined several others in concluding that unfair competition becomes an antitrust violation only when the defendant is a "significant existing competitor," id., the better rule would seem to require a showing that the *plaintiff*'s existence plays a significant role in the competitive process. If the unfair elimination of the plaintiff has an effect on the extent of rivalry in a market, then antitrust intervention is warranted.

In *Lessig v. Tidewater Oil Co.*,[17] the Ninth Circuit took a similar, though not quite so extreme, position as the district court in *Mt. Lebanon*, holding that Tidewater had illegally attempted to monopolize by using improper means to eliminate one of its service station dealers. In that case, the jury had found that the dealer was eliminated as part of the defendant's scheme to fix the price of Tidewater gasoline and to exclude rival brands of tires and other accessories from its service stations. The court reasoned that "specific intent itself is the only evidence of dangerous probability the statute requires—perhaps on the not unreasonable assumption that the actor is better able than others to judge the practical possibility of achieving his illegal objective."[18] Although this assumption is often valid, it need not rise to the level of a conclusive presumption; where, as in *Lessig*, the defendant's market share was minimal, there was no basis to infer a dangerous probability of monopolization.

The majority of the circuits reject the approach taken in *Mt. Lebanon* and *Lessig* and instead require the opposite—that each element of attempted monopolization be separately proved. For example, in *United States v. Empire Gas Corp.*,[19] the defendant engaged in a pattern of behavior whereby it would invite rivals to fix prices; when a rival refused, Empire began predatory pricing directed at the rival, and its sales agents informed customers that the rival was going out of business. On some occasions, Empire acquired the rival's supplier in order to apply additional pressure. In at least one instance, the evidence showed, a rival capitulated and agreed to fix prices. Nevertheless, the Eighth Circuit found for the defendant. The court found no evidence that the defendant's intimidation tactics had actually succeeded in the two local markets where its market share approached 50%. In other markets, the defendant's market share was deemed inadequate to create a dangerous possibility of success.

Empire Gas makes sense for those who believe that attempts to monopolize are probably unlikely, are correctable by market forces, and are difficult to distinguish from aggressive competitive conduct. Requiring separate proof of the dangerous probability of success, in particular, serves to filter out cases so as to avoid the risk that courts and juries may be persuaded to impose antitrust liability for unfair conduct that does not really harm competition (*Mt. Lebanon* might be a case in point). This requirement also saves considerable litigation costs where there may be little threat

17. 327 F.2d 459 (9th Cir.), cert. denied, 377 U.S. 993 (1964).

18. Id. at 474. *Lessig* has since been superseded by William Inglis & Sons Baking Co. v. ITT Continental Baking Co., 668 F.2d 1014 (9th Cir. 1981), cert. denied, 459 U.S. 825 (1982), discussed below in subsection (3).

19. 537 F.2d 296 (8th Cir. 1976), cert. denied, 429 U.S. 1122 (1977).

to competition, but the plaintiff hopes to hit the jackpot by undertaking an extensive discovery process designed to uncover some tidbit of improper *mens rea* in the defendant's files.

On the other hand, the majority rule reflects an unduly unskeptical faith in the court's ability to accurately define the relevant market in for determining the dangerous probability of success. In *Empire Gas*, for example, the court noted that the defendant had many competitors, that entry into the market was frequent, and that barriers to entry were minimal (one needed only a supply of gas, a truck, and a storage tank).[20] But *Empire Gas* did not take account of more recent economic insights about the success of a strategy aimed at developing a credible reputation as a predator, especially if the defendant's goal is price leadership, not exclusion of all rivals.[21] Indeed, the evidence that Empire Gas' scheme succeeded in raising prices in three locales where its market share did not even approach 50% suggests that conventional means of market definition may not have accurately measured the likelihood that Empire Gas' monopolistic scheme would succeed. Thus, in cases like *Empire Gas*, we may get closer to the truth by viewing structural evidence (such as market share) more skeptically in the face of evidence of that clear misconduct on the part of someone with clearly evil intent. Those skeptical of aggressive antitrust enforcement usually assume that firms behave in economically rational ways. Why would Empire Gas engage in a pattern of blatantly predatory conduct if it believed that new entry would prevent it from recouping its losses through future monopoly pricing?

International Distribution Centers, Inc. v. Walsh Trucking Co.[22] illustrates the problem with taking a rigid position on these issues. In the year following commencement of the litigation, the plaintiff's market share was 50%, the defendant's was 17%, and there was evidence that other firms had entered the market. The plaintiff maintained that it need not demonstrate a dangerous likelihood of success, in light of clear proof of the defendant's anticompetitive acts and exclusionary intent (Walsh Trucking's president told the plaintiff's chief executive that "he was determined to completely obliterate" the plaintiff and that "he couldn't wait to mount [the rival chief's] head on his wall"[23]). The court correctly rejected that position. A defendant's intent is highly relevant to the likelihood of success, because a firm in the indus-

---

20. Id. at 305.

21. See, e.g., Janusz Ordover & Daniel Wall, Proving Predation after *Monfort* and *Matsushita*: What the New "New Learning" Has to Offer, Antitrust, p.5 (Summer 1987).

22. 812 F.2d 786 (2d Cir.), cert. denied, 482 U.S. 915 (1987).

23. Id. at 789.

try is probably better qualified than a federal judge to determine the vagaries of the particular market. But an intent to eliminate a particular competitor (especially where, as here, the evidence suggests the possibility of personal malice, rather than monopolistic scheming)—which is a business tort—is not the same as an intent to eliminate competition so as to monopolize a market— which violates the Sherman Act.

The court granted judgment n.o.v. in favor of the defendant, finding that Walsh Trucking's monopolization attempt could not possibly succeed because of existing and potential competition. Yet the court noted that the defendant's prices were currently higher than those charged by three existing rivals.[24] If competition was so vigorous, how could the defendant have imposed higher prices? Once again, this analysis suggests that market definition is more difficult and less accurate than those who advocate its use as a filter would have us believe.

(3) The "interactive" approach.

The Ninth Circuit may have ended up with the soundest approach to the standard of proof required in attempted monopolization cases in *William Inglis & Sons Baking Co. v. ITT Continental Baking Co.*[25] In an opinion reflecting a consensus between two judges with opposite antitrust ideologies,[26] the court emphasized that "[e]ach element interacts with the others in significant and unexpected ways."[27]

Thus, on the west coast specific intent may not only be proved by direct evidence, but may also be inferred from the unambiguously anticompetitive nature of the defendant's conduct. However, specific intent alone is insufficient to make out a case of attempted monopolization. As the court noted in *Inglis*:

> [D]irect evidence of intent to vanquish a rival in an honest competitive struggle cannot help to establish an antitrust violation. It also must be shown that the defendant sought victory through unfair or predatory means. Evidence of conduct is thus indispensable.[28]

Similarly, dangerous probability of success can be proved through traditional structural evidence (a near-monopoly share in a properly defined market), but may also be inferred from reliable evidence of improper intent plus impermissible conduct. As the

24. Id. at 792.

25. 668 F.2d 1014 (9th Cir. 1981), cert. denied, 459 U.S. 825 (1982). *Inglis'* facts are summarized in section D(3), supra.

26. The opinion was written by Nixon appointee Joseph Sneed; Kennedy appointee James Browning, who had authored *Lessig*, joined the opinion.

27. Id. at 1027.

28. Id. at 1028 (footnote omitted).

court noted, Justice Holmes' original formulation of the attempt standard in *Swift* contains a key passage: "an intent to bring [about a monopoly] is necessary in order to produce a dangerous possibility that it will happen." [29]   This language suggests that the requirement of dangerous possibility, rather than being a separate element as envisioned in *Empire Gas*, is merely another factor that ensures that the defendant's conduct is sufficiently wrongful in deed and purpose to justify condemnation.   Under *Inglis'* analysis, evidence of specific intent combined with the wrongful acts described in *Empire Gas* would suffice to prove attempt to monopolize.

Finally, as noted above, direct evidence of impermissible conduct may justify a finding of liability, even without equally clear evidence of specific intent.   What constitutes impermissible conduct?   *Inglis* defines it as conduct that amounts to a violation of § 1 or that is "clearly threatening to competition or clearly exclusionary." [30]   Professors Areeda & Turner suggest that this exclusionary element exists where the conduct lacks pro-competitive benefits and thus necessarily reflects the defendant's expectation that monopoly power will result.[31]   But liability may also be imposed under *Inglis* where the defendant's conduct was competitively ambiguous, if the plaintiff can show sufficiently reliable evidence of bad intent and dangerous probability of success.

Empire Gas and *Inglis* illustrate the difference between the Eighth Circuit's "elemental" approach and the Ninth Circuit's "interdependent" approach.   In *Empire Gas*, the defendant had engaged in a deliberate scheme of predatory conduct, but the court still conducted a full analysis of market definition in evaluating the separate element of dangerous probability of success.   *Inglis* suggests that borderline conduct that some might condemn as the wilful maintenance of power by an established monopolist might be tolerated when the defendant lacks such power in order to avoid chilling competitive instincts.   Moreover, where the conduct is not clearly predatory, the fact that market conditions make any actual monopolization by the defendant unlikely strongly suggests that the defendant's conduct is probably not anticompetitive.   The Ninth Circuit would allow an inference of dangerous probability, however, from unambiguously anticompetitive conduct.   This approach properly reflects both the logical proposition that the defendant knew what it was doing, and the historical concern that

29.   Swift & Co. v. United States 196 U.S. 375, 396 (1905) (quoted in *Inglis*, 668 F.2d at 1029 n.8).

30.   668 F.2d at 1028, 1030.

31.   III Phillip Areeda & Donald F. Turner, Antitrust 352 (1978).

the law of attempt should not punish innocent conduct or bad thoughts.[32]

As the Ninth Circuit noted, the *Empire Gas* rule allows those with market shares below 40% to act with impunity.[33] One's faith in the market and one's skepticism about the judicial process must be fairly substantial to prefer imposing such a heavy burden on plaintiffs.

(4) Attempted joint monopolization.

You will recall from section A that monopoly power is defined as the ability to raise prices or exclude rivals,[34] and this section has discussed how misconduct aimed at obtaining this ability violates the attempt to monopolize portion of § 2. *United States v. American Airlines, Inc.*[35] colorfully illustrates how a solicitation to fix prices can rise to the level of attempted joint monopolization under the proper circumstances. In 1982, American and Braniff Airlines both operated hubs out of the Dallas–Fort Worth airport; because of the competitive advantages enjoyed by hubs and FAA restrictions on new entry, other airlines did not pose a real competitive threat in the Dallas market. In the midst of a period of aggressive price and service rivalry between American and Braniff, American President Robert Crandall phoned Braniff President Howard Putnam and invited him to join in a 20% fare hike. According to the court, "Putnam did not raise Braniff's fares in response to Crandall's proposal; instead he presented the government with a tape recording of the conversation."[36]

32. See Petition for Writ of Certiorari, United States v. Empire Gas Corp., 429 U.S. 1122 (1977) (reprinted in Richard Posner & Frank Easterbrook, Antitrust 675–76 (2d ed. 1981)).

33. Greyhound Computer Corp., Inc. v. International Business Machines Corp., 559 F.2d 488, 504 (9th Cir. 1977) (Browning, C.J.), cert. denied, 434 U.S. 1040 (1978).

34. United States v. E.I. du Pont de Nemours & Co., 351 U.S. 377, 391 (1956).

35. 743 F.2d 1114 (5th Cir. 1984), cert. dismissed, 474 U.S. 1001 (1985).

36. Id. at 1115–16. Some colorful highlights from the transcript follow:

Crandall: I think it's dumb as hell for Christ's sake, all right, to sit here and pound the * * * out of each other and neither one of us making a * * * dime.

    * * *

Putnam: But if you're going to overlay every route of American's on top of ... every route that Braniff has—I can't just sit here and allow you to bury us without giving our best effort.

Crandall: Oh sure, but Eastern and Delta do the same thing in Atlanta and have for years.

Putnam: Do you have a suggestion for me?

Crandall: Yes, I have a suggestion for you. Raise your goddamn fares twenty percent. I'll raise mine the next morning.

Putnam: Robert, we—

Crandall: You'll make more money and I will too.

Putnam: We can't talk about pricing.

Crandall: Oh bull * * * Howard. We can talk about any goddamn thing we want to talk about.

All three elements of an attempted monopolization claim seemed to be present in the case. Crandall's conversation clearly showed a specific intent that the two airlines monopolize.[37] Fixing prices with one's principal competitor is clearly anticompetitive conduct. Because economies of scale and governmental regulation meant that Braniff was American's only effective rival on many routes, Crandall's offer, if accepted, posed a dangerous likelihood of success.

The defendant's strongest argument was that while § 2 prohibits attempted monopolization, § 1 does not bar either attempted conspiracies to restrain trade or solicitations to fix prices.[38] The court correctly noted that this argument confused the two sections. Section 1 prohibits the act of conspiracy, whether or not it is successful. Section 2 prohibits acquisition of the power to raise prices or misconduct that comes dangerously close to resulting in the acquisition of such power.[39] Because Braniff's assent was the only act that remained prior to the joint monopolization of the market, the court therefore concluded that American had attempted to monopolize.

Section H: Joint Efforts to Monopolize

(1) Introduction and scope note for readers.

This section discusses the nature of conduct that may violate the prohibition contained in § 2 of the Sherman Act against conspiracies to monopolize, as well as related conduct that may constitute an unfair method of competition in violation of § 5 of the FTC Act. Previous sections of this chapter have discussed the Sherman Act's ban on monopolization by a single firm; the chapter that follows concerns agreements among competitors, focusing on conspiracies that restrain trade in violation of § 1 of the Sherman Act. Because this section devotes considerable attention to § 2, joint efforts to monopolize are discussed in this chapter. Readers unfamiliar with basic concepts of agreement and conspiracy under antitrust law, however, should consider reviewing Chapter 4 before proceeding further here.

In a sense, § 2's prohibition of conspiracies to monopolize is redundant, for any such conspiracy would also restrain of trade

Id.

37. In another part of the conversation, Crandall indicated, "we can both live here and there ain't no room for Delta." Id. at 1118.

38. History buffs will recall United States v. United States Steel Co. (discussed in section A(2) above), where the defendant's unsuccessful efforts to arrange price-fixing cartels were not challenged under § 1, and its perception that it needed to fix prices with its rivals convinced the court that it did not possess monopoly power and therefore could not have committed unlawful monopolization.

39. 743 F.2d at 1122.

and thus violate § 1. However, the courts have articulated a working distinction between the two sections. The Supreme Court has defined monopoly power as the power to "control prices or exclude competition."[1] Attempts by competitors to harm consumers by directly inhibiting price competition have usually been condemned under § 1. Section 2 allegations of conspiracy to monopolize have, instead, typically focused on anticompetitive conduct that directly excludes competitors, thereby indirectly harming consumers by allowing the conspirators either to fix prices more easily (or more stealthily) or simply to engage in oligopoly behavior that allows them to raise prices and profits. In sum, § 1 concerns competitors' agreements to limit competition among themselves, while § 2's conspiracy prohibition concerns agreements to limit competition between the conspirators and third parties.

(2) Conspiracy to monopolize: basic doctrine.

American Tobacco Co. v. United States[2] sets forth the basic doctrine governing conspiracies to monopolize and illustrates the differences between that offense and conspiracies to restrain trade. Like attempted monopolization, and unlike actual monopolization, a conspiracy to monopolize requires a specific intent to monopolize. In *American Tobacco*, the Court affirmed the trial court's further definition of the § 2 offense as the

> joint acquisition or maintenance by a member of a conspiracy ... of the power to control and dominate interstate trade and commerce in a commodity to such an extent that they were able, as a group, to exclude actual or potential competitors.[3]

In addition, the Court rejected the defendants' argument that actual exclusion of competitors was an element of the offense. Rather, a conviction under § 2 could be based on evidence that the principal corporate defendants—American Tobacco, Liggett & Myers and R.J. Reynolds—controlled 68–75% of national cigarette production and 80% of the higher-priced cigarette market, so long as there was sufficient evidence to allow the jury to find that the defendants had acted jointly in order to monopolize the market.[4]

1. United States v. E.I. du Pont de Nemours & Co. ("*Cellophane*"), 351 U.S. 377, 391 (1956).

2. 328 U.S. 781 (1946).

3. Id. at 785 (emphasis deleted).

4. Id. at 797–98. See Interstate Circuit, Inc. v. United States, 306 U.S. 208 (1939) and its progeny, discussed in Chapter 4, section F, concerning the jury's ability to infer a conspiracy from circumstantial evidence, including parallel conduct by the defendants. A jury's ability to make such inferences should be the same for conspiracies to restrain trade as well as conspiracies to monopolize.

Rejecting the defendants' claim that they were unconstitutionally being punished twice for the same conspiracy (the government prosecuted the case criminally [5]), the Court held that "§§ 1 and 2 of the Sherman Act require proof of conspiracies which are reciprocally distinguishable from and independent of each other." [6] In affirming the jury's verdict on the § 2 count, the Court relied on evidence that each defendant maintained large inventories of cigarettes, and that each regularly bid up the price of cheaper tobaccos used to manufacture inexpensive "ten-cent" cigarettes, without ever explaining how they intended to use the cheap tobacco. This conduct would not have supported a § 1 price-fixing allegation. Maintaining large inventories tends to increase incentives to cheat on an agreed upon price, thus making price-fixing more difficult to achieve.[7] Likewise, bidding up the price of cheap tobacco, or acquiring such tobacco with no intent to use it in manufacturing, has no direct effect on the price the defendants charge for their higher-priced products. Rather, this conduct was designed to make it more difficult for other rivals to compete with the defendants. Section 2 thus condemns joint efforts to maintain an oligopoly among the conspirators, even in the absence of proof that the oligopolists actually conspired to set prices.

The Second Circuit's opinion in *United States v. Consolidated Laundries Corp.*[8] also illustrates the special nature of conspiracies to monopolize. In that case, the defendant linen supply firms (1) allocated customers among themselves, (2) agreed not to deal with each other's customers, and (3) jointly drove non-cooperating linen suppliers out of business.[9] As discussed in Chapter 4, the first two aspects of this conspiracy violated § 1,[10] yet the court observed that this evidence, standing alone, would not be sufficient to prove a violation of § 2. The third aspect—joint exclusion of non-cooperating rivals—was deemed necessary to establish a specific intent to monopolize.

5. Professor Lawrence Sullivan has suggested that the government may have proceeded criminally because it could not devise an injunctive remedy that would be economically sensible. Antitrust 363 (1977).

6. 328 U.S. at 788.

7. See Chapter 4, section F for a discussion of how concerted practices that facilitate price agreements violate § 1.

8. 291 F.2d 563 (2d Cir. 1961).

9. The court's opinion does not include specific details about the type of exclusionary conduct involved, other than an allusion to the indictment's allegations of an agreement to "buy out competing non-member linen suppliers in order to compel them to join the conspiracy or to exclude them from the industry," id. at 567, and an oblique reference to "predatory practices against independent linen suppliers in order to compel them to join the conspiracy or be put out of business." Id. at 575.

10. See Chapter 4, section E.

The *Consolidated Laundries* defendants also argued that the government had failed to establish a dangerous probability that their conspiracy would be successful in monopolizing a relevant market. The court distinguished conspiracy to monopolize from both attempted monopolization (which requires a dangerous probability of success) [11] and actual monopolization (which requires monopoly power in a properly defined market).[12] "[W]here the charge is conspiracy to monopolize," the court explained, "the essential element is not the power, but the specific intent, to monopolize." [13] This approach is consistent with the criminal law's general approach to conspiracy, which punishes defendants once they have agreed to pursue illegal ends even if they have not yet come close to attempting or completing an illegal act. As Professor Donald Turner has explained, if "defendants are attempting to drive someone out of the market by foul means rather than fair, there is ample warrant for not resorting to refined analysis" of the economics of the relevant market.[14]

(3) Parallel exclusionary conduct as an unfair method of competition.

Chapter 4, section F discusses how the Federal Trade Commission Act's ban on unfair methods of competition might be used to condemn parallel conduct by competing firms that has the effect of restraining trade, even absent evidence that would allow the FTC to find or infer an agreement or conspiracy.

In re Kellogg Co.[15] was an unsuccessful effort by the FTC staff to proscribe what is often referred to as a "shared monopoly." A shared monopoly is an oligopoly that is maintained by exclusionary conduct by the dominant firms, although there is no basis to find or infer an agreement among the firms to jointly engage in anticompetitive behavior. The staff targeted the ready-to-eat cereal market, dominated for years by three large firms (Kellogg, General Foods, and General Mills). They alleged that these three had maintained their tight oligopoly by anticompetitive parallel conduct. If a single firm with the combined market share of the three respondents had maintained its dominance through anticompetitive conduct, the firm would be liable for monopolization under § 2. If the three oligopolists had maintained their dominance by agreeing with each other to engage in exclusionary conduct, they would be guilty of conspiracy to monopolize under *American Tobacco*. The FTC staff's basic theory was that similar

11. See section G above.

12. See section B above.

13. 291 F.2d at 573.

14. Antitrust Policy and the *Cellophane* Case, 70 Harv. L. Rev. 281, 305 (1956).

15. 99 F.T.C. 8 (1982).

parallel conduct engaged in by the three oligopolists constituted an unfair method of competition in violation of § 5 of the FTC Act. To remedy the respondents' market dominance, the staff sought the divestiture of plants and mandatory exclusive licensing of trademarks (giving some new company, for example, the sole right to make "Rice Krispies") so that the industry would be transformed into one with seven viable competitors.[16] The administrative law judge dismissed the complaint, and by a 3–1 vote the FTC refused to hear the staff's appeal.[17]

The "shared monopoly theory" underlying the complaint was that § 5 is violated where (1) an industry is highly concentrated; (2) the market's competitive performance is poor; (3) barriers to entry are high and (4) new entries are deterred by exclusionary conduct of industry members.[18] The first three elements were clearly present in *Kellogg*. The top three firms controlled 80% of the market. The evidence suggested high sustained profits and minimal price competition. There had been virtually no entry for years. More controversial, however, were the following allegations of exclusionary conduct: (a) the proliferation of brands and artificial attempts to differentiate similar brands; (b) misleading advertising to suggest that respondents' cereals were different from those of the smaller manufacturers; (c) detailed shelf-space recommendations to grocers made by Kellogg, and acquiesced in by the others, which had the effect of restricting smaller brands and eliminating cereals of small regional producers; and (d) an absence of discounts and a pattern of price increases initiated by one respondent and followed by the others.

The shared monopoly theory was endorsed unconditionally only by Commissioner Michael Pertschuk in dissent. He believed

16. This sort of restructuring is likely to significantly increase economic performance. In contrast, suppose an industry had five firms with respective market shares of 40, 20, 20, 15 and 5 percent, and a firm needed a market share of approximately 15% to meaningfully compete with the others. Breaking up the dominant firm so as to create an industry with six firms may not be worth the effort. See III Phillip Areeda & Donald Turner, Antitrust Law 377–78 (1978). Creating a seven-firm cereal industry would not involve scale diseconomies, at least according to one study. Paul Scanlon, Oligopoly and "Deceptive" Advertising: The Cereal Industry Affair, 3 Antitrust L. & Econ. Rev. 99, 106 (Spring 1970).

17. The complaint had initially issued on a 3–2 vote of the Commission in 1972. After the administrative law judge dismissed the complaint and an appeal was filed, the new director of the FTC's Bureau of Competition (now-Representative Thomas Campbell) sought to withdraw the appeal because he believed that the shared monopoly theory was unsound antitrust doctrine that punished success. See 99 F.T.C. 283–84 (separate statement of Bailey, C.).

18. 99 F.T.C. at 281 (Pertschuk, C., dissenting).

Requiring evidence of poor economic performance as an essential element of a shared monopoly case is justified by the relatively weakness of oligopoly theory, compared to monopoly theory, as an accurate predictor of performance. See Areeda & Turner, supra note 16, at 372–77.

that the theory was not only sound, but also the only effective tool for breaking up stagnant oligopolies harmful to consumers.[19] Commissioner David Clanton endorsed the theory in the abstract, but limited its application. Unless the respondents had engaged in predatory behavior, Clanton argued, relief should be limited to enjoining specific anticompetitive practices. Where oligopolies are maintained by exclusionary conduct, he reasoned that restructuring an industry is very costly and "carries with it too great a risk of wrong or imperfect judgments." Moreover, he believed that conduct remedies against a persistent oligopoly are more likely to restore competition over time than is true in the single-firm monopoly context.[20] Commissioner Patricia Bailey also endorsed the theory in the abstract, while questioning the remedy. She found substantial reason to doubt that the benefits to consumers of improved competition would outweigh the costs of divestiture when combined with the loss of the economies of scale enjoyed by the three respondents.[21] Moreover, she believed that the FTC should adopt such a novel theory with far-reaching economic consequences with only clear evidence of congressional approval (in fact, leading members of Congress had been criticizing the case from the outset).[22] If the antitrust laws are comfortable restructuring an industry dominated by a monopolist who has committed clearly exclusionary acts, it does not seem too great a step (especially in the context of § 5, which has no treble-damage or private litigation liability) to order similar relief when similar conduct is used to maintain a tight and non-performing oligopoly. To suggest that new antitrust theories not envisioned in 1914 can only be implemented with approval of today's Congress is inconsistent with the intent of the FTC Act's drafters, as shown by their use of a broad and flexible term like "unfair methods of competition." Thus, Commissioner Bailey's separation of powers concern misses the mark.

Moreover, Commissioner Bailey's complaint about the "novelty" of the shared monopoly theory is probably overstated because the theory is comparable to general theories of monopolization. At the extremes, of course, there is a significant difference between ordering structural relief in an industry dominated by one firm with 90% of the market and in a pure oligopoly of four equally sized firms. But in the real world, monopolists' market shares seldom approach 90%, and oligopolies—including the cere-

---

19. 99 F.T.C. at 281–83.

20. Id. at 275.

21. Id. at 287.

22. Id. at 288. Chairman James Miller III joined the order of dismissal without separate comment. In a previ-ous order, however, he had indicated his agreement with the Director of the Bureau of Competition (whose views are described in note 17, above). 98 F.T.C. 893–94 (1981).

al industry—often do have a dominant firm or leader. Moreover, cases where a monopolist raises prices above competitive levels through unilateral acts and those where the dominant firm in an oligopoly secures price agreements with a few leading rivals often shade together into a gray area. Thus, permitting structural relief in shared monopoly cases helps avoid turning monopolization litigation into fights over form rather than substance.

The key difficulties in a shared monopoly case are defining and identifying the type of exclusionary acts that would support a divestiture remedy. Maintaining the analogy between a § 2 monopolization case and a § 5 shared monopoly case would basically allow the FTC to condemn "wilful oligopolization" of a market. Thus, the same type of conduct that would violate § 2 if engaged in unilaterally by a monopolist would be unlawful if engaged in uniformly, even without agreement, by oligopolists. However, as noted in the earlier sections discussing such conduct,[23] only generically predatory behavior (a deliberate sacrifice of short-term revenues for long-term monopoly profits) constitute unlawful monopolization under § 2 of the Sherman Act.[24] The problem with *Kellogg* is that it is not easy to see how the cereal companies' conduct was generically predatory.

First, as Commissioner Clanton emphasized, new brands of cereal were not introduced "primarily as a blocking device to discipline competitors,"[25] but as self-sustaining products that generated significant consumer demand. As the staff noted, the respondents' strategy of filling every plausible product niche prevented any new entry in response to market changes. New brand proliferation is best analogized to a monopolist's continual expansion to meet demand, condemned by Judge Hand in *Alcoa*. When the *Kellogg* case was originally brought by the FTC staff, then, it had some force. But by 1980 the FTC had limited *Alcoa* and held that increasing production to meet demand is not "wilful maintenance."[26] Second, Kellogg apparently did not couple its shelf-space recommendations with implicit or explicit threats to withhold products from grocers who disregarded its advice;[27] even if Kellogg's recommendations did have significant exclusionary ef-

---

23. See sections B and F, above.

24. This is perhaps what Commissioner Clanton meant when he sought to distinguish predatory and non-predatory conduct. Given the general misuse of the word "predatory," however, see section D, his meaning is not entirely clear.

25. 99 F.T.C. at 277.

26. Compare United States v. Aluminum Co. of America, 148 F.2d 416, 431 (2d Cir. 1945), with E.I. du Pont de Nemours & Co. (TiO$_2$), 99 F.T.C. 653 (1980). These cases are discussed in section A(4), above.

27. See 99 F.T.C. at 144 (initial decision).

fects,[28] a cease and desist order barring shelf-space recommendations could have been issued. Finally, respondents' refusal to discount and parallel price increases represent no more than classic oligopoly pricing. Just as monopoly pricing does not violate § 2, pure oligopoly pricing should not be held to violate § 5.

A critique of the application of the shared monopoly theory in *Kellogg* does not necessarily mean that the FTC is without authority to restructure the cereal industry. Just as some have advocated using § 5 to restore competition to a monopolized market without regard to "fault" on the part of the monopolist,[29] the FTC Act could be used to similarly restructure concentrated industries. This is the point, however, where Commissioner Bailey's concerns about separation of powers may be most appropriately targeted. Such an approach would be without precedent or even close analogy—and for years Congress has considered and failed to act on bills mandating deconcentration.[30] Critics of the shared monopoly theory have strong arguments that the number of industries that are concentrated, capable of efficient restructuring, and likely to remain concentrated for the next decade (the probable length of litigation) absent relief is probably so small that empowering the FTC to look for them (with the attendant risks of error) is not advisable.

---

28. Clanton noted that a leading economist, one of the staff's expert witnesses, believed that the shelf-space recommendations did not play a significant role in the respondents' maintenance of their oligopoly. *Id.* at 278 (citing Richard Schmalensee, Entry Deterrence in the Ready–to–Eat Breakfast Cereal Industry, 9 Bell J. Econ. 305, 307 n.4 (1978)).

29. See section A(5) above.

30. See S. 3832, 92d Cong., 2d Sess. (1972), reintroduced as S. 1167, 93d Cong., 1st Sess. (1973), reintroduced with minor modifications as S. 1959, 94th Cong., 1st Sess. (1975).

CHAPTER 4: AGREEMENTS AMONG COMPETITORS

Agreements among rival firms, or "horizontal agreements," [1] pose the greatest threat to the competitive process. In fact, it was the proliferation of these agreements—in the form of price-fixing cartels and large trusts established to monopolize markets—that led to the adoption of the Sherman Act.[2]

Generally, these agreements create a substantial risk of bringing about all the social harms the antitrust laws are designed to prevent. Agreements among rivals to fix prices or reduce output are the principal means by which firms in non-monopolized markets can cause an inefficient allocation of societal resources. By raising prices, cartels force consumers to pay more for desired goods and services than would be necessary in a free marketplace. Cartels also limit the pricing freedom of individual entrepreneurs. Finally, cartels abuse the economic power they possess, to the detriment of the consumer and the ordinary citizen.

Admittedly, cartels do not invariably cause the same social and economic harms that result from monopoly power. The members of some cartels, for example, may not be able to agree on a price. By "cheating" on an agreed upon price, firms may end up in a price war as vigorous as any that would occur without a cartel. In other ways, however, cartels may be more harmful than monopolies, for the agreed upon price must be high enough to be profitable for the laziest carteleer as well as the most efficient.

Nevertheless, we have seen in the prior two chapters that benefits can result from agreements among competitors (where the restraint on competition is ancillary to a lawful purpose, such as the sale of a business) as well as from the possession of monopoly power (where the monopolist has superior skill). Horizontal agreements are so varied, and proving the presence of market power through the typical means of market definition is so complex, that the courts have endeavored to develop short-cuts to distinguish permissible from impermissible combinations among rivals.

---

1. Economists and antitrust lawyers refer to agreements among firms at the same stage of production as "horizontal." Agreements among firms at different stages of production (e.g. between a supplier and customer, or between a manufacturer, its wholesaler, and retailers) are called "vertical agreements" and are considered in Chapter 5.

2. Act of July 2, 1890, ch. 647, 26 Stat. 209, codified at 15 U.S.C. § 1–8.

Unfortunately, the judiciary has not done a particularly good job of articulating the standards it has used in drawing these distinctions. Indeed, if the Supreme Court were in the business of providing accurate information about legal doctrine, its opinions in this area could justify a finding of liability under § 5 of the FTC Act for unfair and deceptive acts or practices. In cases involving horizontal restraints, the Court frequently makes contradictory statements, overrules precedent without acknowledging that it is doing so, and describes its mode of analysis in a way that appears to be at variance with what it is really doing.

This chapter will attempt to sort out what the Court says about horizontal agreements and what it usually does. The discussion begins with three sections concerning the paradigm agreement among competitors—price fixing. First, the chapter traces the history of three conflicting modes of analysis developed to determine when price-related horizontal agreements are unlawful. Second, the development of the oft-misunderstood "per se rule" against price fixing is examined. Third, the modern price-fixing cases are analyzed and criticized, and an alternative means of understanding these decisions is set forth, along with a summary that suggests how to maintain fidelity to both Supreme Court precedent and reasoned analysis. After a brief digression to consider the special case of agreements among rivals in the "learned professions," the chapter proceeds to discuss specific types of horizontal agreements.

Section A: The Development of Three Conflicting Modes of Analysis

In the quarter century following adoption of the Sherman Act in 1890, the federal courts adopted three conflicting modes of analysis to determine the lawfulness of horizontal agreements under § 1. First, Justice Rufus Peckham attempted to distinguish between agreements that "directly" restrained trade, all of which were illegal under § 1, and agreements that did not "directly" restrain trade, which were lawful. Second, Judge William Howard Taft read the congressional condemnation of "restraints of trade" as incorporating into federal antitrust law the common law concept of the same name. Taft then sought to reconcile the various common law decisions into a coherent approach, providing that restraints ancillary to a lawful purpose and necessary to achieve that purpose were lawful and other restraints were illegal. Third, Justice Louis Brandeis refined a "rule of reason" applied in earlier Supreme Court decisions so as to permit judges to review all the facts surrounding a particular agreement and then to reach their own conclusion as to whether the agreement aided or harmed "competition."

(1) Justice Peckham and "direct" restraints of trade.

United States v. Trans–Missouri Freight Association[3] was the first of a series of restraint of trade opinions written by Justice Peckham. The case involved a fairly classic price-fixing agreement. Eighteen railroads that controlled most of the traffic west of the Mississippi River met regularly to set the rates charged for transporting goods by rail. The defendants argued that their prices were reasonable and that rate agreements were necessary to avoid "ruinous competition" in the railroad industry. Although Peckham seemed to reject each of these contentions on the merits,[4] the opinion's key holding was that the defendants' arguments about reasonableness were legally irrelevant, for "all contracts in restraint of trade" were prohibited by the literal language of § 1.[5] In so holding, he specifically and emphatically rejected the view that the Sherman Act meant to proscribe only those contracts that were void as unreasonable at common law. All restraints, reasonable or unreasonable, were illegal, he wrote. He then promptly contradicted himself, however, noting in the same opinion that a restrictive covenant ancillary to the sale of a business "might not be included" in the congressional ban on "every" restraint of trade.[6]

Justice Edward White wrote a forceful dissent for four members of the Court. First, he cited a number of state court decisions to support his view that contemporary courts did not consider reasonable agreements to be "restraints of trade."[7] In any event, White argued that when Congress uses familiar common law phrases like "restraint of trade," the courts should construe them in light of the common law.[8] White also invoked the canon of statutory construction that counsels against interpreting legisla-

---

3. 166 U.S. 290 (1897).

4. The Court reasoned that determining the of a reasonableness of a price is too difficult for the judiciary, id. at 331–32, and that cartels are not likely to solve rate wars and come at too high a price for consumers. Id. at 338–39. In United States v. Trenton Potteries Co., 273 U.S. 392 (1927), discussed in detail in section B(1) below, the Court expressly rejected the defense that a "reasonable" fixed price is lawful. In United States v. Socony–Vacuum Oil Co., 310 U.S. 150 (1940), discussed in detail in section B(2) below, the Court expressly rejected the defense that a

price-fixing agreement can serve the public interest by preventing "ruinous competition."

5. 166 U.S. at 328. Section 1 provides in relevant part that "[e]very contract, combination in the form of trust or otherwise, or conspiracy, in restraint of trade or commerce among the several States, or with foreign nations, is declared to be illegal."

6. Id. at 328–29.

7. Id. at 348–51.

8. Id. at 353.

tion to reach results clearly not contemplated by Congress,[9] which would have been violated here had Peckham not inserted the qualification about restrictive covenants. In White's view, the defendants should have been permitted to demonstrate that their cartel was a reasonable response to excessive competition in the railroad industry, and that their rates were reasonable.

The following Term gave Justice Peckham the opportunity to write three antitrust opinions in an attempt to extricate himself from *Trans–Missouri* 's contradictory statements that all contracts in restraint of trade were illegal but that restrictive covenants might not be unlawful. Only contracts whose restraint on trade was "direct and immediate" were prohibited by the Sherman Act, he explained in these cases. In the first of these cases, *Hopkins v. United States*,[10] a group of cattle brokers fixed commissions and employees' salaries and refused to share information about the local market with outsiders. The inevitable effect of the agreement was to keep the defendants' commissions high and their costs (salaries) low, and to limit the ability of outsiders to ruin this cozy agreement by entering the market. Peckham's majority opinion overturned an injunction prohibiting the agreement on the grounds that, although the sale of livestock constituted interstate commerce, the performance of brokerage services did not (in that day and age).[11] Hence, a restraint on services performed at the Kansas City Livestock Exchange was not a restraint on interstate commerce.[12] Similarly, in *Anderson v. United States*,[13] Peckham permitted an agreement among cattle purchasers to deal only among themselves because their association was open to all and thus involved no "direct" restraint of trade.

Hopkins and *Anderson* would be no more than interesting legal history had Peckham not applied this doctrine more generally in the third case decided that Term. In that case, *United States v. Joint Traffic Ass'n*,[14] another railroad cartel vigorously urged the Court to reconsider *Trans–Missouri* 's literalist interpretation

---

9. Id. at 354–55.

10.   171 U.S. 578 (1898).

11. Supreme Court decisions of that era adopted a much narrower definition of interstate commerce subject to congressional regulation. In United States v. E.C. Knight Co., 156 U.S. 1 (1895), for example, the Court held that the Sherman Act did not apply to the acquisition of virtually all the sugar refineries in Philadelphia because "manufacturing" was not commerce. For the past half century, the Court has rejected this narrower approach and has interpreted the Commerce Clause to give Congress broad power to regulate. Wickard v. Filburn, 317 U.S. 111 (1942). See generally 1 Ronald Rotunda, John Nowak & J. Nelson Young, Constitutional Law § 4.8 (1986). Consistent with the modern approach, *E.C. Knight* was expressly overruled in 1948. Mandeville Island Farms, Inc. v. American Crystal Sugar Co., 334 U.S. 219 (1948).

12. *Hopkins*, 171 U.S. at 603.

13.   171 U.S. 604 (1898).

14.   171 U.S. 505 (1898).

of the Sherman Act. Responding to the defendants' argument that a literal construction was unreasonable, Peckham observed that non-competition covenants, mergers, and the designation by rivals of a joint selling agent would all be permissible under his reading of the Sherman Act because they did not "directly" restrain trade.[15]

Unfortunately, Peckham's method of determining whether or not an agreement directly restrains trade remains opaque.[16] Perhaps the language in *Trans–Missouri* that reveals Peckham's extreme Jeffersonian hostility to new methods of business (whether benign or malign) that threaten the traditional livelihood of "small dealers and worthy men"[17] best explains his view as to what constitutes a direct "restraint of trade." Perhaps his understanding of the adverse economic impact railroad cartels have on consumers influenced his judgment in *Trans–Missouri* and or *Joint Traffic*. Alternatively, Peckham may have drawn on the English common law tradition that condemned restraints only if they involved coercion; because the cattle merchants in *Hopkins* and *Anderson* were free to join or quit the cartel, and because the cartel had none of the quasi-governmental features of the two railroad agreements, it did not restrain trade.[18] Followers of Peckham's jurisprudence are left free to condemn or approve horizontal agreement, under the general "direct/indirect" rubric, without significant doctrinal guidance.

(2) Judge Taft and the common law.

The second mode of analysis used in § 1 cases was set forth by Judge William Howard Taft in his masterful opinion for the Sixth Circuit in *United States v. Addyston Pipe & Steel Co.*[19] In condemning a cartel of pipe makers that had allocated customers among themselves by designating one real bidder for each job and arranging for the others to submit phony high bids, Taft cleverly used the opinion to conclude, despite his position as a lower court judge, that Justice Peckham's mode of analysis was simply wrong. The defendants sought to distinguish *Trans–Missouri* on the theory that railroads were subject to stricter governmental regulation and had a greater impact on the public interest than pipe sellers.

---

15. Id. at 567–68.

16. Peckham's retreat in *Joint Traffic* from *Trans–Missouri*'s literal condemnation of all restraints of trade was something of a vindication for Justice White, who noted in his dissent in *Trans–Missouri* that Peckham's "asserted exception [for ancillary restraints] not only destroys the rule which is relied on [the literal reading of § 1], but it

rests upon no foundation of reason." 166 U.S. at 352.

17. Id. at 323.

18. See William Page, Ideological Conflict and the Origins of Antitrust Policy, 66 Tulane L. Rev. 1, 44–48 (1991).

19. 85 Fed. 271 (6th Cir. 1898), aff'd, 175 U.S. 211 (1899).

Of course, nothing in Justice Peckham's literal interpretation of the Sherman Act supported such a distinction, but it gave Taft the opening he needed. He began by indicating that the case could be decided on the authority of *Trans–Missouri*, but proceeded to accept *arguendo* the defendants' efforts to distinguish that case and then held, contrary to *Trans–Missouri*, that Congress did *not* intend § 1 to literally prohibit every contract, but rather to make criminal and tortious the formation of contracts that were void as unreasonable restraints of trade at common law.[20] Taft interpreted the common law to permit restraints of trade ancillary to a lawful purpose and reasonably necessary to accomplish that purpose.[21] Contracts that satisfied this standard were lawful, but contracts that did not were prohibited by § 1. Because the pipe cartel had no "main purpose" other than restraining trade, Taft concluded that the better view among the common law cases would void the agreement.[22]

Addyston Pipe's focus on whether horizontal agreements are necessary for a lawful purpose can be applied so as to be consistent with each of the conflicting goals of antitrust law. Significant disagreements will, of course, arise in defining what constitutes a "lawful purpose." The efficiency-oriented judge will insist that lawful purposes be limited to those that permit the parties to lower the costs of production and distribution. Those concerned with wealth transfers will ask whether the agreement to which the restraint is ancillary actually redounds to the benefit of consumers. Those with non-economic concerns will approve only those agreements that increase equality of opportunity and decentralize the market structure.[23] Although *Addyston Pipe*'s mode of analysis does not materially aid in resolving these basic disputes about antitrust policy, it at least provides a framework for courts to analyze the issues in a forthright manner.

In *Addyston Pipe*, Taft took an indirect swipe both at Peckham's contentless distinction between those agreements that constitute a "direct" trade restraint and those that do not and at White's contentless standard of reasonableness. Taft was particu-

---

20. Id. at 278–79.

21. Id. at 283.

22. Shortly after the Supreme Court affirmed of Judge Taft's decision, the members of the pipe cartel merged into one company; the government did not challenge the merger. For a possible explanation of the government's decision, see the discussion of Appalachian Coals, Inc. v. United States, 288 U.S. 344, 376 (1933), in section B(3) below.

23. Where a contract lowers costs for the parties to the agreement but excludes participation by small firms, it might be considered lawful by the Chicago school but not the Jeffersonians. Conversely, these competing visions will reach conflicting conclusions where an agreement designed to enable small firms to continue participating in the market has the predictable effect of reducing vigorous price competition among rivals.

larly critical of a common law decision that had upheld an agreement among three rivals to eliminate competition among themselves by dividing England into three territories, one reserved for each of them.[24]   By abandoning the anchor of the common law's distinction between ancillary restraints and unlawful ones, Taft warned that this approach and other similar decisions [25] would "set sail on a sea of doubt, and ... assume[d] the power to say, in respect to contracts which have no other purpose ... than the mutual restraint of the parties, how much restraint of competition is in the public interest, and how much is not." [26]

(3) The "rule of reason."

Unfortunately, however, the Supreme Court has never expressly adopted Taft's approach.   Instead, beginning in 1918 with *Chicago Board of Trade v. United States*,[27] the Court has used a third analytical mode.   In *Chicago Board of Trade*, the Court upheld the Board's "Call Rule," whereby competing grain dealers agreed that any grain in transit to Chicago that was purchased after the end of the special afternoon "Call" session would be sold at the closing price.   Unlike Justice Peckham, Justice Louis Brandeis concluded for the majority that § 1 could not be read literally because *every* contract restrains trade.   Brandeis agreed with Taft that the proper basis for distinguishing between lawful and unlawful contracts was not Peckham's *ipse dixit* declaration that a benign contract was not a "restraint," but instead required an evaluation as to whether the contract "unreasonably" restrained trade.   However, unlike Taft, Brandeis refused to base this departure from the literal statutory language on congressional intent, or to look to the common law of contracts to define reasonable and unreasonable restraints.   Rather, *Chicago Board of Trade* set forth what is now the classic open-ended standard for determining the legality of restraints of trade: "whether the restraint imposed is such as merely regulates and perhaps thereby promotes competition or whether it is such as may suppress or even destroy competition." [28]

Brandeis went on to mandate a full inquiry into the "facts peculiar to the business to which the restraint is applied," and the history, purpose, and effect of the restraint.   *Chicago Board of Trade* makes clear, however, that the defendants' intent is relevant only because it may shed light on an agreement's effect.   A benign intent, the Court made clear, does not save an anticompeti-

24. 85 Fed. at 284 (citing Wickens v. Evans, 148 Eng. Rep. 1201 (1829)).

25. Taft also rejected several precedents relied upon by White's dissenting opinion in *Trans–Missouri*.

26. Id.

27. 246 U.S. 231 (1918).

28. Id. at 238.

tive agreement.[29]   Rather, if the parties' motives are benign, it becomes somewhat more likely that the effect will be benign as well because the defendants' experience as actual participants in the marketplace will enable them to correctly predict the impact of their agreement.

Unfortunately, Justice Brandeis' open-ended inquiry provided little more assistance in distinguishing lawful and unlawful agreements than had Justice Peckham's declaration that those contracts he considered benign did not directly restrain trade. *Chicago Board of Trade* did not define "competition," a term that can mean entirely different things to those with differing views of the goals of antitrust. For example, the challenged Call Rule could be approved under Brandeis' analysis because it made the grain market work more efficiently, and thereby promoted an efficient allocation of resources. Alternatively, although the potential "victims" of the rule included farmers and grain dealers who might have been able to receive a higher overnight bid for grain in transit, in fact the rule brought more of that grain into the Board's regular trading sessions,[30] created a public market for grain in transit, and allowed rural grain dealers to sell their product with better information about marketplace conditions.[31] Thus, the rule did not appear to effect a wealth transfer harmful to consumers. Similarly, because creating this public market aided country dealers (small, independent entrepreneurs) and distributed the grain-in-transit business among a larger number of Chicago purchasers, the rule fostered a more decentralized and deconcentrated market structure.[32]

Chicago Board of Trade remains a favorite of both litigators and academics because it can be cited authoritatively for almost any position, and thus sets sail on the very sea of doubt that Judge Taft warned about. The Court's refusal to adopt the *Addyston Pipe* mode of analysis is particularly disappointing because an opinion upholding the Call Rule could have been written under Judge Taft's approach. Because the antitrust laws favor reliance on the marketplace to determine price, quality, and quantity,

---

29. Id.

30. Sellers that might otherwise have traded overnight would wait for the regular session in hopes that the price would exceed the call price.

31. Id. at 240–41.

32. Judge Robert Bork has suggested that the rule may have been a self-serving device adopted by the majority of Board of Trade members to take away some of the large, efficient dealers' overnight business. Antitrust Paradox 158–59 (1978). Whether or not these larger firms were more efficient, trading at prices other than the closing price of the Call gave them a decided informational advantage over the many smaller dealers and farmers. To achieve the benefits of competition, market actors must have access to similar information. Rules that correct problems of "asymmetric information" thus allow society to reap the full benefits of competition.

rules or agreements that make a market work more effectively are permissible. The Court could have found that the Call Rule was ancillary to this lawful purpose.

Between *Addyston Pipe* and *Chicago Board of Trade* came two companion Supreme Court decisions, *Standard Oil Co. v. United States* [33] and *United States v. American Tobacco Co.*,[34] that played a major role in antitrust history, although subsequent Court decisions have deprived their holdings of much doctrinal significance. The cases involved the dissolution of two of the major trusts that had been the object of the Sherman Act some twenty years earlier. Tremendous public attention focused on what construction the Court would give to the Sherman Act in ruling on these two highly publicized cases. The business community had been both confused and alarmed by Justice Peckham's suggestion that "every" restraint of trade was illegal under the Sherman Act. Naturally, they favored the "rule of reason" advocated by Justice White, who would have allowed price-fixing cartels if competition was excessive and the fixed prices were reasonable.[35]

The results in *Standard Oil* and *American Tobacco* were not controversial: in both cases, the Court unanimously sustained trial court decisions finding that the defendants had unlawfully restrained trade and monopolized their respective industries. In finding that Standard Oil had violated § 1, however, now-Chief Justice White's majority opinion construed the statutory phrase "restraint of trade" by using the same phraseology—"the rule of reason"—that had appeared in his *Trans–Missouri* dissent. White thereby effectively overruled the majority holding in *Trans–Missouri* that "every" restraint of trade, reasonable or unreasonable, violated § 1, and set the stage for the *Chicago Board of Trade* standard that is still in force today. Contradicting the earlier view he had espoused in his *Trans–Missouri* dissent, however, White held that a price-fixing agreement between Standard Oil and its rivals was properly subject to a conclusive presumption of unreasonableness.[36]

Justice Harlan wrote a stinging dissent, and delivered from the bench an even more stinging attack on the majority (not found in his written opinion), which accused the Court of "judicial legislation":

33. 221 U.S. 1 (1911).

34. 221 U.S. 106 (1911).

35. See generally IX Alexander Bickel & Benno Schmidt, History of the Supreme Court of the United States 86–199 (1984).

36. 221 U.S. at 65.

Lest anyone doubt the effect of the decree, consider how much combined economic power the oil companies that were part of the Standard Oil Trust would enjoy today: Exxon (Standard of New Jersey), Mobil (Standard of New York), Amoco (Standard of Indiana), Sohio (Standard of Ohio), and Chevron (Standard of California).

when men having vast interests are concerned, and they cannot get [Congress] to pass the legislation they desire, the next thing they do is to raise the question in some case, to get the court to so construe the Constitution or the statutes as to mean what they want it to mean.[37]

Such rhetoric was illustrative of the reaction many had to the opinion, and it led the progressive Congress to enact the Clayton Act and the Federal Trade Commission Act out of concern that conservative federal judges would use the rule of reason to allow abuses of economic power by private firms.

In reality, the rule of reason articulated by Chief Justice White in *Standard Oil* and *American Tobacco* was quite different from both the rule of reason he had advocated in his *Trans–Missouri* dissent (which permitted powerful firms that controlled an entire industry to justify price fixing on the grounds that too much competition was unreasonable) and the open-ended, look-at-anything rule of reason set forth by Justice Brandeis in *Chicago Board of Trade*. Instead, White set forth a three-pronged rule of reason. First, certain agreements were "conclusively presumed" to be illegal because their "inherent nature" was to injure the public. Second, agreements that were not inherently anticompetitive were nevertheless unreasonable if their "evident purpose" was to restrict competition. Third, agreements were unreasonable if their "inherent effect" was to restrain trade.[38]

Indeed, William Howard Taft suggested (after losing the 1912 presidential election and returning to Yale Law School as Kent Professor of Law) that, despite Harlan's vitriol, a careful analysis showed that *Standard Oil* really had not changed antitrust law much at all. Taft observed that, in both *Trans–Missouri* and *Joint Traffic*, Peckham had expressly "excluded from the operation of the statute all restraints which would be reasonable at common law." [39] He further noted that White adopted a rule of reason test in *Standard Oil* because he believed that Congress intended the phrase "restraint of trade" to be interpreted consistently with the common law,[40] and, as Taft had said years before in *Addyston Pipe*, the common law permitted contracts in restraint of trade where the restraint was ancillary and necessary to a lawful purpose.[41]

37. Bickel & Schmidt, supra note 35, at 109.

38. 221 U.S. at 179.

39. The Anti–Trust Act and the Supreme Court 63 (1914).

40. In *Standard Oil*, White had written: "It is certain that those terms [in the Sherman Act], at least in their rudimentary meaning, took their origin in the common law." 221 U.S. at 51.

41. Taft noted that Justice Harlan, whose *Standard Oil* dissent so fervently defended Peckham's absolutist position, had joined Taft's common law-anchored

As a means of analysis, *Addyston Pipe* remains more faithful to the common law, and appears to be more workable than *Standard Oil*, because it obviates the need to determine which restraints are "inherently" anticompetitive and how much "inherent effect" makes a contract unreasonable. In any event, White's formulation in *Standard Oil* was replaced only five years later by Brandeis' rule of reason standard, which has been used by the courts ever since.

Thus, by the early part of the century, the federal courts had developed three conflicting modes of analyzing horizontal agreements. The first, which has apparently been discredited by its implicit rejection in *Addyston Pipe* and flat contradiction in *Chicago Board of Trade*, condemned agreements that judges found directly "restrained trade" and tolerated agreements that did not directly "restrain trade," without providing any content to the verb "restrain." The second, articulated by Judge Taft in *Addyston Pipe*, directed courts to evaluate whether the agreement was ancillary and necessary to a lawful purpose. If so, the parties were not "unreasonably" restraining trade, the contract would have been enforceable under the common law of contracts, and thus Congress did not intend to proscribe the agreement under § 1. If not, the contract would have been void under the common law and Congress intended to condemn it under the Sherman Act. The third mode likewise permits courts to uphold reasonable restraints while condemning unreasonable ones. As set forth in *Chicago Board of Trade*, however, this test does little to guide the determination as to whether a restraint is reasonable.

Section B: The Evolution of Per Se Condemnation of Certain Horizontal Restraints

(1) Establishing the per se "rule": *Trenton Potteries.*

The open-ended "rule of reason" adopted in *Chicago Board of Trade* has proven inadequate in two important respects. First, the cost of inquiring into every relevant aspect of a challenged restraint proved too burdensome for plaintiffs, even for the government. Second, this third mode of analysis provided no real basis for distinguishing between agreements that regulate and thereby promote competition and those that suppress competition. Over the past decades, the Supreme Court has forthrightly endeavored to address the first problem by creating a category of re-

approach as the Circuit Justice presid-   39, at 72.
ing in *Addyston Pipe*. Taft, supra note

straints so likely to suppress competition that they can be condemned without full consideration of their history, purpose, and effect (the so-called "per se" rule). Unfortunately, the Court's inability to articulate a coherent basis for resolving the central question raised by *Chicago Board of Trade*—whether a restraint promotes or suppresses competition—has resulted in case law that ultimately provides little guidance in determining when to apply the time-saving per se rule of presumptive illegality.

This section traces the development of the doctrine that price-fixing agreements are subject to automatic condemnation under the Sherman Act. The section that follows then discusses recent cases that attempt—ultimately without success—to permit agreements that "regulate or perhaps promote competition" to escape per se condemnation without jeopardizing the entire concept of presumptive illegality.

In *United States v. Trenton Potteries Co.*,[1] the defendants, who controlled 82% of the market for what the Court politely referred to as "vitreous pottery fixtures produced in the United States for use in bathrooms and lavatories," had agreed to maintain uniform prices and to sell only to designated wholesalers. The trial court instructed the jury, in apparent contradiction to the rule of reason inquiry mandated by *Chicago Board of Trade*, to find the defendants guilty if the government had proved the price-fixing arrangement. Under the court's instructions, the jury was not permitted to fully inquire into the reasonableness of the fixed price, the intent of the parties, or the actual economic effect of the agreement. Nevertheless, the Supreme Court affirmed the defendants' conviction under § 1.

Trenton Potteries held that price-fixing cartels are conclusively unreasonable and therefore illegal under the Sherman Act.[2] The Court's reasoning in reaching this conclusion is instructive, for it relied heavily on institutional concerns. The majority argued that even price-fixing agreements that set a reasonable price are too difficult to monitor, for the "reasonable price fixed today may through economic and business changes become the unreasonable price of tomorrow." Moreover, determining whether a fixed price was reasonable was not an appropriate task for federal judges because such questions could only be answered "after a complete survey of our economic organization and a choice between rival philosophies."[3]

---

1. 273 U.S. 392 (1927).

2. Id. at 398.

3. Id. at 397–98. Cf. United States v. L. Cohen Grocery Co., 255 U.S. 81 (1921) (invalidating World War I statute that criminalized charging "any unjust or unreasonable" price for "necessaries" as an unconstitutional delegation to the judiciary).

As was the case in *Chicago Board of Trade*, the Court could have reached the same result using the second mode of analysis described above. The Court could have concluded, as Judge Taft did in *Addyston Pipe*, that price-fixing agreements are not ancillary to any lawful purpose. *Trenton Potteries'* explanation as to why price fixing is undesirable could thus have complemented Judge Taft's conclusion that fixing even a reasonable price was not a lawful purpose under the common law. But the Court preferred to continue applying *Chicago Board of Trade*'s third mode of analysis, which does not constrain the Court in the way that the common law might. Under this analysis, the Court remains free to determine, based on the Justices' own personal philosophies, what is reasonable and what is not. Exercising this power, *Trenton Potteries* determined that price fixing is per se illegal.

(2) The apex of per se condemnation: *Socony–Vacuum.*

If courts can dispense with *Chicago Board of Trade*'s time-consuming, open-ended inquiry for "price-fixing" arrangements, what constitutes "price fixing?" The Supreme Court attempted to answer that question in *United States v. Socony–Vacuum Oil Company.*[4] Unlike the toilet-maker defendants in *Trenton Potteries*, the major oil companies indicted in *Socony* did not actually agree to a specific price for oil.[5] Oil was freely sold in the marketplace, but it was customary to sell most oil under long-term contracts, which set prices based on a formula that relied heavily on the "spot market price"—that is, the price at which oil was sold for immediate delivery to meet unexpected needs.[6] The spot market price directly involved less than 5% of total oil sales, but given the customary practices in the industry, it actually affected the contract price for 80% of the oil sold in the Midwest.

The problem confronting the oil companies was that the spot market price was significantly affected by distress sales, which occurred when small independent refiners sold surplus oil for which they had no storage capacity.[7] Because these distress sales caused periodic crashes in the spot market, the defendants entered into the agreement challenged in *Socony*: each of them agreed to select one or more independent refiners as a "dancing partner" and to assume responsibility for purchasing the partner's excess oil supply.[8] Under this agreement, the independents would not have to sell at desperation prices to get rid of their inventory, the

4. 310 U.S. 150 (1940).   7. Id. at 171.
5. Id. at 222–23.   8. Id. at 179.
6. Id. at 193–94.

spot market would not crash, and the price of oil sold under long-term contract would be stabilized.

Writing for the Court, Justice William O. Douglas concluded that this agreement constituted price fixing. In so holding, he wrote in broad strokes, asserting that

> [a]ny combination which tampers with price structures is engaged in an unlawful activity. Even though the members of the price-fixing group were in no position to control the market, to the extent that they raised, lowered, or stabilized prices they would be directly interfering with the free play of market forces.[9]

The Court further held that "[u]nder the Sherman Act a combination formed for the purpose and with the effect of raising, depressing, fixing, pegging, or stabilizing the price of a commodity in interstate or foreign commerce is illegal *per se*."[10] Douglas thus extended *Trenton Potteries*, which had involved a cartel that controlled 82% of the market, and expressly ruled that a conspiracy formed with the intent of fixing prices is per se illegal even without proof of any actual effect on price.[11]

The breadth of *Socony*'s language cannot be overstated. When its holding that any horizontal agreement that has an apparent effect on prices is price fixing is combined with *Trenton Potteries*' holding that price fixing is conclusively presumed to be unreasonable, virtually any form of horizontal agreement may be banned. But *Socony* seems be another case, like *Trans–Missouri*, where the Court issued a broad holding that it did not really intend and that was later followed by confusing retreats. For example, although Justice Douglas persuasively distinguished the oil companies' conspiracy from the Call Rule sustained in *Chicago Board of Trade*,[12] a literal reading of the key *Socony* holdings appears to encompass the Call Rule—after all, the rule did have the effect of stabilizing the price of grain in transit.

---

9. Id. at 221.

10. Id. at 223.

11. Id. at 224 n.59.

12. As Douglas noted, the oil companies' agreement had both the purpose and effect of setting a floor on oil prices, id. at 222–23, whereas there was no evidence that either the purpose or effect of the Call Rule was to raise or lower prices. *Chicago Board of Trade*, 246 U.S. at 238. Moreover, the price at which the defendants in *Socony* purchased oil from their "dancing partners" was determined at their own discretion. *Socony*, 310 U.S. at 179–80. In contrast, the price fixed by the Call Rule was the closing price at the end of the prior day, which was determined in an open market. *Chicago Board of Trade*, 246 U.S. at 238. Finally, the artificially fixed spot oil price had a direct impact on the price at which most oil was sold in the Midwest. *Socony*, 310 U.S. at 198. Yet there was no evidence that the price of grain in transit had any significant effect on the prices at which most of the grain was traded in Chicago. *Chicago Board of Trade*, 246 U.S. at 240.

(3) **Struggling to apply** *Socony.*

In holding that sharply falling prices caused by distress sales of surplus inventory did not justify price fixing, Justice Douglas' opinion in *Socony* effectively overruled the Court's earlier decision in *Appalachian Coals, Inc. v. United States,*[13] where Chief Justice Charles Evans Hughes had sustained a plan that created an exclusive selling agent for almost 200 coal mine owners. Hughes had noted that the industry was afflicted by distress sales of surplus coal, which he characterized as "injurious and destructive practices"[14] that "demanded correction."[15] *Socony* restored the sound doctrine, articulated by Judge Taft in *Addyston Pipe,* that elimination of "excessive" competition cannot be a lawful purpose under the antitrust laws.

Socony's broad language condemning any "combination which tampers with price structures" was unnecessary, however, to justify rejecting the defense that "excessive" competition required creation of a price-fixing cartel. Douglas' rejection of that defense followed from the results in both *Trans–Missouri* and *Addyston Pipe,* where carteleers likewise sought to justify their conduct by suggesting that competition would not work in their industry. But applying the *Addyston Pipe* mode of analysis would have condemned the conspiracy in *Socony* without creating a doctrine more expansive than could be reliably defended in subsequent opinions. The oil companies' agreement was not ancillary to any lawful purpose, because its principal goal was to avoid ruinous competition and financial disaster for the participants. As Douglas noted, this justification could be offered by every cartel. Moreover, the notion that competition can be sufficiently "ruinous" to be against the public interest is flatly contrary to the national policy favoring competition and embodied in the Sherman Act.[16] As Peckham observed, "[c]ompetition ... is the general rule which governs all the ordinary business pursuits and transactions of life. Evils, as well as benefits, result therefrom.... The time may come when the companies will be relieved from the operation of [the antitrust laws], but they cannot, by combination and agreements among themselves, bring about this change."[17] When the evils of ruinous competition outweigh the benefits of economic

13.   288 U.S. 344 (1933).

14.   Id. at 360.

15.   Id. at 372.

16.   310 U.S. at 221.

17.   *Trans-Missouri,* 166 U.S. at 337.

Some industrialized nations permit the formation of "crisis cartels" in times of economic hardship. But often these cartels are just one part of a concerted effort by government, industry, and organized labor to restructure an industry to meet modern conditions. This type of partnership, with workers and government bureaucrats participating in making investment and business decisions for an industry, is usually considered unacceptable by the American business community.

rivalry (if, for example, sunk costs like railroad rights-of-way and track are so high that rival lines could not possibly recoup their investment), Congress always has the option of exempting the industry from the antitrust laws and subjecting it to some other form of price regulation.[18]

Had *Appalachian Coals* been decided under the *Addyston Pipe* mode of analysis instead of the rule of reason, the mine owners' agreement might still have passed muster without creating a troubling digression in antitrust doctrine. The challenged plan was justified as a means to sell *more* coal, not less, through "better methods of distribution, intensive advertising and research, and the achievement of economies of marketing." [19] Integrating distribution operations to provide better marketing than each small firm could provide individually serves a lawful purpose, just as mergers are lawful agreements to end competition under the common law.[20] The only real question in *Appalachian Coals* should have been whether an agreement among 73% of the producers in eight Appalachian coal districts was overinclusive. Modern, sophisticated joint-venture analysis (see section I(2), below) might call into question the permissibility of the agreement, although the severe competition that the defendants faced from coal producers in other areas and from producers of alternative

---

18. The government also has tools other than antitrust exemptions to remedy problems caused by ruinous competition. For example, the overproduction of depleting natural resources that occurred in *Socony* could have effectively been stopped by strict federal regulation of production. (Such a plan was struck down by the Supreme Court in 1935 because Congress had not sufficiently cabined the discretion of the executive branch administrator, *Panama Refining Co. v. Ryan,* 293 U.S. 388 (1935), but Congress could have remedied that problem with a more detailed authorizing statute.) Moreover, in both *Appalachian Coals* and *Socony*, a major cause of "distress" sales was the absence of facilities to store excess coal and oil. Government-funded storage facilities might have done more to legitimately stabilize prices in those industries than any cartel agreement.

19. 288 U.S. at 359.

20. In *Appalachian Coals*, Chief Justice Hughes had also reasoned that because the defendants could probably have merged without violating the antitrust laws, reducing competition among them while maintaining their independence should also be permitted. 288

U.S. at 376. *Addyston Pipe* likewise recognized that mergers were lawful at common law, and that the resulting decrease in competition between the merging companies was ancillary to the lawful purpose of integrating the economic operation of the merging companies. 85 Fed. 271, 280 (6th Cir. 1898). But, *Addyston Pipe* concluded, price fixing among the same firms was unlawful because there were no benefits comparable to those resulting from a merger to weigh against the "naked" cartel agreement. Id. at 282.

The economic rationale for permitting mergers is considered in detail in Chapter 6. For present purposes, suffice it to note that mergers allow firms to integrate their operations and sales forces and thus, at least potentially, to manufacture better products at lower cost than each firm could do on its own. Thus, although the pipe cartel was barred by the Sherman Act, the government permitted the defendants to merge following the judgment in *Addyston Pipe*. 2 Simon Whitney, Antitrust Policies: American Experience in Twenty Industries 7 (1958).

fuels suggests that the combination may have been permissible. Unfortunately, in 1933 the Supreme Court was not interested in performing this kind of analysis.

What explains the sharply differing approaches, coming just seven years apart, taken by Chief Justice Hughes and Justice Douglas? Hughes wrote at the height of the Depression, when the Justices' personal views no doubt reflected society's shaken faith in free enterprise. Douglas wrote as the nation was gearing up for World War II and pulling its way out of the Depression, with a restored faith in competition. Recall that the absence of any coherent standards in the first mode of analysis (where Justice Peckham distinguished between illegal "direct" restraints of trade and lawful "indirect" restraints) allowed Peckham to tolerate blatant cartel behavior that did not offend his economic values (price fixing and limiting competition among cattle brokers in the *Hopkins* and *Anderson* cases), but to condemn equally anticompetitive railroad cartels with little analysis (in the *Trans–Missouri* and *Joint Traffic* cases). Similarly, the lack of coherent standards from *Chicago Board of Trade* permitted Chief Justice Hughes to opine that an agreement among competitors aimed at fighting off the ravages of the Depression did not offend his values, while a similar plan could be condemned seven years later in *Socony* when the attitudes of the Justices had changed once again.

Socony also directly contradicted another key holding of *Appalachian Coals* by accepting the government's argument that any plan that "affects" prices is illegal even though it did not "fix" them. In *Appalachian Coals*, Chief Justice Hughes had observed that a "cooperative enterprise, otherwise free from objection, which carries with it no monopolistic menace, is not to be condemned as an undue restraint merely because it may effect a change in market conditions."[21] Hughes emphasized that the defendants there did not eliminate other sources of competition. In contrast, although the government had actually proved that the defendants enjoyed market power in *Socony*, Justice Douglas went out of his way to note that such proof was unnecessary where defendants conspire with the purpose of tampering with prices.[22]

Justice Douglas was of course correct in rejecting the oil companies' contention in *Socony* that their conduct should not be viewed as price fixing because there was no actual agreement as to price. As the facts of *Socony* demonstrated, the conspiracy had the same economic effect on price as would an explicit agreement to set a floor on the price for oil in the spot market. To require a full rule of reason trial whenever a horizontal agreement leaves

21. 288 U.S. at 373–74.   22. 310 U.S. at 221.

some competition remaining in the market would significantly hinder meritorious suits against cartels. *Socony*'s progeny demonstrate that ingenious competitors could easily inflict the very harms caused by price fixing if only the most blatant forms of fixing prices were deemed illegal per se. Examples of cases correctly condemning horizontal agreements as illegal per se even though they that did not involve express price fixing include *National Macaroni Manufacturers Ass'n v. FTC*,[23] where manufacturers faced with a shortage of wheat agreed to lower the quality of their products by using less desirable wheat instead of bidding up the price of the more expensive grain, and *Catalano, Inc. v. Target Sales, Inc.*,[24] where beer retailers agreed to use uniform terms of credit.

Socony correctly recognized that the ease of evasion makes the area of horizontal restraints one where precisely drawn legal rules are not appropriate. Thus, horizontal agreements that "tamper" with prices are properly viewed with suspicion. Justice Douglas' error was in applying the per se rule as soon as an agreement is deemed to fall within the broad category of agreements that "stabilize" or "tamper with" prices. The language of *Socony*, of course, provides for no defense based on ancillarity. The enduring wisdom of *Addyston Pipe*, however, subsequently led courts to adopt standards that incorporate the concept of ancillarity, but that are confusing both in language and substance so as to appear faithful to precedent while preserving desirable horizontal restraints.

Section C: The Modern Confusion— Where Are We Now?

(1) *BMI*: The retreat from *Socony*.

The Court's opinion in *Broadcast Music, Inc. v. Columbia Broadcasting System* [1] (*BMI*) ushered in "the modern confusion" surrounding restraints of trade. In *BMI*, the court revised *Socony* and began articulating a legal standard that is at odds with its true method of analyzing the cases. The Court has engaged in this deception because it wishes to preserve the *Chicago Board of Trade* mode of analysis, which tests all restraints by asking whether they "promote" or "suppress" "competition," but realizes that it must conclusively presume that certain practices are unreasonable. A careful examination of the reasoning and results in recent cases reveals, however, that the modern Court has effective-

---

23. 345 F.2d 421 (7th Cir. 1965).   **1.** 441 U.S. 1 (1979).

24. 446 U.S. 643 (1980).

ly returned to the *Addyston Pipe* method of analyzing restraints, sustaining those that are ancillary and necessary to accomplishing a lawful purpose.

For years, BMI and its co-defendant, the American Society of Composers, Authors and Publishers (ASCAP), represented competing composers and other holders of copyrighted musical works who jointly licensed their work to networks, radio stations, juke box operators, and other users of copyrighted music. Both BMI and ASCAP offered buyers a choice between purchasing a blanket license for all works within their repertoire (for a fee based on the buyer's total revenue) or a program license allowing use of all their works on a specific program (for a fee based on the program's revenue).[2] Because the licenses were non-exclusive,[3] buyers could also secure copyrights by negotiating individually with composers.[4] Unhappy with these three options,[5] CBS challenged the blanket license scheme under the antitrust laws, claiming that these licenses constituted per se illegal price fixing.

The logic and language of *Socony* would have supported a verdict for CBS. The blanket license constituted an agreement among competing composers to license their copyrighted works for a fixed price, and *Socony* had held that price-fixing arrangements were conclusively unreasonable—in fact, that any agreement that fixed, stabilized, or tampered with price was price fixing. Contrary to *Socony*, however, the Court held without dissent [6] that the term "price fixing" was instead "a shorthand way of describing certain categories of business behavior to which the per se rule has been held applicable,"[7] which the majority opinion generically described as agreements that were "plainly anticompetitive."[8] *BMI* stated that no conspiracy can be condemned as per se illegal without a prior judicial determination that the restraint lacks "redeeming virtue."[9]

During the 39–year period between *Socony* and *BMI*, the Court had never suggested that the per se rule against price fixing was so qualified. To be sure, the Court had utilized the "lacks redeeming virtue" test in determining whether to apply the per se

2. Id. at 5.

3. Exclusive licenses granted to BMI and ASCAP had been enjoined on antitrust grounds shortly after World War II. United States v. American Soc'y of Composers, Authors and Publishers, 1950–1951 Trade Cas. (CCH) ¶ 62,595 (S.D.N.Y. 1950).

4. *BMI*, 441 U.S. at 11.

5. CBS preferred to purchase licenses only for those compositions actually used in its programs. Presumably,

such a license would have cost less than a blanket license.

6. Justice John Paul Stevens dissented on other grounds.

7. Id. at 9.

8. Id. at 8.

9. Id. at 9. The Court reiterated this position in Catalano, Inc. v. Target Sales, Inc., 446 U.S. 643, 650 (1980).

rule to *other* types of restraints.[10] In the first such case to invoke this test, the Court had described the per se rule as an exception to *Chicago Board of Trade*'s broad rule of reason that applied to restraints with no redeeming virtue, and added that price fixing was among the practices that fell within this category.[11] In *BMI*, however, Justice Byron White turned this precedent on its head. Price fixing was no longer a subset of virtueless restraints; instead, in order to establish "price fixing," the plaintiff now had to show that the defendant's conduct was virtueless.

If the Court has jettisoned *Socony*'s definition of price fixing as an agreement that tampers with price structures, then when do courts depart from the rule of reason analysis set forth in *Chicago Board of Trade*? *BMI* indicated that courts must inquire whether "the practice facially appears to be one that would always or almost always tend to restrict competition and decrease output." [12]

If the Court were actually using that standard, antitrust doctrine would be seriously flawed, for several reasons. First, *BMI* provided no guidance to help judges make this determination whether a practice "almost always" harms competition and reduces output. Although the standard is an understandable reaction to the rigidity of *Socony*'s ban on all horizontal agreements tampering with price, it provides no clear limit on a defendant's ability to demand a rule of reason trial unless the trial judge— who is not necessarily sophisticated in antitrust or economics—can confidently say that the challenged conduct is anticompetitive. Second the Court could not really have meant to adopt a conjunctive test, requiring that the restraint both restrict competition *and* decrease output; if the *Trenton Potteries* cartel had fixed prices at "reasonable levels," as the defendants claimed, there would have been no reduction in output, but the Court could not have intended to approve that behavior. Finally, equating competition with output ignores the possibility that in some circumstances cartels can serve to transfer wealth from consumers to the carteleers without any significant effect on output. For example, suppose that identifiable groups of consumers place significantly different values on a product, and that arbitrage is infeasible. A cartel can engage in price discrimination by charging higher prices to the group that is willing to pay more, and charging prices at the competitive level (or allowing competition without price fixing) for

10. These cases, discussed in Chapter 5, include *Northern Pacific Railway* (tying agreements lack redeeming value and are per se illegal), and *White Motor Co.* and *Sylvania* (vertical non-price restraints have redeeming value and are not per se illegal).

11. Northern Pacific Railway Co. v. United States, 356 U.S. 1, 5 (1958).

12. 441 U.S. at 19–20.

the patronage of the other consumers. Under these circumstances, consumers in the first group pay more, but overall output is the same as it would be in a competitive market.[13]

Fortunately, it does not appear that the Court actually meant to apply the standard set forth in *BMI*. In explaining why the blanket license challenged there did not "facially appear" to restrict competition, Justice White's majority opinion did not first look to see whether the plaintiffs had shown that the practice appeared to almost always restrict competition. Rather, he turned immediately to the defendants' justifications, noting that the license "accompanies the integration of sales, monitoring, and enforcement against unauthorized copyright use." [14] He also emphasized that the blanket license was really a new product that could not be offered by the defendants individually.[15] Finally, he concluded that the defendants' collective fixing of the price for a blanket license "was an obvious necessity." [16] Thus, although the standard set forth in *BMI* suggests that the plaintiff must initially demonstrate facial harm to competition, White's actual analysis appears to be more consistent with *Addyston Pipe* : (a) the plaintiff must show a horizontal agreement affecting price; (b) the court will then look to the defendant's justifications and will sustain restraints necessary to accomplish lawful purposes; and (c) integrating sales and copyright enforcement activities, providing a new product, and price agreements essential to supply of the new product all constitute lawful purposes.

Should White's analysis have ended the Court's scrutiny of BMI's blanket license? The majority said no, but then refused to determine the reasonableness of BMI's practice of offering only blanket and program licenses and remanded the case to the court of appeals.[17] In his concurring opinion, Justice Stevens argued that the record before the Court was sufficient to justify a funding that the arrangement was unreasonable. He reasoned that BMI and ASCAP dominated the industry, and that they charged fees that were "patently discriminatory" because they were based on the buyer's ability to pay, instead of "factors—such as the cost, quality, or quantity of the product—that normally affect price in a competitive market." [18]

---

13. Another example occurs when competition permits consumers to obtain products at far below the maximum amount they would be willing to pay (i.e., there is substantial consumer surplus and demand is inelastic), but new technology allows a cartel to charge higher prices for the same product. An example might be a decision by the owners of professional football teams to shift all their games to pay cable television.

14. 441 U.S. at 20.

15. Id. at 21–23.

16. Id. at 20.

17. Id. at 25 & n.44.

18. Id. at 30–32.

Despite Stevens' arguments, BMI's practices were ultimately exonerated in the lower courts, on the theory that buyers dissatisfied with blanket licenses could obtain musical licenses directly (albeit at some increased transactions costs).[19] Unfortunately, the courts failed to recognize that, once an agreement is found necessary to produce a new product or to integrate economic activity, the defendants are in reality forming a joint venture, and the agreement should be analyzed as such. Among the inquiries made in joint venture analysis (explored in detail below in section I) is the question whether the venture is overinclusive—i.e., whether on balance society would be better off with five or six licensing agencies instead of only two. This question, which the lower courts ignored in analyzing BMI's licensing scheme, may have led them to a different conclusion.

(2) The retreat from *BMI*.

The Court's decision the following year in *Catalano, Inc. v. Target Sales, Inc.*[20] confirms that *BMI* did not really mean to limit the per se rule as much as its broad language might have suggested. In *Catalano*, competing liquor wholesalers had agreed not to extend credit to customers. They justified their agreement on the theory that smaller firms could more easily compete without having to extend credit, and that limiting price competition to retail prices made prices more "visible." [21] Accepting this argument, the Ninth Circuit held that the agreement was subject to the rule of reason.[22] However, unlike *BMI*, the defendants were not entering into a joint venture to produce or distribute their liquor or to create a new product that could not be created by the defendants individually. The Supreme Court reversed in a unanimous per curiam opinion. Citing *Socony*'s broad language, the Court found that the agreement tampered with prices and was therefore per se illegal.[23] Given the plausibility of the defendants' arguments and the probable existence of competition as to price, albeit not as to credit terms, it is difficult to believe that all nine Justices really thought that the restriction *plainly* restricted competition *and* decreased output *and* lacked *any* redeeming value.

The Court's 4–3 decision in *Arizona v. Maricopa County Medi-*

19. See, e.g., Buffalo Broadcasting Co. v. American Soc'y of Composers, Authors and Publishers, 744 F.2d 917 (2d Cir. 1984), cert. denied, 469 U.S. 1211 (1985); Columbia Broadcasting System, Inc. v. American Soc'y of Composers, Authors and Publishers, 620 F.2d 930 (2d Cir. 1980), cert. denied, 450 U.S. 970 (1981); National Cable Tele-vision Ass'n v. Broadcast Music, Inc., 772 F.Supp. 614 (D.D.C.1991).

20. 446 U.S. 643 (1980).

21. Id. at 649.

22. 605 F.2d 1097 (1979).

23. 446 U.S. at 646.

cal Society [24] is an archetypical example of the modern confusion. In that case, the majority held that the state was entitled to summary judgment against the defendants, a group consisting of 70% of Phoenix doctors who had entered into an agreement setting the maximum prices to be charged for their services to patients with health insurance. Justice Stevens' majority opinion purported to apply the *Chicago Board of Trade* mode of analysis, using a standard that appears unworkable, but his actual analysis approximates the *Addyston Pipe* standard. In setting out the relevant law, the opinion is clearly reminiscent of *Chicago Board of Trade*. First, Stevens explained that, although the literal language of § 1 prohibits every contract, the section should be interpreted to bar only unreasonable contracts because "Congress could not have intended" a literal reading. Second, he noted, determining reasonableness normally requires that the courts look at all the circumstances of the case. Third, because such an inquiry can be very costly, he observed that the courts will apply a conclusive presumption of unreasonableness "[o]nce experience with a particular kind of restraint enables the Court to predict with confidence that the rule of reason will condemn it." [25]

The incoherent and confusing nature of *BMI*'s verbal formulation is evident from *Maricopa*'s attempt to apply the *BMI* standard to the doctors' maximum price fixing scheme. Drawing on the Court's prior decisions,[26] Justice Stevens first identified several reasons why maximum price fixing should be deemed per se illegal: (1) a Madisonian concern with substituting the "perhaps erroneous judgment" of the defendants for the marketplace; (2) a Jeffersonian concern that maximum price fixing "cripples the freedom of traders"; (3) an economic concern that maximum price levels "may" prevent practitioners from offering high-priced, high-cost services valued by consumers; and (4) an economic concern that maximum price levels "may" be minimum price levels in disguise.[27] Stevens then refused to consider the defendants' prof-

---

24. 457 U.S. 332 (1982). Justices Blackmun and O'Connor did not participate.

25. Id. at 343–44.

In contrast to *Maricopa*, *Addyston Pipe* rejects a literal interpretation of § 1 because the legislative history strongly suggested that Congress intended to incorporate the common law rules governing contracts in restraint of trade, and instead asks the focused question whether the challenged restraint is ancillary and necessary to

some lawful purpose. See section A(2) above.

26. Kiefer-Stewart Co. v. Joseph E. Seagram & Sons, Inc., 340 U.S. 211 (1951); Albrecht v. Herald Co., 390 U.S. 145 (1968).

27. *Maricopa*, 457 U.S. at 347–49.

A price ceiling can also arbitrarily curtail innovation by depriving firms of the option of pricing higher (perhaps selectively) and using the funds for research and development.

fered justifications for the agreement, because to do so would be inconsistent with per se illegality.[28]

A court faithfully applying the verbal standards set forth in *BMI* and *Catalano,* and purportedly followed in *Maricopa,* would not have concluded that the doctors' arrangement should be condemned as per se illegal. The practice does not facially appear to be one that will almost always be anticompetitive; indeed, absent some evidence that it limits innovation, denies consumers high-price, high-cost services, or really serves as a minimum price-fixing scheme, the agreement presents at most only the *risk* of being anticompetitive. Moreover, there is no indication the Court concluded that the practice lacked potentially redeeming value, for the majority expressly refused to consider that question.

Maricopa makes much more sense when viewed through an *Addyston Pipe* lens. Even accepting the defendants' argument that a fee schedule agreed to by independent doctors provided consumers "a uniquely desirable form of health coverage that would otherwise not exist," [29] the majority concluded that it was not necessary for the *doctors* to set the fees.[30] Insurance companies or other independent entities could achieve the same result— a viable insurance program for fee-for-service medicine—without the anticompetitive risks of price fixing.[31]

Addyston Pipe 's analysis justifies harsh treatment for maximum price-fixing agreements. The risks alluded to by Justice Stevens are significant; whether or not they are "facially anticompetitive" or economically "obscene",[32] there is no reason to take those risks when the horizontal agreement at issue is not necessary to accomplish any lawful purpose.

(3) A structured rule of reason analysis.

Broadcast Music, on close analysis, suggests an antitrust doctrine in chaos. The Court failed to identify precisely what sort of conduct is per se illegal, and failed to provide any guidelines, other than the open-ended rule of reason under *Chicago Board of Trade,* for how lower courts should evaluate restraints not subject to per se condemnation. *National Collegiate Athletic Ass'n v. Board of Regents of the University of Oklahoma* [33] clarifies these two key

28. Id. at 351.

29. Id.

30. Id. at 352.

31. Id. at 353–54. One could quibble with the propriety of Justice Stevens' resolution of this issue at the summary judgment stage, in light of Justice Powell's forceful contention in dissent that

schedule setting by insurance companies is much more costly. Id. at 357.

32. Cf. Miller v. California, 413 U.S. 15 (1973) (deeming pornography obscene only if it lacks any redeeming social or artistic value).

33. 468 U.S. 85 (1984).

questions. Like *Maricopa*, this case reflects the modern confusion, and understanding of the Court's actual holding comes more easily by using Judge Taft's mode of analysis instead of Justice Brandeis'.

The litigation involved a challenge to an NCAA plan whereby member schools (all sponsors of major college football programs) sold the rights to televise their football games exclusively through NCAA contracts. The Court found that the plan precluded member schools from conducting independent price negotiations and placed an artificial limit on output—the number of games shown each Saturday. Writing for the majority, Justice Stevens noted that a horizontal arrangement that fixed prices and limited output would "ordinarily [be] condemned as a matter of law under an 'illegal per se' approach." [34] Nevertheless, the Court rejected per se condemnation. In explaining the Court's decision to judge the restraint under a rule of reason, Justice Stevens wrote that the "critical" factor "is that this case involves an industry in which horizontal restraints on competition are essential if the product is to be available at all." [35]

Significantly, the Court did not follow *BMI*'s verbal standard. The Court did not inquire as a preliminary matter whether the agreement raised prices or reduced output. Indeed, given the district court's thorough findings that the agreement *did* raise prices and reduce output,[36] the *BMI* test might have led the Court to find that the practice was illegal per se. Nor did the Court reach any conclusion as to whether the NCAA's challenged television plan, as opposed to the NCAA itself, had any redeeming economic value. Instead, given that *some* restraints agreed to by member schools were ancillary to the lawful purpose of creating the product known as college football, the Court concluded that a rule of reason inquiry was appropriate to allow a more careful exploration as to whether the NCAA's television plan was one of those ancillary restraints.

Rather than embarking on the open-ended rule of reason analysis suggested by *Chicago Board of Trade*, however, the *NCAA* opinion proceeded along a path that has become known as a "structured rule of reason" that focuses on analyzing the defendants justifications and the "fit" between these ends and the means chosen to achieve them.[37] The Court rejected the key argument made by the NCAA—that there was no evidence that

---

34. Id. at 100.

35. Id. at 101.

36. See id. at 95–96.

37. See, e.g., Eleanor Fox and Lawrence Sullivan, Antitrust–Retrospective and Perspective: Where Are We Coming From? Where Are We Going?, 62 N.Y.U. L. Rev. 936, 955 (1987) (citing *NCAA*, 468 U.S. at 98–104).

the organization had market power. Justice Stevens' majority opinion responded that "the absence of proof of market power does not justify a naked restriction on price or output." [38] Of course, if the NCAA plan was such a "naked restriction," why wasn't it per se illegal? Stevens explained that, under *his* view of the rule of reason, the defendant had the burden of showing "some competitive justification even in the absence of a detailed market analysis." [39]

Turning to the NCAA's justifications, the Court dismissed the defendant's attempt to analogize the case to *BMI* because, unlike price fixing ancillary to the issuance of a blanket license, the television plan was not necessary to produce college football.[40] The Court also rejected the NCAA's claims that the plan was needed to protect the live gate attendance of non-televised games and to promote competitive balance among member schools. The Court scrutinized the factual record and found that the plan did not accomplish either of these objectives.[41] In sum, Justice Stevens employed the rule of reason in an orderly manner to consider and reject, either in theory or on the facts of the case, each of the NCAA's efforts to justify its plan as necessary to some legitimate purpose. Thus, the plan was held to be an unreasonable restraint of trade in violation of § 1.

(4) Litigating amid the confusion.

Despite this analytical confusion, the Supreme Court has yet to expressly reject the *Chicago Board of Trade* method of analysis, or to admit that it is really following *Addyston Pipe*. Thus, a linguistic translation is necessary to enable those litigating cases involving horizontal agreements to maintain both accuracy and fidelity to the language in the United States Reports. First, litigators should ask whether the agreement tampers with or stabilizes prices. If not, a rule of reason inquiry is required (cite *Chicago Board of Trade* [42]). If so, "per se" analysis is triggered (cite *Socony* [43]). Continuing with the per se analysis, the second step is to determine whether the agreement furthers any lawful purpose. If not, it is per se illegal, and the analysis ends (cite *Catalano*,[44] and distinguish *BMI* as involving a lawful purpose). If so, the third step is to inquire whether the agreement is necessary to accomplish a lawful purpose. When an obvious less restrictive alternative makes it clear that the agreement is not *necessary* to a lawful purpose, the agreement is "per se illegal" and the inquiry

---

38. *NCAA*, 468 U.S. at 109.

39. Id. at 110.

40. Id. at 114.

41. Id. at 115–17.

42. 246 U.S. 231 (1918).

43. 310 U.S. 150 (1940).

44. 446 U.S. 643 (1980).

ends (cite *Maricopa* [45]). Where the question of necessity is less clear, the fourth step is to conduct a trial under the "rule of reason" label (cite *NCAA* [46]).

This translation should hold attorneys in good stead, as long as the defendants are not members of the "learned professions." For those defendants, the Court has articulated another set of verbal standards that it has then proceeded to ignore. Those cases are considered in the next section.

Section D: The "Learned" Professions

The same sort of linguistic dexterity that antitrust lawyers must learn in order to correctly analyze horizontal restraints generally must be performed, with somewhat different verbal rules, when analyzing horizontal restraints involving parties who comprise what has traditionally been referred to as the "learned professions." In cases involving doctors, attorneys, and dentists, the Supreme Court has suggested that different rules apply to professionals and therefore that the per se analysis discussed in the prior sections is not applicable. Close scrutiny of the opinions, however, again reveals that the Court is merely applying the same principles first set forth by Judge Taft in *Addyston Pipe* to the particular facts and circumstances of the cases involving the professions.[1]

In *Goldfarb v. Virginia State Bar*,[2] the Supreme Court held that the defendant's fee schedule, combined with the threat to discipline attorneys who habitually charged lower fees, constituted price fixing in violation of the Sherman Act. Although the Court

45. 457 U.S. 332 (1982).

46. 468 U.S. 85 (1984). Cf. Massachusetts Bd. of Registry in Optometry, 110 F.T.C. 549, 604 (1988), where the FTC explained its horizontal restraint methodology in similar terms.

During the Reagan administration, the Department of Justice issued guidelines for horizontal restraints in international business that might have domestic implications. See Antitrust Enforcement Guidelines for International Operations, 4 Trade Reg. Rep. (CCH) ¶ 13,109 (1988). The approach taken in these guidelines differs from that suggested by this treatise and by the FTC. Under the Justice Department's guidelines, once the Antitrust Division finds that a restraint is not "naked," it next seeks to determine whether the restraint creates or enhances market power. As seen in Chapter 3, this is a difficult task. Moreover, because the common law prohibited agreements among competitors that were not necessary to a lawful purpose, regardless of market power, *Addyston Pipe* suggests that the Justice Department's approach is not the best way to apply § 1. On the other hand, a market power "filter" is preferred by those with great faith in the market, little faith in the ability of the adjudicatory process to determine the competitive effect of particular practices, albeit greater faith in judges' ability to correctly define relevant markets. See Frank Easterbrook, The Limits of Antitrust, 63 Texas L. Rev. 1, 9, 19 (1984).

1. See section A(2) above.

2. 421 U.S. 773 (1975).

thus established that the learned professions were "trades" subject to § 1, it suggested that the special nature of the professions meant that "a particular practice, which could properly be viewed as a violation of the Sherman Act in another context, [should] be treated differently" here.[3]

Armed with this precedent, the defendant in *National Society of Professional Engineers v. United States*[4] asserted that an agreement among member engineers not to engage in competitive bidding was "reasonable." Specifically, the defendants claimed that vigorous price competition in engineering services would lead to low-cost contracts that endangered the public safety. The Court treated this argument just as it had the oil companies' argument in *Socony*[5] that vigorous price competition in the spot oil market would ruin the industry and harm the public interest—it rejected it out of hand. *Professional Engineers* thus makes clear that courts may not consider the defense that unrestricted competition for professional services is not in the public interest.[6] The majority concluded that the only justification for the prohibition on competitive bidding challenged in that case would be one that showed how the restraint had "a positive effect on competition."[7]

The Court's refusal to allow federal judges to determine whether competition for professional services serves the public interest is sensible for the same reasons that *Addyston Pipe* and *Socony–Vacuum* opposed similar judicial inquiries in cases involving other industries. Protecting against the sale of low quality or even potentially unsafe goods or services, whether or not offered by professionals, is probably best left to either marketplace forces or direct government regulation. Suppose, for example, that toy manufacturers decide not to use lead paint in children's toys. Because the safety hazards of lead are easily understood, no agreement is necessary to accomplish this purpose; instead, each toy maker could begin producing lead-free toys and advertise that fact. Consumers wishing to protect their children from lead poisoning would purchase the lead-free products. Alternatively, especially where safety or health defects are less patent (airplane safety problems, for example), direct government regulation remains preferable to private agreements. Private agreements always pose the risk of eliminating competition to avoid non-existent health and safety risks. Were antitrust doctrine otherwise, the respondents in *National Macaroni Manufacturers Association v.*

3. Id. at 788 n.17.

4. 435 U.S. 679 (1978).

5. United States v. Socony–Vacuum Oil Co., 310 U.S. 150 (1940).

6. 435 U.S. at 696.

7. Id. at 693 n.19.

FTC[8] could have claimed that their agreement requiring that macaroni be made with only 50% of high-quality wheat, which has imposed because of a wheat shortage, was really motivated by a concern that low-quality wheat was healthier to eat! In any event, if special circumstances justify replacing competition by private agreement, Congress can always amend the antitrust laws.[9]

The difficulty ordinary consumers may have in discerning the quality and value of professional services has led to two areas where the professions are given greater leeway than are other defendants. The first arises where a professional society sets ethical standards that have the effect of increasing the reliability of (and hence the demand for) its members' services. For example, in *Vogel v. American Society of Appraisers*,[10] the appraisers agreed not to charge fees based on a percentage value of the property to be appraised. Such a fee structure, the society argued, would create a conflict of interest between the appraisers' desire for high fees and an accurate appraisal of the property's value. The Seventh Circuit rejected a per se challenge to the agreement, even though the appraisers had "tampered" with price.

The result seems sensible. The appraisers' rule, rather than restricting the use of appraisal services due to artificially high prices, may actually promote the use of such services. The defense raised in *Vogel* was thus very different from that rejected by the Court in *Professional Engineers*. *Vogel* appears to be what *Professional Engineers* had in mind when it said that professional societies may adopt ethical norms that "serve to regulate and promote" competition. By contrast, the engineers' argument was "a far cry" from this principle[11] because they did not seriously claim that a no-bidding rule would mean that more projects would be turned over to engineers; rather, they argued that the decrease in prices and quality that would result from competition was unacceptable according to some generalized view of the public interest.

8. 345 F.2d 421 (7th Cir. 1965).

9. Indeed, Congress has exempted the insurance industry from antitrust liability in most circumstances. See the McCarran–Ferguson Act. 15 U.S.C. § 1012(b). Following American Medical Ass'n v. FTC, 638 F.2d 443 (2d Cir. 1980), aff'd by an equally divided court, 455 U.S. 676 (1982), several attempts were made to legislatively bar FTC scrutiny of professional activities; these efforts were never successful.

10. 744 F.2d 598 (7th Cir. 1984).

11. *Professional Engineers*, 435 U.S. at 696.

Using language that Judge Taft could have written himself, *Professional Engineers* also permits rivals to agree to restraints related to product safety where "they have no anticompetitive effect and ... they are reasonably ancillary to the seller's main purpose of protecting the public from harm or itself from product liability." Id. at 696 n.22.

The second area in which the professions are accorded greater leeway involves the regulation of deceptive practices. *Professional Engineers* expressly permitted the defendant to continue to regulate its member in this area, and the Second Circuit likewise held in *American Medical Association v. FTC* that the AMA had a "unique" role to play in ending deceptive advertising and oppressive solicitation practices.[12] Because deception on the part of professionals, especially those who provide health care or legal services, may cause irreparable damage, and because the complexities of the profession give private groups greater expertise than can be marshalled by government regulators, the courts give rival professionals greater latitude in entering into horizontal agreements to regulate deception.

In *FTC v. Indiana Federation of Dentists*,[13] the most recent Supreme Court case to focus on the unique issues affecting agreements among rivals in the learned professions, the Court confirmed what seemed apparent from earlier cases: these restraints will not be quickly disapproved under the per se rule formulated in *Trenton Potteries* and *Socony*. Rather, even after the government demonstrates that an agreement significantly restricts price competition, the defendants will be allowed to put on their case and try to establish justifications for the agreement.[14] Nevertheless, the Court condemned the dentists' agreement to refuse to comply with insurance companies' demands that they submit x-rays as a condition of reimbursement. The Court's analysis paralleled *Addyston Pipe*: the FTC prevailed because it showed that the agreement posed a significant risk to price competition and was not ancillary to a lawful purpose. The Court's refusal to characterize the dentists' agreement as per se illegal amounted, in short, to professional courtesy. As lawyers, we will give fellow professionals their full day in court, although the ultimate result will be no different than if the agreement were among tradespeople.

Despite its deceptive language, *Indiana Federation of Dentists* is useful in a broader context by demonstrating that the rule of reason analysis articulated in *Chicago Board of Trade* can be shortened, even when the defendants' conduct does not fall into the category of per se illegality. The FTC did not expressly find that the dentists' agreement had any impact on price, or that the defendants held market power. Nevertheless, the Court sustained a finding of unreasonableness based on two key pieces of evidence

---

12. 638 F.2d 443, 452 (2d Cir. 1980), aff'd by an equally divided court, 455 U.S. 676 (1982).

13. 476 U.S. 447 (1986).

14. Id. at 458 ("we have been slow to condemn rules adopted by professional associations as unreasonable *per se* ").

presented by the FTC: economic theory and evidence concerning other markets. Economic theory suggested that consumers would be better off if the dentists were not permitted to conspire; those dentists who unilaterally refused to provide x-rays to insurers would be denied reimbursement and would lose patients to those willing to cooperate with the insurance companies. Evidence from other markets where the FTC knew competition was working showed that rival dentists, anxious to offer insurance coverage for their patients, cooperated with insurance companies in submitting x-rays. Allowing the government and private plaintiffs to combine theory and comparative analysis to prove that the defendants' conduct harmed competition significantly lightens their burden.

A review of antitrust cases concerning agreements among professionals demonstrates several pervasive themes about antitrust jurisprudence. The Court seems unable to clearly articulate the analytical method it is employing, purporting to employ a full-blown inquiry into all facets of a restraint when it is really applying the common law requirement that any competition-restraining agreement be ancillary to some lawful purpose. Of greater importance is the Court's clear message that, in determining what are the lawful objects of concerted trade restraints, competition is the policy and any arguments to the contrary must be directed to Congress, not the judiciary.

Section E: Agreements to Divide Markets

(1) Why market division is bad.

Cartels can suppress competition by means other than agreements that fix, raise, or lower prices: they can divide customers among themselves, and agree not to compete for the patronage of those allocated to their rivals. Specific customers can be allocated to specific sellers; alternatively, customers can be allocated by the time of year when the purchase is made. The most common type of customer allocation, however, is a territorial division of the market whereby each carteleer reserves a particular geographic area for itself. Whatever their form, market division schemes have the effect of allowing each firm to set its price without the threat of rivalry from its co-conspirators.

The economic power that a market division scheme confers leads to the same social harms that the antitrust laws properly condemn if caused by illegal monopolization or price-fixing schemes. A firm that eliminates competition via market division can reduce output to inefficient levels, raise prices to exploit consumers, and exercise arbitrary power over its allocated consumers. In addition, conspirators can more easily spot and retaliate against new entrants, thus interfering with Jeffersonian concepts of equal economic opportunity. In some ways, indeed, market division schemes are more insidious than price-fixing agreements. A firm that enters into a price-fixing agreement can, after all, still engage in non-price competition—by offering, for example, products of higher quality or better or quicker service. By contrast, a market division scheme eliminates *any* competition among the carteleers.

National Ass'n of Window Glass Manufacturers v. United States,[1] an early case that upheld an agreement among makers of hand-blown glass to operate only during half the year, illustrates another way in which market division agreements harm consumers and society by protecting inefficient carteleers. Price-fixing cartels may agree to lower prices, or may eventually become ineffective altogether, when more efficient members of the cartel (i.e., those with lower costs) seek to establish a lower price than their less-efficient conspirators. In contrast, a market division scheme allows each firm free reign within its designated area and thus permits inefficient firms to pass on their higher costs (as well as a monopoly surcharge) to their unfortunate customers. For example, the agreement in *Window Glass* allowed less efficient glass makers to stay in business; without the agreement, these firms would have faced more competition for scarce labor, and ultimately would have lost out to their more efficient rivals.[2]

Window Glass is a classic example of the open-ended nature of the rule of reason established by *Chicago Board of Trade*. That case, you will recall, held that § 1 claims should consider all relevant facts and determine whether the defendants' agreement "suppressed" or "merely regulated" competition.[3] *Chicago Board of Trade* represented a departure from the more anchored approach advocated by Judge William Howard Taft in *Addyston Pipe*, which focused on whether the challenged restraint would have been voided under the common law.[4] Justice Oliver Wendell

---

1. 263 U.S. 403 (1923).

2. It is conceivable that all hand-blown glass makers were equally efficient, but that the agreement was necessary lest bidding on scarce labor drive all of them into bankruptcy. Even this scenario would not justify the glass manufacturers' agreement, however, because it involves a frontal attack on the value of competition in the industry. Essentially the same argument was made by the railroads in *Trans–Missouri* (see section A(1)) and by the engineers in *Professional Engineers* (see section D); the Court has consistently rejected this defense as inconsistent with the Sherman Act's policy of letting competition allocate goods and services.

3. Chicago Board of Trade v. United States, 246 U.S. 231 (1918), discussed above in section A(3).

4. United States v. Addyston Pipe & Steel Co., 85 Fed. 271 (6th Cir. 1898), aff'd, 175 U.S. 211 (1899), discussed above in section A(2).

Holmes, Jr., immediately moved to the rule of reason analysis in *Window Glass* and found that the glass manufacturers' agreement met his personal standard of reasonableness. Although the Court was doubtless motivated by a Jeffersonian desire to tolerate agreements that allowed less efficient firms to remain in business, *Window Glass* is a case where each of the other competing goals of antitrust dictates the opposite result. Allowing inefficient firms to operate leads to a misallocation of society's resources; the firms will necessarily charge higher prices than their more efficient counterparts,[5] and consumers will therefore be exploited; and important decisions about where laborers work are determined not by the impersonal hand of the market but by the discretionary power of the defendant trade association. Moreover, there was no suggestion that the glass manufacturers' agreement was necessary to avoid a monopolistic or oligopolistic industry that would make consumers worse off. Holmes did not analyze the issues in this manner, of course; the case demonstrates how the rule of reason allows for unarticulated judicial decisionmaking in the guise of antitrust analysis.[6]

5. Actually, the peculiar facts in *Window Glass* suggest that none of the hand-blown glass makers could have raised their prices because they operated at such a cost disadvantage vis-a-vis automated glass manufacturers; Holmes said that they stayed in business merely "by the sufferance" of the automated manufacturers and by working longer hours. 263 U.S. at 412. In fact, it is unclear how defendants stayed in business at all. In any event, the general proposition stated in the text remains true for most industries.

6. Cf. 1 Holmes–Pollock Letters 163 (1941) (letter of April 23, 1910) ("I don't disguise my belief that the Sherman Act is a humbug based on economic ignorance and incompetence.")

Although market division agreements are properly condemned under the antitrust laws, it would not be unreasonable for policymakers to tolerate such agreements under some circumstances in order to serve a variety of social and economic goals. For example, market division agreements like that at issue in *Window Glass* might be seen as a useful way to protect workers from dramatic developments in technology that save labor costs and thus result in layoffs. Even in such cases, however, market division agreements aimed at "rationalizing" the workforce should probably be combined with job retraining programs, government supervision of firm investments aimed at making the industry competitive, and a host of other affirmative industrial policies. Of course, this scheme runs counter to the policies of competition reflected in the Sherman Act and therefore would require affirmative congressional legislation; judges should not take it upon themselves to construct industrial policy by approving anticompetitive agreements absent legislative sanction.

Similarly, under European law, firms may petition competition authorities for permission to divide markets as part of specialization agreements. See Eleanor Fox & Lawrence Sullivan, Antitrust 350 (1989). For example, in Fine Papers, Commission Decision 72/291, O.J. L 182/24 (Aug. 10, 1972), the Commission of the European Community granted an exemption from the EC's equivalent of § 1 (Article 85 of the Treaty of Rome, which prohibits agreements "which have as their object or effect the prevention, restriction or distortion of competition") so as to allow five French cigarette companies to agree that each would specialize in a different type of cigarette paper. The Commission approved the agreement because economies of scale would allow each company to manufacture its special product at

(2) **Development of per se condemnation.**

Subsequent to *Window Glass Manufacturers*, of course, the Supreme Court decided the *Socony* case; in condemning any restraint that tampered or stabilized prices as illegal per se, the Court strongly suggested that Justice Holmes' antitrust jurisprudence was no longer good law. *Timken Roller Bearing Co. v. United States*[7] could have given the Court an opportunity to clarify the law regarding market division schemes and, in the process, perhaps the entire mode of analysis governing horizontal restraints. The case involved an agreement entered into by an American company, a related British corporation, and a jointly owned French subsidiary, to avoid competing among themselves in those three countries. The defendants argued that their agreement was ancillary to the lawful purpose of protecting their shared trademark. Based on the district court's finding that the dominant purpose of the arrangement was to stifle competition and its own conclusion that the agreements were broader than necessary for trademark protection, the Court could have used the *Addyston Pipe* methodology to condemn the agreement. Instead, the Court held that "regardless" of the purpose or overbreadth of the agreement, the evolving doctrine condemning price-fixing restraints as illegal per se "plainly establish[es] that agreements providing for an aggregation of trade restraints such as those existing in this case are illegal under the Act."[8]

lower cost than if each tried to sell the entire range of cigarette papers, and substantial competition from German, Italian, and Austrian rivals would force the French firms to pass the cost savings along to consumers in the form of lower prices.

Such an agreement would not appear to survive scrutiny under the Sherman Act. Those defending the agreement would necessarily have to argue that competition yielded a socially undesirable result—the very argument the Court rejected in *Trans–Missouri and Professional Engineers*. Moreover, if Professor Michael Porter is correct about the importance of domestic rivalry (see Chapter 1), allowing a firm to become the American "specialist" in a particular area, and thus to face competition only from foreign sources, may put a damper on the competitive pressure to innovate. However, it may be appropriate for Congress to follow the European model and authorize a regulatory agency to approve such agreements on a case-by-case basis if the parties can demonstrate significant production efficiencies *and* a competitive market structure that will encourage innovation and force the affected firms to pass any cost savings on the their customers.

7. 341 U.S. 593 (1951).

8. Id. at 598 (citing, among other cases, United States v. Socony–Vacuum Oil Co., 310 U.S. 150, 223–24 & n.59 (1940).

Timken also wrestled with the question whether corporations with overlapping shareholders can conspire with each other under § 1. This knotty issue troubled the courts for years. Recently, however, the Supreme Court has simplified the issue by holding that corporations with the same ownership cannot be co-conspirators under § 1. Copperweld Corp. v. Independence Tube Corp., 467 U.S. 752 (1984). Whether affiliated corporations can conspire with one another depends on whether they have a unity of interest. In a case like *Timken*, where the British company was effectively controlled by one in-

Timken involved agreements among rivals who all sold the same brand of roller bearings. That intrabrand market division was per se illegal when agreed to by rival retailers was made clear in *United States v. General Motors Corp.*[9] As we shall explore in detail in a later chapter,[10] a manufacturer may have legitimate pro-competitive reasons for independently deciding to limit the territories in which retailers may sell its product. *General Motors* made clear, however, that these reasons do not justify allowing retailers to agree among themselves to limit competition in the retail sale of one brand of a product.[11] Thus, in that case, the Court found that an agreement between competing Southern California Chevrolet dealers and General Motors to inhibit discount pricing was per se illegal. This result is sound for several reasons. First, an agreement among retailers poses a significant risk to competition. If a manufacturer believes that retail competition should be limited, it doesn't need a cartel of its dealers to coerce it to do so. Second, determining the market power of a brand name, particularly in a market characterized by substantial advertising and brand loyalty, is a difficult question that the courts should avoid unless the challenged agreement plausibly is necessary to accomplish a lawful (i.e., pro-competitive) purpose.

The Court found it easy to apply the distinction between illegal "horizontal" market division schemes and arguably lawful "vertical" market divisions in *General Motors*. A scheme agreed to by the dealers, as was the case there, was horizontal. A scheme implemented unilaterally by GM would have been vertical. But suppose GM was not a separate company, but instead had been a joint venture wholly owned by independent, competing retailers? In two subsequent cases, the Court held that a market division agreement among such joint venturers constitutes per se illegal horizontal market division.

United States v. Sealy, Inc.[12] struck down an agreement among competing mattress manufactures that created mutually exclusive territories where each could use their jointly owned Sealy trademark. *United States v. Topco Associates, Inc.*[13] condemned an agreement among competing grocers that effectively allocated territories for the use of the Topco label, a jointly produced private label for items like canned goods and paper products. The Topco agreement essentially allowed any member to veto the sale of Topco products by other members within 100

---

dividual, the American company was publicly traded in this country, and the French company was jointly owned by the other two, *Copperweld* suggests that a conspiracy could be shown.

9. 384 U.S. 127 (1966).

10. See Chapter 5, sections A–C.

11. 384 U.S. at 130.

12. 388 U.S. 350 (1967).

13. 405 U.S. 596 (1972).

miles of its store. The *Sealy* defendants sought to analogize their agreement to a vertical territorial arrangement imposed by an independent manufacturer upon its dealers,[14] but the Court rejected the analogy: "Sealy, Inc., is an instrumentality of the licensees for purposes of the horizontal territorial allocation. It is not the principal." [15] The Court likewise dismissed Chief Justice Burger's effort to analogize the Topco agreement to the unilateral use of a private brand label by a large supermarket chain (such as A & P or Safeway).[16]

Actually, *Topco* provides an excellent illustration of why agreements among joint venturers are properly considered horizontal. Suppose that the twin cities of Champaign–Urbana have one Safeway store, which is located in Champaign, and that a business consultant recommends to Safeway executives that another store be opened in Urbana. Some of the Champaign Safeway's customers might begin patronizing the new Urbana store, but Safeway can nevertheless be expected to expand if doing so would increase the overall number of Safeway customers. Any objections the manager of the Champaign Safeway might raise because she feared losing business in her store would be quickly overruled. In contrast, suppose that Champaign has a single Eagle store that is part of the Topco venture, and that a business consultant recommends to the Big Bear Stores chain (another member of the Topco venture) that it could profitably open a store in Urbana. Even if the overall number of customers patronizing the two Topco-affiliated stores would increase, Eagle would veto the plan if it would lose any of its Eagle customers to the new Big Bear store. Thus, although Justice John Harlan correctly observed in his *Sealy* dissent that agreements among joint ventures are similar to vertical restraints in that their primary impact is to diminish intrabrand rivalry,[17] the agreement at issue in *Topco* was more like a horizontal cartel and less like a vertical agreements because it permitted less efficient retailers to shield themselves from intrabrand competition, even if consumers would have benefitted from that competition.

The rest of *Topco*'s analysis reflects the inherent flaws in the general way the Court has approached horizontal restraints since *Chicago Board of Trade*. After properly characterizing the Topco agreement as horizontal, the Court next considered whether horizontal territorial restraints, like horizontal price fixing, should be

---

14. See White Motor Co. v. United States, 372 U.S. 253 (1963) (remanding such a vertical restraint case to the trial court for evaluation under the rule of reason). The case is discussed in Chapter 5, section C.

15. 388 U.S. at 354.

16. See 405 U.S. at 623 n.11 (Burger, C.J., dissenting).

17. 388 U.S. at 359.

considered illegal per se. For the reasons noted at the beginning of the section, the Court correctly equated these two types of cartel activities. But Justice Thurgood Marshall then went on to characterize the grocers' agreement as a "naked restraint[ ] of trade with no purpose except stifling competition." [18] This was clearly incorrect, for the agreement was ancillary to the lawful purpose of allowing Topco members to effectively compete with the large national supermarket chains. Marshall needed to overlook this aspect of the Topco arrangement because, under the *Chicago Board of Trade/ Socony–Vacuum* paradigm, his only options were to condemn the arrangement with no further analysis or to require a full rule of reason trial even though the agreement appeared to be overly restrictive.

In erroneously concluding that the restriction on competition among Topco members could not be justified in order to enhance competition between Topco members and the national supermarkets, Marshall's opinion demonstrates another flaw in the *Chicago Board of Trade* approach. In his view, courts cannot "weigh, in any meaningful sense, destruction of competition in one sector of the economy against promotion of competition in another sector." [19] Thus, destruction of competition in one "sector" was conclusively unreasonable (since "unreasonable" is, under *Chicago Board of Trade*, whatever the Court says it is) and therefore illegal.

Marshall is literally correct when he writes that courts cannot easily balance the lessening of competition in one "sector" of the economy against the benefits of increased competition in another, and when he states that private parties like Topco should not have the discretionary power to determine the "respective values of competition in various sectors of the economy." [20] The problem with his opinion is that, for consumers, there is only one sector of the economy at issue here—grocery stores. The same consumers who would suffer if Topco unduly lessened competition among its members (as Topco actually did in that case) would benefit from a less restrictive Topco arrangement that gave them a real choice between purchasing name and private label brands of groceries from Topco members, A & P, or Safeway. An antitrust standard that permits joint agreements necessary to enhance interbrand competition thus benefits consumers, efficiently allocates resources, and enhances economic opportunities for small independent entrepreneurs.

18. 405 U.S. at 608 (quoting *White Motor*, 372 U.S. at 263).

19. Id. at 609–10.

20. Id. at 611.

Judge Taft, whose analysis in *Addyston Pipe* was anchored in the common law, would have recognized the fallacy of Justice Marshall's conclusion. The common law permitted mergers on the theory that the loss of competition between the newly merged parties was outweighed by the new firm's enhanced ability to compete against other rivals. Similarly, non-competition covenants between partners or between employers and employees were clearly permissible under the common law, again based on the notion that the competition eliminated by the covenant was outweighed by the increased competition between the parties and others.

Use of the *Addyston Pipe* mode of analysis would have allowed the Court to condemn the Topco arrangement without having to flatly mischaracterize the joint venture as a naked restraint. Applying *Addyston Pipe*, the Court would have credited the defendants' argument that a partial combination of separate grocery chains to enable them to compete with the large national chains was a lawful, pro-competitive purpose. Next, the Court would have determined that giving every grocer a veto on intra-brand competition was clearly broader than necessary to achieve that lawful purpose. The principal justification for limiting competition among Topco members was that such competition might inhibit members from aggressively promoting the Topco brand in their areas for fear that another member would "free-ride" on their advertising and take away their customers. As the district court held on remand in *Topco*, the free rider problem could be resolved by a variety of agreements less restrictive than an absolute veto.[21] Similarly, in private litigation following *Sealy*, the jury was permitted to consider the legality of less restrictive agreements, and a judgment against Sealy was upheld only after careful consideration of evidence that its restrictions were still broader than necessary to protect the legitimate interests of its licensees.[22]

21. The district court allowed Topco to assign each member "primary areas of responsibility" and to require those who sold outside their areas of responsibility to pay a pro rata share of legitimate advertising and promotion costs for those areas. 1973 Trade Cas. (CCH) ¶ 74,485 (N.D. Ill.), aff'd per curiam, 414 U.S. 801 (1973).

A recent telephone call to a food marketing executive found that, 25 years after the defendants claimed that their exclusive territories were essential for the cooperative to function, Topco is still alive and well. Topco has apparently solved the free rider problem that arises when one Topco member enters another's market area by providing the new entrant with identical products packaged under a different trademark; the new entrant thus gets all the benefits of Topco's purchasing without encroaching on any promotion or loyalty the established Topco member has built up in the area.

22. Ohio-Sealy Mattress Mfg. Co. v. Sealy, Inc., 585 F.2d 821 (7th Cir. 1978), cert. denied, 440 U.S. 930 (1979). The jury was told that market allocation is per se illegal, although primary responsibility clauses, location clauses (limiting the locations from which licensees

(3) Post-*Topco* cases.

In two recent opinions, two noted academic critics of *Topco* who are now federal appellate judges have cut back on the breadth of Justice Marshall's opinion. Judge Richard Posner, writing in *General Leaseways, Inc. v. National Truck Leasing Ass'n*,[23] and Judge Frank Easterbrook, writing in *Polk Brothers, Inc. v. Forest City Enterprises, Inc.*,[24] appear to suggest that *Topco*'s formalistic analysis should be replaced with that of *Addyston Pipe*.

Judge Posner's approach in *General Leaseways* seems the most satisfactory. The defendants in that case were competing companies that lease and repair trucks. Their agreement required each company to operate only within a designated territory, but then to perform emergency service on trucks leased by the other signatories to the agreement that happened to break down in its territory; the other company would then reimburse the firm doing the repair work. Relying on language in *Broadcast Music* that suggested that the per se rule is limited to "facially" anticompetitive conduct, Posner reexamined the whole area of horizontal restraints.[25] He found the defendants' conduct in this case more egregious than that at issue in *Topco* and thus sustained a preliminary injunction against the territorial limitation. He suggested that a territorial scheme might have been justified in *Topco* in order to prevent one grocer from "free riding" off of the promotional investment made by another grocer in a particular territory.[26] He distinguished *General Leaseways*, however, because the repair work at issue there was a service for which each firm could, and did, easily receive reimbursement from its rivals.

can sell their mattresses), and pass-over payments (requiring a firm that sells in another licensee's area of primary responsibility to compensate the licensee for a pro rata share of promotional or service expenses) are not illegal unless used to achieve market division. The jury was then told that these less restrictive alternatives would be illegal if they served to "limit or restrict, 'in any substantial way, the geographic areas in which products may be sold.'" Id. at 827 (quoting trial court's instruction). This instruction may have been a bit too favorable to the plaintiffs. A perfectly legitimate restriction narrowly tailored to prevent free rider problems might substantially restrict a firm's ability to pursue a strategy of discounting by saving on promotional or service expenses incurred by its intrabrand rival. The rest of the court's analysis, however, sensibly considers the particular restraints at issue and explains how each of them, while permissible in theory, were overbroad and hence operated to perpetuate the original market division scheme condemned by the Supreme Court. Id. at 828–30.

23. 744 F.2d 588 (7th Cir. 1984).

24. 776 F.2d 185 (7th Cir. 1985).

25. 744 F.2d at 595 (citing Broadcast Music, Inc. v. Columbia Broadcasting System, Inc., 441 U.S. 1, 19–20 (1979)). *Broadcast Music* is discussed above in section C(1).

26. Given his admiration for efforts to eliminate free riders that is typical of the Chicago school, Posner appears to have overlooked the fact that private-brand labels—the goods at issue in *Topco*—are by definition lower-priced goods that are not extensively promoted by the sellers.

Thus, Posner properly condemned the territorial allocation as illegal per se because it was clearly broader than necessary to achieve the legitimate purpose of creating a nationwide system of truck repairs.

Even when "free riding" problems exist, *Topco*'s defenders might criticize Posner's approach on the grounds that balancing the elimination of free riding against the harm caused by reducing competition among the parties to the agreement is precisely the "ramble through the wilds of economic theory" that *Topco* wanted judges to avoid.[27] But, as we shall see in the next chapter, the Supreme Court expressly sanctioned this type of balancing in cases analyzing the reasonableness of a vertical restraint.[28] Moreover, common law courts have been engaging in this kind of balancing for years. Determining whether a particular non-competition covenant is overbroad requires the courts to judge whether the restriction strikes a reasonable balance between the need to encourage new entrants to acquire existing companies or to hire confidential employees and the public's desire for competition.[29] Sound application of *Addyston Pipe* is no less workable in cases involving exclusive territories than in those involving other horizontal agreements; indeed, it remains the most sensible way for judges to discriminate between restraints that serve consumers' interests and those that do not.

In *Polk Brothers*, a home appliance store (Polk) and a lumber/hardware store (Forest Park) agreed to share a single building in exurban Chicago. Because they sold complimentary items, they hoped to attract more customers to the location then either could attract alone. Polk would not have entered into the promise but for Forest Park's agreement not to sell home appliances in competition with Polk. Applying *Addyston Pipe* to these facts, Judge

27. See 405 U.S. at 610 n.10.

28. Continental T.V., Inc. v. GTE Sylvania, Inc., 433 U.S. 36, 54–57 (1977). Indeed, dicta in National Collegiate Athletic Ass'n v. Board of Regents, 468 U.S. 85 (1984) ("*NCAA* "), suggests that the Court believes this kind of balancing would apply in horizontal restraint cases as well. Although *Topco* summarily rejected the defendant's attempt to justify its restraints on the grounds that they would help members compete more effectively with Safeway, A & P, and other giants in the industry, *NCAA* noted that unspecified "forms of collective action might [have been] appropriate in order to enhance [the NCAA's] ability to compete" were it not for the fact that the NCAA faced no

competition from substitute groups. Id. at 115 n.55. The FTC has seemingly followed *NCAA* 's instructions, for the Commission recently approved a horizontal agreement between two major college football conferences that limited competition between them; the agreement presumably allowed the two conferences to compete more effectively against the other 60–odd major college football programs. Mike Dodd, Pac–10, Big Ten get double dose of good news, USA Today, June 5, 1990, at 9C (FTC notifies conferences that it has dropped investigation into their joint television football contract). The *NCAA* case is discussed above in section C(3).

29. See Chapter 2.

Easterbrook correctly permitted the agreement,[30] although his general mission to minimize antitrust liability for defendants led him to depart from Judge Taft's analysis in several important respects.

In order to justify applying *Addyston Pipe*, Judge Easterbrook had to explain initially why the horizontal agreement was not per se illegal. Without mentioning *Topco*, he relied on *NCAA* for the proposition that per se analysis is not appropriate "[w]hen cooperation contributes to productivity through integration of efforts"— i.e., when rivals are combining for some lawful purpose. Citing both *Addyston Pipe* and *NCAA*, *Polk Brothers* next suggested that the rule of reason requires courts to distinguish between "naked" and "ancillary" restraints. The opinion adds a significant clarification to *Addyston Pipe* by insisting that the propriety of the contract's broader purpose, to which the challenged restraint is ancillary, must be evaluated as of the time the agreement was made.[31]

Unfortunately, *Polk Brothers* then departed from *Addyston Pipe* and the common law of contracts on which Judge Taft's opinion relied. First, Judge Easterbrook wrote:

> Covenants of this type are evaluated under the Rule of Reason as ancillary restraints, and unless they bring a large market share under a single firm's control they are lawful. See *United States v. Addyston Pipe Co.*[32]

Later, he asserted:

> The first step in any Rule of Reason case is an assessment of market power.... [Cf.] *NCAA* (only "naked" arrangements may be condemned without proof of market power). Unless the firms have the power to raise price by curtailing output, their agreement is unlikely to harm consumers, and it makes sense to understand their cooperation as benign or beneficial.[33]

These are not accurate restatements of *Addyston Pipe*. Covenants that are, to quote *Polk Brothers*, "part of a larger endeavor whose success they promote" are ancillary to a lawful purpose; but under *Addyston Pipe*, they are still illegal if they are broader than necessary to achieve that purpose. The classic covenant not to compete illustrates the difference between the approaches endorsed by Judge Taft and Judge Easterbrook. A covenant that accompanies the sale of a business and its goodwill is clearly ancillary, but it is still unreasonable if overbroad. Suppose that

---

30. 776 F.2d at 189 (citing *Addyston Pipe*, 85 Fed. at 280–83).

31. 776 F.2d at 188–90.

32. Id. at 189.

33. Id. at 191 (citations omitted).

the plaintiff baker in *Mitchel v. Reynolds*[34] had been prevented from competing for twenty years, rather than for the five-year term the court found reasonable? Common law judges, and Judge Taft, would have held the agreement unreasonable. If the quoted excerpts from *Polk Brothers* were followed, the plaintiff would lose unless he could show that the market for bakers in St. Andrews parish gave his rival market power. Judge Easterbrook's sleight of hand to impose his own minimalist views of antitrust policy[35] is particularly unfortunate because it was totally superfluous to the result in the case: the record established that the non-competition covenant was absolutely necessary in order to bring about the building-sharing agreement.

Both *General Leaseways* and *Polk Brothers* make an important contribution to antitrust jurisprudence by recognizing that *Topco*'s reasoning is inconsistent with sound antecedents (such as *Addyston Pipe*) as well as important subsequent decisions (such as *Broadcast Music* and *NCAA*). If defendants really can show that a territorial market division is necessary to produce or distribute a new or improved product, the Court is likely to, and should, distinguish *Topco* so as to limit "per se" condemnation to overbroad restraints.

Section F: Conscious Parallelism and Proof of Conspiracy

(1) Basic concepts.

The conduct challenged in the cases described so far in this Chapter involved fairly clear agreements among rivals: the legal issue in those cases was whether the agreements were "in restraint of trade" for purposes of § 1. This section discusses the proof necessary to demonstrate that the defendants actually entered into an agreement, in order to satisfy § 1's requirement that the restraint of trade result from a "contract, combination, or conspiracy." This section also considers the extent to which the Federal Trade Commission can exercise its somewhat broader powers under § 5 of the FTC Act to reach anticompetitive oligopolistic conduct where an agreement cannot be proved.

For most criminal conspiracies, the parties' underlying unilateral acts are also illegal. Four bank robbers who agree to simultaneously hold up four banks have entered into a conspiracy; if they independently rob different banks at the same time, they are still guilty of felony bank robbery. In contrast, four sellers who agree

---

34. 1 P. Wms. 181, 24 Eng. Rep. 347 (K.B. 1711).

35. See generally Frank Easterbrook, The Limits of Antitrust, 63 Texas L. Rev. 1 (1984).

on prices have violated § 1, but if the same four independently decide to charge the same price for their goods, their conduct is perfectly lawful. The Sherman Act properly condemns conspiracies despite the legality of the underlying acts because joint action increases the conspirators' economic power, enables them to eliminate competition, and lessens their individual autonomy and choice in how they sell their products.

In a market with a large number of firms, each company will realize that it can increase its own sales by lowering its price; even a staid firm will envision that *some* firm will cut its prices. Thus, either out of fear that someone else will act first, or simply to obtain the brief momentary advantage from being the first price-cutter, all are likely to keep their prices at the competitive level, absent some overly collusive behavior.

In contrast, oligopoly theory demonstrates that firms in markets with few sellers can keep prices above the competitive level without an express agreement among rivals to fix prices. In industries with few sellers and little threat of new entry, no firm has an incentive to cut prices in order to attract more business. Although a firm that does so might see a brief increase in sales, its discount will quickly be matched by its rivals, leaving it with the same market share as before the discount—and with less revenue to show for it. If a "price leader" raises prices, however, its rivals realize that they can either follow suit or maintain the current prices and watch the leader bring its prices back down; they all know that they can price at the higher level without losing market share to their rivals. Understanding the predictable behavior of their rivals allows firms in oligopoly markets to set prices that creep above the competitive level. Thus, where an oligopoly exists, firms can raise price and reduce output even though there is no spoken or express agreement. Without proof of an agreement, however, this type of oligopolistic behavior may not fall within the language of § 1. Because oligopoly pricing [1] has many of the same adverse social effects as cartel pricing (inefficient allocation of resources, exploitation of consumers, and concentration of economic power in a few hands) commentators have suggested that where such pricing is not effected by an agreement, the structure of the market should be directly attacked, either under novel theories of monopolization or under new legislation.[2]

Oligopoly theory is relevant to a number of areas of antitrust doctrine. This section analyzes the circumstances when parallel

---

1. For purposes of this treatise, "oligopoly pricing" refers to interdependent pricing by oligopolists that results in higher prices and/or lower output than would exist in a competitive market.

2. See Donald Turner, The Definition of Agreement Under the Sherman Act: Conscious Parallelism and Refusals to Deal, 75 Harv. L. Rev. 655 (1962).

behavior—typically by oligopolists—can be condemned as a conspiracy in restraint of trade even absent direct evidence of overt collusion. The following section then discusses the situations when an agreement among rivals to exchange information becomes unreasonable because it will be used to facilitate oligopoly pricing. Chapter 6, section A, focuses on mergers that reduce the number of firms in a market to such an extent that the risk of oligopoly pricing is unacceptably increased.

(2) The standard for proof of agreement.

Interstate Circuit, Inc. v. United States,[3] still the leading case governing proof of agreement, involved the distribution of motion pictures in the southwest. Distributors licensed their films to exhibitors, which operated the movie theaters. At the time, exhibitors tended to feature either first-or second-run films. Although there was no direct evidence of an agreement, Interstate Circuit, a first-run exhibitor, was found guilty of conspiring with six major distributors to require second-run exhibitors to raise their prices and limit their showing of double features. The Supreme Court affirmed the conviction, recognizing that evidence of a conspiracy is rarely proved directly and may be shown by circumstantial evidence.[4]

Specifically, the Supreme Court found five factors present that permitted the finding of conspiracy. First, the distributors engaged in parallel conduct: each required second-run exhibitors to raise prices and limit the number of double features. Second, each distributor was made aware that Interstate Circuit was asking all distributors to impose these limits on second-run theaters. Third, each distributor was unlikely to have engaged in this conduct without some assurance that all the others would do likewise. If Paramount, for example, had agreed to impose these onerous restrictions on second-run theaters while MGM did not, the latter would have gained a significant competitive advantage in the second-run market. Fourth, there was no credible explanation, other than conspiracy, why the distributors would all have imposed these restrictions. Finally, the conduct was a sharp deviation from "traditional business patterns." The Court assumed that traditional patterns of business represented a competi-

---

3. 306 U.S. 208 (1939).

4. Id. at 221. At the time, violations of § 1 were misdemeanors; after 1974, however, criminal violations of § 1 became felonies that could lead to substantial jail and financial penalties. Pub. L. No. 93–528, § 3, 88 Stat. 1708. As a result, many government conspir-

acy prosecutions are now able to use direct evidence—testimony of one of the conspirators who turns state's evidence. Nevertheless, the inferences approved in *Interstate Circuit* are still highly relevant for private litigation as well as for some government cases.

tive market. Thus, dramatic, unexplained deviations were signs that the market was no longer working competitively.[5]

The foregoing are not elements of a conspiracy; they are factors to consider. Ultimately, proof of conspiracy requires evidence that the defendants conducted themselves in a manner consistent with the way they would act if they were in fact conspiring, and, most important, *inconsistent* with the way they would act if they were competing against each other.

American Tobacco Co. v. United States[6] is illustrative. In that case, the jury convicted three major tobacco companies of conspiring, based on circumstantial evidence. First, the defendants suddenly increased their prices in the midst of the Great Depression, even though "[n]o economic justification for this price raise was demonstrated."[7] Then, less than two years later, the three companies simultaneously embarked on a price war against lower-priced competitors. The court of appeals, in sustaining the jury's verdict, noted the implausibility of the defendants' explanations that any price hike had to be followed lest their rivals obtain greater revenues for advertising, yet any price cut also had to be followed lest their rivals gain market share.[8] Because the defendants' conduct was inconsistent with independent competitive behavior, the jury's finding of a conspiracy was upheld.

Conscious parallelism is insufficient to prove a conspiracy, because while parallel conduct is consistent with cartel behavior, it is also consistent with competition. Indeed, in a perfectly competitive market, all firms will sell at the identical price. Thus, some evidence inconsistent with independent competitive behavior is required. This point is illustrated by *Theatre Enterprises v. Paramount Film Distributing Corp.*[9] In that case, the defendant motion picture distributors uniformly refused to grant a first-run license to the plaintiff, a suburban exhibitor. The defendants persuaded the jury that they had each reached this decision independently because it was more profitable to show first-run films in downtown theaters. Their conduct was thus consistent with the way they would act if they were competing.[10]

---

5. 306 U.S. at 221–26.

6. 328 U.S. 781 (1946).

7. Id. at 805.

8. American Tobacco Co. v. United States, 147 F.2d 93, 114 (6th Cir. 1944). Although the Supreme Court favorably discussed this aspect of the Sixth Circuit's opinion, certiorari was granted only on the question of the elements necessary to prove a conspiracy under § 2 of the Sherman Act. 328 U.S. at 784. See Chapter 3, section H(2).

9. 346 U.S. 537 (1954).

10. See also Pevely Dairy Co. v. United States, 178 F.2d 363 (8th Cir. 1949), cert. denied, 339 U.S. 942 (1950) (where federal regulation set the prices paid to farmers, union contracts led to standardized labor costs, and products were standardized by local health ordinances, evidence of parallel prices was

In *Ambook Enterprises v. Time, Inc.*,[11] by contrast, the Second Circuit found that the defendant media companies' parallel refusal to grant a discount for advertisements prepared in-house rather than by ad agencies was the result of a conspiracy. The court reasoned that there was no explanation, "save continuity and fear of reprisal," [12] why each media company would resist increasing its business by granting discounts for in-house operations that performed the same service as the outside agencies. Noting that the market was not oligopolistic, the court expressed skepticism that such a uniform policy would be adhered to by hundreds of media companies absent an agreement. The court also observed that the plaintiff's evidence included proof of veiled threats by an ad agency executive that Time would lose business if it granted discounts for in-house ads and Time's expressed realization that actions displeasing to ad agencies could result in lost revenue. Accordingly, the court reversed a grant of summary judgment in favor of the defendants and held that a jury could find that their parallel conduct was "coerced" by the ad agencies. Time's conduct made little sense absent the knowledge that Newsweek would follow, and Time's fear of reprisal was necessarily premised on some form of tacit or explicit collusion among the leading ad agencies. For example, it is difficult to see how advertising giant J. Walter Thompson could refuse to place ads for a leading client in Time magazine due to pique at Time's extension of the standard discount to in-house industries, without the confidence that the other leading ad agencies would do likewise; otherwise, Thompson's clients would soon shift to less peevish agencies.

(3) Summary judgment and proof of agreement.

In order to survive a motion for summary judgment, the plaintiff must establish that there is "a genuine issue of material fact" as to whether the defendants entered into an illegal conspiracy.[13] In *Theatre Enterprises*, for example, the case could not be disposed of on summary judgment because of an unresolved factual question essential to determining the existence of a conspiracy. The defendants in that case claimed that they had independent

insufficient to support conviction for fixing milk prices even though the record also showed that the defendants consulted as to pricing).

Pevely demonstrates how government regulation can often retard aggressive price competition. Another example is the taxing cigarettes at a flat rate. If taxes were based on a percentage of the purchase price (an "ad valorem" tax), every price cut would be matched by a tax reduction and the incentives for

price competition would increase. See William Nicholls, Price Policies in the Cigarette Industry ch. 29 (1951).

11. 612 F.2d 604 (2d Cir. 1979), cert. dismissed, 448 U.S. 914 (1980).

12. Id. at 614.

13. Matsushita Electrical Industrial Co. v. Zenith Radio Corp., 475 U.S. 574, 585–86 (1986).

reasons for refusing to do business with the plaintiff—that the plaintiff's theatre in the suburbs would attract less business. The plaintiff, on the other hand, alleged that it had offered to provide financial guarantees that would have made a suburban license more profitable; the defendants challenged the bona fides of these offers.[14] Suppose, however, that the plaintiff is unable to provide evidence that the defendants' parallel conduct is consistent with conspiracy and inconsistent with their independent interests? In such cases, the rule appears to be that the jury is not allowed to infer an agreement. Hence, the defendants are entitled to either summary judgment or a directed verdict.

The difficulty in this area concerns the quantum of evidence the plaintiff must produce to allow a jury to infer the existence of an agreement. Those seeking guidance from the Supreme Court find a series of decisions of bewildering inconsistency. As noted above, Court purports to apply a standard that requires the plaintiff to show evidence consistent with conspiracy and inconsistent with competitive, non-collusive behavior. *Theatre Enterprises* seems to make clear that, if the plaintiff makes such a showing, the jury is allowed to resolve any factual disputes between the parties. Under the general rule for summary judgment provided for in the Federal Rules of Civil Procedure, summary dismissal of the plaintiff's claim is appropriate only if the plaintiff has failed to provide any genuine evidence to support a conspiracy claim.[15] Unfortunately, the justices have allowed their views concerning the likelihood that certain types of antitrust claims will ultimately prove meritorious to have an unarticulated effect on their analysis of supposedly neutral summary judgment rules. This lack of judicial candor has led to confusing doctrine.

Poller v. Columbia Broadcasting System, Inc.[16] is a landmark case concerning summary judgment in antitrust cases, although the circumstantial evidence offered to prove a conspiracy did not involve consciously parallel rivals. The complaint in that case alleged that CBS had terminated its affiliation with the plaintiff and had purchased a rival UHF television station[17] in Milwaukee as part of a conspiracy with the rival UHF station to eliminate UHF competition. The plaintiff's evidence included the termination and affiliation decisions; CBS' subsequent termination of the rival UHF station in favor of a new VHF affiliate; a CBS vice president's deposition statement that "it would be the kiss of

14. 346 U.S. at 540.

15. Fed. R.Civ. P. 56.

16. 368 U.S. 464 (1962).

17. For readers whose television experience does not precede cable, UHF (ultra high frequency) stations broadcast over the air on channels 14–83. In most major markets, networks such as CBS prefer to broadcast on VHF (very high frequency) channels 2–13.

death to UHF" if NBC or CBS dropped an affiliation; the plaintiff's demonstrated success as a UHF affiliate; and CBS' economic interest in eliminating UHF because of the network's sizable investment in VHF.[18] The defendant's executives denied any anticompetitive motive; they also contended that CBS had conspired with no one but had unilaterally exercised its contractual right to select its own affiliate. The Court held that summary judgment was inappropriate because there was a crucial question as to CBS' motive.

As in other areas, the justices' differing approaches to this issue reflected their different perspectives on antitrust law. Justice Tom Clark's majority opinion reflects the view that business executives often conspire to restrain trade and that proof of such conspiracies is difficult. In contrast, Justice John Harlan began his dissenting opinion by frankly noting his perception that "this is one of those cases, not unfamiliar in treble-damage litigation, where injury resulting from normal business hazards is sought to be made redressable by casting the affair in antitrust terms." [19] Thus, it is no surprise that Clark was more willing to draw inferences from the plaintiff's circumstantial evidence than was Harlan.

Both the majority and the dissent seemed to be applying reasonable standards. The majority held that "summary procedures should be used sparingly in complex antitrust litigation where motive and intent play leading roles, the proof is largely in the hands of the alleged conspirators, and hostile witnesses thicken the plot." [20] The majority correctly emphasized the importance of allowing jurors to evaluate the credibility of the witnesses when factual disputes exist as to motive and intent. This is particularly important in conscious parallelism cases where the key focus is on whether the defendant's conduct was the result of an independent decision in a competitive market. On the other hand, Harlan correctly noted that summary judgment was appropriate if "the depositions and affidavits which were before the District Court disclosed to a practical certainty" that there was no illicit motive.[21]

The real issue in *Poller* was whether there were any facts supporting the plaintiff's claim that the termination was part of a scheme to eliminate UHF competition. Justice Harlan seems to have the better of the argument if, as his dissent maintained, the plaintiff produced no evidence to controvert CBS' showing that (1) it had valid independent reasons to take advantage of a new FCC

18. 368 U.S. at 469–72.   20. Id. at 473.

19. Id. at 474.   21. Id. at 476.

rule and acquire its own Milwaukee UHF outlet; (2) it purchased the rival station, albeit with inferior facilities, for a fraction of the price of purchasing the plaintiff because the plaintiff's price was too high; and (3) it believed that the plaintiff would be able to continue operating either as an independent or as an affiliate of ABC or the DuMont network.[22] The majority did not respond to these points. Rather, it seemed to recognize that the plaintiff's only hope of winning the case was to persuade the jury to infer liability solely from the non-credible assertion of innocence made by CBS officials. As Justice Harlan correctly observed, this sort of evidence is insufficient to sustain a verdict.[23]

There are a number of possible explanations for the majority's willingness to find relevant facts in dispute. First, the Court may have acted out of a misguided concern about the defendant's superior access to information. Proper administration of discovery, however, would have allowed the plaintiff to determine if the defendant had a plausible, non-conspiratorial explanation for the challenged conduct, and then to identify factual issues that contradicted the defendant's explanation.[24] Second, the majority may have felt that CBS' action, even if unilateral, should be actionable under the antitrust laws. If so, the Court was improperly abusing summary judgment doctrine as a means to accomplish *sub silentio* a substantive change in antitrust doctrine that the justices were unwilling to acknowledge openly. Third, the majority may have believed that a plaintiff should not be required to present evidence to refute the defendant's non-conspiratorial statements. In other areas (such as proof of damages for proven violations[25]), the Court has expressly reduced the plaintiff's burden for such policy reasons. But if the Court were motivated by these concerns in *Poller*, it should have said so directly. Finally, the majority may have felt that Poller was really victimized by a conspiracy, but that the record did not reflect the material issues that would prove Poller's case because of poor lawyering.[26] Appellate judges, however, need to resist the temptation to secure just results by distorting procedural rules.

22. Id. at 478, 480–83.

23. Id. at 480 (citing Dyer v. Mac-Dougall, 201 F.2d 265 (2d Cir. 1952)).

24. But see First National Bank of Arizona v. Cities Services Co., 391 U.S. 253 (1968) (affirming summary judgment for the defendant even though trial judge blocked any opportunity to depose defendant's key employees).

25. See Bigelow v. RKO Radio Pictures, Inc., 327 U.S. 251 (1946).

26. Perhaps additional evidence that was not in the record would have showed that CBS' decision to purchase the inferior facilities of Poller's rival did not make sense absent a conspiracy, or would have cast doubt on CBS' claim that it thought Poller would continue to operate without the CBS affiliation.

The next significant summary judgment opinion, *First National Bank of Arizona v. Cities Services Co.*,[27] did little to clarify the law. The petitioner there was the executor of the estate of Gerald Waldron, an oil entrepreneur. Waldron was acting as an intermediary in an effort to market Iranian oil—a difficult task because at that time seven major multinational oil companies were boycotting Iranian oil to protest the Iranian government's expropriation of their property.[28] Waldron alleged that Cities Service backed out of a deal to purchase Iranian oil as part of the multinational conspiracy, but a divided Supreme Court affirmed an award of summary judgment in favor of the defendant.[29]

Like *Poller*, the case turned on the defendant's motives for declining to do business with the plaintiff. In the lower courts, Waldron claimed that Cities Service had been induced to join the multinational conspiracy by financial incentives. The defendant responded that it had found an alternative source for its oil (sold to it by co-defendant Gulf Oil from Kuwait), that it had been pursuing this oil before the Iranian boycott began, and that the threat of complicated international litigation over the legality of the nationalization of the Iranian oil fields had given it an independent reasons for avoiding business with Waldron. According to the majority, Waldron's allegations that Cities Service had been bought off were refuted by "overwhelming evidence that no such payoff was ever made or promised to it in return for an agreement not to deal with Waldron, a showing which [Waldron] has in no way rebutted."[30] As the dissent correctly observed, though, Waldron had not been allowed to depose key witnesses employed by the defendants. Moreover, the majority expressly refused to consider the plaintiff's claim that Cities Service had been coerced into joining the conspiracy to boycott Iranian oil by threats of economic reprisals, because it reflected a drastic change in the theory of the plaintiff's case while the litigation was in the Supreme Court.[31]

Unlike the sensible and clear standard used by Harlan in his *Poller* dissent, which authorized summary judgement in cases

27. 391 U.S. 253 (1968).

28. The expropriation was the work of a leftist government that subsequently was replaced by the authoritarian regime of the Shah; many have accused the CIA of masterminding the coup that ousted the leftist government. See, e.g., Francis Boyle, World Politics and International Law 188 (1985).

29. Justice Marshall's majority opinion was joined by Justices Harlan and Stewart, who dissented in *Poller*, and by Justices White and Fortas, who joined the Court only after *Poller* was decided. Of the four justices from the *Poller* majority who remained on the Court, Chief Justice Warren and Justices Black and Brennan dissented in *Cities Services* and Justice Douglas did not participate.

30. 391 U.S. at 286.

31. Id. at 280 n.16.

where uncontroverted evidence disclosed the absence of illegal motive "to a practical certainty," Justice Thurgood Marshall's majority opinion in *Cities Service* used a variety of ambiguous and contradictory verbal formulations to justify summary judgment. At one point, the majority opinion argued that the record "contains an overwhelming amount of . . . contrary evidence of Cities' motives." [32] At another point, though, the Court observed that it found Waldron's claim that Cities Service had been bought off "insupportable." [33] In a third portion of the opinion, the Court suggested that it was applying *Interstate Circuit* and found no evidence consistent with conspiracy *and* inconsistent with competition.[34] These statements are particularly disconcerting because the majority did sensibly hold that summary judgment should be awarded because of "the absence of any significant probative evidence tending to support the complaint," [35] a standard that seems the most applicable to the facts of *Cities Service*.

One might try to reconcile *Poller* and *Cities Service* on the grounds that CBS did have an economic incentive to conspire to drive the plaintiff out of the market, whereas Cities Service had no incentive to join an international boycott of oil. This distinction is somewhat artificial, however, because the Supreme Court refused to permit Waldron to show coercion as an incentive. Moreover, CBS' unrefuted explanation for its behavior seems no less persuasive than Cities Service's defense. Unfortunately, more recent decisions do not clarify this area of law.

(4) *Matsushita* : the confusion continues.

The Supreme Court's most recent foray into this area involved controversial and lengthy litigation brought by two American television manufacturers against their major Japanese rivals, alleging a conspiracy to set predatorily low prices in order to drive the American firms out of business.[36] The plaintiffs in *Matsushita Electric Industrial Co. v. Zenith Radio Corp.*[37] argued that the Court could infer the presence of a predatory pricing conspiracy from evidence that the defendants had (1) conspired to raise prices in Japan; (2) conspired to fix prices in the United States at non-predatory levels; (3) conspired to limit retail competition in Japanese televisions in the United States; and (4) actually lowered

32. Id. at 277.

33. Id. at 279.

34. Id. at 280.

35. Id. at 290.

36. Predatory pricing is discussed in detail in Chapter 3, section D. For present, simplistic purposes, a predator sacrifices current revenues in order to change the market so that it can recoup its losses in the future through monopoly profits.

37. 475 U.S. 574 (1986).

prices in the U.S. below their agreed-upon levels.[38]

The court of appeals concluded that the evidence was sufficient to create a jury question on the issue of conspiracy, relying on four factors to deny the defendants' motion for summary judgment. First, the court noted that the Japanese market was susceptible to collusion, due to trade barriers and vertical integration in Japan. Second, the defendants had excess capacity and thus had an economic incentive to increase sales in the U.S. Third, the defendants had conspired in other respects, and finally, they had actually undercut their minimum price agreement.[39]

The Supreme Court reversed. The Court correctly summarized the law governing antitrust conspiracies by holding that a plaintiff must present evidence that "tends to exclude the possibility" that the defendants' conduct was independent [40]—in other words, evidence inconsistent with the way the defendants would act if they were conspiring. Applying that standard to the facts, the Court concluded that the four factors relied on by the court of appeals were insufficient to avoid summary judgment. The fact that the Japanese market was oligopolistic and that the defendants conspired on other terms did not necessarily mean that they conspired to engage in predatory pricing. The fact that each had excess capacity suggested that they would want to compete vigorously with the plaintiffs, but did not necessarily mean that they would compete predatorily. Similarly, the fact that the defen-

---

38. Although the first three conspiracies were in restraint of trade, the plaintiff could not recover any damages under § 1. The Court held that the jurisdiction of the United States' antitrust laws does not extend to an agreement made in Japan by Japanese firms to raise prices in Japan. The other two conspiracies in the United States had the effect of raising the price of television sets in this country, thus *benefiting* any rival who was not part of the conspiracy rather than harming it. For example, Zenith (one of the plaintiffs) could have responded to *higher* prices for Japanese televisions by either raising its prices as well or by keeping its prices lower and increasing sales.

The dissent argued that the certain expert testimony concerning the effect in America of the defendants' conspiracy in Japan was sufficient to warrant a trial. Specifically, an economist testified that the effect of the defendants' output restrictions in Japan was to increase the number of televisions available for sale in the United States, and the effect of the defendants' market division scheme in the United States was to allow each Japanese firm to compete more aggressively against American rivals without fear of also having to fend of its fellow nationals. See id. at 601– 03 & nn.2–3 (White, J., dissenting). The majority correctly found this testimony insufficient. The damage suffered by the plaintiff because of these two violations were simply the need to compete at lower prices and against more aggressive rivals. This is not the sort of injury that the antitrust laws are designed to protect, and thus the plaintiffs injury was not "antitrust injury" sufficient to warrant damages under § 4 of the Clayton Act. For a detailed discussion of antitrust injury, see Chapter 6, section D.

39. In re Japanese Electronic Products Antitrust Litigation, 723 F.2d 238, 303–16 (3d Cir. 1983), rev'd, 475 U.S. 574 (1986).

40. 475 U.S. at 588 (citing Monsanto Co. v. Spray–Rite Service Corp., 465 U.S. 752, 764 (1984)).

dants cheated on a minimum price-fixing cartel was just as consistent with competition as it was with conspiratorial predation.

Had the Court stopped there, the case would have added little to precedent. However, Justice Lewis Powell's majority opinion went on, suggesting a new standard for summary judgement motions in antitrust conspiracy cases: "if the factual context renders [plaintiffs'] claim implausible—if the claim is one that simply makes no economic sense—[plaintiffs] must come forward with more persuasive evidence to support their claim than would otherwise be necessary." [41] The sentence sets out two distinct standards. It is one thing to say that a claim is implausible, and another to say that it makes no economic sense. As Justice Byron White aptly wrote in dissent:

> If the Court intends to give every judge hearing a motion for summary judgment in an antitrust case the job of determining if the evidence makes the inference of conspiracy more probable than not, it is overturning settled law. If the Court does not intend such a pronouncement, it should refrain from using unnecessarily broad and confusing language.[42]

If a claim really makes *no* economic sense, then the plaintiff may properly be required to put forth evidence explaining why the defendants would act in the irrational manner alleged by the plaintiff. But given the diversity of economic theories, many claims may be sincerely viewed by different judges or economists as implausible.

Matsushita itself illustrates the problem this broader meaning creates. Justice Powell opined that "there is a consensus among commentators that predatory pricing schemes are rarely tried, and even more rarely successful." [43] As an empirical description of the views of academic commentators, this statement is simply false.[44] Under the broad reading of *Matsushita*, virtually every predatory pricing claim can now be dismissed on summary judgment because an allegation of predation is "implausible" according to some economic theories. Indeed, in finding no evidence to support the plaintiff's predatory conspiracy claim, the Court excluded from evidence key expert testimony offered by the plaintiff that the defendants sold their products in the American market at substantial losses. Evidence of parallel below-cost pricing, combined with all the other evidence of conspiracy, would probably have been sufficient to raise a triable issue about whether the defendants' behavior was inconsistent with a non-conspiratorial market. But the Court instead concluded that because "the ex-

41. Id. at 587.

42. Id. at 601.

43. Id. at 589.

44. See Chapter 3, section D.

pert opinion of below-cost pricing has little probative value in comparison with the economic factors ... that suggest that such conduct is irrational," the testimony was insufficient to defeat the defendants' summary judgment motion.[45] If a majority of the Supreme Court can completely misstate the "consensus" of commentators concerning economic theory, district judges should not be entrusted with the power to terminate cases based on their own perhaps erroneous view of that theory.

Today, perhaps more than ever, federal judges are inclined to share Justice Harlan's perspective that many plaintiffs try to shove square-pegged business disputes into the round hold of federal antitrust law. History reflects, however, a congressional purpose in enacting the Sherman Act to encourage private antitrust litigation as a means of enforcing the law, and that in enacting the Clayton and FTC Acts Congress displayed its concern that judges would frustrate effective antitrust enforcement. Unfortunately, the current confusion in summary judgment litigation makes it easier for judges appointed by Presidents Reagan and Bush, no less than those appointed by Presidents Cleveland, McKinley and Taft, to demonstrate their hostility by rejecting many claims, both meritorious and non-meritorious, before they get to the jury.

Fortunately, however, a recent majority formed by an eclectic coalition of justices appointed by Presidents Kennedy, Nixon, Ford, Reagan, and Bush joined an opinion by Justice Harry Blackmun (who dissented in *Matsushita*) that seems to limit the ability of pro-defendant judges to unduly take cases away from a jury by the use of summary judgment. In *Eastman Kodak Co. v. Image Technical Services, Inc.*,[46] the Court reversed a summary dismissal of claims that Kodak had unlawfully attempted to monopolize and had engaged in an illegal tying arrangement. The defendant's case rested in large measure on an argument, similar to that made by the Japanese television manufacturers in *Matsushita*, that their conduct could not be anticompetitive because a strategy designed to lessen competition would make no economic sense. The Court endorsed the narrower reading of *Matsushita* suggested above: "*Matsushita* demands only that the nonmoving party's inferences be reasonable in order to reach the jury.... If the plaintiff's theory is economically senseless, no reasonable jury could find in its favor, and summary judgment should be granted."[47] Many of the insights by Chicago school economists and

---

45. Id. at 594 n.19.

46. 112 S.Ct. 2072 (1992). Justice Blackmun's majority opinion was joined by Chief Justice Rehnquist and Justices White, Stevens, Kennedy and Souter.

Justices O'Connor, Scalia and Thomas dissented.

47. Id. at 2083.

lawyers may convince federal judges that a plaintiff's claim is probably wrong (or "implausible"), but not "economically sense-less." In such cases, *Kodak* seems to require that the defendant submit its arguments for the jury's consideration.

(5) Base point pricing.

One distinct type of conscious parallelism case involves allegations that competitors utilize particular pricing schemes in order to promote oligopoly pricing. Where competitors agree to use these so-called "facilitating practices," their conduct will be enjoined as a violation of § 1 of the Sherman Act.[48] In the late 1970s, parallel conduct that facilitated oligopoly pricing came under tough scrutiny from the antitrust authorities. The FTC found that such parallel practices constituted unfair methods of competition in violation of § 5 of the FTC Act. The judicial results were mixed. In two major decisions, the courts of appeals reversed the Commission's determination, and one Justice Department initiative resulted in a consent decree, thus limiting its precedential value.

One facilitating practice that has received extensive judicial scrutiny is the parallel use of "delivered pricing." Among the various ways that goods can be priced are "F.O.B. (Free on Board) mill pricing" and "delivered pricing." An F.O.B. mill price is the price of the good as loaded on to a truck, train, or boat adjacent to the seller's plant: the purchaser assumes possession at the seller's plant and is then responsible for transportation. A delivered price is the price as delivered to the buyer's plant: the seller is responsible for transportation.

FTC v. Cement Institute [49] condemned an industry-wide agreement among cement manufacturers to use delivered prices. The agreement in that case was particularly egregious. The defendants ensured that the cartel would stay together by targeting non-cooperating rivals with very low prices; they avoided disputes over changing conditions by agreeing not to build new plants; they prevented cartel cheating by shipping by rail and actively discouraged shipment by ship or truck. In addition, the defendants submitted sealed bids for government contracts that were identical to the sixth decimal point. Nevertheless, there was no proof of any actual agreement among the defendants to fix prices. The Supreme Court easily upheld the FTC's finding that the agreements the defendants had clearly made—including the agreement to use delivered prices—were themselves restraints of trade

48. The most common form of agreement on facilitating practices involves exchanges of price information through trade associations. These agreements are discussed below, in section G.

49. 333 U.S. 683 (1948).

because they were "a means to bring about uniform prices and terms of sale." [50]

"Base point pricing" is a form of delivered pricing where the price does not include the actual cost of transportation from the seller's plant to the buyer but the artificial cost of transportation from a given "base point" to the buyer. For example, the steel industry traditionally used Pittsburgh as its base point; all steel was priced as if it had been sold from Pittsburgh. A Chicago firm that purchased steel from a mill in Gary, Indiana would pay a "phantom freight" charge reflecting the cost of transportation from Pittsburgh to Chicago. On the other hand, the Gary plant would "absorb" the actual cost of freight selling to a buyer close to Pittsburgh.

Base point pricing occurs almost exclusively in industries where three factors are present: (1) the cost of transportation is significant relative to the price of the product; (2) the product is sold via price lists, rather than through individual negotiations between buyer and seller; and (3) firms are geographically spread out across the country. Firms in these industries can use base point pricing to exploit consumers in two respects. First, uniform transportation costs make it easier for firms to coordinate pricing. Spotting a discount, or matching a competitor's price, becomes more difficult if a firm must not only compare the cost of producing the good but also the cost of shipment by different modes of transportation. Second, base point pricing facilitates price discrimination.

Because transportation costs are high, without base point pricing each firm would have a natural advantage over customers located nearby; they can thus raise their prices to these customers up to the cost of transportation from the closest rival. Moreover, base point pricing gives firms the option of taking a lower profit and competing for the patronage of customers closer to the base point, without having to change their price lists and thereby cut the prices to current customers. To illustrate, a Gary, Indiana steel mill using a Pittsburgh base point will be able to charge a "phantom freight" charge to its Chicago customer, while competing with a Pittsburgh plant for the patronage of an Ohio customer. If the Ohio customer were paying transportation, the Gary company would have to revise its entire price list downward in order to compete with the closer Pittsburgh mill. But in so doing, the Gary company would sacrifice its ability to charge a higher price to its customers in Chicago. Base point pricing thus allows the Gary company to charge discriminatorily higher prices in Chicago and lower prices in Ohio.

50. Id. at 708.

This potential for price discrimination explains why firms might independently choose to engage in base point pricing. Thus, absent an agreement to use delivered prices (which would be illegal under *Cement Institute*), the Ninth Circuit correctly held in *Boise Cascade Corp. v. FTC* that the Commission must prove that the parallel use of base point pricing "actually had the effect of fixing or stabilizing prices" in order to establish an unfair method of competition.[51] The Commission challenged southern plywood manufacturers' parallel practice of quoting only a delivered price that included its mill price plus an amount equal to rail freight from Portland, Oregon. If the respondents were ordered to offer F.O.B. mill pricing, they might decide to maintain high list prices for closer customers and forego the opportunity to compete for more distant patrons. Under these circumstances, base point pricing actually helps consumers: the closer customers would be exploited under either type of pricing, but at least distant customers would get some competition under a base point scheme. On the other hand, ordering the respondents to offer F.O.B. mill pricing would benefit consumers where the FTC could show that the respondents would probably respond by lowering list prices in order to compete for distant patrons (suppose, for example, that nearby purchasers accounted for only 20% of respondents' business).

It is not clear that this type of proof would meet *Boise Cascade* 's requirement that the Commission show an actual effect on prices, but it should. Not only does base point pricing, in this situation, harm consumers, but it can significantly distort the efficient allocation of resources in three ways. First, as a result of base point pricing, a California lumber company might pay the same price for Louisiana plywood as Oregon plywood. If the Louisiana manufacturer's mill price were set so that it could compete for the business of California customers, using a Pacific Coast delivered price, it is necessarily imposing a monopoly overcharge on New Orleans customers. This results in less lumber being purchased in New Orleans—an inefficient allocation of resources. Second, base point pricing can lead to inefficient transportation practices. Because plywood is all sold at a delivered price including rail costs from Oregon, a California buyer might

---

51. 637 F.2d 573, 577 (9th Cir. 1980).

Ironically, private plaintiffs were able to prove that the plywood manufacturers had conspired to fix prices. In re Plywood Antitrust Litigation, 655 F.2d 627, 633–34 (5th Cir. 1981), cert. dismissed sub nom., Weyerhaeuser Co. v. Lyman Lamb Co., 462 U.S. 1125 (1983). In addition to parallel adoption of a base point system, the record in that case showed frequent communication among the parties regarding pricing practices. This was deemed sufficient to support the jury's finding a § 1 violation. In addition, the private plaintiffs, unlike the FTC, presented expert economic testimony in support of their case. Id. at 637 n.2.

order from a Louisiana manufacturer while a Texas buyer will order from a Washington state plywood manufacturer. Finally, a long-standing base point pricing scheme causes economically inefficient incentives for plant location by buyers and sellers. A manufacturer of pre-fabricated houses, for example, might locate in Oregon just to get low delivered prices on plywood, even though it might find it otherwise more efficient to be in southern California. A plywood manufacturer might find it more profitable to locate near its buyers, even if it were more efficient to locate near its raw materials, in order to take advantage of phantom freight.[52] The combination of consumer exploitation and inefficient resource allocation should suffice to support a finding that a practice is an unfair method of competition.

The Ninth Circuit's opinion makes a different argument about the benefits of base point pricing: the court found that the pricing scheme at issue in *Boise Cascade* was not anti-consumer because southern buyers "frequently expressed a preference for receiving quotations in terms of West Coast freight." [53] This may have been true because in the short run, buyers prefer the benefits of easily comparable prices; it is only over time that the elimination of a uniform pricing scheme can be expected to increase price competition. The short-term preferences of individual buyers should not, therefore, preclude a finding of anticompetitive effect.

The Ninth Circuit's decision in *Boise Cascade* was colored by the history of the FTC's treatment of parallel base point pricing. In an earlier case, *Triangle Conduit & Cable Co. v. FTC*,[54] the Seventh Circuit court upheld an FTC finding that parallel use of a base point system is an unfair method of competition where each firm knows that the others will use the formula and that the formula will allow them to avoid price competition. The case set off a "storm of protest from Congress and industry," [55] and the Commission responded to congressional inquiries by declaring in 1949 that *Triangle Conduit* applied only to "conspiracy situations." [56]

Nevertheless, the FTC is free to depart from this precedent if it clearly explains its reasons for doing so.[57] Even if the 1949 statement precludes the FTC from restricting base point pricing absent collusion, the Commission ought to be able to modify that

---

52. Thanks to my economics department colleague Larry DeBrock for these insights.

53. 637 F.2d at 580.

54. 168 F.2d 175 (7th Cir. 1948).

55. *Boise Cascade*, 637 F.2d at 576.

56. Id. (quoting Interim Report on the Study of the Federal Trade Commission Pricing Policies, S. Doc. No. 27, 81st Cong., 1st Sess. 62–63 (1949)).

57. Motor Vehicle Mfrs. Ass'n v. State Farm Mut. Auto. Ins. Co., 463 U.S. 29, 42 (1983).

precedent in order to protect consumers from specific practices that result in higher prices.

In sum, base point pricing schemes involve, at least, parallel decisions by competitors not to offer their goods for sale on an F.O.B. mill basis. Where a firm's customers are geographically dispersed, absent collusion the firm's efforts to increase market share will cause the firm to deviate from base point pricing, because sales at prices that include "phantom freight" will be quickly undercut by rivals. In these situations, evidence of adherence to a base point system is both consistent with conspiracy (facilitating price coordination) and inconsistent with competition. *Interstate Circuit* suggests that a court may even find this evidence alone sufficient to justify the inference of conspiracy.[58]

(6) Other facilitating practices.

United States v. General Electric Co.[59] illustrates the doctrinal and remedial difficulties that arise when § 1 is used to condemn facilitating practices in oligopolistic industries. In 1962, a price-fixing investigation in the large turbine generator market culminated in a consent decree that prohibited the three domestic manufacturers from exchanging price information. A decade later, the government filed suit against the two remaining firms in the market, General Electric and Westinghouse, observing that there had been no price competition between the two firms since 1963. The complaint alleged that, beginning in 1963, the defendants had adopted and published identical pricing policies and had strictly adhered to those policies. When these detailed pricing formulas were combined with each defendant's "price protection plan" that guaranteed buyers the benefit of any discounts it had given to other buyers within a six-month period, the government claimed that each firm could be confident that the other would not engage in discounting. Without admitting liability, the defendants settled.

As a doctrinal matter, the government's theory in *General Electric* demonstrates how "plus" factors can join with consciously parallel conduct to permit the inference of an agreement. The case involved identical behavior by duopolists, who each used very detailed pricing formulas in a market where previously an actual

---

58. See National Lead Co. v. FTC, 227 F.2d 825, 834 (7th Cir. 1955). The court noted that where virtually all firms sell "at identical prices, without regard to differences in shipping costs," the "pricing structure seems so arbitrary and artificial as to negative an inference of innocent parallel behav-ior." In light of evidence that the defendants in that case talked to each other about the benefits of base point pricing, an inference of tacit prearrangement was required there.

59. 1977-2 Trade Cas. (CCH) ¶ 61,-659-60 (E.D. Pa.1977).

conspiracy to fix prices had been suspected. *General Electric* can thus be analogized to a case involving evidence of secret motel room meetings among competitors, which likewise can provide the "plus" to conscious parallelism.[60]

Moreover, if G.E. and Westinghouse had been engaged in vigorous rivalry, they probably would not have found it in their independent self-interest to reveal highly detailed pricing formulae. Vigorous rivals seek to increase their own market share by cutting prices to consumers. Although consumers wish to know the actual prices they (and perhaps their rivals) are receiving, buyers do not have a particularly strong interest in the detailed formulae that underlie the bottom-line price. On the other hand, a seller's revelation of its pricing formula to its own rivals inhibits its ability to steal customers away from others, because it allows rivals to quickly match price cuts. Thus, absent some special explanation, firms who are competing rather than cooperating would not be expected to make the kind of announcements made by G.E. and Westinghouse. On the other hand, public dissemination of general pricing information may well be consistent with independent self-interest, and thus absent the particular facts of this case, the government would have had a difficult time proving that this aspect of the defendants' parallel conduct was contrary to their independent self-interest.

Determining the appropriate remedy to prevent practices that facilitate tacit collusion raises further problems. The consent decree in *General Electric* properly enjoined publication of the defendants' highly detailed pricing formulae.[61] It also barred the parties from offering a "price protection" policy. That provision of the decree involves clear trade-offs: consumers clearly prefer such a policy in the short run, although over the long term buyers would benefit from vigorous price competition. Most troublesome was the decree's requirement that each defendant's price lists be

---

60. See, e.g., Bray v. Safeway Stores, Inc., 392 F.Supp. 851, 857 (N.D. Cal. 1975).

61. In contrast, enjoining the public announcement of actual sale prices has been criticized:

> The public announcement of a pricing decision cannot be twisted into an invitation or signal to conspire; it is instead an economic reality to which all other competitors must react. The government has not shown that either defendant intended its pricing moves to be a signal of its willingness to take specific additional pricing actions.

United States v. General Motors Corp., 1974–2 Trade Cas. (CCH) ¶ 75,253, 97,-671 (E.D. Mich.1974).

The court also noted that, unlike other defendants whose parallel conduct led to inferences of conspiracy, Ford and General Motors, the defendants in that case, had legitimate reasons for independently engaging in the challenged behavior, and that top executives from each company had credibly explained the non-collusive motives underlying for the conduct. Id. at 97,670–71.

"based on [its] own individually determined criteria and costs" and not on "the prices in any price book, price list, or compilation of prices in effect" during the 14-year period of parallel pricing.[62] This amounts to a directive that each defendant must ignore the obvious reaction of its rival, which is contrary to the way that both common sense and economic theory suggest duopolists will behave.[63]

These remedial problems will not often trouble judges in the Second Circuit, however. That court's decision in *E.I. du Pont De Nemours & Co. v. FTC ("Ethyl")*[64] rejected any antitrust liability for parallel use of facilitating practices—even under the FTC Act's ban on unfair methods of competition. In *Ethyl*, the FTC found that the four oligopolists that produced leaded antiknock compounds for automobile gasoline violated § 5 by the parallel use of four facilitating practices. In addition to the use of delivered prices, each firm included a "most favored nation" clause in contracts with customers, promising to extend to each customer any discount given to any other buyer; promised to advise buyers of price changes 30 days in advance; and adopted a policy of publicity announcing all price changes in advance. Economic theory suggests that each of these practices will facilitate oligopoly pricing. Most favored nation clauses create a strong disincentive for a firm to cut prices in order to gain more business: in order to do so, the firm would also have to cut prices for all current customers even though they are willing to pay the higher price. Advance price announcements make it much more likely that price cuts will not be profitable, because by the time a firm's new price becomes effective, it will likely be matched by other firms' price cuts; all firm realize this in advance, and therefore they will probably simply forego price cutting.

In an effort to satisfy the requirements for a § 5 violation set forth in *Boise Cascade* (proof of an actual effect on prices), the FTC noted in *Ethyl* that the industry was a tight oligopoly with stable market shares and steady prices, despite each firm's excess capacity.[65] Economic theory suggests that this excess capacity should have led to aggressive discounting and unstable market shares, as each firm sought to expand its own output. Because prices and shares remained relatively steady, with no apparent explanation, the FTC reasoned that the parallel practices must be facilitating tacit collusion. This evidence was not enough for the Second

---

62. 1977–2 Trade Cas. at 72,718.

63. This is precisely the type of remedy that Professor Donald Turner criticized in his influential law review article, supra note 2.

64. 729 F.2d 128 (2d Cir. 1984).

65. Due to environmental regulations prohibiting the use of leaded gasoline in almost all new automobiles, demand for their product was rapidly dwindling.

Circuit. The court could simply have rejected the FTC's reasoning, given its finding that "substantial price and non-price competition" existed during the period subject to complaint (including discounts off list price, secret discounts, and numerous "free" services), and it could have credited the defendants' expert testimony that oligopoly pricing can easily be achieved without any of the allegedly "facilitating" practices challenged by the government.[66] Instead, the court sharply limited the Commission's authority under § 5, disagreeing with *Boise Cascade*'s holding that the FTC can prevail by showing a stabilizing effect on price. Absent an actual violation of the Sherman or Clayton Act, the court held, the Commission must find that the conduct at issue was collusive, coercive, predatory, or exclusionary, or that it was done with an anticompetitive purpose or for no legitimate purpose.

The result in *Ethyl* may have been influenced by the history of the challenged practices. Each of them had been initiated by Ethyl at a time when it operated as a monopolist in the industry, and the court naturally questioned how a practice could facilitate oligopoly pricing if it was initiated when Ethyl had no rivals with whom to collude. But the fact that these practices did not *create* oligopoly pricing does not suggest that they did not help *maintain* anticompetitive behavior. Moreover, as the Supreme Court has made clear, § 5 was intended to give the FTC broad powers to halt conduct that conflicts with the "policies" of the antitrust laws,[67] and one of the Sherman Act's key policies is to ensure that markets be characterized by vigorous competition. Pure conscious parallelism is tolerated under the Sherman Act for two reasons: (1) the language of § 1 cannot fairly be read to apply when there is no agreement; and (2) a workable remedy is impossible. This logic suggests that facilitating practices should not be tolerated under the FTC Act: (1) the language of § 5 does not require an agreement; and (2) enjoining specific practices is an easy remedy.

Ethyl's limitation of the FTC's powers to define unfair methods of competition is also inconsistent with the history and purpose of § 5. As the court correctly noted, the "term 'unfair' is an elusive concept, often dependent upon the eye of the beholder," [68] but the question is who is the beholder. The FTC Act was passed in part because Congress feared that the libertarian-oriented judiciary of the time would adopt an unduly crabbed interpretation of the Sherman Act; Congress therefore wanted an agency that would be more politically responsive than the judiciary to deter-

---

66. 729 F.2d at 132–34. Indeed, this was the position of Judge J. Edward Lumbard, who wrote a separate opinion concurring in the result. Id. at 142.

67. See FTC v. Sperry & Hutchinson Co., 405 U.S. 233 (1972); FTC v. Brown Shoe Co., 384 U.S. 316, 321 (1966).

68. 729 F.2d at 137.

mine competition policy. (Recall that the FTC Act was passed in 1914, at the height of the *"Lochner"* era of judicial activism favoring the rights of business.) For the judiciary, 70 years later, to narrowly restrict the FTC Act out of concern that a broad reading would "permit arbitrary or undue government interference with the reasonable freedom of action that has marked our country's competitive system" [69] seems, to quote Yogi Berra, like "deja vu all over again."

(7) Intra-corporate conspiracy and the single entity doctrine.

Thus far, this section has considered whether the parallel conduct of admittedly independent actors constitutes a "contract, combination, or conspiracy" for purposes of § 1 of the Sherman Act. This subsection discusses the converse issue: when the defendants' business relationship with each other is so interrelated that they are not independent actors, so that agreements among them do not fall within the scope of § 1. For example, no one suggests that § 1 is violated when the Vice President for Sales and her regional managers all agree on the price of products sold by a major corporation; or that the Smith & Jones law firm acts illegally when partners Sara Smith and Jane Jones set on hourly rates for the firm's attorneys.

Fortunately, this is one area of antitrust law where prior chaos has now substantially been clarified by the Supreme Court. *Copperweld Corp. v. Independence Tube Corp.*[70] held that a parent corporation and its wholly owned subsidiary were not legally capable of conspiring with each other for purposes of § 1.[71] The Court noted that the Sherman Act draws a basic distinction between concerted and unilateral activity. The former is condemned under § 1 if it has the effect of unreasonably restraining trade; the latter is proscribed under § 2 only if its effect is to attempt or maintain an unlawful monopoly. Writing for the majority, Chief Justice Warren Burger cogently explained why the Sherman Act treats concerted behavior more strictly:

> Concerted activity inherently is fraught with anticompetitive risk. It deprives the marketplace of the independent centers of decisionmaking that competition assumes and demands. In any conspiracy, two or more entities that previously pursued

---

69. Id.

70. 467 U.S. 752 (1984).

71. The decision effectively overruled precedents that applied a case-by-case approach in determining whether a parent and its subsidiary could conspire for § 1 purposes. Under this approach, the courts looked at a variety of factors, including the degree of separation between the officers, headquarters, and day-to-day operations of the parent and the subsidiary. Id. at 773 n.18.

their own interests separately are combining to act as one for
their common benefit. This not only reduces the diverse
directions in which economic power is aimed but suddenly
increases the economic power moving in one particular direction.[72]

Based on this important distinction, few thought that § 1 applied
to agreements among officers or employees of the same company
or to internally coordinated conduct of a corporation and its
unincorporated division.[73]

For the same reasons, the Court properly concluded that a
parent and its wholly owned subsidiary have a

> complete unity of interest. Their objectives are common, not
> disparate.... They are not unlike a multiple team of horses
> drawing a vehicle under the control of a single driver..... If
> a parent and a wholly owned subsidiary do 'agree' to a course
> of action, there is no sudden joining of economic resources
> that had previously served different interests." [74]

The facts of *Copperweld* demonstrate the soundness of the
Court's conclusion. The plaintiff, the owner of Independence
Tube, had previously worked for Regal Tube Co., an unincorporated division of Lear Siegler, Inc. Copperweld purchased the assets
of Regal Tube and transferred them to a wholly owned subsidiary
corporation that was also named Regal Tube Co. When Independence Tube went into business in competition with Copperweld's
Regal Tube subsidiary, the defendant sent letters to potential
customers warning that the owner of Independence Tube might be
subject to liability for stealing trade secrets he had learned during
his tenure at Regal. Independence Tube sued, claiming that the
letters were the result of concerted conduct between Copperweld
and its subsidiary. The impact of the letters (which might have
been actionable as business torts) would have been no different if
Regal Tube had been an unincorporated division of Copperweld.
The Court rightly held that antitrust law has no business discour-
aging the organization of divisions into corporate subsidiaries.
Moreover, the decision to send out these letters did not represent a
combination of previously separate interests that, but for the
conspiracy, would have behaved in a more competitive way.

In dissent, Justice John Paul Stevens argued that a rule of
reason analysis ought to be used to determine when intra-corpo-
rate conspiracies are actionable under § 1. However, his opinion
suggested only two categories of cases where § 1 liability should
attach: where the formation of the relationship between the

72. Id. at 768–69.   **74.** Id.
73. Id. at 771.

parent and the subsidiary lessens competition; and where affiliated corporations engage in predatory or exclusionary behavior.[75] Although Stevens correctly noted that the first situation was the prime concern of the framers of the Sherman Act, it was not affected by the majority's holding. If the *formation* of the affiliation among corporations is anticompetitive, that formation remains unlawful under § 1. In *Copperweld*, however, no one challenged the defendant's acquisition of Regal Tube; rather, it was conduct by the now affiliated corporations that was at issue. As for the second situation, § 2 properly condemns predatory or exclusionary behavior by a single firm that constitutes attempted or actual monopolization. It is true, as discussed in Chapter 3, section H(1), that these two provisions leave a gap for anticompetitive, non-collusive conduct that does not threaten to monopolize, but there is no sound reason to impose greater liability on firms that happen to be organized into separate corporations than on those that are not. Justice Stevens indicated that two affiliated corporations might pose a greater threat of anticompetitive conduct, but he provided no support for this assertion.[76] Moreover, he did not explain how the letters sent by Regal and Copperweld would have been less threatening if they had come from only the parent, or if Regal had been an unincorporated division.

The majority in *Copperweld* properly limited its holding by distinguishing *United States v. Timken Roller Bearing Co.*[77] In that case, affiliated corporations based in the United States, Britain, and France were found to have conspired in violation of § 1. The American-based corporation owned 30% of the British corporation's stock and half of the French corporation. In order to effectuate the agreements, the American firm needed to secure the cooperation of the British investor who owned much of the remaining stock. Thus, there was no unity of interest among the affiliated corporations; absent the agreement between the American corporation and the British investor, the corporations might well have behaved differently. *Copperweld*'s discussion of *Timken* provides the basis for lower courts to determine the scope of § 1 in cases involving agreements among affiliated corporations: the outcome should turn on the unity of interest among the corpora-

---

75. Id. at 789. Stevens' dissent was joined by Justices William Brennan and Thurgood Marshall.

76. This critique is supported by Stevens' one example—the case where two affiliated corporations operate a newspaper and a radio station and the latter uses its monopoly power to refuse to deal with patrons of a rival newspaper. See 467 U.S. at 795 & n.29 (citing Law-rence Sullivan, Antitrust 327 (1977)). These facts are identical to those of Lorain Journal Co. v. United States, 342 U.S. 143 (1951), where the Court found a violation of § 2.

77. 467 U.S. at 764–65 & n.10 (citing 83 F.Supp. 284, 311–12 (N.D. Ohio 1949), aff'd as modified, 341 U.S. 593 (1951)).

tions. Section 1 should therefore apply whenever business realities and fiduciary duties required by corporate law suggest that, absent an agreement, affiliated corporations might be expected to engage in competition that would benefit consumers.

Section G: Information Exchanges

Agreements among competitors to exchange information are not illegal in and of themselves. Their anticompetitive potential lies in their usefulness in facilitating coordinated pricing. Therefore, when an agreement to exchange information has the necessary tendency or ultimate effect of dampening competition, it unreasonably restrains trade. Because many of these exchanges and ventures so obviously benefit competition, however, they have always been analyzed under the rule of reason, even though they appear to tamper with price competition.

Information exchanges can damper price competition in any number of ways, but typically they enable competitors to coordinate pricing in two ways: by facilitating express or tacit agreements on price, and by detecting cheating on an agreed price. (For purposes of this section, students should ignore the moral lesson that "cheating" is bad. Rather, "cheating" on a cartel—i.e., a firm's decision to lower its price or otherwise engage in competition in violation of a tacit or express non-competition agreement with rivals—helps the competitive process and consumers, and thus is encouraged by antitrust law.)

(1) Early cases.

The information exchange condemned by the Supreme Court in *American Column & Lumber Co. v. United States*[1] featured aspects that both facilitated agreement and detected cheating. The trade association's "manager of statistics" constantly exhorted the defendant lumber companies to cut output, and each company reported estimates of its own future production, certainly creating a climate conducive to agreement. In addition, exclusive use of F.O.B. mill pricing and standardized grading facilitated agreement because agreeing on a price is easiest when firms sell standardized products.[2] When transportation costs and varying product quality are introduced, firms will have different perceptions of their own self-interest and agreement becomes more difficult. For example, lumber companies can more readily agree on the F.O.B. mill price

---

1. 257 U.S. 377 (1921).

2. See id. at 409–12. F.O.B. pricing does not include the cost of transporting the product to the buyer.

for objectively rated "Grade A" oak than on F.O.B. mill and delivered prices for subjectively rated "top quality" oak.

In two subsequent cases, the court condemned similar exchanges of information that facilitated price agreements. In the first case, *United States v. American Linseed Oil Co.*,[3] the government successfully challenged an agreed-upon regional price differential that standardized pricing decisions and thus facilitated price agreement. Likewise, the Court prohibited a number of practices in *Sugar Institute, Inc. v. United States*[4] that facilitated maintenance of publicly announced prices. These included standardizing sales by agreeing not to vertically integrate[5] and simplifying the terms of sale that each rival needed to match by agreeing not to offer quantity discounts or long-term contracts. The agreements in these three cases demonstrate how competitors can significantly facilitate price coordination without having to expressly agree on prices.

The companies' activities in *American Column & Lumber* were also condemned because each company submitted reports to the trade association that disclosed price cuts and identified specific buyers, thus hindering any attempt to cheat on the cartel.[6] Whether prices creep above the competitive level because of an express agreement or because of oligopolistic interdependence, the primary motive for cheating is to increase sales in the short period before the rest of the industry realizes the discount has occurred and matches it. Immediately reporting information about specific sales dramatically shortens this time lag, thereby reducing the value of cheating.[7] An even more dramatic effort to halt cheating was similarly disapproved in *Sugar Institute*, where the defendants agreed to stick to announced prices.[8]

Justice Oliver Wendell Holmes Jr. dissented in *American Column & Lumber* on the ground that increasing the amount of information in a free marketplace is desirable.[9] Indeed, a stock exchange is a paradigmatic example of a free market characterized by the total exchange of information. The majority respond-

3. 262 U. S. 371 (1923).

4. 297 U.S. 553 (1936).

5. Vertical integration occurs when manufacturers also perform wholesale and/or retail functions. If some, but not all, the firms in an industry are vertically integrated, it becomes more difficult to agree on price. The internal price which a manufacturer changes itself is obviously subject to fudging by a cheater, and it is more difficult to compare one firm's wholesale price to another firm's retail price than to compare and agree upon prices at the same level of distribution.

6. 257 U.S. at 411.

7. Indeed, many information exchanges began following the 1912 publication of Jerome Eddy's book, The New Competition, which endorsed immediate disclosure of all sales as a means of deterring secret price cuts.

8. 297 U.S. at 601–02.

9. 257 U.S. at 412.

ed that the information exchanged by the lumber companies went far beyond "the amount of stock held, the sales made and the prices received, by every other member of the group, thereby furnishing the data for judging the market, on the basis of supply and demand and current prices."[10]   Rather, the disclosure of projections of future behavior, the fact that the recipients of the information were primarily other sellers instead of buyers, and the pleas for coordinated behavior clearly distinguished this agreement from an open market or exchange.   Thus, the majority seemed to create a useful safe harbor for trade associations, at the same time that it evoked *Addyston Pipe* by suggesting that the challenged agreement was broader than necessary to achieve the legitimate purposes of the information exchange.

Justice Louis Brandeis also dissented in *American Column & Lumber*.   His opinion is striking for its lack of concern with consumers.   In Brandeis' view, there was no attempt to coerce any of the entrepreneurs involved and therefore no restraint of trade.[11] Despite the government's proof that the information exchange was intended to and did raise prices, Brandeis stressed the fact that the information provided by the trade association was very valuable to smaller firms without access to up-to-date market data; larger firms could probably have learned about market conditions in other ways.   Thus, the exchange "create[d] among producers equality of opportunity."   Finally, Brandeis contrasted the pro-enforcement attitude towards § 1 with the lax view contemporary courts and the Justice Department were taking toward mergers, concluding that the principal effect of the government's lawsuit would be to centralize economic control in the hands of big business.[12]   Although Brandeis made some good points (particularly his last argument), he failed to justify his decision to prefer Jeffersonian concerns when they clearly result in an inefficient allocation of resources, higher prices for consumers, and the exercise of discretionary power by lumber firms.   As Judge Robert Bork has observed, "nobody is smaller than the individual consumer.   If you want to favor the small guy, the consumer is that guy."[13]

10.   Id. at 398.

11.   Id. at 414–15.

12.   Id. at 418–19.

13.   *Paradox* Revisited: Interview with Robert H. Bork, Antitrust (Summer 1989) at p.17.

Justice Brandeis' views would be consistent with a populist consumer position if, in fact, banning on the exchange of information would drive smaller firms out of business and thus allow the remaining large firms to raise prices to higher levels.   Such a scenario, though, was not suggested by Brandeis and appears to have been unlikely, given the many firms in the industry.

The Court has not disapproved of every exchange of information to come before it. In *Maple Flooring Manufacturers Ass'n v. United States*, the Court upheld an information exchange among flooring producers.[14] Justice Stone's majority opinion in that case demonstrates an unfortunate inconsistency in applying antitrust principles. Although the Court properly distinguished its prior precedents because the defendant flooring producers had not exchanged immediate and detailed information about specific sales,[15] the defendants had exchanged information that included data about average costs and freight rates from Cadillac, Michigan to 6,000 destinations. The Court sustained this exchange even though information about average costs tends to standardize pricing and facilitate agreement. Similarly, the freight information tended to encourage delivered base point pricing, which, as discussed in section F(5), can both facilitate agreement and raise prices by permitting price discrimination. Moreover, the history of the challenged agreement included a prior, but then discarded, agreement among the defendants to fix prices at average cost plus 10% profit plus the arbitrary freight rate from Cadillac, Michigan.

Correctly restating, but incorrectly applying, the rule of law set down in *American Linseed*, the Court held that information could not be exchanged where the "necessary tendency"[16] was to destroy price competition, but sustained the flooring manufacturers' information exchange anyway. Indeed, the Court said, such exchanges were lawful even if "the ultimate result of their efforts may be to stabilize prices or limit production through a better understanding of economic laws and a more general ability to conform to them."[17] Although *Maple Flooring*'s sanctioning of the dissemination of average cost and freight rates is highly questionable, the Court's observation was headed in the right direction. In a competitive market, information helps buyers and sellers trade at a price that is efficient and does not exploit either party's lack of knowledge. The price will indeed become "stabilized" at the true market-clearing level; absent information, ignorant buyers will pay more and ignorant sellers will obtain less than the market price for their products. In competitive markets, the exchange of significant market data therefore furthers rather than impedes the efficiency and consumer protection goals of antitrust as well as promoting the Jeffersonian concept equal of opportunity. Yet, as the prior cases demonstrate, in markets susceptible to collusion, information exchanges can be used to

14. 268 U.S. 563 (1925).
15. Id. at 567–68, 573–74.
16. Id. at 578.
17. Id. at 584.

facilitate agreements and detect cheating.[18]

(2) The current rule of reason.

An oft-cited footnote in *United States v. United States Gypsum Co.* sets forth the standard that governs information exchanges: they are evaluated under the rule of reason, with the structure of the industry featured as the most prominent factor to be considered. In addition, exchanges of specific types of information that "have the greatest potential for generating anticompetitive effects"—that is, those that most clearly facilitate price coordination or deter cheating—will be condemned even in industries where collusion may be unlikely.[19]

United States v. Container Corp. of America,[20] though decided prior to *Gypsum*, is a good case study for applying of the rule of reason. In *Container Corp.*, Justice William O. Douglas' majority opinion condemned an agreement among rival box makers to disclose the specific prices they quoted to potential buyers. The Court concluded that this type of information had led to price matching rather than price cutting, and that continued entry into the market suggested the existence of monopoly profits and collusion.[21] Justice Thurgood Marshall's dissenting opinion emphasized another piece of economic data relevant to industry structure—that entry into the container market was easy.[22] Thus, the Justices' views on the structure of the market strongly influenced their reactions to the case. *Gypsum* later explained the significance of market structure: "[p]rice concessions by oligopolists generally yield competitive advantages only if secrecy can be

---

18. The same day *Maple Flooring* was decided, the Court also upheld an information exchange in Cement Mfrs' Protective Ass'n v. United States, 268 U.S. 588 (1925). In that case, the disclosure of information served to protect cement manufacturers against the one-sided contracts prevalent in the industry that gave contractors the option of accepting or rejecting the promised cement depending on fluctuations in the market price. This was a case where the market was not working due to a one-sided lack of information, and the Court properly viewed the information exchange as a reasonable means to correct what economists call "information asymmetry." This case is also discussed below in section H(2).

19. 438 U.S. 422, 441 n.16 (1978). The principal holding in *Gypsum* was that § 1 imposes different standards of liability in civil and criminal cases.

While proof of intent is unnecessary in a civil suit, a defendant cannot be convicted of a criminal violation of § 1 unless the government proves that the conduct was "undertaken with knowledge of its probable consequences" and had an anticompetitive effect. Id. at 445.

In rejecting the defendants' contention that their anticompetitive information exchange was justified by their desire to comply with the Robinson–Patman Act, the Court also clarified the standards for the "meeting competition" defense available under § 2(b) of that statute. Id. at 448–60. This defense is discussed in Chapter 7, section F(3).

20.   393 U.S. 333 (1969).

21.   Id. at 336–38.

22.   Id. at 342.

maintained; when the terms of the concession are made publicly known, other competitors are likely to follow and any advantage to the initiator is lost in the process."[23]

(3) Economic considerations in applying the rule of reason.

The courts' ability to identify which markets are susceptible to collusion and which are already characterized by actual collusion will thus significantly affect their ability to meaningfully evaluate exchanges of information that do not substantially facilitate agreement or deter cheating—such as information about past sales (with some lag time) and current inventory. Judge Richard Posner has set forth a useful checklist of factors to consider in such cases, with the caveat that the presence or absence of none of then should be considered dispositive.[24]

Factors suggesting that a market is susceptible to collusion, and thus that information exchanges are more likely to result in coordinated pricing, include:

Few sellers and many buyers. The fewer the sellers, the easier to agree on price and the more comfortable each seller is that no one will cheat. A few powerful buyers can disrupt a cartel by playing firms off against one another; this can not happen when buyers are numerous and each individual sale therefore becomes less important.

Consumers are not price sensitive at the competitive level. If substitute products are produced by those outside the cartel, the cartel will fail, for buyers will respond to higher prices by taking their business elsewhere.

New entry takes a long time. Otherwise, new firms can respond to higher prices by quickly entering the market, undercutting the cartel and gaining a large share of the market.

Goods are bought and sold in standard, frequent patterns. Where transactions vary, it is more difficult for rivals to agree on terms, and management of a cartel becomes more complex. In markets characterized by major, infrequent transactions, firms have a greater incentive to cheat to get the "big sale".

Manufacturers' costs are similar. If rivals all have the same costs, each manufacturer's profit-maximizing monopoly price will be identical. Where costs are dissimilar, the low-cost producers will want to charge a lower price in order to increase their sales. For example, if Firm A spends $8 to manufacture a product and

---

23. 438 U.S. at 456.

24. See Richard Posner & Frank Easterbrook, Antitrust 335–40 (1981).

Firm B spends $13, Firm A might be happy charging $13 (a with $5 monopoly profit) and be unwilling to lose sales by pricing at a higher level. This type of disparity can therefore disrupt a cartel.

The product is standardized.   Again, standardized products facilitate agreement among carteleers. Where products are differentiated, each firm will try to fudge by charging less on its "low-grade" product, and maintaining high price levels thus becomes more difficult.

Identical degree of vertical integration.   When some firms own their own retail outlets and others do not, cheating becomes easier. If the cartel agrees on a set wholesale price, the integrated firms can simply charge a lower retail price and claim that their wholly fictional internal wholesale price conformed to the price-fixing agreement. Alternatively, the non-integrated firms can cheat on the agreed-upon price and falsely claim that their independent distributors are responsible for the lower retail price in the market.

Most competition is based on price.   Where non-price considerations play a significant role in consumers' purchasing decisions, a price-fixing agreement becomes more difficult. Carteleers will have to spend a substantial amount of money competing with each other on better service, more reliable quality control, or other non-price factors. Coordinating the same degree of service, for example, is much more difficult than coordinating prices.

Demand is static or declining.   Where demand is rising, firms have is less incentive to bother with the time and risk of an illegal price-fixing agreement because higher demand will lead to higher prices and profits anyway.

Posner proposed that these nine factors be considered in determining whether structural considerations make an industry susceptible to collusion, thus raising antitrust concerns about information sharing agreements. In addition, he has suggested several indicators to be used in determining whether collusion, either explicit or tacit, is actually occurring in the market. These indicators include:

Stable market shares.   Cartels are typically not found in industries where the division of market shares is dynamic, with obvious winners and obvious losers, because cartels are unlikely to agree to allow some members to gain and others to lose.

Persistent price discrimination.   If firms are consistently charging some purchasers higher prices than others, some form of collusion is probably occurring. If Firm A charges a higher price to a particular consumer in a competitive market, Firm B will usually come along and undercut that price.

Stable price variations or identical bids. These phenomena are obviously less likely to occur in a competitive market.

In sum, a rule of reason analysis governs agreements among competitors to exchange information about their businesses. Although sharing certain highly sensitive information (e.g., identification of specific buyers, projections of future production plans) is usually condemned because it is so likely to reduce price competition, the exchange of other information in a competitive market may actually foster competition by providing sellers and buyers with better information. On the other hand, the exchange of almost any information can significantly facilitate price agreements in an oligopolistic industry prone to collusion. Thus, the courts examine the structure of the market to determine whether, on balance, an exchange of information is likely to promote vigorous competition or facilitate express or tacit collusion.

Section H: Group Boycotts

We return to another type of horizontal restraint that courts have designated for per se analysis—agreements among competitors not to deal with others, a.k.a. concerted refusals to deal, a.k.a. group boycotts.[1] As is true with many other doctrines, the early group boycott cases involved blatant conduct that all schools of antitrust ideology would condemn, although those earlier decisions were grounded primarily in non-economic concerns, while recent decisions attempt to distinguish between lawful and unlawful conduct primarily on economic grounds.

What is a boycott? The term covers a broad variety of conduct involving joint refusals to deal with others. In *St. Paul Fire & Marine Insurance Co. v. Barry,*[2] the Court defined the term as "a method of pressuring a party with whom one has a dispute by withholding, or enlisting others to withhold, patronage or services from the target."[3] It includes the "enlistment of third parties in an agreement not to trade, as a means of compelling capitulation by the boycotted group."[4] Some boycotts target

1. The term "boycott" originated in 1880 when Irish peasants, following three years of bad harvests and the British House of Lords' rejection of tenant protection measures, called a meeting and agreed to cease all dealings with Captain Boycott, a land agent who paid starvation wages and evicted any who protested. See Louis Schwartz, John Flynn & Harry First, Free Enterprise and Economic Organization: Antitrust 530 (6th ed. 1983).

2. 438 U.S. 531 (1978).

3. Id. at 541. *Barry* involved an antitrust suit against several insurance companies. The Court was construing a section of the McCarran–Ferguson Act which provided that the Act's general antitrust exemption for insurance companies did not apply to "boycotts." 15 U.S.C. § 1013(b).

4. Id. at 544.

rivals in an effort to drive them out of the market, so that the boycotters can keep the business for themselves. A boycott need not, however, necessarily be aimed at one of the conspirators' competitors.[5] Other boycotts involve refusals to sell except on certain terms, thus targeting customers for exploitation in the same way that price fixing exploits them.

Boycotts tend to defy easy categorization. Where a boycott is primarily directed at enforcing a price-fixing arrangement, it is usually analyzed as price fixing would be.[6] Whenever members of a joint venture limit access to the venture, the limit technically involves a concerted refusal to deal with the excluded firms'. These arrangements are analyzed separately in the following section.

(1) Development of per se illegality.

Montague & Co. v. Lowry[7] involved the most reprehensible type of group boycott. In that case, the plaintiff was not permitted to join the defendant trade association, and the members of the trade association refused to do business with the plaintiff. In fact, the trade association members refused to do business with anyone except at agreed upon prices, and agreed to boycott any manufacturers that sold to non-members. In finding a violation of § 1, the Supreme Court emphasized a pervasive Madisonian fear of the discretionary power inherent in this agreement, rather than any concerns about inefficiency in the market. The defendants pointed out that the affected market was small; the Court rejected this argument with a seemingly unqualified ban on these type of agreements. "The amount of trade in the commodity is not very material," the Court wrote, because of the potential that the exclusionary effects would increase if the cartel were allowed to flourish.[8]

The development of the law governing group boycotts tracked the development of the law against price fixing in terms of the rejection of defendants' alleged justifications for their boycotts. You will recall that *Addyston Pipe* declared price fixing illegal, *Trenton Potteries* held that price fixing is illegal even if the set price is "reasonable," and *Professional Engineers* held that price fixing is illegal even if vigorous rivalry disserves the public inter-

5. Id. at 543.

6. See sections A through C, above. FTC v. Indiana Federation of Dentists, 476 U.S. 447 (1986), involved a concerted refusal by dentists to provide x-rays to insurance companies. It seems to have been analyzed as a price-fixing case, although it could be considered a group boycott as well. It is analyzed in section D, above.

7. 193 U.S. 38 (1904).

8. Id. at 46.

est.[9] Similarly, the Court has held that a boycott is illegal even if it is designed to enforce an underlying agreement the parties believe is reasonable. In *Paramount Famous Lasky Corp. v. United States*,[10] the Court condemned an agreement among the major motion picture distributors to refuse to do business with theatre owners except pursuant to a standard contract that contained, *inter alia*, a mandatory arbitration clause. Especially today, few would disagree with the notion that private alternative dispute resolution is highly desirable. But the Court properly rejected the view that antitrust courts should make a *post hoc* determination of the reasonableness of a contract term implemented by the force of a boycott, rather than the force of competition. If mandatory arbitration clauses are appropriate in a certain industry, each firm can independently insist on such clauses.

Just as literal price fixing can be lawful when necessary to create a market or a new product, the per se rule may also be inapplicable when a joint refusal to deal is necessary in order to achieve a pro-competitive result. The Ninth Circuit may have been getting at this point in *Joseph E. Seagram & Sons, Inc. v. Hawaiian Oke & Liquors, Ltd.*,[11] although its analysis was not clear and unfortunately the opinion did not discuss or distinguish *Paramount Famous Lasky*. Two rival liquor distillers, the House of Seagram and Barton, agreed to replace Hawaiian Oke, the exclusive Hawaiian distributor for several of their products, with McKesson, another distributor. Although McKesson was an established distributor who already handled some of Seagram's products, both Seagram and Barton wanted McKesson to open a new distribution subsidiary, with different sales personnel, to market the items in question. Because liquor is generally marketed through exclusive distributors, the necessary effect of the decision was to refuse to deal further with Hawaiian Oke.

In reversing the jury's verdict in favor of the plaintiff and instituting judgment n.o.v. for the defendants, the court emphasized that individual firms are free to select their own distributors.[12] However, the antitrust concern in that case was that Seagram and Barton made a *joint* decision to switch distributors. Under *Paramount Famous Lasky*, the court should therefore have asked why each could not have independently determined whether to terminate Hawaiian Oke and sign with McKesson. The answer, though, is suggested in the court's recitation of the facts: the nature of the industry was such that the new separate distribution company McKesson would establish needed to handle a number of

9. See sections A(2), B(1) and D, above.

10. 282 U.S. 30 (1930).

11. 416 F.2d 71 (9th Cir. 1969), cert. denied, 396 U.S. 1062 (1970).

12. Id. at 79–80.

lines of liquor. Apparently, the Seagram's products at issue were name-brand, high-profit lines, while Barton's were lower-priced brands. Thus, Seagram and Barton could not have independently determined to switch to McKesson's new sales force because the new force would not have been viable unless they both joined together. Assuming that both Seagram and Barton faced vigorous competition from other distillers who used distributors other than those controlled by McKesson (the court fails to discuss this at all), the joint decision appears necessary to the pro-competitive result of creating a new sales force in Hawaii.

Just as *Paramount Famous Lasky* tracks *Trenton Potteries* in rejecting a post hoc determination of reasonableness, the Court's decision in *Fashion Originators' Guild of America v. FTC*[13] parallels *Professional Engineers* in rejecting an argument that restricted competition was socially preferable to unrestrained rivalry. The Court enjoined an agreement among style designers not to do business with any retailer that sold products made by "style pirates"—firms that copied fashions and designs from the original and then made and sold their copies at a discount. The Court explained that the boycott had a number of anticompetitive consequences: it limited the outlets to which manufactures could sell and the sources from which retailers could buy; it subjected retailers and manufacturers to the discretionary power of a group boycott; it deprived retailers of freedom of action; and it had the purpose and effect of suppressing competition from style pirates.[14]

Fashion Originators involved an agreement that ended arguably anti-social practices. Although style piracy did not violate federal patent or copyright laws, many states had held that it constituted a business tort. Nevertheless, the Court held that the goal of ending style piracy did not justify concerted efforts to achieve that goal. If competition did not work, Congress could grant fashion designs legal protection—as it had done with patented and copyrighted works.[15]

13. 312 U.S. 457 (1941).

14. *Fashion Originators* is inconsistent with an antitrust approach focusing solely on economic efficiency. The defendant guild represented 176 manufacturers of women's garments. Even if they succeeded in eliminating every style pirate, it is unlikely that any firm with so many competitors could possibly reduce output below, and raise price above, the competitive level. Thus, the Court's objection had to be based on non-efficiency concerns about preserving free choices for consumers and retailers.

15. It is unclear which statute the Supreme Court was interpreting in *Fashion Originators*. The case was brought under § 5 of the FTC Act, which prohibits "unfair methods of competition." Although language in the opinion suggests that the court may have been influenced by the fact that § 5 gives the FTC broader power to strike down anticompetitive conduct, later decisions make clear that *Fashion Originators* sets the standard for group boycotts under § 1 of the Sherman Act. See, e.g., Klor's, Inc. v. Broadway–Hale Stores, Inc., 359 U.S. 207, 212 (1959).

The Court properly left the decision whether to extend protection against copying to Congress. For the economy as a whole, *any* ability to realize monopoly profits from a creative innovation will have *some* positive effect on incentives to innovate. The policy question is whether the benefits of innovation outweigh the disadvantage of monopoly profits. For example, the current patent laws permit inventors to monopolize their products for 17 years. If a patent lasted 30 years, there would clearly be a greater incentive to innovate, but Congress has determined that benefit is not worth the cost of an additional 13 years of monopoly profits. Similarly, it is clear that more innovations in clothing and textile design would have occurred had the Fashion Originators' Guild been allowed to restrict competition; whether these gains are worth the cost are not matters capable of judicial determination.[16]

Moreover, even if protection for style design represents sound social policy, there are persuasive reasons why the Guild should not be allowed to do the protecting themselves (if style piracy were prohibited by Congress, injured Guild members would sue, rather than engage in a private boycott). Madisonian concerns about concerted discretionary power suggest that the appropriate response to anti-social conduct by rivals is to sue them, not to mount a boycott against them. Thus, in *Kiefer–Stewart Co. v. Joseph E. Seagram & Sons*,[17] the Court rejected the defendant liquor manufacturers' effort to justify their group boycott of wholesalers that were allegedly engaged in cartel pricing. The Court directed the defendants to rely on the government or private antitrust litigation if they were injured by the plaintiffs' cartel.

(2) Inferring an agreement to boycott.

Eastern States Retail Lumber Dealers' Ass'n v. United States[18] displayed an early sophistication regarding important concepts of conspiracy and boycott that the Court did not expressly articulate

---

The case also purported to rely on § 3 of the Clayton Act, which also deals with group boycotts. That section makes it unlawful "to make a sale ... on the condition ... that the ... purchaser thereof shall not use or deal in the goods ... of a competitor ...", where the effect ... may be to substantially lessen competition." 15 U.S.C. § 14. Although passage of § 3 may have influenced the evolution of § 1 doctrine, little difference exists between the two standards today and they are considered one for purposes of this discussion. Jefferson Parish Hosp. Dist. No. 2 v. Hyde, 466 U.S. 2, 10–11 (1984).

16. To use an extreme example, suppose that the nation's booksellers conspired to restrict the distribution of books to public libraries. There would doubtless be some marginal increase in profits (as some library patrons would purchase books instead of being "free readers"); it is hard to argue, though, that the benefits to society in terms of the slight increase in the number of books being written would outweigh the harm to the millions of Americans who would no longer be able to read desired books on loan from their libraries.

17. 340 U.S. 211, 214 (1951).

18. 234 U.S. 600 (1914).

until later opinions. In that case, the defendant widely circulated reports to lumber retailers identifying wholesalers that sold directly to ultimate consumers. The government did not have any direct evidence that the retailers had agreed to boycott these wholesalers. Rather, the Court inferred a group boycott from evidence that the reports identified these wholesalers, that the reports were referred to as "blacklists," that they publicized the retailers' objections to direct sales by wholesalers, and that their purpose was to persuade retailers to refuse to deal with these wholesalers.[19]

Having thus inferred the existence of a boycott, the Court affirmed the trial court's conclusion that preventing wholesalers from competing for retail business restrained competition. There was no legitimate justification for excluding wholesalers; in fact, the retailers seemed motivated by fears that—at least for some customers—wholesalers could offer competitive products at lower prices. Like *Montague*, the opinion's brief analysis reflects both economic and non-economic concerns, for the Court also held the boycott unlawful because it tended to prevent retailers from choosing with whom they wished to deal.

Eastern Lumber Retailers concluded that the exchange of information constituted a *concerted* refusal to deal because absent the boycott, some of the retailers would assuredly have continued to deal with wholesalers that offered lumber at reasonable prices.[20] By contrast, *Cement Manufacturers Protective Ass'n v. United States* [21] distinguished *Eastern Lumber Retailers* and concluded that the information sharing at issue there did not lead the members to jointly refuse to deal. In *Cement*, the Court upheld an information exchange disclosing orders placed by cement contractors. The purpose of the exchange was to protect cement manufacturers from a standard industry practice that gave contractors the option of accepting or rejecting promised cement, depending on fluctuations in the market. Because the Court viewed the contractors' practice as akin to fraud, the information exchange could have been perceived as a form of seller protection, rather than the exercise of economic power. Once a manufacturer

---

19. The defendants conceded that "the circulation of this information would have a natural tendency to cause retailers receiving these reports to withhold their patronage from the listed concerns." Id. at 609.

20. The Court emphasized that each lumber retailer had the "unquestioned right to stop dealing with a wholesaler for reasons sufficient to himself." Id. at 614. This individual privilege to refuse to deal was made more explicit in a decision handed down 5 years later, United States v. Colgate & Co., 250 U.S. 300 (1919). *Colgate* and its progeny are discussed infra in Chapter 5, section F.

21. 268 U.S. 588 (1925). The case is also discussed above in section G(1), supra.

learned that a contractor was acquiring excess cement, it would be in its own interest to refuse to deal, regardless what its rivals did.

(3) *Klor's* : accommodating non-economic concerns and justifying per se analysis.

Although *Addyston Pipe* may be the best reasoned opinion in support of making certain horizontal agreements per se illegal, *Klor's, Inc. v. Broadway–Hale Stores, Inc.*[22] may provide the best facts in support of summary condemnation. Broadway–Hale, a large San Francisco department store, secured the agreement of a host of appliance manufacturers to boycott Klor's, a small rival that operated next door to Broadway's then-prime downtown location. Broadway's defense was that the large number of competing retail stores selling appliances made it impossible for the boycott to decrease competition, and that the dispute was thus a "purely private quarrel" of no concern to the antitrust laws. On this basis, the trial court granted the defense motion for summary judgment. The Supreme Court reversed, holding that the concerted exclusion was illegal without regard to its particular effect on competition in a defined market.

Under standard market definition techniques, no one would find that Klor's exit from the market would harm competition. Yet, we might justifiably wonder why Broadway–Hale would bother going to all the trouble of arranging a multi-manufacturer group boycott unless it thought it could secure some competitive advantage from Klor's elimination. Often, especially in this heyday of economic analysis, we are too quick to assume that courts can easily and accurately define the appropriate market, and that the defendants' intent, and particularly their animus, is unreliable evidence of anticompetitive impact. *Klor's* suggests that the opposite may be true in some cases.[23]

---

22.   359 U.S. 207 (1959).

23.   Several other possible explanations for the boycott have been suggested. One is that the appliance manufacturers were all engaging in resale price maintenance and that Broadway–Hale was merely reporting that Klor's was discounting below the manufacturers' set prices. Klor's complaint, however, alleged a conspiracy among Broadway and the various manufacturers. If the defendants were engaged in an *Interstate Circuit* type of conspiracy (one retailer enters into an agreement with a number of manufacturers in order to harm another retailer), then the boycott was not merely vertical price fixing (discussed below in Chapter 5, section B) but a horizontal agreement to boycott the discounter, which is properly condemned as per se illegal. Subsequent lower court cases suggest that if Broadway–Hale had entered into an agreement with only one appliance manufacturer, a group boycott claim would not have been sustained. See, e.g., Oreck Corp. v. Whirlpool Corp., 579 F.2d 126 (2d Cir. 1978) (en banc) (permitting Sears and Whirlpool to agree that latter will not sell to plaintiff).

Others have suggested that Klor's was "free riding" on Broadway–Hale's services, by luring customers who had received helpful (and costly) information from the latter to then come to their store to purchase the identical

Klor's also nicely illustrates the continued importance of the non-economic goals of antitrust, especially where they do not conflict with economic goals. Suppose that the defendants were correct and that Klor's exit really would not hurt competition; rather, suppose that Broadway–Hale organized the boycott because of a personal feud between its downtown manager and Mr. Klor. The Jeffersonian concern with equality of opportunity and the Madisonian fear of discretionary power suggest that Broadway–Hale should not be able to use its economic clout with all the major appliance manufacturers to eliminate a rival, even for personal reasons.[24] It is true that such conduct neither affects the efficient allocation of resources nor exploits consumers, but *Klor's* prohibition on the use of concerted economic power to eliminate rivals helps small firms without harming the marketplace or consumers.

The stark facts of *Klor's* obviously do not exist in every case involving a concerted refusal to deal. Just as some horizontal agreements to fix price are ancillary to lawful purposes, some agreements not to deal with others are necessary to accomplish desirable economic results. These agreements should be upheld despite the Jeffersonian and Madisonian concerns so long as they benefit consumers. For example, when firms form joint ventures and exclude others, a firm challenging the exclusion may allege that the venturers are engaged in a group boycott, but the courts usually do not treat them as per se illegal. The leading case concerning the application of group boycott law to joint ventures, *Northwest Wholesale Stationers, Inc. v. Pacific Stationery & Printing Co.,*[25] is discussed below in section I.

(4) Setting standards and certification.

A discrete set of issues arise when concerted refusals to deal are ancillary to competitors' agreements to set standards and

goods at a discount. E. Thomas Sullivan & Herbert Hovenkamp, Antitrust Law, Policy and Procedure 315 (2d ed. 1989). Even if this were true, Broadway–Hale need not have secured an agreement among the appliance manufacturers to terminate Klor's; each manufacturer should have decided individually whether it wanted to tolerate free riders. (The legality of a vertical agreement between a single manufacturer and Broadway–Hale to terminate Klor's for free riding is discussed in Chapter 5, section C.) Moreover, this hypothesis suggests that Broadway–Hale did have some market power. If, as the defendants claimed, there were "hundreds of other household appliance retailers" in the area, 359 U.S. at 210, then Klor's could not possibly have been the only one "free riding" off Broadway–Hale. The free rider story takes on greater plausibility only if the market is more narrowly defined.

24. Separate concerns arise when concerted economic power is used to further political ends. Such cases require the courts to consider the interests in both competition and free speech; they have resulted in a wholly separate body of law. See Chapter 8, section B.

25. 472 U.S. 284 (1985).

certify products for their industry. Although many products are tested and certified by independent firms (such as Underwriters Laboratories), in many other industries the financial incentives and testing expertise remain with established firms. Agreements among these firms can provide the public with a real service: establishing uniform standards ensures minimum safety and quality standards and can also be essential for efficiency (by standardizing railroad width, for example) or consumer information (by making it easier to compare prices and ingredients). However, agreements can also pose real risks. For example, in *Allied Tube & Conduit Corp. v. Indian Head, Inc.,*[26] a new firm asked the trade association responsible for adopting the National Electrical Code to approve their plastic electrical conduits; the defendant, which manufactured metal pipes, packed the meeting with hundreds of members, and used walkie-talkies to instruct them on how to defeat the request.

Particularly sensitive issues about influencing the government arise in cases like *Allied Tube* where public agencies rely on private trade associations to enact legal requirements for products. When these concerns are not present, the courts have drawn a sensible line between permissible and impermissible standards and certification activity. In *Radiant Burners, Inc. v. Peoples Gas Light & Coke Co.,*[27] the Supreme Court held that an agreement among gas companies to sell natural gas only to customers using boilers approved by the American Gas Association was per se illegal. Although the per curiam opinion is terse, *Addyston Pipe* supports the result. If there are legitimate reasons why individual gas companies may not wish to sell to customers using non-approved equipment, each company can make this decision independently; an agreement is not necessary to achieve that lawful purpose. The Court's later opinion in *Professional Engineers* makes clear that an agreement cannot be justified by concerns that competition might lead to unsafe sales—that is a problem to be remedied by the government, not by private agreement.[28]

Similarly, in *Union Circulation Co. v. FTC,*[29] the Second Circuit sustained an FTC order that prohibited a group of firms which sold magazine subscriptions door-to-door from agreeing to refuse to hire any salesperson who had worked for a rival firm within the past year. The court applied a rule of reason analysis, because the agreement was not directed at controlling manufac-

26. 486 U.S. 492 (1988). The legal issues in this case concerned application of the *Noerr* doctrine, which is discussed in Chapter 8, section B.

27. 364 U.S. 656 (1961).

28. See National Soc'y of Professional Engineers v. United States, 435 U.S. 679 (1978), which is discussed in section D above.

29. 241 F.2d 652 (2d Cir. 1957).

turing or merchandising practices or at excluding competitors. The court noted that the signatories represented a significant segment of the industry, and that the agreement clearly had an anticompetitive effect in the labor market by "freezing" the labor supply. Significantly, the court rejected claims that the agreement was intended to prevent the hiring of salespeople who had engaged in deceptive sales practices with a former employer. The court noted that the agreement could be enforced against any salesperson, and thus "went beyond what was necessary to curtail and eliminate fraudulent practices." [30]

On the other hand, absent a sham (subjective standards really motivated by competitive animus, for example), seals of approval that merely provide information that firms can independently take into account serve a useful purpose without unnecessary agreement. Hence, *Structural Laminates, Inc. v. Douglas Fir Plywood Ass'n* [31] and other lower court decisions have sustained these agreements. Indeed, *Radiant Burners'* per se rule may reflect the Court's recognition that a seal of approval system is always a less restrictive alternative to a group boycott of non-standard products. [32] Hence, no elaborate rule of reason is required. [33] Defendants are in the best position to argue that a standard was legitimately adopted, and is therefore permissible under the rule of reason, when they delegate decision-making to those who do not compete with the applicant.

In many respects, the law concerning group boycotts parallels the law of price fixing. This is obviously as it should be. In a sense, price fixing is but one form of group boycott: firms jointly refuse to do business with others except at the fixed price. Thus, neither the reasonableness of its terms nor its arguably laudable non-competitive motives justify a group boycott. Where a concerted refusal to deal is ancillary to a lawful purpose, however, it may be sustained, so long as it is no broader than necessary to effectuate that purpose.

30. Id. at 657–58.

31. 261 F. Supp. 154 (D. Or. 1966), aff'd, 399 F.2d 155 (9th Cir. 1968), cert. denied, 393 U.S. 1024 (1969).

32. In *Allied Tube*, the Court cited *Radiant Burners* in observing that "private associations promulgat[ing] safety standards based on the merits of objective expert judgments and through procedures that prevent the standard-setting process from being biased by members with economic interests in stifling product competition ... can have significant procompetitive advantages," but that "[c]oncerted efforts to *enforce* (rather than just agree upon) private product standards face more rigorous antitrust scrutiny." 486 U.S. at 501 & n.6 (emphasis added).

33. See Arizona v. Maricopa County Medical Soc'y, 457 U.S. 332 (1982), which is discussed in section C(2) above.

Section I: Joint Ventures

Joint venture analysis provides further proof that the Supreme Court never really meant what it said in *Socony–Vacuum*, when it characterized any horizontal agreement tampering with price as per se illegal.[1] Joint ventures have never been condemned without some detailed analysis of their economic effects. Rather, courts have always recognized that joint ventures have the potential of being extremely beneficial to society and to the competitive process.

What is a joint venture? Because the term has positive connotations, many seek to fit their activities within its rubric.[2] Although there is no judicially accepted definition, a joint venture can be defined as a partial integration of production or distribution functions by firms that previously were separate. Each partner must make a substantial contribution to the venture (although that contribution might consist solely of cash). Joint ventures are thus distinguishable from cartels (where firms do not cooperate to jointly produce or market a product); the joint use of existing facilities (which adds nothing new to the market); and mergers (where firms integrate all their functions).

(1) The pros and cons of joint ventures.

Joint ventures are preferable to mergers for several reasons. First, many mergers do not result in new products or efficiencies; instead, they are consummated because of financial or tax considerations. Joint ventures, in contrast, usually result in new benefits to the economy. Second, while mergers eliminate one or more firms from the marketplace, joint ventures often increase the number of separate actors. For example, the General Motors–Toyota joint venture to produce the Chevy Nova meant that GM, Toyota, and the GM–Toyota joint venture all produce smaller cars. Finally, joint ventures allow smaller companies that do not wish to sacrifice their independence (a laudable objective from a Jeffersonian perspective) to achieve the economies of scale otherwise available only to their larger competitors. Joint ventures thus promote equality of economic opportunity.

Economists have also observed that joint ventures can be preferable to contracts between the parties to cooperate in produc-

1. United States v. Socony–Vacuum Oil Co., 310 U.S. 150, 221 (1940). The case is discussed in section B(2) above.

2. Timken Roller Bearing Co. v. United States, 341 U.S. 593, 597–99 (1951), properly cautioned that defendants (in that case, British and American interests that combined to allocate world markets) whose dominant purpose is to avoid all competition among themselves or with others will attempt to label their project a "joint venture." The case is discussed in detail in section E(2).

ing a product. Contracts can rarely anticipate all contingencies, and they give the parties a chance to behave "opportunistically" (in oversimplified terms, to change the rules of the game later when the other side is unable to do anything about it). Joint ventures can reduce these problems by making the firms partners.

Some joint ventures, however, can result in reduced competition. There are three principal ways in which joint ventures can harm competition. First, the venture can eliminate actual or potential competition among the members. This concern goes to the *formation* of the venture itself; where this problem exists, the antitrust remedy should be to dissolve the venture. Second, where only certain firms are allowed to participate in the venture and members have a significant competitive advantage over non-members, competition from non-members can be substantially reduced or eliminated. This concern focuses on *access* to the venture, and the members are often alleged to have engaged in a group boycott. In these cases, the venture itself would not be prohibited, but the remedy might be to require open or equal access. Finally, because joint ventures involve only partial integrations, it is important to remember that the parties are still competing against each other in other areas. The venturers might therefore enter into *collateral agreements* that restrain competition among themselves or between some of them and third parties. If so, an antitrust suit would not challenge either the formation of or access to the venture, but would ask the court to enjoin the collateral agreements, and to compensate the parties injured by them.

(2) Formation issues.

Formation issues in joint venture cases often implicate the classic trade-off, discussed earlier in Chapter 3, between costly duplication of service and competition. As an economic matter, the competitive price charged by separate competing firms will be lower than the monopoly price charged by a single seller if the rivals' duplicative costs are not significant. Where very significant economies of scale are present, however, consumers and the economy may benefit from creation of a joint venture, because the joint venture's cost savings will be so great that even its monopoly price will be lower than a competitive price charged by less efficient non-cooperating firms. In a world market, for example, the United States might prefer to avoid using duplicative American resources instead of enjoying the benefits of competition among U.S. firms. This preference for cooperation is reflected in the National Cooperative Research Act,[3] considered below. Al-

3. 15 U.S.C. §§ 4301–4305 (1984).

though cooperation may prove beneficial in the short term, however, those concerned with dynamic efficiency balk at ventures that significantly reduce rivalry among domestic firms, because they view domestic rivalry as essential to maintaining the incentive to innovate and the disincentive to sit still.[4]

United States v. Terminal Railroad Ass'n[5] involved a joint venture whose creation reduced competition. Under the guidance of leading robber baron Jay Gould, ownership of the three bridges by which trains could cross the Mississippi River between St. Louis, Missouri and East St. Louis, Illinois was consolidated into one joint venture formed by the dominant railroads. The joint venture proceeded to abuse its power to the disadvantage of non-member railroads, by acts such as fixing prices and charging discriminatory tariffs.

The fact that *Terminal Railroad* arose in the context of an industry subject to extensive regulation by the Interstate Commerce Commission gave the Supreme Court an easy way out of the efficiency/competition trade-off. By refusing to break up the venture and instead ordering that all comers be given fair access, subject to ICC oversight, the Court preserved the economies of scale of the venture while limiting monopolistic exploitation. Where such a regulatory regime is not readily available, however, the courts must choose: they can do nothing and allow the monopoly to continue unfettered; they can regulate the industry on a semi-permanent basis; or they can dissolve the joint venture and restore competition. The last option will usually be preferable.

Even where some cooperation is needed and a joint venture offers clear benefits to the economy, allowing any venture of any size is not necessarily desirable. This point is illustrated by *United States v. Columbia Pictures Industries, Inc. (Premiere)*.[6] In that case, Columbia, Universal, Paramount, and Fox were all dissatisfied with the market power exercised by Home Box Office (HBO), which dominated the market for pay television. Combining with a financial partner (Getty Oil), the four defendants—whose movies accounted for over half of the revenues paid by HBO and other cable networks for cable rights—embarked upon a joint venture, named Premiere, to compete with HBO in providing subscription cable movies. Their agreement provided that the four studios would each grant Premiere the exclusive cable rights

---

4. See Innovation, Rivalry, and Competitive Advantage: Interview with Professor Michael E. Porter, Antitrust (Spring 1991) at 5–10.

5. 224 U.S. 383 (1912).

6. 507 F. Supp. 412 (S.D.N.Y. 1980), aff'd without opinion, 659 F.2d 1063 (2d Cir. 1981).

to their movies for nine months. The district court enjoined the implementation of venture.

The initial portion of the court's analysis, which concluded that the venture was per se illegal, was seriously flawed. Although the court recognized that the venture was "an unusual price-fixing situation" because the partners were agreeing on the prices that they would be paid by their venture, the court nevertheless found that the agreement constituted price fixing.[7] The court thereby took an unduly narrow view of *Broadcast Music*, which rejected per se condemnation for price fixing by rival music composers that was necessary to produce a blanket copyright license for their compositions.[8] Although the license at issue in *Broadcast Music* was subject to continuing judicial scrutiny under a long-standing antitrust decree, the Justice Department had approved the license, and Congress had approved the concept of blanket licensing in the Copyright Act, those factors were not really critical to the Supreme Court's decision in that case. Rather, the key was that the defendants needed to fix prices in order to accomplish their legitimate purposes. Like *Broadcast Music*, the Premiere defendants were combining to offer a new product (a competitive cable movie network), and setting a price for their individual sales was a necessary component of that offering.[9]

The district court's desire to cram the studios' venture into the per se category may have been motivated by its fear that a judicial inquiry into whether the restraints were ancillary to a lawful purpose would entail years of discovery and litigation.[10] Yet the court's alternative holding, which actually examined the restraint under the rule of reason, adopted a sound approach that allowed for relatively summary treatment. The court emphasized that the venture was over-inclusive because its members had received approximately half the revenues paid by network programming services. There was no showing that a new entrant needed exclusive arrangements with four of the six major studios in order to compete with HBO. Moreover, the court concluded that the nine-month exclusivity provision was also broader than necessary to enable a new competitor to enter the market.[11] If, for example, Columbia and Fox were really interested in compet-

---

7. Id. at 426–27.

8. Id. at 427 (distinguishing Broadcast Music, Inc. v. Columbia Broadcasting System, Inc., 441 U.S. 1 (1979)). *Broadcast Music* is discussed in detail in section C(1) above.

9. The court's conclusion that the venture constituted a per se illegal group boycott, id. at 427–29, does not survive the analysis in *Northwest Wholesalers*, discussed below in subsection (3).

10. 507 F. Supp. at 429.

11. Id. at 431.

ing, instead of supplanting HBO as the primary cable movie network, they could have formed a smaller venture.

(3) Access issues: when the rule of reason applies.

In *Associated Press v. United States*,[12] member newspapers agreed to share news stories with each other. The government did not challenge the formation of the venture, but instead attacked the limits on access to the venture, whereby the partners were allowed to veto their rivals' membership. The Court struck down this restriction on membership because it gave members a "competitive advantage."[13] Language in Justice Hugo Black's plurality opinion suggests a per se analysis: citing *Socony*, he upheld the lower court's finding that the restrictions, "on their face, and without regard to their past effect, constitute restraints of trade."[14] Justice Black's analysis, however, indicates that he was really applying a rule of reason. Citing *Standard Oil*,[15] the origin of the rule of reason, he expressly distinguished cases where the venture did not possess economic power, noting that an exclusive story-sharing agreement between two small newspapers would be permissible. Sounding both economic and non-economic themes, Black noted that Associated Press (AP) members controlled 83% of daily newspaper circulation and that rivals could thus be denied equality of economic opportunity because of a rival's veto, without regard to the applicant's "individual 'enterprise and sagacity.' "[16]

The plurality's reliance on AP's market power[17] is apparent in light of a vigorous dissent by Justice Owen Roberts. Roberts argued (with no real dispute from Black) that AP's purpose was to promote the interchange of news and information and (with significant dispute from Black) that the arrangement did not have the effect of restraining competition among newspapers. Roberts pointed out that United Press, the International News Service, and 20–30 smaller reporting agencies were available alternatives to AP, and he cited the district court's finding that AP did not hinder non-member newspapers from obtaining access to the news.[18] If, in fact, rival papers could effectively compete with AP

12. 326 U.S. 1 (1945).

13. Id. at 17.

14. Indeed, Black went out of his way to ignore the trial court's finding, based on undisputed evidence, that the actual effect of the restriction was to impede the growth of rival newspapers. Id. at 12 & n.8.

15. Standard Oil v. United States, 221 U.S. 1 (1911).

16. 326 U.S. at 14.

17. Justice Felix Frankfurter provided the fifth vote to affirm the lower court's judgment against the defendants, but he wrote separately, emphasizing the critical role that the free and open dissemination of news play in our democracy. Of key import, he appears to have conceded *arguendo* that AP faced competition from rival news agencies. Id. at 28–29.

18. Id. at 32, 35–40.

members, then AP's access restrictions would be more akin to the hypothetical exclusive story-sharing agreement between two small papers which Black had approved.

Some have criticized the Court for requiring Associated Press to sell "its property" to others. This argument confuses agreements among competitors with decisions made by a single-entity.[19] If the property really belonged to Associated Press, i.e., if AP were not a joint venture but a separately owned company seeking to maximize overall profits, it might have chosen to accept as many subscribing members as possible. The joint venture, in contrast, was not interested in maximizing profits for AP but for its individual members. Thus, hypothetically, the vast majority of AP members might prefer to permit the *Daily Illini*, the University of Illinois' student newspaper, to join the venture so as to take advantage of both the membership fee it would pay and the insightful stories it would contribute, but the *Champaign–Urbana News–Gazette* might well veto its rival's entry into AP.

Although AP membership conferred a competitive advantage, Professors E. Thomas Sullivan and Herbert Hovenkamp argue that the advantage "accrued from the fact that they produced better news than anyone else."[20] This critique seems to imply that it is both unfair to make AP share its stories with others and bad economic policy to create such a disincentive to quality reporting. Their reasoning is not necessarily correct. The more plausible explanation for AP's "better" reporting was that it could cover more stories because it was simply bigger. Where a joint venture enjoys advantages due to economies of scale, so that breaking up the venture is not attractive, it is difficult to see how judicially mandated access would create inequity or discourage good work.

In *Northwest Wholesale Stationers, Inc. v. Pacific Stationery & Printing Co.*,[21] the Court made clear that the doctrine condemning group boycotts as per se illegal does not apply to concerted refusals to grant access to a joint venture. The Court also gave shape and content to the rule of reason analysis governing access refusals, imposing filters and exceptions to provide more focus than the kitchen-sink approach of *Chicago Board of Trade*.[22] The plaintiff in *Northwest Wholesalers* had been excluded from membership in a purchasing cooperative, and alleged that the exclu-

---

19. Cf. United States v. Topco Associates, Inc., 405 U.S. 596 (1972), discussed in section E(2).

20. Antitrust Law, Policy and Practice 341 (2d ed. 1989).

21. 472 U.S. 284 (1985).

22. For a critique of the open-ended rule of reason contained in Chicago Board of Trade v. United States, 246 U.S. 231 (1918), see Chapter 4, section A(3).

sion constituted a per se illegal group boycott. The Court disagreed. First, the Court narrowly limited its prior decision, *Silver v. New York Stock Exchange*,[23] which had held that excluding a broker from membership in the NYSE was per se illegal if the broker was not provided with due process prior to the exclusion. *Northwest Wholesalers* held that such an obligation was *sui generis* to self-regulating exchanges operating under the Securities and Exchange Act. If the challenged exclusion by the Northwest cooperative was unlawful, the Court wrote, "no amount of procedural protection would save it. If the challenged action would not amount to a violation of § 1, no lack of procedural protections would convert it into a per se violation."[24]

Second, *Northwest Wholesalers* noted that two important features of the group boycotts that had successfully been challenged in prior cases were absent in that case. Justice William Brennan's majority opinion described the prior precedents as limiting per se condemnation to exclusions that harm competitors by "either directly denying or persuading or coercing suppliers or customers to deny relationships the competitors need in the competitive struggle."[25] Brennan also read the prior cases as precluding per se condemnation when the venture puts forth "plausible arguments that [the challenged conduct was] intended to enhance overall efficiency and make markets more competitive."[26]

The opinion nonetheless suggested that certain types of exclusionary conduct would not require a full rule of reason analysis. It noted that plaintiffs could prevail by showing that the exclusion was primarily motivated by non-efficiency concerns or by anticompetitive animus. Such a determination, however, would be part of a rule of reason inquiry.[27] The Court also reaffirmed *Silver*'s holding that, absent special congressional sanction, rivals' exclusion of a competitor would be per se illegal when the rivals' joint venture was dominant or when the exclusion would put the plaintiff at a "severe competitive disadvantage."[28]

The disguised rule of reason analysis that prevailed in *Associated Press*, and the "exceptions" to per se analysis carved out in

23. 373 U.S. 341 (1963).

24. 472 U.S. at 293.

25. Id. at 294 (quoting Lawrence Sullivan, Antitrust 261–62 (1977)).

26. Id.

27. See, e.g., Gamco, Inc. v. Providence Fruit & Produce Building, 194 F.2d 484 (1st Cir. 1952). The defendant in that case was owned by produce wholesalers in Rhode Island, and operated the most favorable storage and shipping facilities along the New Haven Railroad. Demand for leased space exceeded supply, and Gamco's lease was not renewed. Gamco alleged that it was ejected because it was controlled by a large Boston firm, and that concerns about Gamco's creditworthiness were pretextual. The court held that under these circumstances, the defendant had the obligation to come forward with a legitimate justification for its action.

28. 472 U.S. at 295 n.6.

Northwest Wholesalers, demonstrate the artificiality of the dichotomy created by *Chicago Board of Trade* and its progeny between blanket condemnation as per se illegal and open-ended inquiry under the rule of reason. As the following discussion of professional sports leagues indicate, exclusion may be permissible even when the defendants have market power. The focus ought to be the inquiry set forth in the common law, as articulated in *Addyston Pipe*: is the exclusion necessary to accomplish some lawful purpose? Market power is highly relevant to this analysis for two reasons: exclusivity arrangements that might be ancillary to the purpose of allowing a venture to compete more vigorously against rival ventures may not be lawful when the venture does not face substantial competition; and the existence of such power increases the anticompetitive effects of denials of access. Thus, consumers may benefit from AP's exclusivity if it creates a more vigorous battle for news between AP and UP; consumers may be hurt, however, if virtually all the major newspapers are AP members and the net effect of the venture is to stifle new entry. Similarly, a purchasing cooperative's membership decisions should not be subject to antitrust liability if excluded firms can find alternative ways to compete with the cooperative's members; where no alternatives are available, competitive concerns—and the Sherman Act—come into play.

Cases involving professional sports league rules that impose restrictions on member clubs' hiring of players presaged *Northwest Wholesalers* in applying a rule of reason analysis in the context of joint venture activity. The facts of *Molinas v. National Basketball Ass'n*[29] provide an excellent reminder that labels such as "group boycotts" should not be used indiscriminately. In *Molinas*, professional basketball defendant's clubs all agreed not to employ the plaintiff, a former player who admitted that he had gambled on his own team. The district court recognized that a per se approach would lead to the absurd result of condemning every league disciplinary rule. The court upheld the NBA's actions, finding that an anti-gambling rule "seems about as reasonable a rule as could be imagined." The court added that in its view the rule's application to Molinas was reasonable.[30]

In *Smith v. Pro Football, Inc.*,[31] the D.C. Circuit similarly rejected per se condemnation of the National Football League

---

29. 190 F. Supp. 241 (S.D.N.Y. 1961).

30. Id. at 244. It seems inappropriate to make a league's liability for treble damages under the Clayton Act turn on whether a federal judge agrees with its determination that a player is the proper subject of discipline. However, a reasonableness test is useful in preventing clubs from using their monopsonistic power to arbitrarily exclude a player from the game or from using legitimate discipline rules as a pretext to punish a player for other reasons.

31. 593 F.2d 1173 (D.C. Cir. 1978).

rookie draft, whereby teams rotate in selecting college players and agree that only the drafting team will negotiate for the player's services. Although, as discussed in the next subsection, the court ultimately found the draft illegal under the rule of reason, it presaged *Northwest Wholesalers* by holding that the draft was not a "classic" group boycott. The court reached the right result, but articulated the wrong reasons.

The *Smith* court reasoned that group boycotts are not per se illegal unless they are designed to exclude competitors; because players seek to be employed by, and not to compete with, NFL owners, the group boycott rubric did not apply.[32] Excluding rivals, however, is only one way in which firms can conspire to exercise economic power. Where the players have no realistic alternatives, an agreement among league owners that results in only the Washington Redskins bidding for Yazoo Smith's services has the same effect as price fixing, and warrants per se condemnation unless it can otherwise be justified.[33]

The D.C. Circuit also found per se condemnation inappropriate because NFL clubs "are not *competitors* in any economic sense. The clubs operate basically as a joint venture in producing an entertainment product—football games and telecasts."[34] This statement is factually incorrect. NFL teams are separately owned and do not share profits or losses. Absent illegal agreements like the draft, NFL clubs would compete with each other for players, just as they compete for coaches and executives. A team with superior players is likely to win more games, enabling it to charge higher ticket prices and thus to increase its own profitability, separate and distinct from its profitability as a league member.

The court reached the correct result, however, because of the unique nature of sports leagues: each team is dependent on the continuing viability of rival teams. The court thus recognized that "[e]venly-matched teams make for closer games, tighter pennant races, and better player morale." Unlike competing retail stores, relative equality in football teams "maximiz[es] fan interest, broadcast revenues, and overall health of the sports."[35] Thus, agreements among these rivals can potentially increase efficiency and benefit fans; some forms of concerted refusals to deal can therefore allow rival clubs to compete against each other in the business and sporting sense, resulting in a more attractive product

32. Id. at 1182.

33. Cf. National Society of Professional Engineers v. United States, 435 U.S. 679 (1978) (per se illegal for engineers to agree that they will engage in price negotiations with contractors one at a time).

34. 593 F.2d at 1179 (emphasis in original).

35. Id. at 1176.

for fans. Such agreements should be evaluated under the rule of reason.

Because information-sharing agreements among newspapers, buying agreements among retailers, and league rules agreed to by sports teams have clear benefits to consumers, the antitrust laws should not mandate access to these ventures absent some showing of competitive harm. Where the evidence clearly shows that alternatives exist, so that rivals do not need access in order to compete, access limitations cause no real injury to competitors or competition. Even where the denial of access puts rivals at a competitive disadvantage, it may be necessary to a lawful purpose. Exploring the lawfulness of the purpose and the extent to which the exclusion is necessary to accomplish that purpose can be accomplished under a structured rule of reason, as described in the following section.

(4) Access issues: applying the rule of reason.

Not only was the rationale for the court's choice of rule of reason analysis flawed in *Smith v. Pro Football, Inc.*, but its application of the rule of reason also left something to be desired. The court seemed to feel obligated to enter the wilderness of the *Chicago Board of Trade* test, looking at all relevant evidence and balancing the "anticompetitive evils" of the agreement against its "pro-competitive virtue." [36] Correctly observing that the draft significantly restricts a player's bargaining power, the court then sought to weigh this disadvantage against the draft's competitive benefits. In doing so, however, the court adopted an unduly crabbed definition of competition. In its view, "competition" consists solely of encouraging new firms to enter the market and allowing existing firms to offer a product at lower cost.[37] This view, of course, ignores the possibility that an agreement may allow existing firms to offer a superior product at the same cost. The court erred, then, in analogizing the NFL's argument that market restrictions would best serve the public to the argument rejected in *Professional Engineers* that banning competition would protect public safety. The NFL's argument was economic, not social—that consumers would be better of *as consumers* because of the draft. Nonetheless, as more sophisticated subsequent judicial opinions demonstrate, the court again reached the correct conclusion. Because the draft "went beyond the level of restraint reasonably necessary to accomplish whatever legitimate business purposes might be asserted for it," [38] it was properly condemned as unreasonable.

36. Id. at 1183.

37. Id. at 1186–87.

38. Id. at 1183.

United States v. Realty Multi–List, Inc.[39] reflects increased judicial sophistication in applying a structured rule of reason. In that case, the government challenged a by-law adopted by a Georgia realtor's association that limited access to membership and to valuable information about homes for sale. The government particularly targeted provisions that required members to: (1) have a "favorable" credit report and "business reputation;" (2) keep a real estate office open during customary business hours; and (3) pay an initiation fee. Rejecting the government's argument that the by-laws were per se illegal, the Fifth Circuit remanded for further proceedings. First, the court noted that per se analysis was inappropriate because the defendants' cooperative multiple listing real estate service reduced information barriers between buyers and sellers and made the market work more effectively. Second, the court created a "facial unreasonableness" test to "reach and void on its face any significantly restrictive rule of a combination or trade association with significant market power, which lacks competitive justification or whose reach clearly exceeds the combination's legitimate needs."[40]

Applying this test, the court noted that Georgia law extensively regulated real estate brokers, that there was no showing that state regulation was inadequate, and that the credit and reputation provisions were unreasonably vague. The court also struck down the office-hours requirement, because of its discriminatory effect on brokers who operated primarily on evenings and weekends.[41] Finally, the Court recognized that the association could assess an initiation fee based on the cost of including the new member and recovering a pro-rata share of the expenditures for maintaining and developing the multiple listing service, but that a substantially larger fee would be unlawful.

The *Realty Multi–List* approach synthesizes *Addyston Pipe* and *Chicago Board of Trade* by labelling as per se illegal certain acts that clearly are not necessary to achieve a lawful purpose, while subjecting to the rule of reason horizontal conduct whose necessity can only be determined after a fuller inquiry. It departs from *Addyston Pipe*, however, by suggesting that a defendants' market power must be proven before the "facial unreasonableness" standard can be imposed. Under *Addyston Pipe*, agreements among rivals that are broader than necessary to achieve pro-competitive goals are illegal whether or not the defendants

39. 629 F.2d 1351 (5th Cir. 1980).

40. Id. at 1370.

41. Id. at 1380–85. Competition from part-time brokers, often women with substantial domestic responsibilities who seek supplementary household income, can be particularly irksome to established high-cost incumbents. An office-hours requirement works a particular hardship on these rivals.

have market power.[42]   *Realty Multi–List* offers no persuasive explanation for this deviation from *Addyston Pipe*.[43]

While *Realty Multi–List* struggled to incorporate Taft's approach into standard joint venture analysis, Judge Robert Bork's opinion for the D.C. Circuit in *Rothery Storage & Van Co. v. Atlas Van Lines, Inc.* [44] represents a bold effort to remake the law, only partly in Judge Taft's image.   *Rothery Storage* involved a joint venture formed by competing household goods van lines to operate under a common trademark (Atlas), to create a centralized system for setting rates and efficiently routing trucks back and forth throughout the country, to set uniform standards, and to advertise nationally.   Each independent line did its own local promotion and contributed to these national efforts.   The controversy concerned an agreement whereby each firm promised not to compete with the Atlas venture by independently offering household goods transportation services, and to exclude from the venture firms who violated this rule.[45]

Judge Bork conceded that the challenged restriction was literally a group boycott—an agreement among competitors not to compete with a rival.   Nevertheless, the court rejected the antitrust challenge, using a two-step approach.   First, Bork found that "the challenged restraint is ancillary to the economic integration of Atlas and its agents so that the rule of per se illegality does not apply."   Second, the restraint passed muster under the rule of reason "since Atlas' market share is far too small for the restraint to threaten competition or to have been intended to do so." [46] Bork conceded that the plaintiff would have prevailed under *Topco* because the restraint was literally a group boycott.   However, after summarizing Judge Taft's analysis in *Addyston Pipe*, Bork concluded that recent Supreme Court opinions (*BMI, NCAA,* and *Northwest Wholesalers*) had effectively resurrected Judge Taft's approach.

As this chapter indicates, had Judge Bork stopped there, *Rothery Storage* would represent an extremely positive contribution toward ending the "modern confusion" and restoring *Addy-*

---

42. Indeed, although the facts suggested that the defendants in *Addyston Pipe* had economic power, Judge Taft analyzed the case as if they did not. United States v. Addyston Pipe & Steel Co., 85 Fed. 271, 291 (6th Cir. 1898), aff'd, 175 U.S. 211 (1899).

43. For a more complete discussion of market power as a threshold factor under the rule of reason, see the discussion of the *Polk Brothers* case in Section E(3).

44. 792 F.2d 210 (D.C. Cir. 1986), cert. denied, 479 U.S. 1033 (1987).

45. Actually, Atlas' policy was to permit such competition if the rival business was conducted under the auspices of a separate corporation, with a new name, and if no Atlas facilities or services were used in the competing business. Id. at 213.

46. Id. at 214.

ston Pipe to its rightful place as the primary guidepost for analyzing horizontal restraints. As noted above,[47] Taft's approach transcends antitrust ideology, and represents the soundest means of distinguishing between desirable and offensive horizontal agreements, regardless of one's views on the goals of antitrust. Unfortunately, several aspects of *Rothery Storage* confuse and improperly seek to affix Bork's Chicago school imprint into the case law.

One troubling facet of the opinion may simply be due to lack of clarity. Bork wrote that, once an agreement is shown to be ancillary, reviewing courts should immediately proceed to the rule of reason analysis and uphold the agreement if the defendants do not have market power: "Analysis might begin and end with the observation that Atlas and its agents command between 5.1 and 6% of the relevant market."[48] Later, he reasoned that "[o]nce it is clear that restraints can only be intended to enhance efficiency rather than to restrict output, the degree of restraint is a matter of business rather than legal judgment."[49] These two statements could be read to suggest that the defendant can require the plaintiff to bear the difficult burden of proving market power under the rule of reason merely by making some plausible showing of a relationship between the challenged restraint and some other contract. As Judge Patricia Wald correctly observed in a concurring opinion, a true *Addyston Pipe* analysis would find that an overbroad restraint was not ancillary in the first place, thus preventing the defendant from invoking the rule of reason.[50] Although Judge Bork inexplicably failed to clarify this point in response to Judge Wald's observation, both intrinsic and external evidence suggests that Wald accurately captured Bork's meaning.[51]

47. See sections A(2) and C(3) above.

48. Id. at 217.

49. Id. at 229 n.11.

50. Id. at 231 n.4.

51. Part of the confusion may be due to the fact that, while *Addyston Pipe* suggests that reasonable restraints must be "ancillary" to a contract *and* no broader than necessary to achieve the purposes of the contract, Judge Bork conflates the analysis by defining "ancillary" to include the "no broader than necessary" standard.

Of course, the restraint imposed must be related to the efficiency sought to be achieved. If it is so broad that part of the restraint suppresses competition without creating efficiency, the restraint is, to that extent, not ancillary.

Id. at 224. Moreover, in other contexts Judge Bork has made it clear that a restraint which is broader than necessary is "naked" and hence per se illegal. See Antitrust Paradox 279 (to be lawful, agreements among rivals must be capable of increasing the effectiveness of economic cooperation between the parties and must be "no broader than necessary for that purpose"); *Paradox* Revisited: Interview with Judge Robert H. Bork, Antitrust (summer 1989) at 18 ("[I]f you have an actual integration in some sense but the restraint is broader than anything that the integration would justify, to that extent it is a naked restraint. You shouldn't put up with it.").

Rothery Storage also gratuitously attempted to implant the Chicago school's single-minded focus on efficiency onto horizontal restraint doctrine. Bork wrote that courts should inquire only about the effect of the agreement on output. If an agreement seems aimed at increasing output, it "must be designed to make the conduct of the business more efficient. No third possibility suggests itself." [52] Actually, a number of other possibilities suggest themselves. First, competitors might get together to lessen competition among themselves where demand for a good is highly inelastic: output will not decrease even if prices increase. This type of agreement leads to the exploitation of consumers, which many believe to be the chief evil of cartels. Second, rivals might agree to reduce competition in order to facilitate price discrimination—to charge higher prices to some customers and lower prices to those who are more price-sensitive. This type of agreement might even increase output somewhat, but it will still result in a massive wealth transfer from consumers to producers. Finally, venturers might reach agreements that have no effect on output but allow them to exercise discretionary power to exclude others for arbitrary or economically irrational reasons. The exercise of combined economic power for these purposes should also be condemned. Since none of these possibilities actually did suggest themselves in *Rothery*, Judge Bork's dictum was clearly obiter.

(5) Collateral restrictions.

The final major area of antitrust concern surrounding joint ventures relates to collateral restrictions imposed by joint ventures—i.e., those that involve something other than limitations on access. For example, in *Tyson's Corner Regional Shopping Center*,[53] the FTC challenged an agreement between a shopping center development and its "anchor" department store tenants that gave the department stores a compete veto over other tenants. The Commission did not challenge the formation of the joint venture, nor did it claim that rival stores needed to lease property at that particular shopping center in order to compete meaningfully in the market. Rather, the Commission struck down the tenant veto provisions as unnecessary to a lawful purpose. Reasonable restrictions on other tenants that might be necessary to maintain the center's attractiveness would be permissible. But a veto, the Commission reasoned, was inherently likely to deter smaller stores from vigorously competing with the major lessees.[54] This case is an example of "collateral restraints." Simply put, just as *Addyston Pipe* sustained restraints that are ancillary to a lawful

52.   792 F.2d at 221.   **54.**   Id. at 1008.
53.   85 F.T.C. 970 (1975).

purpose and necessary to bring about that purpose, *Tyson's* struck down restraints that are not ancillary and necessary to a lawful purpose.[55]

Even when the parties to a joint venture do not expressly agree on collateral arrangements, otherwise legitimate cooperation may have a "spillover effect" and inhibit vigorous rivalry in areas separate from the joint venture. In *United States v. Minnesota Mining & Manufacturing Co.*,[56] for example, the court condemned a joint venture where four dominant American manufacturers of coating abrasives combined to produce their product at overseas factories, and agreed not to independently export from the United States in competition with the joint venture. Judge Charles Wyzanski distinguished independent decisions to operate overseas factories, and found that the joint venture clearly reduced the number of American exports and therefore restrained foreign commerce. In addition, though, he noted in dicta that

> intimate association of the principal American producers in day-to-day manufacturing operations, their exchange of patent licenses and industrial know-how, and their common experience in marketing and fixing prices may inevitably reduce their zeal for competition *inter sese* in the American market.[57]

Although no case has ever used this reasoning to invalidate an otherwise legitimate joint venture solely because of spillover concerns, one case comes close. In *General Motors Corp. (GM/Toyota)*,[58] the FTC approved with modifications a consent decree that permitted the two automotive giants to form a joint venture to produce small cars in California. As in *Minnesota Mining*, one of the Commission's primary concerns was whether the effect of the venture was to reduce output by the parents. Thus, the FTC order limited the joint venture's annual production to 250,000 cars, lest GM be inhibited from continuing its own production of small cars.[59] The FTC was also concerned that the parties would exchange competitively sensitive information that was unnecessary to the legitimate purposes of the joint venture, and thus restricted the parties' ability to share certain designated informa-

55. The Commission held that Tyson's restraints were illegal per se. Id. at 1011–13. However, the FTC also indicated that it would approve reasonable restrictions, id. at 1009, while condemning those with clear anticompetitive effects that were broader than necessary, thus suggesting that the Commission (like the Supreme Court in *Associated Press*) used per se verbiage to condemn a restraint it found to be unreasonable.

56. 92 F. Supp. 947 (D. Mass. 1950), modified, 96 F.Supp. 356 (D. Mass. 1951).

57. Id. at 963.

58. 103 F.T.C. 374 (1984).

59. Id. at 383 (order limiting output of joint venture); id. at 387 (separate statement of Miller, C.) (explaining rationale).

tion.[60] The three-member majority who approved the decree apparently did not consider seriously the general spillover concern raised by Judge Wyzanski—that the very idea of GM/Toyota cooperation "may inevitably reduce their zeal for competition *inter sese*." In a forceful dissent, however, Commissioner Michael Pertschuk suggested that any benefits resulting from GM's partnership with a Japanese manufacturer (more efficient production of small cars or the opportunity to learn Japanese management techniques) could be obtained with significantly less antitrust risk by forming a venture with a smaller Japanese concern.[61] Pertschuk emphasized that the exchange of competitively sensitive information is inherent in a joint venture, with the inevitable result of reducing competition between the parties.[62] Commissioner Patricia Bailey reached a similar conclusion, noting that she "had trouble accepting this rosy picture of uncompromising competitors who will never be tempted to do each other favors." [63]

(6) Research and development ventures.

Special antitrust issues arise when joint ventures are created to engage in research and development. Congress enacted the National Cooperative Research Act to clarify the antitrust law's treatment of these ventures and to avoid deterring lawful ventures due to unwarranted fears of liability.[64] The Act codified existing law providing that joint ventures are not per se illegal, and provided extensive legislative history to guide the courts in applying a rule of reason.[65] Congress was particularly concerned that American firms remain competitive in developing new and innovative technologies necessary to compete in the international market, and felt that R & D joint ventures were effective ways of maintaining such global competitiveness.

The NCRA focuses primarily on formation issues, and shows the most concern with overinclusive ventures. The Act envisions that ideally American firms will form several competing joint ventures to pursue research and development. In this way, society realizes the benefits of economies of scale and cooperation while preserving the competitive pressure to be the first to produce successful innovations. At the same time, Congress reasoned that information about technology is generally global in scope, so that the "market" for R & D is international. The legislative history

---

60. Id. at 384, 387.

61. Pertschuk rejected the argument that Toyota's cost structure would enable it to produce American cars at significantly lower cost as "speculative" and "highly unrealistic." Id. at 389.

62. Id. at 390.

63. Id. at 395.

64. 15 U.S.C. §§ 4301–4305 (1984).

65. H.R. Conf. Rep. No. 1044, 98th Cong., 2d Sess. 8 (1984) (hereafter "NCRA Conference Rep.").

suggests, therefore, that joint ventures are probably legal it there are approximately five domestic or international firms or ventures with the ability and incentive to perform similar research.[66]

Recent work has suggested, however, that information moves more quickly within a nation's border than throughout the world. Moreover, contrary to the congressional understanding, those concerned with dynamic efficiency argue that a firm's fear of falling behind domestic rivals dwarfs other competitive incentives (international rivalry or the affirmative desire to profit from new inventions) in spurring innovation. Where domestic rivalry is maintained at a vigorous level and cooperation is limited to basic research, firms are more likely to aggressively innovate with the technology developed by the venture; if domestic rivalry declines or cooperation extends into production, concerns about falling behind are mollified and incentives to innovate are reduced.[67]

The NCRA exhibits only limited concern about access issues. In general, the Act seems to prefer that some firms be excluded from a venture, in hopes that they will go out and form their own, competitive R & D ventures. Congress recognized, however, that in some cases the R & D project will necessarily be such a large undertaking that it would be efficient to include almost all competitors within the same venture. In such cases, exclusion may be anticompetitive.[68]

Because R & D ventures almost always involve firms that actually or at least potentially compete in the market for the commercial fruits of their technological research, these ventures raise particular concerns about collateral restraints. The NCRA therefore excludes from its scope any side agreements that are neither related to marketing the proprietary information developed by the venture nor "reasonably required" (cf. *Addyston Pipe*) to prevent misappropriation of any relevant proprietary information.[69] Moreover, courts applying the rule of reason analysis required by the Act must consider the risk of express or tacit "spillover agreements" between the parties to the venture.[70] Firms that cooperate with one another in a venture are less likely to compete vigorously in the finished product market. Thus, a court might be skeptical of an automotive R & D venture between Ford and General Motors, where the benefits of cooperation could be achieved if each of the American giants formed a separate venture with foreign competitors with smaller domestic market shares.

---

66. Id. at 10.

67. See Porter interview, supra note 4, at 7.

68. NCRA Conference Rep. at 10.

69. 15 U.S.C. § 4301.

70. NCRA Conference Rep. at 11.

Whether or not the NCRA applies, agreements among venturers that have the effect of forestalling innovation will be deemed
illegal.   For example, in *Berkey Photo, Inc. v. Eastman Kodak
Co.*,[71] the court found Kodak and General Electric guilty of conspiring to restrain trade when Kodak, the market leader in
cameras, agreed to work with GE, a light-bulb manufacturer, to
develop a new light bulb compatible with Kodak cameras only if
GE would withhold the product for several years.   The court's
holding reflects an implicit empirical prediction that the threat of
antitrust liability would most likely have meant either that Kodak
would have proceeded forthwith in exploring new technologies
with GE, or that GE would have taken its business elsewhere.   In
either case, consumers would receive the benefits of competition—
new technologies brought to market as quickly as possible.   As it
was, consumers had to wait until marketing specialists at Kodak
determined that a previously developed technology had outlived
its usefulness.

———

Joint ventures have the potential to confer a variety of economic and social benefits on consumers and the economy.   These
ventures can threaten competition, however, when their formation
reduces actual or potential competition among the parties, when
access to the venture is critical to competitive success and is
denied to some, or when the parties agree to anticompetitive
collateral arrangements that are not necessary to realize the
benefits of the venture.   With increasing sophistication, the courts
are determining whether these concerns are real or non-existent
in a particular case, using a structured rule of reason designed to
focus the inquiry on the particular risks of harm to consumers and
the economy.

Section J: Private Indirect Purchaser Litigation

(1) Background.

As Judge Taft recognized in *Addyston Pipe*, a central feature
of the Sherman Act was its transformation of the law governing
contracts in restraint of trade: such agreements were no longer
merely void and unenforceable but were now criminal and tortious.[1]   In order to implement the tort element of this transformation, the antitrust laws allow any person "injured in his business
or property" by reason of an antitrust violation to recover treble

---

71.   603 F.2d 263 (2d Cir. 1979), cert.   **1.**   See section A(2), above.
denied, 444 U.S. 1093 (1980).

damages. (This language appears in its current form in § 4 of the Clayton Act).[2]

Allowing private recovery for tort-like damages is not aimed solely at compensating victims of antitrust wrongs. Senator John Sherman also recognized that criminal and civil antitrust enforcement by the Attorney General may not suffice to deter illegal conduct, and he envisioned the private remedy section as a means by which businesses could act as "private attorneys general" to vindicate the public good while they were sought redress for their individual injuries. To encourage such suits, he therefore proposed that successful plaintiffs be awarded multiple damages as well as attorneys fees.[3]

A host of legal issues arise concerning private enforcement under § 4. Generally, these issues are beyond the scope of this treatise. (Typically, time does not permit their discussion in basic antitrust courses, and commentary is best reserved for detailed treatises principally useful to experienced antitrust litigators.)[4] One particular issue of considerable academic as well as practical interest, however, concerns the question of which private plaintiffs should be able to sue when illegally inflated prices are passed through the chain of distribution from a manufacturer to the ultimate consumer.[5]

In *Hanover Shoe, Inc. v. United Shoe Machinery Corp.,*[6] one of United Shoe's customers filed a § 4 "piggybacking" on the government's challenge to the defendant's leasing practices.[7] The plaintiff sought treble damages for losses caused by the unlawful leasing practices. In response, United Shoe argued that the plaintiff was not "injured in his business or property" pursuant to

2. 15 U.S.C. § 15.

3. 21 Cong. Rec. 2457 (1890).

4. These issues include the definition of "business or property" under § 4, see, e.g. Reiter v. Sonotone Corp., 442 U.S. 330 (1979); standing to sue, see, e.g., Blue Shield of Va. v. McCready, 457 U.S. 465 (1982), and Associated General Contractors v. California State Council of Carpenters, 459 U.S. 519 (1983); the applicability of "in pari delicto" and unclean hands defenses, see, e.g., Perma Life Mufflers, Inc. v. International Parts Corp., 392 U.S. 134 (1968); the evidence required to prove damages, see, e.g., Bigelow v. RKO Radio Pictures, 327 U.S. 251 (1946); the availability of contribution in antitrust cases, see Texas Industries, Inc. v. Radcliff Materials, Inc., 451 U.S. 630 (1981); and the interstate commerce requirement, see, e.g., McLain v. Real Estate Bd. of New Orleans, Inc., 444 U.S. 232 (1980); Gulf Oil Corp. v. Copp Paving, 419 U.S. 186 (1974); Burke v. Ford, 389 U.S. 320 (1967).

5. Another litigation issue that this treatise does discuss is the requirement that a plaintiff establish "antitrust injury." This becomes critical in cases involving private merger enforcement, as well as in some other aspects of antitrust litigation. This requirement is considered in detail in Chapter 6, section D.

6. 392 U.S. 481 (1968).

7. See United States v. United Shoe Machinery Corp., 110 F.Supp. 295 (D. Mass. 1953), aff'd, 347 U.S. 521 (1954). The case is discussed in Chapter 3, section F(2).

§ 4 because the entire cost of any overcharge it had unlawfully imposed had been passed on to purchasers of the plaintiff's finished shoes. The Supreme Court rejected this defense.

United Shoe recognized that buyers would be injured if they absorbed the losses entirely, or maintained their own prices by cutting costs or volume. However, it argued that because the cost of shoe machinery represented only about 2% of the price of finished shoes and was borne equally by virtually every shoe manufacturer, and because the shoe manufacturing industry was intensely competitive, it was reasonable to conclude that Hanover Shoe had passed the entire cost down the line. The Court rejected this economic theorizing. As Justice Byron White wrote for the majority, determining what effect a change in prices has on total sales is very difficult "in the real economic world rather than an economist's hypothetical model."[8] Foreshadowing the key reasoning of later cases, the Court also noted that the defendant's argument would apply to all conceivable plaintiffs other than ultimate consumers, and "the buyers of single pairs of shoes would have only a tiny stake in a lawsuit and little interest in attempting a class action." Thus, "those who violate the antitrust laws by price fixing or monopolizing would retain the fruits of their illegality because no one was available who would bring suit against them."[9]

(2) The *Illinois Brick* decision.

In *Illinois Brick Co. v. Illinois*,[10] the state sought treble damages under § 4 because it had been victimized by a price-fixing conspiracy among brick companies. The defendants sold their products at inflated prices to masons; the masons incorporated these inflated prices when they bid to be subcontractors on major public construction projects; general contractors incorporated these inflated subcontract bids in bidding on public projects; and the end result was that a number of projects cost the taxpayers a lot more than they should have. The defendants argued that the principle of *Hanover Shoe* should be applied to plaintiffs as well as defendants—that the plaintiff should not be permitted to argue that the direct purchaser (here, the masons) passed on the cost of higher prices. The Supreme Court agreed. In ruling for the defendants, the Court first concluded that plaintiffs and defendants seeking to invoke the pass-on theory must be governed by identical rules. Second, it held that the *Hanover Shoe* rule was preferable to allowing both sides to make pass-on arguments.

8. 392 U.S. at 493.

9. Id. at 494.

10. 431 U.S. 720 (1977).

The Court gave three reasons why the *Hanover Shoe* rule should apply to both plaintiffs and defendants. First, the Court felt that symmetry was necessary to avoid multiple liability. Without symmetry, both the brick masons and the state could sue the defendants and recover the full amount of the overcharge.[11] Second, the Court was concerned that judicial analysis of pass-on arguments would increase the complexity of antitrust litigation in a manner equally unwarranted in both contexts.[12] Third, and most important, the majority argued that the private attorney general rationale underlying § 4 is best served by keeping all relief in the hands of the direct purchaser. The direct purchaser has the most to gain because its recovery is most direct, but its incentives to sue would be reduced if (a) it must spend the time and money necessary to litigate the pass-on issues, and (b) its recovery will likely be diminished in whole or in part by awards to indirect purchasers.[13] This last argument, which has sparked considerable academic debate and is very difficult to evaluate empirically,[14] is the key to understanding the opposing sides of this issue.

The *Illinois Brick* dissenters, in contrast, believed that the majority's approach "flouts Congress' purpose and severely undermines the effectiveness of the private treble-damages action as an instrument of antitrust enforcement." Specifically, they were concerned that a price-fixer might retain its ill-gotten profits if the direct purchaser chose not to sue: "[i]njured consumers are precluded from recovering damages from manufacturers, and direct purchasers who act as middlemen have little incentive to sue suppliers so long as they may pass on the bulk of the illegal overcharges to the ultimate consumers."[15]

From the dissent's perspective, the first two justifications offered by the majority lose much (though not all) of their force. First, if one does not believe that the policies underlying § 4 are served by concentrating all possible relief in the hands of the direct purchasers, a variety of procedural techniques are available to reduce the risk of duplicative liability by limiting awards to direct purchasers if and when the court awards judgment to

---

11. Id. at 730.

12. Id. at 731–32.

13. Id. at 737–47.

14. Compare Robert Harris & Lawrence Sullivan, Passing on the Monopoly Overcharge: A Comprehensive Policy Analysis, 128 U. Pa. L. Rev. 269 (1979), with William Landes & Richard Posner, Should Indirect Purchasers Have Standing to Sue Under the Antitrust Laws? An Economic Analysis of the Rule of *Illinois Brick*, 46 U. Chi. L. Rev. 602 (1979), and Landes & Posner, The Economics of Passing–On: A Reply to Harris and Sullivan, 128 U. Pa. L. Rev. 1274 (1980).

15. 431 U.S. at 749 (Brennan, J., dissenting).

indirect consumers.[16]   Second, as the government argued in an *amicus* brief supporting the plaintiffs,

> it is one thing to say that [the practical difficulties in proving the extent of passing on] should not be allowed to defeat recovery by a person who clearly paid illegal overcharges (as in *Hanover Shoe*) and quite another to say (as petitioners do) that because a plaintiff in an antitrust case will have a hard time proving his case, he should not even be allowed to try.[17]

Supporters of *Illinois Brick* would respond that the combined self-interest of direct purchasers and plaintiffs' antitrust lawyers will mean that few price-fixers go unpunished.   Critics see direct purchasers enjoying cozy long-term relationships with manufacturers that they are unlikely to want to disturb by filing suit if the overcharge was passed on to someone else.

(3) Exceptions to the bar on indirect purchaser suits.

The Supreme Court has identified several specialized situations where indirect purchasers might be allowed to recover treble damages.[18]   In *Illinois Brick*, the Court noted that the bar on indirect purchaser suits should not apply when the direct purchaser is owned or controlled by the manufacturer.[19]   In its prior *Hanover Shoe* decision, the Court had also indicated that pass-on issues could be raised (for both defensive and offensive purposes) when "an overcharged buyer has a pre-existing 'cost-plus' con-

16. Justice Brennan assumed that a court simultaneously trying cases brought by direct and indirect purchasers would reduce the judgment awarded to the former by the amount awarded to the latter. The risk of multiple liability also exists when direct and indirect purchasers are litigating in different courts, or when one group files suit after an award has already been made in a prior case. Separate contemporaneous suits can be dealt with by transferring jurisdiction to allow for consolidated proceedings and by using statutory interpleader. Given the length of most private price-fixing cases and the four-year statute of limitations, it is unlikely that many plaintiffs will be able to delay filing their claims until another category of purchasers completes its litigation. See id. at 762–65.

17. Brief for the United States, Illinois Brick Co. v. Illinois, 431 U.S. 720 (1977), at 6.

18. *Illinois Brick* has been held inapplicable to suits for injunctive relief under § 16 of the Clayton Act. 15 U.S.C. § 27. Obviously, neither the need to determine the degree of injury nor the risk of multiple liability is present in these cases. See, e.g., Mid–West Paper Prods. Co. v. Continental Group, Inc., 596 F.2d 573, 589–94 (3d Cir. 1979).

19. 431 U.S. at 736 n.16. Subsequent lower court decisions have expounded on this exemption, permitting indirect purchaser suits when the conspiracy includes both horizontal price fixing by the manufacturers and resale price maintenance agreements with the middlemen.   In this situation, the plaintiff consumer technically *is* a direct purchaser (from the middleman-conspirator). See, e.g., Arizona v. Shamrock Foods Co., 729 F.2d 1208 (9th Cir. 1984), cert. denied, 469 U.S. 1197 (1985). To avoid risk of multiple liability, some courts have required joinder of the middleman in such cases. See, e.g., In re Beef Indus. Antitrust Litigation, 600 F.2d 1148, 1161–63 (5th Cir. 1979), cert. denied, 449 U.S. 905 (1980).

tract, thus making it easy to prove that he has not been damaged." [20]

Kansas and Missouri v. Utilicorp United, Inc.[21] gave a narrow construction to the cost-plus exception. In that case, various producers of natural gas allegedly conspired to fix prices. They were sued by two sets of plaintiffs, one representing public utilities (the direct purchasers) and the other consisting of several state attorneys general, who sued on behalf of residential consumers and state agencies (indirect purchasers, who bought gas from the public utilities). The lower courts concluded that *Hanover Shoe* and *Illinois Brick* were fully applicable and thus dismissed the states' complaint. The court of appeals held that the gas producers could not defend against the utilities' claim on the ground that the utilities had passed on the cost of the overcharge to consumers, and the state attorneys general therefore could not pursue their claims on behalf of the indirect purchasers. The states sought review in the Supreme Court, where the judgment was affirmed.

The states made two primary arguments in the Supreme Court. First, they maintained that concerns about the complexity of apportioning damages do not apply in cases involving utilities that are subject to the typical pattern of rate regulation—where the state agency allows regulated firms to pass their costs on to consumers. The Court responded that the utilities might well be damaged even in those cases, both because they might lose business as a result of the overcharge and because they might have been able to raise their rates to the same level even without the overcharge, thus pocketing the additional profit. The first argument has some merit, but the second does not. Consumers may well use less natural gas, even in the short run, when faced with inflated prices; thus, the utilities will lose business (and profit).[22] The Court's other argument, though, requires antitrust judges to assume that state regulators are not doing their jobs. The goal of simplifying antitrust proceedings calls for the opposite assumption.

Second, the states argued that there was no risk of duplicate damages because the utilities' claim for lost profits was not identical to the consumers' claim for the costs of purchasing overpriced gas. The Court did not directly reject this argument, for good reason. Antitrust violations often cause injury at different levels of the marketplace. For example, a decision by psychiatrists,

20. 392 U.S. at 494.

21. 110 S.Ct. 2807 (1990).

22. Even so, the task of estimating the effect of inflated prices on consumer demand is somewhat easier than estimating the amount of the overcharge that will be passed on to consumers compared to the amount that will "eaten" by the middleman.

working in concert with an insurer, to boycott psychologists injures both the psychologists (lost profits) and patients (higher prices for psychotherapeutic services), yet both victims can sue.[23] Rather, the Court emphasized its concern that indirect suits would add increased complexity to antitrust litigation. Specifically, the majority noted that indirect suits weaken private antitrust enforcement by complicating it, and opined that utilities have incentives to sue overcharging suppliers. In making the latter argument, the Court reasoned that state regulators might not allow inflated gas prices if the utilities did not vigorously pursue antitrust claims, and suggested that the utilities could probably keep monies over and above actual damages for themselves.[24]

Cases involving overcharges paid by regulated utilities demonstrate the key analytical role played by the court's assessment of who is the best plaintiff to bring a private damages action. In *Utilicorp*, the utilities were vigorously prosecuting their direct purchaser claims from the outset. The Court viewed them as the best plaintiffs, and therefore did not wish to diminish their incentive to sue by complicating the litigation. In a similar case brought by the Illinois attorney general, in contrast, the utilities did not file their claim until it appeared that the indirect purchasers' action was faltering.[25] In that case, Judge Posner—whose academic writings vigorously defended *Illinois Brick* [26]—wrote the en banc court of appeals opinion holding that the indirect purchasers could pursue their claims.[27] Similarly, Justice Byron White (the author of *Illinois Brick*) wrote the dissent in *Utilicorp*, joined by the three Justices who had dissented in *Illinois Brick*. White's dissent argued that the indirect purchasers *should* be able to sue because the utilities were unlikely to have an incentive to recover the overcharge passed on to consumers.[28]

(4) Indirect purchaser suits under state antitrust law.

In *California v. ARC America Corp.*,[29] a number of direct and indirect purchasers sued a group of cement manufacturers to recover damages caused by price fixing in that industry. The complaints sought recovery under § 4 of the Clayton Act for

23. See, e.g., Blue Shield of Va. v. McCready, 457 U.S. 465 (1982); Virginia Academy of Clinical Psychologists v. Blue Shield of Va., 624 F.2d 476 (4th Cir. 1980), cert. denied, 450 U.S. 916 (1981).

24. 110 S.Ct. at 2816.

25. Illinois ex rel. Hartigan v. Panhandle Eastern Pipe Line Co., 852 F.2d

891, 895 (7th Cir.) (en banc), cert. denied, 488 U.S. 986 (1988).

26. See supra note 14.

27. Id. The defendants subsequently prevailed at trial. 730 F.Supp. 826 (C.D. Ill. 1990), aff'd, 935 F.2d 1469 (7th Cir. 1991).

28. 110 S.Ct. at 2821.

29. 490 U.S. 93 (1989).

violations of the Sherman Act, and also sought recovery for state law violations, which the federal court considered under the doctrine of pendent jurisdiction. The indirect purchasers based their claims on amendments to the state antitrust laws passed in response to *Illinois Brick*.[30] The defendants sought to bar their claims, and the lower courts agreed, holding that the Sherman Act as interpreted in *Illinois Brick* pre-empted state law.

The Supreme Court reversed without dissent,[31] holding that none of the accepted grounds for preemption were applicable. First, the Sherman Act did not expressly preempt state law.[32] Second, Congress intended that the Sherman Act supplement, not displace, a long tradition of state common law and statutory remedies against monopolies and unfair business practices. Finally, nothing in *Illinois Brick* suggested a congressional purpose to limit recovery under state law. The concerns expressed in that decision about introducing undue complexity into federal antitrust litigation have no bearing on a state's decision whether to complicate or simplify its own state court litigation. (The Court specifically noted that federal courts could decline pendent jurisdiction.[33]) And, while allowing indirect purchasers to bring state claims would have some adverse effect on direct purchasers' incentives to pursue Sherman Act claims, the Court dismissed that concern because it had no limiting principle: *any* state law claims could threaten the federal plaintiff's ability to recover by lessening the funds available for settlement or judgment. Nevertheless, the Court noted, concerns about multiple liability have not led to preemption of state causes of action involving conduct that can also be challenged under federal statutes.[34]

---

30. See also id. at 98 n.3 (listing similar statutes in other states).

Similar efforts to overturn *Illinois Brick* in Congress have been unsuccessful. In 1979, the Senate Judiciary Committee favorably reported such legislation by a vote of 9–8, see S. Rep. No. 239, 96th Cong., 2d Sess. 61 (1979), but it has yet to pass either House.

31. Justice White, the author of *Illinois Brick*, wrote the opinion. Justices Stevens and O'Connor did not participate.

32. Cf. National Cooperative Research Act, 15 U.S.C. § 4303(c) (expressly preempting state law for certain research and development joint ventures).

33. See 28 U.S.C. § 1367(c)(2) (giving district courts discretion to decline jurisdiction over state claims where state law issues "predominate").

34. 490 U.S. at 104.

CHAPTER 5: VERTICAL RESTRAINTS

Vertical restraints are agreements between firms at different levels of the chain of distribution, ranging from the original supplier of basic components to the retailer who sells the finished product to the ultimate consumer. Most antitrust litigation challenging vertical restraints has centered on agreements between a manufacturer and its wholesalers and/or retailers that limit the conditions under which the manufacturer's product is available at the retail level. Probably the most controversial debate over antitrust doctrine today concerns vertical restraints. These agreements provoke the sharpest disparity between Chicago school efficiencianados and neo-populist advocates who seek to maintain consumer surplus. Because a lenient policy toward vertical restraints is consistent both with maximizing manufacturers' discretion to conduct their affairs as they see fit and with promoting the interests of small retailers who enjoy the benefits of these agreements, the debate features an ironic alliance between Posnerian conservatives and Brandesian liberals.

Vertical restraints take a number of forms. *Resale price maintenance* (or *vertical price fixing*) involves agreements between a manufacturer and its retailers that fix the minimum price at which retailers will sell the manufacturer's product. Other agreements are classified generally as *non-price restraints* and include various restrictions on the retailer's ability to sell a product to customers other than those designated by the manufacturer. For example, *exclusive territorial agreements* permit the retailer to sell only to customers within a designated geographic area. *Location clauses* permit the retailer to sell to any customer but only from a retail outlet in a designated area. Thus, a location clause would permit a retailer to lure a customer from another area into its store, which would be prohibited under an exclusive territorial arrangement. An even less restrictive non-price vertical restraint is a *profit pass-over clause*. This contractual provision permits a retailer to compete for all business; however, where sales are made outside its designated *primary area of responsibility*, the retailer must compensate the dealer in whose area the sale was made for a pro rata share of the promotional, warranty, or other local investments that the designated has made.

Because one's evaluation of vertical restraints depends so heavily on one's economic and political approaches to antitrust, this Chapter begins with an analysis of the conflicting approaches. Next, three kinds of vertical restraints—resale price maintenance, non-price restrictions, and maximum price fixing—are examined. Two sections that follow then discuss whether and when consignment agreements and refusals to deal constitute lawful unilateral conduct on the part of the manufacturer, and when they represent unlawful agreements in restraint of trade. Finally, this Chapter discusses two types of vertical practices that raise similar antitrust concerns because of their capacity to foreclose competitors from suppliers or markets: tied sales and exclusive dealing arrangements.

Section A: Basic Economic and Political Concepts

(1) The Chicago school approach.

Efficiency advocates generally believe that vertical restraints are rarely anticompetitive and should be treated leniently by the antitrust laws. They conclude that vertical restraints can lead to inefficiencies only in narrow circumstances, if at all. For example, where these restraints are employed by most of the manufacturers in an industry otherwise prone to collusion,[1] they can facilitate a manufacturers' cartel. Where the manufacturers control retail competition, a rebel manufacturer cannot easily explain away discounting at the retail level (where it is most open to detection); thus, cheating on the cartel becomes easier to detect and harder to accomplish. Widespread vertical restraints may also reflect express or tacit collusion by retailers, who use manufacturers as their pawns to jointly reduce retail competition and allow cartel-level profits at the retail level.

On the other hand, efficiency advocates argue that, absent their widespread use in an industry prone to collusion, vertical restraints usually benefit competition. A particular brand of a product might be most effectively marketed on a local level if a retailer engages in heavy advertising or promotional activities or provides point-of-sale services like attractive and informative showrooms or high quality warranty repair service. Yet an individual retailer may be reluctant to invest in advertising, showrooms, or a service department if a competing discount retail outlet can offer the same product at a lower mark-up because it has not incurred these expenses. The discounter, in such a case, would be "free riding" on the full-service retailer's promotional

1. See Chapter 4, section G(3) for a discussion of the clues that Judge Richard Posner suggests are useful in determining a market's propensity for collusion.

activities that benefit both consumers and other retailers. It may therefore be efficient to allow restrictions on retail competition to overcome the reluctance of full-service retailers to invest in promoting a manufacturer's product.[2]

It is important to keep in mind that efficiency analysts approach this issue with a view that private firms should be free to conduct their business as they see fit unless their conduct clearly causes a restriction on output and a consequent misallocation of society's economic resources. In the area of vertical restraints, Chicago school economists argue that a manufacturer maximizes profits by collecting the highest possible wholesale price and then ensuring that the most efficient retail system is implemented. Once its wholesale price has been set, the reasoning goes, the manufacturer prefers the lowest possible retail mark-up because a lower retail price means increased sales and higher manufacturer revenues.[3] This analysis concludes that unless a manufacturer is coerced by a conspiracy of retailers to restrict competition (as discussed in Chapter 4, section E(2), such a horizontal conspiracy would be per se illegal[4]), or unless the use of vertical restraints is widespread in an oligopolistic industry with high entry barriers, we can safely assume that most restraints are efficient and should be tolerated.

(2) Non-economic concerns.

Non-economic concerns about vertical restraints have changed dramatically over time. In the early part of the century, retailers were almost uniformly small independent businesses. Vigorous competition resulted from the entry of larger retail outlets, such as corporate-owned department stores. Vertical restraints often served to protect the smaller retailer from being put out of business by the larger concerns, and thereby promoted equality of economic opportunity. Thus, Louis Brandeis, prior to his appointment to the Supreme Court, unsuccessfully lobbied for legislation amending the Sherman Act to legalize these restraints.[5]

Retailers were better received in the state capitols. California enacted the first state law in 1931 authorizing "fair trade" contracts, which prohibited resale "except at the price stipulated by the vendor."[6] Congress sanctioned these laws by passing the Miller–Tydings Amendment in 1937, which amended § 1 to permit

2. See Richard Posner, Antitrust Policy and the Supreme Court: An Analysis of the Restricted Distribution, Horizontal Merger and Potential Competition Decisions, 75 Colum. L.J. 282, 285 (1975).

3. Id. at 283.

4. United States v. General Motors Corp., 384 U.S. 127 (1966).

5. See Thomas McCraw, Rethinking the Trust Question, in Regulation in Perspective 46–52 (T. McCraw ed. 1981).

6. Cal. Stats. 1931, p. 583.

"contracts or agreements prescribing minimum prices for the resale of trademarked goods" when such contracts were lawful under state law.[7] Congress was particularly concerned that large retail outlets were selling certain items as "loss leaders" to attract business. This practice according to the Senate Committee Report, "operates as a fraud on the consumer, destroys the producer's goodwill in his trade mark, and is used by the large merchant to eliminate his small independent competitor ... [and] unquestionably has had a disastrous effect upon the small independent retailer, thereby tending to create monopoly." [8]

Popular support for fair trade laws continued into the 1950s. The original fair trade laws were ineffective if discounters could obtain a product without signing the manufacturer's no-discount contract. Some states responded with "non-signer" provisions that required all retailers to adhere to fixed prices when any retailer had signed a fair trade contract. In *Schwegmann Brothers v. Calvert Distillers Corp.*,[9] the Supreme Court construed Miller–Tydings to apply only to actual contracts signed by a cooperating retailer, and struck down these "non-signer" provisions. Congress responded with the McGuire Act, again amending § 1 to permit these provisions.[10]

The controversy continues. In the 1970s, faced with growing pressure from a consumer movement opposed to fair trade laws and inflation blamed in part on these laws, most states repealed their fair trade laws and Congress enacted the Consumer Goods Pricing Act, repealing both the Miller–Tydings and the McGuire Acts.[11] More recently, the Reagan Administration issued Vertical Restraint Guidelines that took a very permissive approach to of these restraints; Congress responded with a resolution expressing its view that these guidelines did not reflect "an accurate expression of the Federal antitrust laws or Congressional intent." [12] Today, a Madisonian objection to giving manufacturers discretionary power to fix the kind and level of local retail competition for their products, combined with traditional concerns about maintaining the independent freedom of entrepreneurs, has led advo-

7. 50 Stat. 693 (1937). The amendment was attached as a rider to unrelated legislation affecting the District of Columbia, to overcome opposition from President Roosevelt. Roosevelt was concerned about rising retail prices, and the FTC warned that this legislation would lead to abuse. See I The Legislative History of the Federal Antitrust Laws and Related Statutes 461 (E. Kintner, ed. 1978).

8. S. Rep. No. 257, 75th Cong., 1st Sess. 2 (1937). By contrast, a Canadian commission characterized loss-leader selling as competitive pricing that had no significant anticompetitive effect. Restrictive Trade Practices Commission, Report on an Inquiry into Loss-Leader Selling 249 (1955).

9.   341 U.S. 384 (1951).

10.   66 Stat. 631 (1952).

11.   89 Stat. 801 (1975).

12.   99 Stat. 1136, 1169–70 (1985).

cates of non-economic antitrust goals to oppose most vertical restraints.[13]

(3) Protecting consumers from higher prices.

The desire to protect ultimate consumers from higher prices has resulted in significant skepticism about the benefits of vertical restraints, as well as a belief that these restraints allow manufacturers and dealers to force consumers to pay for unwanted services and promotional activities. Neo-populists argue that at least two scenarios cast doubt on the Chicago school assumption that absent a dealer or manufacturer cartel, any vertical agreement must reflect an efficient system of retail distribution. First, one or more major, high-cost retailers may fear competition from discounters, not because they are afraid that the discounters will free ride on their promotional activities, but merely because they wish to protect their own high mark-ups. These powerful, entrenched retailers (such as anchor department stores that sell a large amount of a manufacturer's product in many different markets) may effectively end vigorous retail competition by independently coercing individual manufacturers. Second, where high-cost retailers offer competing brands of goods and consumers are easily influenced by sales employees (such as buyers of electrical or kitchen appliances), these retailers can force manufacturers to agree to inefficient vertical restraints by threatening to steer customers to other brands.[14]

Vertical restraints can also cause a significant wealth transfer from consumers to the manufacturer by facilitating a scheme whereby retailers provide, at the manufacturer's direction, point-of-sale promotions and services that most consumers do not want. These consumers are "inframarginal"—that is, they would have been willing, if necessary, to pay more for the product than the prior price, and thus they previously enjoyed a significant "con-

13. See, e.g., Lawrence Sullivan, Antitrust 376 (1977).

14. Critics of vertical restraints also question their efficiency when the effect is to facilitate advertising and other promotions that increase product differentiation. The validity of this argument depends on one's view of the desirability of advertising and product differentiation. The critics argue that these business practices provide consumers with little valuable information but serve mainly to create phony brand loyalties, thus allowing firms to raise prices above the competitive level. (For example, Anheuser–Busch, which uses exclusive territories, can raise the price of its Michelob brand super-premium beer by both national and local ads designed to convince consumers, without actually improving its product, that "weekends are made for Michelob.") Defenders of advertising argue that neither policymakers nor courts can identify what advertising information is "valuable" to consumers. If it makes a consumer happy to drink Michelob on weekends, even if they have to pay more to do so, why should this be an antitrust concern? A fuller analysis of this issue accompanies the discussion of the *Procter & Gamble* merger case in Chapter 6, section B(2).

sumer surplus." Suppose, for example, that Sony Trinitron television sets enjoy special brand loyalty among many affluent purchasers, and one million consumers buy these sets each year at a price of $500. Under such circumstances, Sony could agree with selected dealers to restrain retail competition in Sony television sets (through resale price maintenance, exclusive territories, or other agreements) so that the retail price would increase to $600; in return, the dealers would agree to provide attractive showrooms with knowledgeable sales personnel in order to entice more consumers to purchase a Sony. We know from basic economics that, all else being equal, fewer sales will be made if the price rises. Suppose that, sure enough, 200,000 price-sensitive consumers switch to other brands or decide to keep their current set instead of paying $600 for a new Sony. But all else is not equal, for the new showrooms and knowledgeable salespeople attract 200,000 new consumers, who would not have paid $500 for a Sony without these extra amenities. If the cost of the showrooms and personnel is less than $100 per set, Sony and its dealers are better off. From an efficiency point of view, no harm is done, for the same one million televisions are sold. From a consumer perspective, though, 800,000 Sony loyalists are paying $100 more for services they do not want.[15]

Arguably, the antitrust laws should not prohibit vertical restraints that harm inframarginal consumers, because manufacturers can cause similar injury without imposing these restraints. To return to the Sony example, consumers would be equally harmed if Sony unilaterally initiated a national advertising blitz and raised it wholesale price by $100. Because of the administrative impossibility of distinguishing advertising campaigns that actually benefit the majority of consumers by providing useful information from those that harm inframarginal consumers, the antitrust laws properly would not scrutinize Sony's decision in that case. Antitrust doctrine has, however, frequently evaluated and proscribed joint conduct even though administrative reasons prevent scrutiny of similar unilateral behavior. For example, monopoly pricing by a monopolist is not scrutinized, whereas identical pricing by a cartel is a criminal offense. As discussed in section G of this Chapter, a firm with economic power can charge a monopoly price for a very desirable product, but cannot attempt to increase profits or sales by tying the sale of that product to the sale of a separate product. If a principal goal of antitrust doctrine is to maximize the well-being of the majority of Americans, and if the antitrust laws can prevent harm to most consumers by prohibiting certain types of contracts, neo-populists conclude that condemning of

---

15. See generally William Comanor, Vertical Price–Fixing, Vertical Market Restrictions and the New Antitrust Policy, 95 Harv. L. Rev. 983 (1985).

restraints whose net effect is to harm inframarginal consumers is fully justified.

Interestingly, vertical restraints constitute one area where Chicago school adherents appear relatively sanguine about the courts' ability to distinguish between pro- and anticompetitive conduct. They agree with advocates of other antitrust philosophies that harms occur when vertical restraints are imposed by a manufacturer acting as a tool of a group of conspiring dealers.[16] Yet, they argue, such a plan can easily be condemned as a horizontal agreement among retailers. But such an agreement may not be so easy to prove. For example, in 1905 competing retail drug stores settled a civil government complaint charging them with conspiring to fix prices in medicines manufactured by the Dr. Miles company.[17] Six years later, the case reached the Supreme Court in private litigation based purely on a vertical price-fixing theory because the plaintiff was unable to prove a horizontal conspiracy.[18] Perhaps none existed, but perhaps the collusion simply evaded proof. How one resolves this issue will probably turn on which of the scenarios set forth in the preceding paragraphs seems most plausible.

Section B: Resale Price Maintenance

The preceding discussion did not differentiate among the various forms of vertical agreements that manufacturers and retailers might employ. Antitrust law, in contrast, draws a sharp distinction between different types of restraints: although most vertical restraints are judged under the rule of reason, those deemed to constitute price restraints (resale price maintenance) are per se illegal. Evidence that a manufacturer and a dealer agreed that the dealer would maintain a certain price or price level means certain victory for the plaintiff; unlike the approach taken with respect to horizontal restraints, the defendant cannot raise any defenses or justifications.

(1) The per se rule of *Dr. Miles*.

This doctrine of per se illegality was first established by the Supreme Court in its 1911 decision in *Dr. Miles Medical Co. v. John D. Park & Sons Co.*[1] Park, a leading discounter in home

16. See, e.g., Valley Liquors, Inc. v. Renfield Importers, Ltd., 678 F.2d 742, 743 (7th Cir. 1982) (Posner, J.).

17. United States v. National Ass'n of Retail Druggists, No. 10593 (D.C. Ind., May Term 1907).

18. Dr. Miles Medical Co. v. John D. Park & Sons Co., 220 U.S. 373 (1911).

1. 220 U.S. 373 (1911).

medicines, challenged Dr. Miles' elaborate contract system that made it difficult for Park to obtain Dr. Miles' products. Preliminarily, the Court rejected Dr. Miles' claim that its wholesalers and retailers were its consignment agents. The Court found that the consignment agency agreements were really sham transactions, and that the wholesalers and retailers were not truly agents of Dr. Miles.[2]

On the merits, the Court noted that an agreement among the retailers to fix the price of Dr. Miles' products would clearly have been illegal. The Court also observed that the beneficiaries of the resale price fixing were the retailers, rather than Dr. Miles' consumers.[3] The Court therefore concluded that resale price maintenance was per se illegal, and that the public should receive the benefits of retail competition in Dr. Miles' products.[4]

Dr. Miles argued that, because it had the right to choose whether or not to sell its product, it could condition its sales as it saw fit. The Court responded by invoking the property law doctrine of unreasonable restraints on alienation.[5] This doctrine limits a seller's ability to restrict the conditions upon which its property can be resold. Of course, only unreasonable restraints violated the common law of property, but the Court concluded, for the reasons stated above, that the restraints at issue there were unreasonable.

Justice Oliver Wendell Holmes' dissent presaged the Chicago school's argument in favor of resale price maintenance. Because ready substitutes existed for Dr. Miles' medicines, Holmes reasoned, consumers would have taken their patronage elsewhere if they were being harmed by unduly high prices. Thus, he concluded that Dr. Miles' decision to maintain resale prices could be assumed to reflect what was best for consumers.

Chief Justice Charles Evans Hughes' majority opinion did not respond to this economic argument, but instead rested on its analogy to horizontal price fixing among retailers. The Hughes–Holmes debate was a precursor to the modern controversy surrounding the antitrust laws. Hughes, for the majority, saw the antitrust laws as protecting the freedom of independent discounters to price as they saw fit, and skeptically assumed that the resale price maintenance scheme arose out of some exercise of economic power on the part of the dealers. Holmes' dissent saw the antitrust laws as interfering with manufacturers' freedom to

---

2. Id. at 395–98. For a discussion of the legal consequences of genuine consignments, see section E below.

3. Id. at 407.

4. Id. at 406.

5. Id. at 404–05.

price as they saw fit, and assumed that competition in the marketplace would check any attempt to exploit economic power.

(2) Analysis.

At the risk of sounding like a broken record, the question posed by Judge Taft in *Addyston Pipe*—whether an agreement is ancillary and necessary to a lawful purpose—serves to focus the modern debate on the per se illegality of resale price maintenance.[6] Defenders of resale price maintenance (RPM) argue that it is really akin to a joint marketing venture between a manufacturer and its retailers, and is thus always ancillary to a lawful purpose—whether it be attracting high quality retailers, inducing retailers to promote the manufacturer's product aggressively, or providing an incentive for dealers to maintain point-of-sale services. Because without market power RPM cannot possibly harm consumers, these defenders argue that RPM should be analyzed under a rule of reason and that the courts should not bother with determining whether the restraint is necessary.

Critics of resale price maintenance question whether it is inevitably ancillary to any of the lawful purposes cited by its defenders. Many manufacturers use RPM even though their retailers engage in minimal promotion and no point-of-sale services.[7] Their effect is converse to that of horizontal maximum price-fixing agreements (discussed in Chapter 4, section C): RPM skews the market toward non-price competition and away from price competition, even if consumers would prefer the latter. Finally, dealer promotions often do not provide consumers with useful information but merely serve to create illusory differences among product brands that allow manufacturers to raise prices.[8]

6. As Professor Herbert Hovenkamp explains, the focus of the common law was evolving at the turn of the century from trader freedom to consumer protection. The Sherman Act and the Classical Theory of Competition, 74 Iowa L. Rev. 1019 (1989). Indeed, a number of common law precedents sanctioned resale price maintenance. Id. at 1060 n.256 (citing cases). The Supreme Court even enforced one contract that included a resale price maintenance covenant, although the plaintiff's injury was caused not by discounting but by the defendant's breach of another covenant not to sell at all in territories reserved exclusively for the plaintiff. See Fowle v. Park, 131 U.S. 88 (1889). The textual discussion applies the standard articulated in of *Addyston Pipe*, rather than the actual methodology used by the common law courts. As discussed in chapter 4, Judge Taft's opinion in *Addyston Pipe* is to be commended more for its doctrinal soundness than for its fidelity to the various contemporary common law decisions.

7. Manufacturers of boxed candy and blue jeans are notable examples of firms that have engaged in resale price maintenance under these circumstances. See Milton Handler, Harlan Blake, Robert Pitofsky & Harvey Goldschmid, Cases and Materials on Trade Regulation 650–51 (3d ed. 1990).

8. See William Comanor, Vertical Territorial and Customer Restrictions: White Motor and Its Aftermath, 81 Harv. L. Rev. 1419 (1968).

Whatever the standard, should resale price maintenance be judged more harshly than other forms of vertical restraints? Judge Richard Posner thinks not. He argues that RPM not only has potential benefits, but in some respects is less restrictive than exclusive territories. For example, resale price fixing still allows competing retailers to engage in significant non-price competition, whereas exclusive territorial agreements eliminate all intra-brand retail competition within the designated area.[9]

In *Continental T.V., Inc. v. GTE Sylvania Inc.*,[10] the Supreme Court took the opposite view, concluding that resale price maintenance is worse than non-price vertical restraints. The Court reasoned that resale price maintenance, unlike non-price restraints, "almost invariably" reduces price competition among competing brands, not just among the retailers that sell a single brand.[11] In explaining this conclusion, Dean Robert Pitofsky has observed that discounting occurs not only where a manufacturer wants to increase its own market share, but also where retailers put pressure on manufacturers to lower the wholesale price because they are anxious to increase their own sales by offering discounts to retail consumers. Resale price maintenance schemes remove any incentive for retailers to apply this pressure, because the retailers' inability to pass on the discount means that they cannot increase their market share. Moreover, Pitofsky asserts that resale price maintenance is an ineffective way of inducing dealers to perform desired promotional services; he argues that either direct contractual terms requiring such services, or profit pass-over clauses to prevent free-riding, would accomplish the

---

9. The Next Step in the Antitrust Treatment of Restricted Distribution: Per Se Legality, 48 U. Chi. L. Rev. 6, 9 (1981). Another motive, never advanced by defendants or prominently argued by most legal scholars, may underlie certain resale price maintenance schemes. Contrary to fundamental assumptions of basic economics (the higher the price, the fewer the sales), some producers may find that lower prices reduce sales by projecting an inferior image for the product. (This problem did warrant some attention in the 1930s when Fair Trade legislation was enacted, in part to stop the "loss leader" practice of retailers offering certain goods at substantial discounts. See note 8 in section A(2), supra.) Perfume is one obvious example. The disdain for discounting reflected in the challenged termination of the plaintiff Business Electronics Corp. v. Sharp Electronics Corp., 485 U.S. 717 (1988), may be another. In that case, Sharp had entered the market as a low-cost manufacturer of business machines; after enjoying some success in that field, it embarked on an advertising campaign designed to upgrade its image and compete against the more established, expensive manufacturers, and it may have feared that low prices by a discount retailer would soil its image. Thanks to my friend Ron Snider for this insight.

10. 433 U.S. 36 (1977). The case is discussed below in section C(2).

11. Id. at 51 n.18 (citing White Motor Co. v. United States, 372 U.S. 253, 268 (1963) (Brennan, J., concurring)).

manufacturer's legitimate goals in this area.[12]

This debate leads to several possible conclusions about resale price maintenance. One is that RPM is ancillary to a lawful purpose, and thus should always be evaluated under the rule of reason. Another is that RPM schemes are never related to a lawful purpose or one so unlikely to meet that standard that courts should presume them illegal. Yet a third argument was cited by *Sylvania*: congressional actions in recent years demonstrate continued legislative support for the per se rule against vertical price fixing.[13] This fairly strong evidence of congressional intent suggests that, regardless of the policy implications, resale price maintenance should remain per se illegal as a matter of statutory construction.

Section C: Non–price Restraints

(1) Initial approaches.

Fifty-two years after *Dr. Miles*, *White Motor Co. v. United States*[1] gave the Supreme Court its first opportunity to rule on the legality of non-price vertical restraints.[2] In that case, the government challenged White Motor's scheme of assigning specific dealers the exclusive right to sell its trucks within a specified geographic territory, reserving to itself the exclusive right to sell to governmental entities. The syllogistic logic of the government's case was flawless. Horizontal allocations of territories are per se illegal (see *Timken Roller Bearing*);[3] vertical restrictions have the same effect as horizontal agreements among dealers (see *Dr. Miles*),[4] and therefore vertical territorial allocations are per se illegal.

Nevertheless, the government lost. Justice William O. Douglas' majority opinion broke the syllogism by denying the minor premise: vertical restraints are not just like horizontal restraints and do not inevitably have the same effect as dealer cartels, the Court held. In Douglas' view, the Court's horizontal restraint

---

12. The *Sylvania* Case: Antitrust Analysis of Non–Price Vertical Restrictions, 78 Colum. L. Rev. 1, 15–17 (1978).

13. *Sylvania*, 433 U.S. at 51 n. 18. Subsequent to *Sylvania*, Congress passed an appropriations rider preventing the Reagan Justice Department from advocating the overruling of *Dr. Miles*, Pub.L. No. 98–166, § 510 (1983); it reenacted these riders in 1987 and 1988, Pub.L. Nos. 99–1005, § 605, 100–202, § 605, and then adopted a "sense of Congress" resolution that reaffirmed

the validity of the per se rule. Pub.L. No. 99–180 (1985).

1. 372 U.S. 253 (1963).

2. Dr. Miles Medical Co. v. John D. Park & Sons Co., 220 U.S. 373 (1911), held that vertical price fixing was illegal. See section B(1) above.

3. Timken Roller Bearing Co. v. United States, 341 U.S. 593 (1951).

4. 220 U.S. at 408.

decisions reflected an empirical assumption that agreements among competitors have no purpose but to harm competition. In contrast, vertical arrangements are not inherently illegitimate. Rather, a vertical territorial limitation "may or may not" have purposes other than stifling competition. The majority therefore took a cautious approach. The Court opined that non-price restraints "may be too dangerous to sanction or they may be allowable protections against aggressive competitors or the only practical means a small company has for breaking into or staying in business." Because "[w]e need to know more than we do about the actual impact of these arrangements on competition," the majority held, these restraints should be more carefully evaluated under the rule of reason.[5]

The need for both greater tolerance and more careful scrutiny of non-price restraints had been demonstrated several years before *White Motor* in *Packard Motor Car Co. v. Webster Motor Car Co.*[6] In the mid–1950s, Packard was well into a losing effort to remain competitive with the Big Three auto manufacturers when Zell, Baltimore's leading Packard dealer, threatened to quit unless it became Baltimore's only Packard dealer. Packard complied and terminated Webster, which then challenged the exclusive arrangement under § 1. The D.C. Circuit reversed a jury verdict in favor of the plaintiff and directed a judgment for Packard. The court emphasized that Packard faced a small and declining market share, and that the company already had sole distributors in many cities, including several of Baltimore's size.[7] The court could have noted that greater tolerance was also appropriate because Packard needed assurance that at least one dealer in each metropolitan area could sell its cars and make a profit.

The court of appeals also indicated that the fact that the dealer had sought the exclusive arrangement was irrelevant.[8] Experience and hindsight demonstrate that this suggestion is too simplistic. In cases less stark than *Packard*, it may be difficult to determine whether a restriction will boost sales or simply boost dealer prices and profits. Although the fact that the dealer sought protection from competition is not dispositive, sound antitrust policy would permit the courts to condemn exclusive agreements where the evidence suggested that the manufacturer "knuckled under" to a powerful dealer's threats even though its product could have been marketed successfully by several dealers.

---

5. 372 U.S. at 263.

6. 243 F.2d 418 (D.C. Cir.), cert. denied, 355 U.S. 822 (1957).

7. Id. at 420–21.

8. Id. at 421.

(2) *Schwinn's* formalism.

Taking its direction from the Court's decision in *White Motor*, the Antitrust Division's attack on an exclusive territorial system implemented by the Schwinn bicycle company was based on the rule of reason. Culminating in a brilliant Supreme Court brief written by Assistant to the Solicitor General Richard Posner, the government argued that the defendant's system was unreasonable because, *inter alia*, it allowed Schwinn to stifle intrabrand competition by effectively preventing discount retailers from obtaining its product. Intrabrand competition was particularly important, the government argued, because Schwinn was perceived as the "Cadillac" of the industry.[9]

The government won the case, *United States v. Arnold, Schwinn & Co.*,[10] but on grounds far different from those advanced in its briefs. In its opinion, the Court resurrected, and then incorrectly applied, the property law doctrine against restraints on alienation, condemning part, but not all, of the Schwinn plan. Specifically, the Court held that non-price vertical restraints are per se illegal when title has passed to the retailer. However, when the goods have legitimately been consigned to the retailer and title remains with the manufacturer, there is no restraint on alienation and the restrictions were to be evaluated under the rule of reason.[11]

As the Court was later to acknowledge,[12] critics had a field day with *Schwinn*. Its holding that legitimate consignments should be reviewed under the rule of reason was inconsistent with *Dr. Miles* and other precedents, which suggested that restraints a principal places on its agent are not agreements at all for purposes of § 1.[13] *Schwinn*'s decision to bar all exclusive territorial restrictions when title had been transferred as restraints on alienation was also incorrect, for the Court ignored the common law's flexible condemnation of only *unreasonable* restraints. At least in *Dr. Miles*, Chief Justice Hughes had presented a reason (dealer cartels) why the Court felt that vertical price restraints were unreasonable. *Schwinn* failed to explain what had happened in the four years since *White Motor* to change the Court's view of exclusive territorial restraints. Indeed, language in the portion of *Schwinn* that sustained these restraints when part of a legitimate consign-

9. Brief for the United States at 36, United States v. Arnold, Schwinn & Co., 388 U.S. 365 (1967) (No. 66–25) [hereafter "*Schwinn* brief"].

10. 388 U.S. 365 (1967).

11. Id. at 379–80.

12. Continental T.V., Inc. v. GTE Sylvania Inc., 433 U.S. 36, 48 n.13 (1977).

13. See section E below.

ment arrangement indicated that the Court had not actually convinced itself that these agreements were so bad.[14]

(3) *Sylvania* : balancing benefits and harms.

Schwinn's life was short, for in 1977 it was overruled in *Continental T.V., Inc. v. GTE Sylvania Inc.*[15] In so doing, the Court created the current dichotomy between price restraints, which remain illegal per se, and non-price restraints, which are illegal only if a court so finds under the rule of reason. In the majority opinion, Justice Lewis Powell first decided that non-price vertical restraints, in the abstract, had sufficient potential to promote interbrand competition that they deserved careful analysis on a case-by-case basis.[16] This is the same approach, albeit with an opposite result, as that employed by Justice Thurgood Marshall in his earlier *Topco* opinion where Marshall decided, in the abstract, that horizontal market division agreements were so inherently anticompetitive that they should be categorically condemned, even if a particular restraint might not be pernicious.[17]

Sylvania's facts provided an excellent vehicle to justify Powell's conclusion that the challenged restraint ought not be condemned categorically. Sylvania's share of television sales had declined to as low as one or two percent when it began to include location clauses in its distribution agreements.[18] Handy Andy, Sylvania's Sacramento dealer, had done remarkably well in promoting the product, gaining a 15% local market share.[19] The restriction seemed to be having the desirable, pro-competitive impact of increasing sales of Sylvania products and allowing Sylvania to compete more effectively against the larger television manufacturers. It was thus apparent to the Court that vertical restrictions should not be treated the same as their horizontal counterparts: they could simultaneously decrease intrabrand competition among Sylvania dealers and stimulate interbrand competition between Sylvania retailers and retailers of other brands.[20] Thus, a balancing of the harms and benefits was required.[21]

---

14. 388 U.S. at 379–80 (per se condemnation would "severely hamper smaller enterprises resorting to reasonable methods of meeting the competition of giants ... and it might sharply accelerate the trend toward vertical integration of the distribution process").

15. 433 U.S. 36 (1977).

16. 433 U.S. at 57–58.

17. United States v. Topco Associates, Inc., 405 U.S. 596 (1972). See Chapter 4, section E(2) above.

18. 433 U.S. at 38.

19. Id. at 39 n.6.

20. Id. at 51–52.

21. Cf. id. at 57 n.27 (rejecting plaintiff's argument that "balancing intrabrand and interbrand competitive effects" was not a proper judicial function).

Justice Byron White concurred in the judgment, believing that the use of location clauses by a firm like Sylvania that had only a small market share was clearly distinguishable from the rigid territorial restraints imposed by the

Unfortunately, the Court has not revisited this area to clarify how the courts should proceed under the rule of reason to balance reduced intrabrand competition against increased interbrand competition. The result has been considerable doctrinal confusion with the outcome depending in large measure on judicial acceptance of the plaintiff's theory as to why the restraint is unreasonable.

For the Reagan Justice Department, the *only* way that vertical non-price restraints harm competition is by facilitating collusion. By limiting the number of retailers, non-price restraints might facilitate a cartel among the remaining retailers, or make it easier for a pre-existing manufacturers' cartel to detect cheating. As the Department's Vertical Restraints Guidelines [22] correctly observe, vertical restraints will facilitate collusion only if three conditions are met: (1) the use of significant vertical restraints is widespread in the industry (otherwise, any cartel will be defeated by unrestrained retailers selling rival brands); (2) the market is concentrated (otherwise, cartels are unlikely), and (3) there are barriers to entry (otherwise, new firms will enter once prices go up).

Sylvania did not suggest, however, that this is the only scenario under which non-price restraints might harm competition. Indeed, *Sylvania* called for a more open-ended approach when it endorsed a process of balancing the reduced competition for the defendant's brand with the benefits in the larger market. [23]

"Cadillac" of the bicycle industry and condemned in *Schwinn*. Thus, he believed that it was premature for the Court to overrule a precedent of relatively recent vintage. Id. at 67–72. Although Justice White may have been correct as a matter of *stare decisis*, a more careful examination of vertical non-price restraints under the rule of reason represents sound antitrust policy. Vertical restraints are potentially pro-competitive even when imposed by firms that enjoy significant market share or brand loyalty; in fact, in some cases even rigid exclusive territoriality may be necessary to achieve a manufacturer's legitimate marketing objectives.

22. 4 Trade Reg. Rep. (CCH) ¶ 13,105 at 20,581 (1988).

23. The majority opinion noted that "[e]conomists ... have argued that manufacturers have an economic interest in maintaining as much intrabrand competition as is consistent with the efficient distribution of their products." 433 U.S. at 56 (citing Robert Bork, The Rule of Reason and the Per se Concept: Price Fixing and Market Division [II], 75 Yale L.J. 373, 403 (1966), and Richard Posner, Antitrust Policy and the Supreme Court: An Analysis of the Restricted Distribution, Horizontal Merger and Potential Competition Decisions, 75 Colum. L. Rev. 282 (1975)). But the opinion did not endorse this view, which would suggest per se legality, or at least a highly limited rule of reason, rather than the open-ended balancing approach the Court adopted. Rather, the majority recognized that this view was not universally shared. Id. at 56–57. Indeed, manufacturers might adopt inefficient distribution schemes for a number of reasons: to facilitate cartelization; to appease powerful dealers; to increase product differentiation, which may allow prices to rise significantly above cost; or simply to enjoy the quiet life. As Professor Lawrence Sullivan observed, economics does not teach that businesses will always make efficient decisions. Rather, the "only economic

Where neither the manufacturer nor the authorized retailer has market power, any effort by the manufacturer or its retailers to exploit the reduced intrabrand competition will be checked by the availability of substitutes.[24] If the authorized retailer(s) have market power (suppose the major manufacturers permit only the large department stores to handle their sales), non-price restraints can eliminate vigorous price competition among brands, and can channel sales exclusively to high-priced outlets.

Similarly, when vigorous interbrand competition among manufacturers does not exist, consumers benefit from intrabrand competition, and the reduction of this competition therefore warrants careful antitrust scrutiny.[25] Intrabrand competition protects consumers from exploitation in a variety of ways. First, and most notably, where a market features highly differentiated products with strong brand loyalty, the lack of intrabrand competition can lead to higher prices because dealers do not compete with one another for the patronage of brand-loyal consumers and have no incentive to pressure the manufacturer to lower prices so as to increase sales. Second, where products are sold through retailers

law of relevance is that which says that *if* competitive conditions are maintained, the market will tend to select out for favor those firms which make the best decisions." Antitrust 382 (1977) (emphasis in original).

24. 433 U.S. at 52 n.19.

Professor William Comanor has suggested that, regardless of the current level of interbrand competition in a market, vertical restraints encourage promotional activities that have the principal effect of decreasing interbrand competition by increasing product differentiation. Vertical Territorial and Customer Restrictions: *White Motor* and Its Aftermath, 81 Harv. L. Rev. 1419 (1968). Justice Powell rejected this argument in *Sylvania*, calling it "flawed by its necessary assumption that a large part of the promotional efforts resulting from vertical restrictions will not convey socially desirable information about product availability, price, quality, and service." 433 U.S. at 56 n.25. Consider, though, most beer advertising, and the extent to which it conveys information about price, quality, and service, as opposed to biographical sketches of retired athletes and appeals to prurient interest. On the other hand, Comanor's argument raises the troublesome spectre of the government determining what information is useful

to consumers (price? calories?) and what information is not (does beer taste great? is it less filling?).

Justice Powell did not dispute, however, Comanor's further claim that promotional efforts can increase entry barriers. Thus, even assuming Comanor is wrong about the extent to which promotional efforts convey socially desirable information, the harm caused by advertising should at least be considered in evaluating the benefits to interbrand competition cited by the defendant. For example, the interbrand competitive benefits of promotions on behalf of established dealers with significant market shares, especially where designed to attract brand loyalty, may be outweighed by the harms Comanor identified.

25. Congress apparently agrees. Recent legislation included a "sense of the Congress" resolution declaring that the narrow focus of the Reagan administration's Vertical Restraints Guidelines was inconsistent with congressional intent and also, in Congress' view, with current law. The resolution specifically criticized the Department for ignoring harms to intrabrand competition, which Congress felt raised legitimate antitrust concerns that should be considered under the rule of reason. Pub. L. No. 99–180, 99 Stat. 1136, 1169–70 (1985).

that carry several brands, the lack of intrabrand competition can lead retailers to "steer" consumers toward brands whose profit margin is higher.[26] The potential for this consumer deception is significantly reduced if consumers can purchase the same brand from several retail outlets. Third, brand-loyal consumers may be forced to pay for unwanted retail services when intrabrand competition is reduced. In the absence of vertical restraints, other dealers will forego the unwanted services and the accompanying price increases.[27]

On the other side of the balance are the advantages of vertical restraints. In *Sylvania*, Justice Powell identified two related benefits. By reducing or eliminating intrabrand competition from "free riders," vertical restraints encourage retailers both to aggressively promote the manufacturer's product and to provide point-of-sale service (such as quality warranty repair service or knowledgeable sales representatives). Both of these benefits enable the manufacturer to compete more effectively against its rivals.[28]

(4) The lower courts' reluctance to balance harms and benefits.

Where products are highly differentiated from their generic counterparts, or where vigorous interbrand rivalry does not exist because the market is an oligopoly, intrabrand competition is essential to preserve the benefits of competition for consumers. Many lower courts, however, have been so eager to summarily reject claims because of the defendant manufacturer's low market share that they have failed to seriously consider whether significant numbers of consumers will be exploited by reduced intrabrand competition. As a result, virtually no plaintiffs have prevailed under *Sylvania*'s rule of reason.[29]

---

26. This practice is particularly likely for products, such as electronic equipment or household appliances, where sales personnel are well-situated to influence consumer choice.

27. For a more extended discussion of the harmful effects of reduced intrabrand competition on consumers, see section A(3) above.

28. See 433 U.S. at 55.

Sylvania also alludes to the emergence of strict products liability laws as a justification for restricted distribution. Id. at 55 n.23. Although concerns about product safety or effectiveness clearly justify a system of autho-

rized distributors, it is unclear why they support significant restraints on the territories in which these distributors can sell. These concerns would, however, support customer restrictions that prevented retailers from selling the product to consumers who were not qualified to use it safely or correctly (e.g. dangerous toys to children, complex chemical products designed for professional use to untrained consumers).

29. See Douglas Ginsburg, Vertical Restraints: De Facto Legality Under the Rule of Reason, 60 Antitrust L.J. 67 (1991).

In *Valley Liquors, Inc. v. Renfield Importers, Ltd.,*[30] Judge Richard Posner explained the rationale for using a market power "screen" to summarily dispose of vertical restraint cases under the rule of reason. Because it is difficult to balance the harm that a restricted distribution scheme causes to intrabrand competition against its benefits to interbrand competition, he noted many courts have held that "the balance tips in the defendant's favor if the plaintiff fails to show that the defendant has significant market power (that is, power to raise prices significantly above the competitive level without losing *all* of one's business)." A firm without such power, Posner reasoned, cannot exploit consumers by adopting anticompetitive restrictions, and "if it blunders and does adopt such a policy, market retribution will be swift."[31]

Read generously, *Valley Liquors* merely restates the principle announced in *Sylvania* that balancing may be unnecessary "because of the ability of consumers to substitute a different brand of the same product."[32] Nevertheless, consumers purchasing from firms in oligopolistic industries, or from manufacturers that produce a differentiated product with significant brand loyalty, may be subject to exploitation because, respectively, the price level of other brands will also remain above the competitive level or consumer brand preferences make other products less attractive substitutes. Hopefully, the Seventh Circuit would find that the defendant possessed market power in such cases. If, instead, as *Valley Liquors* suggested, the court defines market power as a firm's unilateral power to raise prices (the Supreme Court's definition of *monopoly* power[33]), the market power "screen" will result in the premature dismissal of otherwise meritorious claims.

Unfortunately, the Eighth Circuit has used the market power screen in a way decidedly unfriendly to *Sylvania* and consumers. In *Assam Drug Co. v. Miller Brewing Co.,*[34] the court summarily rejected a challenge to a beer distributor's exclusive territory because of Miller's low market share. Writing broadly that if "Miller lacks market power, the territorial restraints it imposed ... cannot have an anticompetitive effect on interbrand competition,"[35] the court ignored the problems that reduced intrabrand rivalry can cause in industries with an oligopolistic structure and significant brand-name product differentiation.[36] As noted in the

---

30. 678 F.2d 742 (7th Cir. 1982).

31. Id. at 745 (emphasis added).

32. *Sylvania*, 433 U.S. at 52 n.19.

33. United States v. E.I. du Pont de Nemours & Co., 351 U.S. 377, 391 (1956).

34. 798 F.2d 311 (8th Cir. 1986) (aff'g 624 F.Supp. 411 (D.S.D. 1985)).

35. Id. at 319.

36. In an earlier footnote, *Assam Drug* noted that Miller's affidavits in support of its motion for summary judgment asserted that product differentiation is not a significant force in the

prior subsection, even the Reagan administration recognized that vertical restraints can lessen competition in an oligopolistic industry if they are widespread and there are barriers to entry. (Both conditions typically characterize beer distribution.[37]) Because Miller's product is highly differentiated, the opportunity to purchase some other brand is less likely to protect those who look forward to "Miller Time" from the exploitation occasioned by reduced intrabrand competition. Both product differentiation and barriers to entry would receive careful consideration if these cases were analyzed under the rule of reason test mandated by *Sylvania*.[38]

(5) A sensible balancing.

The Ninth Circuit's analysis on remand in *Sylvania* provides a contrasting and superior approach to analyzing non-price restraints.[39] The court's analysis there did not begin and end with a discussion of Sylvania's market share. Although Sylvania's national market share was quite small, its televisions did have a 15% share of the Sacramento market. Assuming that television brands attracted substantial customer loyalty and that the overall markets in both televisions and retail outlets were concentrated, the court appropriately refused to end the analysis there because it could not conclude that vigorous interbrand competition would check any exploitation of consumers.

Rather, the court explicitly adopted the balancing test suggested by Justice Powell's opinion, holding that a "vertical restraint may be reasonable if it is likely to promote interbrand competition without overly restricting intrabrand competition." [40] The court was still able to grant summary judgment for the defendant because it found that undisputed facts demonstrated the reasonableness of Sylvania's distributional restrictions. In so holding, the court emphasized that the restraint prohibiting Conti-

brewing industry and that the industry was highly competitive, and that the plaintiff had failed to present sufficient evidence to raise a genuine issue of disputed fact concerning this claim. Id. at 319 n.20. While this explanation may demonstrate that the Eighth Circuit correctly resolved that particular lawsuit, it does not justify the broad reliance on market power evidence in the text of the opinion.

37. The leading brewers all use vertical restraints. In addition, many states strictly regulate entry into the alcoholic distribution business. See New York by Abrams v. Anheuser-Busch, Inc., 673 F.Supp. 664, 668 (E.D.N.Y. 1987).

38. Indeed, a New York district judge found *Assam* to be inconsistent with *Sylvania* and its Second Circuit progeny, and thus rejected Stroh's and Heileman's argument that their small market shares (8 and 5%, respectively) warranted summary dismissal of the state's challenge to their exclusive distribution schemes. Id. at 667–68.

39. Continental T.V., Inc. v. G.T.E. Sylvania Inc., 694 F.2d 1132 (9th Cir. 1982).

40. Id. at 1137.

nental from opening a Sacramento outlet was a location clause. Location clauses allow discount stores to obtain desired products from wholesalers or even retailers outside their particular territory, whereas rigid exclusive territories eliminate any intrabrand rivalry. Moreover, the restrictions could be changed at any time by Sylvania. Thus, Sylvania did not employ the most restrictive form of restraint.[41]

The court also explored the purposes underlying the restraint, and concluded that Sylvania had not adopted its location clause policy in order to prevent price discounting. The court found no evidence that any other manufacturer had imposed a similar restraint, or that Sylvania had adopted the restriction at the request of other retailers.[42] The plaintiff's theory as to how the restraint would affect interbrand competition—that if it could sell Sylvania products in Sacramento, it could also sell other brands in Sacramento—was correctly rejected.[43]

In directing that non-price restraints be analyzed under the rule of reason, the Supreme Court's opinion in *Sylvania* cited

---

41. The Supreme Court's opinion in *Sylvania* refused to draw distinctions among the various types of non-price vertical restraints, noting that location clauses were neither the most nor the least restrictive plans Sylvania could have imposed. 433 U.S. at 58 n.29. Fairly read, the language does not proscribe the courts from determining the reasonableness of a restraint by looking, in part, at the existence of less restrictive alternatives. Rather, this discussion was in the context of holding the per se rule inapplicable to all non-price vertical restraints.

Despite the court of appeals' characterization of Sylvania's location clause, it appeared to be fairly restrictive. Consumers who did not wish to patronize Sylvania's only Sacramento dealer had to travel two hours to San Francisco in order to buy a Sylvania television. The court's ruling thus demonstrates that even fairly restrictive agreements can pass muster under a proper balancing analysis.

42. In *Valley Liquors*, Judge Posner seemed to minimize the relevance of the question whether the manufacturer unwillingly imposed the restraint on the dealers or acquiesced in restrictions sought by the dealers. 678 F.2d at 743–44. That discussion, however, was in the context of the plaintiff's claim that the arrangement constituted a per se illegal horizontal conspiracy among rival distributors to eliminate the plaintiff. In that context, the possibility that the manufacturer "may have had reasons for terminating Valley that were independent of the desires of [other distributors] to be rid of the competition of a price cutter," id., suggested that a rule of reason analysis was appropriate. This discussion does not indicate, however, that the fact that the manufacturer terminated Valley at the request of other dealers would be irrelevant when analyzing a case under the rule of reason.

43. This theory is akin to the concerns raised by exclusive dealing arrangements, considered in section H below, that manufacturers may be foreclosed from access to the outlets necessary to market their products if dominant firms prevent them from utilizing existing retailers. This is one area where market structure should play a dominant role: even if the products were differentiated or the market was oligopolistic, other television manufacturers would not have been foreclosed by the actions of Sylvania, which had only a small share of the market, especially because, as the court of appeals noted, Sylvania's restrictions were not prevalent in the industry.

Chicago Board of Trade as the venerable standard for analysis.[44] That standard requires a broad inquiry determining the competitive effect of a challenged restraint. The Ninth Circuit's approach in *Sylvania* fulfills this mandate, yet demonstrates that defendants can prevail, even on summary judgment, despite the detailed inquiry the court must make into (1) whether vigorous interbrand competition at both the manufacturer and dealer level will prevent any exploitation of reduced intrabrand competition; (2) how severe the restriction is (i.e., the harm to intrabrand competition); (3) what defendant's intent was in imposing the restraint (i.e., the potential benefit to interbrand competition); (4) how prevalent the restraint is in the industry (i.e., the potential harm to interbrand competition); (5) whether the plan reflects an acquiescence to dealer pressure; and (6) how persuasive is the plaintiff's theory of competitive harm.

The Ninth Circuit's opinion in *Sylvania* suggests that *Valley Liquors* may have overemphasized the difficulty of performing the balancing test mandated by the Supreme Court. In many cases, the defendant's product will face vigorous interbrand competition from products that consumers will view as genuine substitutes and there will be no evidence that the restraints were imposed to eliminate discounters.[45] In others, the evidence will clearly show that the restraint was necessary to successfully promote the defendant's product or to ensure that quality services were provided at the retail level. In these two situations, judgment can be rendered easily for the defendant. In other cases, a manufacturer with significant market power, the purveyor of a highly differentiated product with brand loyalty, or one or more oligopolists will impose a restraint that is clearly more restrictive than necessary to accomplish the defendant's stated purposes (thus suggesting that the proclaimed benefits are pretextual and some anticompetitive motivation underlies the restraint's implementation). No elaborate balancing is necessary here either, for the restraint would appear to be unreasonable. Only in the relatively rare event that these various factors conflict would a court need to engage in extensive balancing.

(6) The role of non-economic concerns.

Sylvania is also important jurisprudentially for an oft-quoted footnote that seemingly discarded the use of non-economic goals as

44. 433 U.S. at 49 n.15 (citing Chicago Board of Trade v. United States, 246 U.S. 231, 238 (1918)).

45. As Richard Posner once insightfully observed, it would be futile for a firm to eliminate price cutters if in the consumer's mind adequate substitutes existed for the defendant's product. Any patronage that high-priced retailers lost to discounters would simply be lost instead to the purveyors of these other brands. See *Schwinn* Brief, supra note 9, at 36.

legitimate pillars of antitrust doctrine. In the court of appeals, Chief Judge James Browning had argued that exclusive territorial restraints ought to be illegal because they interfered with the independence of small retailers.[46] The Supreme Court rejected this argument, declaring that "an antitrust policy divorced from market considerations would lack any objective benchmarks."[47] This holding has been sharply criticized. In his concurring opinion, Justice White responded that, like it or not, non-economic concerns informed the Congress that enacted the antitrust laws and must therefore be given effect. White scolded the majority for focusing solely on economic efficiency:

> while according some weight to the businessman's interest in controlling the terms on which he trades in his own goods may be anathema to those who view the Sherman Act as directed solely to economic efficiency, this principle is without question more deeply embedded in our cases than the notions of "free rider" effects and distributional efficiency borrowed by the majority from the "new economics of vertical relationships."[48]

Professor Eleanor Fox has also attacked Powell's premise that an inquiry limited to economic efficiency is less value-laden and more objective than one including non-economic concerns.[49]

Both of these criticisms are well-founded, but they really go to the breadth of Justice Powell's generalization, rather than to the specifics of his response to Judge Browning's argument in the court below. The Supreme Court correctly held that Madisonian fears about discretionary power cannot be balanced in any rational way against the benefits to consumers and competition created by a pro-competitive vertical restraint, as Sylvania's appeared to be.[50] Justice White, after all, did not dissent from the judgment that a restraint imposed by a small company that still left some room for intrabrand competition should be judged under the rule of reason. But harmonizing the various goals of antitrust probably does not call for per se treatment of exclusive territorial restraints, even if imposed by firms with market power. White

46. GTE Sylvania Inc. v. Continental T.V., Inc., 537 F.2d 980, 1019 (9th Cir. 1976) (dissenting op.).

47. 433 U.S. at 53, n.21.

48. Id. at 68–69.

49. The Politics of Law and Economics in Judicial Decision Making: Antitrust as a Window, 61 N.Y.U. L. Rev. 554 (1986).

50. Of course, if a manufacturer can find effective ways of achieving its marketing goals short of exclusive territories or location clauses, then Madisonian goals could be accommodated by finding these restraints illegal. And even one concerned solely with economic efficiency should condemn restraints that are inevitably broader than necessary to achieve the plausible efficiencies.

cited no evidence to suggest that location clauses or other less restrictive schemes will always be effective in ensuring that dealers will provide desired services; even the limited per se rule he advocated could therefore harm consumers solely to protect the Jeffersonian independence of entrepreneur-dealers. Populists, as well as efficiencianados, would reject this interpretation of the Sherman Act because it privileges a few dealers over millions of consumers.

Thus, even if discretionary power ought to be minimized unless to do so would harm consumers, and even if the entire enterprise is heavily laden with personal value judgments (as this treatise has repeatedly argued), non-economic concerns do not justify per se treatment of vertical restraints. Justice Powell's footnote is unfortunate, then, not in the context of *Sylvania*, but in other cases where non-economic goals can be achieved without harming consumers.[51]

(7) Natural retail monopolies.

Vertical restraints can even be appropriately sustained under the rule of reason in some cases where there is no interbrand competition. In *Omega Satellite Products Co. v. City of Indianapolis*,[52] for example, the court rejected a challenge to a city's decision to grant exclusive cable franchises rather than allowing the plaintiff to serve various apartment complexes with a cable connected to its own satellite dish. In an opinion by Judge Posner, the court held that the city could legitimately grant exclusive franchises because cable service is a natural monopoly.

Omega Satellite correctly held that exclusive distribution agreements should be lawful in a natural monopoly market. The difficult question, though, is what constitutes such a market. The commonly accepted *legal* definition of natural monopoly comes from Judge Learned Hand's *Alcoa* opinion—a market that is "so limited that it is impossible to produce at all and meet the cost of production except by a plant large enough to supply the whole

---

51. The non-economic concerns valued by Justice White could play a role, however, in tilting the balance in close cases. Where the record shows that a restriction has a decidedly mixed impact on consumers with evidence suggesting harm to some consumers and no clear benefit to interbrand competition, a court seeking to harmonize the competing goals of antitrust could justifiably find the restrictive scheme unreasonable.

The major policy objection to such an approach is its *in terrorem* effect, given that imposing unreasonable restraints may expose a manufacturer to treble-damage liability. Thus, the best course might be to leave it to the FTC to proscribe restraints that warrant condemnation only because of non-economic concerns under § 5 of the FTC Act, where remedies are limited to cease and desist orders.

52. 694 F.2d 119 (7th Cir. 1982).

demand."[53]   Because Posner's approach to antitrust is concerned solely with efficiency, he chose instead the *economic* definition of natural monopoly—a market where it is less costly to have a single company than to have several.[54]   This focus, however, ignores the prices that consumers pay.   Consumers are better off with several alternatives than with an exclusive franchisee, even if each alternative provider's costs are slightly higher than those of the putative monopolist.   As a result, *Alcoa*'s definition is superior: natural monopoly considerations should apply only when competition among multiple firms simply cannot exist over any length of time.

The fact that Omega was interested in serving selected customers meant that *it* thought it could cover its costs of production without building a network capable of serving the entire territory. The case may therefore have fallen into one of several scenarios where consumers are harmed by an exclusive cable franchise.

First, a market may be a "natural oligopoly."   To paraphrase *Alcoa*, the market may be so limited that it is impossible to meet the costs of production, except by a plant large enough to supply a significant part of the demand—perhaps 20–30% of the market— and therefore the market can support only 3–5 firms.   These firms would be unlikely to drive each other out of business by slicing their prices down to cost; they would be more likely to engage in oligopoly pricing that will creep above the competitive level.   Still, consumers are better off so long as their costs are not significantly higher than those of a putative monopolist, and their interdependent pricing does not closely approach the monopoly price.   In this situation, consumers would prefer competition among cable franchisees.

Second, in a dynamic market, new technology may be developed that changes the cost structure.   For example, Omega's effort to enter the market was due to the recent development of inexpensive satellite dishes that could support smaller-scale cable distribution.   Consumers who can benefit from new technology will prefer the resulting competitive choices.

Third, the economic definition of natural monopoly assumes that the product or service is homogenous, i.e., that consumers will see all substitutes as fungible.   But competition in a service such as cable television is likely to be differentiated, with firms seeking to increase market share not simply by lowering price but also by offering different services attractive to various segments of the

---

53.   United States v. Aluminum Co. of America, 148 F.2d 416, 430 (2d Cir. 1945).

54.   694 F.2d at 126.

marketplace. Thus, multiple firms can successfully stay in business.

This is not to say that *Omega Satellite* was wrongly decided. The case arose in the specialized context of an exclusive territory granted not by a private firm with market power, but by a city council elected by the consumers themselves. Unfortunately, the court's analysis does not distinguish this context, however, from the grant of an exclusive territory by Home Box Office or ESPN.

(8) Dual distribution.

In mandating that vertical territorial restrictions be analyzed under the rule of reason, *Sylvania* expressly reaffirmed the Court's prior holding that the same sort of agreement made by competing dealers would have been classified as horizontal and per se illegal.[55] Left unanswered by this dichotomy are cases involving dual distribution—where manufacturers distribute their products in competition with their restricted dealers. Although plaintiffs usually seek to characterize these agreements as horizontal, the lower courts tend to treat these cases as vertical agreements under the rule of reason. Although this approach seems correct, a sound rule of reason analysis must take into account the special nature of dual distribution.

To illustrate, in *Copy–Data Systems, Inc. v. Toshiba America, Inc.,*[56] the plaintiff was originally given an exclusive distributorship for Toshiba office copying equipment in three geographic markets. Eventually, Toshiba took over and began distributing its equipment itself in each of these markets in lieu of Copy–Data. The district judge characterized this as a horizontal territorial allocation scheme, but the Second Circuit reversed. The court of appeals correctly noted that all the pro-competitive reasons why a manufacturer might want to impose vertical restraints are equally applicable when the manufacturer finds it more efficient to distribute its own product in some areas.[57] In addition, the court observed that Toshiba could not exploit any reduction in intrabrand competition through higher prices because the market was dominated by Xerox and was being flooded by new manufactur-

---

55. See 433 U.S. at 58 n.28 (italics omitted):

> There may be occasional problems in differentiating vertical restrictions from horizontal restrictions originating in agreements among the retailers. There is no doubt that restrictions in the latter category would be illegal per se, see, e.g., United States v. General Motors Corp., 384 U.S. 127 (1966); United States v. Topco Associates, [405 U.S. 596 (1972)], but we do not regard the problems of proof as sufficiently great to justify a per se rule.

56. 663 F.2d 405 (2d Cir. 1981).

57. Id. at 409–10.

ers.[58] Finally, the court held that an inquiry into the purposes and impact of the dual distribution scheme would only be appropriate under a rule of reason theory, which Copy–Data had expressly waived.

The principal anticompetitive harm arising from genuine dual distribution schemes [59] is that they facilitate price discrimination. To return to an example used in Chapter 3,[60] a manufacturer of orange polyester clothing will find that it can sell its wares for higher prices in college towns like Champaign, Illinois, Syracuse, New York, and Clemson, South Carolina where orange is one of the school colors. In the absence of vertical restraints, arbitrageurs will buy the clothing in Indiana or Pennsylvania and ship it to the high-demand areas, thus driving down the price. By reserving these three towns for direct selling, the manufacturer can maintain discriminatory high prices because sporting goods stores in these areas will not be able to acquire the products at a lower price. In such cases, dual distribution may prove harmful to consumers.

Section D: Maximum Price Fixing

(1) Evaluating the case against maximum price fixing.

In *Albrecht v. Herald Co.*,[1] the Supreme Court held that the St. Louis Globe–Democrat's plan to place a ceiling on the price their independent distributors could charge subscribers for newspapers was a per se violation of § 1.[2] The Court's decision purports to be anchored in both precedent and policy, although careful scrutiny reveals that neither claim is persuasive.

Two precedents guided the Court's decision. First, the Court relied on *Dr. Miles'* holding that a manufacturer could not agree with its distributors on the minimum price at which its product was sold.[3] *Dr. Miles* reasoned that because dealers could not lawfully agree on a minimum price, the manufacturer could not agree with its dealers on a minimum price. Following the same

---

58. Id. at 410. Actually, this is a good argument for finding the restraint reasonable, not for refusing to apply a per se rule. A price-fixing conspiracy among several independent Toshiba dealers would be per se illegal even if the defendants could show that Xerox would have crushed any attempt to implement a monopolistic pricing scheme.

59. There are significant risks of cartelization when rivals combine in a form that resembles dual distribution. In United States v. Sealy, Inc., 388 U.S. 350, 354 (1967), the Court properly rejected efforts to characterize these restraints as "vertical."

60. See Chapter 3, section E(2).

1. 390 U.S. 145 (1968).

2. See section F(1) for a discussion of how and why the Court found the scheme to be an agreement.

3. Dr. Miles Medical Co. v. John D. Park & Sons Co., 220 U.S. 373 (1911), is discussed in section B(1) above.

logic, *Albrecht* explained, distributors could not set a maximum price either,[4] and therefore a manufacturer could not agree with its dealers on a maximum price. The problem with this reasoning is that four years earlier, the Court had expressly rejected this logical syllogism in *White Motor*, noting that vertical restraints are different in character from horizontal restraints.[5] *White Motor* held that fuller analysis of the policy implications surrounding vertical restraints (in that case, non-price restraints) was necessary before any of these restraints warranted per se condemnation. Thus, *Dr. Miles* and its progeny do not support prohibiting the Globe–Democrat's scheme without consideration of the policy implications. As Justice John Harlan noted in his *Albrecht* dissent, "to conclude that no acceptable justification for fixing maximum prices can be found simply because there is no acceptable justification for fixing minimum prices is to substitute blindness for analysis." [6]

The other precedent relied on by the *Albrecht* majority was *Kiefer–Stewart Co. v. Joseph E. Seagram & Sons*,[7] which condemned as per se illegal an agreement between the defendants, two liquor distillers, and the plaintiffs, their distributors, that established maximum resale prices. But *Kiefer–Stewart* involved both a horizontal and a vertical agreement. At trial, the distillers sought to justify their scheme by claiming that Kiefer–Stewart and its fellow liquor retailers were colluding to raise the price of liquor.[8] Acting individually, the Court wrote, each distiller could lawfully have refused to deal with the carteleers. But the Court focused on the agreement between the two distillers to stop selling to particular customers (those who would not accept their maximum price scheme).[9] *Kiefer–Stewart* is therefore distinguishable.

4. This holding was subsequently confirmed in Arizona v. Maricopa County Medical Soc'y, 457 U.S. 332 (1982), discussed in Chapter 4, section C(2) above, but earlier precedents such as United States v. Socony–Vacuum Oil Co., 310 U.S. 150 (1940) (any agreement that stabilizes or tampers with price is per se illegal), had already suggested this was the law.

5. White Motor Co. v. United States, 372 U.S. 253 (1963), is discussed in section C(1) above.

Dissenting in *Albrecht*, Justice Harlan drew an important distinction between the Globe–Democrat's maximum price fixing and Dr. Miles' minimum price fixing: in *Dr. Miles*, the defendant appeared to be acquiescing in the minimum price demands of retailers, while the Globe–Democrat was not likely doing its retailers' bidding by imposing a price ceiling in *Albrecht*. 390 U.S. at 157–58.

6. 390 U.S. at 157.

7. 340 U.S. 211 (1951).

8. The relevant events took place shortly after World War II; the defendants were seeking to hold prices to the levels set by the government during wartime price controls. See Note, The Per Se Illegality of Price-fixing—Sans Power, Purpose, or Effect, 19 U. Chi. L. Rev. 837, 838–39 (1952).

9. 340 U.S. at 214. The distillers, Seagram's and Calvert, were owned by the same company. After Copperweld Corp. v. Independence Tube Corp., 467 U.S. 752 (1984), their agreement would

Although the *Albrecht* majority recognized that "[m]aximum and minimum price fixing may have different consequences in many situations,"[10] it gave four reasons why maximum vertical price fixing is anticompetitive. Each of these arguments has merit, but ultimately they do not provide sufficient justification for per se condemnation. They appear to ignore a number of very plausible scenarios where maximum price fixing is pro-competitive, and they fail to explain why these pro-competitive scenarios are likely to exist so rarely that they can safely be ignored.

First, the Court noted that maximum price fixing, "by substituting the perhaps erroneous judgment of the seller for the forces of the competitive market, may severely intrude upon the ability of buyers to compete and survive in that market."[11] This point is essentially the traditional Madisonian argument against discretionary power. While this concern has validity in many cases, it has far less force when the distributor is itself a monopolist or has greater bargaining power than the manufacturer. In these situations, maximum price fixing may, to paraphrase the Court, substitute the perhaps erroneous judgment of the seller for the monopoly power of the buyer.

Second, the Court observed that "[m]aximum prices may be fixed too low for the dealer to furnish services essential to the value which goods have for the consumer or to furnish services and conveniences which consumers desire and for which they are willing to pay."[12] This concern is the mirror image of one described in the previous discussion of minimum resale price maintenance: whereas the latter channels competition toward non-price competition (elaborate showrooms) and away from price competition (discounts), maximum price fixing has the opposite effect. Recent antitrust doctrine recognizes that a manufacturer in a truly competitive market should be allowed to impose restraints necessary to implement a marketing strategy that stresses non-price competition.[13] Similarly, a manufacturer in a truly competitive market should be permitted to impose restraints necessary to effect a discount pricing strategy. Consumers in a competitive market will therefore be able to choose from a plethora of brands, some which of will be priced higher and feature substantial non-price amenities, while others will be "bare bones" discounts. Where a manufacturer faces vigorous brand rivalry

not be considered a conspiracy. But at the time, the law provided that agreements between sister companies were deemed horizontal restraints. United States v. Yellow Cab Co., 332 U.S. 218 (1947). For a discussion of the intra-enterprise conspiracy doctrine, see Chapter 4, section F(7).

10. 390 U.S. at 152.

11. Id.

12. Id. at 152–53.

13. Continental T.V., Inc. v. GTE Sylvania Inc., 433 U.S. 36 (1977).

and retailers face less rigorous competition, maximum price fixing may be the only way for the manufacturer to increase its market share though discounting; otherwise, the distributor will be able to raise prices because it has less competition at the retail level. Thus, the kind of marketing strategy condemned by *Albrecht* seems to be precisely what the antitrust laws want to encourage in competitive markets.

Third, the Court found that "[m]aximum price fixing may channel distribution through a few large or specifically advantaged dealers who otherwise would be subject to significant non-price competition." [14] This scenario is quite anticompetitive, and where it exists, maximum price fixing should be prohibited. But, as the Court has observed in the non-price area, vigorous interbrand competition severely limits a manufacturer's ability to exploit any reduction in intrabrand competition.[15] Similarly, where retail competition is vigorous, other brands will be available to dealers that offer higher-priced, higher-quality services, and these dealers can provide "significant non-price competition" to the large discount houses.

Finally, the Court also correctly noted that what purports to be maximum price fixing can merely be a cover for minimum price fixing.[16] This concern is valid, but the Court did not explain why it needed to condemn every maximum price scheme, regardless of the degree of interbrand competition in the market and the variation among the defendants' actual prices, just because some of these schemes may be efforts to evade *Dr. Miles.*

In addition to the four reasons provided in *Albrecht*, one plausible reading of the facts in *Atlantic Richfield Co. v. USA Petroleum Co.*[17] suggests another anticompetitive effect of maximum price-fixing schemes. Atlantic Richfield (ARCO) is an integrated oil company; it drills, refines, and sells oil for retail, both through its own outlets and through independent franchisees. In addition to competing with the other major independent oil companies, ARCO faces competition at the retail level from independent discount operations such as USA Petroleum. ARCO allegedly engaged in a predatory campaign against USA Petroleum, using maximum price fixing to force its retailers to join the predation. If ARCO's prices were below cost, it would have been guilty of predatory pricing under § 2 (assuming that its market share was high enough). Alternatively, ARCO may have engaged in "limit pricing," i.e., a targeted sacrifice of some, but not all, of its short-

---

14. 390 U.S. at 153.

15. *Sylvania*, 433 U.S. at 52 n.19.

16. 390 U.S. at 153.

17. 495 U.S. 328 (1990). The legal issue in *ARCO*, whether USA Petroleum suffered "antitrust injury," is discussed below in subsection (3).

term profits in discrete geographic areas in order to drive firms with lesser capital (like USA Petroleum) out of business in those areas and to establish a reputation as a predator elsewhere. This "generic" predation would probably not violate § 2,[18] but would be per se illegal under *Albrecht* if implemented through a price agreement between the manufacturer and its dealers.

If there were no sound reasons to tolerate maximum vertical price-fixing arrangements, these policies might justify the holding in *Albrecht*. However, the facts of the two cases the Supreme Court has decided in this area demonstrate maximum price fixing's pro-competitive potential.

(2) Scenarios where vertical maximum price fixing can be pro-competitive.

Albrecht may well have been a situation where vertical maximum price fixing was pro-competitive. In making that determination, one key issue is whether the distribution of newspapers is a "natural monopoly," that is, a function that is best performed for any given block of home subscribers by only one firm. Newspaper delivery is generally thought to be a natural monopoly,[19] but even if this assumption is incorrect, natural monopolies in retailing or distribution surely exist in our economy. When a manufacturer faces a retail monopolist, consumers are clearly better off if the manufacturer is allowed to set a maximum resale price. Economists call this scenario the "serial monopoly problem," because no matter what price the manufacturer charges, the retail monopolist will hike the retail price to get its own share of monopoly profits. By imposing a maximum price, the manufacturer can limit the retail price and restrict the monopoly profits available at the retail level.[20]

---

18. See Chapter 3, section D(4).

19. See Herbert Hovenkamp, Vertical Integration by the Newspaper Monopolist, 69 Iowa L. Rev. 451, 452–54 (1984). My colleague from the University of Illinois' Business School, Mark Roszkowski, strongly doubts that this is true. He notes that in many cities competing firms collect the trash despite the repetition involved in visiting different homes on the block. Given the low fixed costs involved in distributing papers, it may well be that prices would fall if three or four separate firms offered to deliver the morning paper. See Vertical Maximum Price Fixing: In Defense of *Albrecht*, 23 Loy. U. Chi. L.J. 209, 232–34 (1992).

20. *Albrecht* did not discuss the natural monopoly issue; rather, the court of appeals held that a price ceiling was necessary to protect the public from exploitation by dealers who had monopolies by virtue of the exclusive territory given them by the Globe–Democrat. The Supreme Court rejected this argument, because it had just held in United States v. Arnold, Schwinn & Co., 388 U.S. 365, 373 (1967), that these exclusive territorial arrangements were themselves illegal. *Albrecht*, 390 U.S. at 153–54.

Because exclusive territories are now judged under the rule of reason and will therefore be lawful in many instances, see Continental T.V., Inc. v. GTE Sylvania Inc., 433 U.S. 36 (1977), several com-

The serial monopoly problem is especially acute in the atypical business like newspapers, where much of the publisher's revenue comes from advertising. In this situation, the publisher has a particular interest in boosting circulation; the best way to accomplish that goal is to hold down subscription rates. Not only is maximum price fixing pro-competitive in such cases, but *Albrecht* causes decidedly anticompetitive results. As a result of *Albrecht*, virtually every newspaper in the country has begun to use agents or employees rather than independent entities to distribute its issues. Thus, while *Albrecht* has done nothing for the consumers' pocketbooks, it has interfered with the Jeffersonian goal of preserving independent newspaper delivery firms.

The second situation in which maximum price fixing is pro-competitive is illustrated by another plausible reading of the facts in *Atlantic Richfield Co. v. USA Petroleum Co.*[21] ARCO may have decided to encourage its retailers to match the retail prices of discounters in order to compete more effectively against independents like USA Petroleum and thereby to increase its market share. To induce its retailers to lower their prices, ARCO offered them discounts and eliminated credit-card sales. Suppose that ARCO was intent on competing for price with the independents (while some of its brand-name rivals were content to charge more and rely on brand loyalty), and was willing to lower its wholesale price in order to enable its retailers to engage in price competition. The only way ARCO could ensure that its independent franchisees passed on the lowered wholesale price to consumers, rather than simply pocketing it and maintaining higher prices, was to set a maximum price.[22]

mentators have suggested that *Albrecht*'s per se condemnation of maximum price fixing is no longer appropriate in those cases where it is ancillary to a lawful scheme of non-price restraints. See Jack Walters & Sons Corp. v. Morton Building, Inc., 737 F.2d 698 (7th Cir. 1984) (Posner, J.), cert. denied, 469 U.S. 1018 (1984); Robert Pitofsky, The Sylvania Case: Antitrust Analysis of Non–Price Vertical Restrictions, 78 Colum. L. Rev. 1, 16 n.59 (1978).

21. 495 U.S. 328 (1990).

22. Cf. Newberry v. Washington Post Co., 438 F.Supp. 470, 481–82 (D.D.C. 1977) (unlawful under *Albrecht* for defendant to raise wholesale price charged to plaintiff by the same amount that plaintiff had increased retail price charged to consumers). But see Lewis Service Center, Inc. v. Mack Trucks, Inc., 714 F.2d 842 (8th Cir. 1983), cert. denied, 467 U.S. 1226 (1984).

What USA Petroleum was really complaining about was not the low maximum price fixed by ARCO, but the relationship between that price and the higher wholesale price which it was charged by ARCO. See Roszkowski, supra note 19, at 230 n.136. The proper antitrust standards concerning this type of a "price squeeze" is discussed in Chapter 3, section E(3).

Care must be used in evaluating ambiguous vertical relationships in the petroleum industry. The Petroleum Marketers Protection Act, 15 U.S.C. § 2801 et seq., provides a variety of procedural protections that limit the ability of oil companies to terminate relations with a franchised dealer. Some conduct apparently designed to force dealers from the market may constitute an effort to

A starker example is provided by *Jack Walters & Sons Corp. v. Morton Building, Inc.*[23] Morton advertised its products in a local newspaper, telling consumers that they could buy the goods at Jack Walters and other named retail outlets. The advertisements listed the prices at which Morton's products were sold, and Morton required its retailers to charge no more than the advertised price. If Morton could not place a ceiling on its retailers' prices, it would at a minimum face considerable consumer ill will and would potentially face liability for deceptive advertising. Prohibiting maximum price fixing in such cases would also deter manufacturers from engaging in aggressive price competition.[24]

In some instances, therefore, maximum price fixing appears to be necessary to achieve legitimate business purposes. Although non-price restraints may well be effective alternatives to minimum resale price maintenance, there are no clearly less restrictive alternatives to maximum price fixing in cases involving either serial monopolies or discounting manufacturers. Thus, whether one limits per se condemnation to restraints that are almost always anticompetitive,[25] or tolerates competition-limiting arrangements when necessary to achieve a lawful purpose,[26] *Albrecht* seems wrongly decided. Moreover, unlike *Dr. Miles*, there is no evidence that Congress supports continuation of the per se rule articulated in *Albrecht*.[27] Thus, unless the Court wants to take a very strict view of *stare decisis*, it should consider overruling that decision.

(3) Guerilla warfare on *Albrecht*: antitrust injury.

The concept of "antitrust injury," explained in detail in a later chapter,[28] limits the ability of private parties to prevail in antitrust litigation unless they can show that their injury resulted from the anticompetitive aspect of the defendant's misconduct. The concept, which has its roots in established tort principles of causation, prevents misuse of the treble-damage remedy by those

evade this statute, rather than any attempt to monopolize or harm consumers.

23. 737 F.2d 698 (7th Cir.), cert. denied, 469 U.S. 1018 (1984).

24. As discussed in the following subsection, the court dismissed the case on procedural grounds.

25. See Broadcast Music, Inc. v. Columbia Broadcasting Systems, 441 U.S. 1, 8 (1979), discussed above in Chapter 4, section C(1).

26. United States v. Addyston Pipe & Steel Co., 85 Fed. 271 (6th Cir. 1898),

aff'd, 175 U.S. 211 (1899), discussed above in Chapter 4, section A(2).

27. Legislation recently reported by the Senate Judiciary Committee that would codify *Dr. Miles* specifically excepts from per se condemnation agreements to set, change, or maintain maximum resale prices. The Committee Report specifically recognizes the benefits of allowing newspaper publishers to engage in maximum price fixing. S. Rep. No. 42, 102d Cong., 1st Sess. 17–18 (1991).

28. See Chapter 6, section D.

who are not the victims that Congress intended to protect. Unfortunately, this concept has been applied inconsistently, with some courts limiting a victim's ability to recover because of judicial hostility to the plaintiffs' substantive claims.

Jack Walters & Sons Corp. v. Morton Building, Inc.[29] appears to have correctly invoked the doctrine to dismiss charges that Morton illegally fixed a maximum price for its goods. As discussed in the prior subsection, Morton imposed the price ceiling to ensure that consumers were charged the price that appeared in Morton's newspaper advertisements. Apparently, the plaintiff did not allege that the advertised price was too low to allow retailers to furnish essential services, or that Morton was channeling all distribution to large dealers and protecting them from the plaintiff's non-price competition, or that the ceiling was really a cover for minimum price fixing. The only other anticompetitive harm of maximum price fixing was that it curtails the discretionary power of sellers. But Walters admitted that it would not have had the discretion to charge a higher price because it faced competition from direct sales from Morton.[30] Thus, Walters' injury resulted from its need to compete with others, not from any anticompetitive aspect of Morton's practices.

Jack Walters stands in contrast to the Supreme Court's recent decision in *Atlantic Richfield Co. v. USA Petroleum Co.*[31] In that case, the plaintiff argued that its injury was due to conduct the antitrust laws were clearly intended to forbid—low prices set by ARCO in an effort to drive the plaintiff from the market. Thus, if the Court has been sympathetic to the defendant, the sound analytical course would have been to overrule *Albrecht*. Rather than explaining why *Albrecht*, was rightly decided, Justice William Brennan's majority opinion assumed *arguendo* that the decision was correct, while recognizing that a substantial amount of scholarly authority argued that vertical maximum price fixing can be pro-competitive.[32] The Court then reinstated the trial court's order of summary judgment in favor of the defendant, on the ground that USA Petroleum had not suffered "antitrust injury." The Court thereby misused the principle in a misguided effort to limit the perceived damage caused by *Albrecht*'s continuing vitality.

Because of *Albrecht*'s per se rule, ARCO was guilty of violating § 1 regardless of the plaintiff's theory of competitive harm. The doctrine of antitrust injury would, however, have barred

29. 737 F.2d 698 (7th Cir.), cert. denied, 469 U.S. 1018 (1984).

30. Id. at 713 (Swygert, J., concurring).

31. 495 U.S. 328 (1990).

32. Id. at 335 n.5, 343 n.13.

Union Oil from recovering any profits it lost as a result of ARCO's discounting scheme. Union Oil would not have been injured by the anticompetitive aspects of ARCO's scheme, but by its pro-competitive aspects.

USA Petroleum, however, claimed that ARCO's scheme to hold prices down to "artificially low levels" had injured it and other independents and had threatened them with extinction. Nevertheless, the Court concluded that USA's failure to allege that ARCO had engaged in below-cost pricing made ARCO's scheme pro-competitive. As Justice John Paul Stevens pointed out in dissent, though, ARCO's advertised gasoline might sell for a penny more than USA's unadvertised product in a free market, and both firms could make a reasonable profit. But if ARCO forced its stations to lower their price by 2¢, it could drive USA out of the market. "The fixed price would be lower than the price that would obtain in a free market," Stevens explained, "but not so low as to be 'predatory' in the sense that a single actor could not lawfully charge it under 15 U.S.C. § 2." [33] In effect, USA claimed that it was the victim of a limit pricing scheme by ARCO.

You may recall from Chapter 3 that limit pricing (pricing that is above cost but is generically predatory because it represents a sacrifice of the defendant's short-term revenues in the hopes of securing long-term monopoly profits) can be anticompetitive, but it is *not* illegal. Although limit pricing can harm competition, the courts have been unwilling to condemn it because of the risk that doing so would chill legitimate incentives to discount. [34] But if *Albrecht* is still good law, then it is not necessary to distinguish limit pricing from legitimate discounting, or to worry about chilling incentives to discount, because presumably *Albrecht* has already barred maximum price fixing. Thus, as Stevens correctly observed, "[p]redatory pricing by a conspiracy, rather than a single actor, may result from more than pricing below an appropriate measure of cost." [35] *ARCO* thus encourages manufacturers, knowing they can be sued only by the government, their own franchisees, or consumers, to set maximum prices without fear that their rivals will haul them into court. The term "guerilla warfare" is a polite way to describe such an invitation to illegality.

Section E: Consignment Arrangements

The typical vertical agreement discussed in this chapter involves restrictions placed by a manufacturer or seller on the

33. Id. at 347.

34. See the discussion of Barry Wright Corp. v. ITT Grinnell Corp., 724 F.2d 227 (1st Cir. 1983), in Chapter 3, section D(4).

35. 495 U.S. at 354 n.12.

conditions of resale by a wholesaler or retailer. The agreements usually involve goods that are sold by one firm to another, for ultimate resale to consumers. Consignment arrangements are a special type of vertical relationship. In the typical consignment, the reseller obtains physical custody of the product and then sells it to the ultimate consumer on behalf of the manufacturer. A consignee is really an agent of the manufacturer, rather than an independent actor. As an agent, the consignee must follow the manufacturer's instructions about the terms of the sale, including price.

Consignment arrangements are highly desirable means of effecting certain retail transactions. Retailers may be unwilling to purchase and resell certain goods, such as art objects, where the demand for the product is either thin or speculative. By selling on consignment, the original producer retains the risk of economic loss if the product does not sell. Because the good is still owned by the consignor, there is no more a resale price maintenance agreement when the consignee conforms to the specified price than there is when a Sears & Roebuck cashier insists on charging customers the price marked on a screwdriver.[1]

Thus, when the manufacturer in *Dr. Miles Medical Co. v. John D. Park & Sons Co.*[2] argued that its agreements with wholesalers and retailers were genuine consignments, the Court assumed that, if so, the agreements would not violate the Sherman Act, because there is no price fixing agreement when an agent follows its principal's directions. The Court noted, however, that although many of Dr. Miles' medicines were "consigned" to "wholesale agents" and then reconsigned to "retail agents," some products were sold outright from one wholesaler to another. Dr. Miles sought to fix the price of its products in both situations.[3] The Court found the outright sales to constitute retail price fixing; indeed, the facts of the case suggest that the scheme was not a legitimate consignment arrangement at all.

Pursuant to *Dr. Miles*, the government filed suit in *United States v. General Electric Co.*,[4] challenging GE's extensive scheme to control resale prices on electric lights (the sales of which GE dominated, with a 69% market share). Like Dr. Miles, GE defended the suit on the ground that its products were sold by genuine

---

1. Indeed, forbidding legitimate consignment arrangements may simply force manufacturers to change their distribution schemes by vertically integrating rather than using independent agents. See Morrison v. Murray Biscuit Co., 797 F.2d 1430, 1437 (7th Cir. 1986) (Posner, J.). Such a result would not only be inefficient (Judge Posner's concern), but would also be inconsistent with the goal of preserving the independence of small businesses.

2. 220 U.S. 373 (1911).

3. Id. at 398.

4. 272 U.S. 476 (1926).

consignments to over 21,000 agents (who also happened to be independent retail merchants). In an opinion written by Chief Justice William Howard Taft, the Court noted that GE maintained title and assumed the risk of loss from fire, flood, obsolescence, and price decline.[5] Likewise, Taft found "nothing in the form of the contracts and the practice under them which makes the so-called B and A agents anything more than genuine agents of the company."[6] The Court concluded that these "genuine contracts of agency" did not violate the Sherman Act, "however comprehensive as a mass or whole in their effect."[7]

The Court again faced the tension between the need to preserve consignment arrangements and its desire to avoid creating a huge loophole in this area of the law in *Simpson v. Union Oil Co.*[8] Union consigned gasoline to Simpson, fixing the price and retaining title, although Simpson was responsible for securing insurance and bearing the risk of loss. The plaintiff was terminated as a retailer when it sold the gasoline for less than the price specified by Union Oil. The Court found that this consignment arrangement achieved resale price maintenance in violation of the Sherman Act and was therefore illegal.

Although, the Court noted, the producer of a rug or painting could legitimately require a consignee to sell at a fixed price, consignments are illegal when "used as a cloak" to avoid the antitrust laws.[9] Unfortunately, Justice William O. Douglas' majority opinion did not identify the factors that distinguished Union's gasoline from an artist's painting. The Court did, however mention two important points: coercion and the vast size of the distribution system. Specifically, the Court wrote that the retailers were "coercively laced into an arrangement under which their supplier [was] able to impose noncompetitive prices on thousands of persons whose prices otherwise might be competitive."[10] But the Court's lack of clarity led Justice Potter Stewart to sharply dissent. He noted that *General Electric* had expressly upheld a virtually identical consignment scheme for the sale of light bulbs. Although the *Simpson* majority attempted to distinguish *General Electric* on the grounds that GE's light bulbs has been patented, Stewart wrote that "no one has ever considered [the patent] relevant to the holding in that case that bona fide consignment agreements do not violate the antitrust laws 'however comprehensive as a mass or whole in their effect.'"[11]

---

5. Id. at 483.

6. Id. at 484.

7. Id. at 488.

8. 377 U.S. 13 (1964).

9. Id. at 18.

10. Id. at 21.

11. Id. at 27–28 (quoting *General Electric*, 272 U.S. at 488).

Obviously, any doctrine that subjects some relationships which are nominally consignments to the scrutiny of § 1 will create greater uncertainty than a bright-line rule that all bona fide consignments are lawful. However, sound doctrine in this area necessarily requires a balancing of the legitimate reasons why manufacturers use consignment arrangements when it is efficient to do so against the concern that such arrangements may reduce retail competition and ultimately victimize consumers. Recall that consignment arrangements are desirable because they facilitate the sale of products that retailers would not purchase at wholesale prices. Thus, where retailers are willing to buy the product at its wholesale price, it is difficult to envision what lawful interest the manufacturer has in insisting on a consignment sale. An artist offering to sell a painting for $500 and to give the gallery a 20% commission is unlikely to object if the gallery owner wishes to pay $400 to purchase the painting it outright.

Moreover, the typical consignment involves special or unique goods, which explains why the manufacturer is often unable to find retailers willing to purchase the product outright at a wholesale price. In contrast, where there is widespread demand for the product by consumers, numerous otherwise independent firms are likely to be willing to assume the risk of purchase and resale. The consumers' interest in retail competition in such cases outweighs the manufacturer's interest in a consignment arrangement that appears unnecessary to facilitate the sale of its product.

There are, of course, plausible reasons why a firm would want to coerce a large number of retailers into using consignment agreements. Consignment agreements can facilitate retailer promotion efforts (by avoiding vigorous price competition and "free riding"), cartel pricing by manufacturers, or efforts by the manufacturer of a prestige product to maintain a "high price image" for its product. These rationales, however, are identical to those that might be employed by vertical price fixers. Thus, it is not surprising that Judge Posner, a leading critic of *Dr. Miles*, has opined that *Simpson* is limited to consignments that have no "function other than to circumvent the rule against price fixing." [12] Posner argues that any bona fide consignment should be lawful. His views were also expressed by Justice Stewart in *Simpson*. But Stewart lost.

Section F: Refusals to Deal

Difficult antitrust questions arise when a manufacturer refuses to deal with a distributor or retailer, and the purpose or effect

---

12. Morrison v. Murray Biscuit Co., 797 F.2d 1430, 1436 (7th Cir. 1986).

of the refusal is to maintain resale prices at levels dictated by manufacturers.   Like consignments, the critical issue concerns when such a termination constitutes an agreement at all for purposes of § 1.

(1) The *Colgate* decision and its erosion.

Shortly after *Dr. Miles* outlawed vertical price fixing, the Supreme Court held in *United States v. Colgate & Co.*[1] that a manufacturer could lawfully announce a suggested resale price and then refuse to deal with those who failed to comply.   Significantly, the Court's decision was based on its conclusion that this behavior does not constitute an agreement.   In cases involving pure horizontal conduct, the courts have held that an agreement can be inferred when one firm fixes its price and announces its intent to maintain that price as long as its rivals do likewise, and its rivals consistently follow the same pricing pattern.[2]   Similarly, the indictment in *Colgate* alleged that the defendant had violated § 1 by implementing a comprehensive scheme of fixing retail prices for its soap and toilet articles.   Colgate not only announced that no sales would be made to those who did not adhere to its list prices, but also secured assurances from offending dealers that they would adhere to the price list in the future.   The district court dismissed the indictment, and the government sought Supreme Court review under a writ of error.   The procedural context of the case is important because it required the Supreme Court to accept the trial judge's interpretation of the indictment.[3]   The Court agreed with Colgate that the trial judge had construed the indictment to allege only that Colgate had specified resale prices and refused to deal with any one who failed to maintain them.[4]   With this interpretation in mind, the Court concluded that, absent a monopolistic purpose or effect, the Sherman Act

> does not restrict the long recognized right of trader or manufacturer engaged in an entirely private business, freely to exercise his own independent discretion as to parties with whom he will deal.   And, of course, he may announce in advance the circumstances under which he will refuse to sell.[5]

Colgate has engendered a good deal of doctrinal confusion because its legal analysis was seriously flawed.   In issuing the indictment against Colgate, the government did not allege a *contract* (i.e., a legally binding and judicially enforceable pact) in restraint of trade.   Rather, as the district court noted, the indict-

---

1.   250 U.S. 300 (1919).
2.   See Chapter 4, sections F(1) and (2) above.
3.   See 250 U.S. at 304–05.

4.   Id. at 306.
5.   Id. at 307.

ment alleged a "*combination* in restraint of such trade and commerce, because [Colgate] *agrees* with [its] wholesale and retail customers, upon prices claimed by them to be fair and reasonable, at which the same may be resold, and declines to sell [its] products to those *who will not thus stipulate as to prices.*" [6] The district court went on to find the Sherman Act inapplicable to this sort of combination. The district court thus ruled for the defendant, not because there was no "agreement" in the abstract sense, but because the case presented the " 'threshold' " issue of " 'how far one may control and dispose of his own property.' " [7]

Had the Supreme Court focused on the same issue, it might well have reached the same result—construing the broad words of the Sherman Act ("combination in restraint of trade") so as to be consistent with a judicial policy of allowing manufacturers the right to choose with whom they will do business. This course would have been preferable because, by the district court's own terms, there was a meeting of the minds between Colgate and its retailers, even if it did not result in a binding contract. Surely if Colgate told its *rivals* that it would sell at $1 if they did likewise, and over the course of time no one charged less than $1, the Court would have found a trade-restraining combination even though no rival was legally obligated to maintain the $1 price. Because *Colgate* thus insisted that conduct which was clearly a combination was not a combination, it has misfocused the inquiry and created repercussions that are still being felt today.

In a series of decisions from the 1920s through the 1960s, the *Colgate* doctrine was consistently eroded. The Court found that *Colgate* did not apply where, for example, (1) an agreement to maintain resale prices was either expressed or could be "implied from a course of dealing;" [8] (2) a manufacturer terminated a dealer but then reinstated the dealer when it promised to adhere to the suggested prices in the future; [9] and (3) the manufacturer secured the agreement of intermediate wholesalers that they would terminate discount retailers. [10]

The erosion of *Colgate* reached its apex in *United States v.*

---

6. See id. at 304–05 (emphasis added) (reprinting district court opinion).

7. Id. at 305 (quoting district court).

8. United States v. Schrader's Son, Inc., 252 U.S. 85 (1920).

9. FTC v. Beech–Nut Packing Co., 257 U.S. 441 (1922). Strictly speaking, *Beech–Nut* did not affect *Colgate* because the government alleged an unfair method of competition in violation of § 5 of the FTC Act, as opposed to a combination in restraint of trade in violation of § 1 of the Sherman Act. But in historic context, the Supreme Court perceived *Beech–Nut* as part of the judicial narrowing of *Colgate*. See United States v. Parke, Davis & Co., 362 U.S. 29, 40–44 (1960).

10. United States v. Bausch & Lomb Optical Co., 321 U.S. 707 (1944).

Parke, Davis & Co.[11]   The Court refused to apply *Colgate* and
instead found a violation of § 1, reasoning that the Parke, Davis
scheme "plainly exceeded the limitations of the *Colgate* doctrine
and under [earlier precedents] effected arrangements which violated the Sherman Act."   In addition to publicly its threatening to
terminate sales to discount retailers, Parke, Davis announced that
it would terminate any wholesaler that refused to help enforce the
scheme, it received assurances from a large drug store chain that
the chain would abide by Parke, Davis' prices, and it visited
various retailers to assure each that their rivals would be cooperating in maintaining resale prices.[12]

As Justice Potter Stewart noted in a separate concurrence,
there was thus ample evidence of an illegal combination to maintain resale prices.[13]   However, *Parke, Davis* makes clear that,
although some of the earlier decisions continued to look for
evidence of an "agreement," *Colgate* really reflects more a manufacturer's privilege than a finding of insufficient evidence of
agreement.   Justice William Brennan's majority opinion held that

> an unlawful combination is not just such as arises from a
> price maintenance *agreement*, express or implied; such a
> combination is also organized if the producer secures adher-
> ence to his suggested prices by means which go beyond his
> mere declination to sell to a customer who will not observe his
> announced policy.[14]

Given the defendant's conduct, this holding may have been
unnecessary to the result in *Parke, Davis*, but its privileged-based,
rather than agreement-based, approach was probably essential to
the decision in *Albrecht v. Herald Co.*[15]   In that case, the Court
held that the St. Louis Globe–Democrat entered into a combination within the meaning of § 1 when it terminated Albrecht for
violating the paper's maximum price rules and then designated
Kroner as the new distributor.   The Court found that a combination existed between the Globe–Democrat and Kroner because
"Kroner knew that [the paper] was giving him the customer list as
part of a program to get [Albrecht] to conform to the advertised
price, and he knew that he might have to return the customers if
[Albrecht] ultimately complied with [the paper's] demands."
Moreover, the majority observed, Albrecht could have alleged an
illegal agreement between *himself* and the Globe–Democrat "as of

11. 362 U.S. 29 (1960).
12. Id. at 45–46.
13. Id. at 49.
14. Id. at 43 (emphasis in original).

15. 390 U.S. 145 (1968). The Court's
substantive holding that maximum
price-fixing agreements are per se illegal is discussed in section D(1).

the day he unwillingly complied with [the paper's] advertised price."[16]

Clearly, the Globe–Democrat's conduct went beyond a mere refusal to sell and thus the privilege did not apply. It is difficult, however, to see how Albrecht or Kroner went any further than the hundreds of retailers who likewise adhered to Colgate's prices for fear that otherwise they might be replaced by someone else.

Colgate's privilege is clearly unsound as a matter of economic policy. Whatever one thinks of resale price maintenance, its economic impact is the same whether enforced by explicit written contracts or by a *Colgate*-protected refusal to deal. *Colgate* thus has no place in an "economically rational" antitrust doctrine. It is therefore somewhat ironic that efficiency-minded defenders of resale price maintenance have made such a strong argument in favor of this manufacturer's privilege, for the privilege is really based on non-economic concerns—protecting the a "Jeffersonian" right of individual entrepreneurs to select with whom they will do business.

(2) *Colgate's* resurrection.

Because *Colgate's* distinction between price restraints enforced by explicit contract and those enforced through a manufacturer's threat to terminate discounters makes no economic sense, the FTC made efforts to limit its reach. In *Russell Stover Candies*,[17] the Commission considered a test case where the complaint clearly alleged no more than the "Doric simplicity"[18] of complaint and termination that was seemingly protected by the *Colgate* privilege. The Commission held that searching for "plus" factors that would enable a terminated discounter to circumvent the privilege was a waste of time. Instead, the FTC confined the privilege to the initial selection of dealers, and prohibited manufacturers from conditioning continued dealing on retailers' adherence to a price list.[19]

16. Id. at 150 & n.6. This dictum has since been directly contradicted in Monsanto Co. v. Spray–Rite Service Corp., 465 U.S. 752 (1984), which is discussed in the next subsection.

17. 100 F.T.C. 1 (1982), rev'd, 718 F.2d 256 (8th Cir. 1983).

18. Cf. George W. Warner & Co. v. Black & Decker Mfg. Co., 277 F.2d 787, 790 (2d Cir. 1960) (the Supreme Court's decisions leave a "narrow channel through which a manufacturer may pass even though the facts would have to be of such Doric simplicity as to be somewhat rare in this day of complex business enterprise").

19. 100 F.T.C. at 46.

The Commission rejected an alternative argument raised by its staff—that Russell Stover's policy constituted a horizontal agreement between complying retailers. Russell Stover's policy appears to meet the standard set forth in Interstate Circuit, Inc. v. United States, 306 U.S. 208 (1939): the dealers engaged in parallel conduct; they were aware that Russell Stover had invited their rivals to maintain list prices; each

This steady descent toward elimination of the *Colgate* doctrine was braked by the Eighth Circuit and subsequently reversed by the Supreme Court. First, the court of appeals reversed the FTC's *Russell Stover* decision.[20] The commission had concluded that a combination exists when would-be discounters adhere to a manufacturer's suggested prices solely to avoid termination. Although such adherence literally represents a meeting of the minds, an inquiry into what constitutes an agreement has never been the real focus of the *Colgate* doctrine. Thus, the court of appeals was probably correct in refusing to effectively overrule Supreme Court precedent, giving the Commission the option to seek further guidance on certiorari (an option which the Commission did not exercise, given a change in its leadership).

The full reversal of *Colgate*'s erosion came in *Monsanto Co. v. Spray–Rite Service Corp.*[21] Spray–Rite, a family-run discount distributor, bought agricultural chemicals in large quantities and sold at a low margin. Monsanto, which manufactured corn and soybean herbicides in competition with several larger firms, declined to renew Spray–Rite's distributorship. A jury found that the termination was part of a conspiracy between Monsanto and its other distributors to maintain retail prices. The Seventh Circuit affirmed, based on evidence that a number of competing Monsanto retailers had complained about Spray–Rite's price-cutting and testimony of a Monsanto official that Spray–Rite was terminated because of those complaints. Evidence that a manufacturer terminated a discount retailer "in response to" or "following" complaints by other distributors is sufficient to allow a jury to find a conspiracy, the appeals court held.[22]

was aware that its rivals was likely to maintain list prices because of the threat of termination; and each would be hurt competitively by adhering to Russell Stover's to list prices unless the others also complied with the price schedule. See the discussion above in Chapter 4, section F(2). Nevertheless, the Commission rejected this argument. It correctly reasoned that this logic would transform any vertical restraint into an agreement among conspirators, and would also subject manufacturers and dealers to liability for a system of suggested list prices that was frequently but not inevitably followed. 100 F.T.C. at 38–40. This discussion demonstrates why tests for identifying horizontal agreements should not be used in determining § 1's application to refusals to deal that arise in a vertical context.

20. Russell Stover Candies, Inc. v. FTC, 718 F.2d 256 (8th Cir. 1983).

21. 465 U.S. 752 (1984).

22. Spray–Rite Service Corp. v. Monsanto Co., 684 F.2d 1226, 1238, 1239 (7th Cir. 1982). Part of *Monsanto*'s confusion may lie in the court of appeals' failure to distinguish between terminations that chronologically followed complaints by rival deals and terminations that were caused by rivals' complaints. The Supreme Court also refused to recognize the difference between terminations "following" or "in response to" complaints, 465 U.S. at 759 n.4, although the former seems plainly to provide no evidence of agreement while the latter seems plainly to demonstrate some combination of economic forces. See subsection (3), below.

The Supreme Court rejected this ruling, opting instead to fully protect the manufacturer's prerogatives under *Colgate* to refuse to deal and its right under *Sylvania* to impose non-price restraints on its dealers.[23] Taking about a 160-degree turn from *Parke, Davis*, Justice Lewis Powell's majority opinion reaffirmed *Colgate*'s holding that a "manufacturer can announce its resale prices in advance and refuse to deal with those who fail to comply. And a distributor is free to acquiesce in the manufacturer's demand in order to avoid termination."[24]

Demonstrating again that any talk of "agreement" makes little sense in this context, *Monsanto* went on to affirm the jury verdict despite its reaffirmation of *Colgate*. The Court observed that the evidence showed more than mere termination in response to dealer complaints. First, Monsanto had invited and secured assurances of future price adherence from several other distributors, which was plainly illegal under earlier precedents. Second, the Court indicated, the jury could reasonably have inferred a conspiracy from the concededly "ambiguous" evidence of a distributor's newsletter, which could be read to indicate that competing retailers had agreed not to discount and that Monsanto had promised not to discount in its own retail sales. Third, and most perplexing, the Court indicated in a footnote that an agreement could be inferred from the fact that Monsanto's threat to terminate the plaintiff came during the shipping season, when herbicide was scarce and Monsanto "was able to use supply as a lever to force compliance."[25] Basic concepts of agreement or combination simply cannot justify relying on any of these three pieces of evidence to distinguish *Monsanto* from the standard case where repeated complaints about price cutting lead to a discounter's termination.

Why was *Monsanto* such a mess? The explanation harkens back to *Colgate*, where the Court insisted on mucking about in an abstract discussion about the meaning of the term "combination" for purposes of § 1, when it was really construing the Sherman Act to effectuate its own view of sound policy. Justice Powell, who had written in *Sylvania* that non-price restraints were to be evaluated under the rule of reason, accepted the argument made by the chief of the Reagan Administration's Antitrust Division, William Baxter, that non-price vertical restraints should not only

---

23. Id. at 763. See Continental T.V., Inc. v. GTE Sylvania Inc., 433 U.S. 36 (1977).

24. Id. at 761. *Monsanto* thus swept away the FTC's attempt to narrow *Colgate* in *Russell Stover*. This reaffirmation of *Colgate* also appears to overrule *sub silentio Albrecht*'s privileged-based holding that a retailer cannot take over an account from a rival that refused to comply with the manufacturer's price schedule without itself violating § 1.

25. Id. at 765 n.10.

be judged under the rule of reason, but should also be affirmatively encouraged. Any broad rule condemning complaints by dealers, Powell reasoned in *Monsanto*, would have a chilling effect on
these desirable non-price communications. *Monsanto* thus encourages manufacturers to use their wholesalers and retailers to
monitor and report the pricing activities of potential discounters,
even though *Parke, Davis* suggested that a manufacturer that
involved its wholesalers in monitoring retail prices would forfeit
Colgate's protection. In effect, then, *Monsanto* created a special
evidentiary rule expanding the *Colgate* privilege in order to encourage dealers and manufacturers to communicate about non-
price restraints.

(3) *Monsanto*'s further perversion of "agreement."

Unfortunately, *Monsanto* did far more than resuscitate an
eroded manufacturer's privilege to choose its dealers and preserve
its options under *Sylvania*. In an effort to preserve the fiction
that *Colgate*-protected conduct does not constitute an "agreement," Justice Powell continued *Colgate*'s "tradition" by further
distorting the definition of an agreement. *Monsanto* reflects a
willingness to make it much harder to prove a price fixing case in
order to avoid any inhibition on communications relating to non-
price restrictions, as well as a strong distrust of juries to accurately determine the factual disputes in this type of case.

Monsanto purported to apply in the vertical context the standard *Interstate Circuit* established for proving a horizontal agreement—conduct that is consistent with conspiracy and inconsistent
with independent action.[26] However, the Court rejected the argument that a conspiracy could be inferred based on evidence that a
retailer was terminated "in response to" complaints from rival
distributors.[27] In other words, even if the evidence showed that
the manufacturer would not have terminated the plaintiff absent
the complaints, and did so *only* because of the complaints, the
conduct would still be independent. What could be a clearer
showing of conduct that meets *Interstate Circuit*'s requirement of
evidence consistent with conspiracy and inconsistent with competition?

Monsanto further explained that an agreement requires a
"common scheme" and a "unity of purpose."[28] Some lower courts
have thus held that where a complaining dealer seeks to terminate its rival because of price competition, and the manufacturer
knuckles under in order to preserve the complaining distributor's

---

26. Id. at 760–64. Cf. Interstate Circuit, Inc. v. United States, 306 U.S. 208
(1939), discussed above in Chapter 4,
section F(2).

27. Id. at 763.

28. Id. at 764.

business, there is no agreement because each defendant is acting from a different purpose.[29] This reasoning would suggest that the *Interstate Circuit* conspiracy did not include the exhibitor, the real wrongdoer in the case! (You may recall that Interstate Circuit, the exhibitor, secured promises from movie distributors to require second-run movie houses to raise prices.) The movie distributors all acquiesced in Interstate Circuit's demands because they wanted to maintain the powerful exhibitor's good will. Interstate Circuit did not have a "unity of purpose" with its co-conspirators—it made the demands in order to decrease retail competition. Clearly, the fact that each conspirator has a different motive for agreeing to lessen competition should not exempt the conduct from § 1 scrutiny. Perversely, the result of this sort of reasoning is that the most egregious vertical restraints—those imposed by a manufacturer at the insistence of a dealer in order to insulate the dealer from vigorous competition—are immunized from Sherman Act liability, while the most beneficial restraints—those imposed by a manufacturer who learns from a dealer that a rival dealer is not providing the quality of retail services the manufacturer desires in order to vigorously compete—are reviewed under § 1 because in the latter case the manufacturer and complaining dealer have a "unity of purpose." [30]

The record in *Monsanto* suggests the shortcomings of the Court's desire to avoid hindering non-price restraints by making it more difficult to prosecute vertical price-fixing conspiracies. Although it affirmed the jury verdict in favor of the plaintiff, the Court was no doubt somewhat hostile to the complaint, emphasizing that Monsanto had only a small share of the "market." [31] Indeed, as noted in section C above, many courts would find this market share sufficiently low that they would grant summary judgment to Monsanto were the case being tried under the rule of reason. Closer analysis suggests, however, that the story was more complex. If farmers considered rival brand chemicals to be adequate substitutes for Monsanto's products, then business Spray–Rite had taken from Monsanto's high-priced dealers could be expected to simply be diverted instead to a discount dealer carrying another brand of chemicals if Spray–Rite went out of business. So why would Monsanto's dealers bother complaining?

---

29. See, e.g., Garment District, Inc. v. Belk Stores Services, Inc., 799 F.2d 905 (4th Cir. 1986).

30. See, e.g., McCabe's Furniture, Inc. v. La–Z–Boy Chair Co., 798 F.2d 323 (8th Cir. 1986). The defendant nevertheless prevailed in that case because the court found insufficient evidence that the the plaintiff was terminated due to its low prices, as opposed to its failure to maintain "legitimate nonprice standards." Id. at 329–30.

31. 465 U.S. at 756 (Monsanto sales accounted for 15% of corn herbicide sales and 3% of soybean herbicide sales).

One possibility is that the jury erred in finding a price-fixing conspiracy, and that the complaining dealers were mainly upset Spray–Rite was free-riding on their promotional efforts. Two more anticompetitive explanations are also plausible, however. One is that Monsanto enjoyed significant brand loyalty, so that farmers would not shift to other products; but, if so, Monsanto did not command a small share of the "market." Another possibility is that Spray–Rite was the only discount dealer of any brand in the geographic area (the other brands were sold only by high-priced dealers). In either case, Spray–Rite's elimination really had a detrimental effect on competition. These possibilities remind us again of the difficulties surrounding market definition and the benefits of condemning all restraints unnecessary to the achievement of pro-competitive or efficient purposes.

The more one believes that vertical agreements are not only to be tolerated but actually to be encouraged and the more one distrusts the judicial process, especially juries, the more one agrees with the current line of cases. Fundamentally, the purpose of even the most beneficial restraint is to limit intrabrand competition in order to spur dealer promotion or services. Dealers are primarily concerned with ensuring that their investment in promotion and services will be rewarded, and not undercut by discount competitors. Thus, the distinction between suspicious complaints ("Spray–Rite is discounting and undercutting our resale price scheme") and benign ones ("Spray–Rite isn't spending enough time promoting the product") can become blurred. Moreover, a broad rule protecting retailers that are improperly terminated for discounting inevitably will also protect retailers terminated for poor sales or other legitimate reasons. It seems sensible, then, not to allow juries to infer an agreement simply because a retailer is terminated following complaints from its rivals. Where the terminated dealer can, however, prove a causal link between the termination and *price* complaints, refusing to allow juries to draw proper inferences smacks of a special treatment for antitrust defendants inconsistent with our jury-based system of dispute resolution.

An illustrative case reflecting the courts' unwillingness to allow juries to resolve disputed fact questions in antitrust litigation is *McCabe's Furniture, Inc. v. La–Z–Boy Chair Co.*[32] In that case, the defendant terminated McCabe after receiving complaints from McCabe's rival retailer, Opferman. At trial, one of the defendant's executives testified that McCabe was terminated because it failed to advertise, display, and service La–Z–Boy furniture. Opferman testified that his concerns were based primarily

32. 798 F.2d 323 (8th Cir. 1986).

on McCabe's failure to advertise and service La–Z–Boy products (i.e., that McCabe was free-riding on Opferman's promotional efforts and then gaining customers by undercutting Opferman's price). The defendant also showed that, although it suggested retail prices, it did not strictly enforce them, and even Opferman sold below the suggested price. In support of its price-fixing claim, however, the plaintiff not only proved that Opferman complained about price, but also that prior to termination, La–Z–Boy had urged McCabe to raise its prices. In contrast, the plaintiff noted, there was no evidence that La–Z–Boy had asked McCabe to advertise or improve its displays or servicing.

The jury believed the plaintiff, but the court of appeals granted judgment n.o.v.. The appeals court espoused the correct legal standard—whether there was any evidence that " 'tends to exclude the possibility that the manufacturer and nonterminated dealer' were motivated by nonprice concerns in reaching their agreement" [33]—but it did not actually apply this test. Although the court claimed that "[t]here is simply no evidence that La–Z–Boy's natural price concerns were more than a mere byproduct of the central agreement to maintain legitimate nonprice standards," [34] this statement simply ignores the evidence that La–Z–Boy's sole advice to McCabe concerned prices. The real explanation for the court's decision was its desire to follow *Monsanto*'s instruction that cases involving "highly ambiguous" evidence should not go the jury.[35]

The foregoing analysis suggests that the Court's vertical restraint doctrine has gone down the wrong path by relying on the rules used to identify the existence of horizontal agreements. Unless they are involved in a joint venture, rivals are not supposed to have ongoing relationships or effective channels of communication; communication between suppliers and retailers is, however, an ordinary and expected occurrence. Instead of continuing along this path, the Court should acknowledge the real basis of the *Colgate* doctrine: the desire to preserve for non-economic reasons, a manufacturer's privilege to choose those to whom it wishes to sell. Where this policy is inapplicable, the privilege should be unavailable and those who succeed in having their dealers maintain resale prices through threats of termination should be subject to Sherman Act liability.

(4) Dealer terminations and *price* restraints.

La-Z-Boy's extreme distrust of juries is clearly reflected in the Supreme Court's most recent pronouncement on this subject, *Busi-*

---

33. Id. at 330 (quoting *Monsanto*, 465 U.S. at 764) (citation omitted).

34. Id.

35. See *Monsanto*, 465 U.S. at 764.

ness Electronics Corp. v. Sharp Electronics Corp.[36] Sharp, a manufacturer of office products, terminated the plaintiff following complaints from Hartwell, the plaintiff's retail competitor. Expressly
finding that *Dr. Miles* needed to be narrowed and vertical restraints should be encouraged,[37] *Sharp* held that even if a plaintiff
overcomes *Monsanto* and proves that the manufacturer and complaining dealer agreed to terminate the plaintiff because of price
cutting, *Dr. Miles* does not apply absent evidence of a further
agreement that the complaining retailer will maintain the suggested resale prices.[38] Thus, even if a discounter is able to
overcome the reinvigorated *Colgate* hurdle, *Sharp* makes it much
more difficult to avoid the daunting task of winning under the
rule of reason.

Of course, those who believe that *Dr. Miles'* ban on resale
price maintenance is unsound may applaud any narrowing of that
doctrine. Absent such candor, Justice Antonin Scalia's reasoning
for the majority in *Sharp* is extremely unpersuasive. Any agreement between a manufacturer and a complaining dealer to terminate a discount retailer *because of price cutting* (as the jury found
occurred in *Sharp*) inherently involves an implied agreement that
the complaining dealer will maintain its higher prices following
the termination. Why else would the dealer have complained?
Why else would the manufacturer have agreed to terminate the
discounter?

It is not enough for Chicago school devotees that non-price
vertical restraints are evaluated under the rule of reason rather
than the per se rule. In order to affirmatively encourage non-
price restraints and communications between dealers and manufacturers about those restraints, they have successfully persuaded
the Court to legalize conduct that constitutes price fixing under
standard antitrust analysis. *Sharp* is extreme, even accepting an
antitrust policy of encouraging communications regarding non-
price restraints; such a policy might require clear evidence of
price-related complaints, and proof of a causal link between a
termination and the plaintiff's pricing behavior—two obstacles
that the plaintiff seemed to overcome in *Sharp*. Other than as a
cynical attempt to wage guerilla warfare on *Dr. Miles*, which the
Court may be reluctant to overrule for fear of Congress' reaction,[39]
the only rationale that explains *Sharp* is the majority's concern
that juries are unable to distinguish between legitimate non-price

---

36.   485 U.S. 717 (1988).

37.   Id. at 724.

38.   Id. at 733.

39.   See *Paradox* Revisited: Interview with Judge Robert H. Bork, Antitrust (Summer 1989) at 19 ("I'd rather

the Court didn't strike down the rule
against vertical price fixing for the time
being, at least, because I am afraid Congress would come back and solidify it by
statute,").

restraints and price agreements that remain illegal under *Dr. Miles*, and that uncertainty about jury verdicts will "chill" highly desirable communications aimed at restricting intrabrand competition.

That Justice Scalia's majority opinion and Justice John Paul Stevens' dissent in *Sharp* take divergent paths is not surprising when one considers the different mindsets with which each approached the case. Scalia would characterize vertical restraints as desirable business strategies designed by manufacturers to effectively promote their products. In his view, Sharp's acquiescence to pressure from Hartwell to adopt a scheme aimed primarily at promoting Hartwell's profit margin, rather than increasing Sharp's sales, was an unlikely scenario that required clear proof.[40] Stevens, in contrast, saw intrabrand competition among retailers as important to consumers, and believed that the checks and balances of interbrand competition must be proved, not assumed.[41] Scalia expressed considerable doubt that juries could accurately distinguish between pro- and anticompetitive restraints;[42] Stevens was much more sanguine about juries' ability to get at the truth.[43] Most fundamentally, *Sharp* exemplifies the divergent value judgments discussed in Chapter 1: Scalia thought that markets almost always work well and that the courts do not; Stevens thought that the courts are capable of making the right decisions and that agreements among firms do not invariably enhance efficiency.

Both *Monsanto* and *Sharp* invoked Justice Powell's teaching in *Sylvania* that antitrust doctrine should make economic sense and should not be based on pure formalities.[44] By the Court's own admission, though, *Dr. Miles* is a formality, and *Colgate* is no less one.[45] In some cases, resale price maintenance may be less restrictive of competition than non-price restraints, and a manufacturer's announcement of price limits accompanied by coercive threats of termination may be more pernicious than express vertical agreements. Each of these four strategies, however, can be used either for good (to induce dealers to aggressively promote a product or offer point-of-sale services) or for evil (to facilitate a manufacturer or dealer cartel or to force consumers to pay for profitable but unwanted services). By continuing to wage guerilla war on *Dr. Miles* while resuscitating *Colgate*, the Court has vigorously continued the very formalism it has condemned.

---

40. 485 U.S. at 727 n.2.

41. Id. at 748–51.

42. Id. at 727–28.

43. Id. at 751–52.

44. *Monsanto*, 465 U.S. at 762; *Sharp*, 485 U.S. at 728 (both citing *Sylvania*, 433 U.S. at 51).

45. *Monsanto*, 465 U.S. at 761–62.

Section G: Tying Arrangements and Related Practices

(1) Definition and statutory basis for liability.

Tying arrangements (or "tied sales") occur when a seller conditions the purchase of one good or service on the buyer's purchase of another good or service.[1] (The product the buyer wants to buy is called the "tying" product. The product the purchaser is forced to buy in order to acquire the tying product is the "tied" product.) These arrangements differ from other vertical restraints in that they often involve the seller and the ultimate consumer; the other agreements discussed in this chapter primarily involve manufacturers and their distributors. Nevertheless, tying arrangements are considered here because they can threaten competition by foreclosing vertical relationships—by preventing a manufacturer from finding adequate distribution outlets for its product or by preventing a retailer from acquiring adequate supplies to sell. They raise additional consumer-oriented concerns as well: non-economic concerns about denying consumers the freedom to choose, and economic concerns about enabling sellers to hide the true cost of a product and to engage in price discrimination.

Unlike many practices prohibited by the courts under the broad rubric of "unreasonable restraint of trade," tying arrangements have been specifically condemned by Congress. The Clayton Act, passed in 1914 with the strong recommendation of President Woodrow Wilson, responded to concerns expressed in the 1912 Democratic Party platform. The platform criticized the Supreme Court for "depriving [the Sherman Act] of much of its efficiency" and called for "the enactment of legislation which will restore to the statute the strength of which it has been deprived by such interpretations."[2] These concerns were fueled in part by the Supreme Court's sharply divided opinion in *Henry v. A.B. Dick Co.*,[3] which upheld the defendant's requirement that any owner of its patented stencil-duplicating machine purchase only its paper,

---

1. Two other common commercial transactions fall within this definition of a tied sale: the requirement that a lessee acquire multiple patents or copyrights under a "block" or "package" license; and the requirement that retailer purchase the supplier's full line of products in order to sell any of them (known as "full-line forcing").

2. These platform excerpts are quoted in Felix Levy, The Clayton Law—An Imperfect Supplement to the Sherman

Law, 3 Va. L. Rev. 411, 414–15 (1916). See generally Victor Kramer, The Supreme Court and Tying Arrangements: Antitrust as History, 69 Minn. L. Rev. 1013 (1985).

3. 224 U.S. 1 (1912). The majority reasoned that A.B. Dick could suppress the patent entirely, in which case no ink sold by others would be used on its machines; thus, the defendant had the right to condition sales in order to increase its profits. This argument is

ink, and other supplies. The House version of the Clayton Act criminalized and outlawed all exclusive dealing and tying arrangements involving goods.[4] Many senators objected to such a broad prohibition; they argued that exclusive arrangements might be desirable in some circumstances (if, for example, a new entrant in the cereal business wanted its dealers to push its product to the exclusion of cereals made by the dominant Quaker Oats[5]) and preferred that the newly formed Federal Trade Commission be delegated authority to condemn as an unfair method of competition any tying and exclusive dealing arrangements that were anticompetitive. On the other hand, some senators expressed concern that *A.B. Dick* allowed patent holders to unfairly exploit consumers.[6] Thus, the Senate modified the House version by limiting condemnation to tying arrangements involving patented products. The conference committee reached a compromise between the House and Senate bills. The result of that compromise, § 3 of the Clayton Act, bars a seller from conditioning the sale of a good on the purchaser's forbearance from purchasing a competitor's products, where the effect may be to lessen competition.

Taking note of § 3, the Court expressly overruled *A.B. Dick* in *Motion Picture Patents Co. v. Universal Film Manufacturing Co.*[7] In that case, the Motion Picture Patents Co. required licensees that used its patented movie projectors (for which there were no substitute products in the market) to use film covered by film patents owned by the company (there were substitutes for these products). Without reaching the question of the application of § 3, the Court held that the policies reflected in the Clayton Act showed that this tying arrangement constituted patent misuse. Thus, the court rejected the patent holder's infringement suit against the licensee, and refused to prohibit the licensees from using alternative suppliers for film.

Justice Oliver Wendell Holmes, Jr. dissented. Holmes agreed with the majority in *A.B. Dick* that because a patent holder could withhold its product from the market entirely, it was free to impose whatever conditions it chose on the use of that product.[8] In overruling *A.B. Dick*, the majority in *Motion Picture Patents* correctly rejected this argument. Whatever the propriety of

considered in detail in subsection (2c) below, in connection with Motion Picture Patents Co. v. Universal Film Mfg. Co., 243 U.S. 502 (1917), the case that ultimately overruled *A.B. Dick*

4. See H.R. 15,657, § 4, 63d Cong., 2d Sess. (1914), reprinted in 2 The Legislative History of the Federal Antitrust Laws and Related Statutes 1729 (Earl Kintner ed. 1978).

5. 51 Cong. Rec. 14,253 (1914) (statement of Sen. Cummins).

6. Id. at 14,091–95 (statement of Sen. Reed).

7. 243 U.S. 502, 518 (1917).

8. Id. at 519–20.

Holmes' approach under some theory of natural law,[9] it makes no sense under any theory of antitrust. "Conditions of sale" can harm allocative and dynamic efficiency and exploit consumers by creating a greater wealth transfer than would result solely from the sale of a patented or special product. The owners of all products, patented or unpatented, have the right to withhold their products from the market entirely, but surely that does not give them the right to condition sales on their ability to conspire with rivals to fix prices.

Similarly, the Court did not accept *A.B. Dick*'s reasoning that a patent holder will not be able to impose unreasonable conditions because "the public is always free to take or refuse the patented article on the terms imposed. If they be too onerous or not in keeping with the benefits, the patented article will not find a market."[10] This argument, if accepted, would undermine the entire rationale for the antitrust laws. If cartels set prices too high or if a firm unlawfully acquires a monopoly and raises prices, economic exploitation will always be limited by the willingness of consumers to pay the price charged. The fact that consumers may be willing to pay more for less does not mean that society should tolerate the resulting allocative inefficiency, harm to the more numerous class of voters known as consumers, and aggregation of power in the hands of the defendants.

The first significant Supreme Court opinion to actually apply § 3 was *United Shoe Machinery Corp. v. United States*.[11] In that case, the defendant imposed a number of restrictions on its lessees'

---

9. Holmes suggested that his approach "has become a rule of property that law and justice require to be retained." Id. at 520.

10. 224 U.S. at 34.

11. 258 U.S. 451 (1922). This case was the government's *third* attempt to challenge United Shoe's monopoly. In United States v. Winslow, 227 U.S. 202 (1913), the government did not attack United Shoe's tying practices directly, but instead challenged the combination of three separate companies that formed the United Shoe monopoly. Writing for the Court, Justice Holmes sustained the merger because the separate firms made complementary machines and thus did not compete with each other. For a fuller discussion of *Winslow*, see Chapter 6, section A(2). In United States v. United Shoe Machinery Co., 247 U.S. 32 (1918), the government argued that United Shoe's tying arrangements constituted re-straints of trade in violation of § 1 of the Sherman Act. The Court upheld the arrangements as lawful prerogatives of the holder of the patent. In the case discussed in text, which was brought under § 3 of the Clayton Act, the Court emphasized that the latter statute specifically applied to tying arrangements involving any commodity, "patented or unpatented," and thus held that the government's defeat in the Sherman Act litigation did not preclude further Clayton Act litigation. 258 U.S. at 458–60. For an extensive discussion of the government's final effort, which successfully argued that United Shoe had unlawfully monopolized in violation of § 2 of the Sherman Act, see United States v. United Shoe Machinery Corp., 110 F.Supp. 295 (D. Mass. 1953), aff'd per curiam, 347 U.S. 521 (1954), see Chapter 3, section F(2), above.

right to use its machines in conjunction with complementary machines obtained from rival machinery companies. For example, a shoe manufacturer was not permitted to use a United Shoe machine if the manufacturer used a rival company's machine for certain other operations on the same shoes; United Shoe retained the right to cancel the lease or to charge higher fees if a lessee used certain machines from other sources; and rental rates included a royalty on all shoes made by the manufacturer, whether or not they were produced on United Shoe machines. The Supreme Court held that § 3 invalidated these restrictions. Justice William Day explained: "While the clauses enjoined do not contain specific agreements not to use the machinery of a competitor of the lessor, the practical effect of these drastic provisions is to prevent such use." [12]

The Clayton Act's prohibition applies only to "commodities." Therefore, in *Times–Picayune Publishing Co. v. United States*,[13] the government invoked § 1 of the Sherman Act to challenge the paper's requirement that advertisers purchase space in both the larger Times–Picayune and its sister evening daily, the States. The Court held that, although the government could prevail in a § 3 case by showing *either* the defendant's "monopolistic position in the market" *or* a restraint of a significant volume of commerce in the tied product, both "ingredients" must be present in a § 1 case.[14] Since the Times–Picayune's market share was only 40%, the government's § 1 claim failed.

The holding incorrectly purported to be based on a reading of prior cases, and provided no additional rationale for applying a heightened standard in § 1 litigation.[15] If a tying arrangement

12. 258 U.S. at 457.

13. 345 U.S. 594 (1953). Other aspects of the opinion are analyzed below in subsections (3c) and (3d).

14. 345 U.S. at 608–09.

15. The opinion thus demonstrates the wisdom of the authors of the Clayton Act, who felt the need to adopt specific provisions prohibiting certain anticompetitive conduct for fear that the Supreme Court would unduly narrow § 1 of the Sherman Act.

Times–Picayune cited five cases in support of its conclusion that the Sherman Act imposed a significantly higher standard of proof than the Clayton Act. Id. at 606–08. FTC v. Gratz, 253 U.S. 421 (1920), reversed an FTC order pursuant to § 5 of the FTC Act. The majority opinion in that case did not discuss the proper standards of liability

under the Sherman or Clayton Acts; in fact, the FTC had expressly found § 3 of the Clayton Act inapplicable. Id. at 424. United Shoe Machinery Corp. v. United States, 258 U.S. 451, 457–58 (1922), held that the lessening of competition required under § 3 could be inferred automatically from the defendant's "dominant position" in the market. *United Shoe* did not consider the applicability of § 1, and thus provided no support for *Times- Picayune*'s conclusion that the same evidence could not have supported an inference of restraint of trade under the Sherman Act. FTC v. Sinclair Refining Co., 261 U.S. 463 (1923), involved a small firm that clearly possessed no economic power. Thus, no lessening of competition could be shown. International Business Machines Corp. v. United States, 298 U.S. 131 (1936), was another § 3 case that

has the effect of "substantially lessening competition" for purposes of the Clayton Act, the arrangement also unreasonably restrains trade for purposes of the Sherman Act. Fortunately, the distinction drawn in *Times–Picayune* between the Clayton and Sherman Acts does not appear to survive the Court's decision in *Northern Pacific Railway Co. v. United States.*[16]

Without explicitly rejecting *Times–Picayune*, *Northern Pacific* held that an anticompetitive effect in the tied market was inevitable whenever a tying arrangement was successfully imposed.[17] And, as discussed below, the Court also held that a plaintiff could prove "monopolistic" control simply by showing "sufficient economic power to impose an appreciable restraint on free competition in the tied product."[18] Thus, after *Northern Pacific*, satisfying the effects-based test of § 3 seems sufficient to justify a finding of liability under § 1. The Court has subsequently stated that the standards applied under § 1 of the Sherman Act have now effectively merged with those applied under § 3 of the Clayton Act, although § 3 remains useful as an expression of congressional concern about the competitive harms that tying arrangements can cause.[19]

(2) What's wrong with tied sales?.

(2a) Extending a monopoly and non-economic concerns.

Some early cases condemned tying arrangements because they enabled the defendant to extend its monopoly power from the tying product to the tied good. For example, in *Carbice Corp. of America v. American Patents Development Corp.*,[20] another patent misuse case, the Dry Ice Corporation manufactured solid carbon dioxide (dry ice) and specially lined cabinets for refrigerating foods (mostly ice cream) that were chilled by the dry ice. Dry Ice sold both its ice and its cabinets on the condition that they only be used together; it then sued Carbice Corporation for contributory patent

did not occasion any discussion of Sherman Act standards. Finally, International Salt Co. v. United States, 332 U.S. 392 (1947), did find a tied sale violative of § 1, but the tying product was a patented item that the Court held automatically provided proof of monopolistic control. Thus, Sherman Act standards for cases involving non-monopolistic defendants simply were not discussed in any of the precedents *Times–Picayune* purported to rely on.

16. 356 U.S. 1 (1958).

17. Id. at 5–6, 10–11.

18. Id. at 11. See subsection (3c) below.

19. Jefferson Parish Hosp. Dist. No. 2 v. Hyde, 466 U.S. 2, 10–11 (1984). Contrast the congressional concerns with tied sales, which were deemed sufficient to warrant an explicit prohibition in the Clayton Act, with Justice O'Connor's concurrence in *Hyde*, which opined that tying is economically harmful only in rare cases. Id. at 36–38.

20. 283 U.S. 27, supplemented on other grounds, 283 U.S. 420 (1931).

infringement because Carbice sold its own dry ice with the knowledge that consumers would use its ice in conjunction with the Dry Ice cabinets.[21] The Court rejected the complaint, because no patent rights had been violated: "Dry Ice Corporation has no right to be free from competition in the sale of solid carbon dioxide."[22] Otherwise, the Court feared, "the owner of a patent for a product might conceivably monopolize the commerce in a large part of unpatented materials used in manufacture."[23]

However, other cases that condemned tying arrangements suggested that the defendant's ability to monopolize all sales in the tied product or to increase its monopoly profits was not essential to a finding of illegality. For example, in *International Salt Co. v. United States*,[24] the Court held that § 1 was violated by the defendant's insistence that purchasers of its patented machines for inserting salt into canned goods also buy its salt. Surely, there were so many other uses for salt that International could not possibly have monopolized the salt market. Moreover, International's contracts specifically allowed buyers to purchase the salt elsewhere if they found a better price, thus suggesting that the tied sale would not increase International's profits. Sellers of canned foods will only pay so much to purchase salt and insert it into cans. The defendant can obtain that maximum amount by imposing a monopoly price on the patented good. But once that "single monopoly price" has been charged, the "turnip" has been squeezed dry: there are no further monopoly profits the defendant can extort by raising the price of salt.

In developing the law governing tying arrangements, the Court was not, however, primarily concerned with whether or not the arrangement allowed the seller to increase monopoly profits. This concern is, of course, directly relevant to whether the practice harms overall societal efficiency. But the Court's decisions focus on other antitrust goals. *International Salt* held that it was illegal to "foreclose competitors from *any* substantial market."[25] (This policy is different from focusing on whether the rival has been completely foreclosed from the market, which is considered in the next subsection.) The Court believed that salt sellers should compete on the merits, and that one company should not be

---

21. If you find the terms "dry ice" (the generic product) and "Dry Ice" (the company) confusing, so do I; if enough of us do, the latter will be considered a generic trademark and everyone will be allowed to use it (as has happened with previous trademarks like escalator, aspirin, and thermos, but not with other trademarks like formica, which is considered the non-generic trademark for laminated fiberboard).

22. Id. at 33.

23. Id. at 32.

24. 332 U.S. 392 (1947).

25. Id. at 396 (emphasis added).

disadvantaged because it did not also happen to be selling a desirable second product.

Similar concerns were expressed in *Northern Pacific Railway Co. v. United States.*[26] In that case, the defendant had received millions of acres of land to facilitate its construction of a railroad from Lake Superior to Puget Sound. It sold or leased the farmland, often including "preferential routing" clauses that required farmers to ship their products over its railroad, unless another railroad offered a better deal. In condemning the tied sale, the Court expressly objected to the denial of freedom of choice for consumers.[27] A policy focused on efficiency would not be concerned that consumers were forced to buy a product from one seller, so long as they were not paying a monopoly price. *Northern Pacific* reflects instead Madisonian concerns about discretionary power.[28]

The increasing dynamism of high technology markets provide another justification for *International Salt*'s holding that sellers may not foreclose rivals in the sale of the tied product. Requiring the sale of the tying product alone will stimulate further innovation by rivals in a high technology tied product. Even if the defendant cannot charge more for a package than for the separate pieces, the tying arrangement allows the defendant to stifle innovation in the tied product if there are few opportunities to sell that product alone.[29]

(2b) Exclusion of rivals.

The Court revisited the issue of tying arrangements in *Jefferson Parish Hospital District No. 2 v. Hyde,*[30] where an anesthesiologist challenged East Jefferson Hospital's practice of requiring all surgery patients at the hospital to use Roux and Associates for anesthetic services. The Court held that tied sales are unlawful

---

26. 356 U.S. 1 (1958).

27. Id. at 10–11.

28. Although the "single monopoly price" theory set forth above suggests that Northern Pacific's tying arrangement did not transfer wealth from consumers to the defendant, the lack of free choice also offends populist concerns inherent in the antitrust law. The populist vision of antitrust, you will recall from Chapter 1, is premised on the notion that the Sherman Act was passed by a Congress elected by voters who were largely consumers. These consumers can be expected to favor a law that preserves their freedom to choose a product for reasons of taste or personal preference, even if the

seller offers the tied product at the competitive price.

Like Justice Brandeis (see Chapter 1), Justice Black saw no conflict between non-economic goals and efficiency. In *Northern Pacific*, he expressed the view that tied sales " 'serve hardly any purpose beyond' " lessening competition. Id. at 6 (quoting Standard Oil Co. v. United States, 337 U.S. 293, 305–06 n. 5 (1949)).

29. My thanks for this insight to Shane Greenstein, my colleague from the University of Illinois Department of Economics.

30. 466 U.S. 2 (1984).

when they exclude rivals or increase entry barriers. If others can not offer the tying product, the defendant obtains a monopoly in both the tied and the tying products, thus excluding those who sell only in the tied market. Moreover, entry becomes more difficult because any potential rival must sell in both markets in order to compete. The Court found no illegality in *Hyde*, though, because rival anesthesiologists could practice in a number of other New Orleans hospitals.

(2c) Price discrimination.

Where the tied sale is not accompanied by an escape clause for the buyer who finds a better price, (such as the one in *International Salt*,) the tying arrangement can be used to price discriminate. Many of the illegal ties condemned by the Supreme Court seem to fall in this category. For example, *International Business Machines Corp. v. United States*[31] concerned the sales practices of IBM, the market leader with 80% of the sales of tabulating machines. IBM sold its machines at less than the monopoly price, but insisted that purchasers use high-priced IBM punch cards. Thus, high-volume users (who would have been willing to pay more for the machine) paid more than low-volume users (who would not have been willing to pay very much for the machine). Absent the tie, IBM would have been faced with two less profitable choices. If it kept its price low to attract the low-volume users, it would forego the monopoly profits available from high-volume users, who were willing to pay more. (IBM could not charge the latter group a higher price because if it charged a higher price to high-volume users, they could simply use arbitrage to acquire their machines cheaply via a smaller purchaser.) On the other hand, if IBM kept its price high, it would lose the patronage of the low-volume user.[32] The tying arrangement thus enabled IBM to price discriminate, resulting in a lessening of competition sufficient to render the arrangement illegal under § 3.

Another apparent use of tied sales to price discriminate was *Eastman Kodak Co. v. Image Technical Services, Inc.*[33] Kodak adopted a policy that prevented its customers or third parties from acquiring replacement parts for its photocopying machines

---

31. 298 U.S. 131 (1936).

32. Tying not only makes price discrimination more commercially feasible, but also allows the seller to avoid antitrust liability under the Robinson–Patman Act. That statute, which is considered in detail in Chapter 7, would subject IBM to potential liability if it sold the same tabulating machine at different prices. However, IBM sold all its machines for a low price and all its punch cards at a high price, and the Robinson–Patman Act's prohibition on price discrimination thus was not implicated (even though the effective cost to a high-volume user was higher).

33. 112 S.Ct. 2072 (1992).

through arbitrage, and then conditioned the sale of these parts on the buyers' agreement to use Kodak servicepeople or their own employees, rather than independent service firms such as Image Tech. Larger buyers, the Court found, were more likely to (a) have the capability of servicing their own machines and (b) have the sophistication to anticipate, when deciding to purchase equipment, the true long-term costs of servicing. Kodak's policy thus allowed it to charge higher prices for services for those smaller customers who could not service their own machines and might be unaware of true long-term costs, while maintaining the patronage of these larger buyers at a lower effective price.[34]

Zenith Radio Corp. v. Hazeltine Research, Inc.[35] illustrates how tied sales that lead to price discrimination can harm dynamic efficiency. Hazeltine licensed its patented television and radio components to Zenith on the condition that Zenith pay a royalty based on its total revenue from television and radio sales, regardless of whether the licensed patents were used in the products sold. The condition was discriminatory because it recovered more from highly profitable concerns, and the Court enjoined it. The Court reasoned that Hazeltine was attempting to recover revenue from unpatented products.[36] As a result, Zenith lost any incentive to find a cheaper or better component because it paid the same royalty to Hazeltine whether or not it used a Hazeltine part. Thus, the cost of producing Zenith televisions increased, consumers paid higher prices, and innovation was stifled.

Price discrimination via tied sales is most defensible where it permits the manufacturer to offer its product at a low price to low-volume users. In these cases, tied sales expand output and more efficiently allocate resources. Moreover, the lower prices might be essential for small firms to survive, and thus might help maintain a deconcentrated market structure. Smaller users who are risk-averse and are not sure how much they will use a product might also benefit from a tied sale: they might be willing to purchase the product at a low cost even if it turns out that they do not really use it.

Three arguments suggest, however, that the antitrust laws should, on balance, condemn tied sales that are designed to permit price discrimination. First, as a matter of statutory interpretation, the legislative history of § 3 shows a clear congressional intent to condemn tying by patent holders and others with monopoly power. Second, a firm cannot charge higher prices to some customers and lower prices to others if the consumers in the first category can shift their patronage to alternative sellers. Because

34. Id. at 2086–87.   **36.** Id. at 139–40.
35. 395 U.S. 100 (1969).

a firm therefore needs some degree of economic power in order to practice price discrimination, allowing discriminating techniques like tied sales creates an incentive for firms to engage in inefficient, monopolistic acts to obtain this economic power. Most important, where tying arrangements foreclose competition, they stifle dynamic efficiency by allowing the monopolist the comfort of a two-market monopoly. As a result, innovation is likely to be retarded.[37]

(2d) Consumer choice.

Tied sales can also force consumers to purchase goods they do not want at all. This form of exploitation is a variation on the price discrimination scenario discussed in the previous paragraph: those consumers who value a product more than others are effectively forced to pay a higher price.[38] To illustrate, suppose that an electronics store ties the sale of a Sony Trinitron (previously priced at $500) to the purchase of high fidelity headphones (priced at $100), for which the store can extract some monopoly profits. Those consumers who would buy each product separately are not affected by the tie. Others might have little interest in the headphones, but value the television so highly that they would have paid $600 for it alone. The tied sale allows the retailer to keep the patronage of price-sensitive television buyers who like headphones, while exploiting those with particular brand loyalty to Sony.

For unexplained reasons, the *Hyde* majority did not seem troubled by this aspect of tying arrangements. Writing for the Court, Justice John Paul Stevens opined that when "a purchaser is 'forced' to buy a product he would not have otherwise bought even from another seller in the tied-product market, there can be no adverse impact on competition because no portion of the market which would otherwise have been available to other sellers has been foreclosed."[39] This analysis would be correct if "competition" is harmed only when rival sellers are denied the opportunity to compete on the merits. But concern for rivals should be only one goal of competition; another important goal should be the

---

37. There are however, response to these points (which is what makes the issue so difficult). In enacting § 3, Congress rejected a total ban on tied sales, proscribing only those with a competition-lessening effect. Thus, arrangements considered today to be pro-competitive should be lawful. As to policy, the greater opportunity for monopoly profits may spur superior skill and efficiency as well as exclusionary conduct. Similarly, the two-stage monopoly may encourage rivals to try to innovate in both markets, rather than accepting the defendant's monopoly in the tying product.

38. Economically, this scenario results in price discrimination against "inframarginal consumers" just like other vertical restraints: this issue is discussed above in section A(3).

39. 466 U.S. at 16.

protection of consumers from exploitation. Competitive markets allow consumers the freedom to choose what to buy, and from whom. To the extent that a firm with economic power deprives consumers of these options, the antitrust laws should be available to protect those who, after all, elected the Congress that enacted the Sherman Act.

(2e) Consumer awareness.

Hyde also found tying arrangements harmful because they hide or make it more difficult for consumers to identify the products' true price.[40] Thus, consumers cannot fully appreciate the effective price charged to them; if they did know, they might want to switch. To illustrate, consider a variation on a tied sale— the common practice of allowing only one beer company to sell overpriced beer at baseball games. If Richard Posner were to think about venturing from his chambers up to Wrigley Field, he might carefully consider in advance the ticket price and the number of beers he anticipated consuming, and then decide whether the outing was worthwhile. Most of us, however, are likely to decide first whether we can afford the ticket; once we get in the stadium and are hot and thirsty, we will go ahead and buy the beer, even though, had we considered the full cost of the day's activity, we might have stayed home. We would prefer competition among beer vendors.

The harm caused by hiding the true costs to consumers was the key to the Court's condemnation of a tied sale in *Eastman Kodak Co. v. Image Technical Services, Inc.*[41] Kodak tied the sale of replacement parts to its photocopying machines to repair and maintenance services for those machines, thus excluding independent service firms from the market. It argued that its policy could not harm consumers because any effort to raise price or lower quality in parts or services would result in a loss of customers to its rivals in the photocopying equipment market. The Court instead found that many consumers—like the hypothetical Cubs fan—would not accurately anticipate the long-term cost of replacement parts and servicing when making the initial purchase of equipment. These consumers are subject to later exploitation when—like the hot, thirsty fan in the Wrigley Field bleachers— they need follow-up goods or services and must turn to Kodak.[42]

---

40. Id. at 15 & n.24.

41. 112 S.Ct. 2072 (1992).

42. Id. at 2085–87.

Justice Antonin Scalia's dissent did not seem to appreciate this point. Scalia observed that Kodak could lawfully have tied both replacement parts and service to the original sale of its equipment, because the tying product would then be the equipment and Kodak clearly had no economic power in the equipment market. Id. at 2095. But tying products as part of the initial sale

The finding that Kodak's tied sale hid the true cost of services from consumers is also significant because the Court's judgment was based on evidence of actual consumer behavior, rather than economic theory. The dissent argued that "a rational consumer considering the purchase of Kodak equipment will inevitably factor into his purchasing decision the expected cost of aftermarket support." [43] The majority, however, credited evidence that many consumers could not accurately ascertain the long-term costs of aftermarket support, as well as the fact that many purchasing entities (including many public agencies) use different departments to purchase initial equipment and subsequent services. [44]

(2f) Facilitating cartel pricing.

An additional economic harm of tied sales that has not received substantial judicial attention has been suggested by economists reviewing the *Northern Pacific Railway* case. Requiring buyers of the tying product to give the seller a right to match any rival's price on the tied product will expose any cheating on the cartel, thus facilitating price fixing. [45] Another case that may support this cartel theory is *International Salt*. Apparently, International Salt's major competitors also tied sales of their patented salt machines to purchases of salt, subject to an escape clause if the buyer could find a better price. [46]

On the other hand, a firm can sometimes use tying arrangements to cheat on the cartel agreement, thus benefiting consumers. For example, package sales were used by airlines that wanted to compete for market share despite agreeing on minimum prices (price fixing used to be lawful when sanctioned by government regulators). Airlines would offer "fly-drive" packages at rates far below those available to consumers who separately purchased an airline ticket and rented a car. [47] This illustration suggests that tied sales are not invariably anticompetitive. Rather, as the next subsection demonstrates, tying is illegal only where the plaintiff can establish five elements that indicate a likelihood of harm to competition. [48]

would have made it more difficult for Kodak to hide the true long-term costs of servicing.

43. Id. at 2097 (Scalia, J., dissenting).

44. Id. at 2086.

45. See F. Jay Cummings & Wayne Ruther, The *Northern Pacific* Case, 22 J. L. & Econ. 329 (1979).

46. See, e.g., Morton Salt Co. v. G.S. Suppiger Co., 314 U.S. 488 (1942) (finding that such an arrangement imposed by Suppiger constituted patent misuse).

47. See, e.g., Robert's Waikiki U-Drive, Inc. v. Budget Rent–A–Car Systems, Inc., 491 F.Supp. 1199 (D. Hawaii 1980).

48. Yet another harm was articulated by Justice O'Connor in her *Hyde* concurrence: tying arrangements can

(3) The elements of an illegal tying arrangement.

According to black-letter law, tying arrangements are per se illegal. The rule originated in *International Salt Co. v. United States*,[49] where the Court condemned as "per se" illegal the defendant's requirement that purchasers of its patented machine for inserting salt into canned goods also promise to buy its salt. Actually, this is a gross distortion of the term "per se," for tying arrangements are not per se illegal unless a court applies a five part test that resembles a well-structured rule of reason analysis. *Jefferson Parish Hospital District No. 2 v. Hyde*[50] set out the five elements of a successful tying claim: (1) the tie must affect more than a de minimis amount of interstate commerce; (2) where the tying arrangement is not express, buyers must in fact have been coerced into buying the tied product as a condition of buying the tying product; (3) the two products must be "separate;" (4) the defendant must have economic power in the tying market; and (5) there must not be any valid business justifications for the tied sale.[51] The first element is mechanical;[52] the latter four will each be discussed in turn.[53]

(3a) Coercion.

Where a contract or term of sale explicitly requires the buyer to purchase both the tying and tied products, the element of coercion is necessarily present. As noted above, two reasons to

help a regulated monopolist evade government control of its pricing. 466 U.S. at 36 n.4. For example, suppose that I am willing to pay at least $30 per month for local phone service, but the Illinois Commerce Commission only allows Illinois Bell to charge me $20. If permitted by law, Illinois Bell could require me to purchase a pencil each month as a condition of obtaining phone service, and could charge me $10 for the pencil; I would go along because I would still be receiving phone service at a price I was willing to pay.

49. 332 U.S. 392 (1947).

50. 466 U.S. 2 (1984).

51. The term "elements" is used loosely here. It may be that, as a matter of pleading and proof, the fifth element is really an affirmative defense.

52. In Fortner Enterprises, Inc. v. United States Steel Corp., 394 U.S. 495, 501–02 (1969), the Court found the first element satisfied because the plaintiff had purchased $190,000 worth of goods from the defendant.

53. Although, as noted above in subsection (2d), *Hyde* did not expressly identify protection of consumers' freedom of choice as a reason for prohibiting tying arrangements, *Hyde*'s five-pronged standard provides consumers with the protection they need. Consumers' freedom of choice is limited only when the tied products are truly separate products and the seller has economic power. Forcing consumers to purchase left shoes as a condition of buying right shoes is not a real limit on consumer options. Likewise, if the seller has no economic power, consumers can exercise their freedom of choice to switch to substitute products. Finally, the kind of business justifications approved in *Hyde* should outweigh free choice issues and the tied package should be permitted to stand because these justifications benefit consumers in the long run by enhancing the quality and availability of the product.

condemn tying arrangements are because they deny the defendant's rivals the fair opportunity to compete on the merits for patronage in the tied product, and because they deny consumers freedom of choice. Thus, when the tie is explicit, the plaintiff need not prove that other products are equal or superior to the defendant's, or that consumers would necessarily have purchased other products absent the tie.[54] If, in fact, the defendant's product is superior and consumers would have purchased both the tying and tied products from the defendant, the defendant is free to untie the sale and achieve the same result.

A sale may be tied, however, even though the buyer is not legally obligated to purchase the tied product in order to obtain the tying good. *United Shoe Machinery Corp. v. United States*[55] established that it is sufficient that business realities "practically compel"[56] the use of the tied product. In that case, the defendant leased a variety of shoe machines and prohibited their use on shoes that had been made in part with any rival's shoe machine. Thus, United Shoe's lessees realistically had to purchase all their machines from the defendant.

Similarly, *Bogosian v. Gulf Oil Corp.*[57] reversed a district court's summary dismissal of plaintiff service stations' claims that the defendant oil companies were unlawfully tying their leases to an agreement to sell only their brand of gasoline. Although no contractual provision expressly forbad the sale of competing brands, each defendant required that its pumps and tanks be used only for its own brand of gasoline;[58] when combined with short-term leases that could be terminated if the plaintiffs installed separate tanks for separate brands, and minimum purchase quotas that effectively precluded selling separate brands, the Third Circuit concluded that the "practical economic effect" was the same as a tie.[59]

---

54. See Bogosian v. Gulf Oil Corp., 561 F.2d 434, 449–50 (3d Cir. 1977), cert. denied, 434 U.S. 1086 (1978).

This rule has an enormous practical effect on antitrust litigation. Requiring proof that an explicit tie forced consumers to purchase an unwanted product would necessitate independent proof concerning each purchase and thus would significantly lessen the likelihood that plaintiffs could challenge tying arrangements through class actions.

55. 258 U.S. 451 (1922).

56. Id. at 458.

57. 561 F.2d 434 (3d Cir. 1977), cert. denied, 434 U.S. 1086 (1978).

58. This practice had been upheld by the Supreme Court in FTC v. Sinclair Refining Co., 261 U.S. 463 (1923). See subsection (3c) below. *Sinclair* involved a challenge to the widespread use of this practice by oil companies, but the FTC targeted a small company without economic power. Bogosian's complaint included allegations of conspiracy among the oil companies and the defendants were major oil companies who controlled a majority of the leases for gasoline stations in the relevant market. 561 F.2d at 454.

59. Id. at 452.

In contrast, *Kentucky Fried Chicken Corp. v. Diversified Packaging Corp.*[60] upheld KFC's requirement that its franchisees purchase paper products from independent suppliers only with KFC's written approval, because there was no real coercion and hence no tie. The Fifth Circuit noted that KFC had approved nine independent suppliers, who provided no commissions or payments to KFC, and that the franchise agreement obligated KFC not to "unreasonably withhold" approval. The court observed that the principal evils of tying arrangements—foreclosing competitors and denying choice to buyers—were not present given that KFC franchisees had ten approved suppliers from which to choose from.[61]

Absent a contractual obligation, actual coercion is necessary to establish a violation of either § 1 of the Sherman Act or § 3 of the Clayton Act. A lesser standard will suffice, however, to establish an unfair method of competition in violation of § 5 of the FTC Act. In *Atlantic Refining Co. v. FTC*[62] and *FTC v. Texaco, Inc.*,[63] the Supreme Court upheld FTC orders prohibiting oil companies from receiving a 10% commission on tires and other accessories ordered by their retailers from certain tire manufacturers in return for the oil companies' efforts to "encourage" their dealers to select those particular tire companies. The Commission found that the oil companies' bargaining power over their dealers rendered any such encouragement "inherently coercive."[64] The broad discretion entrusted to the Commission under the FTC Act permits that expert agency to find "inherently coercive" situations unlawful, although courts and juries cannot so find under the Sherman and Clayton Acts.[65]

(3b) Separate products.

Almost all products have two or more elements, yet it is not a tied sale for Nike to offer left shoes only in tandem with right shoes or for Chevrolet to offer an automobile chassis only in tandem with an engine. Rather, tied sales involve products that are really separate. The test is consumer-oriented: would consumers value competition for goods in the tied market alone? Unless fashions dramatically change, few consumers who purchase Nike tennis shoes for their left feet want a competitive choice among sellers of shoes for their right feet. My brother-in-law is among a minority who, having purchased an auto chassis, might prefer competitive choices among engines; most of us would

60. 549 F.2d 368 (5th Cir. 1977).
61. Id. at 378.
62. 381 U.S. 357 (1965).
63. 393 U.S. 223 (1968).
64. Id. at 228–29.

65. On similar facts, the court in Belliston v. Texaco, Inc., 455 F.2d 175 (10th Cir.), cert. denied, 408 U.S. 928 (1972), found no violation of § 1 or § 3.

not think of buying the engine elsewhere and assembling the car ourselves.

In determining when two products are truly separate, *Hyde* cited with approval the approach taken by the influential district court opinion in *United States v. Jerrold Electronics Corp.*[66] In that case, Jerrold had pioneered technology in community television antenna systems[67] and refused to sell the components for its system separately. The district judge rejected Jerrold's contention that its system was a single product. In so holding, the judge correctly focused on several key factors. First, firms other than Jerrold sold the products separately, thus suggesting that consumers valued competition in the tied market. Second, Jerrold priced the goods individually, rather than as a package. If the products were really inseverable (like left and right shoes), separate pricing would not be feasible. Third, Jerrold's "packages" were customized, suggesting a bundling of separate products rather than one single product.[68]

The majority in *Hyde* found that general surgical services constituted a separate product from anesthesiological services because patients still might prefer competition or choice among anesthesiologists even after they selected a particular hospital. The Court noted that others offered hospital services separately, allowing surgeons to make their own arrangements for anesthetics (subject to a competency requirement that had to be met in order to gain staff privileges) and that hospitalization and anesthetic services were billed separately.[69]

Writing for three others, Justice Sandra Day O'Connor advocated a narrower definition of the separate products requirement, as one of several ways in which she sought to limit the reach of the antitrust prohibition on tying. She maintained that products are not separate if consumers would want to purchase the tied product only if they were also purchasing the tying product. Because no law-abiding consumer seeks to be anesthetized without being hospitalized, Justice O'Connor concluded that *Hyde* did not involve a tied sale. She adopted this standard because, she reasoned, if the buyer was going to purchase the tying product anyway, the seller could exploit the full monopoly profit from that

---

66. See 466 U.S. at 23 (citing 187 F.Supp. 545 (E.D. Pa.1960), aff'd per curiam, 365 U.S. 567 (1961)).

67. The earliest cable systems were suited particularly for rural communities. A large antenna was built on a mountain and connected via cable to each home.

68. 187 F. Supp. at 559. The judge went on to find that Jerrold had a legitimate business justification for its tied sale. See subsection (3d) below.

69. 466 U.S. at 23.

sale; no further exploitation could take place if consumers were forced to buy the tied product from the same seller.[70]

O'Connor's test is flawed in three respects. First, in cases (unlike *Hyde*) where the buyer pays one price for the package sale, O'Connor's test ignores the argument that tied sales hide the true cost to the consumer. Second, it ignores consumers' non-economic interest in free choice. Finally, even if a tied sale merely requires the buyer to pay the seller a competitive price for the tied product, O'Connor ignores the long-term societal harm of having only one purveyor of the tied product. As Judge Hand wrote and recent economic studies confirm, monopoly is a narcotic and rivalry a stimulant to industrial progress.[71] Because the only hospital in town could charge a full monopoly price for an operation, O'Connor would permit it to force patients to use only their chosen anesthesiologists.

In *Kodak*, the Court reaffirmed its view that products or services are separate when there is sufficient consumer demand to justify firms providing one item without the other.[72] The Court found that the sale of replacement parts, as well as the provision of repair and maintenance services, to Kodak photocopying machines each constituted separate products. The very "development of the entire high-technology service industry is evidence of the efficiency of a separate market for service."[73] The Court specifically rejected the approach taken by Justice O'Connor in *Hyde*, noting that this logic would immunize tied sales for any aftermarket, including cameras and subsequent film purchases, computers and software, or automobiles and tires.[74]

One area where the courts have been reluctant to apply these standards for determining separate products is that of credit sales. Indeed, in *United States Steel Corp. v. Fortner Enterprises, Inc. (Fortner II)*,[75] Chief Justice Warren Burger wrote in a concurring opinion that the desirability of allowing firms to compete by offering below-market credit to purchasers who bought their products suggested that such arrangements should be deemed to involve only a single product.[76] There is no sound basis, however, for distinguishing credit sales from other forms of competition involving two separate products. The majority's approach in *Fortner II* seems superior: the Court acknowledged that credit and the underlying good constituted separate products, but concluded

---

70. Id. at 39–40.

71. United States v. Aluminum Co. of America, 148 F.2d 416, 427 (2d Cir. 1945); Michael Porter, Competitive Advantage of Nations 662–69 (1990).

72. 112 S.Ct. 2072, 2080 (1992).

73. Id.

74. Id.

75. 429 U.S. 610 (1977).

76. Id. at 622–23.

that economic power in the credit market was so unlikely that credit sales were not realistically going to be subject to condemnation as an illegal tie.[77]

Perhaps because of the confusion that results when a "per se" offense includes a "business justification" defense, some courts have suggested that only a single product is involved where a tying arrangement is necessary for the seller to effectively market its product. For example, in *Principe v. McDonald's Corp.*,[78] the Fourth Circuit permitted McDonald's to require its trademark licensees to lease land purchased by McDonald's for their restaurants.[79] The court reasoned that no tied sale was involved because the products were not truly separate. The products at issue in *Principe* seem separate because franchisees were forced to take an unwanted lease to obtain a desired trademark license, and they would have preferred competition in the market for leases. Although the court correctly rejected the plaintiff's effort to characterize the franchise as an unnecessary aggregation of separate products tied to the McDonald's name, the better analytical approach would have been to sustain the tying arrangements because it had business justifications (discussed in subsection (3d) below), rather than distort the *Hyde* analysis of separate products.

(3c) Economic power in general.

The defendant must have economic power in the tying product in order to inflict any of the harms that have been identified as resulting from tying arrangements. Without some power, a firm cannot exclude existing rivals from the market. Consumers who do not wish to buy both products from the defendant can obtain them separately elsewhere. Without power, the defendant cannot price discriminate, for those who would otherwise pay the high price will also shop elsewhere. If the defendant is hiding the true costs of its products in a competitive market, its rivals will point this out in order to increase their sales.

Moreover, manufacturers who do not enjoy economic power have a compelling argument that they should be allowed to compete against each other using strategies like package sales. For example, in *FTC v. Sinclair Refining Co.*,[80] the Supreme Court upheld the defendant's requirement that underground tanks and

77. This aspect of *Fortner II* is discussed in subsection (3c), below.

78. 631 F.2d 303 (4th Cir. 1980), cert. denied, 451 U.S. 970 (1981).

79. See also Dehydrating Process Co. v. A.O. Smith Corp., 292 F.2d 653 (1st Cir.), cert. denied, 368 U.S. 931 (1961), where the court found that a storage silo and a grain unloading device constituted a single product because seven years of experience with selling the products separately showed a 50% malfunction rate when the unloader was used with other brands of silos.

80. 261 U.S. 463 (1923).

pumps it sold to retail dealers use only Sinclair gasoline. The FTC had condemned the widespread use of this tying arrangement in the gasoline industry as an unfair method of competition, but the Court noted that the tying product—the tanks and pumps— were not expensive and could easily be acquired elsewhere. More- over, retailers were free to sell rival brands of gasoline, so long as they used different pumps to do so. As the Court observed, the arrangement not only posed no threat to competition, but actually helped competition: it allowed smaller firms to enter the market by purchasing the pumps and tanks (which Sinclair sold at low prices to encourage the purchase of its gasoline).

How much power is enough to make a tied sale unlawful under the Clayton Act? *Times–Picayune Publishing Co. v. United States* [81] held that the defendant must possess "monopolistic" or "dominant" control, which was not shown there by evidence that the defendant operated two of the three daily newspapers in New Orleans. *Northern Pacific Railway Co. v. United States* [82] mod- ified this standard, clearly rejecting the need to prove monopoly power. Rather, the Court wrote, the plaintiff must demonstrate that the defendant has "more than sufficient economic power to impose an appreciable restraint." [83] The Court concluded that the railway did have economic power there, in part because the "very existence of this host of tying arrangements is itself compelling evidence of the defendant's great power, at least where, as here, no other explanation has been offered for the existence of these restraints [and the restrictions] conferred no benefit on the pur- chasers or lessees." [84]

This reasoning seems sound. If a defendant is (1) coercing buyers to (2) purchase two separate products and there is (3) no business justification for the tying arrangement, it seems reason- able to infer that buyers are putting up with this (keep in mind that if buyers have other options or are freely choosing a package, the coercion element is not met) because the seller has economic power. Justice Harlan's dissent in *Northern Pacific* suggests, however, that applying this reasoning to the facts of that case may have been improper. He noted that the vast majority of Northern Pacific's lands were close to its rail lines, and that farmers would therefore be expected to use those lines as a matter of course; when combined with the clause allowing farmers to use other lines that offered better service or lower rates, Harlan persuasively questioned how much coercion existed. [85] But if, in Harlan's words, a seller uses "tying clauses which would be likely to result

81. 345 U.S. 594, 611–13 (1953).

82. 356 U.S. 1 (1958).

83. Id. at 11.

84. Id. at 7–8.

85. Id. at 16–17.

in economic detriment to vendees or lessees," [86] then it would be proper to infer economic power.

The Court reaffirmed its move away from the "dominance" standard of *Times–Picayune* in *United States Steel Corp. v. Fortner Enterprises (Fortner II)*,[87] applying the *Northern Pacific* standard to reach a different result. In that case, U.S. Steel's credit subsidiary offered very favorable loans (below market interest, 100% financing) to those who bought their prefabricated homes, which were offered at above-market prices. The issue was whether the credit subsidiary possessed economic power; the Court held that it did not. Citing *Northern Pacific*, the Court concluded that attention must be focused on whether the seller's control of the tied product gives it the power either to raise prices or "to require purchasers to accept burdensome terms that could not be exacted in a completely competitive market." [88] The Court noted that U.S. Steel's credit subsidiary enjoyed no particular advantages over other major lenders, and therefore found that the "unusual credit bargain offered to Fortner proves nothing more than a willingness to provide cheap financing in order to sell expensive homes." [89] Thus, unlike *Northern Pacific*, the buyers *were* getting a benefit from the package sale. *Fortner II* thus stands for the sound proposition that economic power will not be inferred simply from the existence of the tying arrangement unless the entire deal makes consumers worse off than they would be in a competitive market.

Fortner II came after a trial developed the facts set forth above. The case had previously reached the Court on appeal from an order granting summary judgment to U.S. Steel *(Fortner I)*.[90] *Fortner I* reiterated the teaching of *Northern Pacific* that a total monopoly is not essential to demonstrate economic power. Rather, the key is whether *some* buyers can be forced to "accept a tying arrangement that would prevent free competition for their patronage in the market for the tied product." [91] Given the procedural posture of the case, the Court hypothesized facts that would suffice to demonstrate the defendant's economic power: U.S. Steel might have unique economies of scale, or banking regulations might

---

86. Id. at 19.

87. 429 U.S. 610 (1977).

88. Id. at 620.

89. Id. at 622.

90. Fortner Enterprises, Inc. v. United States Steel Corp., 394 U.S. 495 (1969).

91. Id. at 504. This approach seems correct, even if it was colored by the Court's overly simplistic view that "the presence of any appreciable restraint on competition provides a sufficient reason for invalidating the tie." This view was based on the Court's opinion that "tying arrangements generally serve no legitimate business purpose that cannot be achieved in some less restrictive way." Id. at 503.

preclude rival lenders from offering 100% financing. The Court cautioned, though, that uniqueness "confers economic power only when other competitors are in some way prevented from offering the distinctive product themselves." [92]

Similarly, *Hyde* required a showing that the defendant's power be sufficient to force consumers to buy something they would not buy in an unrestrained market. The Court concluded that East Jefferson Hospital did not have this power. The hospital attracted only 30% of the residents of the parish. There was no evidence suggesting that these patients could not take their patronage elsewhere if they preferred to receive anesthesiological services from someone other than Dr. Roux and his colleagues. In sum, the Court said, no one was forced into a tying arrangement.[93]

Hyde listed three situations where market power could be inferred in future cases: a high market share, a unique product, or a product protected by a patent or copyright.[94] The first example is self-explanatory. Unique products may a subset of products with high market shares—if a product is truly unique, it has a 100% share of its own market. But the Court may have meant this second example to encompass a more subtle concept: a product can be unique for purposes of the tied sale, although not necessarily unique in conventional market definition terms. If the arrangement requires multiple or subsequent purchases of the tied product, the buyer may be unaware of the true costs of the sale at the outset, and thus find itself "locked in" to an arrangement, even though the buyer had numerous options at the outset.

This situation was directly presented to the Court in *Eastman Kodak Co. v. Image Technical Services, Inc.*,[95] where the Court confirmed that a seller has economic power when its consumers cannot easily switch their patronage because they are "locked in" to the defendant's product. Kodak insisted that purchasers of replacement parts for its photocopying machines either repair their own machines or use Kodak servicepeople. When independent service firms alleged that this policy was an illegal tied sale, Kodak persuaded the district court to summarily dismiss the case because Kodak lacked economic power in the tying market. Kodak had no economic power in the sale of original equipment, and thus Kodak argued that it could not raise prices in services or parts above the competitive level because any effort to exploit

92. Id. at 505 n.2.

93. 466 U.S. at 26–27.

94. Id. at 17–18. Concurring in the result, Justice O'Connor wrote that it is a "common misconception" that one of these three factors *suffices* to show market power; she argued that "it is also possible that a seller in these situations will have no market power." Id. at 37 n.7.

95. 112 S.Ct. 2072 (1992).

consumers would be checked by a rapid shift of patronage to its rivals.

Applying *Hyde*'s test that "appreciable economic power in the tying market ... is the power 'to force a purchaser to do something that he would not do in a competitive market,' " [96] the Court found Kodak's argument flawed factually and theoretically. The factual problem with Kodak's position was that the plaintiffs provided evidence that service fees had risen for Kodak customers but Kodak's sales had not apparently declined.[97] The Court also accepted the plaintiff's theory for why Kodak had "appreciable economic power" vis-a-vis Kodak customers, notwithstanding the absence of power in the broader equipment market: consumers cannot accurately ascertain the total cost of the "package" of equipment, parts, and servicing when deciding which machine to purchase, and once a machine is purchased the consumer is "locked in" to the parts and service for that specific brand because it is very costly to switch to a new machine.[98]

A similar phenomena may have been present in *Northern Pacific*. Although the dissent suggested that the railroad's tracts of land were not significantly different from those owned by other lessors in the area,[99] farmers might have had great difficulty evaluating the true cost of being bound to ship their products on the Northern Pacific during the entire length of the lease. Farmers are unlikely to leave their farms simply to obtain full choice on which railroad to ship their crops. Thus there are sound reasons why consumers would favor interpreting the Sherman Act to prohibit these arrangements absent demonstrated justifications.

(3c–1) Economic power: intellectual property.

In suggesting that market power could be inferred from a patent or copyright, *Hyde* cited *United States v. Loew's, Inc.*[100] *Loew's* held that six major motion picture distributors violated § 1

---

96. Id. at 2080 (quoting *Hyde*, 466 U.S. at 14).

97. Id. at 2085.

98. Id. at 2085–87.

Kodak attempted to rebut this argument by suggesting that its equipment rivals will correct this information deficiency by pointing out any Kodak effort to exploit consumers through higher prices for parts or services. The Court rejected this rebuttal, observing that it was unlikely that Xerox and IBM (who, with Kodak, controlled virtually the entire market) would provide this information rather than adopt similar policies themselves. Id. at 2086 n.21.

Moreover, even in a competitive market, any one competitor may not have a sufficient incentive to inform consumers of Kodak's exploitive scheme because any shift in patronage would have to be shared with all rivals in the market. Id. (citing Howard Beales, Richard Craswell & Steven Salop, The Efficient Regulation of Consumer Information, 24 J.L. & Econ. 491, 503–04, 506 (1981)).

99. 356 U.S. at 16 (Harlan, J., dissenting).

100. 466 U.S. at 13–14 (citing 371 U.S. 38 (1962)).

by "block booking" their movies with television stations—i.e., conditioning the sale of desirable feature films with unwanted films. (The Court's example was packaging "Gone With the Wind" with "Getting Gertie's Garter.") Rejecting the defendants' argument that they lacked economic power because feature films constitute only 8% of television programming, the majority held that the "requisite economic power is presumed when the tying product is patented or copyrighted." [101] This holding is of dubious validity.

This presumption of economic power is based on a flawed analogy, is inconsistent with other precedent, makes little sense, and was unnecessary to the result in *Loew's*. In creating this presumption, Justice Arthur Goldberg relied on the doctrine of patent misuse, pursuant to which the courts refuse to enforce patents that the patentee has misused through a tied sale. Goldberg reasoned that because the existence of a patent sufficed to justify the conclusion that tying the patented and unpatented product constituted misuse, cases involving antitrust challenges to tied sales involving patented goods should take a similar approach. He then concluded that by their nature patented products are sufficiently distinctive that any tying arrangement involving them would have anticompetitive consequences.[102] A judicial decision to withhold enforcement of a patent (perhaps akin to the unclean hands doctrine in equity) does not, however, necessarily carry over to antitrust policy. As the Court observed in *Walker Process Equipment, Inc. v. Food Machinery & Chemical Corp.*,[103] a patent may signify a truly unique invention, but consumers may find many substitutes for that invention in the marketplace.

A sounder approach would ask the pragmatic question posed in *Northern Pacific Railway* and *Hyde* : can the seller force the buyer to purchase unwanted products? In *Loew's*, widespread coercion was occurring, and there was little doubt that television stations were being forced to take unwanted films and show them (thus preempting other motion pictures that consumers preferred). Little analysis would have been required to demonstrate the requisite economic power.

A recent Ninth Circuit decision showed this kind of sophisticated pragmatism, in refusing to extend *Loew's* to trademarked products. In that case, *Mozart Co. v. Mercedes–Benz of North America, Inc.*,[104] the plaintiff challenged Mercedes' requirement that its franchised dealers use only replacement parts supplied by

---

101. 371 U.S. at 45 (citing International Salt Co. v. United States, 332 U.S. 392 (1947)).

102. Id. at 46.

103. 382 U.S. 172 (1965).

104. 833 F.2d 1342 (9th Cir.1987), cert. denied, 488 U.S. 870 (1988).

Mercedes. Mercedes was allowed to tie its trademark license to the purchase of parts in part because its lacked economic power. The court correctly reasoned that a trademark only protects the name or symbol and does not itself confer economic power. Such power needed to be established based on the product itself. The court also observed that, in looking at the power attributable to the product itself (Mercedes automobiles), the district court erred in concentrating on consumers (many of whom regard a Mercedes as unique) instead of the buyers who were allegedly "coerced" by the tie—franchisees. The correct analysis, the court held, should focus on whether car dealers' opportunities to sign up with another manufacturer were such that Mercedes could force unwanted products on its franchisees.[105]

(3d) Business justifications.

The careful analysis required in evaluating the prior elements should suffice to demonstrate that the "per se" ban on tied sales is a complete misnomer. Rather, "structured rule of reason" would better describe the judicial practice in these cases. Just as modern analysis of horizontal restraints allows for judicial recognition that even rivals may need to cooperate, the courts explore the justifications offered for tied sales, and permit them when necessary to achieve a legitimate objective. Like the horizontal restraint cases dating back to *Addyston Pipe*, however, the courts will not allow firms to defend tied sales that are unnecessary to achieve the desired result.

Thus, *Hyde* reaffirmed language in *International Salt Co. v. United States* [106] that a defendant may insist on a tied sale when the quality of the tied product affects the operation of the tying product. However, as *International Salt* had previously indicated, the tying arrangement is not justified where the defendant can set quality standards for the tied product. Thus, although International Salt could legitimately require that its machines be used only with rock salt that was 98.2% pure, the Supreme Court refused to sanction the tying arrangement because the defendant could not claim "that the machine is allergic to salt of equal quality produced by anyone except International." [107] Similarly in *Hyde*, Jefferson Parish Hospital had a legitimate interest in ensur-

---

105. Id. at 1346–47. The district court in *Mozart* was not alone in erroneously focusing on ultimate consumers. In *Susser v. Carvel Corp.*, 332 F.2d 505 (2d Cir. 1964), cert. dismissed, 381 U.S. 125 (1965), the court found that Carvel's trademark did not indicate economic power because of Carvel's relatively low market share. While con- sumer opinion may be strong evidence that Carvel had no ability to exploit potential franchisees, it does not conclusively demonstrate the lack of such power.

106. 332 U.S. 392 (1947).

107. Id. at 398.

ing that anesthesiologists were available 24 hours a day, but the facts did not show that excluding Hyde was necessary to secure round-the-clock coverage.[108]

Lower courts have suggested that tying arrangements may be lawful in order to maintain quality control in several franchising situations where a seller licenses its trademark to independent retailers, who offer the same product to the consuming public. (McDonald's is perhaps the best-known example of a universally recognized trademark that stands for a certain kind of fast food sold at a certain range of prices in a restaurant with clean bathrooms.)

Principe v. McDonald's Corp.[109] upheld McDonald's practice of requiring its franchisees to lease property purchased by its real estate subsidiary. The Fourth Circuit listed several reasons why McDonald's found it necessary to own its own restaurants: to ensure that McDonald's outlets were placed in the most strategic locations, carefully selected by McDonald's corporate personnel; to permit quick and easy transfer of franchises when one franchisee retired, died, or was terminated; and to guarantee that franchisees could be selected based solely on management potential rather than real estate expertise or wealth.[110] The court's reasoning is another variation on the familiar theme that McDonald's restraint of trade was not unreasonable because it was ancillary and necessary to the lawful purpose of effectively marketing its highly successful fast-food chain.[111]

In *Mozart*,[112] the Ninth Circuit held that Mercedes could lawfully insist that its dealers purchase only authorized repair parts because monitoring compliance with quality standards was expensive. In this way, Mercedes could protect consumer expectations that its licensed dealers would maintain a high level of quality. Similarly, in *Warriner Hermetics, Inc. v. Copeland Refrigeration Corp.*, the Fifth Circuit allowed Copeland, a manufacturer of refrigerator components, to show that franchise agreements requiring its authorized dealers to buy only Copeland parts "con-

---

108. 466 U.S. at 25–26 n.42.

109. 631 F.2d 303 (4th Cir. 1980), cert. denied, 451 U.S. 970 (1981).

110. Id. at 310.

111. See also Pick Mfg. Co. v. General Motors Corp., 80 F.2d 641 (7th Cir. 1935), aff'd per curiam, 299 U.S. 3 (1936). *Pick* upheld GM's requirement that its dealers use only GM parts. Noting that the restriction did not apply to the many independent repair shops that were available to work on GM cars, the court expressly found that the restraint was no broader than necessary to achieve GM's legitimate goals of ensuring that its trademarked services were done at a satisfactory level of quality and meeting consumer expectations that an official GM dealer would use official GM parts.

112. 833 F.2d at 1351.

stitute the least restrictive techniques available for preserving the goodwill associated with the Copeland trade-mark." [113]

In *Siegal v. Chicken Delight, Inc.,*[114] by contrast, the Ninth Circuit prohibited the defendant from requiring franchisees to buy cooking machinery, dip and spice mixes, and paper packaging only from Chicken Delight itself. The jury found that the defendant could provide specifications for these items, and therefore could maintain the desired uniformity without a tied sale. The court of appeals suggested, however, that the tie would have been permissible if the only way for the defendant to control quality would have been to disclose trade secrets.[115] Thus, presumably Chicken Delight could have required its franchisees to purchase a secret recipe; it would not be forced to face the dilemma of disclosing such a recipe or risking widely varying seasoning for its chicken.

Another valid business justification for tying arrangements, as set forth in *United States v. Jerrold Electronics Corp.,*[116] applies to new market entrants. In that case, one of the first sellers of cable television insisted on a package sale that included all the products necessary for cable reception. Although quality specifications might have been feasible, the defendant persuaded the district court that, because the product was new, consumers would blame Jerrold for any malfunction in their reception, even if it was caused by a faulty part sold by someone else. The court also found that Jerrold had reasonably concluded that it could not effectively service the entire system if unauthorized components were included. The use of unauthorized components thus posed a significant risk of faulty reception, which would decrease demand for Jerrold's new product. As *Hyde* emphasized, though, this exception is available only while the defendant actually is a new entrant in the market. Once its reputation is established, consumers should be free to acquire parts elsewhere.[117]

Jerrold properly rejected, however, the defendant's argument that the tied sale was necessary to allow the defendant to recover its investment in the best available "head end" equipment (the principal receiver of television transmissions and related components that convert the reception into a signal to be sent via cable to each home). Although the court expressed some sympathy with Jerrold's complaint that other companies which had not made this investment were taking advantage of Jerrold's invention by profitable selling unauthorized components, the court noted that Jerrold

113.   463 F.2d 1002, 1016 (5th Cir.), cert. denied, 409 U.S. 1086 (1972).

114.   448 F.2d 43 (9th Cir. 1971), cert. denied, 405 U.S. 955 (1972).

115.   Id. at 51 n.9.

116.   187 F. Supp. 545 (E.D. Pa.1960), aff'd per curiam, 365 U.S. 567 (1961).

117.   466 U.S. at 23.

could recover its investment by selling its quality equipment at a high price and competing on the merits as to the other equipment.[118]

The Supreme Court's earlier decision in *Times–Picayune Publishing Co. v. United States* suggests another justification—that a tying arrangement may be permissible when it reduces the defendant's overhead cost. In that case, the newspaper insisted that advertisements be published in both of its newspapers, thereby substantially reducing its expenses.[119] If the costs of joint sales are much lower, however, the publisher's pricing scheme can reflect that fact, by offering a substantial discount price for a joint purchase while charging a higher price for individual ads.[120] *Times–Picayune* has questionable precedential value because the Court rejected a "per se" analysis subsequently adopted in *Northern Pacific* and refined in *Hyde*.

Finally, the special case of patent ties has led to special legislation that effectively recognizes a business justification where the tied sale is necessary to allow the patent holder to recover any value for its invention. Two cases illustrate the problem. *Mercoid Corp. v. Mid–Continent Investment Co.*[121] concerned the marketing of a "combination patent" for a home heating system. This type of patent rewards an inventor whose innovation was to combine various pre-existing components in a novel way. Mid–Continent (and its licensee, Minneapolis–Honeywell) required any user of its combination patents to use unpatented Honeywell switches as well. When Mercoid sold switches for use as part of Mid–Continent's patented combination system, Mid–Continent sued for contributory patent infringement. The Court held that "the owner of a patent may not employ it to secure a limited monopoly of an unpatented material used in applying the invention," even when the unpatented material is an integral part of the patented system.[122]

The law requires the typical patent holder to obtain its reward directly through the sale or license of its patented product, not indirectly by offering its product at a low price and selling unpatented complementary products at high prices. For certain kinds of patents (such as combination patents), however, the

118. 187 F. Supp. at 560–61.

119. 345 U.S. 594, 623 (1953).

120. Where the cost savings are so great that no one would realistically want to purchase the items separately, consumers have no interest in competition in the tied product, and *Hyde* would conclude that the sale is of a single product.

121. 320 U.S. 661 (1944).

122. Id. at 664 (citing Motion Picture Patents Co. v. Universal Film Mfg. Co., 243 U.S. 502 (1917), and Carbice Corp. of America v. American Patents Development Corp., 283 U.S. 27 (1931)).

patent holder may not be able to feasibly sell its patent directly, or to police those who would use its patent without paying for it.

Congress responded to *Mercoid* by enacting special legislation that allows a patent holder to sue for contributory infringement when the infringer makes an unpatented product (other than a staple article, like dry ice), "knowing the same to be especially made or especially adopted for use in an infringement of such patent." [123] Relying on the statute, the Court effectively overruled *Mercoid* in *Dawson Chemical Co. v. Rohm & Haas Co.* [124] Rohm owned a patent on the process for applying the herbicide propanil (the herbicide itself was unpatented). Dawson sold propanil to farmers, knowing that they would use the Rohm process to apply it to their crops. The Court held that the statute allowed Rohm to tie the sale of propanil to the sale of its patented process, and to recover for contributory infringement from unlicensed vendors of propanil. Given the expense of monitoring individual farms, how else could Rohm ensure that its patented process was not being infringed? [125]

(4) Rule of reason.

If the five elements of a "per se" case are not met, *Hyde* requires that the tied sale be analyzed under a broader rule of reason that focuses on whether the widespread use of tying arrangements throughout the industry will either preclude free consumer choice or prevent new firms from entering one market without also entering the other. [126] This analysis is virtually identical to that the courts use when analyzing exclusive dealing contracts under the rule of reason. These agreements are discussed in section H, below. [127]

---

123. 35 U.S.C. § 271(c).

124. 448 U.S. 176 (1980).

125. See Peter Maggs, New Life for Patents: Chakrabarty and Rohm & Haas Co., 1980 Sup. Ct. Rev. 57.

126. *Hyde* concluded that although it was theoretically possible that the tying arrangement between the hospital and the anesthesiologists may limit entry into the anesthesiology market, the evidence did not support that theory. Indeed, Jefferson Hospital's financing of Roux' capital expenditures at the hospital demonstrates that tying arrangements actually facilitate new entry where the hospital selects a new firm, rather than an established one, as its exclusive anesthesiologist. The Court also noted that, given the number of other hospitals in the area, any pa-

tient or surgeon who preferred services from someone other than Roux could simply go to another hospital. 466 U.S. at 29–31 & nn.48,50.

127. As discussed in section H(1), a rule of reason focus on foreclosing rivals looks not only at the effect of the defendant's contracts, but the cumulative effect of exclusive contracts in the market. See FTC v. Motion Picture Advertising Service Co., 344 U.S. 392 (1953) (exclusive dealing contract illegal even though defendant only has 40% market share, because similar contracts used by other top firms foreclosed 75% of the market). Under a rule of reason analysis, then, *Kodak* would have condemned the exclusion of independent service firms if the record showed that Kodak's two other large rivals, IBM and

(5) Reciprocal buying.

A reciprocal dealing arrangement is a variant of a tied sale. For example, in *Waugh Equipment Co.,*[128] the respondent was able to significantly increase the sales of its draft gears to railroads by promising buyers that its parent company, Armour & Co., would transport its meat products over the purchasing railways' lines. The FTC condemned this agreement as an unfair method of competition in violation of § 5 of the FTC Act. The Commission's decision is consistent with the non-economic objections to tied sales that motivated the Court in *International Salt.*[129] Although neither Waugh's draft gears nor Armour's meats probably had sufficient economic power to earn monopoly profits, the reciprocal deal injured competition in two ways: it deprived the railroads of their free opportunity to select the best draft gears; and it denied Waugh's rival gear suppliers an equal opportunity to compete on the merits.

In *Betaseed, Inc. v. U & I, Inc.,*[130] the Ninth Circuit held that coercive reciprocal contracts were to be analyzed as tying arrangements. Betaseed alleged that it was unable to sell seeds to farmers, because U & I, which was the only local processor of sugarbeets (and thus the only purchaser realistically available for farmers) insisted that it would only process beets grown from U & I seeds. The terms of the U & I contract allowed farmers to purchase seeds from rival seed producers if they met quality standards, but Betaseed alleged that no objective standards had been established and that this provision was a sham. The court reversed an order granting summary judgment to the defendant, and remanded the case so that the district court could analyze the elements set forth in *Hyde*: separate products, coercion, economic power, and business justification. The appellate court reasoned that the competitive harm occasioned by coerced reciprocity is similar to that caused by tying arrangements.[131] Reciprocity erodes the buyer's freedom to select goods based on price, quality and service, forecloses rivals from the market unless they also have the leverage necessary to engage in reciprocity, and raises entry barriers (to effectively compete with U & I, Betaseed would not only have had to develop competitive seeds, but also construct a local beet processing plant).

Some actual agreement to engage in reciprocal dealing must be established for the arrangement to violate § 1. In *United*

Xerox, employed similar exclusionary policies.

128. 15 F.T.C. 232 (1931).

129. See subsection (2a) above.

130. 681 F.2d 1203 (9th Cir. 1982).

131. Id. at 1220–21.

States v. General Dynamics Corp.,[132] the government claimed that the defendant—one of the country's leading defense contractors—conditioned purchases of products from suppliers upon the suppliers purchase of carbon dioxide from its subsidiary, Liquid Carbonic. To support its complaint, the government showed that Liquid Carbonic's sales presentations systematically included references to General Dynamics' willingness to use its vast purchasing power, and introduced statistical evidence that the its reciprocal buying program was effective. The district court rejected this count of the government's complaint, reasoning that the business Liquid Carbonic attracted could have been the result of the mere presence of reciprocity power and the desire of General Dynamics' suppliers to "curry favor." [133] Thus (except for one minuscule contract that affected an insubstantial amount of commerce), the suppliers might have unilaterally desired to buy from Liquid Carbonic.

The court seemed to employ the right standard. To prove an illegal reciprocal agreement, the plaintiff must either identify an explicit agreement or present evidence permitting the inference that the parties agreed to reciprocate. In determining whether circumstantial evidence permits such an inference, antitrust precedents require that the plaintiff negate the possibility that unilateral conduct explains the market behavior.[134] But the court's conclusion is more questionable: how likely is it that a supplier unilaterally decided to "curry favor" with General Dynamics, when Liquid Carbonic's sales representatives had explicitly told them that buying Liquid Carbonic would lead General Dynamics to purchase more of their products? Internal memoranda showing that General Dynamics had specifically targeted those from whom it made sizable purchases for sales pitches from Liquid Carbonic provided further evidence that the statistical evidence of reciprocity could not be explained by unilateral behavior.[135]

The proof problems that arise in inferring reciprocity agreements may not have significant practical impact, however, as illustrated by the district court's treatment of the government's second count in *General Dynamics*. In that count, the government alleged that the defendant had acquired its Liquid Carbonics subsidiary with the intent to employ reciprocity tactics, and thus that the acquisition restrained trade in violation of § 1 and § 7 of the Clayton Act.[136]

132. 258 F. Supp. 36 (S.D.N.Y. 1966).

133. Id. at 66.

134. See, e.g., Interstate Circuit, Inc. v. United States, 306 U.S. 208 (1939),

which is discussed in Chapter 4, section F(2).

135. See 258 F.Supp. at 43.

136. The Supreme Court has also held that acquisitions raising signifi-

Tying arrangements demonstrate the multi-faceted nature of antitrust law. The courts have recognized that they can harm competition in a number of ways. Certain tying arrangements may misallocate societal resources by eliminating competition and/or increasing entry barriers. Tied sales can also hurt consumers by raising prices and/or by denying consumers the free opportunity to choose those whom they wish to patronize. The courts have also recognized that forcing consumers to purchase two separate products from a single seller denies the seller's rivals the equal opportunity to compete on the merits (price, service, quality). In responding to these concerns, the courts have not followed the approach they have taken in horizontal restraint cases and embarked on the confusing path of strictly condemning certain broad categories of conduct and effectively immunizing other practices. Rather, despite misnaming the elements of illegality as a "per se rule," the courts have actually established a sophisticated, "structured rule of reason" that effectively separates efficiency-enhancing tying arrangements, or those that threaten no competitive harm, from those that are anticompetitive. Courts analyzing other antitrust problems would be well-advised to follow this more sophisticated approach to antitrust analysis.

Section H: Exclusive Dealing

(1) Current law: the focus on foreclosure.

Exclusive dealing contracts require a firm to buy all its supplies from a single source.[1] They typically involve promises by a retailer that it will exclusively stock one manufacturer's brand of a particular product.[2] For example, a malt shop might agree to sell only Coca–Cola soft drinks, or a donut manufacturer might agree to buy all its sugar from one manufacturer. As the Attorney General's antitrust committee observed in 1955, the key antitrust issue in such cases is whether the contracts effectively "foreclose" access to retail markets for actual or potential rival manufacturers, or foreclose access to sources of supply for actual

cant risks of reciprocity violate § 7. FTC v. Consolidated Foods Corp., 380 U.S. 592 (1965), is discussed in Chapter 6, section B(4).

1. As with other vertical restraints, antitrust coverage is limited by the *Colgate* privilege, which allows a seller to unilaterally refuse to deal with a buyer who does not purchase exclusively from the seller. See section F, above.

2. The promise can be either express or implied. Roland Machinery Co. v. Dresser Indus., Inc., 749 F.2d 380, 392 (7th Cir. 1984).

or potential rival retailers.[3] At the same time, exclusive dealing contracts can permit obvious efficiencies. A guaranteed source of supply or patronage often induces firms to make desirable investments. Like exclusive territories, exclusive dealing arrangements can also encourage local promotional activities for a distant manufacturer's product and can justify a manufacturer's investment in training retailers.

Exclusive dealing contracts were the principal object of § 3 of the Clayton Act.[4] Section 3 requires the plaintiff to present evidence that the probable effect of the contract will be to decrease competition.[5] Section 3 of the Clayton Act applies only to sales, leases, or contracts of sale, and only covers "goods, wares, merchandise, machinery, supplies or other commodities." Those who wish to challenge transactions not falling within the scope of § 3 must claim that the exclusive dealing arrangement constitutes a restraint of trade in violation of § 1 of the Sherman Act. Courts have held that § 1, like § 3, requires proof of a probable competition-lessening effect.[6] Thus, the two standards have become identical.

The cases establishing the antitrust rules governing exclusive dealing contracts may be less interesting for their holdings than for their jurisprudence, which is discussed below in subsection (4). In *Standard Oil Co. of California v. United States* (*Standard Stations*),[7] the Court held that § 3 was violated whenever exclusive dealing foreclosed a significant dollar volume of commerce. Regardless of the effect on competitive rivalry or the ability of firms to compete, the Court held it illegal to contractually tie up a large amount of business. This holding was effectively overruled, however, by *Tampa Electric Co. v. Nashville Coal Co.*[8] *Tampa Electric* now sets forth the general standard: exclusive dealing

---

3. Report of the Attorney General's National Committee to Study the Antitrust Laws 146–47 (1955).

4. The section provides that
it shall be unlawful for any person ... to lease or make a sale ... of goods ... or other commodities, whether patented or unpatented ... or fix a price charged therefore, or discount from, or rebate upon, such price, on the condition, agreement or understanding that the lessee or purchaser shall not use or deal in the goods ... or other commodities of a competitor or competitors of the lessor or seller, where the effect ... may be to substantially lessen competition....

15 U.S.C. § 14.

5. Standard Fashion Co. v. Magrane–Houston Co., 258 U.S. 346, 356 (1922).

6. See, e.g., Twin City Sportservice, Inc. v. Charles O. Finley & Co., 676 F.2d 1291, 1302 (9th Cir.), cert. denied, 459 U.S. 1009 (1982), which expressly applied the standards that had been developed in cases evaluating the legality of exclusive dealing under § 3 of the Clayton Act to litigation brought under § 1 of the Sherman Act.

7. 337 U.S. 293, 314 (1949).

8. 365 U.S. 320, 328–29 (1961).

contracts are unlawful where they significantly foreclose the opportunity for rivals to enter or remain in the market.

A key factor in applying this standard is what percentage of the relevant market—according to *Tampa Electric*, "the market area in which the seller operates, and to which the purchaser can practically turn for supplies" [9]—the exclusive dealing contract forecloses to others. Thus, in *Standard Fashion Co. v. Magrane–Houston Co.*,[10] the Supreme Court prohibited a garment manufacturer that enjoyed a 40% market share from engaging in exclusive dealing because many small towns were large enough to support only one retailer.

Importantly, antitrust analysis of exclusive dealing contracts looks at the cumulative effect of all such contracts; the law does not simply focus on the effect of the particular contract at issue. Thus, in *FTC v. Motion Picture Advertising Service Co.*,[11] the Court sustained an FTC cease and desist order that barred the defendant from entering into contracts with 40% of the movie theatres in a 27–state area whereby the theatres agreed not to show commercial advertising from any other ad agency. The Court focused not solely on the 40% of the theatres that were bound by the respondent's agreements, but also on the fact that four firms with a combined market share of 75% all used exclusive dealing contracts. Similarly, in *Standard Stations*,[12] the Supreme Court condemned exclusive dealing arrangements by Standard Oil Co., the industry leader. Although Standard Oil controlled only 16% of the retail gasoline market, the top seven firms all used exclusive dealerships and controlled about two-thirds of the market. (As discussed above, however, this was not the basis for the Court's decision). In contrast, *Tampa Electric* upheld a requirements contract that obligated Tampa Electric to buy all the coal it needed for one of its generating stations from Nashville Coal, because Tampa Electric's purchases pre-empted less than 1% of the coal market.[13]

In addition to market share, the courts examine the length of the contract in determining whether exclusive dealing forecloses entry. Thus, *Motion Picture Ads* suggested that even widespread use of one-year exclusive dealing contracts by the dominant sellers would be lawful.[14] Similarly, where exclusive dealing contracts foreclose a manufacturer from retail outlets, but entry into retailing is easy (or where a retail entrant appears cut off from sources of supply, but it is easy to enter the manufacturing end of the

9. Id. at 327.

10. 258 U.S. 346 (1922).

11. 344 U.S. 392 (1953).

12. 337 U.S. 293 (1949).

13. 365 U.S. at 333.

14. 344 U.S. at 395–96.

business), exclusive dealing arrangements should pose no serious threat of foreclosure because a potential entrant can simply enter both markets simultaneously. In sum, where a firm's ability to compete is not foreclosed, because of the small cumulative market share of those with exclusive contracts or the short duration of these contracts, § 3 is not violated.

Tampa Electric correctly held that exclusive dealing that results in significant foreclosure of manufacturers or retailers may have the effect of substantially lessening competition in violation of § 3, because significant foreclosure can harm competition in several ways. To illustrate, suppose that both the tire and truck manufacturing industries are dominated by a few firms, and that exclusive dealing is prevalent. New firms that might instill some vigorous rivalry into the truck market may not be able to enter because they can not obtain a reliable supply of tires. Even one major exclusive dealing arrangement may set off a rapid trend toward significant foreclosure. If, hypothetically, Mack Truck were to sign an exclusive arrangement with Goodyear Tire Co., oligopoly pricing among the remaining tire companies would become easier, tire prices would increase, other truck manufacturers would have greater incentive to enter exclusive dealing arrangements, and so on.

However, the law's focus on foreclosure demonstrates that efficiency is not the only concern: equal opportunities to compete and free consumer choice also play a role. In a case like *Standard Fashion*, where the defendant had exclusive arrangements with a number of general stores that were the only retail outlets in town, exclusivity may actually have kept prices down in those areas. A monopoly retailer will be able to charge consumers a monopoly price. Standard Fashion by contrast, presumably offered a lower wholesale price to monopoly retailers in order to gain exclusive rights; economic theory suggests that some (though not all) of the savings were passed on to consumers.[15] Nonetheless, prohibiting the exclusive arrangements in *Standard Fashion* accommodates the various goals of antitrust law, when one considers the effects on equal opportunity for new entrants, the preference of many consumers for choice among brands, and the fact that the economic effect in other markets was to maintain an oligopoly (four firms controlled 90% of the market).[16]

Tampa Electric's foreclosure test thus seems to reasonably accommodate the competing aims of antitrust policy. Focusing on

---

15. See Robert Bork, Antitrust Paradox 307 (1977).

16. See Harlan Blake & William Kenneth Jones, Toward a Three-Di- mensional Antitrust Policy, 65 Colum. L. Rev. 421, 441–43 (1965).

the share of the market foreclosed sensibly considers rivals' abilities to obtain supplies and outlets. Where there is little foreclosure, then, the exclusive dealing arrangement creates little risk of monopoly pricing, and thus resource allocation will not be distorted. Consumers are unlikely to be victimized by high prices or absence of choice when a significant share of the market remains unforeclosed. Firms can choose whether to deal exclusively or non-exclusively, rather than having one means of doing business imposed on them, and, by definition, small firms are not foreclosed from the market. This approach seems superior to *Standard Stations*, which condemned contracts affecting a large dollar volume without regard to an effect on anyone's ability to compete.

(2) What role for efficiencies?.

Seizing an opportunity to imprint his views upon the Federal Reporter (no matter how unnecessary to the result), Judge Richard Posner's opinion reversing a grant of preliminary relief to the plaintiff in *Roland Machinery Co. v. Dresser Industries, Inc.*[17] makes proof of a § 3 violation more difficult. The litigation arose when Dresser, a manufacturer of farm implements, exercised its right to terminate its dealership agreement with Roland after Roland also agreed to sell products made by Komatsu, one of Dresser's rivals. Posner first concluded that the trial judge erred in finding that Roland would go out of business during the pendency of the litigation unless the termination was enjoined. Because, absent this finding, the hardship was equally balanced, Roland was required to prove that it would likely prevail on the merits of the § 3 claim to win preliminary relief. Roland's proof was not sufficient. The court of appeals reversed the trial court's decision that circumstantial evidence justified an inference that Roland and Dresser had agreed to deal on an exclusive basis.[18] Section 3 applies only to sales made "on the condition, agreement or understanding" that the buyer will not deal in the goods of a competitor. The conclusion that there was no such agreement between Roland and Dresser should, of course, have ended the case.

Nevertheless, the court went on to opine about the plaintiff's chances at trial, assuming that Roland had been able to show an exclusive agreement. In so doing, Posner announced a two-pronged test for § 3 cases. Not only must the plaintiff show, consistent with *Tampa Electric*, that at least one significant competitor has actually been foreclosed, it must also show that "the probable (not certain) effect of the exclusion will be to raise prices

---

17. 749 F.2d 380 (7th Cir. 1984).   18. Id. at 392.

above (and therefore reduce output below) the competitive level." [19] Nothing in prior precedents required plaintiffs to perform a full market power analysis in order to win a § 3 exclusive dealing case.

This dictum is consistent with Posner's focus on efficiency as antitrust's sole goal: absent evidence that output will decline, the allocation of societal resources will not be affected. Posner's test would permit 11 equally-sized firms in an otherwise atomistic industry to enter into separate exclusive dealing arrangements with retailers, thus foreclosing the rest of their rivals from the market. (As we will see in Chapter 6's merger analysis, antitrust law predicts that a market with 11 firms is sufficiently competitive that prices are unlikely to exceed the competitive level.) The harm to other independent entrepreneurs and consumers' loss of free choice are irrelevant to a Chicagoist, even if these injuries are in no way necessary to achieve whatever goals were intended by the exclusive agreements.

Roland Machinery 's deviance from established precedent does, however, expose what some would consider a major analytical shortcoming in the case law. By focusing exclusively on foreclosure issues, the law from *Standard Fashion* through *Tampa Electric* does not appear to engage in the process of balancing anticompetitive harms against efficiency benefits that characterizes the post-*Sylvania* cases dealing with other non-price restraints [20]. The exclusive dealing precedents suggest, for example, that the courts would strike down long-term exclusive dealing agreements entered into by five manufacturers in a market with difficult entry, regardless of the cost savings that resulted from the arrangements. *Roland Machinery's* requirement that the plaintiff show an effect on price or output allows consideration of these efficiencies.

Unless applied with care, however, this doctrinal contribution is not only inconsistent with the non-economic reasons to promote atomistic industries, but it may also harm consumers. Consumers benefit from efficiencies only when the resulting market structure is sufficiently competitive that firms pass the cost savings along to consumers in the form of lower prices or higher quality. Thus, the proper focus of the *Roland Machinery* test should be on price, and not on output. To illustrate, let us assume that Dresser had a large market share and entered into an exclusive relationship with Roland that resulted in cost savings. There is a significant risk that these cost savings would not be passed on to consumers

---

19. Id. at 394.

20. As detailed above in section C(2), Continental T.V., Inc. v. GTE Sylvania Inc., 433 U.S. 36 (1977), adopted such a balancing test for restricted distribution arrangements other than price fixing.

unless (a) the retail market was competitive (otherwise, Roland would pocket the cost savings itself) and (b) the equipment market was competitive (otherwise, Roland and Dresser would share the cost savings but would not be forced by competitive rivalry to share their efficiencies with consumers). In determining the degree of competition in both the "upstream" and the "downstream" markets, the plaintiff should be able to use the standards applied under § 7 of the Clayton Act in evaluating the legality of mergers to draw inferences about the likelihood that an exclusive dealing contract will decrease competition under § 3 of the Clayton Act (both sections use the same operative phrase—"where the effect ... may be to substantially lessen competition or to tend to create a monopoly"). Thus, if *Roland Machinery*'s test is to be adopted, the plaintiff should still prevail in a case where five firms in an industry with entry barriers enter into exclusive dealing contracts, unless the defendants can demonstrate that the cost savings resulting from the contracts are so significant that prices will not rise, despite the foreclosure effects.[21]

As with other rule of reason cases, courts considering efficiencies must also examine whether the defendants could obtain the desired efficiencies through an obvious less restrictive alternative. For example, in *Twin City Sportservice, Inc. v. Charles O. Finley & Co.*,[22] Finley, the owner of the Oakland Athletics baseball team, breached a 15–year exclusive contract with Twin City for concession services. The court upheld a finding that the breach was permissible because the contract violated § 1. Exclusivity was justified because Twin City had made substantial investments in facilities at the ballpark, and the court did not suggest that the ball club was required to license two or more concessionaires in its stadium. Rather, the court condemned the length of the contract as unreasonable because it exceeded the time needed to recapture the concessionaire's investment.[23]

Excessively exclusive terms like these should create suspicions that efficiency is not the real motive for the arrangement, even if an initial examination of market structure suggests that the contract does not threaten competition. Ultimately, however, *Tampa Electric* teaches that if the market is defined correctly, an exclusive dealing arrangement poses no competitive threat unless a significant percentage of the market is foreclosed. Procedurally, this approach suggests that where evidence of market definition clearly rules out significant competitive risks, the court need not

---

21. See Alan Fisher, Frederick Johnson & Robert Lande, Price Effects of Horizontal Mergers, 77 Calif. L. Rev. 777 (1989), discussed in the introduction to Chapter 6.

22. 676 F.2d 1291 (9th Cir.), cert. denied, 459 U.S. 1009 (1982).

23. Id. at 1304.

ask whether the arrangement is necessary; where there are any reasonable grounds to doubt how accurately market structure data describes the level of rivalry in the market, unduly broad agreements can lead courts to suspect that something may be amiss. To illustrate, a court might initially think that stadium concessionaires compete in the broad market for beer and sodas. Because firms in competitive markets have no incentive to agree to excessive exclusivity, if a 15–year lease was clearly longer than necessary, this may suggest that the market might be limited to metropolitan stadia or perhaps an even narrower market.

(3) The lesser standard applied under § 5 of the FTC Act.

As discussed earlier, the absence of criminal or treble damage liability for violations of the FTC Act and the assumed expertise of administrative agencies suggest that the FTC can condemn borderline cases without fear of chilling legitimate competition, and may make the Commission more willing to consider complex economic issues that the courts may prefer to avoid. In *FTC v. Brown Shoe Co.*,[24] the Supreme Court unanimously held that the Commission has the discretion to find an unfair method of competition in violation of § 5 of the FTC Act on evidence skimpier than that necessary to prove a violation of § 1 of the Sherman Act or § 3 of the Clayton Act. Although the only evidence described in the Court's opinion that supported the FTC's conclusion was that Brown was the country's second largest shoe manufacturer and had effectively required franchisees to limit their trade with other shoe manufacturers, the Court held that the FTC acted within its authority under § 5 to stop a violation in its incipiency.

If the FTC's § 5 jurisprudence really represented a careful exercise of its expertise, this holding might be defensible. However, the Commission's opinion in *Brown Shoe* suggests that the FTC read § 5 to subject exclusive dealing arrangements to virtual per se condemnation under a standard that closely resembles the discredited *Standard Stations* test (which condemned any foreclosure of a significant volume of sales).[25] The FTC did not provide any explanation, expert or otherwise, why banning exclusive agreements that foreclose any volume of sales is the best way to prevent unfair foreclosure. Because the FTC refused to exercise its expert judgment in analyzing the facts of the case, its

---

24. 384 U.S. 316 (1966).

25. See 62 F.T.C. 679, 709 (1963) (rejecting any economic justification for exclusive dealing); id. at 715 (finding a § 5 violation based on the foreclosure of a "significant number of retail shoe stores"); id. (finding Brown's exclusive dealing arrangement to be akin to tying arrangements, which are "inherently anticompetitive").

analysis of whether Brown Shoe violated § 5 did not discuss why the respondent's franchise agreements, which strongly discouraged franchisees from selling rival brands, needed to be enjoined, given that Brown's national market share was minuscule and its franchisees constituted only a small fraction of the nation's 70,000 retail shoe outlets. Nor did the Commission explain how Brown's conduct could bloom into the type of foreclosure that would be unlawful under *Tampa Electric*'s interpretation of § 3 of the Clayton Act (which requires substantial foreclosure of rivals from retail outlets).

Perhaps Chairman Paul Rand Dixon's opinion was just inartfully drafted; he did turn to an economic analysis of the industry in determining the appropriate remedy. In that portion of the opinion, he found a trend towards vertical integration in the industry and a "tendency to dry up otherwise available sales outlets to independent shoe manufacturers." He also discovered that smaller manufacturers were "faced with a diminishing number of retail outlets as a practical matter," a problem exacerbated by Brown's practice of including the most select group of retailers in its franchise program.[26] Had the FTC's analysis of whether Brown violated § 5 included a specific prediction that Brown's plan would transform the industry into one characterized by widespread exclusive dealing, its citation to Supreme Court decisions endorsing the Jeffersonian goal of promoting "an organization of industry in small units which can effectively compete"[27] might have been a legitimate exercise of its § 5 authority.[28]

Any expert FTC assessment of possible trends in the industry must also carefully evaluate the actual role that exclusive dealing contracts play in contributing to that trend. If the contracts will play an integral role in increasing concentration, § 5 condemnation may be warranted. Where industry concentration is increasing anyway, exclusive dealing contracts may well provide a way to preserve a relatively *de* concentrated market. While exclusive

26. Id. at 718–19.

27. Id. at 720 & n.38 (citing United States v. Aluminum Co. of America, 148 F.2d 416, 429 (2d Cir. 1945), which is discussed above in Chapter 3, section A(4), and Brown Shoe Co. v. United States, 370 U.S. 294 (1962), which is discussed below in Chapter 6, sections A(3) and C(3).

28. The FTC's expertise may also be questioned in light of the remedy it eventually imposed in *Brown Shoe*. Brown Shoe had never prohibited retailers from selling other brands; rather, it gave them valuable inducements

to encourage them to carry only Brown Shoe products. Many retailers objected that a ban on exclusivity would have resulted in a termination of these valuable inducements. Accordingly, the FTC order simply prohibited Brown Shoe from collecting monthly reports, which was one way the manufacturer monitored compliance. As one commentator concluded, "whatever one's point of view it is clear that nothing was accomplished by bringing this case." John Peterman, The Federal Trade Commission v. Brown Shoe Company, 18 J.L. & Econ. 361, 393 (1975).

dealing contracts may foreclose rivals without outlets, they tend to help rivals that have established outlets maintain their ability to compete, and may therefore forestall concentration in markets where large firms are increasing their market share.

To illustrate, compare the beer distribution system in the United States and the Netherlands, where taverns serve all varieties of beers, with the "closed" system in Britain and Germany, where pubs and beerhouses often sell only one particular brand of lager or ale. The beer market in the United States is dominated by a few major brands, and in the Netherlands by two. In contrast, a number of sellers compete in Britain and Germany. One explanation may be that "tied houses" (taverns with exclusive dealing arrangements with a single brewer) tend to compete on quality and thus promote brand loyalty, while the "open" system used in the United States leads to aggressive price competition, giving an advantage to a few large firms that enjoy economies of scale.

(4) Jurisprudential themes.

Apart from their holdings, the language and reasoning contained in the various opinions in *Standard Stations* and *Tampa Electric* make these cases landmarks in antitrust jurisprudence. In the majority opinion in *Standard Stations*, Justice Felix Frankfurter recognized that exclusive dealing contracts can be efficient, but nevertheless concluded that any evaluation of their economic effect was beyond judicial competence. Thus, he construed § 3 as imposing a virtual per se ban on exclusive dealing, requiring only that the plaintiff prove that a significant dollar volume of sales had been foreclosed to rivals.[29]

Frankfurter's opinion is not the only antitrust ruling inconsistent with precedent, but it may win the Oscar. *Standard Fashion* had clearly held that § 3's requirement of a "probable" lessening of competition obligated the courts to predict the likely competitive effect of an exclusive dealership.[30] Other § 3 precedents had expressly supported a rule of reason approach, which has always included an evaluation of competitive effects.[31] Moreover, Frankfurter's attempt to extend the Court's apparent per se condemnation of tying agreements to exclusive dealing contracts is difficult to understand in light of his own view that tying arrangements are rarely beneficial while exclusive dealing contracts have

29. 337 U.S. at 314.

30. 258 U.S. at 356–57.

31. In both Pick Mfg. Co. v. General Motors Corp., 299 U.S. 3 (1936) and FTC v. Sinclair Refining Co., 261 U.S. 463 (1923), the Court had held that § 3 did not condemn the particular exclusive requirements at issue because the share of the market foreclosed was not sufficient to lessen competition.

obvious efficiencies.[32] Finally, construing a statute that called for proof that the exclusive dealing arrangement "may ... substantially lessen competition" to simply require a foreclosure of a significant volume of sales ignores the legislative history of § 3. The competitive effect clause was added in Conference Committee as a compromise between the House, which sought to ban all exclusive dealing arrangements, and the Senate, which preferred to leave the entire matter to the FTC except for a ban on exclusive deals on patented goods.[33]

A close runner-up for faithlessness to precedent would have to be *Standard Stations'* sequel, *Tampa Electric*. In expressly rejecting the plaintiff's argument that the exclusive contract was illegal because it foreclosed a significant amount of business (measured in terms of dollars), Justice Tom Clark flatly overruled *Standard Stations*, without so acknowledging.

Justice Frankfurter's opinion in *Standard Stations*, like Justice Thurgood Marshall's per se condemnation of exclusive territories in *Topco*,[34] ironically sounded a theme now echoed by the Chicago school. Felix Frankfurter, Thurgood Marshall, and Robert Bork have all displayed a sharp distrust of the courts' ability to make factual determinations on a case-by-case basis about restraints that, in theory, can either help or harm competition. Instead, they have all attempted to apply broad generalizations to the restraints, despite theory's teaching that accurate generalizations are necessarily indeterminate. Frankfurter and Marshall would condemn almost all vertical restraints; Bork would uphold them.

Justice Robert Jackson's dissent in *Standard Stations*[35] reflects a preference for possibly imperfect factual analysis over simple but inaccurate rules. Like Justice Lewis Powell in *Sylvania*,[36] Jackson assumed that courts can and should weigh the benefits to overall competition derived from these contracts against any restraints they impose. Jackson would therefore have followed § 3 precedent and inquired into the actual competitive effect of the contracts.

Justice William Douglas' dissent in *Standard Stations* reflected two other recurrent themes of antitrust jurisprudence. Douglas recognized that exclusive dealing contracts in the oil

32. 337 U.S. at 305–06.

33. See William Lockhart and Howard Sacks, The Relevance of Economic Factors in Determining Whether Exclusive Arrangements Violate Section 3 of the Clayton Act, 65 Harv. L. Rev. 913, 933–40 (1952).

34. United States v. Topco Associates, Inc., 405 U.S. 596 (1972), which is discussed in Chapter 4, section E(2).

35. 337 U.S. at 321.

36. Continental T.V., Inc. v. GTE Sylvania Inc., 433 U.S. 36 (1977).

industry might well foreclose new entrants. But he also realized that in the 1950s the retail level of the oil industry consisted of thousands of small businesses. Because merger and monopoly laws had not been enforced with the Jeffersonian fervor that Douglas favored, he feared that the major oil companies could and would respond to *Standard Stations* by vertically integrating— taking over their own retail operations in order to maintain the desired exclusivity. As a result, entrepreneurs seeking to own service stations would lose their independence, which, Douglas believed, was at odds with the basic Jeffersonian tenet of the antitrust laws.[37]

Douglas' decision is not significant only for its articulation of the Jeffersonian antitrust goal. Preserving independent gasoline dealers in an industry foreclosed to many new refiners or would-be gasoline dealers was, in Douglas' view, the lesser evil. Thus, because other aspects of antitrust law were not to his liking (he was probably correct in predicting, for example, that the law would not put an end to vertical integration that would wipe out independent service stations), he was willing to wage guerilla warfare on antitrust doctrine by distorting it in this case. This means to an end approach is ironically similar to today's efforts by Chicago school opponents of *Dr. Miles*, who distort conspiracy theory and the *Colgate* doctrine to permit more manufacturer control of retail prices than would otherwise be possible.

---

37. 337 U.S. at 319–21. Douglas cited with approval Justice Louis Brandeis' similar views. Id. at 317 n.4, 318 n.7. See also American Column & Lumber Co. v. United States, 257 U.S. 377, 413–19 (1921) (Brandeis, J., dissenting).

CHAPTER 6: MERGERS

By definition, mergers put an end to any actual or potential competition between the merging firms. As such, a literal reading of § 1 of the Sherman Act might prohibit all mergers as contracts to restrain trade. From the outset, however, the antitrust laws borrowed from the common law's more lenient treatment of mergers: mergers were one of the specific categories of agreements that could constitute "reasonable" restraints trade under the common law because some mergers can be quite beneficial to society.[1] On the other hand, not all mergers are benign. Indeed, Congress enacted § 7 of the Clayton Act in 1914 because it was concerned that the Sherman Act did not adequately protect the public against harmful mergers, and then significantly strengthened it in 1950 with amendments passed as part of the Celler–Kefauver Act. As amended, § 7 prohibits any merger or acquisition "where in any line of commerce or ... in any section of the country, the effect of such acquisition may be substantially to lessen competition, or to tend to create a monopoly."[2]

Mergers can benefit society in a number of ways. They can allow firms to take advantage of economies of scale. For example, some manufactured goods can be produced at a lower cost per unit in a larger plant; likewise, merging into larger entities and thus spreading the cost of overhead over more a greater number of employees might allow service industries (lawyers, accountants, etc.) to lower costs. Economies of scope, or synergies, can also be created by merging two firms with complementary strengths and weaknesses. For example, if a firm with a modern, efficient plant but an inept sales force merges with another firm that has an old, decrepit plant and aggressive marketers, the result may be a newly strengthened rival that can efficiently get quality products to consumers. Similarly, acquisitions allow more competent corporate executives to obtain control of physical assets being misused by poor management. In each of these cases, a merger leads to a more efficient use of society's resources. Where the industry remains competitive after the merger, the forces of rivalry will ensure that consumers receive the benefits of this efficiency through lower prices, higher quality, or both.

1. United States v. Joint Traffic Ass'n, 171 U.S. 505 (1898); United States v. Addyston Pipe & Steel Co., 85 Fed. 271, 281 (6th Cir. 1898), aff'd, 175 U.S. 211 (1899).

2. 15 U.S.C. § 18.

You will recall from Chapter 4 that, according to the Supreme Court, the common law approved reasonable non-competition covenants because they facilitate the sale of good will in a business.[3] Allowing an entrepreneur to preserve and market the value of the good will accrued in developing a business (by promising not to compete with the buyer for a reasonable period) creates an incentive to create good will. Similarly, mergers provide the same long-run benefit to consumers by encouraging an entrepreneur to develop a successful business and then, through merger, to sell the business to another firm at a substantial profit.

Mergers have a negative effect on consumers and society primarily when they are simply poor business decisions. One economic study suggests that on balance, most mergers do not, achieve efficiencies and that their overall effect is to waste money that the acquiring company could have been better spent on other things.[4] Of course, the hindsight knowledge that many mergers are not efficient is not directly helpful in shaping antitrust policy, absent some way of identifying in advance those mergers destined for failure. However, whether or not one believes this study will affect one's view of how aggressive or lenient the government's overall merger policy should be.

In any event, § 7 does not condemn mergers "where the effect may be to waste societal resources"; rather, the law prohibits combinations that may have the effect of lessening competition. Thus, the proper focus of merger doctrine is on a merger's effect on rivalry in the marketplace. The legislative history of the 1950 amendment to the Clayton Act suggests four principal ways in which mergers can substantially lessen competition.[5] *First*, a merger can eliminate a firm that itself was a *substantial factor in competition*. With the elimination of a particularly aggressive rival from the industry, some or all of the remaining firms can more safely avoid price cutting or innovation. *Second*, the size of the merged firm can be so large as to give that firm a *decisive advantage* over its rivals. This congressional concern could mean several different things. A firm's size and resulting competitive advantages may give it sufficient economic power that Congress feared that it could unilaterally succeed in raising prices to consumers. Alternatively, Congress may have wanted to ban mergers that create a large, efficient firm that is able to out-compete smaller rivals because of a Jeffersonian concern that

---

3. National Soc'y of Professional Engineers v. United States, 435 U.S. 679, 688–89 (1978).

4. See David Ravenscraft & F.M. Scherer, Mergers, Sell–Offs, and Economic Efficiency (1987).

5. H.R. Rep. No. 1191, 81st Cong., 1st Sess. 8 (1949).

competition between a large number of firms ought to be preserved for its own sake. *Third,* one or more horizontal mergers may *eliminate an undue number of rivals* from the industry. This concern receives the most attention in merger law. The theory here is that the presence of a large number of firms in a market results in aggressive competition and lower prices; with fewer rivals, it is easier for the remaining firms to actively collude on prices, to engage in oligopoly pricing based on the knowledge of how their competitors are likely to respond, or simply to feel less pressure to innovate. *Fourth,* vertical mergers (i.e., mergers between suppliers and their purchasers) can *deprive rivals of a fair opportunity to compete* in the same way that exclusive dealing contracts can harm competition—by denying independent rivals sources of supply or outlets for their products.

As elsewhere, one's view of the appropriate antitrust approach to horizontal mergers is a function of one's ideological attitude about the goals of antitrust, one's quasi-empirical sense of the extent to which markets with relatively few firms can function in a competitive manner, and one's assessment of the government's ability to easily identify the existence (or lack thereof) of competitive harm. For many years, the ideological debate raged between those who sought to foster a Jeffersonian concern with preserving atomistic industries and those who sought to allow most mergers to proceed in order to maximize the efficient allocation of resources. The legality of many mergers turned on which of these two views prevailed: modern technological improvements often allowed firms to take advantage of economies of scale that enabled them to offer better products at lower prices, but only by substantially reducing in the number of firms in the market.

More recently, however, a new ideological dialectic has entered antitrust debates, between those who are solely concerned with efficiencies and those who seek to ensure that consumers are not forced to pay higher prices. Mergers often simultaneously lower costs for the merging firms and enable the firms remaining in the market to raise price. Efficiency advocates who want to maximize societal wealth, regardless of its distribution, approve of mergers that save resources and enrich shareholders, even if consumers are exploited. Neo-populists, on the other hand, have no qualms about condemning such mergers, without any careful balancing of harms and benefits. As they point out, any such balancing of the benefits realized by shareholders against the harms suffered by consumers is quite difficult, and cost savings are unlikely to outweigh the predictable harm to consumers unless those harms are severely discounted.[6] Neo-populists also oppose

---

6. See, e.g., Alan Fisher, Frederick Johnson & Robert Lande, Price Effects of Horizontal Mergers, 77 Calif. L. Rev. 777 (1989).

such mergers on utilitarian grounds—more people are hurt by them and, in a democracy, the predominant majority of Americans are consumers who want the antitrust laws to protect *them*.

Antitrust ideology matters most, however, only in extreme cases, where, at the time of the merger, it is clear that a merger would cause a simultaneous reduction in costs and an increase in price. In other cases, though, the advocates of a merger claim that the deal will clearly reduce costs and dismiss the forecast of higher prices as speculative, while opponents of the merger argue that cost-saving claims are exaggerated and that economic theory suggests a high probability of higher prices. Thus, one's faith in the reliability of legal standards to determine when an "undue number of rivals" have been eliminated and in the ability of government agencies and judges to determine whether efficiency claims are valid can become more important than ideology.

In considering the trade-offs between the potential costs and benefits of particular mergers, it is important to keep in mind that government merger policy involves the enforcement of a statute. Despite recently imposed limits on the ability of private parties to challenge mergers under § 7,[7] the law governing mergers law in this country is like our other antitrust laws: it is enforced through the courts by litigation brought by the government or private parties. American merger policy, then, must be one capable of judicial management through the adversarial process of litigation.

Section A: Horizontal Mergers

The principal concern arising when competitors merge is that the resulting market structure will be insufficiently competitive to force prices down to the competitive level. Every school of anti-trust thought would therefore prohibit mergers that result in oligopolistic behavior, for the same reason that everyone agrees about the evils of price fixing.[8] Where prices are not competitive, because of express agreement, hidden agreement, or oligopolistic interdependence, resources are inefficiently allocated, consumers are exploited, and discretionary power to raise prices or limit innovation is placed in the hands of oligopolists. Moreover, the presence of only a few firms in an industry often means that, because of economies of scale or greater access to capital, these firms will be large in size, yeomen entrepreneurs will be discouraged, and opportunities to enter the market will therefore be limited. Insufficient pressure by competitors can also result in

---

7. See section D, below.   **8.** See introduction to Chapter 4.

reduced innovation and product quality, as oligopolists enjoy the quiet life. Unfortunately, there is no agreement as to how many firms are necessary to maintain aggressive competition.

(1) How many firms does a market need?.

One initial source of dispute concerns the question whether the competitiveness of a market structure is more like age (with each year, one gradually grows older; with each merger, a market gradually becomes less competitive) or like virginity (one either is a virgin or is not; a market either has enough firms to be competitive or it does not). Some cases decided by the Warren Court at the apex of Jeffersonian populism suggest the former view: the Court condemned one merger because it would set off a trend that would transform the industry from one with hundreds of firms to one with, at worst, twenty large entities.[9] In a few limited areas, Americans continue to share this view—witness the support for family farms and localized banking.[10]

Most economists believe, however, that markets with some minimum number of firms will generally behave competitively and do not warrant antitrust concern. Two related economic theories suggest that consumers will often be harmed if the number of firms in the market becomes too small. First, the fewer the number of firms, the easier it is for those in the market to collude on prices, to keep a watchful eye on each other to prevent cheating, and to hide the conspiracy from the government. Second when a firm sets prices in an oligopoly market, it can accurately predict how its rivals will react: price cuts will quickly be matched, and thus will not result in increased market share; price increases can be rolled back if not matched, or can be followed to the mutual benefit of all concerned, without the need for an explicit agreement.

Of course, economists disagree as to how many firms are necessary to avoid collusion and oligopoly pricing. Moreover, high concentration is not a sufficient condition for secret price fixing and oligopoly pricing; some firms with few rivals do engage in fierce rivalry. F.M. Scherer believes that ten to twelve firms are necessary.[11] Robert Bork has written that two or three firms

---

9. Brown Shoe Co. v. United States, 370 U.S. 294 (1962) (merger increased Brown Shoe's market share to 5%). See also United States v. Von's Grocery Co., 384 U.S. 270 (1966) (concern about merger trends that reduced the number of grocery stores in a metropolitan area from 5,300 to 3,800).

10. In contrast, many European countries have six or fewer nationwide banks.

11. F.M. Scherer, Industrial Market Structure and Economic Performance 199 (2d ed. 1980).

suffice.[12] The Department of Justice effectively considers markets with more than five or six relatively equal firms sufficiently competitive to permit rivals to merge.[13]

(2) The Sherman Act and merger policy.

The Supreme Court's treatment of horizontal mergers under § 1 of the Sherman Act seemed to validate the concerns about the judiciary's lax antitrust enforcement that led to passage of the Clayton Act. Indeed, in *Northern Securities Co. v. United States*,[14] the Court held by only the barest majority that § 1 even applied to anticompetitive mergers. In that case, the Court concluded that the formation of a holding company to purchase the stock of large, parallel railroads was a "combination in restraint of trade." The majority explained:

> If such a combination be not destroyed, all the advantages that would naturally come to the public under the operation of the general laws of competition, as between the Great Northern and the Northern Pacific Railway Companies, will be lost, and the entire commerce of the immense territory in the northern part of the United States between the Great Lakes and the Pacific at Puget Sound will be at the mercy of a single holding corporation...."[15]

12. Antitrust Paradox 221–22 (1977). Professor John Kwoka has done several studies suggesting that the existence of three rivals of approximately equal strength is the key to competitive performance. Thus, in his view, the merger of two smaller firms in an industry dominated by two larger ones would be desirable. Does the Choice of Concentration Really Matter?, 29 J. Indus. Econ. 445 (1981).

13. 4 Trade Reg. Rep. (CCH) ¶ 13,104 (1992). The Justice Department uses a measure called the Herfindahl–Hirschman Index (HHI) to determine the competitive structure of a marketplace. The index is computed by taking the market share of each firm in the market, squaring those numbers, and adding them all together. Thus, the HHI for a market with five companies, each of which has a 20% share of the market, would be 2000 ($20^2=400$; $400+400+400+400+400=2000$). The HHI is sensitive to dominance by a few firms. Thus, the HHI for a market with five firms, where the top two firms each had a 35% market share and the three remaining each had 10% would

be 2750 ($35^2=1225$, $10^2=100$; $1225+1225+100+100+100=2750$).

Despite the language of the Justice Department guidelines, which are considered in detail below, the Department's effective policy during the Reagan administration was to tolerate mergers where the HHI after the merger did not exceed 2000, and the Bush administration's new guidelines presume competitive harm only where a merger significantly increases the HHI above the 1800 level. Id. at 20,573–6.

14. 193 U.S. 197 (1904).

15. Id. at 327–28.

There was some evidence that the principal strategy behind the creation of the Northern Securities holding company was not the horizontal merger of the Northern Pacific and the Great Northern, for they were controlled by two robber barons (J.P. Morgan and James Hill) who were business allies. Rather, the two men agreed to the plan because they both wanted to gain control of the Chicago, Burlington & Quincy Railroad, thus giving them control of access from Chicago to the west.

Justice Oliver Wendell Holmes, Jr. authored a vigorous dissent, which garnered four votes.[16] He suggested that the common law did not consider mergers "contracts" in restraint of trade, and that the statutory ban on "combinations" in restraint of trade was only meant to bar "combinations to keep strangers to the agreement out of the business." [17]

Holmes also argued that the effect of the merger-to-monopoly challenged by the government was no worse than if a single railroad company had built both lines. As a statutory matter, such reasoning would eviscerate most of the Sherman Act—the anticompetitive effect of many cartels and mergers could be replicated by a monopolist. On policy grounds, Holmes' argument is even more objectionable. A merger deprives society of a pre-existing independent competitor, and with one bold stroke can eliminate competition and its benefits for consumers. Internal growth by a single firm is much less likely to eliminate competition.[18]

The framers of the Sherman Act did not understand, as we do today, that mergers can simultaneously increase market power and efficiency. Although that misunderstanding may have led to judicial opinions condemning horizontal agreements that affected prices, even if consumers would benefit through lower costs and lower prices,[19] it also resulted in an inability to appreciate the long-term harm of reduced competition, even where a merger might be efficient. For example, in *United States v. Winslow* [20], the Court held that the merger of three separate companies to

The three railroads ultimately agreed to a similar merger plan in 1960. By then, however, railroad mergers were immune from the antitrust laws, subject instead to regulatory approval by the Interstate Commerce Commission. The ICC, over the objections of the Antitrust Division of the Department of Justice, approved the merger. See United States v. ICC, 396 U.S. 491 (1970). See generally Richard Posner & Frank Easterbrook, Antitrust 396–97 (2d ed. 1981).

16. Holmes' anti-antitrust coalition became a majority in Standard Oil Co. v. United States, 221 U.S. 1 (1911). See Chapter 3, section A(2) above.

17. 193 U.S. at 404. Cf. Norcross v. James, 140 Mass. 188, 2 N.E. 946, 947 (1885) (Holmes, J.) (non-competition covenant could not be enforced against successor in interest to covenantor; it did not "touch and concern" real property but was only a personal agreement between the contracting parties). Holmes

may have been correct about the classic common law, but at the time of the Sherman Act's enactment, state courts were moving towards condemning voluntary restraints as public threats. See Herbert Hovenkamp, The Sherman Act and the Classical Theory of Competition, 74 Iowa L. Rev. 1019 (1989).

18. See Chapter 3, section A(4) above.

19. See United States v. Socony–Vacuum Oil Co., 310 U.S. 150, 221, 223 (1940), discussed in detail in Chapter 4, section B. For a more recent application of this principle, see Columbia Broadcasting System, Inc. v. American Society of Composers, Authors and Publishers, 562 F.2d 130, 140 (2d Cir. 1977) (blanket license providing new and unique product to television networks held per se illegal), rev'd, 441 U.S. 1 (1979).

20. 227 U.S. 202 (1913).

form the United Shoe Machinery Corporation did not violate § 1.
The Court noted that the merger would lower costs in the short
term (the new firm was going to build a large, efficient plan to
centralize operations), and would not harm consumers because the
three merging companies all produced complementary products
under patent. Justice Holmes' opinion for a unanimous Court
ignored, however, the long run; in fact, it took three more lawsuits before the government was able to break up United Shoe's
monopoly.[21]

The Supreme Court's Sherman Act merger jurisprudence,
culminating in *United States v. Columbia Steel Co.*,[22] led to the
revision and strengthening of § 7 of the Clayton Act as the
primary anti-merger statute. In *Columbia Steel*, the majority
upheld the acquisition by United States Steel, the nation's largest
steel manufacturer, of the assets of a smaller regional competitor.[23] The Court found that the merger was not an unreasonable
restraint of trade even if, taking the most favorable view of the
government's evidence, the merger would allow the company to
control 24% of the market. Although earlier railroad merger
cases had suggested that trade was restrained whenever two
substantial competitors merged,[24] *Columbia Steel* instead articulated an open-ended rule of reason that required consideration of (1)
the market shares of the merging firms; (2) the "strength of
remaining competition"; (3) "whether the [merger] springs from
business requirements or purpose to monopolize"; (4) trends in the
industry; and (5) consumer demands.[25] In applying these factors
to approve the acquisition, the majority emphasized recent new
entry into the market, the significant number of local competitors,
the ability of outside rivals to compete because of the customized
character of many orders, and the relatively small amount of
direct competition between the merging parties. The opinion
suggests that, when these factors are considered, the merger did
not constitute an unreasonable restraint of trade because the
industry would not become monopolistic.[26]

The Court rejected the railroad precedents as "so dissimilar"
to the steel acquisition as to "furnish little guidance".[27] Although

21. A description of United Shoe's antitrust saga is summarized in note 11 in Chapter 5, section G.

22. 334 U.S. 495 (1948).

23. Section 7 was not applicable in *Columbia Steel* because, prior to 1950, that section did not apply to mergers where the acquiring firm purchased the assets, rather than the stock, of the acquired concern. One of the principal purposes of the Celler–Kefauver amend-

ments in 1950 was to plug this loophole in the Clayton Act.

24. See, e.g., United States v. Southern Pacific Co., 259 U.S. 214 (1922); United States v. Union Pacific Railroad, 226 U.S. 61 (1912).

25. 334 U.S. at 527.

26. Id. at 529–30.

27. Id. at 531.

the Court did not elaborate,[28] presumably this view was based on the fact that, for many consumers, the railroad mergers resulted in a monopoly. In essence, *Columbia Steel* held that even though a merger of significant competitors in a concentrated market might lessen competition by increasing the likelihood of oligopoly pricing, such an effect did not constitute an unreasonable restraint of trade. The open-textured list of factors to be considered under the rule of reason were not analyzed (by the majority or the dissent) with oligopoly pricing in mind. Rather, based on the railroad cases, the U.S. Steel acquisition of Columbia was challenged because the elimination of competition between any two significant rivals was thought to constitute, in and of itself, an unreasonable restraint of trade.[29] The Court also refused to read § 1 to apply to potential competition mergers.[30]

The four dissenters unsuccessfully advocated a virtual per se rule against horizontal mergers. Citing Justice Louis Brandeis' classic work, *The Curse of Bigness*, Justice William O. Douglas' dissent took aim at the notion that "sound business reasons" justify horizontal mergers among substantial competitors.[31] Brandeis wrote that the "economies of monopoly are superficial and

28. Particularly troubling for those seeking more aggressive antitrust enforcement was the Court's comment that it would not "examine those cases to determine whether we would now approve either their language or their holdings." Id.

29. Cf. United States v. First Nat'l Bank & Trust Co. of Lexington, 376 U.S. 665 (1964). In that case, Justice Douglas (who barely missed securing a majority in *Columbia Steel* for a per se rule against large horizontal mergers), wrote for five Justices, holding that *Columbia Steel* "must be confined to its special facts." Id. at 672. Douglas reinstated as § 1 doctrine the language of the railroad cases: "where merging companies are major competitive factors in a relevant market, the elimination of significant competition between them, by merger or consolidation, itself constitutes a violation of § 1 of the Sherman Act." Id. at 671–72. Justices Brennan and White concurred, arguing that the *Columbia Steel* factors condemned the acquisition by the leading bank (with a 40% market share) of the fourth largest bank (with a 12% share). Id. at 673.

Consistent with the majority's reasoning in *Columbia Steel*, Justices Harlan and Stewart dissented, emphasizing the "strength of the remaining competition" (four other banks had significant market shares). Id. at 677–79. The dissenters overlooked economic theory predicting that firms in a highly concentrated market—where five firms had over 90% of the assets, the leader had 52%, and the second largest firm had 17%—was more likely to engage in oligopoly pricing than where six firms controlled the market and the leader had 40% share.

30. These mergers, which are challenged based on the fear that the acquisition will stifle potential future competition between the two merged firms, are discussed in detail in section B, below.

Lessening of potential competition was perhaps the strongest part of the government's case in *Columbia Steel*, in that of 2,400 jobs bid on by United States Steel and almost 6,400 jobs bid on by the acquired firm, Consolidated, in a ten-year period, both companies bid in competition with one another on only 166 contracts. 334 U.S. at 515 n.13.

31. Id. at 534 & n.1.

delusive. The efficiency of monopoly is at the best temporary." [32]
Moreover, Brandeis argued, "experience teaches us that whenever
trusts have developed efficiency, their fruits have been absorbed
almost wholly by the trust themselves." [33] Although Douglas'
proposal in *Columbia Steel* to condemn any significant horizontal
merger may seem simplistic now, it is difficult to view the American steel industry today without questioning the wisdom of the
more "sophisticated" pro-merger policy followed since World War
II.

   Nonetheless, Douglas' concern about virtually any horizontal
merger is unwarranted. Where the parties to a merger still face
vigorous competition from other firms, economies of scale or other
efficiencies are unlikely to be absorbed wholly by the merging
firms. On the other hand, many have overlooked Brandeis' argument and are too quick to support mergers simply because short
term efficiencies may result, without regard to how these efficiencies will benefit society. For example, recent work has suggested
that dynamic efficiency and innovation are significantly stifled by
mergers that lessen vigorous domestic rivalry.[34]

   The solicitous view toward major industrial mergers reflected
in *Columbia Steel* appears to offend the goals of dynamic economic
efficiency, populist protection of consumers, and maintenance of
small business entities. The Court's historic treatment of mergers
is an argument for Justice Douglas' position; the Court demonstrated that it simply was not capable of performing the "sophisticated" merger analysis suggested by a rule of reason. However,
although one of the principal purposes of the 1950 congressional
amendments to § 7 was to overrule *Columbia Steel*,[35] Congress did
not adopt Douglas' position. Rather, in re-enacting § 7's "substantially lessening competition" standard for mergers, Congress again
delegated to the Court the task of determining the lawfulness of
major horizontal mergers—though perhaps with slightly greater
specificity than the "rule of reason" test applied under the Sherman Act.[36]

(3) Applying Celler–Kefauver in the legacy of Jefferson.

   As noted in the introduction to this Chapter, the Celler–
Kefauver amendments reflected a congressional intent that the
antitrust laws be able to more aggressively stop undesirable merg-

32. Louis Brandeis, The Curse of Bigness 105 (1934).

33. Id. at 120.

34. See Michael Porter, The Compet-itive Advantage of Nations 662–63 (1990).

35. S. Rep. No. 1775, 81st Cong., 2d Sess. 4–5 (1949); H.R. Rep. No. 1191, 81st Cong., 1st Sess. 11–12 (1949).

36. For a discussion of the evils of mergers identified by the authors of the Celler–Kefauver amendments in 1950, see the introduction to this Chapter.

ers. Congress sought to achieve this result by changing the statutory language of § 7 of the Clayton Act to close some loopholes in its coverage,[37] and by creating legislative history to guide the courts in determining when mergers had the effect of "substantially lessening competition." The congressional attitude was Jeffersonian: the word "competition" was used in a socio-political context rather than an economic one, focusing on preserving the small entrepreneur and avoiding the ill effects of big business (and resulting big labor) on initiative and individuality. As Derek Bok's careful study concluded, "[t]o anyone used to the preoccupation of professors and administrators with the economic consequences of monopoly power, the curious aspect of the debates is the paucity of remarks having to do with the effects of concentration on prices, innovation, distribution, and efficiency."[38]

The first Supreme Court case to apply the amended § 7 was *Brown Shoe Co. v. United States*,[39] which condemned Brown's acquisition of its rival, Kinney Shoe Co. The Court read the congressional amendments to § 7 as neither adopting nor rejecting any particular tests for determining what constituted a "substantial" lessening of competition or which markets constituted "lines of commerce"—the two key statutory terms.[40] Chief Justice Earl Warren's majority opinion therefore seized the opportunity to adopt a decidedly Jeffersonian bent to the Clayton Act. The Court could have easily found that the merger unlawful because it lessened competition in more than 100 local markets where the acquisition gave Brown over 30% of the market. Instead, the Court found that § 7 was violated even in markets where Brown's market share would be only 5%. In so holding, the Court emphasized its concern with the trends toward concentration in the industry.[41] In amending § 7, Congress was clearly concerned about waves of mergers that transformed atomistic industries into ones where only large firms could compete. Brown's acquisition of Kinney, the Court feared, would significantly contribute to this trend in the shoe industry.[42] Even if the merger led to efficiencies permitting lower costs to consumers, the Court read § 7 as preserving the ability of the Jeffersonian entrepreneur to remain in the marketplace.[43]

---

37. The original § 7 only applied to purchases of stock, not assets. The competitive effects test in the original statute also focused on lessened competition "between the corporation whose stock is so acquired and the corporation making the acquisition." The amendments removed both these limitations on the scope of the section.

38. Section 7 of the Clayton Act and the Merging of Law and Economics, 74 Harv. L. Rev. 226, 236 (1960).

39. 370 U.S. 294 (1962).

40. Id. at 320–21.

41. Id. at 332, 343–45.

42. Id. at 334, 343–45.

43. Id. at 344.

The introduction to this Chapter listed a number of reasons why mergers might benefit society, including economics of scale, synergies, and the ability of entrepreneurs to sell their businesses. *Brown Shoe* seemed to recognize instead only two legitimate reasons for mergers: to permit the acquisition of a failing company (which could not possibly be a competitive force anyway), and to allow two small firms to realize efficiencies that would enable them to compete more effectively with industry giants.[44]

Another Warren Court case, albeit one brought under the Sherman Act, illustrates the Jeffersonian ideology reflected in Congress' intent that § 7 proscribe mergers giving firms a "decisive" advantage. In *United States v. First National Bank & Trust Co. of Lexington*,[45] the Court condemned a merger between First National, the leading local bank (with a 40% market share), and Security Trust, the fourth largest bank (with a 12% share). Justice Douglas' majority opinion relied on testimony from rivals that "the consolidation will seriously affect their ability to compete effectively."[46] The Court viewed the merger as creating a bank that would not face effective rivalry because of two factors: the "image" of "bigness" that would attract customers and the additional services the new company could offer.[47]

Because of his almost exclusively Jeffersonian focus on preserving small firms, Justice Douglas was probably too quick to reject the benefits consumers would realize as a result of the new bank's extra services. But the holding is defensible from a long-term consumer perspective. As Brandeis observed, the long-term efficiency benefits of mergers are somewhat speculative (I would bet that over time the other banks ended up offering the same services); meanwhile, the harm to consumers caused by the lack of effective price restraints on First National, the greater ease with which First National could exercise price leadership (the top 4 firms controlled 83% of the market), and the reduced pressure on First National to continue to innovate, all suggest Celler–Kefauver's wisdom in condemning even efficiency-enhancing mergers

---

44. Id. at 346.

45. 376 U.S. 665 (1964).

46. Id. at 669.

47. This faithfulness to congressional intent was ironic. Prior to United States v. Philadelphia National Bank, 374 U.S. 321 (1963), there was some question as to whether the Clayton Act applied to bank mergers. *Lexington Bank* was therefore filed under the Sherman Act. In applying the Jefferso-nian standards of the Celler–Kefauver amendments to a Sherman Act case, Douglas' opinion does not appear to be consistent with the Court's decision in *Columbia Steel*. Cf. 376 U.S. at 673 (Harlan, J., dissenting) (arguing that the *Lexington Bank* merger would have been lawful under the rule of reason set forth in *Columbia Steel*). For a discussion of *Lexington Bank's* fidelity to *Columbia Steel*, see note 29 supra.

that give a "decisive" advantage.[48]

Two other significant Warren Court merger cases [49] reflect the Jeffersonian view that "competition" means "many competitors" with an equal opportunity to compete. In *United States v. Pabst Brewing Co.*,[50] the Court found that the defendant's acquisition of Blatz Brewing substantially lessened competition in three different geographic markets, including a national market where the firms' combined market share was 4.49%, because the merger was part of a significant trend of acquisitions that were transforming the beer industry from one characterized by many independent local and regional firms to one dominated by a few large national firms. In *United States v. Von's Grocery Co.*,[51] the government challenged the acquisition of the 12th largest supermarket chain in Los Angeles by the fourth largest chain. Justice Hugo Black wrote:

> Congress sought to preserve competition among many small businesses by arresting a trend toward concentration in its incipiency before that trend developed to the point that a market was left in the grip of a few big companies. Thus, where concentration is gaining momentum in a market, we must be alert to carry out Congress' intent to protect competition against ever increasing concentration through mergers.
>
> The facts of this case present exactly the threatening trend toward concentration which Congress wanted to halt.[52]

The evidence in that case revealed that the number of supermarkets in L.A. had decreased from over 5,365 to 3,818. Citing Justice Rufus Peckham's concern that combinations "driv[e] out of business the small dealers and worthy men whose lives have been

---

48. The efficiency / competition trade-off appeared to be particularly stark concerning trust services. By acquiring Security Trust, First National would have controlled 94.8% of all trust assets.

Lexington Bank is an example of lengthy antitrust litigation with questionable results. Shortly after the Supreme Court's decision, Congress enacted the Bank Merger Act of 1966, 12 U.S.C. § 1828(c), establishing a slightly modified standard for bank acquisitions that did not constitute monopolization under § 2 of the Sherman Act. The government argued that this merger violated § 2, but the district court disagreed. Pending appeal, the parties settled the case when First National promised not to make further acquisitions

for ten years. See United States v. First Nat'l Bank & Trust Co. of Lexington, 280 F.Supp. 260 (E.D. Ky. 1967), aff'd per curiam sub nom., Central Bank & Trust Co. v. United States, 391 U.S. 469 (1968).

49. A third case, United States v. Continental Can Co., 378 U.S. 441 (1964), which is discussed below in subsection (8) in connection with market definition, added little to the law concerning the prima facie case. It condemned a merger that resulted in a 25% market share in a concentrated market where there were trends to concentration.

50. 384 U.S. 546 (1966).

51. 384 U.S. 270 (1966).

52. Id. at 277.

spent therein" [53] and Judge Learned Hand's view that one of the purposes of the antitrust laws "was to perpetuate and preserve, for its own sake and in spite of possible cost, an organization of industry in small units which can effectively compete with each other," [54] Black prohibited a merger resulting in a 8.9% share of a market tending toward concentration.[55]

Justice Potter Stewart wrote a sharp and memorable dissent in *Von's*. The most famous portion of his opinion accused the majority of taking an unprincipled approach in merger cases. Reviewing the Court's precedents, he wrote that the "sole consistency that I can find is that in litigation under § 7, the government always wins." [56] Actually, there is some consistency in the Warren Court precedents: they suggest that horizontal mergers are unlawful when they either (1) create a merged entity with an undue market share (30%); [57] (2) eliminate a particularly aggressive rival from competition; [58] or (3) eliminate a firm of any significant size from a market that has shown a trend to concentration. Justice Stewart and many others might object to the soundness of the third principle on policy grounds, but, as a matter of statutory interpretation, the Court can look to several sources for support: the tremendous emphasis given by the sponsors of the Celler–Kefauver Act to stopping trends to concentration; the four votes Justice Douglas' dissent in *Columbia Steel* received for what amounted to a per se ban on significant mergers; and references in the legislative history indicating that Congress sought to overrule the majority opinion in that case.

The Warren Court's reading of § 7 was not, of course, the only reasonable construction of that statute, and Justice Stewart's policy attack on the substantive holding in *Von's* is more persuasive. Stewart correctly noted that what really troubled Justice Black was the supermarket revolution that was transforming the entire retail grocery industry. This revolution was not attributable to mergers, but to the greater availability of automobiles and changing demographics. While Mom & Pop grocery stores were declining in number, the number of chain grocery stores was not, Stewart observed. Thus, antitrust policy was not effectively serving any real Jeffersonian goals by blocking these mergers; indeed, by denying firms operating small chains the opportunity to sell

53. United States v. Trans–Missouri Freight Ass'n, 166 U.S. 290, 323 (1897).

54. United States v. Aluminum Co. of America, 148 F.2d 416, 429 (2d Cir. 1945).

55. 384 U.S. at 274 & n.7.

56. Id. at 301.

57. See United States v. Philadelphia Nat'l Bank, 374 U.S. 321 (1963), which is discussed in subsection (4) below.

58. See United States v. Aluminum Co. of America (Rome Cable), 377 U.S. 271 (1964), which is discussed in subsection (5) below.

their businesses, the Warren Court was actually reducing incentives for independent entrepreneurs in a dynamic market.[59]

Brown Shoe and *Pabst* were arguably closer cases. The trend to concentration in the shoe and beer industries threatened to transform markets that had previously been regional into ones where national advertising was a competitive necessity; although economies of scale were not significant as long as shoes and beer were sold close to home, only a few major firms could seriously compete on a national level. The decisions in *Brown Shoe* and *Pabst* reflect the non-economic judgment that preserving large numbers of small firms is worth the cost in efficiency; the quasi-economic value judgment that national advertising does not really provide significant benefits to consumers and thus that the efficiency gains are probably not all that significant; and the economic judgment that consumers suffer because few of the efficiency gains achieved are passed on to consumers as the forms engage in oligopoly pricing.

Although new "micro-breweries" have entered the upscale beer market in the past few years, giving local options to affluent yuppies, it is by no means clear that beer drinkers are better off in the modern world of Spuds McKenzie, Bob Uecker, and "Why Ask Why? Drink Bud Dry!" than they were with fierce regional competition thirty years ago. Despite *Pabst*, however, the antitrust laws did not succeed in stemming the tide to concentration in the beer industry. Although some of this can be blamed on ineffectual § 7 enforcement, a major cause of increased concentration during the 1960s and '70s was the internal growth of major breweries.[60] Section 7 ought not apply where blocking the merger will not slow inevitable industry trends to concentration.

(4) Structural economics and the prima facie case.

Although *Brown Shoe* indicated that market share was the primary sign of economic power, the Court blocked the merger at issue there, even though it resulted in only a 5% market share, because a careful review of the shoe retailing industry led to the conclusion that the market was being transformed into an oligopoly by a pattern of acquisitions by large national chains. In *United States v. Philadelphia National Bank*,[61] the Court sought to avoid the need for a detailed inquiry into the history of each industry by setting forth an alternative rule of presumptive illegality:

59. For an argument, based on a narrower market definition, that the Von's merger violated § 7 on standard economic grounds, see subsection (8) below.

Ross Antitrust Law UTS—12

60. See Stanley Ornstein, Antitrust policy and market forces as determinants of industry structure: case histories in beer and distilled spirits, 26 Antitrust Bull. 281 (1981).

61. 374 U.S. 321 (1963).

[A] merger which produces a firm controlling an undue percentage share of the relevant market, and results in a significant increase in the concentration of firms in that market is
so inherently likely to lessen competition substantially that it
must be enjoined in the absence of evidence clearly showing
that the merger is not likely to have such anticompetitive
effects . . . .

  . . . . Without attempting to specify the smallest market
share which would still be considered to threaten undue
concentration, we are clear that 30% presents that threat.[62]

The case, which involved a merger between the second and third
largest commercial banks in Philadelphia, did not afford the Court
a good opportunity to explain what type of evidence a defendant
could present to show that the merger would be unlikely have
anticompetitive effects. However, relying on legislative history
suggesting that § 7 should be interpreted in light of other provisions in the Clayton Act,[63] the Court did cite a § 3 case for the
proposition that the lessening of competition standard turned to
some extent on outsiders' ability to enter the market.[64] In *Philadelphia National Bank*, governmental regulation resulted in significant entry barriers to commercial banking. The case did,
however, allow the Court to reject one common defense that the
parties made to refute the presumption of illegality—the defendants' suggestion that the merger created efficiencies by allowing
expansion to the suburbs. The Court observed that each firm
could accomplish the same result through internal growth, and
expressed a clear preference for internal expansion over merger.[65]

  The defendants in *Philadelphia National Bank* also invoked
in the "little guys ganging up on the giants" defense recognized in
Brown Shoe, arguing that the merger would allow them to compete more effectively for huge commercial accounts with the New
York banks. In a significant holding, the Court rejected the idea
that § 7 allowed a substantial lessening of competition in one
market (commercial accounts for smaller Philadelphia-area merchants, who could not look outside the metropolitan area for

62. Id. at 363–64.

63. Id. at 365 (citing H.R. Rep. No.
1191, 81st. Cong., 1st Sess. 8 (1949)).

64. Id. at 366 (citing FTC v. Motion
Picture Advertising Serv. Co., 344 U.S.
392 (1953)).

65. Id. at 370. To illustrate why the
law prefers internal expansion, consider
United States v. Bethlehem Steel Corp.,
168 F.Supp. 576 (S.D.N.Y. 1958), which
barred Bethlehem's acquisition of its rival, Youngstown Steel. Bethlehem argued that Chicago needed more steel,
that Youngstown lacked the capital to
expand, and that Bethlehem would not
open new facilities in the Chicago area.
Four years after the merger was rejected, Bethlehem began building a new
steel plan in northern Indiana. Today
it is one of the more efficient large
American steel plants. See F.M. Scherer, Industrial Market Structure and
Economic Performance 546 (2d ed.
1980).

banking services) in order to permit the merging firms to compete in a second market.[66] This holding was based on statutory interpretation as well as administrability concerns. Section 7 prohibits mergers that lessen competition "in *any* line of commerce ... in *any* section of the country," the Court pointed out, not mergers whose net effect on the American economy may be to lessen competition. Moreover, the Court found that balancing the benefits large customers would realize if an additional firm competed with the New York banks against the harm inflicted on smaller firms deprived of competition in the Philadelphia market was beyond judicial competence.[67]

Philadelphia National Bank's doctrine of presumptive illegality obviously makes more sense to those who distrust the courts' ability to identify lessened competition on a case-by-case basis than to those who prefer the open-ended rule of reason approach used by the Court in *Columbia Steel* the last major Sherman Act merger case. What level of concentration should trigger the presumption depends on two discrete considerations. First, those who believe that a market "needs" ten to twelve firms to avoid collusion and oligopoly pricing will favor a lower threshold than those who believe that two or three firms are sufficient.[68] Second, and paradoxically, those who believe that the courts should allow defendants to rebut the presumption by presenting evidence that a merger will result in cost savings may favor a lower threshold than those who believe that courts should not assess efficiency claims.[69]

(5) Eliminating aggressive rivals.

The government's challenge in *United States v. Aluminum Co. of America (Rome Cable)*[70] gave the Court the opportunity to apply Congress' directive that § 7 should be used to block mergers where

66. 374 U.S. at 370–71.

67. Id. Similarly, the Court rejected the argument that the merger would, on balance, benefit the economy in the Philadelphia region. Such an argument is both contrary to the language of § 7 and beyond judicial competence. Cf. National Soc'y of Professional Engineers v. United States, 435 U.S. 679 (1978), discussed in Chapter 4, section D above, a case interpreting § 1 of the Sherman Act, where the Court refused to allow rivals to agree to restrain trade based on arguments that the restraint served the public interest.

68. See subsection (1) above.

69. For example, Professors Phillip Areeda and Donald Turner believe that the courts should presume that any merger resulting in a market share of 13–14% is illegal, but then should examine a broad range (though not all conceivable) efficiency claims and permit the merger to go forward where the defendant demonstrates that it is efficient. IV Antitrust Law ¶ 907 (1980). Others who argue that efficiency considerations should not be examined favor a much higher threshold. See Fisher, Johnson & Lande, supra note 6, at 817 (efficiencies should be ignored where post-merger HHI is significantly above 1800).

70. 377 U.S. 271 (1964).

the acquired firm was a "substantial factor in competition." [71] Although the defendant's post-merger market share approached the 30% mark, it would have been difficult to find that the merger met *Philadelphia National Bank's* second requirement for presumptive illegality—a significant increase in concentration—because Rome Cable's market share was so small. (Alcoa had a 27.8% share in one market, Rome Cable 1.3%.) Rather, in finding the merger unlawful, the Court emphasized that the market was concentrated (nine firms controlled 95.7% of the market; the HHI was 2354), and that Rome Cable was a particularly aggressive and independent rival, despite its small market share. [72]

The government's 1992 merger guidelines add an important new consideration to the analysis of mergers where the acquired firm's independence played a "substantial" role in maintaining competition. In a market where the existing firms sell differentiated products, the merger of two firms whose products are quite similar might lead to unilateral price increases because the products made by the remaining firms are sufficiently dissimilar that many customers will not shift their patronage. [73]

(6) Merger guidelines, the prima facie case, and trends to concentration.

Philadelphia National Bank and *Rome Cable* represent the last word from the Supreme Court on what constitutes a prima facie case in § 7 merger litigation. Although *United States v. General Dynamics Corp.* [74] significantly expanded the arguments defendants can raise in rebutting the prima facie case, [75] the Court's opinion still cited all the Warren Court precedents with approval in finding that the government had made out a prima facie statistical case attacking the merger. But few practitioners act as if the Warren Court decisions are still the law. Rather, largely influenced by the reality that clearance from the Justice Department or the FTC is equivalent to a finding of legality, firms have placed tremendous reliance on the government's merger guidelines. [76] These guidelines reflect the post-*General Dynamics* view (considered in detail in subsection (11), below) that the prima facie case can often be refuted.

In describing the mergers that it considers illegal, however, the Justice Department uses an approach similar to, but slightly

71. See H.R. Rep. No. 1191, 81st Cong., 1st Sess. 8 (1949).

72. 377 U.S. at 280–81.

73. Merger Guidelines — 1992, § 2.21, reprinted at 4 Trade Reg. Rep. (CCH) ¶ 13,104, at 20,573–8.

74. 415 U.S. 486 (1974).

75. See subsection (11) below.

76. See note 73 supra.

more refined than, the Court's approach in *Philadelphia National Bank*. As discussed above, that decision presumed that any merger that increased concentration in already concentrated markets was illegal. The merger guidelines use a measure of concentration called the Herfindahl–Hirschman Index (HHI).[77] Under the guidelines, mergers that either significantly increase concentration in moderately concentrated markets[78] or modestly increase concentration in heavily concentrated markets[79] raise "significant competitive concerns" that warrant careful scrutiny, and mergers are presumptively illegal when they significantly increase concentration in heavily concentrated markets.[80]

The guidelines emphasize that "market share and concentration data provide only the starting point for analyzing the competitive impact of a merger,"[81] although they do not purport to affect the burden of production or the burden of proof encompassed by doctrines like *Philadelphia National Bank*'s presumption of illegality if the merger is challenged in court under § 7.[82] Specifically, the guidelines take the position that evaluation of a merger's competitive effect should focus on two principal harms caused by anticompetitive mergers: (1) that they facilitate the ability of the firms remaining in the market to engage in "coordinated interaction," including "tacit or express collusion" (i.e., including both price fixing and oligopoly pricing); and (2) that they increase the economic power unilaterally exercised by the merging firms. As to the first harm, coordinated interaction, the guidelines call for a close look when conditions are conducive to reaching terms of agreement, and ask in such cases whether the firms will able to detect those who "cheat" on any such agreement and retaliate

77. Id.

78. A market whose HHI falls between 1000 and 1800 is considered moderately concentrated. (A market with six equally sized firms has an HHI of 1667.) The guidelines define a significant increase as one that increases the HHI in the market by 100 or more. (Mergers between firms with market shares of 25% and 2%, 10% and 5%, or 7.1% and 7.1% result in an HHI increase of approximately 100 and thus fall into this category.)

A convenient short-cut to determine the increase in the HHI caused by a merger is to multiply the market share of the acquiring firm times that of the acquired firm, and then again times two. For example, a merger between firms with shares of 10% and 5% would increase the HHI by 100 (10 x 5 x 2).

The merger guidelines provide an algebraic proof that this short-cut works. See id. at p. 20,573–5 n.18.

79. A market whose HHI exceeds 1800 is considered heavily concentrated. (An industry where the market leader has 30%, the next firm has 20%, and five other firms each have 10% would have an HHI of 1800). The guidelines define a modest increase as one that increases the HHI in the market by 50 points. (Mergers between firms with market shares of 12% and 2.1%, 8% and 3.1%, or 5% and 5% fall into this category.)

80. 1992 Guidelines, supra note 13, §§ 1.51(b) and (c).

81. Id., § 2.0.

82. Id. § 0.1.

against them. The second harm, unilateral market power, is most likely to occur in markets with differentiated products, where the acquired firm sells one of the closer substitutes for the acquiring firm's product.

The one major area where the guidelines depart from the case law concerns trends to concentration: this is simply not a factor in the Department's analysis.[83] The omission is objectionable on a host of grounds. It totally ignores the overriding congressional concern in enacting Celler–Kefauver—to forestall the emergence of concentrated markets.[84] No judge or antitrust enforcer faithful to Congress' policy concerns can fail to distinguish an acquisition that is part of a trend to concentration from an isolated merger in an industry that poses no risk of concentration. In addition, failing to consider trends is not only inconsistent with the Jeffersonian goal of preserving small businesses, but it is also unwise from an economic perspective. One or more mergers can transform an industry from one where economies of scale are slight and many firms are flourishing to one where economies of scale are significant and an oligopoly takes control (either through merger or the eventual exit of small firms coupled with the internal growth of larger firms).

Care must be used in this area. Because a possible trend to concentration could justify condemning mergers where the market structure would otherwise suggest no serious threat to competition, courts should be fairly certain that the merger is likely to ignite or perpetuate similar mergers, and that the resulting market structure is likely to increase the market power of those who remain. As noted above, these conditions are likely to lead to higher prices for consumers unless the cost savings are huge.[85] Moreover, stopping only the merger that brings the HHI over 1800 unfairly rewards, and unwisely encourages, firms to merge well before the merger is economically efficient; despite the congressional concern about locking the proverbial barn door before all the horses get out, the guidelines tell firms to get their own horses out of the barn now, because they never know when the door will close.

---

83. The last merger case considered by the Supreme Court expressly reaffirmed and emphasized the role that trends to concentration play in helping the government establish its prima facie case. United States v. General Dynamics Corp., 415 U.S. 486, 496–98 (1974).

84. Indeed, even the discredited Sherman Act analysis used by the Court prior to Celler–Kefauver included trends to concentration as one factor to be considered. See United States v. Columbia Steel Co., 334 U.S. 495, 527 (1948).

85. Fisher, Johnson & Lande, supra note 6.

(7) Recent developments concerning the prima facie case.

Since *Philadelphia National Bank*, judges have become more sophisticated and sensitive to economic arguments in favor of mergers. *Hospital Corp. of America v. FTC*[86] reflects both the continuing vitality of *Philadelphia National Bank* as well as this increased sophistication. In that case, the FTC had determined that the Hospital Corporation's acquisition of two hospitals in Chattanooga violated § 7. The merger increased Hospital Corporation's market share from 14% to 26% and reduced the number of independently managed hospitals in the market from eleven to seven. The merger also increased the market share of the top four firms from 79% to 91%.

In sustaining the Commission's finding, Judge Richard Posner's opinion for the court held that FTC findings are entitled to particular weight in § 7 proceedings. Although the opinion clearly indicates the court's agreement with the FTC on the merits, it also suggests that an FTC order blocking or unscrambling a merger is entitled to greater deference on appeal than is a judgment in a § 7 case that arose in some other context.[87] As the court explained, "[o]ne of the main reasons for creating the Federal Trade Commission and giving it concurrent jurisdiction to enforce the Clayton Act was that Congress distrusted judicial determination of antitrust questions." Moreover, one of the FTC's primary responsibilities is to draw "inferences of competitive consequence" from largely undisputed facts. The court therefore upheld the FTC's conclusions because there was "plenty of evidence to support" them; "whether we might have come up with a different prediction on our own is irrelevant." [88]

In determining that Hospital Corporation's acquisition might substantially lessen competition, the FTC did not simply rely on the significant increase in concentration that the merger caused in an already concentrated market. In addition, the Commission noted that the demand for hospital services is highly inelastic—people are unlikely to quickly switch hospitals because of small but significant price exploitation. It also found that the local hospitals had a tradition of cooperation, which would make it easier to actually fix prices. And finally, it observed that the hospitals had the ability and incentive both to lobby the federal

86. 807 F.2d 1381 (7th Cir. 1986), cert. denied, 481 U.S. 1038 (1987).

87. These other contexts include suits filed by the Department of Justice, state attorneys general, or private parties under § 7, and preliminary injunction suits brought by the FTC under § 13(b) of the FTC Act to enjoin the consummation of a merger while the Commission fully considers the issue. For a discussion of the latter, see note 93 below.

88. 807 F.2d at 1386.

government and to negotiate with insurers to frustrate insurance companies' efforts to control hospital costs.[89] These findings were highly relevant because they bolstered the structural evidence showing the merger's likely anticompetitive effect. The FTC's opinion appears to reflect a recognition that market share information provides a limited basis for concluding that a merger is likely to increase market power, and that additional facts allow a more confident prediction that a merger will indeed have a harmful effect.

Although the Seventh Circuit approved the FTC's conclusions, once again Judge Posner could not resist adding dicta. He wrote the following cryptic sentence: "When an economic approach is taken in a § 7 case, the ultimate issue is whether the challenged acquisition is likely to facilitate collusion."[90] This language seems to suggest that § 7 has only one goal—to protect consumers from higher prices. Perhaps the introductory clause is meant to reconcile the sentence with the Warren Court's populist decisions, which were not based on an economic approach. But even as limited to economics, Posner's statement is incorrect. One way that mergers can substantially lessen competition is by stifling the fear of being left behind, which is the greatest spur to technological innovation. Mergers of this sort should be condemned even if price collusion is unlikely.[91]

A more traditional view of merger policy was recently expressed by Judge Gerhard Gesell in *FTC v. Coca–Cola Co.*[92] In that case, he granted a preliminary injunction enjoining Coke's acquisition of Dr. Pepper, pending full adjudication before the FTC.[93] The merger would have increased the market share of the

89. Id. at 1387–89.

90. Id. at 1386.

91. See Porter, supra note 34. For example, Porter found that domestic, rather than international, rivalry provides a key incentive to innovate. Potential competition from foreign firms may limit the ability of American firms to collude, but a merger of two of the few remaining American firms in an industry may reduce the immediate need to innovate and keep ahead of the crowd.

92. 641 F. Supp. 1128 (D.D.C. 1986), vac'd and rem'd mem., 829 F.2d 191 (D.C. Cir. 1987). Judge Gesell was a distinguished antitrust practitioner prior to his appointment.

93. Under § 13(b) of the FTC Act, 15 U.S.C. § 53(b), the FTC may authorize its attorneys to seek a federal court injunction blocking a merger until the Commission can fully analyze the acquisition under its own procedures (trial before an administrative law judge, appeal to the Commission, review by the circuit court of appeals). Because the FTC's procedures can take several years, issuance of an injunction will often cause the parties to scuttle the deal.

As *Hospital Corp. of America* illustrates, when a case comes before the court of appeals following a full hearing and decision by the FTC, the Commission's judgment is entitled to substantial deference. In contrast, Judge Gesell gave little deference to the FTC's judgment in *Coca–Cola* because it did not reflect a final decision but merely an authorization to staff, without full comment, to proceed with preliminary litigation.

leading carbonated soft-drink manufacturer from 37.4% to 42%, in a market where Coke and its leading rival, PepsiCo (with 29%), dwarfed the competition. Evidence beyond the numbers, however, pointed in different directions. Soft drink manufacturers sell their products through local bottlers, who purchase flavored syrup from the manufacturer, combine the syrup with carbonated water, bottle or can the beverage, and then distribute it to wholesalers and retailers. The court found that economies of scale required a local bottler to maintain at least a 15–20% share to compete effectively, and that Dr. Pepper often combined with Seven–Up, Royal Crown, and other smaller brands to enable a third bottler to effectively compete with the Coke and Pepsi distributors.[94] The challenged merger would have increased Coke's incentives to integrate Dr. Pepper distribution into its own system, harming the ability of these smaller bottlers to compete with Coke and Pepsi. Moreover, the court concluded that significant entry barriers existed, as evidenced by the large sums of money and substantial time needed to build a brand name and overcome existing consumer preferences, and by Procter & Gamble's inability, despite its tremendous resources as a conglomerate, to significantly expand the sales of Orange Crush and Hires Root Beer.[95] On the other hand, competition between Coke and Pepsi was extremely vigorous, and there was no evidence that it would be lessened in any way by this merger. Because the merger would not "lessen competition," the defendants argued, it did not violate § 7.

In the end, the court declined to rely on this conflicting evidence. It recognized that the merger would result in "one less independent factor in the market to challenge the dominance of Coca–Cola Company." More important, the court held, § 7 "was not designed to support a particular economic theory; it was directed at what Congress in the exercise of its own common sense perceived." Thus, because the defendants had introduced no "clear and specific" evidence to counter the government's structural argument, *Philadelphia National Bank* would condemn this merger, which significantly increased concentration in a heavily concentrated industry, without further speculation about the actual economic effect of the proposed acquisition.[96]

(8) Market definition: judicial highlights and lowlights.

The judicial effort to analyze horizontal restraints using techniques such as per se condemnation, the doctrine of ancillary

---

94. Perpetual exclusive territories are often granted to local bottlers in the soft drink distribution industry. 641 F.Supp. at 1134, 1136. These arrangements are exempted from antitrust scrutiny by special legislation, the Soft Drink Interbrand Competition Act, 15 U.S.C. § 3501.

95. 641 F. Supp. at 1137.

96. Id. at 1138–39.

restraints, and a "structured rule of reason" may reflect a desire to avoid defining relevant markets. This reluctance is justified in the case of cartel conduct given the high probability that the challenged behavior will be anticompetitive. Although Justice Douglas may have preferred a per se-type analysis for mergers,[97] it would have been inappropriate. Most mergers take place in industries where there is no risk harm to competition, mergers do have real benefits for society, and the legislative history of § 7 shows that Congress wanted to permit mergers that allowed smaller firms to compete more effectively with larger concerns. Thus, market definition plays an essential role in merger analysis.

In the first exposition of market definition after § 7 was amended in 1950, *Brown Shoe Co. v. United States*[98] provided oft-cited black letter law listing the relevant factors the courts should examine. Recognizing that Congress set forth no single standard, the Court held that the courts should be guided by "practical indicia," such as "[1] industry or public recognition of a submarket as a separate economic entity, [2] the product's peculiar characteristics and uses, [3] unique production facilities, [4] distinct consumers, [5] distinct prices, [6] sensitivity to price changes, and [7] specialized vendors."[99] Although this list seems fairly comprehensive, the open-textured nature of the analysis requires judges to apply these standards to particular cases with care.

United States v. Philadelphia National Bank[100] represents a sensitive and thoughtful approach to market definition. The Court found the relevant line of commerce (product market) there was the "cluster of services" known as commercial banking.[101] Some services offered by commercial banks (such as checking accounts) were not offered by any other type of business. The Court correctly excluded savings banks from the market. Although savings banks competed with commercial banks for savings deposits, convenience and perhaps irrational customer habits led many to refuse to patronize savings banks despite superior interest rates;[102] moreover, savings institutions did not offer commercial loans. Although small loan companies competed in the lending market, their cost disadvantages were such that the Court

97. See United States v. Columbia Steel Co., 334 U.S. 495, 534 (1948) (dissenting opinion), discussed above in subsection (2).

98. 370 U.S. 294 (1962).

99. Id. at 325. Although *Brown Shoe*'s criteria purport to define "submarkets" of actual markets, the Court made it clear that products considered distinctive under these criteria could "constitute product markets for antitrust purposes," id., and the Court has subsequently referred to the *Brown Shoe* criteria in identifying product markets. See United States v. Continental Can Co., 378 U.S. 441, 449 (1964).

100. 374 U.S. 321 (1963).

101. Id. at 356.

102. Id. at 357.

also properly excluded them from the market. As Judge Hand observed in *Corn Products*, firms with cost advantages do not face effective substitutes, at least within the range of their cost advantage.[103]

The Court also held that the relevant section of the country (geographic market) was the Philadelphia metropolitan area. The Court noted that, for most individual and small commercial patrons, this was the area where they could realistically turn for alternatives. Because banking is a highly regulated service that is not subject to arbitrage, the fact that large corporations could look to New York or elsewhere for banking services should competition in Philadelphia suffer did nothing for smaller folk.[104]

The other major Warren Court merger cases do not fare as well under analytical scrutiny. Rather, they often involved market "gerrymandering," where the Court, in an effort to condemn the merger, failed to sensibly identify relevant product geographic markets.[105] These decisions are particularly unfortunate because, in many cases, more defensible market definitions would still have allowed the government to prevail.

In *Brown Shoe*, for example, the Court held that shoes of different quality, which sold for different prices, should not automatically be excluded from the same market, and that "price/quality" differences were relevant in merger analysis. The Court then concluded, without explanation, that the district court had correctly held that Brown's medium-priced shoes competed against Kinney's low-priced product.[106] The key focus *should* be on consumer behavior. For some products, most consumers are both price- and quality-sensitive. If so, a rough equilibrium will be established between superior, high-priced products and inferior, low-priced items. If price increases for either product will lead to significant shifts to the other product, both should be considered to be in the same market. For other products, consumers are not as price-sensitive, and the price they pay is determined more by their income. Thus, the affluent will not likely shift from luxury automobiles to sedans, regardless of the relative prices of a Mercedes and a Buick; the middle class will not be able to afford a Mercedes even if the relative price becomes a real bargain. *Brown Shoe* suggests that Brown's medium-priced shoes were close enough to Kinney's low-priced shoes to make them substitutable,

---

103. United States v. Corn Products Refining Co., 234 Fed. 964 (S.D.N.Y. 1916). This case is discussed in Chapter 3, section C(2).

104. 374 U.S. at 359 (citing Tampa Elec. Co. v. Nashville Coal Co., 365 U.S. 320, 327 (1961)).

105. See United States v. Pabst Brewing Co., 384 U.S. 546, 555–56 (1966) (Harlan, J., concurring).

106. 370 U.S. at 326.

but an express analysis of consumer preference would have been more satisfying.[107]

United States v. Aluminum Co. of America (Rome Cable)[108] represents the high-water mark for market gerrymandering. The merger at issue there involved the acquisition by a major aluminum concern of a company that sold some aluminum cable but specialized primarily in copper cable. The Court found that buyers differentiated between insulated cable (used primarily underground) and bare cable (used principally for high-voltage transmission lines). Thus, each constituted a relevant line of commerce. Because price changes in copper did not seem to significantly affect sales of aluminum, and vice versa, the Court sensibly concluded that, although some inter-metal competition existed, aluminum cable comprised a line of commerce (a submarket) separate from copper cable. The only way to get the two firms' combined market share to approach the 30% mark of presumptive illegality established by *Philadelphia National Bank*, however, was to combine bare and insulated aluminum cable into one market. This the Court did, despite the clear evidence that the two products served totally different uses. The majority reasoned as follows: bare aluminum cable is a separate market; all cable is a separate market; insulated aluminum cable differs from insulated copper cable; therefore, bare and insulated aluminum cable is a separate market.[109] Although the Court purported to call this reasoning "a logical extension of the District Court's findings," [110] there is simply no logic to it. As Professor Lawrence Sullivan has aptly analogized, this analysis could be used to condemn a merger between the dominant seller of pistachio ice cream and the leading purveyor of grapefruit sorbet because it would lessen competition in the "pistachio-grapefruit" market.[111]

In addition, the Court's holding was probably unnecessary to block the merger. Insulated aluminum cable was clearly a relevant line of commerce. That market was moderately concentrated,[112] and combining Alcoa's 11.6% share of that market with Rome's 4.7% share led to a significant increase in concentration.[113] In light of Rome's position as an aggressive competitor and the trends to concentration in the industry (the record showed that

---

107. The Court's geographic market analysis—finding that shoe stores on the outskirts of cities are in the same market as downtown retailers—might also appear incorrect. But given the district court's factual finding that these stores "effectively compete" with each other, it appears to be legally sound. Id. at 336–39.

108. 377 U.S. 271 (1964).

109. Id. at 274–77.

110. Id. at 277 n.4.

111. Antitrust 608 (1977).

112. The top nine firms had a market share of 88.2%. The HHI was approximately 1350.

113. The merger increased the HHI by 109.

Alcoa's interest in the merger was a reaction to other industry mergers), the Court could have concluded that the merger lessened competition in the insulated aluminum cable market. Moreover, although the Court found that copper and aluminum were not entirely effective substitutes, some competition between the two still existed. Because Rome was so effective in selling copper, the Court could also have found that the merger would further reduce the already diminishing competition between copper and aluminum products.

The 1963 Term was not a good one for market analysis, for a few months later the Court held in *United States v. Continental Can Co.*[114] that the merger of a leading can company and a leading bottle manufacturer lessened competition in a market defined as all glass and metal containers. Noting the dynamic competition over time between these two types of containers, the Court properly rejected arguments that cans and bottles were not competitive. With an illogic that seemed infectious that Term, though, the Court decided not to include other potentially competitive container products, like plastic, based on the conclusory assertion that glass and can submarkets would exist in any broader market.[115] Of course, glass and can submarkets would exist, but how does that excuse excluding plastic from a glass-can submarket? The Court did not answer that question.

Again, this odd market definition was not necessary to condemn the merger. Indeed, this was not the government's argument before the Court. Instead, the Justice Department alleged that where two industries are both concentrated (as were the glass and can industries), and some inter-industry competition exists, mergers between leading firms should be prohibited because of their dampening effect on potential inter-industry competition. The government conceded that competition from other types of containers should be considered. However, at the time of the suit (1959), plastic containers represented an insignificant amount of commerce: sales of plastic containers totaled only $40 million, in contrast with $1.4 billion in sales of metal and $830 million in sales of glass. Thus, the government reasonably argued that plastic "could have little impact on the vast competition" between metal and glass.[116]

Continental Can also reveals the weakness in the formulaic approach of precisely defining the relevant market in order to assess whether a merger will substantially lessen competition in "any line of commerce." It would have been inaccurate to treat

114.　378 U.S. 441 (1964).

115.　Id. at 457–58.

116.　Brief for the United States at 25 n.24, United States v. Continental Can Co., 378 U.S. 441 (1964) (No. 367).

Continental and Hazel–Atlas (the acquired glass firm) either as strict rivals or as firms operating in separate markets. The acquisition posed less of a competitive risk than if Continental had acquired another can company, and much more of a risk than if Hazel–Atlas manufactured a wholly unrelated product. A more "gestalt" focus on dynamic efficiency and innovation would be more sensible in cases where mathematical certainty seems inappropriate.

The Court's decision in two cases decided several years later— *United States v. Pabst Brewing Co.*[117] and *United States v. Von's Grocery Co.*[118]—cannot similarly be faulted for defining the market incorrectly. Instead, they simply failed to engage in any of the economic analysis necessary to define a relevant geographic market. The district court in *Pabst* rejected the government's § 7 claim because the national market shares of the two merging beer breweries were too small and the government had failed to show that either Wisconsin or the Wisconsin–Illinois–Michigan area, where the two breweries' sales were concentrated, constituted a relevant market. The Supreme Court reversed: "Certainly the failure of the government to prove by an army of expert witnesses what constitutes a relevant 'economic' or 'geographic' market is not an adequate ground on which to dismiss a § 7 case." [119] Although expert witnesses might not be necessary, Justice Black's opinion for the majority did not explain why failing to provide *any* proof is not fatal to the government's claim. Similarly, *Von's* concluded without analysis that the relevant market was grocery stores in the Los Angeles area. The majority did not respond to Justice Stewart's observation that few customers will travel all over such a massive metropolitan area for a better supermarket bargain, and that within a short driving radius, the two firms had little competitive overlap.[120]

Again, the Court did not need to forego market definition in order to rule in favor of the government in either *Pabst* or *Von's*. In *Pabst*, the Solicitor General argued that the district court had clearly erred in finding that beer breweries had no significant locational advantages, in terms of either shipping costs or brand loyalty. Thus, the government claimed, new entry into Wisconsin was unlikely to check a limited price hike by the established firms in that state.[121] To be sure, this assertion was seriously contested by defense counsel, but antitrust law would have been better

117. 384 U.S. 546 (1966).

118. 384 U.S. 270 (1966).

119. 384 U.S. at 549.

120. 384 U.S. at 281 (dissenting opinion).

121. Brief for the United States at 35, United States v. Pabst Brewing Co., 384 U.S. 546 (1966) (No. 404).

served if the result-oriented court had simply accepted the government's argument.

The Court had an even more persuasive alternative rationale in *Von's*. The government's theory in that case did not rely on the Jeffersonian concerns that led the majority to condemn the small merger in a market of almost 4,000 firms. Rather, the government argued that small grocery stores really did not engage in price competition with larger supermarket chains; thus, the latter constituted a separate submarket. The record established that concentration among the leading supermarkets was significantly increasing. The government also produced evidence that the ten major chains had 43.6% of the L.A. market, and that major chains carefully studied the prices charged by other chains—and not prices charged by the 4,000 smaller stores—to maintain price competitiveness.[122] Moreover, the government suggested that entry and expansion by smaller operators were "sharply limited" because shopping-center owners preferred established large chains.[123] Defining a narrower market and considering the trends to concentration, the Von's–Shopping Bag merger may well have lessened competition among larger supermarket chains. Again, this conclusion is not unassailable, but it is much more defensible than the market definition selected by the Court.

Justice Stewart also attacked the *Von's* majority for defining the geographic market to include the entire area of greater Los Angeles. The record showed that most shoppers patronized a grocery store within a ten-minute drive of their homes.[124] Because most of Von's stores were in the southwestern part of L.A., while Shopping Bag concentrated on the northeastern part of the city, Stewart concluded that the acquisition was principally a market-extension merger (buying a firm in order to expand into a new area) rather than a merger among competitors.[125] Although the Court did not respond to this argument, a careful analysis focusing on supply factors may justify the majority's geographic market definition. Recall that the paradigmatic question in horizontal merger analysis is which firms currently constrain the defendant's pricing and marketing decisions. If Shopping Bag could easily have moved into southwestern L.A., then Von's must have viewed it as a current rival. The merger would have ended this rivalry.

The Court's inexactness in *Pabst* and *Von's* reflected a clear desire to condemn these mergers for non-economic reasons. If the flaw in the two mergers was their tendency to transform the beer

122. Brief for the United States at 32–35, United Stated States v. Von's Grocery Co., 384 U.S. 270 (1966) (No. 303).

123. Id. at 40.

124. In today's Los Angeles, multiply by three.

125. 384 U.S. at 295–96.

and grocery industries into markets where small firms could not meaningfully compete, then Justice Black was correct that economically defined relevant markets are not essential. Black's approach, however, elevates the Jeffersonian preference for atomistic markets over any efficiency or consumer concerns. Some economic analysis was necessary to put the Court in a position where it could reach an intelligible decision on the extent to which protecting small firms would harm consumers or efficiency.

(9) Market definition: the merger guidelines.

Given the morass found in the cases, the government's merger guidelines offer real improvements in market definition doctrine. The guidelines focus on consumers and sellers. The government evaluates a proposed market definition by asking whether all the firms in the market could profitably raise prices by 5% for one year—a "small but significant and nontransitory" increase in price (or SSNIP)—without losing too much business to other firms.[126] If the answer is yes, then the market is a valid product and geographic market because outside firms are not in effective competition. If the answer is no, the market definition is not accurate and must be expanded because the other firms that customers would begin patronizing are true rivals and must be considered in determining market shares.

The SSNIP test is a concrete application of the Supreme Court's reasonable interchangeability test, which was used in the *Cellophane* case to define a relevant market for purposes of § 2 of the Sherman Act.[127] It has the same flaw, in that it fails to identify oligopoly markets where existing firms have already set prices so far above the competitive level that a further SSNIP would, indeed, be unprofitable. Where little competition currently exists, some might argue that another merger can not substantially *lessen* competition; but a significant merger in such an oligopoly market can further stabilize the cartel and remove nonprice competition in the form of hard-to-detect services as the basis for rivalry.[128] The guidelines attempt to address this flaw, by indicating that the government will look at the effect of a SSNIP

---

126. The 1982 guidelines officially quantified the SSNIP at 5%. See 4 Trade Reg. Rep. ¶ 13,102, § II–A, at 20,-533. Although the 1992 guidelines do not specify the 5% level, this does not reflect a change in policy. See Interview with Janusz Ordover, Antitrust (Summer 1992), at 13.

127. United States v. E.I. du Pont de Nemours & Co., 351 U.S. 377, 394, 404 (1956). For another extensive discus-

sion of market definition, see the discussion of this case and others in Chapter 3, section C.

128. Compare William Baxter, Responding to the Reaction: The Draftsman's View, 71 Calif. L. Rev. 618, 623 & n.35 (1983) with E. Thomas Sullivan & Herbert Hovenkamp, Antitrust Law, Policy and Procedure 741–42 (2d ed. 1989).

above prevailing prices "unless premerger circumstances are strongly suggestive of coordinated interaction, in which case the [government] will use a price more reflective of the competitive price." [129]

Significantly, the guidelines pursue a different approach when price discrimination exists. Reflecting a concern about consumer exploitation, rather than a sole focus on efficiency, the guidelines suggest that markets will be defined more narrowly when the firms in an industry can identify and sell at different prices to certain buyers, who do not view other products as substitutes and thus will not shift patronage in the face of a price hike.

The guidelines draw a curious distinction, however, between two types of potential entrants to a market. Firms are considered part of the relevant market if they would respond to a SSNIP by entering the market within one year and could do so without incurring significant expenditures that could not be recovered when they left the market ("sunk costs"). On the other hand, firms that would have to incur these significant costs in order to enter, but whose entry is nonetheless likely to deter anticompetitive behavior among the existing firms in the market, are excluded from the market, but their existence is analyzed separately as part of the general consideration of entry barriers. [130]

The guidelines continue to focus solely on economic power in terms of the ability to increase price, and to assume that foreign and domestic firms are equally able to prevent the leading firms from colluding or engaging in oligopoly pricing. The guidelines thus implicitly reject a recently articulated view that mergers may lessen competition primarily by reducing the remaining firms' incentive to aggressively innovate, and that the existence of vigorous domestic rivalry—as distinct from competition from foreign firms—is essential to promote innovation. [131] Domestic rivalry should also be preferred to the foreign variety when the foreign competitors are located in countries without tough antitrust standards prohibiting cartels. Although the Sherman Act technically applies to collusion occurring overseas that has a direct and foreseeable impact on United States commerce, successfully prosecuting foreign companies is often problematic. It makes little sense to permit American firms to be consolidated with or purchased by foreign concerns if the latter can then agree with

---

129. 1992 Guidelines, supra note 13, § 1.11.

130. Compare id. § 1.32, ("Firms That Participate Through Supply Response.") with id., § 3, ("Entry Analy-

sis"). For a discussion of entry barriers, see subsection (12) below.

131. See Porter, supra note 34, at 117–22.

impunity to raise prices to American consumers.[132]

(10) The failing company defense.

When amending § 7, Congress expressly sanctioned one type of horizontal merger between two major firms—a merger designed to save a failing firm.[133] In *Citizen Publishing Co. v. United States*,[134] the defendants sought to invoke the failing firm defense to justify a "joint operating agreement" between the two daily newspapers in Tucson, pursuant to which the newspapers would maintain independent editorial staffs, but would completely merge their business operations, including pricing for subscriptions and advertising. But the Supreme Court held the agreement illegal because the parties failed to meet the strict standards established for this defense: the acquired firm must be facing imminent bankruptcy, and the buyer must be the only available (i.e., least anticompetitive) purchaser.[135] The government now routinely requires the acquiring firm to retain investment bankers and provide them with a substantial incentive to locate such a purchaser before the latter requirement is satisfied.

Although at first glance it may appear that any merger involving a failing firm cannot possibly lessen competition, in reality this defense does not reflect consumer-oriented goals. The most pro-competitive approach would require firms to attempt to reorganize through Chapter 11 of the Bankruptcy Code, but so few reorganizations are successful that the time delay would often mean that there was nothing left to acquire.[136] The second best approach from a purely competitive point of view, in most cases,[137] would be to require the failing firm to liquidate. The firm's market share would likely be distributed among the remaining firms, rather than going entirely to the acquiring party. The legislative history of § 7 makes clear, however, that Congress did

---

132. This concern has decreased somewhat recently due to increased attention to cartels by foreign competition laws.

133. See H.R. Rep. No. 1191, 81st Cong., 1st Sess. 6 (1949); S. Rep. No. 1775, 81st Cong., 2d Sess. 7 (1950).

134. 394 U.S. 131 (1969).

135. Id. at 137–38.

136. *Citizen Publishing* was somewhat more optimistic that companies reorganized in bankruptcy would "often emerge[ ] as strong competitive companies," and the Court therefore suggested that defendants must also show that the prospects for reorganization are dim in order to invoke the failing company

defense. Id. at 138. Recent statistics show, however, that fewer than 20% of the firms filing for bankruptcy complete a successful reorganization. See, e.g., Robert Rasmussen, The Efficiency of Chapter 11, 8 Bankr. Dev's J. 319, 322 (1991). See also Michael Bradley & Michael Rosenzweig, The Untenable Case for Chapter 11, 101 Yale L.J. 1043, 1075 & n.75 (1992). (Thanks to my colleague Charles Tabb for these bankruptcy insights.)

137. For some ideas on when it might be efficient to allow an existing firm to acquire all the assets of a failing firm, see Sullivan & Hovenkamp, supra note 128, at 793–94.

not endorse this approach because of non-efficiency concerns for shareholders and employees.

Non-efficiency concerns also led Congress to modify *Citizen Publishing* as it applies to newspapers. Pursuant to the Newspaper Preservation Act,[138] the Attorney General is allowed to authorize these "joint operating agreements" when he finds that one or both newspapers are in "probable danger of financial failure." The legislation effectively recognizes that, in most markets, the chances that a failing firm will pull itself out of its problems, successfully reorganize, or will be acquired by a firm posing less of a threat to competition justify waiting until bankruptcy is imminent before tolerating an otherwise anticompetitive merger. On the other hand, the desire to maintain a diversity of editorial voices does not warrant risking the total collapse of a failing newspaper.

(11) Questioning the statistical evidence supporting the prima facie case.

United States v. General Dynamics Corp.[139] established that a company's acquisition of a non-failing firm can withstand a § 7 challenge, even if *Philadelphia National Bank*'s standard of presumptive illegality seems to be met, where the defendant directly refutes the government's prima facie case. *General Dynamics* is the only substantive horizontal merger case decided by the Supreme Court since Chief Justice Earl Warren retired. Significantly, Justice Stewart's majority opinion reaffirmed the view expressed in *Philadelphia National Bank* that the government can prevail "on a showing of even small increases of market share or market concentration in those industries or markets where concentration is already great or has been recently increasing."[140] In *General Dynamics*, the government had introduced statistical evidence showing that the acquisition gave the merged firm[141] a combined market share of 23.2% in Illinois and 12.4% in a larger geographic market known in the industry as the Eastern Interior Coal Province. According to the majority, the evidence demonstrated "not only that the coal industry was concentrated among a

138. 15 U.S.C. § 1801.

139. 415 U.S. 486 (1974).

140. Id. at 497.

141. The challenged merger was a complicated transaction. Material Service Corporation operated its mining activities directly and also through an affiliate company, Freeman Coal Mining Corporation. Through incremental stock purchases, Material Service gradually obtained control of United Electric Coal Companies. Material Service, which then controlled both Freeman and United Electric mines, was in turn acquired by General Dynamics, a large diversified corporation. Id. at 488–90. The Court's opinion discusses the merger in terms of its horizontal component—the merger of Freeman and United Electric.

small number of leading producers, but that the trend had been toward increasing concentration." The Court based this conclusion on data showing that the four- and ten-firm concentration ratios were 75% and 98% in Illinois, and 63% and 91% in the Province.[142] The Court expressly noted that, in an already concentrated market tending to become even more concentrated, a combined market share of even 12.4% would, under the Court's precedents, "have sufficed to support a finding of 'undue concentration' *in the absence of other considerations.*"[143] The Court sustained the judgment for the defendants, however, because they had demonstrated that the government's statistical evidence did not reflect market realities.

The Court acknowledged that statistics showing the percentage of current sales made by each firm in a market are usually reliable indicators of the future market strength of the combined firm.[144] However, coal mining firms tended to enter into long-term contracts with major electric utility companies. As a result, General Dynamics owned few uncommitted coal reserves. Were prices to go up in the industry, United Electric (the acquired firm) had so few uncommitted reserves that it could not possibly respond as a competitive force.[145] The majority therefore held that the correct measure of competitive strength was the amount of one's uncommitted reserves; under this measure, United Electric's market share would have been too small to make out a prima facie § 7 case.[146]

Justice Stewart's analysis may not be entirely consistent with the Court's precedents (as Stewart himself noted in his *Von's* dissent,[147] the dynamic competition in the Los Angeles grocery market suggested that the government's statistics did not paint a fully accurate picture of competition). But the result seems sensi-

---

142. Id. at 494.

143. Id. at 497–98 (emphasis added).

144. Id. at 498.

145. Id. at 502–03.

146. The majority rejected the government's argument that an independent United Electric could respond to industry price increases by increasing output, i.e., by mining deep coal reserves it still owned. Noting that deep mining required different technology and expertise than the strip mining United Electric engaged in, the Court observed that there had been new entry into deep coal mining in recent years, and the merger therefore did not lessen competition by eliminating the "mere possibility that United Electric, in common with all other companies with the inclination and the corporate treasury to do so, could some day expand into an essentially new line of business." Id. at 509. In contrast, the dissenters agreed with the government, pointing out that United Electric had exploited deep mining reserves up until five years prior to the merger. Unlike other companies, the dissent noted, United Electric had a "thriving coal-marketing structure," and expansion was "merely a matter of regaining the expertise it once had to extract reserves it already owned for sale in a market where it already had a good name." Id. at 525 (Douglas, J., dissenting).

147. 384 U.S. at 301.

ble as a matter of antitrust policy: statistics do not always reliably measure the extent of competition in a market. When some other statistics (in this case, reserves) more accurately describe a market, they should be used. What other factors should be considered remains open after *General Dynamics*, although the opinion reflects the Court's recognition that predictions of increased market power based solely on structural evidence are inherently imperfect.[148]

Another example of a case where market realities refuted the government's statistical prima facie case is *United States v. Citizens & Southern National Bank*.[149] In that case, the Court upheld the merger of Citizens, the dominant bank in the Atlanta area, with a number of smaller banks. Prior to an amendment to Georgia banking law, Citizens was barred from owning branch banks in the Atlanta suburbs, but took advantage of a loophole in the law to sponsor smaller banks, in which it owned a 5% interest. Citizens agreed to underwrite these banks (thus assuring them regulatory approval), chose their chief executives and directors, selected their locations, conducted their audits, ensured that customers received identical services at each bank, and "suggested" interest rates and service charges. The Supreme Court affirmed the district judge's conclusion that the acquisitions would not reduce competition "for the simple reason that ... no real competition had developed or was likely to develop" between Citizens and the smaller banks, and therefore there was no "realistic prospect that denial of these acquisitions would lead the defendant banks to compete against each other."[150]

---

148. The *General Dynamics* majority may also be faulted for focusing on long-term contracts entered into after the merger had already occurred. The Court noted that evidence of post-acquisition behavior should be accorded little weight, lest firms tailor such conduct to fend off an antitrust challenge and then engage in anticompetitive behavior later with impunity. It also held that post-acquisition changes in the entire structure of an industry are properly considered at the time of trial. 415 U.S. at 504–05. Suppose, for example, that two leading word processing firms merged, the government challenged the suit, and then on the eve of trial IBM announced its entry into the personal computer/word processing market. It would be silly to disregard the economic significance of such a change in the market. But the dissenters properly noted that the majority failed to apply its own insights to the *General Dynam-*ics facts. The defendants' principal evidence—that United Electric's reserves were all committed—involved business decisions made *after* the merger. Id. at 524.

Evidence of post-acquisition behavior may have been critical to *General Dynamics*, but it is unlikely to be a major concern in future cases. Since the 1976 passage of the Hart–Scott–Rodino Act, 15 U.S.C. § 15c, large firms that wish to acquire control of other companies must notify the government in advance of the merger. As a result, most acquisitions are considered and either cleared or challenged before they even occur. Thus, far fewer cases involve already merged companies where post-acquisition evidence may exist.

149. 422 U.S. 86 (1975).

150. Id. at 121.

The government argued that the absence of price competition between Citizens and its affiliated banks should not be a relevant factor in the § 7 litigation, because this phenomena indicated that the parties had been violating § 1 of the Sherman Act. The Court disagreed, holding that, rather than being an unreasonable restraint of trade, the purpose and effect of Citizens' sponsorship of these banks were to defeat a restraint of trade caused by Georgia's anticompetitive anti-branching law.[151] Most important, however, the Court agreed that if the government had been correct, "making the evil permanent through acquisition or merger would offend the Clayton Act."[152] Thus, *Citizens & Southern* suggests that, even after *General Dynamics*, defendants in § 7 litigation cannot justify a merger on the grounds that no competition currently exists among the leading firms in the market.

Two Seventh Circuit decisions point in different directions on the question whether evidence of a firm's overall financial weakness is sufficient to refute the government's prima facie case after *General Dynamics*. There is some facial appeal to this defense in that an acquired firm's "weak financial reserves (like United Electric's weak coal reserves in *General Dynamics*) would not allow it to be as strong a competitor as the bald statistical projections indicate."[153] But given the rationale for imposing stringent requirements for the failing company defense, the same court appropriately backed away from allowing acquisition's of *flailing* companies when acquisitions of *failing* companies would not be permitted. The court pointed out that the acquisition of a weak company "in effect hands over its customers to the financially strong, thereby deterring competition by preventing others from acquiring those customers, [and] making entry more difficult."[154]

(12) Entry barriers.

One of the recurring issues in antitrust cases concerns "doubt administration"—who wins when neither side can really prove that it is right? Language in *Philadelphia National Bank* suggests that the government prevails when a merger gives a firm control of an "undue share" of a relevant market,[155] but the issue has not been revisited recently. Nowhere is this issue more

151. Id. at 119–20.

152. Id. at 121.

153. United States v. International Harvester Co., 564 F.2d 769, 773 (7th Cir. 1977).

154. Kaiser Aluminum & Chemical Corp. v. FTC, 652 F.2d 1324, 1339 (7th Cir. 1981). See also Daniel Rashin, Note, Horizontal Mergers After *United States v. General Dynamics Corp.*, 92 Harv. L. Rev. 491, 511 (1978).

155. 374 U.S. at 363 (evidence "clearly showing" that the merger is not likely to have anticompetitive effects is necessary to rebut presumption of illegality that arises when a merger "produces a firm controlling an undue percentage share" of the relevant market).

pivotal than in cases where the court must determine the effect of conditions of entry on the government's prima facie case.

In *United States v. Waste Management, Inc.*,[156] the Second Circuit held that the ease of entry must be considered in determining whether a merger lessens competition. Evidence of easy entry truly refutes the government's prima facie case: the presumption that two firms with large market shares could combine to exercise economic power is clearly incorrect when other firms are likely to enter the market should competition be lessened. The key question, however, is what constitutes entry barriers. In answering this question, the Chicago school approach, which favors limited antitrust intervention in the market, seeks to identify conditions that would prevent an equally efficient firm from entering the market. If these conditions do not exist, Chicago school adherents conclude that there are no entry barriers. Other economists have identified ways that firms can raise barriers to new entry (such as by developing a reputation for selected predation) even if physical barriers to entry (huge capital requirements, etc.) are low.[157]

Where the government proves a prima facie case, the defendant should have the burden of showing that entry is sufficiently easy, and (more important) is sufficiently recognized as easy by others, that the merged firm and its remaining rivals are unlikely to attempt to lessen competition. This shifting of the burden is consistent with *General Dynamics'* view that statistics are sufficient to allow the government to establish a prima facie case, but that the defendant may show that these statistics are unreliable.

Waste Management approved the merger of two firms, with a combined market share of 48.8%, because the court found insufficient barriers to entry into the Dallas market for waste collection from commercial customers. Although this result may have been correct, the facts highlighted by the court, while suggestive of easy entry, should not have been considered sufficient to refute the government's prima facie case. The court relied on the absence of physical barriers: the cost of purchasing a truck and entering the market was quite low, and a number of firms operating in neighboring Fort Worth could have entered the market if prices rose too much.[158] However, the court ignored the implications of the district court's finding that, while many companies had entered the industry and a few had grown in size, most new entrants remained small or disappeared entirely. If entry was so easy, why

156. 743 F.2d 976 (2d Cir. 1984).

157. Compare George Stigler, The Organization of Industry 67–70 (1968) ("Stiglerian" barriers), with Joe Bain, Barriers to New Competition 1–13 (1962) and Janusz Ordover & Daniel

Wall, Proving Predation after *Monfort* and *Matsushita*: What the New "New Learning" Has to Offer, Antitrust, Summer 1987, at 5 ("strategic" barriers).

158. 743 F.2d at 983.

was it so difficult to sustain that entry? Most significant, the court rejected the government's argument that brand loyalty constitutes an entry barrier.[159] The court seemed to consider it unfair to "punish" the defendant by finding entry barriers that may have been caused by superior skill and efficiency. Just as in the monopoly context, however, courts must separately analyze the distinct questions whether the defendants have economic power and whether they have done anything illegal.[160] Regardless of why entry barriers exist, the government's prima facie case cannot be refuted if they do. To take *Waste Management*'s point to its logical extreme, would we allow Coca–Cola and Pepsi–Cola to merge because the major barrier to entry into the cola market— brand loyalty—was created by years of effective marketing of perfected trade secrets? [161]

(13) Other factors refuting statistical evidence.

FTC v. Elders Grain, Inc.[162] establishes that the defendant bears the burden of clearly refuting the government's statistical case. In that case, the Seventh Circuit sustained a preliminary injunction barring the merger of two of the six industrial dry corn suppliers. First, the court observed that the buyers in this market were few, large, and sophisticated, perhaps implying that they could take care of themselves. After making this statement, however, the court proceeded to ignore it. As the court noted, § 7 requires a prediction about competition, and "doubts are to be resolved against the transaction";[163] the characteristics of the defendant's buyers therefore merits consideration only when the plaintiff's prima facie case is marginal (moderately concentrated markets, moderate increases in concentration). The greater the market concentration, the more confidence the court has that the merger is likely to create or increase market power.

Elders Grain also suggested that excess capacity in the market was a factor that might refute the government's prima facie case. Judge Posner's opinion for the court then immediately

159. Id. at 984.

160. See Chapter 3, section B(2). Compare E.I du Pont de Nemours & Co. (TiO$_2$), 96 F.T.C. 653 (1980) (evidence that respondent's unilateral increase of prices in order to finance plant expansion and modernization shows that respondent has monopoly power, although such power was not abused) with United States v. United States Steel Corp., 251 U.S. 417 (1920) (evidence that defendant tried to obtain agreement with rivals on prices shows that defendant does not have monopoly power, al-though such conduct was clearly anti-competitive).

161. In reality, firms seeking to compete with the two cola giants would also face the considerable hurdle of con-structing a competitive system for dis-tributing their beverages, but the point made in text illustrates the flaw in *Waste Management*'s reasoning.

162. 868 F.2d 901 (7th Cir. 1989).

163. Id. at 906.

demonstrated, however, why this factor is really irrelevant. Excess capacity may lead to aggressive price cutting (thus suggesting that competition will be vigorous in the market,) or it "may be a symptom of cartelization rather than a cure for it" (indicating that the current market is not competitive and suggesting that the remaining firms may well continue this pattern).[164] Because it cuts both ways, the prima facie case was not refuted.

The government's merger guidelines consider a number of factors that affect the significance of statistical data.[165] Most troublesome is their suggestion that the government is more likely to challenge a merger where the product is homogenous and undifferentiated. The guidelines correctly note that prices are more easily set where all rival products are similar than where they differ in price and quality. But the guidelines ignore the strategic effects of lessened competition in a differentiated market. An oligopoly may find it more profitable to agree to offer differentiated products and take the modest monopoly profits that come from selling a product without a close substitute. The larger the number of firms in a market, the more likely one of them will decide to make money by direct price competition, rather than by offering a different product at an elevated price. Horizontal mergers that concentrate differentiated markets decrease this potential. (How often do national beer companies advertise prices, for example?) [166]

A major unresolved question about merger defenses is whether the courts will permit an otherwise unlawful merger because the defendants demonstrate that the efficiencies created by the merger outweigh any lessening of competition. The legislative history of § 7 suggests that efficiency defenses should be recognized only when small firms wish to merge to compete more effectively against larger concerns.[167] One approach, taken by the Justice Department in its 1982 guidelines, is to set the threshold for presumptive illegality sufficiently high that we can assume that, except in extraordinary cases, efficiencies can be achieved by acquisitions falling under the threshold.[168] An alternative approach advocated by Professors Areeda and Turner is to set a very low threshold (post-merger market share of 13–14%), but then to

164. Id. at 906.

165. See 1992 Guidelines, supra note 13, § 2.

166. Theoretically, a merger that facilitates the ability of the remaining firms to continue to differentiate their products gives each some power to unilaterally raise their own prices, an anticompetitive effect that warrants extensive attention from the 1992 guidelines.

But the discussion about unilateral price increases by a seller of a differentiated product does not mention this scenario. See id., § 2.21.

167. See Brown Shoe Co. v. United States, 370 U.S. 294, 319 n.34 (1962).

168. See § V–A of the 1982 Guidelines, reprinted at 4 Trade Reg. Rep. (CCH) ¶ 13,102, at 20,542 (1992).

consider efficiencies as a defense.[169] The current guidelines seem to moot the point: they will consider efficiencies, but only where the parties show that those efficiencies cannot be realized by means short of the merger.[170] Because this standard is so difficult to achieve, virtually no mergers are cleared on this basis.

As a matter of theory, of course, an efficiency defense is consistent, if not required, by an antitrust policy motivated solely by a desire to achieve an efficient allocation of resources. By definition, such a policy should not prohibit mergers where the net effect is to increase efficiency. If a prima facie case is shown, however, structural economics teaches that rivalry is probably lessened; even if the merger leads to cost savings, they are unlikely to be passed on to the consumer through lower prices. Thus, a consumer-oriented antitrust policy would reject an efficiency defense. As Senator Sherman noted, some trusts may have lower costs, but they should nevertheless be condemned because these costs are not passed on to the consumer.[171] Neo-populist scholars have argued that efficiencies should not be considered because a merger that simultaneously increases market power and lowers costs will result in higher prices to consumers unless the cost savings are enormous.[172] In the litigation context, however, this argument assumes that prices will increase whenever a prima facie case is shown. The prima facie case is an inexact prediction, however, with doubts resolved against the transaction. Often, the available evidence concerning market structure and other industry characteristics makes it impossible to predict with a high degree of confidence that the merger will in fact exploit consumers through higher prices. Where the evidence of efficiency is very strong, consumers may benefit if the risk that the merger will result in higher prices is less clear.

In any event, both the case law and current government practice insist that any efficiencies must relate to the same relevant market where competition may be lessened; merging firms may not defend a merger that substantially lessens competition in one market by citing efficiencies that will occur elsewhere.[173]

---

169. Areeda & Turner, supra note 69, at 25.

170. 1992 Guidelines, supra note 13, § 4.

171. More recently, the FTC rejected an efficiency defense in part because the respondent's dominant market share made it unlikely that market forces would force it to pass the cost savings on to consumers. American Medical Int'l, Inc., 104 F.T.C. 1, 220

(1984) (citing Lawrence Sullivan, Antitrust 631 (1977)).

172. See, e.g., Fisher, Johnson & Lande, supra note 6, at 816–18.

173. See, e.g., United States v. Philadelphia National Bank, 374 U.S. 321, 370–71 (1963) (merger lessened competition for individuals and small businesses in Philadelphia; Court rejects argument that merger will create efficiencies in market for large corporate accounts in Philadelphia and New York).

Section B: Potential Competition & Conglomerate Mergers

(1) Legal background.

If the government's record of success in challenging horizontal mergers during the 1960s was so impressive that Justice Stewart could complain that the only consistency in the § 7 case law was that the government always won,[1] the opposite could surely be said about the government's efforts during the subsequent two decades to attack potential competition and conglomerate mergers—mergers between two firms that are currently neither rivals nor in a supplier-customer relationship. For those who believe that the antitrust laws serve goals other than allocative efficiency, the doctrines developed since the early 1970s are particularly disappointing, for they ignore a host of other serious policy concerns.[2]

Actually, the judiciary's hostile response to government challenges to mergers involving those who are not in actual competition with each other has a rich lineage, dating back to litigation under the Sherman Act. In *United States v. Winslow*,[3] the Supreme Court held that the Sherman Act did not apply at all to potential competition mergers. The defendants in that case owned patents for various different machines used to manufacture shoes, and merged their separate businesses into one concern, the United Shoe Machinery Company. Noting that each firm had lawful patents, making it a monopolist of its own product, Justice Oliver Wendell Holmes' majority opinion reasoned that because "they did not compete with one another, it is hard to see why the collective business should be any worse than its component parts."[4] The Court failed to consider that each defendant was particularly well situated to compete in making other machines (especially when the patents expired) and that the merger forestalled any future competition in the industry. It is no surprise

1. United States v. Von's Grocery Co., 384 U.S. 270, 301 (1966) (Stewart, J., dissenting).

2. For an articulation of these concerns, see The Small and Independent Business Protection Act of 1979: Hearings on S. 600 Before the Subcomm. on Antitrust, Monopoly & Business Rights of the Senate Comm. on the Judiciary, 96th Cong., 1st Sess. (1979). Supporters of supplemental antitrust legislation cite a number of negative social, and political, and economic effects caused by conglomerate mergers. These include lost jobs and reduced local control over the economy, id. at 2 (remarks of Sen. Kennedy); increased corporate political power, id.; capital devoted to acquisitions that could be redirected to job and plant creation, id. at 9 (remarks of Sen. Metzenbaum); and increased discretionary power of large firms, id. at 15 (statement of FTC Chairman Michael Pertschuk).

3. 227 U.S. 202 (1913).

4. Id. at 217.

that the new entity, United Shoe, became the focus of monopolization litigation in later years, and maintained monopoly power through the 1950s.[5]

When Congress responded to the overall judicial hostility to the antitrust laws by enacting the Clayton Act in 1914, it did not address *Winslow*'s crabbed construction of the Sherman Act as applied to potential competition mergers. Section 7 of the Clayton Act, as originally enacted, only barred mergers whose effect was to substantially lessen competition "between the corporation whose stock is so acquired and the corporation making the acquisition."[6] Thus, the Clayton Act, as well as the Sherman Act, was thought to apply only to horizontal mergers. This view continued through the post-World War II era, when the Supreme Court again refused to block a merger under § 1 even though it a lessened potential competition.[7]

Prior to passage of the Celler–Kefauver Amendments in 1950, the FTC had opined that § 7 did not apply to non-horizontal mergers, and until 1949 the government had never challenged a non-horizontal merger under § 7. The House Report on the Celler–Kefauver bill emphasized that one of its purposes was to "make it clear that the bill applies to all types of mergers and acquisitions, vertical and conglomerate as well as horizontal."[8] Nonetheless, the Supreme Court subsequently held, in a 4–2 decision, that the original § 7 applied to *any* merger with a competition-lessening effect.[9]

(2) Non-economic concerns about conglomerate mergers.

One of the key benefits of competition is that major business decisions are effectively made by the "invisible hand" of the marketplace rather than by the whim and discretion of a few powerful people. Louis Brandeis adhered to the Madisonian desire to check power by dispersing it, and thus advocated enactment of the Clayton Act in hopes that it would avoid the prospect that one person's mistakes could cause great economic hardship.[10]

5. For a discussion of the government's four attacks on the United Shoe monopoly, see note 11 in Chapter 5, section G.

6. Clayton Act, Pub. L. No. 63–212, ch. 323, § 7, 38 Stat. 730, 731–32 (1914).

7. United States v. Columbia Steel Co., 334 U.S. 495 (1948), discussed in detail in section A(2), above.

8. H.R. Rep. No. 1191, 81st Cong., 1st Sess. 11 (1949).

9. United States v. E.I. du Pont De Nemours & Co., 353 U.S. 586, 590–92 (1957) (holding a vertical merger unlawful). The case is discussed in section C(1).

10. Brandeis testified: "You cannot have true American citizenship, you cannot preserve political liberty, you cannot secure American standards of living unless some degree of industrial liberty accompanies it." Clayton Act: Hearings on S. 98 Before the Senate

Conglomerate acquisitions centralize economic power in the hands of fewer corporate giants, rather than dispersing power among many economic actors, thus subjecting many more workers, shareholders, and consumers to the whim and discretion of powerful corporate executives. Because they have large numbers of employees and make extensive purchases of goods and services, huge firms can potentially exercise dominant political power as well as compel government intervention to protect them from failure. Conglomeration is also inconsistent with the Jeffersonian goal of preserving citizen entrepreneurs. These entrepreneurs have a greater stake in the society, and thus are more effective participants in politics. As Justice William O. Douglas wrote, "a nation of clerks is anathema to the American antitrust dream." [11]

Conglomerate mergers also decrease local control of local economic institutions. The resulting geographic centralization of economic power has a number of undesirable consequences. Out-of-state business executives are more likely to respond to short-term bottom line concerns, making layoffs and plant closings more likely. Conglomerate corporations have more opportunities to invest than do local business magnates, and therefore may demand a higher rate of return in order to justify continued operation. For example, IT&T may need an annual profit of 20%, while the prior owner of the plant might have been happy to stay in business with 12%. As a result, under the guise of efficiency, plants are closed, workers are displaced, and society faces the economic and social costs of economic dislocation (retraining, unemployment, and welfare benefits) when the prior firm might well have been able to stay in business.

The high-water mark for aggressive Justice Department litigation advancing these concerns came in a series of challenges to acquisitions made by one of America's leading conglomerates. In *United States v. International Telephone & Telegraph Co.*,[12] the district court wrote an extensive opinion rejecting one of these challenges—to IT&T's purchase of Grinnell.[13] The court began by noting that a conglomerate that acquired the dominant competitor in an oligopolistic market would violate § 7 if the merger were to

---

Committee on Interstate Commerce, 62d Cong., 1st Sess. 1155 (1911).

11. United States v. Falstaff Brewing Corp., 410 U.S. 526, 543 (1973) (concurring opinion). Justice Douglas raised a host of non-economic disadvantages of conglomeration in a stirring opinion. Robert Bork has referred to similar arguments made by populist economist Walter Adams as "more poetry than analysis." See Antitrust &

Trade Reg. Rep. (BNA) No. 880, at A–22 (Sept. 14, 1978).

12. 324 F. Supp. 19 (D. Conn. 1970), appeal dismissed, 404 U.S. 801 (1971).

13. At the time, IT&T was the 9th largest industrial corporation in the country, and Grinnell was 268th. (Yes, this is the same Grinnell found to have unlawfully monopolized in the 1960s. See chapter 3, section B(2).)

further entrench the dominant firm through increased barriers to entry and intimidation of smaller firms.[14] However, the court found, while Grinnell was the leading manufacturer of automatic sprinklers and power water pipes, it had significant rivals in each market and its largest market share (with one small exception) was 25%. Significantly, the court found that acquisition by IT&T would not confer any particular advantages on Grinnell that would deter entry by others or discourage smaller rivals from aggressively competing.[15]

Most significant was the court's rejection of the government's non-economic claim that the merger should be blocked because it contributed to the general trend toward economic concentration. Section 7, the court reasoned, requires proof of a lessening of competition in a specific line of commerce in a particular section of the country. "To ask the Court to rule with respect to alleged anticompetitive consequences in *undesignated lines of commerce* is tantamount to asking the Court to engage in judicial legislation," the trial judge wrote.[16]

Unfortunately, this was not the best case to test the government's theories. In challenging a merger between two huge corporations, the government did not target an acquisition that would substantially increase the number of "clerks" vis-a-vis the number of yeoman entrepreneurs. The complaint did not allege that distant IT&T executives would lessen competition by running the company differently than had Grinnell management. Although subsequent events may confirm non-economic concerns about the political power of conglomerates like IT&T,[17] the complaint did not proceed on that theory. In short, the government's suit gave the court little in the way of a coherent theory by which to attack a conglomerate merger on non-economic grounds.

Judicial insensitivity to non-economic concerns has continued. Consider the beer industry, for example. In 1966, the Court's finding in *Pabst* that the defendant's acquisition of Blatz lessened competition appeared principally concerned with avoiding the transformation of the beer industry from a regional one to one

---

14. 324 F. Supp. at 24.

15. The court contrasted FTC v. Procter & Gamble Co. 386 U.S. 568 (1967), and its progeny, which are discussed below in subsection (4).

16. 324 F. Supp. at 52 (emphasis in original).

17. IT&T made a substantial campaign contribution to underwrite the 1972 Republican National Convention, after which White House officials attempted to interfere with the Antitrust Division's prosecution of the case. It is unclear whether or not they succeeded: the government's legal theories were novel, the facts were not ideal from the government's perspective, and the settlement eventually agreed to was fairly favorable to the government. For a reprint of choice Nixon tapes concerning the incident and a discussion of the settlement, see Eleanor Fox & Lawrence Sullivan, Antitrust 843–50 (1989).

dominated by nationally advertised brands.[18] Because of these
generalized concerns about the industry's transformation, the
Court held that no proof of specific harm in a precisely defined
market was necessary. By 1973, however, the Court was willing
to consider only economic factors in approving Falstaff's efforts to
enter the New England beer market by acquiring the region's
largest independent firm.[19] Indeed, when the government challenged the merger of a dominant Seattle bank with an established
bank in eastern Washington, arguing that the merger would
transform the state's banking industry from a regional one to one
dominated by statewide institutions, the Court expressly rejected
Pabst's suggestion that a merger can violate § 7 without proof of
harm in a precisely drawn economically relevant market.[20] In
sum, if tomorrow's paper announced the merger of AT&T, Ford,
and Exxon, it is difficult to see how the antitrust laws would pose
an obstacle.

As a result, legislators considered amending the Clayton Act
in the late 1970s to prohibit acquisitions by the largest American
corporations without requiring evidence of lessened competition in
a defined market.[21] Some of the legislation's supporters favored
creating a presumption that mergers exceeding a certain absolute
dollar volume were illegal, allowing an affirmative defense where
the defendant could demonstrate either clear efficiencies or an
actual increase in the market's competitive structure. Even aggressive antitrust enforcers such as then-FTC Chair Michael Pertschuk had difficulty with this approach, arguing that litigation
brought under the proposed statute would be "complex and unworkable." The FTC advocated an alternative "cap & spin-off"
approach that would flatly ban all conglomerate acquisitions,
unless the company subsequently divested a similar volume of
assets.[22] This disagreement—even among antitrust "hawks"—
combined with strenuous opposition from business groups arguing
that many conglomerate mergers were efficient, doomed the legislation to failure.

A major study released after these proposals died suggests
that conglomerate mergers are actually likely to be inefficient.

18. United States v. Pabst Brewing
Co., 384 U.S. 546 (1966). This case is
discussed in detail above in section A(3).

19. United States v. Falstaff Brewing Corp., 410 U.S. 526 (1973). The case
is discussed in detail below in subsection (3a).

20. United States v. Marine Bancorporation, Inc., 418 U.S. 602, 621 n.20
(1974). The case is discussed in detail
in subsection (3b), below.

21. See, e.g., S. 600, 96th Cong., 1st
Sess. (1979).

22. The Small and Independent
Business Protection Act of 1979: Hearings on S. 600 Before the Subcomm. on
Antitrust, Monopoly & Business Rights
of the Senate Comm. on the Judiciary,
96th Cong., 1st Sess. 23 (1979).

Contrary to the business groups' assertions that these mergers represent efforts to use resources efficiently, the study indicates that conglomerate acquisitions are more likely to driven by a combination of other motives—the opportunity for monopoly profits due to a lessening of competition; an increase in profits because the stock market undervalues the acquired firm's assets; enhancement of the power, prestige, and perquisites of senior management when they control a larger corporate empire; and tax advantages.[23]   Although studies such as these may refute laissez-faire arguments against government interference in the marketplace, further legislation is unlikely until a workable scheme for intervention is developed.

(3) Potential competition.

The chief economic theory underlying arguments that conglomerate mergers may cause a substantial lessening of competition in a relevant market is the theory of potential competition. Potential competition theory affects merger analysis in two ways. As we saw in section A(12), a horizontal merger involving one of the few firms in an industry might not lessen competition if entry barriers are sufficiently low that others remain "in the wings" and threaten to enter the market if the remaining firms engage in anticompetitive behavior.   On the other hand, the theory suggests that mergers can lessen competition even if the merging parties are not currently rivals, when the merger eliminates a potential entry that was restraining the existing firms.[24]

23. David Ravenscraft & F.M. Scherer, Mergers, Sell–Offs, and Economic Efficiency (1987).

24. Labeling mergers as "horizontal" or "potential competition" is somewhat arbitrary. Suppose, for example, that the leading firm in a market acquires a firm that currently does not compete in that market, but would be likely to enter in the event of oligopoly pricing. Some would characterize this as a horizontal merger, and would broadly define the relevant market based on supply-side considerations to include the second firm. Others would describe this as a potential competition merger. Thus, several casebooks (and this treatise) treat United States v. Continental Can Co., 378 U.S. 441 (1964) (enjoining merger of leading can manufacturer and a large glass jar maker because of inter-product competition), as a horizontal merger case (see section A(8), above), while other casebooks treat

the decision as a potential competition case.

In light of the obstacles outlined in this section to successfully challenging mergers on potential competition grounds, one alternative tactic is for the plaintiff to allege (contrary to usual practice) that a market is *broader*, so that a merger between the acquiring and acquired firms can be considered horizontal. For example, in Equifax, Inc. v. FTC, 618 F.2d 63 (9th Cir. 1980), the Commission refused to approve a merger between a firm providing mortgage reports for customers interested in the character and status of potential lenders and a firm providing credit reports on the bill-paying status of potential borrowers. The FTC based its finding that the merger was horizontal on the "commonality of production techniques" that made it easy for suppliers of one product to enter the other market in response to laggard competition. Id. at 66. The court of appeals ap-

It is important to distinguish between two theories of potential competition. The "perceived potential competition" theory focuses on the pro-competitive effect that a potential entrant currently has on the firms in a market. The "actual potential competition" theory posits that competition is lessened in the long run when a potential entrant acquires a major incumbent firm, because absent the merger the entrant would have eventually entered the market through internal expansion or by a "toe-hold" merger—that is, the acquisition of a smaller firm currently in the market. In concentrated markets, the addition of a new major firm is obviously pro-competitive; if instead the firm merely displaces an industry leader, no such deconcentration occurs. The Supreme Court has twice expressly reserved the question whether this second scenario qualifies as a substantial lessening of competition for purposes of § 7.[25]

(3a) Perceived potential competition: developing the theory.

United States v. El Paso Natural Gas Co.[26] clearly illustrates why the acquired firm need not be a current rival of the acquiring firm to exercise a strong pro-competitive influence. In that case, Pacific (the acquired company) had never sold a btu of gas in California, but had enormous reserves in surrounding areas, had tried to secure California contracts for some time, and had lost out to the defendant for a contract with a California utility only after El Paso reduced its price by 25%. Concluding that Pacific was a "substantial factor in the California market at the time it was acquired by El Paso,"[27] the Court blocked the acquisition because of the merger's anticompetitive effect in California.

peared to accept this theory, holding that "cross-elasticity of supply is a valid basis for determining that two commodities should be within the same market." It vacated the FTC's order, however, because it found insufficient evidence that mortgage reporters were realistic rivals to credit reporters. The court found no substantial evidence that mortgage and credit reporters use similar techniques or technology, noted that mortgage reports constituted less than 1% of credit reporters' output, and found no substantial evidence that the company providing mortgage reports actually produced credit reports. Id. at 66–67.

25. United States v. Falstaff Brewing Corp., 410 U.S. 526, 537 (1973):

We leave for another day the question of the applicability of § 7 to a

merger that will leave competition in the marketplace exactly as it was, neither hurt nor helped, and that is challengeable under § 7 only on grounds that the company could, but did not, enter *de novo* or through "toe-hold" acquisition and that there is less competition than there would have been had entry been in such a manner.

See also United States v. Marine Bancorporation, Inc., 418 U.S. 602, 639 (1974) (citing *Falstaff*).

26. 376 U.S. 651 (1964).

27. Id. at 658. The evidence supporting the Court's conclusion included a letter from Pacific to its stockholders indicating that a pre-merger "peace treaty" between El Paso and Pacific "means that El Paso's California mar-

A merger can even lessen competition in a market where neither party is currently operating. In *United States v. Penn–Olin Chemical Co.*, for example, the government attacked a joint venture formed by Pennsalt and Olin to build a Kentucky sodium chlorate plant for sales in the southeast.[28] The district court found that the joint venture did not lessen competition because it was unlikely that both defendants would have entered the market separately. The Supreme Court reversed. Writing for the majority, Justice Tom Clark explained that the "existence of an aggressive, well equipped and well financed corporation engaged in the same or related lines of commerce waiting anxiously to enter an oligopolistic market would be a substantial incentive to competition which cannot be underestimated."[29] Thus, the Court held, a § 7 violation could be established by proving that absent the merger, one firm would have entered the market while the other one remained on the sidelines, capable of entering if circumstances warranted.[30]

In remanding so that the district court could determine whether the merger that standard, the Court noted that "[p]otential competition cannot be put to a subjective test." The objective evidence in the case showed that the market was rapidly expanding and that few other corporations had the same "inclination, resources, and know-how" to enter the market as did Pennsalt and Olin, both of which had substantial resources and experience in the industry. In addition, prior to the joint venture, each had "evidenced a long-sustained and strong interest in entering the relevant market area, each had good contacts with consumers in the area, and each had "compelling reasons" for entering. "Unless we are going to require subjective evidence," Clark wrote, "this array of probability certainly reaches the prima facie stage."[31]

On remand, however, the district court relied on subjective evidence found in internal corporate documents, holding that

---

ket will be protected against future competition." Id. at 654.

28. 378 U.S. 158 (1964).

Initially, the defendants argued that a joint venture into a new market was not subject to § 7, which regulates the acquisition of the stock or assets of firms engaged in interstate commerce. Each defendant had bought 50% of the stock of the Penn–Olin Chemical Company, but that corporation was brand new, they argued, and therefore was not "engaged in commerce." The Court rejected this argument. First, given that the 1950 amendments to § 7 had

been drafted to eliminate loopholes in the original version of the Clayton Act, the Court refused to interpret the statute so as to create such a new gigantic loophole. Moreover, the Court observed that the defendants' argument would only lead to wasteful maneuvers, for as soon as Penn–Olin began operations it would become engaged in commerce. Id. at 168.

29. Id. at 174.

30. Id. at 173.

31. Id. at 175.

neither Pennsalt nor Olin would have entered the market absent the joint venture and again dismissing the government's complaint.[32] It is difficult to understand how the district court could have reached this judgment since it appears to fly directly in the face of Justice Clark's admonition to rely on objective evidence. Clark's theory in *Penn–Olin* was that competition was lessened by the removal of a "perceived potential entrant." Olin, for example, was standing "in the wings" as a potential entrant, forcing those already in the market to compete with each other more aggressively, less their lax performance induce it to take the plunge. Because this theory is based entirely on a prediction as to how other firms in the sodium chlorate market would react to objective evidence concerning Olin's intentions, the Supreme Court correctly limited the inquiry to an analysis of this objective evidence. Nevertheless, the Supreme Court affirmed the district court's contrary decision by a 4–4 vote.[33]

The district court's subsequent dismissal of the *Penn–Olin* complaint based on subjective indications that neither defendant would have entered the market does not really address the perceived potential competition question. In theory, if the other firms in the market saw the defendants as the most likely potential entrants, the venture lessened competition even if neither would have entered. However, the use of such subjective evidence, if reliable, may be justified based on another rationale: an actual competitor in hand is worth two potential competitors in the wings.

The Federal Trade Commission's use of objective evidence to block a merger that harmed potential competition was at issue in *FTC v. Procter & Gamble Co.*[34] P & G, a large, diversified manufacturer of low-price, high-turnover household products sold through grocery, drug, and department stores, did not produce liquid household bleach until it acquired Clorox Chemical Co., the nation's leading bleach manufacturer. The court of appeals' rejected the FTC's finding on potential competition because there was no testimony that P & G's management ever intended to independently enter the bleach industry. The Supreme Court reversed, ignoring the lack of subjective evidence and relying instead on objective evidence of potential entry. Specifically, the Court noted that P & G was engaged in an active program of diversification; liquid bleach was a natural avenue for such diversification; and P & G had just successfully entered the market for

---

32. 246 F. Supp. 917 (D. Del. 1965), aff'd by equally divided court, 389 U.S. 308 (1967).

33. 389 U.S. 308 (1967).

34. 386 U.S. 568 (1967).

a related abrasive cleaner.[35]

The propriety of relying on objective evidence was reaffirmed, although somewhat tempered, in *United States v. Falstaff Brewing Corp.*[36] The defendant in that case was the nation's fourth largest beer producer, but did not sell in New England. Concluding that it must become a "national" brewer to compete against its larger rivals, Falstaff acquired Naragansett, the region's leading brewer. The government claimed that Falstaff was actively seeking to extend its sales into New England and, absent this merger, would have entered that market either through internal expansion or through a "toe-hold" merger with a smaller regional brewer. The district court dismissed the complaint based on testimony from Falstaff's management that it would not have entered the market by any means other than a merger with Naragansett. The Supreme Court reversed. According to the Court, the issue

> is not what Falstaff's internal company decisions were but whether, given its financial capabilities and conditions in the New England market, it would be reasonable to consider it a potential entrant into that market.... [I]f it would appear to rational beer merchants in New England that Falstaff might well build a new brewery to supply the northeastern market then its entry by merger becomes suspect under § 7.[37]

In reviewing the objective evidence, the company's actual intentions were relevant, the Court held, but were "not the last word." Rather, the district court should have determined "whether in any realistic sense Falstaff could be said to be a potential competitor on the fringe of the market with likely influence on existing competition."[38]

This subtle chipping away at *Penn–Olin*'s focus on objective evidence provoked a thoughtful concurrence from Justice Thurgood Marshall. He would have held that "where, as here, strong objective evidence indicates that a firm is a potential entrant into a market, it is error for the trial judge to rely solely on the firm's subjective prediction of its own future conduct." Not only should subjective evidence never be the "last word," as the majority held, but trial judges should consider such evidence only when the objective evidence is weak or contradictory *and* there is "a compelling demonstration that a firm will not follow its economic self-interest."[39] Although Marshall's test is perhaps a bit too strong, he correctly questions the reliability of the defendant's self-inter-

35. Id. at 580. This case is also discussed as a conglomerate merger in subsection (4) below.

36. 410 U.S. 526 (1973).

37. Id. at 533.

38. Id. at 534.

39. Id. at 548.

ested protestations, and properly suggests that the defense bear a heavy burden in explaining why its subjective plans do not conform to objective indicators. Moreover, the district court's reliance on subjective evidence overlooks the critical issue—whether Falstaff would be particularly well-placed to enter *de novo* if prices rose significantly.[40]

(3b) Perceived potential competition: applying (and misapplying) the theory.

In *United States v. Marine Bancorporation*, Inc.[41] the Court set out the elements of a perceived potential competition case: (1) the market must be substantially concentrated; (2) the acquiring firm must have the "characteristics, capabilities, and economic incentive to render it a perceived potential de novo entrant"; and (3) the presence of the acquiring firm in the wings must "in fact [have] tempered oligopolistic behavior on the part of existing market participants."[42] The Justice Department's guidelines take a similar approach, quantifying *Marine Banc*'s three requirements with a few additional restrictions. The Antitrust Division will challenge mergers that threaten potential competition only where (1) the market has an HHI exceeding 1800; (2) there are no more than two other entrants who are as likely to enter the market as the defendant; and (3) the acquired firm's market share is at least 5% (though the government might elect not to challenge a merger where the share is in the 5–20% range).[43]

Applying these standards, the Supreme Court rejected the government's challenge to the acquisition by the National Bank of Commerce, Washington's second largest bank, of Washington Trust Bank, a mid-sized bank based in the city of Spokane in eastern Washington, where National had no offices. (Marine Bancorporation, a holding company, owned National's stock.) Justice Lewis Powell, writing for the majority, dismissed the complaint because state banking restrictions made it impossible for National to be an aggressive, major competitor in the Spokane market absent the merger.[44]

40. See Richard Posner & Frank Easterbrook, Antitrust 524 (2d ed. 1981). On remand, the merger was again upheld based on the district court's finding that no one perceived Falstaff to be a potential entrant. United States v. Falstaff Brewing Corp., 383 F.Supp. 1020 (D.R.I. 1974).

41. 418 U.S. 602 (1974).

42. Id. at 625. The third element is discussed below in connection with Ten-

neco, Inc. v. FTC, 689 F.2d 346 (2d Cir. 1982).

43. Merger Guidelines of Department of Justice, 4 Trade Reg. Rep. (CCH) ¶ 13,103, § 4.1 (1984). These provisions of the 1984 guidelines are not affected by the more recent horizontal merger guidelines jointly issued by the Antitrust Division and the FTC. See 4 Trade Reg. Rep. (CCH) ¶ 13,104, at 20,-569 (1992).

44. 418 U.S. at 641–42.

The Court accepted the government's argument that the Spokane market was sufficiently concentrated to subject the merger to the potential competition doctrine (the top three firms controlled 92% of deposits).[45] Nevertheless, the Court held the government failed to prove two key "preconditions" for establishing a pro-competitive effect if National remained in the wings. First, National needed to have "available feasible means for entering the Spokane market other than" by the challenged merger. The Court found that state law prohibited any such entry. Second, the alternative means of entry must "offer a substantial likelihood of ultimately producing deconcentration of that market or other significant pro-competitive effects."[46] Thus, even if, as the government suggested, the defendant could weasel around the state bank entry law, other state regulations would strictly limit National's ability to add branch offices in Spokane, and thus would deny National the means to be a significant pro-competitive force in that market.

Justice Byron White dissented, blasting "the Court's new antitrust majority" for "chipping way at the policies of § 7." White did not agree that National's inability to add branches once it entered the Spokane market deprived it of the ability to compete effectively. Even if limited to one office, White wrote, "[i]t is incredible to me that the presence of a major Seattle bank like [National] in downtown Spokane could or would be ignored by the entrenched banking powers."[47]

Marine Banc thus requires the party challenging a merger on potential competition grounds to navigate through narrow shoals. If the market has few entry barriers, then eliminating one potential entrant will not lessen competition. On the other hand, if the market has very significant entry barriers (as in *Marine Banc*), the merger can not eliminate potential competition because the outside firm was never really posed a threat to enter anyway.

If this obstacle was not difficult enough for the government to overcome, the lower courts have made it worse. In *Tenneco, Inc. v. FTC*,[48] for example, the Commission challenged the acquisition of Monroe, the second largest firm in the highly concentrated

45. Id. at 607 n.2.

46. Id. at 633.

47. Id. at 649. Justices Brennan and Marshall joined White's dissent.

An astute student of mine observed that Washington's restrictive banking laws prevented National from purchasing Washington Trust and then adding additional Spokane branches, whereas Washington Trust would have been free to add more branches in the Spokane area. In light of the limited economic growth in Spokane and National's plans to add additional services for customers, however, the majority apparently felt that National was in an equal or better position to attract Spokane patronage than Washington Trust.

48. 689 F.2d 346 (2d Cir. 1982).

shock absorber market, by Tenneco's Walker division, the nation's leader seller of automobile exhaust systems. The Second Circuit agreed with the FTC that there was "abundant evidence that the oligopolists in the market for replacement shock absorbers perceived Tenneco as a potential entrant." [49] But the court reversed the Commission's order blocking the merger on perceived potential competition grounds because, in the majority's view, the FTC failed to establish *Marine Banc*'s third element—that Tenneco's position in the "wings" actually tempered oligopolistic behavior.

The Commission observed that Gabriel, the industry leader in the shock absorber market, began an aggressive campaign of vigorous rivalry while Tenneco was actively searching for possible entry into that market. The FTC found that this activity could not be adequately explained by

> factors indigenous to the existing replacement shock absorber market, and it inferred from all of the circumstances that [Gabriel's] conduct was at least in substantial part in response to Tenneco's standing at the edge of the market as a competent, efficient, and financial powerful potential competitor.[50]

But the Second Circuit concluded that Gabriel's aggressive conduct was attributable instead to its own precarious downward trend prior to its acquisition in a separate conglomerate merger. The majority gave great credence to testimony from an executive of Gabriel's parent company that Gabriel's actions were not a response to pressure from Tenneco on the wings.[51]

The majority opinion is not simply flawed because, as Judge Walter Mansfield argued in dissent, it violated principles of administrative law by substituting its own fact-finding for FTC findings that were supported by substantial evidence (although this violation is particularly poignant in light of the Commission's origins in congressional dissatisfaction with the judicial interpretation of the antitrust laws).[52] Because the evaluation of any merger requires informed inferences when the issue concerns how market behavior is perceived by others, applying any standard other than de novo review should lead to the acceptance of a factfinder's conclusion that a recognized potential entrant has the requisite pro-competitive effect on a market when an oligopolist suddenly improves its economic performance at the same time the potential entrant appears to be actively considering entry.

49. Id. at 355.

50. Id. at 361 (Mansfield, J., dissenting).

51. Id. at 356–57.

52. See Hospital Corp. of America v. FTC, 807 F.2d 1381, 1384 (7th Cir. 1986), cert. denied, 481 U.S. 1038 (1987).

More fundamentally, however, *Tenneco* calls into question the wisdom of *Marine Banc*'s requirement that a plaintiff prove that the existence of the perceived potential entrant in fact restrained the exercise of market power. Such a requirement is arguably contrary to precedent: no such burden was imposed in *Procter & Gamble*. Moreover, as a matter of policy, the basic structural paradigm that underlies § 7 assumes that the removing of *any* competitive factor from an oligopolistic market illegally lessens competition. When the government wishes to block a horizontal merger between two of the six firms in an oligopolistic industry, for example, it need not introduce any specific evidence about the acquired firm's effect on competitive behavior in the market; that effect is inferred from oligopoly theory.[53] Similarly, where four firms control over 90% of the market and the acquiring firm is one of the few perceived potential entrants, the government should not be required to prove, as *Tenneco* held, that the acquiring firm itself "actually tempered the conduct of oligopolists in the market." [54]

Tenneco should be distinguished from a case like *Penn–Olin*, where the challenged acquisition involved *two* potential entrants. Merger cases always involve predictions, and the "bird in the hand" theory suggests that we should be reluctant to sacrifice the certainty of one new entrant because of the possibility of two new entrants—unless the risks of eliminating potential competition are particularly strong. Absent strong evidence that Tenneco's acquisition of Monroe would produce significant benefits to consumers that would be lost if the merger were enjoined, however, a balanced antitrust doctrine would have inferred pro-competitive effect from Tenneco's presence in the wings. Such an inference could be refuted, of course, if the defendant proved (contrary to the FTC's explicit findings in *Tenneco*) that other factors nullified

53. The legislative history of § 7 identified, as separate bases for a finding that a merger substantially lessened competition, the removal of a firm that was a "substantial factor" in the market and a merger that resulted in the elimination of an "undue" number of rivals. H.R. Rep. No. 1191, 81st Cong., 1st Sess. 8 (1949).

54. 689 F.2d at 355.

Tenneco's insistence on substantial evidence that a potential entrant actually exercised a pro-competitive effect from the wings was not dictated by *Marine Bancorporation*. Indeed, in an earlier opinion concerning actual potential competition, the Second Circuit suggested that *Marine Banc*'s requirement

that de novo or toehold entry result in pro-competitive effects can, as this treatise has suggested, be inferred "since typically in an oligopolistic situation the entry of a large firm as a new competitor necessarily has significant pro-competitive effects." BOC Int'l, Ltd. v. FTC, 557 F.2d 24, 27 (2d Cir. 1977) (citing Ford Motor Co. v. United States, 405 U.S. 562, 587 (1972) (Burger, C.J., concurring and dissenting); Stanley Robinson, Antitrust Developments: 1973, 74 Colum. L. Rev. 163, 183–84 (1974); and Donald Turner, Conglomerate Mergers and Section 7 of the Clayton Act, 78 Harv. L. Rev. 1313, 1383 (1965)). *BOC International* is discussed below in subsection (3c).

the anticompetitive effect of eliminating the potential entrant. This showing should be similar in nature to the showing that the defendant in a horizontal merger case would make, after *General Dynamics*, to refute the plaintiff's prima facie case.

(3c) Actual potential competition.

As noted above, the Supreme Court has yet to address the validity of § 7 challenges to mergers based on the theory of actual potential competition—that, absent the merger, one of the merging parties would have entered the market in competition with the other party by expanding internally or by acquiring a smaller firm, thus enhancing competition more so than would the challenged merger.[55] In the absence of Supreme Court precedent, the lower courts have refined the standard to be applied in actual potential competition cases.

In *BOC International, Ltd. v. FTC*,[56] the Second Circuit set forth the two key questions to be resolved in cases proceeding under this theory: (1) Would the acquiring firm otherwise have entered the market through internal expansion or a toehold acquisition? (2) Would such an alternative means of entry have had pro-competitive effects within the relevant market? Although the court suggested that an affirmative answer to the second question could be inferred from the oligopolistic nature of the market, it reversed the FTC's finding that British Oxygen's acquisition of Airco, the third largest American industrial gas producer, violated § 7.[57] The Commission had found that at the time of the merger, "there was a 'reasonable probability' that [British Oxygen] would have eventually entered the U.S. industrial gases market by internal expansion, or its equivalent, but for the acquisition of Airco."[58] The Second Circuit remanded because there was no indication of the time frame within which this entry might occur. To succeed on an actual potential competition theory, the court held, the Commission must point to substantial evidence supporting the conclusion that entry was reasonably probable within the "near future."[59]

---

55. See note 25 above and accompanying text.

56. 557 F.2d 24, 26–27 (2d Cir. 1977).

57. The FTC conceded that British Oxygen did not exercise any pro-competitive pressure from the "wings" prior to the merger.

58. Id. at 28 (citing In re British Oxygen Co., 86 F.T.C. 1241, 1360 (1975)).

59. Id. at 29. The FTC succeeded on an actual competition theory in Yam-

aha Motor Co. v. FTC, 657 F.2d 971 (8th Cir. 1981). In that case, the court of appeals sustained the Commission's findings that a joint venture between Brunswick and Yamaha substantially lessened competition in the American outboard-motor market. Brunswick was the second largest firm in a highly concentrated market (the top two firms controlled 85% of the market; the top four controlled 98.6%); objective evidence demonstrated that Yamaha was a viable potential entrant; and Yamaha's

In *Tenneco, Inc. v. FTC*,[60] a divided Second Circuit panel further increased the FTC's burden in actual potential competition cases. The court agreed with the Commission that the replacement shock absorber market was concentrated, that Tenneco had actively considered entering the market, and that it clearly possessed adequate financial resources to become a significant market factor. However, because there was no evidence that Tenneco had subjectively considered de novo entry, the court set aside the Commission's order blocking its acquisition of Monroe, a major incumbent. After *Tenneco*, firms that might otherwise consider entering a market will simply fail to make a record of any serious consideration of internal expansion, secure in the knowledge that the absence of such evidence will keep them from being labeled a potential entrant. *Tenneco* cannot be squared with *Penn–Olin*'s holding that a potential competition theory cannot be tested based on subjective evidence.

(4) Other economic harms caused by conglomerate mergers.

Although there have been few successful § 7 challenges to conglomerate acquisitions, such mergers can cause significant economic harm. Three principal types of harm have received judicial and scholarly attention in addition to those reflected in potential competition theory. First, the acquisition of a large firm can intimidate potential entrants and discipline rivals that are contemplating aggressive competition by the threat of retaliation, thus *entrenching* the power of the conglomerate firm. Second, conglomerate control of companies in related businesses can create the potential for unfair *reciprocity* agreements, where one subsidiary agrees to do business with a third party if the third party will patronize another subsidiary. Third, where conglomerates compete in different markets, *mutual forbearance* may deter effective rivalry: for example, Conglomerate A may be reluctant to have its hotel subsidiary start a price war against a hotel subsidiary owned by Conglomerate B, for fear that Conglomerate B will retaliate by having its computer software company target Conglomerate A's computer subsidiary for aggressive rivalry.

In *FTC v. Procter & Gamble Co.*,[61] the Court relied on concerns about entrenchment to invalidate the acquisition of Clorox, the nation's leading bleach manufacturer, by P & G, a conglomerate

stature and financial strength, as well as the brand name recognition its other products, would have an "obvious procompetitive effect leading to some deconcentration" were Yamaha to enter the market. Id. at 979.

60. 689 F.2d 346 (2d Cir. 1982).

61. 386 U.S. 568 (1967).

that was the nation's leading advertiser. The Court affirmed the FTC's finding that "the substitution of Procter with its huge assets and advertising advantages for the already dominant Clorox would dissuade new entrants and discourage active competition from the firms already in the industry due to fear of retaliation by Procter." [62] The Court also relied on some post-merger evidence suggesting that P & G had engaged in selective predation to prevent new entry.[63]

In a sophisticated concurring opinion, Justice John Harlan argued that the economic efficiencies produced by a conglomerate merger must be weighed against its anticompetitive consequences.[64] The FTC's conclusions about P & G—that it currently influenced the bleach market and would likely enter the market in the future were predictions. In light of the prophylactic nature of § 7, these predictions should suffice to establish a prima facie case for illegality. If the defendants were able to show, however, that the merger will definitely result in efficiencies, the FTC and the courts ought to consider taking the efficient bird in the hand.

If a balancing approach is taken, what efficiencies count in favor of a merger? Obviously, speculative claims of future efficiency should be discounted, in light of the general policy to resolve doubts in § 7 cases against the transaction. Significantly, Justice Harlan rejected P & G's argument that the merger should be permitted because it would create efficiencies in advertising. His position was correct, for several reasons. An efficiencies defense is designed to promote the antitrust goal of efficiently allocating society's resources; therefore, the fact that P & G might receive a better deal from media companies because of its buying power simply reflects a wealth transfer to P & G rather than a resource savings that should be weighed on the plus side of a merger. Moreover, as the FTC had found in its decision, sustained advertising often raised entry barriers, had questionable benefits for competition, and little beneficial effect on prices.[65] For example, Clorox' advertising campaign enabled it to obtain a 48% market share even though it sold its bleach at prices equal to or

62. Id. at 575.

63. When Purex, a distant second to Clorox in the liquid bleach market, attempted to enter the Erie, Pennsylvania market, P & G subjected it to a selective price war. Purex withdrew, and then acquired an existing firm in Erie in order to expand its geographic coverage. Id. at 579 n.3. This result is contrary to the antitrust laws' preference for internal expansion.

64. Id. at 597.

65. Procter & Gamble Co., 63 F.T.C. 1465, 1581–82 (1963). See also Donald Turner, Advertising and Competition, delivered before the Briefing Conference on Federal Controls of Advertising and Promotion in Washington D.C. (June 2, 1966), reprinted in part in Milton Handler, Harlan Blake, Robert Pitofsky & Harvey Goldschmid, Cases and Materials on Trade Regulation 971–74 (2d ed. 1990).

greater than those charged for other brands of the chemically identical product.[66] In contrast, neither Clorox or any other major advertiser was able to dominate sales in bulk to industrial buyers.[67] Thus, a dominant advertiser's acquisition of a major firm in an oligopolistic market is a prima facie violation of the Clayton Act.[68]

Even if P & G's acquisition of Clorox created efficiencies more beneficial to society than consumer advertising, a good argument can be made in support of *Procter & Gamble*'s holding that conglomerate mergers violate § 7 where the evidence strongly supports a conclusion that the merger is likely to entrench the dominant firm's power. As a matter of statutory construction, the legislative history indicates that an efficiency that gives the merged firm a "decisive advantage" over its rivals lessens competition within the meaning of Celler–Kefauver.[69] As a matter of policy, proponents of the Jeffersonian, dynamic efficiency and neo-populist goals of antitrust all support this construction. Allowing P & G to entrench Clorox' dominance would give Clorox an advantage that deprived small businesses of equality of opportunity; would serve as a "narcotic" to innovation; and, because of P & G's entrenched power, would more likely deprive consumers of the benefits of whatever efficiencies resulted from the merger. On the other hand, those who are sanguine about the marketplace and skeptical about antitrust intervention argue that using § 7 to block "entrenching" mergers creates too great a risk of deterring efficient, cost-saving mergers. In addition, they question whether courts and agencies can accurately determine when the defen-

---

66. 386 U.S. at 571.

67. Turner, supra note 65, at 973.

68. One's perspective on *Procter & Gamble* may be influenced by one's view of advertising. Skeptics find the case an apt and archetypical (if not representative) case study: advertising enables Clorox to charge more than other firms that sell chemically identical products. This example suggests that brand loyalty is often the result of advertising that manipulates consumers into making irrational choices. From this perspective, Justice Harlan is correct that efficiencies in advertising are not to be rewarded; sound antitrust policy would steer P & G toward independent entry and head-on competition with Clorox. The contrary view, however, is that brand loyalty is usually the result of a superior product, and advertising provides essential information to allow consumers to select the product that best serves their needs. Advertising, its proponents argue, also promotes competition—by allowing new brands to inform consumers of their existence and, even when practiced by a dominant firm, by creating a demand for new products that can be captured in part by other firms. See generally Posner & Easterbrook, supra note 40, at 514–15. From this perspective, a merger that allows less costly (and thus more) advertising is beneficial; moreover, if P & G's advertising efficiencies were so significant as to give it a "decisive" advantage if it acquired Clorox, the merger is not anticompetitive because those same efficiencies would allow P & G to quickly displace Clorox as the dominant firm if it entered de novo.

69. See H.R. Rep. No. 1191, 81st Cong., 1st Sess. 8 (1949).

dant's advantages are "decisive" and/or when they are unlikely to reflect real resource savings for the economy.[70]

The second economic harm caused by conglomerate mergers—that they can lessen competition within the meaning of § 7 by creating a probability that the newly merged entity will engage in anticompetitive reciprocal buying practices—has also been endorsed by the Supreme Court.[71] In *FTC v. Consolidated Foods Corp.*,[72] the Commission found that a leading food wholesaler and retailer violated § 7 by acquiring Gentry, one of two dehydrated garlic duopolists. The FTC's theory was that Consolidated would use its purchasing power as a leading wholesaler to convince food processors who used garlic as a raw ingredient to patronize Gentry instead of other equally priced brands. This conclusion was supported by post-acquisition evidence that Consolidated had indeed used its leverage to increase Gentry's sales.[73] The FTC feared that this "reciprocity" would pose a significant barrier to deconcentration of the dehydrated garlic market, which was then dominated by two firms.

Concerns about reciprocal dealing make sense in theory, and the Court took the easy way out by "honoring" the decision of the FTC, "whose expertise Congress trusts."[74] Absent a highly deferential approach, though, the correct result in *Consolidated Foods* is less clear. As Justice Potter Stewart noted in his concurrence, it is unlikely that a large wholesale operator like Consolidated would stop handling a popular brand name product simply because the brand's owner declined to use Gentry's garlic. It is more plausible, however, that Consolidated would use this threat against food processors that used lesser-known brands, or those that sold their products for resale under private labels.[75]

---

70. V Phillip Areeda & Donald Turner, Antitrust ¶¶ 1102–1109 (1980).

71. Similarly, a merger could lessen competition if its likely result was to increase the new firm's ability to engage in anticompetitive tying arrangements—forcing consumers to buy products previously made by one of the merging parties in order to obtain products previously made by the other. As discussed in Chapter 5, section G, these arrangements may violate § 1 of the Sherman Act. Just as § 7 acts as a prophylactic to bar mergers where the effect may be to facilitate price fixing in violation of the Sherman Act, it likewise acts to prevent any significant risk that a merger may facilitate unlawful tying arrangements.

72. 380 U.S. 592 (1965).

73. Id. at 598.

74. Id. at 600.

75. In condemning Consolidated's acquisition of Gentry, the FTC relied on the food processors' testimony that they would give their onion and garlic business to Gentry in the interest of reciprocity if it could match the price and quality of its rivals' products, and the admission by Gentry's president that a rival (Basic) offered a superior product but that Gentry had managed to increase its onion sales and limit the decline in garlic sales despite the inferiority of its product. In re Consolidated Foods Corp., 62 F.T.C. 929, 955–60 (1963).

In cases involving weaker evidence, lower courts have rejected the notion that a merger is illegal merely because

A more trenchant criticism of the FTC's approach is that it was unnecessary. Even if the merger was likely to lead to reciprocal buying practices, how hard would they be to detect and directly prohibit as an unfair method of competition? [76] Moreover, what may appear to be a reciprocal buying arrangement may instead be a secret price cut. Suppose, for example, that Gentry sold dehydrated garlic to food processors, who then sold their food to Consolidated (Gentry's new parent). Where no coercion is evident, this two-way deal might facilitate Gentry's sale of high-priced garlic and Consolidated's purchase of processed food at a premium, thus effectively giving food processors a discount. Because the antitrust law favors this type of "cheating" in highly concentrated markets, the courts and the FTC need to exercise care in applying reciprocity theory in § 7 cases.[77]

The third economic harm created by conglomerate mergers—"mutual forbearance"—has not received extensive judicial attention. The theory here is that firms that compete with each other in two or more concentrated markets are less likely to institute aggressive rivalry because of the prospect of retaliation. Oligopolists already are deterred from vigorous competition because of the likelihood that price cuts or quality increases will quickly be met by rivals, with market shares remaining stable while profits decrease. Even if a firm overcame this obstacle and decided to obtain whatever short-term advantages might arise from aggressive rivalry, it would fear that its competitors would not only respond in that market, but would also initiate a price war in some other oligopolistic market. Thus, conglomerates are less likely to engage in this sort of pro-competitive behavior.[78]

it creates the opportunity for reciprocity. In United States v. International Telephone & Telegraph Corp. (Grinnell), 306 F.Supp. 766, 781–83 (D. Conn. 1969), for example, not only was there no evidence of any reciprocal dealing, but the defendants showed that the individuals responsible for making purchases from Grinnell did not have a supplier relationship with IT&T and that IT&Ts profit-center concept (executives from each subsidiary were rewarded based on the performance of their own subsidiary) was not conducive to reciprocity. See also United States v. International Telephone & Telegraph Corp. (Canteen), 1971 Trade Cas. (CCH) ¶ 73,619 (N.D. Ill.1971).

76. Recall Atlantic Refining Co., v. FTC, 381 U.S. 357 (1965), discussed in Chapter 5, section G(3a), which held that Atlantic violated the FTC Act by subjecting its gasoline dealers to "inher-

ent coercion," compelling them to purchase tires from a specified tire company.

77. However, coercion ought not be an essential element of a reciprocity challenge to a conglomerate merger. Widespread efforts by others to "curry favor" with the newly enlarged conglomerate by offering reciprocal trading lessens competition on the merits between conglomerate subsidiaries and their rivals. Absent a pro-competitive justification (like disguised discounting), this should provide an adequate basis for concluding that a conglomerate merger violates § 7.

78. Posner and Easterbrook may well be right that this sort of retaliation can really be explained only as a form of predatory pricing. See Posner & Easterbrook, supra note 40, at 934. But given the difficulties proving that pric-

Another harm caused by conglomerate mergers that has received virtually no judicial or scholarly attention was suggested at a hearing several years ago by Representative John Seiberling, a veteran member of the House Monopolies Subcommittee. He claimed that a highly leveraged acquisition of a healthy, profitable competitor in a concentrated market (presumably with barriers to entry) violates § 7 where the new debt burden would prevent the company from increasing output in the face of price hikes by other firms.[79]

Where markets are concentrated, each oligopolist has the option of responding to gradually rising prices by following the others or by initiating a price war. Basic antitrust theory suggests that the more firms there are in the market, the greater the chance that one of them will decide to compete rather than go along with the crowd. Thus, a horizontal merger that reduced the number of firms from six to five would substantially lessen competition. The Seiberling theory suggests that the economic effect is the same when one of the six companies is acquired by a non-rival under a financing scheme whereby all available capital must be used to service the debt. In these circumstances, the acquiring firm is much less likely to choose either to engage in price competition by adding new capacity or to compete on quality by increasing spending on research and development; the number of firms likely to initiate aggressive rivalry has therefore been reduced from six to five. Application of § 7 to debt-increasing mergers is sensible, of course, only if debt-laden firms are, in fact, less likely to compete aggressively than those that have pools of retained earnings. Skeptics of antitrust enforcement doubt the government's ability to accurately predict the vigor with which a firm will compete after a merger. Because this theory is so novel (no prior cases have found a merger unlawful under § 7 because the post-merger firm was *weaker*), perhaps it ought be applied only where the acquired firm was a significant competitive force in the marketplace prior to the merger and facts uncovered during the investigation provide the government with a confident basis for concluding that the firm will lose this vigor after the transaction has been consummated.

---

ing practices constitute attempted monopolization in violation of § 2 (see Chapter 3, section D), blocking conglomerate mergers where mutual forbearance likely is consistent with the prophylactic goal of § 7.

79. Actually, Representative Seiberling proposed that a firm's efforts to engage in a hostile takeover of another healthy firm in a concentrated market should be subject to injunction under § 7, a point refuted by several witnesses. See Antitrust Division of the Department of Justice, Oversight Hearings Before the House Subcomm. on Monopolies & Commercial Law, Comm. on the Judiciary, 99th Cong., 1st Sess. 20, 25 (1985). However, the broader question remains whether a completed merger that significantly increased the acquiring firm's debt burden would be unlawful.

Mergers or acquisitions can harm competition even if the merging parties were not formerly rivals or involved in a vertical relationship. When a likely entrant into a non-competitive market acquires a major firm in that market, instead of entering by expanding internally or by merging with a smaller firm, competition is lessened because the existing firms no longer need to fear new entry and because the possibility that the firm's independent entry would restore more competitive vigor to the marketplace is lost. When a plaintiff challenges a merger using this potential competition theory, it claims that one of the merging parties exercised an important role in deterring anticompetitive conduct, even though it was not part of the market in question. Ironically, this is the same argument defendants use to fend off challenges to horizontal mergers: they argue that the merger should be permitted because other firms that are not currently part of the market remain as potential entrants and deter anticompetitive conduct. Unfortunately, the government has a poor track record in potential competition cases, but the courts have increasingly found this argument persuasive when raised by defendants.[80]

Section C: Vertical Mergers

The Celler–Kefauver amendments to § 7 of the Clayton Act were clearly intended to have a significant effect on the antitrust law's treatment of vertical mergers—that is, acquisitions involving two firms in a supplier-customer relationship. As originally enacted, § 7 condemned only mergers that lessened competition "between the acquiring and acquired firms." The 1950 amendments not only broadened § 7 so as to make the section clearly applicable to vertical mergers, but evinced a clear desire to impose standards stricter than those applied under the Sherman Act.[1] In particular, the legislative history shows two overriding quasi-economic concerns about vertical mergers: that such mergers deny firms a "fair" opportunity to compete on the merits and that they contribute to trends to concentration that deprive competitive industries of their atomistic character.

(1) A "fair" opportunity to compete.

A good example of the fairness principle at work is *United*

80. See Mark Leddy, Entry Issues in Merger Analysis, 54 Antitrust L.J. 1257, 1258 (1985).

1. A full discussion of the differences between the two statutes is found in section A of this chapter.

States v. E.I. du Pont De Nemours & Co. (du Pont/GM).[2] From 1917 to 1919, du Pont acquired a substantial interest in General Motors (23% of the outstanding stock). In the Court's words,

> [t]he primary issue is whether du Pont's commanding position as General Motors' supplier of automotive finishes and fabrics was achieved on competitive merit alone, or because its acquisition of the General Motors' stock, and the consequent close intercompany relationship, led to the insulation of most of the General Motors' market from free competition.[3]

The Court noted that du Pont did not have a large share of the GM business until these stock purchases. Internal du Pont documents suggested that the purchases were not solely for investment purposes (profit from dividends or capital gain), and other evidence indicated that du Pont subsequently focused its sales on GM as opposed to other automotive companies. Thus, the Court concluded that "du Pont purposely employed its stock to pry open the General Motors market to entrench itself as the primary supplier of General Motors' requirements for automotive finishes and fabrics." The Court reasoned that "free competition is obviously furthered when no supplier has an advantage over his competitors from an acquisition of his customer's stock." [4]

Vertical mergers possess the same potential for harm as exclusive dealing contracts (discussed in Chapter 5, section G). As specified in the legislative history of the 1950 amendments to § 7, firms using either practice can substantially lessen competition, "depriving their rivals of a fair opportunity to compete," [5] by foreclosing access to basic materials or to retail outlets. The majority and dissenting opinions in *du Pont/GM* present two different versions of foreclosure, however. Justice William Brennan's majority opinion held that a substantial share of the market had been foreclosed, apparently focusing on the large volume of automobile finishes and fabrics purchased by General Motors annually. Justice Harold Burton correctly observed in dissent that the government did not show that du Pont's rivals were in any way foreclosed from selling identical products used for other purposes in other industries.[6] In short, there was no showing that du Pont's rivals were foreclosed from the market as a result of the defendant's cozy relationship with GM. The goal of equal economic opportunity is not impeded simply because du Pont's competitors lost access to one particular, albeit large, account.

2. 353 U.S. 586 (1957).

3. Id. at 588–89.

4. Id. at 606–07.

5. H. R. Rep. No. 1191, 81st Cong., 2d Sess. 8 (1949).

6. 353 U.S. at 654.

Thus, *du Pont/GM*'s holding rests on a broader definition of fairness: the Court read the antitrust laws as requiring GM to make its purchasing decisions on "competitive merit alone." [7] In so doing, the Court drew on two non-economic concerns—an extreme version of the Jeffersonian concern with equality of economic opportunity (firms do not have an equal opportunity if they can not sell their product because a rich rival bought stock in a customer) and a Madisonian concern with lessening discretionary power (if GM was not owned by du Pont, its decisions would be dictated by the market).[8]

Du Pont/GM is interesting for two other reasons as well. The case was filed prior to enactment of Celler–Kefauver, and thus was brought under the original version of § 7, which barred only mergers that lessened competition between the acquired and acquiring firms. Because du Pont and GM were not competitors, the defendants argued, § 7 did not apply. The Court held otherwise, ruling that the original § 7 was violated whenever it appeared reasonably likely that the acquisition would result in a restraint of commerce. Whatever the merits of that holding as an interpretation of § 1 of the Sherman Act,[9] it is simply wrong as to the Clayton Act. Du Pont's stock acquisition was a classic partial vertical merger. One of the main purposes of Celler–Kefauver was to amend § 7 to cover vertical mergers, because the FTC had previously opined that § 7 did not apply to non-horizontal mergers, and until the filing of the *du Pont/GM* complaint in 1949 the government had never challenged a non-horizontal merger under § 7.[10]

The other significant ruling was that the competitive effect of the stock acquisition was to be evaluated at the time of the suit (after World War II, when GM's market share approached 50%), rather than at the time of the acquisition (after World War I, when GM's share approximated 11%). Although the constant fear

7. Id. at 589.

8. As Donald Dewey observed, the stock acquisition probably had only a negligible impact on consumers, in terms of the price of automobiles. Rather, "the target of the *du Pont— General Motors* case was the discretionary authority of certain members of the du Pont family; the principal consequence of the case was the transfer of some part of this authority to the higher management of General Motors." The New Learning: One Man's View, in Industrial Concentration: The New Learning 10–13 (Goldschmid, Mann & Weston eds. 1974).

9. According to Justice Burton's dissent, the government's basic contention was that the stock purchase violated the Sherman Act, and the government's Clayton Act claim warranted mention only in the closing pages of the Justice Department's brief and for a few minutes of oral argument. 353 U.S. at 609. The majority opinion acknowledged the Sherman Act claim but did not decide it in light of its holding for the government on the Clayton Act allegations. Id. at 588 n.5.

10. Id. at 615 (Burton, J., dissenting).

of possible government action might chill investment, that policy concern must be weighed against the benefits of allowing suits at a later time: (a) the competitive evil may not be apparent at the time of the acquisition; (b) the government may wisely allow a borderline transaction to proceed, if "unscrambling" the merger is feasible in the future, until it can fully assess the effects of the merger; or (c) changes in enforcement policy may mean that an acquisition is viewed more skeptically at a later date. Resolution of this policy dispute is best left to Congress (which declined to enact a statute of limitations for antitrust suits serving equitable relief).[11] If a particular defendant suffers significant prejudice because of the delay in filing suit and there is no good cause for the delay, a court may well take this into account in fashioning (or even withholding) equitable relief.

Another case illustrating the Court's concern with fairness is *United States v. Yellow Cab Co.*[12] A shrewd businessman, Morris Markin, was the controlling stockholder of the Checker Cab Manufacturing Corporation, a leading maker of taxicabs. Markin arranged a vertical merger with its customers in several major cities. First, he merged the leading taxicab companies in Chicago, Pittsburgh, and Minneapolis, as well as a major New York City cab company, with Checker subsequently controlling these companies. The government alleged that Checker then insisted that its subsidiaries purchase Checker vehicles. The district court dismissed the complaint, and the government appealed. The theory of the complaint, according to the Court, was that Checker obtained dominant power over the local taxicab firms, excluded other taxicab manufacturers from an overwhelming share of the market in at least three cities, forced the local companies to pay more for cabs than they otherwise would have, and thus raised prices to consumers.[13] The Court remanded for a trial on the government's theory.[14]

The Court's economic reasoning seems questionable. The opinion does not explain why Checker's rivals were foreclosed from the market (which, for auto manufacturers, was probably nationwide) simply because they could not sell their cabs in a few cities. Nor is it clear how taxi fares were affected by the higher prices: if a vertically integrated monopolist can get away with charging higher prices (because, as was true in Chicago, for example, the number of licensed taxicabs was strictly limited), it

11. See 15 U.S.C. §§ 15, 16.

12. 332 U.S. 218 (1947).

13. Id. at 224–25.

14. See 80 F.Supp. 936 (N.D. Ill. 1948) (rejecting government's proof at trial), aff'd, 338 U.S. 338 (1949).

will do so anyway, regardless of what price it charges itself for taxicabs.[15]

Once again, the Court's dominant concern appeared to be fairness. "By excluding all cab manufacturers other than [Checker] from that part of the market represented by the [local cab companies], the appellees effectively limit the outlets through which cabs may be sold in interstate commerce," the Court declared.[16] The wrong in this partial exclusion can only be that each cab manufacturer is entitled to compete "on the merits" for the business of local cab companies rather than be subjected to Checker Cab's discretionary power.

(2) From fairness to foreclosure: *Columbia Steel.*

As detailed in section A, a major impetus in amending § 7 was the Supreme Court's decision in *United States v. Columbia Steel Co.*[17] That decision, involving the merger of U.S. Steel's Columbia subsidiary with Consolidated Steel, had both horizontal and vertical components.[18] The vertical component was that Consolidated was a major fabricator of finished steel products and needed to purchase "rolled steel" from other manufacturers. The government's theory was that the merger unlawfully excluded U.S. Steel's rivals from supplying rolled steel to Consolidated.

The Court focused solely on foreclosure, and concluded that vertical mergers are not illegal under § 1 "until the effect of such control is to unreasonably restrict the opportunities of competitors to market their product."[19] The record provided ample evidence that the merger would not have this effect. The Court found that Consolidated accounted for only 3% of the demand for rolled steel in the relevant 11-state geographic market; that Consolidated's former suppliers could easily shift their production to sell other products to other customers; and that post-war development of the steel industry opened further business opportunities for the defendant's competitors.[20]

The government properly invoked *Yellow Cab* as precedent for a broader view of foreclosure. In *Yellow Cab*, the facts did not demonstrate that the effect of Checker's vertical merger was to restrict the opportunity of other automobile companies to sell their taxicabs to other local taxicab companies. Like *Yellow Cab*, the government focused on the fairness principle—a substantial

15. The situation is very different if the firm is subject to rate regulation based on its costs. See subsection (4b) below.

16. 332 U.S. at 226.

17. 334 U.S. 495 (1948).

18. The horizontal aspect is discussed in section A(2).

19. 334 U.S. at 524.

20. Id. at 527–30.

amount of rolled steel would not be sold "on the merits" after the
merger. The Court disingenuously distinguished that opinion
because there the government had alleged that the mergers were
part of a scheme to monopolize.[21] The majority opinion in *Columbia Steel* thus ignored the broader fairness issues raised in other
opinions.

(3) Foreclosure and fairness after Celler–Kefauver.

The leading vertical merger opinion issued by the Warren
Court, *Brown Shoe Co. v. United States*,[22] began its analysis by
recognizing that "the size of the share of the market foreclosed"
was an important consideration in evaluating whether a vertical
merger lessened competition.[23] In that case, however, Brown Shoe
manufactured 4% of shoes in this country, and Kinney Shoe's
retail market share was only 2%. How could such a merger
possibly foreclose any shoe manufacturer from finding retail outlets or any retailer from obtaining products to sell?

For some, the answer to that question is that the merger could
not possibly have had an anticompetitive effect.[24] An alternative
explanation, implied by Chief Justice Earl Warren's majority
opinion and more fully articulated by Professors Harlan Blake and
William K. Jones, is that the acquisition, although not likely to
foreclose anyone when viewed in isolation, was a significant example of a trend to concentration that needed to be "nipped in the
bud." Blake and Jones correctly observe that the antitrust laws
should view vertical mergers more stringently than exclusive
dealing contracts because the latter can easily be enjoined once
they reach the stage where they begin to have real foreclosure
effects. Mergers, by contrast, are very difficult to unscramble.[25]
Brown Shoe's critics might respond to Blake and Jones by arguing
that their worst case scenario of the trends in the shoe industry
would be 20–25 vertically integrated firms like Brown Shoe, each
with a 4–5% share of the market. What would be the harm
there?

There are two answers to this question, neither satisfactory to
some. A non-economic "Jeffersonian" answer, advanced by Chief
Justice Warren, is that the antitrust laws care about the transformation of an industry from one characterized by thousands of
independent shoe manufacturers and retailers to a vertically inte-

21. Id. at 520–23.

22. 370 U.S. 294 (1962).

23. Id. at 328.

24. See IV Phillip Areeda & Donald Turner, Antitrust Law 314 (1980) ("the

reasoning and the result in *Brown Shoe* seem indefensible").

25. Towards a Three–Dimensional Antitrust Policy, 65 Colum. L. Rev. 422, 453–57 (1965).

grated market with only 20–25 firms. In a famous statement, Warren wrote:

> [W]e cannot fail to recognize Congress' desire to promote competition through the protection of viable, small, locally owned businesses. Congress appreciated that occasional higher costs and prices might result from the maintenance of fragmented industries and markets. It resolved these competing considerations in favor of decentralization. We must give effect to that decision.[26]

An economic answer is that Kinney was the largest retail outlet for those manufacturers of non-branded shoes that did not advertise nationally. Thus, the merger foreclosed a major outlet for these firms. Moreover, Brown's acquisition of Kinney's retail stores may have made Brown less willing to furnish its product to independent retailers, which relied on nationally advertised brand names to sell their shoes locally. In short, the likely result of transforming the industry would be the elimination of independent firms on both the manufacturing and retail levels, not because they were unable to produce or sell quality shoes at competitive prices, but because they were unable to wage large-scale national advertising campaigns.

Thus, *Brown Shoe* is best read not to condemn vertical mergers foreclosing relatively small market shares, but instead as a case that effectuates the intent of the 81st Congress that mergers not cause the transformation of the general character of an industry. This reading of *Brown Shoe* is consistent with the approach taken by both the FTC and the Second Circuit in *Freuhauf Corp. v. FTC.*[27] The Commission found that the merger of Kelsey, a leading wheel maker and Freuhauf, one of its major customers and the nation's leading builder of truck trailers, would foreclose a maximum of 5.8% of the market for heavy duty wheel production. If *Brown Shoe* required the condemnation of mergers of any size, those numbers would warrant a conclusion that Freuhauf violated § 7. Instead, the Court distinguished *Brown Shoe*, noting that the merger would not make entry more difficult by increasing scale economies, and that the merger was not "part of an existing or prospective trend toward vertical integration."[28] Indeed, the FTC's theory of illegality was based not on *Brown Shoe* but on entirely different grounds. The Commission agreed that the small market share would not ordinarily foreclose rival truck trailer manufacturers who currently bought wheels from Kelsey; Freuhauf's rivals had sufficient alternatives that they would not be forced to rely on Kelsey. Rather, the FTC argued that, in the

---

26. 370 U.S. at 344.   **28.** Id. at 359.
27. 603 F.2d 345 (2d Cir. 1979).

event of shortages, Kelsey would be likely to favor its parent Freuhauf, and this favoritism would harm competition. The court rejected this "special foreclosure theory" as unsupported by the evidence.[29]

(4) Economic effects of vertical mergers.

In enacting Celler–Kefauver, Congress did not have a particularly sophisticated explanation of its hostility to vertical mergers. Non-economic, quasi-economic, and pseudo-economic analysis played some influence. In focusing on foreclosure, Congress did not appear to consider precisely how rivals are foreclosed by a merger that removes even 20% of sales from the market. For example, if U.S. Steel was operating at capacity, forcing its Consolidated subsidiary to buy its steel would mean foregoing sales to independent fabricators that would then be available to rivals. Nonetheless, there are strong reasons to condemn some vertical mergers on purely economic grounds.

(a) Upstream mergers lessen competition among remaining independent sellers.

Suppose that downstream firms (e.g., auto manufacturers) faced oligopoly pricing from upstream firms (e.g., steel makers). Under those circumstances, GM might find it profitable to buy Republic Steel, thus assuring itself of a source of steel without having to pay super-competitive prices. GM's purchases from Republic might mean that Republic would no longer sell to the other auto manufacturers. Indeed, the price the others would have to pay for steel would rise even higher as the number of firms in the steel oligopoly grew smaller. The other auto makers would then have an incentive to buy steel makers as well, soon eliminating all independent steel companies.[30]

(b) Evasion of monopoly rate regulation.

Suppose that a regulated firm (e.g., a taxicab company) wanted to evade rate regulation, increasing its rates above the level where it received reimbursement for its costs plus a reasonable return on investment. The firm might merge with a supplier (e.g.,

29. Id. at 354–55.

30. Those solely concerned with allocative efficiency might find nothing inherently wrong if independent steel companies were eliminated. However, in this scenario, mergers would not be made because the auto companies can manufacture steel more efficiently, but only so the auto makers can avoid oligopolistic exploitation. If, for example, a Ford–Bethlehem Steel merger was so inefficient that it would actually increase steel costs by 5%, Ford is still better off consummating the merger if the steel oligopolists were charging Ford a 10% monopoly profit prior to the merger. The economy, however, is not better off if steel companies are run inefficiently.

a manufacturer of taxicabs), and then arrange for its supplier-parent to charge high costs for its product (taxicabs). The high costs would then be passed on to the consumer.[31]

(c) Facilitating collusion at the upstream level.

Widespread vertical integration facilitates collusion by manufacturers because price cuts are easier to detect. (This argument is similar to the argument against resale price maintenance.) The vertical acquisition of a retailer that is particularly aggressive at negotiating for low wholesale prices is especially likely to facilitate collusion.

On the other hand, when vertical integration is not common, collusion becomes more difficult if one or two firms do vertically integrate. The non-integrated firms may seek to fix a wholesale price, but the wholesale price is meaningless for the integrated firms because they are charging it to themselves. Thus, they can easily cheat on the manufacturers' cartel.

(d) Downstream integration facilitates price discrimination.

Integrating into retail allows a manufacturer to price discriminate without having to worry about arbitrage among its independent retailers. For example, a firm might manufacture a product that is sold in both boutique and discount stores, and might wish to charge the boutique a higher price. Rather than paying a high wholesale price, boutique owners will buy the goods indirectly from a discount retailer, keeping the high mark-up for themselves. Owning its own boutiques enable the manufacturer to sell to the boutiques' customers at a high price, keep the profits for itself, and continue to earn something from wholesale sales to discount retailers.[32]

(e) Increasing entry barriers by requiring two-stage entry.

Although early judicial condemnation of the "foreclosure" caused by vertical mergers was based on Jeffersonian concerns with equal economic opportunity, foreclosure can harm efficiency as well. Like exclusive dealing contracts, vertical mergers deprive independent sellers or retailers of sources of supply or outlets for their products. Where vertical relationships are widespread (because of mergers or long-term contracts), a new entrant is forced to provide for its own supply, or develop new retail outlets. Where entry into both stages of the market is not easy, this

---

31. See, e.g., United States v. AT&T, 552 F.Supp. 131, 228 (D.D.C. 1982) (barring price-regulated local telephone monopolists from manufacturing their own equipment), aff'd sub nom. Maryland v. United States, 460 U.S. 1001 (1983).

32. The vertical merger also avoids potential liability under the Robinson-Patman Act, which, may occur if the manufacturer sells the same product to boutiques and discount houses at different prices. See Chapter 7.

additional obstacle to entry may pose a significant deterrent to those who might otherwise compete in a particular market, and result in reduced output if the market is currently concentrated.

(f) Forcing other firms to operate at inefficient scale.

Suppose that vertical mergers involving other firms foreclosed a downstream firm (e.g., a maker of steel pipes) from a steady source of supply from the upstream market (e.g., manufacturers of raw steel). Even if building one's own upstream plant (e.g., a steel mill) was possible, the only efficient way to run the plant might be at a scale much larger than necessary to meet the needs of the downstream firm. Thus, the downstream firm would either have to operate its own plant inefficiently, or enter at two stages and go into the business of selling off surplus products (e.g., extra steel) to others.

(g) Benefits of vertical mergers.

This is not to say that all vertical mergers are harmful. After all, almost all economic functions involve some vertical integration. A law firm, for example, has employees who provide legal advice, type written documents, and xerox and deliver materials. Like exclusive dealing relationships, vertical integration can assure a steady and reliable source of supply, thus allowing firms to plan and invest in major capital development. Mergers can also lower transaction costs and minimize the risks of opportunistic behavior. In a sense, the upstream firm acts as the partner of the downstream firm in getting a desirable product to consumers. It may be cheaper to arrange the partnership within one firm, rather than by contract. For example, an industrial firm may find it easier to own the source of key raw materials, as well as a fleet of trucks to transport the materials, instead of constantly searching around for the "best buys." Moreover, retailers may be unwilling to invest heavily in promoting a particular brand for fear that they may not be allowed to sell the brand at some later date; a manufacturer that owns its retail operations will have no such hesitancy about investing in its own product.

Vertical mergers can also eliminate the problem of serial monopolies. A serial monopoly problem exists when consumers must pay a price that gives monopoly profits to both the manufacturer and the retailer. A merger allows the manufacturer to take its own monopoly profits without forcing consumers to pay a monopoly price to the retailer as well. Thus, as is the case with horizontal mergers, fully analyzing a vertical merger's effect on competition defies simplistic rulemaking.

(5) Merger guidelines.

In contrast to the legislative history's emphasis on denying competitors a "fair opportunity to compete," the case law's focus on trends to concentration, and the foregoing multi-faceted analysis of the possible economic effects of vertical mergers, the treatment of such mergers in the Reagan administration's 1984 merger guidelines is a paradigm for limited enforcement.[33] Outside regulated markets, the guidelines theorize that there are only two ways for vertical mergers to harm competition: by increasing barriers to entry or by facilitating collusion. To increase barriers to entry, the guidelines hypothesize, (1) the merger must create so much foreclosure that a rival must enter both markets to compete; (2) it must be significantly more difficult to enter both markets than just one; and (3) the existing market must be concentrated (i.e., the Herfindahl index must exceed 1800). To facilitate collusion, (1) vertical integration must be widespread, and (2) the market must be concentrated.

As a matter of economic theory, the guidelines' analysis of the conditions necessary for these two specific economic harms to occur seems reasonable. But the conclusion that otherwise the Justice Department will consider vertical mergers lawful is more troubling. Those who are more skeptical of markets and less skeptical of judicial fact-finding may prefer a more open-ended policy that seeks to ascertain what is really going on in a particular industry. In addition, those who are less dogmatic on the question of antitrust goals may wish a fuller analysis of the merger's real impact on the industry before accepting the conclusion that the merger will not harm competition, especially where it constitutes a trend-setting acquisition that will substantially transform the nature of competition within the market. The Justice Department and the FTC have done a fairly rigorous job at identifying those horizontal and vertical mergers that facilitate collusion, increase single-firm market power, or create competition-lessening entry barriers. The guidelines would be significantly improved, then, if the Justice Department would apply the same rigor to identifying when vertical mergers deny rivals a fair opportunity to compete, facilitate trends to concentration, or cause many of the other economic harms discussed above.

---

33. 4 Trade Reg. Rep. (CCH) ¶ 13,-103, § 4.2 (1984). These guidelines still reflect the policy of the Bush administration, notwithstanding issuance of new guidelines governing horizontal mergers. See Merger Guidelines—1992, 4 Trade Reg. Rep. (CCH) ¶ 13,104, at 20,569 (1992).

Section D: Antitrust Injury in
Private Merger Litigation

(1) Background and key concepts.

The vast majority of lawsuits challenging mergers under § 7
of the Clayton Act are brought by government agencies. The
federal agencies, in particular, have the advantage of the Hart–
Scott–Rodino pre-merger disclosure statute, which requires companies over a certain size to report information relating to a merger
to the FTC or the Justice Department prior to consummating the
deal.[1] Many state attorneys general also have resources available
to enforce the antitrust laws, and often they can use compulsory
process to reduce litigation costs. Few private companies, however, are willing or able to expend the resources necessary to
investigate and litigate in order to block mergers they oppose.
The plaintiffs' antitrust bar usually works on a contingent-fee
basis, receiving a specified percentage of treble damage awards.
Damages are difficult to obtain in merger litigation, and, if a
merger is challenged prior to consummation, the successful plaintiff will be awarded an injunction blocking the merger and, at best
an hourly attorneys fee.

Nonetheless, § 4 of the Clayton Act allows persons injured
"by reason of anything forbidden in the antitrust laws" to recover
treble damages,[2] and § 16 permits any person to sue for injunctive
relief "against threatened loss or damage by a violation of the
antitrust laws."[3] Thus, some private lawsuits are brought challenging mergers on antitrust grounds.

The Supreme Court has imposed an additional and substantial
limitation on private firms' ability to challenge mergers, by rigorously construing the "by reason of" and "loss or damage by"
phrases in §§ 4 and 16. This limitation is usually referred to as
the requirement that plaintiffs show "antitrust injury." As applied in merger cases, the antitrust injury doctrine is best understood by recognizing that many mergers violative of § 7 will
simultaneously harm and help competition. Indeed, mergers can
even be largely pro-competitive but nevertheless unlawful because
of the legal presumptions created by substantive merger law. A
party could conceivably suffer an economic injury because of the
pro-competitive aspects of a particular merger, but the concept of
antitrust injury provides that only those injured by the anticompetitive aspects of an unlawful merger can proceed with a § 7
challenge.

To illustrate, suppose that Company A acquires its rival,
Company B, in part to allow A to take advantage of a modern fleet

1. Hart-Scott-Rodino Antitrust Improvements Act, 15 U.S.C. § 18a.

2. 15 U.S.C. § 15.

3. 15 U.S.C. § 26.

of trucks owned by B that can more efficiently transport their product to market. If there are only two other firms in the entire market, the merger probably violates § 7 because of the increased risk that the three firms remaining in the industry will engage in express or tacit collusion. The independent trucking company that previously serviced Company A will also be hurt because it will lose a major customer, but the trucker's loss is not "antitrust injury" because it was not injured by the anticompetitive aspect of the merger.

Important policy concerns underlie the antitrust injury requirement. Most countries view merger policy as a complex political and economic question involving significant prosecutorial discretion.[4] Americans who share this view look with disfavor on private challenges to mergers that, after enactment of the Hart–Scott–Rodino pre-merger reporting statute, the FTC or the Antitrust Division has "cleared." Especially when the plaintiff is a competitor, they believe that private litigation is almost always designed to block pro-competitive mergers, and therefore advocate that the antitrust injury requirement should be rigorously employed to minimize private § 7 litigation. At the other extreme, proponents of vigorous § 7 enforcement have viewed the Reagan administration's record with disgust. They see § 7 as a statute to be enforced by the courts to block unlawful mergers, whether or not the executive thinks they ought to be enjoined, and they favor private enforcement because it provides some modicum of protection. Even if the federal antitrust authorities were aggressively enforcing the law, their limited resources might preclude effective enforcement, especially in cases involving smaller, localized mergers.[5] Because, from this perspective, any merger violating § 7 ought to be enjoined, the motives of the party bringing the action are irrelevant; indeed, those who believe in the private attorney general concept are not at all troubled by a case where a competitor is willing to finance litigation to block an unlawful merger for reasons having nothing to do with competition.

4. For example, the British Office of Fair Trading must get approval from the Trade Minister before referring an anticompetitive merger to the Monopolies and Merger Commission.

5. Consider the following hypothetical: Firm A is the only manufacturer of minibikes and distributes its product through retail stores owned by Firm X. Firm A then acquires Firm B, which owns retail stores that sell recreational bicycles; prior to the merger, B was planning to open a new plant to make minibikes. Aside from the governmental authorities, Firm X is probably the only party with a financial incentive to challenge merger, which denies consumers the benefits of competition in the manufacture of minibikes. But, as the cases discussed in this section appear to hold, X would not suffer antitrust injury and thus could not succeed with its antitrust claim. See Richard Posner & Frank Easterbrook, Antitrust 548–49 (2d ed. 1981).

(2) Suits by victims of enhanced competition.

If a hypothetical senator working on drafting the Clayton Act wanted to persuade her colleagues to include an antitrust injury limitation in the statute, she would be hard pressed to invent a more convincing factual scenario than *Brunswick Corp. v. Pueblo Bowl-O-Mat, Inc.*[6] Brunswick, a leading manufacturer of bowling supplies, sold on credit to bowling alleys; it began a series of bowling alley acquisitions in the early 1960s when many of its customers went bankrupt. Pueblo, a rival bowling alley operator, challenged these mergers under § 7. Although Pueblo's legal theory was that Brunswick's size gave it the ability to lessen competition by driving smaller competitors out of business,[7] its proof of injury was based entirely on the fact that Pueblo's profits would have increased had Brunswick allowed the defaulting alleys to close instead of buying and continuing to operate them in competition with Pueblo. In other words, Pueblo's complaint was that Brunswick's acquisitions provided too much competition.

Since the *Schoolmaster's Case*,[8] courts have rejected the notion that economic injury arising from greater competition is actionable. Accordingly, the Court dismissed Pueblo's suit on the ground that its injuries did not arise "by reason of" a violation of the antitrust laws. Justice Thurgood Marshall's unanimous opinion suggested that had Pueblo offered any evidence that Brunswick had "abused its deep pocket by engaging in anticompetitive conduct," damages attributable to that conduct could be recovered under § 4.[9] Thus, private parties who can trace their injury to the anticompetitive aspects of the challenged merger can vindicate their rights under the antitrust laws.

(3) Equitable relief against feared predatory conduct.

Cargill, Inc. v. Monfort of Colorado, Inc.,[10] was a suit for injunctive relief brought under § 16 by Monfort, the country's fifth largest meat packer, to challenge the merger of the second and third largest firms. It differed from *Brunswick* in two important respects. First, Monfort sought no money damages but only injunctive relief; while § 4's treble damages provision requires actual injury to one's business or property, § 16 authorizes injunc-

6. 429 U.S. 477 (1977).

7. Such a theory finds support in the legislative history of the Celler–Kefauver Act, which indicated that a merger might substantially lessen competition if "the relative size of the acquiring corporation had increased to such a point that its advantage over competitors threatened to be 'decisive.'" See H.R. Rep. No. 1191, 81st Cong., 1st Sess.

8 (1949) (cited in Brown Shoe Co. v. United States, 370 U.S. 294, 321 n.36 (1962), which is discussed above in section A(3).)

8. Y.B., 11 Hen. IV, f.47, pl. 21 (Ct. Com. Pleas 410). See Chapter 2.

9. 429 U.S. at 490.

10. 479 U.S. 104 (1986).

tive relief in cases of threatened injury without requiring evidence
of business or property loss. Second, at trial Monfort proffered a
sophisticated theory explaining how the merger would lessen
competition and how Monfort would be injured by the anticompetitive aspects of the merger. These differences did not persuade
the Court, however. It concluded that the same antitrust injury
requirement applies to § 4 damages suits and § 16 injunctive
cases, and that Monfort, like Pueblo, was really harmed only from
the increased competition.

The majority's statutory interpretation argument noted that
the legislative history of § 16 shows Congress' intent to authorize
equitable relief as a supplement to § 4's legal remedies. "It would
be anomalous," Justice William Brennan wrote, "to read the
Clayton Act to authorize a private plaintiff to secure an injunction
against a threatened injury for which he would not be entitled to
compensation if the injury actually occurred." [11] The fact that
many mergers have both pro-competitive and anticompetitive aspects should also suggest caution before any private party is
allowed to file a § 7 challenge; otherwise, there may be too many
opportunities for those harmed by the pro-competitive aspects of
an acquisition to challenge the merger. In addition, the threat of
private § 7 litigation and the delay caused even by an expedited
hearing on a request for preliminary relief may allow a rival to
strategically block a pro-consumer merger that would eventually
be found lawful.[12] Many merger agreements are not consummated when the parties face the uncertain prospect of § 7 litigation.[13]
Even those who do not wish to rely exclusively on federal executive officials to enforce § 7 may thus have reason to pause before
allowing a firm whose injury does not arise from the anticompetitive aspect of a merger to tie the acquisition up in court.

At trial, Monfort argued that the merger would enable Cargill
to strategically bid up the price of cattle (the input) while maintaining the price of boxed beef (the output). If proven, this
argument suggests that Monfort would be injured because the
merger would allow Cargill to engage in predatory behavior,
which is clearly an anticompetitive aspect of the merger. Based
on the record, however, Monfort had to concede in the Supreme

11. Id. at 112.

12. The federal antitrust agencies operate under strict time limits when exercising their authority to pre-clear large mergers. Hart–Scott–Rodino Antitrust Improvements Act, 15 U.S.C. § 18a.

13. In an *amicus* brief filed in support of Cargill, the federal agencies sug-

gested that the case reached the appellate level due to an atypical provision in the merger agreement that did *not* allow the parties to withdraw from the agreement in the event of antitrust litigation. Brief for the United States and the Federal Trade Commission, Cargill, Inc. v. Monfort of Colorado, Inc., No. 85–473, at 22 n.32.

Court that "its viability would not be threatened" by this strategy, only that its profit margin would be lowered.[14] By thus admitting that Cargill's strategy did not involve sacrificing short-term profit in return for long-term monopoly returns, Monfort conceded that Cargill was not engaging in predatory behavior. (Indeed, one who sacrifices short-term profit in return for increased market share is *competing*.) Thus, the Court concluded that the case was indistinguishable from *Brunswick*, and that Monfort was really complaining about more competition, not less. Justice Brennan noted that even Jeffersonian concerns about protecting small business were not implicated by Cargill's merger, in light of the fact that Monfort was unable to prove at trial that the merger would drive other firms out of business.[15]

Nevertheless, the Court's treatment of Monfort's theory demonstrates a "naive dichotomy" between efficient mergers and those that increase market power. Often, mergers will fall into both categories, and a rival firm may simultaneously suffer injuries because the merging parties are able to operate more efficiently and because they have a strategic plan to hinder others from competing in the marketplace, at least for a segment of customers.[16]

The Reagan Justice Department asked the Court to go a step further, and bar any competitor challenges alleging that a merger would lessen competition by facilitating predatory pricing. The Department argued that the predation is so rare that the Court should never allow private litigation to hold up mergers, most of which have already been cleared by the government. The Court refused to accept this argument. Even though predation may be rare, it does exist, the Court explained, and it "would be novel indeed for a court to deny standing to a party seeking an injunction against threatened injury merely because such injuries rarely occur." [17]

Unfortunately, however, dictum in Brennan's opinion may accomplish much of what the Justice Department wanted. Even if Monfort had advanced a predation claim, Brennan suggested that it could not possibly have succeeded because Cargill's post-merger market share was only 21% and its post-merger capacity was only 28%. Absent claims of collusive predation, Brennan wrote, Cargill did not have a credible predation theory.[18] As noted in Chapter 3, however, there are several theories that plausibly

14. 479 U.S. at 115 n.10.

15. Id. at 116 n.11.

16. See Oliver Williamson, Delimiting Antitrust, 76 Geo. L.J. 271, 294–95 (1987).

17. 479 U.S. at 121.

18. Id. at 119 n.15.

describe how strategic predatory behavior by a firm with a market share in the 20–30% range can succeed in lessening competition. Because the issue was not before the Court, the majority overlooked these new insights of economic theory.[19]

Subsequent to *Cargill*, the Second Circuit has permitted private § 7 litigation in two separate contexts. In one case, where the merger would have given the defendant an 84% market share, the court found the risk of predatory conduct sufficiently high to warrant a finding of antitrust injury.[20] In the second case, where the defendant wished to purchase most, but not all, of the acquired firm's stock, the court found that the minority shareholders in the acquired firm would suffer antitrust injury if, as they claimed, the defendant planned to reduce output and raise prices by curtailing production in the partially owned acquired firm while reaping monopoly profits in its wholly owned subsidiary.[21] Thus, the plaintiffs would suffer because of the anticompetitive aspects of the acquisition.

19. See the discussion in Chapter 3, section B(3) of Dimmitt Agri Industries, Inc. v. CPC International, Inc., 679 F.2d 516 (5th Cir. 1982), cert. denied, 460 U.S. 1082 (1983) (defendant, the price leader in a tight oligopoly market, initiated predatory pricing scheme to eliminate non-cooperating rival, thus allowing remaining firms to return to oligopoly pricing). New economic explanations of strategic behavior conclude that a predator need not "drive[ ] its rivals into bankruptcy with the sledgehammer of below cost prices" if the "rival is gently convinced that its resources would be better spent elsewhere." See, e.g., Janusz Ordover & Daniel Wall, Proving Predation After *Monfort* and *Matsushita*: What the New "New Learning" Has to Offer, Antitrust, Summer, 1987, at 7. Nothing in Ordover & Wall's review of strategic behavior suggests that a predator needs a monopoly share of the market, especially where it uses techniques like selective price cut-

ting to build a reputation as a feared predator, to create entry barriers, or to punish those who would deviate from oligopoly pricing.

20. R.C. Bigelow, Inc. v. Unilever N.V., 867 F.2d 102 (2d Cir.), cert. denied, 493 U.S. 815 (1989).

Bigelow also illustrates that market definition is not a precise, noncontroversial science. The plaintiff claimed that the merger of its two major competitors would substantially lessen competition in the national herbal tea market. The FTC cleared the merger, apparently because it believed that the manufacturers of regular, caffeinated tea provided a sufficient market check on producers of herbal, decaffeinated tea to assuage any competitive concerns.

21. Consolidated Gold Fields PLC v. Minorco, S.A., 871 F.2d 252 (2d Cir. 1989).

CHAPTER 7: PRICE DISCRIMINATION

Section A: Introduction to Price Discrimination and the Robinson–Patman Act

(1) What is price discrimination?

One of the real benefits of a free market is what economists call "consumer surplus"—that is, many consumers are able to buy goods and services for less than the maximum price they would be willing to pay. This maximum price is referred to as a "reservation price" by economists. Sellers, of course, would prefer to eliminate consumer surplus, to charge higher prices to those willing to pay more.

Consider a local tavern, for example. Surely, there would be a wide variety of answers if the patrons honestly disclosed the maximum amount they would pay for a glass of beer. Yet taverns, like most sellers, find themselves unable to price discriminate for a number of reasons. First, the tavern cannot easily distinguish those patrons willing to spend $4 for a beer from those who will abstain if the cost exceeds $2. In the real world, buyers will not honestly disclose their "reservation price." Second, even if a seller could differentiate between Maurice Moderation and Betty Boozer, the process of arbitrage will block the discrimination scheme. In exchange for a few french fries, Maurice will be happy to make a trip to the bar to procure a $2 beer for Betty, saving her almost $2. Third, in a competitive market, rivals firms will bid down the price for all buyers. Thus, even if the bartender were wise to Maurice's tricks, Betty would find another bar where all patrons were charged $2.

Price discrimination can exist, however, in a number of instances. First, where services are involved, the seller can often prevent arbitrage. In the *Grinnell* case, the seller of burglar and fire alarms was able to charge higher prices to those who needed its particular high-tech service.[1] Arbitrage was not possible in that case: one firm could not buy a custom-made alarm system from Grinnell and then resell it to another business. Second, price discrimination can occur where a firm is a monopolist vis-a-vis some buyers, but faces competition for the patronage of others. A buyer who can credibly threaten to take its patronage to an out-

---

1. United States v. Grinnell Corp., 384 U.S. 563 (1966), is discussed above in Chapter 3, section C(2).

of-town seller might get a lower price from the local monopolist than another buyer who realistically does not have that alternative.

Third, price discrimination exists even in competitive markets, where sellers may all cater to a powerful purchaser that can contribute significantly to their total sales. To illustrate, one of my longtime friends is a donut and cake maker in Los Angeles, a competitive market. A large chain like 7–11 commands a lower price than an individual convenience store. Part of the cost differential can be explained by the cost savings inherent in large volume "runs." [2] But part of the lower price reflects my friend's willingness to accept a lower profit margin above the cost of the materials and labor used to produce the 7–11 order because that order guarantees him such a large sale. He would be unwilling to price below the amount necessary to cover all his costs (including reasonable profit) for small sales because they will not individually contribute significantly to defraying his overhead.

Price discrimination can also be a normal response to changes in the marketplace. Consider a manufacturing firm with a plant in Champaign–Urbana (located almost midway between Chicago and St. Louis) that charges the same market price to buyers in both metropolitan areas. Suppose that a major St. Louis rival ceases production, and that transportation costs prevent the Chicago firms from selling in St. Louis. Prices will go up in St. Louis, and the Champaign plant will respond by price discriminating— charging and selling more to St. Louis buyers than to Chicago buyers. Gradually, the redirection of sales from Chicago to St. Louis will raise prices in Chicago and lower prices in St. Louis, and soon prices in the two areas will again be the same. Because this is precisely how markets are supposed to work in response to fluctuations in supply and demand, this type of pricing must be carefully distinguished from the price discrimination that raises antitrust concerns.

Price discrimination means very different things to economists and lawyers. As a matter of technical economics, price discrimination occurs where the ratio between price and cost differs from one buyer to another. To greatly oversimplify for purposes of this introduction, as a matter of law, price discrimination is any difference in price that is not justified by either specific and provable differences in costs or the need to meet competition. For example, suppose that my friend sells donuts to small stores for 36¢, and it that costs him 30¢ to mix, bake, wrap, box and

2. See section E of this Chapter for a discussion of cost justification as a legal defense to price discrimination.

deliver each of those donuts; in addition, suppose that he sells donuts to large supermarket chains for 30¢, and that those donuts can be produced and delivered at a cost of only 25¢ because of economies of scale. An economist would say that there is no price discrimination: each donut is sold at a 20% mark-up. As discussed below in subsection E, this may or may not be unlawful price discrimination (depending on whether or not my friend can justify the difference). On the other hand, if a seller charges the same price to two different sellers, the law would find no price discrimination even if the cost of production is different. For example, many mail-order firms absorb the cost of delivering goods into the purchase price. These firms therefore charge the same price to customers who live next door and to those who live across the country, although the cost of the sale is much lower in the first case. An economist would say that these sales are discriminatory, but the law does not.

(2) The history of price discrimination legislation.

Section 2 of the 1914 version of Clayton Act expressly outlawed certain forms of price discrimination. The original version of § 2, like § 3's provision concerning tying arrangements and § 7's provision governing mergers, required a showing that the challenged conduct "may have the effect of substantially lessening competition." In addition, the original § 2 expressly permitted quantity discounts. This provision seemed adequate to meet Congress' principal concern at the time—to prevent geographic price discrimination (charging different prices in different areas) as a means of selective predatory pricing, a practice used by the large trusts whose existence led to passage of both the Sherman Act and the Clayton Act.[3]

In the 1920s and 1930s, large retail store chains began to obtain significant market shares. These chains not only threatened their direct competitors—smaller retail outlets—but also a number of wholesalers and distributors who acted as intermediaries between manufacturers and small retailers, and who were often by-passed by the chains.[4] A Federal Trade Commission

3. H.R. Rep. No. 627, 63d Cong., 2d Sess. 8 (1914). Price discrimination that reduces competition between the seller and its rivals causes "primary-line injury." This type of price discrimination is discussed below in section B.

4. Indeed, the general counsel of the United States Wholesale Grocers Association, H.B. Teegarden, is credited as the chief drafter of the Robinson–Patman Act, see United States Dep't of Justice, Report on the Robinson–Patman Act 114 (1977), and the legislation was initially called the "Wholesale Grocers Protection Act." Hugh Hansen, Robinson–Patman Law: Review and Analysis, 51 Fordham L. Rev. 1113, 1123 (1983). According to a leading Robinson–Patman scholar, "[t]hroughout the hearings, Mr. Teegarden functioned as Mr. Patman's factotum—drafting, analyzing, and explaining for

study found that the chain stores' success was attributable in part to the lower prices they received from manufacturers as a result of their superior bargaining leverage vis-a-vis their smaller competitors (although supporters of the Robinson–Patman Act overlooked the Commission's conclusion that the chain stores' growth was due primarily to operating efficiencies [5]). The combination of two provisions in the original Clayton Act—the burden of proving a probability of lessened competition and the exemption for quantity discounts—meant that the original statute was not very responsive to this type of price discrimination.[6] Quantity discounts were one of the main ways in which larger buyers received favored treatment; in many cases, it would be difficult to show that a particular discriminatory sale, or even the elimination of a particular victim of discrimination, would cause a general injury to competitive conditions. Thus, "the design of the Robinson–Patman amendments was to facilitate proof of the substantive violation while narrowing the availability of statutory exceptions for justifying price differentials challenged under the Act." [7]

Support for these amendments to the Clayton Act came from a politically powerful coalition of retailers, wholesalers, and distributors, which were suffering as a result of the Great Depression and feared increased rivalry from large chain stores that operated their own distribution systems. Their efforts culminated in passage of the Robinson–Patman Act in 1936. In support of his legislation, Representative Wright Patman voiced the concern that large retail stores would eventually control the market; [8] certainly the transformation of a market from one of entirely small local stores to one dominated by a few national chains would constitute a lessening of competition. The Senate Committee report explained, however, that the competition-lessening standard in the original version of § 2 was "too restrictive, in requiring a showing of general injury to competitive conditions" and that a focus on

the legislators." Frederick Rowe, Price Discrimination Under the Robinson Patman Act 12 n.38 (1962).

5. The FTC estimated that 85% of the price differences between chain and non-chain stores could be attributed to the chain stores' ability to operate with lower costs. FTC, Final Report on the Chain Store Investigation 55 (1934). Some have suggested that even this figure is too low because the FTC's methodology considered "preferential," rather than "efficient," prices that were lower because a chain store maintained its own warehouse or did not require payment of a brokerage fee. See, e.g., M.A. Adelman, Price Discrimination as

Treated in the Attorney General's Report, 104 U. Pa. L. Rev. 222, 232 (1955).

6. Price discrimination that reduces competition between the various buyers of the discriminating seller causes "secondary-line injury". This type of price discrimination is discussed below in section C.

7. Report of the Att'y General's Nat'l Comm. to Study the Antitrust Laws 156 (1955).

8. Hearings Before the House Comm. on the Judiciary on Bills to Amend the Clayton Act, 74th Cong., 1st Sess. 5–6 (1935).

competitors as well as competition was a necessary prophylactic. Only through harm to competitors can competition be lessened, the Committee observed, and "to catch the weed in the seed will keep it from coming to flower."[9] The new legislation therefore barred price discrimination not only if it lessened competition but also if its effect was to "injure, destroy, or prevent competition" between the beneficiary and the victim of the differential pricing.[10]

The legislation's opponents, and most commentators, viewed the Robinson–Patman bill as pure special interest legislation. Whatever the validity of this criticism in real political terms, the bill's supporters officially denied it, insisting that the legislation implemented the venerable Jeffersonian antitrust goal of preserving equal economic opportunity for all and emphasizing that real "physical economies" were not to be disturbed.[11] These responses suggest that, even in 1936 (or perhaps, given the Depression, especially in 1936), the prevailing congressional vision of the economy was one where artificial and unfair practices, rather than economies of scale, provided the dominant explanation for the growth of big business. Moreover, in an era of high unemployment and massive numbers of bankruptcies, economic survival rather than an optimally efficient allocation of resources seemed an overwhelming priority.[12]

To be sure, the bill's sponsors recognized that economies of scale did exist and did explain *some* cases of increased industrial concentration. Thus, the legislation specifically permits differen-

---

9. S. Rep. No. 1502, 74th Cong., 2d Sess. 4 (1936).

10. The Act provides in part:

That it shall be unlawful for any person engaged in commerce, . . . either directly or indirectly, to discriminate in price between different purchasers of commodities of like grade and quality, where either of the purchases involved in such discrimination are in commerce, . . . and where the effect of such discrimination may be substantially to lessen competition or tend to create a monopoly in any line of commerce, or to injure, destroy, or prevent competition with any person who either grants or knowingly receives the benefit of such discrimination, or with customers of either of them.

15 U.S.C. § 13(a).

11. The House Committee report wrote:

In conclusion, your committee wishes to correct some important misapprehensions, and even misrepresen-

tations, that have been broadly urged with regard to the probable effect of this bill. There is nothing in it to penalize, shackle, or discourage efficiency, or to reward inefficiency. . . .

Any physical economies that are to be found in mass buying and distribution, whether by corporate chain[s] . . . or by [cooperatives]—and whether those economies are from more orderly processes of manufacture, or from the elimination of unnecessary [expenses]—none of them are in the remotest degree disturbed by the bill.

H.R. Rep. No. 2287, Pt. 1, 74th Cong., 2d Sess. 17 (1936).

12. Hansen, supra note 4, at 1120 (1983). The Act was introduced shortly after the Supreme Court struck down the National Recovery Act, which would have immunized industries from antitrust liability for many forms of cooperation aimed at economic survival.

tial pricing "which make[s] only due allowance for differences in the cost of manufacture, sale, or delivery resulting from differing methods or quantities in which such commodities are to such purchasers sold or delivered." [13] The Act, can therefore be seen as an effort to distinguish between price differentials resulting from efficiencies and those resulting from the exercise of buyer power or other arbitrary reasons, albeit with a preference for resolving any doubts in favor of condemnation.

Interpreting the Robinson–Patman Act in this manner not only gives effect to what its sponsors declared to be the public interest underlying the Act, but also best reconciles its goals with the pro-consumer bent of the Sherman and Clayton Acts. Rather than viewing the price discrimination statute as "an act of Congressional schizophrenia, an anticompetitive island situated in an otherwise turbulent sea of pro-competitive efficiency and maximization of consumer welfare," [14] each of the antitrust statutes should be construed in a manner that gives effect to coherent congressional purposes. This means, as some courts have recognized, that the Robinson–Patman Act should be interpreted to "protect small retail businesses against favoritism toward their larger competitors." What Congress sought to prohibit was not all advantages secured by large buyers, but instead those secured "solely by virtue of the size of the buyer's appetite." [15] A coherent interpretation faithful to the legislative intent not only means that the Robinson–Patman Act is not an "anticompetitive island" but also requires recognition that, as noted in Chapter 1, the Sherman and Clayton Acts do not constitute a sea of "efficiency"; rather, they seek to protect consumers from exploitation and to provide for an equality of economic opportunity, as well as promoting an efficient allocation of societal resources. The judiciary's fidelity, or lack thereof, to this balanced congressional policy preference—to protect small businesses from buyer power or arbitrary favoritism but not from harm due to inefficiency—will be discussed throughout this Chapter.[16]

13. 15 U.S.C. § 13(a). This provision is discussed in detail in subsection E. The Act's inclusion of a cost justification defense represented a compromise, as is evident from the variety of speeches made by the bill's supporters that seemed to suggest that small grocery and retail outlets should be preferred to chain stores for entirely non-economic reasons. See, e.g., 80 Cong. Rec. 8128 (1936) (statement of Rep. Shannon) (condemning chain stores because, unlike small family-run outlets, they sell "every article under the sun and keep[ ] open 18 hours on Sunday as well as the day before, the Sabbath of Moses"); id. at 8136 (statement of Rep. Moritz) (noting that his family was able to survive only because of credit extended by local family-run stores).

14. Boise Cascade Corp. v. FTC, 837 F.2d 1127, 1138 (D.C. Cir. 1988).

15. Id.

16. One provision of the Robinson–Patman Act, which is rarely enforced, reflects an insight about industrial structure that was well recognized by

Unfortunately, the quality of the judiciary's interpretation of the Act has been quite poor. Admittedly, the courts have properly rejected the approach used in interpreting the Sherman and Clayton Acts—a common law-like interpretation of the broadly worded provisions in those statutes consistent with the judges' own views of "restraint of trade" or "competition." The courts have recognized that it is inappropriate to adopt such an approach for a more detailed statute like the Robinson–Patman Act—especially in light of Congress' rejection of the FTC's proposal that, instead of enacting the Robinson–Patman Act, Congress simply issue a broadly worded condemnation of "unfair or unjust" price discrimination. However, the courts also seem to have foresworn the traditional method of construing a statute to give effect to the public policies underlying it. Rather than interpreting the statute in light of the congressional concern that price discrimination reflected the unjustified exercise of economic power by powerful rivals or buyers,[17] the courts have alternatively thrown up their hands and reached decisions favoring small businesses regardless of the overall consequences or, reacting to prior decisions in that vein, narrowly construed the Act to limit its damage, but also to limit its ability to meaningfully eradicate buyer power.

(3) Pros and cons of price discrimination legislation.

Any evaluation of the Robinson–Patman Act must begin by considering the evils of price discrimination that the legislation is supposed to remedy. First, as was recognized by the original Clayton Act, and discussed earlier as part of the analysis of predation,[18] selective discriminatory pricing—maintaining price levels in most markets and slashing them against specifically targeted rivals—can be an effective tool for eliminating or disciplining one's competitors. Second, as recognized by the Robinson–Patman Act, price discrimination can facilitate a trend toward

---

the Sherman Act's authors, seemingly ignored by Chicago school advocates of minimal antitrust enforcement, and reinvigorated by neo-populists, whose prime focus is on lowering costs to consumers rather than efficiency. The Act authorizes the FTC to outlaw quantity discounts in specific industries even if they are cost-justified, "where it finds that available purchasers in greater quantities are so few as to render [such discounts] unjustly discriminatory or promotive of monopoly." 15 U.S.C. § 13(a). This provision recognizes that significant efficiencies that cut costs do not benefit consumers if they lead to increased concentration of the industry that allows the remaining firms to price

at monopoly or oligopoly levels. See Chapter 6, section A(13). The FTC invoked this provision only once—to establish a maximum quantity discount for automobile tires—but its decision did not survive judicial review. B.F. Goodrich Co. v. FTC, 134 F.Supp. 39 (D.D.C. 1955), aff'd, 242 F.2d 31 (D.C. Cir. 1957).

17. Report of President Nixon's Task Force on Productivity and Competition, 413 Antitrust & Trade Reg. Rep. (BNA) X-1 (June 10, 1969).

18. See the discussion above in Chapter 3, section D(1).

increasing the power of certain large, favored buyers at the expense of smaller rivals who are unable to obtain goods at the same cost. Third, price discrimination helps enable a firm with market power to obtain monopoly profits by charging a higher price to some buyers and a lower price to others. These increased monopoly profits are socially undesirable for three reasons: (a) they transfer wealth from consumers willing to pay the higher price to the seller; (b) by making monopolies more attractive, they increase firms' incentive to engage in inefficient, exclusionary conduct in order to obtain monopoly power; and (c) because price discrimination requires that the seller separate its patrons based on willingness to pay, they encourage all sorts of inefficient behavior on the part of buyers to exploit and evade the discrimination.[19]

Even if price discrimination is a real disease, there are several arguments suggesting that the Robinson–Patman Act's cure is worse. First, although much of the political impetus for the Act came from the desire to help small businesses, a 1977 Justice Department study concluded that the statute has provided no real protection for small-scale entrepreneurs. For example, despite active enforcement of the Act, grocery chains expanded their market share from 36% to 63% during the period from 1939 to 1972.[20] Moreover, § 2(c) of the Act, which addresses brokerage allowances, has been construed to limit the ability of small firms to match the buying power and efficiencies of their larger rivals through cooperative buying ventures.[21] The Act advantages large buyers in a number of ways: a large order may be sufficiently valuable that a seller will undergo the expense of insuring that any discount is legally justified under a Robinson–Patman defense, while the seller would not go to similar lengths for smaller buyers; larger buyers can turn to overseas sellers for discounts; large buyers can integrate backwards and produce their own inputs,

19. For example, the airline industry price discriminates between business and vacation travelers. (As discussed below in subsection (4), airlines are not subject to the Robinson–Patman Act because an airline ticket is not a "commodity.") But because airlines cannot precisely categorize each traveler, they use a proxy—whether the travel involves staying over a Saturday night. Sometimes, the price differential is so high that business travelers purchase two round-trip tickets, each with a Saturday layover. For example, a colleague of mine who needed to travel from Champaign to Philadelphia for a Thursday meeting purchased one round-trip ticket leaving Champaign on Wednesday and returning Sunday, and another leaving Philadelphia on Friday and returning from Champaign on Sunday. He used the front-end of both tickets and threw away the return tickets. If either return flight was full, he kept another passenger off that flight. This is not an efficient way to allocate airplane seats.

20. See Dept. of Justice Report, supra note 4, at 181.

21. See section G(2), below.

rather than relying on independent sellers.[22]

Second, the Act encourages oligopoly pricing. In industries controlled by a few large firms, no one is likely to announce widespread price reductions because to do so would simply start a price war: rivals would match the lower prices and none of the firms would gain an increased market share. In these industries, the temptation to gain market share leads instead to *selective* price cutting, which may eventually ripen into real price competition. But the Robinson–Patman Act prohibits selective price cutting.[23] Similarly, where the competitive price level in one locale is lower than elsewhere in the country, a new entrant exposes itself to liability for undercutting an established firm; the entrant faces no legal liability for assuming a role as a price follower in the oligopoly.

Third, the Act inhibits retail price wars. Absent the Act, an aggressive retailer seeking to increase sales might pressure its wholesalers to give it special discounts, promising in return to take a lower profit margin itself and push greater volume. The Act makes such conduct illegal.[24]

Fourth, although price discrimination allows a monopolist to charge higher prices to some customers, it may also allows it to charge lower prices to other customers, increasing the monopolist's overall sales. If airlines were prohibited from differentiating between the most price-sensitive vacation travelers and businespeople, for example, they would probably eliminate the "supersaver" rates. This response would hurt the more price-sensitive consumers, and also decrease sales of airline tickets.

Fifth, although price discrimination often unfairly transfers wealth from consumers to businesses, issues of distributive justice are not so clear-cut because on many other occasions the discrimination favors those with less money. A classic example is airline price discrimination, which favors families on vacation over busi-

22. See Robert Varde Keunzel & H. Steven Schiffres, Making Sense of Robinson–Patman: The Need to Revitalize its Affirmative Defenses, 62 Va. L. Rev. 1211, 1215 (1976).

23. Ironically, when oligopolists refrained from selective price cutting by including "most favored nation" clauses in contracts, which promise each buyer that it will receive the same discounts as any other buyers, the government has charged them with engaging in anticompetitive conduct in violation of § 5 of the FTC Act. See E.I. du Pont De Nemours & Co. v. FTC ("*Ethyl* "),

729 F.2d 128 (2d Cir. 1984), discussed in Chapter 4, section F(6). An economic historian noted that the railroads likewise supported legislation prohibiting them from engaging in price discrimination. Gabriel Kolko, Railroads and Regulation 94–101 (1965).

24. Recall that one of the arguments against resale price maintenance is that it also removes the incentive for an aggressive retailer to pressure wholesalers to cut the wholesale price. See Chapter 5, section B(2).

ness travelers. Senior citizen or student movie discounts are another example.

Sixth, compliance with the Act results in the wasteful expenditure of resources. The legal and accounting costs a firm must incur to ensure compliance are significant. Moreover, businesses may make less efficient manufacturing and distribution decisions in order to avoid Robinson–Patman violations.[25]

(4) Statutory elements of § 2(a).

The principal ban on price discrimination appears in § 2(a) of the Robinson–Patman Act. (Subsection (b) of the Act addresses defenses, and subsections (c) through (f) contain additional prophylactic protections to prevent evasion of the provisions of § 2(a)). It is important to contrast the Robinson–Patman Act's detailed provisions with those found in the other antitrust statutes, which are marked by the generality of their terms. The Sherman Act bars combinations "in restraint of trade" and "monopolization"; the Clayton Act proscribes specific business activities, but only where the effect may be to substantially reduce "competition." Indeed, the FTC originally recommended similar treatment for price discrimination. Its proposed legislation would have amended the FTC Act to empower the agency to determine and proscribe "unfair or unjust discrimination in price." But Congress rejected this proposal in favor of the more detailed provisions of the Robinson–Patman Act. Section 2(a) has seven key statutory elements, which are described below.

Interstate commerce

The Sherman Act prohibits conspiracies "in restraint of trade or commerce among the several states." The Supreme Court has broadly construed this jurisdictional requirement to cover any commerce that Congress may lawfully regulate under the Commerce Clause. In contrast, the Robinson–Patman Act applies only where "either of the purchases involved in such discrimination are in commerce." [26] Thus, in *Gulf Oil Corp. v. Copp Paving Co.,*[27] the Supreme Court distinguished Sherman Act precedents and read

---

25. Hansen, supra note 4, at 1188–89. To illustrate, a bathtub manufacturer sold discounted tubs to Sears that were one inch shorter and 2 3/4 inches narrower than other bath tubs and had no soap dishes. Perhaps, as skillful defense counsel successfully persuaded the FTC, the Sears version was designed for the price-conscious "do-it-yourself" shopper and was truly of a different grade and quality than the typical bathtub; perhaps, on the other hand, the manufacturer went to great manufacturing and legal expense so as to avoid violating of the Act. Universal–Rundle Corp., 65 F.T.C. 924, 954–55 (1964), vacated on other grounds, 382 F.2d 285 (7th Cir. 1967).

26. Compare 15 U.S.C. § 1 with id., § 13(a).

27. 419 U.S. 186 (1974).

the Robinson–Patman Act more restrictively, requiring that the goods involved in either the favored or the disfavored purchase must cross state lines in moving from the seller to the buyer. In that case, the defendants were California concrete manufacturers that sold their goods to California contractors for use on interstate highways in California. Given the extensive amount of interstate travel on these roads, the Sherman Act would clearly have applied if, for example, the defendants had fixed prices. Although the concrete sales "affected" interstate commerce, the Court held that the Robinson–Patman Act did not apply because none of the sales were "in" interstate commerce.[28]

Earlier, however, the Court held in *Standard Oil Co. v. FTC*,[29] that the discriminatory prices Standard charged for oil within Michigan was governed by the Act because the oil was within a "stream of commerce." The oil in question was located, when a customer ordered it, at Standard's marine terminal at River Rouge, Michigan, and was sold to customers in Detroit. The Supreme Court rejected the defendant's jurisdictional claim, holding that oil obtained from fields in Kansas, Oklahoma, Texas and Wyoming and then refined in Indiana was within the "stream of commerce" and hence "in" commerce. The temporary storage of the product at River Rouge did not, the Court reasoned, "deprive the gasoline of its interstate character."[30]

Price discrimination

In *FTC v. Anheuser–Busch, Inc.*,[31] the Supreme Court adopted a broad and literal interpretation of the Act's declaration that it is unlawful "to discriminate in price." According to the Court, this language requires only that the plaintiff show an actual difference in the prices charged for two sales.[32] The case involved the defendant's selective lowering of beer prices in St. Louis while increasing prices nationwide. Anheuser–Busch argued that the Act did not prohibit this price differential because the favored and disfavored buyers (local distributors in St. Louis were "favored" and local distributors elsewhere were not) did not compete with each other. The Court rejected the argument. It noted that the St. Louis price war appeared to be part of Anheuser–Busch's efforts to discipline rival brewers in St. Louis, precisely the type of primary-line injury that was targeted by the original Clayton Act. Clearly, the Robinson–Patman Act was intended to expand, not

---

28. Cf. Moore v. Mead's Fine Bread Co., 348 U.S. 115 (1954) (Act allows suit brought against New Mexican firm by in-state rival that was victimized by the defendant's decision to selectively cut prices to New Mexican buyers while maintaining higher prices in Texas).

29. 340 U.S. 231 (1951).

30. Id. at 238.

31. 363 U.S. 536 (1960).

32. Id. at 549.

limit, the prohibition on price discrimination, and the Court therefore refused to adopt the defendant's reading of the statute, which would have confined its scope to secondary-line injury.[33]

The courts have taken a common sense approach in defining "price." Thus, the Act has been held to apply where a commodity is sold to two buyers at identical prices, but one receives significantly better terms for return, longer warranty service, free services, or other similar benefits.[34] However, the Act specifically provides that "nothing ... shall prevent price changes from time to time where in response to changing conditions affecting the market." Thus, even dramatically different prices are not discriminatory if the market has changed in the period between two sales.

Note that this definition of price discrimination does not cover a number of practices that are discriminatory from an economist's point of view. Consider the use of tied sales to price discriminate, which violates the Sherman Act.[35] For example, IBM sold its machines at low prices but required consumers to use its high-priced punch cards. This scheme effectively allowed IBM to charge a higher price for the machine to high-volume users and a lower price to low-volume users, even though the cost of making each machine was identical. Because each machine and each card were sold at the same price, however, the Robinson–Patman Act does not condemn this practice.

Purchasers

The Act specifically bars discrimination "between different purchasers." The courts have construed this provision to require a difference in price in two actual sales. Offers, licenses, and leases therefore are not covered by § 2(a). Nor can a purchaser complain if it was disfavored vis-a-vis a subsidiary of the seller.

Some courts have also read this provision to require that the plaintiff be one of the defendant's purchasers. For example, in *Klein v. Lionel Corp.*,[36] the defendant sold to Klein via a wholesaler, while selling directly to Klein's competitor. The Third Circuit dismissed Klein's price discrimination claim because he was an indirect purchaser. This holding does not seem to be a sound interpretation of either the statutory language or the policy underlying the Act. Section 2(a) makes it "unlawful for any person ... to discriminate in price between different purchasers."

33. Id. at 542–44.

34. See III Earl Kintner & Joseph Bauer, Federal Antitrust Law 189 (1983) (detailing cases).

35. See, e.g., International Business Machines Corp. v. United States, 298 U.S. 131 (1936), which is discussed in Chapter 5, section G(2c).

36. 237 F.2d 13 (3d Cir. 1956).

Klein's action was based on § 4 of the Clayton Act, which awards treble damages to "any person who shall be injured in his business or property by reason of anything forbidden in the antitrust laws." If Lionel was charging different prices to different customers, then it was engaged in price discrimination and, if ultimately proved illegal, that conduct injured Klein. Moreover, the principal purpose of the Robinson–Patman Act was to prevent small retailers from being victimized by their larger rivals' exercise of power. If larger firms could evade the Act by purchasing directly from the manufacturer, the legislation would have little impact.[37]

Nevertheless, *Lionel* was correctly decided. The defendant had not sold at different prices to different purchasers: the price offered to Klein's chain store rivals, like Sears and Strawbridge & Clothier, was identical to the price Lionel charged to Klein's supplier.[38] As noted in the introduction to this Chapter, economic price discrimination occurs both when similarly situated buyers are charged different prices and when differently situated buyers (here, wholesalers and retailers) are charged identical prices. Nonetheless, the latter practice does not violate § 2(a).

Commodities

The Act applies only where buyers of "commodities" are treated differently, thus excluding sales of services, real estate, or intangible property rights (such as advertising time). Although firms can more easily engage in price discrimination in selling services than they can in selling commodities (because of the difficulty of arbitrage in the former case), one explanation for the exclusion of services is the Robinson–Patman Act's concern with socio-political fairness, not economics. Discrimination is unequal treatment—for example, the Equal Protection Clause commands that similarly situated people be treated alike.[39] Buyers of commodities are similarly situated; because services are usually customized, disparate treatment in the sale of services does not create the same political antagonism as discrimination in the sale of goods.[40] In addition, the intangible nature of services adds substantial complexity to the question whether two purchasers have received "like grade and quality," as well as to the determination

37. The "indirect purchaser" doctrine does not apply where the facts show that the defendant exercises an inordinate control over the intermediary. See, e.g., Kraft–Phenix Cheese Corp., 25 F.T.C. 537 (1937).

38. Cf. Krug v. International Telephone & Telegraph Co., 142 F.Supp. 230 (D.N.J. 1956) (distinguishing *Lionel* in case where defendant sold to wholesaler at a *higher* price than that charged to large retailers.

39. City of Cleburne v. Cleburne Living Center, 473 U.S. 432, 439 (1985).

40. See Corwin Edwards, The Price Discrimination Law 2–3 (1959).

of the seller's costs.[41]

Like grade and quality

In order to qualify as price discrimination, the commodities at issue must, according to § 2(a), be "of like grade and quality." This requirement is inherent in the very concept of discrimination. It is only discriminatory to sell the same thing at different prices. Selling different goods at different prices is therefore beyond the scope of the Act.

There are still significant interpretive questions that arise in applying this standard. The issue in *FTC v. Borden Co.*,[42] for example, was whether a nationally advertised brand of milk was of the same grade and quality as identical milk packaged under a house brand. The Supreme Court said yes. Literally, of course, the milk was the same. It may be, as the court of appeals found on remand, that the price differential between branded and generic milk simply reflected consumer preferences for the advertised brand and thus gave no buyer a competitive advantage.[43] Thus, the price difference may not have had the requisite effect on competition (see the last item in this listing of elements, below). But the decision whether to proscribe sales that fall within the literal definition of price discrimination should properly come as part of the analysis of the merits, not at the threshold. As the Court noted, these "transactions are too laden with potential discrimination and adverse competitive effect to be excluded from the reach of § 2(a) by permitting a difference in grade to be established by the label alone or by the label and its consumer appeal." [44]

Justices Potter Stewart and John Harlan dissented, disagreeing with the majority on the facts as well as the law. With respect to the facts, the dissent claimed that Borden took extensive quality-control precautions to insure that a flawed Borden brand product did not reach consumers, while these precautions were not taken for the private brand milk Borden prepared.[45] If the dissent were correct, the two products were not of like grade and quality. As the majority noted, however, if Borden could prove this difference in quality "it is unlikely that the case would be here" [46]—presumably because Borden would have prevailed

---

41. Perhaps for similar reasons, the Uniform Commercial Code's article governing sales does not apply to services. U.C.C. § 2–102. The "Baby FTC Acts" enacted by some state legislatures do, however, proscribe price discrimination in the sale of services. See, e.g., Or. Rev. Stat. § 646.040.

42. 383 U.S. 637 (1966).

43. Borden Co. v. FTC, 381 F.2d 175 (5th Cir. 1967).

44. 383 U.S. at 644.

45. Id. at 651.

46. Id. at 644 n.5.

either on this threshold question or by showing that the price differences reflected the higher cost of quality control.[47]

With respect to the law, the *Borden* dissenters argued that "the consumer's belief, measured by past satisfaction and the market reputation established by Borden," was sufficient to make Borden's brand a superior "grade and quality" to private label milk.[48] But this argument allows defendants to create artificial brand distinctions in order to evade the Act's requirements. Therefore, the concept of "quality" is properly defined more narrowly to refer to physical differences, and consumer appeal should be considered only when inquiring whether the discrimination lessened competition or injured the disfavored buyers' ability to compete.

In focusing on physical differences, "like grade and quality" has been defined to refer to "objective physical characteristics" that affect marketability. For example, in *Quaker Oats Co.*,[49] the defendant used different processes to make different types of oat flour, but the cost of producing each of them was the same. Nonetheless, the defendant charged a lower price to Gerber, which wanted only flour made by a particular type of process not desired by other buyers. The FTC concluded that the flour sold to Gerber was not of like grade and quality as the oat flour made by the other processes. In another decision demonstrating the consumer-oriented focus of this element, the FTC held that shower curtains with a variety of patterns (and therefore with somewhat different physical characteristics) were all of the same grade and quality where they sold at retail for comparable prices.[50]

A narrower view of "like grade and quality," albeit one that maintains a consumer-oriented focus, was the basis for the Seventh Circuit's holding in *A.A. Poultry Farms, Inc. v. Rose Acre Farms, Inc.* that the defendant did not violate the Robinson–Patman Act.[51] The court held that eggs sold by Rose Acre as "specials" were not necessarily of the same grade and quality as other eggs, although the actual product was physically identical. The court explained that "special" contracts guaranteed the buyer a specific quantity of a specific grade of egg, but the timing of delivery was left to Rose Acre's discretion. These contracts were particularly advantageous in dealing with perishable goods like

---

47. See section G for a discussion of the cost justification defense.

48. 383 U.S. at 651.

49. 66 F.T.C. 1131 (1964).

50. See Joseph A. Kaplan & Sons, Inc., 63 F.T.C. 1308, 1347–48 (1963),

modified on other grounds, 347 F.2d 785 (D.C. Cir. 1965).

51. 881 F.2d 1396 (7th Cir. 1989), cert. denied, 494 U.S. 1019 (1990). For a discussion of Judge Frank Easterbrook's lengthy dicta concerning predatory pricing, see Chapter 3, section D(6).

eggs, for they allowed Rose Acre to dispose of overstocked eggs of particular grades. Analogizing to a service that is not covered by the Act, the court said that egg specials are not like other eggs for the same reason that an airline ticket for a 5:00 p.m. flight is not the same as a ticket for a 6:00 a.m. flight, and an airline seat reserved two weeks in advance is not the same as a ticket entitling the passenger to fly stand-by.[52]

Goods used or resold in the United States

The statute is explicitly limited to sales "where such commodities are sold for use, consumption, or resale within the United States." This provision therefore removes international price discrimination from the scope of the Act. This type of discrimination was not a concern of the Robinson–Patman Act's sponsors. Where prices are higher in the United States than overseas, American consumers suffer but merchants are not affected in their rivalry with one another, because they all pay the same uniformly high wholesale price. Foreign firms might cause primary line injury to their American rivals by selling at low costs here, but Congress had already sought to remedy this problem through the Anti–Dumping Act of 1921.[53]

Prohibited effect on competition

As noted above, the Robinson–Patman Act specifically amended the Clayton Act to supplement the nature of the effects prohibited by original statute. As amended, § 2(a) of the Act prohibits price discrimination where its effect "may be substantially to lessen competition" *or* "to injure, destroy, or prevent competition with any person who either grants or knowingly receives the benefit of such discrimination, or with customers of either of them." These standards are discussed in detail below. Section B analyzes discriminations that injure the disfavored buyer's ability to compete with the discriminatory seller, and section C analyzes discriminations that injure the disfavored buyer's ability to compete with other customers of the discriminatory seller.

(5) Recovery of damages in private litigation.

Private plaintiffs usually want to recover damages, not only because damages are trebled under § 4 of the Clayton Act, but also because injunctive relief is often less effective. This is especially true in Robinson–Patman cases because the Act preserves the seller's right to unilaterally refuse to deal with whomever it

---

52. Id. at 1407–08.

53. 42 Stat. 11. The statute was repealed in 1979. Pub. L. No. 96–39, 93 Stat. 193. Other anti-dumping provisions in current law can be found at 19 U.S.C. § 1671 et seq.

chooses.[54]   Nevertheless, *J. Truett Payne Co. v. Chrysler Motors Corp.*[55] demonstrates that proving damages is significantly more difficult than proving a violation of the Act. In that case, a car dealer in Birmingham, Alabama sued Chrysler for injuries caused by an allegedly discriminatory bonus/rebate program Chrysler offered its dealers. Had Truett Payne received the bonuses to which it believed it was entitled, Chrysler would have had to pay it more than $81,000. In addition, the plaintiff's market share dropped from 27% to 23% in one year, which Payne attributed to the discriminatory bonus. However, there was no evidence that Payne rivals that received the full bonuses had passed them on to consumers in the form of lower prices, and the link between the decline in Payne's market share and Chrysler's rebates was thus somewhat attenuated.

A jury verdict in favor of the plaintiff was reversed by the court of appeals, who instructed the trial judge to dismiss the complaint. The Supreme Court by-passed the question whether Chrysler violated § 2(a), finding that the plaintiff had failed to provide sufficient evidence to warrant the award of damages. The Court unanimously rejected Payne's argument that plaintiffs are entitled to "automatic damages" simply by virtue of proving unlawful price discrimination.[56] The standard for Robinson–Patman liability is a prophylactic one, the Court noted. Plaintiffs can prevail by showing that the effect *may be* to lessen competition generally or to injure competition between the victim and the beneficiary of the discrimination. In contrast, § 4 of the Clayton Act, which authorizes the recovery of damages, applies only to a person "who *shall be* injured in his business or property by reason of anything forbidden in the antitrust laws."

54. Section 2(a) contains a proviso that "nothing herein contained shall prevent persons ... from selecting their own customers...."

55. 451 U.S. 557 (1981).

56. In a footnote, Justice William Rehnquist dismissed the plaintiff's reliance on language in Bruce's Juices v. American Can Co., 330 U.S. 743, 757 (1947), that clearly suggested damages should automatically be awarded. In that case, Justice Robert Jackson wrote that if a plaintiff "could establish that the prices [the defendant] charged were discriminatory so that they violated the Act," it could, "despite petitioner's plaint on the difficulty of proving damages, ... establish its right to recover three times the discriminatory difference without proving more than the illegality of the prices." Although Rehnquist was literally correct that "the statement is merely dictum, since the only issue before the Court was whether a violation of § 2(a) could be used as an affirmative defense to void a contract," 451 U.S. at 563 n.3, his dismissal of *Bruce's Juices* is a bit misleading. The statement may not have been necessary to the holding, but it may well have been necessary to support Jackson's reasoning. *Bruce's Juices* was a 5–4 decision, and Jackson's argument for automatic damages was clearly intended to demonstrate that his decision to deprive Robinson–Patman victims of an affirmative defense did not frustrate effective enforcement of the antitrust laws.

The majority nevertheless vacated the appeals court decision, noting precedents allowing antitrust plaintiffs to use somewhat weaker or more speculative evidence in proving injuries.[57] The Court recognized that the plaintiff's evidence was weak, but noted that these precedents only apply to proof of damages against defendants found to have violated the law, and the appeals court had not yet passed on Chrysler's liability. Thus, over the dissent of four justices who felt that the plaintiff's case did not warrant any further consideration, the Court remanded for consideration of liability.[58] Even the majority admitted, however, that the plaintiff's case was particularly weak because of its inability to show that the favored buyers were able to lower retail prices and thus divert business from the plaintiff. Although the plaintiff argued that a disfavored purchaser could be injured, even if retail prices are not affected, because it matches the price of its favored competitors but spends less on advertising and capital expenditures, it is unclear whether Truett Payne actually showed that it suffered *any* injury in its ability to compete with its rivals, and the Court declined to decide whether evidence of lost sales was a necessary element to proof of damages in a Robinson–Patman case.

Section B: Primary Line Injury

(1) What is primary line injury and how does it work?

Primary line injury occurs when the effect of offering goods at different prices to different purchasers is to injure the seller's rivals.[1] Thus, for example, Standard Oil allegedly built its monopoly by selectively cutting prices to eliminate competitors, while maintaining high price levels elsewhere.

57. Although a full examination of the evidence necessary to prove damages is beyond the scope of this treatise, the Supreme Court has recognized that "damage issues in [antitrust] cases are rarely susceptible of the kind of concrete, detailed proof of injury which is available in other contexts." Zenith Radio Corp. v. Hazeltine Research, Inc., 395 U.S. 100, 123 (1969). Thus, "just and reasonable" inferences of damage are permissible because a more demanding standard of proof "would enable the wrongdoer to profit by his wrongdoing at the expense of his victim." Bigelow v. RKO Radio Pictures, 327 U.S. 251, 264 (1946).

58. Over the four-year existence of the challenged bonus program, the dis-

senters noted, the plaintiff's market share actually increased by 1%. 451 U.S. at 570. On remand, the appellate court held that the plaintiff had not shown "sufficient evidence of either violation, injury, or damages." Chrysler Credit Corp. v. J. Truett Payne Co., 670 F.2d 575, 578 (5th Cir.), cert. denied, 459 U.S. 908 (1982).

1. Any discriminatory scheme involves a "favored buyer" and a "disfavored buyer." When price discrimination has the effect of injuring competition between these buyers, instead of between the seller and its rivals, it creates "secondary line injury." Secondary line injury is discussed below in section C.

From the earliest days of antitrust enforcement, it was well
established that selective, predatory price cutting could constitute
monopolization or attempted monopolization in violation of § 2 of
the Sherman Act. But following the Supreme Court's announcement of a rule of reason in the *Standard Oil* case,[2] legislators
feared that a hostile judiciary would not effectively carry out
congressional intent. Thus, the Clayton Act[3] specifically prohibited certain types of conduct, including discriminatory pricing. Although Congress added provisos making clear that conduct was
prohibited only where its effect may be to substantially lessen
competition, the drafters of the Clayton Act felt (probably wrongly, in hindsight) that this phrase would ensure more effective
enforcement.[4]

The Robinson–Patman Act's condemnation of primary line
discrimination is fully consistent with the approach taken in the
legislation it technically amends—the Clayton Act. By 1936,
Congress was not only dissatisfied with what a hostile judiciary
might do with § 2 of the Sherman Act, but was also concerned
that the Clayton Act's requirement that the effect of the selective
pricing may be to substantially lessen competition was too severe.
Seeing the need for a prophylactic test, Congress enacted § 2(a) of
the Robinson–Patman Act, which allows a plaintiff to prevail upon
a showing that the discrimination either lessened competition *or*
injured the ability of individual firms to compete with the defendant.

If Congress was concerned about protecting small firms from
unfair competition and adopted the detailed provisions of the
Robinson–Patman Act because it did not trust the judiciary, its
fears have proven to be well-grounded. The principal cases applying the Robinson–Patman Act to primary line discrimination
exemplify the poor job the judiciary and the Federal Trade Commission have done in interpreting the Act. Some of these cases
simply demonstrate a lack of sophistication about how discrimination can harm competition between the defendant and its rivals.
Others suggest that the courts have thrown up their hands and
reached absurd results, guided only by a dim view that the Act
was intended to help smaller businesses. Finally, recent cases
have all but construed its provisions out of existence, demonstrating disrespect for both the Act and earlier precedents.

2. Standard Oil Co. v. United States, 221 U.S. 1 (1911), discussed above in Chapter 3, section A(2).

3. 38 Stat. 730 (1914).

4. H.R. Rep. No. 627, 63d Cong., 2d Sess. 8 (1914).

(2) **Price discrimination to discipline rivals.**

In *Anheuser–Busch, Inc. v. FTC,*[5] the Seventh Circuit reversed the FTC's finding of unlawful price discrimination, concluding that Anheuser–Busch's pricing scheme was merely designed to "forthrightly [meet] its robust competition in the St. Louis market."[6] The petitioner's leading product, Budweiser, is a "premium" beer that sold at a higher price than rival brands. Like most brewers, Anheuser–Busch (A–B) increased prices nationwide in 1953 following renegotiation of an employee wage contract. In St. Louis, however, A–B's rivals did not pass their increased wage costs on to consumers, and so Budweiser did not increase in price in that area. By January of 1954, A–B began to slash the price of Budweiser in St. Louis, so that by June of that year, it sold for the same price as inferior non-premium beers. Anheuser–Busch's market share in St. Louis soared, from 12.5% of the market in 1953 to 39.3% in early 1955. At that point, A–B hiked the price of Budweiser by 45¢ per case; its rivals followed by raising their prices 15¢ per case, thus restoring the traditional differential between Budweiser and rival brands. A–B's market share then dropped down to 17.5%.[7]

The court's reversal of the FTC can best be understood by contrasting Anheuser–Busch's behavior with the archetypical villain in primary line cases—Standard Oil. Unlike Standard Oil, Busch did not seem intent on, or capable of, eliminating its competitors and achieving monopoly power. Each rival continued to earn profits while Budweiser's price was falling.[8] A–B's terrific gain in market share was only temporary, the court emphasized. Moreover, A–B had a legitimate explanation for cutting prices only in St. Louis. Elsewhere, the brewer had to deal through distributors, who were unwilling to pass wholesale price reductions on to retailers. In St. Louis, however, A–B dealt directly with retail liquor outlets, and thus could be assured that its price decreases would be reflected in increased market share.

The court of appeals properly observed that the Robinson–Patman Act is concerned about the effect on competition, not competitors; mere shifts of business between competitors is not a proscribed evil under § 2(a). Rather, the Act is concerned with "substantial impairment of the vigor or health of the contest for business."[9] On these facts, the court correctly concluded that the discriminatory pricing did not "injure competition with" A–B. Nor did the discounts have the effect of substantially reducing competi-

---

5. 289 F.2d 835 (7th Cir. 1961).

6. Id. at 842.

7. Id. at 837.

8. Id. at 839.

9. Id. at 840.

tion by eliminating competitors, in the sense of enabling A–B to unilaterally exercise monopoly power. Nevertheless, the effects prohibited by the Act's "substantially lessen competition" standard should include not only monopolization, but also the use of selected, targeted pricing to retaliate against rivals that do not follow the defendant's lead in increasing prices. The court seemed oblivious to this possibility, at one point distinguishing A–B's conduct from that at issue in earlier cases, where "the motive for the price cut was vindictive and the effect was punitive." [10]

Similarly, the Commission's decision upholding the administrative law judge's finding of a violation ignored this type of competitive harm, notwithstanding the ALJ's observation that A–B's president had admitted that the two purposes of its discriminatory pricing scheme were to gain market share and to punish its St. Louis rivals for failing to pass on the increased wage costs.[11] Rather, foreshadowing *Utah Pie* (discussed in subsection (4) below), the Commission focused on competitors, not competition, in holding that the sharp loss of business suffered by two of A–B's rivals was sufficient to show "a general adverse effect on the market." [12] (This holding was reversed by the Seventh Circuit.) As made clear in the discussion of predatory behavior challenged under § 2 of the Sherman Act,[13] A–B's selective, discriminatory pricing was far safer to implement than across-the-board cuts, for the losses were felt in a minimal area while the benefit of gaining credibility as a feared predator extended nationwide. The fact that rival brewers were able to remain profitable in the midst of a price war is further evidence that higher costs did not mandate A–B's price hike in March, 1955. The most plausible explanation for the increase was that A–B figured that its rivals had learned their lesson. It appears that A–B figured correctly.

(3) The diversion of business test.

In *Samuel H. Moss, Inc. v. FTC*,[14] a distinguished panel of the Second Circuit (Judges Learned and Augustus Hand and Charles Clark) accepted the Commission's argument that price discrimination lessens competition, or injures competition with the seller, when the lower prices tend to prevent rivals "from taking business

---

10. Id. at 842.

11. 54 F.T.C. 277, 292 (1957).

12. Id. at 300. Actually, modern antitrust analysis might support the FTC's conclusion, albeit not the reasoning. The Herfindahl–Hirschman Index (HHI), which measures the strength of competition in a market, was 2746 in December 1953 and 2952 in March

1955. This change represents a significant increase in concentration in a market that was already highly concentrated. For a fuller discussion of the HHI, see Chapter 6, section A(6).

13. See Chapter 3, section D(1).

14. 148 F.2d 378, 379 (2d Cir.), cert. denied, 326 U.S. 734 (1945).

away from the [defendant] which they might have got, had the [defendant] not lowered his price below what he was charging elsewhere." Thus, armed only with evidence that on eight occasions Moss had cut its price to particular buyers, and that its rivals were unable to match its discounted price,[15] the Commission and the court of appeals found a § 2(a) violation.

Congressional debates on the Robinson–Patman Act featured spirited attacks on the legislation by opponents, who argued that it was fundamentally anticompetitive and designed solely to protect special interests—i.e., small businesses that preferred not to face aggressive competition. The sponsors denied these accusations, maintaining that the Act's specific prohibitions were necessary prophylactics to preserve the competitive process. *Moss* represents an era where the FTC and reviewing courts believed the dissenting legislators, and assumed the worst about the sponsors (based, perhaps correctly, on an assessment of the political forces supporting the bill), and interpreted the Act to effectuate the opponents' nightmare, rather than the sponsors' disclaimers. Permitting a finding of primary line injury based solely on lost business seems a plausible way of protecting competitors, but it is obviously a ludicrous means of preserving either a competitive market structure or an equal opportunity for all to compete on the merits, regardless of size.

The FTC later retreated from *Moss* in *Dean Milk Co.*[16] The respondent there was charged with violating § 2(a) by selling milk to large buyers in Louisville at lower prices than those available to smaller buyers, and by charging lower overall prices in some neighboring cities than in Louisville. Chairman Paul Rand Dixon (a protege of Senator Estes Kefauver, a leading antitrust populist) emphasized that the legislative history of both the original Clayton Act and the Robinson–Patman amendments to § 2 demonstrated that a finding of predation is not necessary to establish primary line injury.[17] Nevertheless, Dixon noted that recent judicial decisions had not found a § 2(a) violation where the actual effects of primary line territorial discrimination were limited to a temporary diversion of business and minor loss of sales and profits, and where there was no indicia of predation.[18] In an effort

15. 36 F.T.C. 640, 648–49 (1943).

16. 68 F.T.C. 710 (1965), rev'd in part, 395 F.2d 696 (7th Cir. 1968).

17. Id. at 744–49. Dixon noted that during Senate consideration of the Clayton Act, criminal penalties were deleted, a defense for good faith efforts to meet competition was added, and, most significant, language requiring proof of

an intent "to destroy or wrongfully injure the business of a competitor" was removed from the bill.

18. Id. at 749. See, e.g., Minneapolis–Honeywell Regulator Co. v. FTC, 191 F.2d 786 (7th Cir. 1951), cert. dismissed, 344 U.S. 206 (1952), which reversed an FTC cease and desist order where the respondent's share of the

to move in this direction, the FTC held that injury to competition could be established in the absence of predation by proof that the defendants' rivals lost a significant amount of profits or business, "*provided that* these immediate actual effects portend either a financial crippling of those competitors, a possibility of an anti-competitive concentration of business in larger sellers, or a significant reduction in the number of sellers in the market." Absent these long-term effects, injury to competition is not shown even if rivals continue to see lower profits or business diverted to the respondent. The FTC noted that the elimination of a single rival will be sufficient to prove injury to competition in markets where there are few firms or where there is a reasonable possibility that continued discrimination will lead to further concentration of the market, and that lost profits will suffice to show injury if the result is that rivals are unable to expand facilities or use aggressive sales or advertising campaigns. The key inquiry in primary line cases, however, is whether the challenged price discrimination "actually lessens or may lessen the ability of local firms to compete" with a national seller.[19]

In dissent, Commissioner Phillip Elman commended the majority for moving in the right direction, and emphasized that price discrimination resulting in a diversion of business can be affirmatively pro-competitive in a number of situations. First, in order to enter a new geographical market, a firm established elsewhere might need to offer its product at promotional prices that would divert business its way. Second, a national seller might cut prices in one area in an effort to gain market share, although it would be unwilling to start a nationwide price war. Alternatively, that seller might engage in discriminatory pricing in taking on a dominant local or regional competitor.[20]

These insights support Dixon's proviso, which requires some evidence of actual or potential harm to the competitive process in order to establish a § 2(a) violation. But Elman's further statement that "illegality must—as in any Clayton Act case—be based on the long-term, probable, foreseeable effects on competition of the respondent's conduct, not merely its immediate short-range impact on competitors,"[21] requires elaboration. Elman may simply have intended to restate the majority's proviso. But his suggestion that Robinson–Patman cases are governed by the same standard as cases brought under other sections of the Clayton Act (which require that the effect may be to significant lessening of competition) is wrong as a matter of statutory interpretation: it

---

market decreased while its rivals' shares increased.

19. 68 F.T.C. at 750–51.

20. Id. at 804–05.

21. Id. at 797 (citation omitted).

ignores the Robinson–Patman Act's express addition of the injury to competition standard as a supplement to the competition-lessening standard of the Clayton Act.   Under the language added by the Robinson–Patman Act, § 2(a) is violated where the discrimination injures the ability of rivals to compete with the defendant, even if it has not yet had a "long-term, probable, foreseeable effect" on competition.

Whatever Elman's doctrinal differences with the majority, his *Dean Milk* dissent painted a very different version of the facts. The majority found that Dean Milk violated § 2(a) by establishing a quantity discount program in Louisville that gave it approximately 40% of the wholesale milk business—primarily through sales to supermarkets.   According to the majority, the result was a significant weakening in the competitive position of local dairies: one local firm was acquired by Bowman, one of Dean Milk's national rivals, and two others merged together and were then acquired by another outside concern.[22]   On the other hand, Elman noted that most of Dean's increased market share came at the expense of another national firm, and that the significant loss in profits suffered by Dean's smaller Louisville rivals may well have been due, as Dean claimed, to predictable losses that occurred when Dean's rivalry ended their pre-existing price-fixing conspiracy.[23]

Similarly, evidence that Dean Milk cut prices in smaller towns near Louisville below those charged in the city, resulting in the elimination of five small town dairies, demonstrated an injury to competition to the majority.   Elman, by contrast, pointed out that Dean never gained more than 2% of the market in one of the smaller cities, that general price levels in the areas surrounding Louisville were persistently below those in effect in the city (so that Dean needed to discriminate in order to compete), that strongly entrenched local competitors were not threatened by Dean's entry, and that the loss of a few businesses over an eight-year period of time was probably due to normal attrition.[24]

On appeal, the Seventh Circuit reversed the FTC's finding of illegality.[25]   The court held that the Commission erred in inferring

22. Id. at 768. Cf. FTC v. Dean Foods Co., 384 U.S. 597 (1966) (describing subsequent merger between Dean Milk and Bowman).

23. 68 F.T.C. at 821. The argument was not, Elman emphasized, that unlawful price discrimination is justified as a response to a price-fixing cartel, but that a decline in profitability following the break up of such a cartel cannot be attributed to price discrimination.

24. Commissioner Mary Gardiner Jones dissented along lines similar to those elaborated on by Elman. Id. at 822.

25. Dean Milk Co. v. FTC, 395 F.2d 696 (7th Cir. 1968). The court sustained a related finding that Dean Milk

injury from evidence that Dean's rivals lost business and profits in
the small towns around Louisville. Historically, a quart of milk
had been one cent cheaper in these small towns than in Louisville,
and Dean maintained that one cent differential between its prices
in Louisville and in the surrounding areas. The court feared that
prohibiting this territorial price differential would discourage mul-
ti-market sellers from entering new markets, and concluded that
it was not required by § 2(a).[26] Moreover, the court faulted the
FTC for failing to explain how the price differential, as opposed to
significant technological changes in the dairy industry, had caused
the demise of those firms that had left the market during the
period of discrimination. Similarly, the court rejected the FTC's
finding of a causal nexus between Dean's quantity discounts in
Louisville and the increased concentration of the market in that
city, suggesting several other equally plausible explanations for
the injury to competition the FTC identified.[27] In sum, the FTC's
doctrinal analysis—requiring evidence of lost business plus a
showing that the long-term effect of the discrimination would hurt
rivals' ability to compete—was not reversed, but supplemented by
a requirement that the Commission cogently link the challenged
discrimination to the identified injury.

(4) The injury to competition standard gone awry.

Utah Pie Co. v. Continental Baking Co.[28] surely ranks among
the handful of worst antitrust decisions in American history. In
finding that a discriminatory pricing scheme violated the Robinson–Patman Act, the Supreme Court effectively required national
businesses engaged in oligopoly pricing to maintain their high
prices rather than compete where they found tough local rivals.
The challenged pricing scheme actually improved competition and
posed no threat to the continued vitality of the "victim"—the local
market leader. The Court's decision can be explained only by the
most unthinking, simplistic logic: the Robinson–Patman Act helps
small businesses, the defendants took profits away from a small
business, therefore the defendants violated the Act.

had engaged in unlawful secondary line discrimination.

26. Id. at 702.

27. Id. at 708–14. The court found that the bulk of Dean's increased mar-ket share in Louisville came from its lawful decision to uniformly reduce the price of its homogenous milk, and from various supermarkets' decision to add certain of Dean's products to their shelves (which did not replace any prod-ucts sold by Deans' rivals). Likewise, its rivals' losses were attributed to ris-ing costs incurred by smaller dairies; the existence of a price-fixing conspira-cy among Dean's rivals that allowed Dean to undercut a supra-competitive price level; and the general growth of supermarkets, which hurt rival dairies that had relied on home delivery sales for a significant part of their market share.

28. 386 U.S. 685 (1967).

The defendants in the case, Continental, Carnation, and Pet Milk, all sold frozen dessert pies nationwide. They each supplied Salt Lake City retailers from plants in California. Because of significant cost advantages, Utah Pie's locally based plant was able to enter the market and began charging prices significantly below those set by the three defendants. By 1958, Utah Pie commanded two-thirds of the market. At that time, the defendants began to offer significant discounts on their product in Salt Lake City, charging lower prices in that area than elsewhere. By 1961, the plaintiff's market share had declined to 45%. But, because the market was growing so rapidly, Utah Pie's sales still increased from $353,000 in 1958 to $589,000 in 1961, and the company's net worth doubled.[29]

The Supreme Court sustained the jury's verdict in favor of the plaintiff.[30] According to the Court, the two key facts that supported the verdict were the existence of price discrimination and the fact that this discrimination "contributed to what proved to be a deteriorating price structure over the period covered by this suit." [31] But the Court failed to explain how the lowering of prices substantially lessened competition or injured Utah Pie's ability to compete with the defendants—the two effects proscribed by § 2(a).

With respect to the discriminatory pricing's effect on competition, Justice Potter Stewart noted in dissent that, when one compares Utah Pie's "quasi-monopolistic" 66.5% market share in 1958 to the market structure in 1961, "the 1961 situation has to be considered more competitive than that of 1958." [32] With respect to the discriminatory pricing's effect on the plaintiff's ability to compete with the defendants, the Court said that eventually Utah Pie would become a "less effective competitive force" if its profit margins continued to decline.[33] This prediction is groundless— when a dominant firm's profits decline because of competition from new or more vigorous rivalry, there is no basis to predict any injury to the firm's ability to remain competitive. Surely, AT&T suffered losses when it lost its long-distance telephone monopoly, but no one seriously thought those losses would continue. To say that Utah Pie's ability to compete with the defendants was injured simply from reduced profits converts § 2(a)'s "injury to competition" standard into a blanket prohibition of any differential pricing that takes business away from rivals. If Congress wanted to condemn every discriminatory price that caused any injury, it would simply have not added the "injury to competition" proviso;

29. Id. at 689.

30. The jury had rejected another count of Utah Pie's complaint that alleged a price-fixing conspiracy among the three defendants.

31. Id. at 690.

32. Id. at 705.

33. Id. at 699–700.

rather, it would have imposed an outright ban on price discrimination, requiring the plaintiff to produce evidence of injury under the general provisions of § 4 of the Clayton Act in order to recover damages. Thus, *Utah Pie* effectively read both competitive effects standards out of § 2(a).

From an antitrust policy perspective, *Utah Pie*'s holding facilitates oligopoly pricing. When national oligopolies face competition from a regional firm, they should be encouraged to decrease prices in that area and engage in real competition.[34] To be sure, the antitrust laws should condemn predatory responses— those that sacrifice short-term revenues in order to recoup long-term monopoly profits. But where lower prices do not seriously threaten the viability of the regional rival, it seems bizarre to condemn them.

Admittedly, *Utah Pie* did conclude that the defendants had engaged in "predatory pricing," but this holding is seriously flawed. Two errors in the Court's analysis bear mention. First, in finding predation, the Court noted that the defendants' prices fell below their total costs.[35] As the discussion of predation in Chapter 3 indicates, however, pricing at a level below total cost and above variable cost may be legitimate in some contexts. In fact, it makes particular sense for oligopolists. These firms are likely to have excess capacity because their high prices reduce demand. It therefore seems eminently sensible to lower prices in selected areas of the country to a level still in excess of variable costs, while maintaining excess profits elsewhere. Unlike targeted predation, the effectiveness of such price discrimination does not depend at all on the oligopoly's ability to eliminate competition and recoup monopoly profits later.

Second, the Court relied on evidence of the defendants' predatory intent. As has been done in other antitrust contexts,[36] the Court properly explored the record to identify credible evidence of the defendant's intent to lessen competition in the Salt Lake City frozen dessert market, or intent to injure Utah Pie's ability to compete with them. Because firms in the market are most likely to know the consequences of their own actions, such evidence

34. Economists refer to this practice as "Ramsey pricing." Because Utah Pie's entry did not change the market outside of Salt Lake City, there was no reason to think that the three defendants would change their behavior nationwide. Thus, the two viable policy options were to encourage them to compete in Utah, or to require them to maintain a uniform oligopoly price across the country. In neither case would consumers outside of Utah benefit from competition; but allowing Ramsey pricing would at least allow customers in Utah to benefit from rivalry, as long as the lower prices did not threaten Utah Pie's ability to remain in the competitive fray.

35. Id. at 696 n.12, 701.

36. See the discussion in Chapter 3, sections B(3) and D(3).

would be admissible to show a reasonable likelihood that the defendants accomplished one of § 2(a)'s proscribed effects. Indeed, reliance on such evidence may actually be desirable if it permits a fact-finder to distinguish between competitive and anticompetitive local price cutting without undertaking an exhaustive economic analysis of all the surrounding circumstances.[37] But it is critically important in conducting this inquiry for courts to distinguish unlawful predatory intent (a purpose to eliminate or discipline competitors and thereafter raise prices) from lawful competitive intent (a purpose to increase market share at the expense of one or more rivals by, among other things, accepting a reduced profit margin). The evidence of unlawful intent relied on by the Court consisted of internal Pet Milk memos describing Utah Pie as an "unfavorable factor" that posed a "check" on Pet's pricing in Salt Lake City and an incident involving industrial espionage.[38] But this evidence provides no help to the fact-finder in determining whether, as the Court found, the defendants wanted to eliminate Utah Pie, or, as the defendant contended, they simply recognized the need to compete aggressively against a pesky local rival.

Given the insubstantial evidence of predation, the Court's holding in *Utah Pie* effectively endorsed a line of FTC cases decided prior to *Dean Milk*, which held that a "diversion of business" to a price discriminator from its rivals makes out a § 2(a) violation.[39] As a leading commentator observed, "[t]o equate the diversion of business among rival sellers with injury to competition is to indict the competitive process itself."[40]

(5) The pendulum swings the other way.

Utah Pie has been severely criticized by almost every commentator.[41] In addition, the judicial reaction has been what one court described as "civil disobedience."[42] Yet subsequent decisions have fared no better than *Utah Pie* in giving effect to congressional intent. Rather, motivated by an inappropriate focus on allocative efficiency, recent decisions give short shrift to Congress' perception of a need for a prophylactic statute designed to preserve competition while nipping predatory schemes in the bud.

37. Dean Milk Co., 68 F.T.C. 710, 807 (1966) (Elman, C., dissenting).

38. 386 U.S. at 696–97.

39. See Frederick Rowe, Price Discrimination Under the Robinson–Patman Act 151–52 (1962) (citing cases).

40. Id. at 162.

41. For a sampling, see, e.g., III Phillip Areeda & Donald Turner, Antitrust Law 189–91 (1978); Robert Bork, Antitrust Paradox 386–89 (1978); Herbert Hovenkamp, Economics and Federal Antitrust Law 188–89 (1985); Lawrence Sullivan, Antitrust 686–87 (1977).

42. A.A. Poultry Farms, Inc. v. Rose Acre Farms, Inc., 881 F.2d 1396, 1404 (7th Cir. 1989) (Easterbrook, J.).

A typical recent example is the FTC's split decision in *General Foods Corp.*[43] The ultimate outcome of the case was not in serious dispute. General Foods was accused of violating the Robinson–Patman Act by selectively discounting the price of its Maxwell House coffee in order to head off efforts by industry giant Procter & Gamble to expand sales of its Folger's brand in the eastern United States. The majority was "unable to find any prospect of injury to competition from the events described in the record."[44] The principal effects of the discriminatory pricing, the majority found, were to lower prices and improve the quality of coffee. The concurrence likewise concluded that no predatory strategy was likely to succeed against a firm with Procter & Gamble's resources.[45]

The troublesome aspect of the case is that the FTC used it as a vehicle to rewrite the standards for primary line discrimination. The majority correctly observed that because the monopolization provisions of the Sherman Act and the primary line discrimination provisions of the Robinson–Patman Act are "directed toward the same goal—the protection of competition—it follows that the *inquiries* under each should be the same."[46] What does not follow, however, is the majority's suggestion that the *standard* for liability should likewise be the same.[47] The majority acknowledged that the Sherman Act's requirement of proof of a dangerous probability of success set a higher "threshold of competitive harm" than the "reasonable probability" standard imposed by the Robinson–Patman Act, but then expressed agreement with language in a Ninth Circuit opinion suggesting that "the analytical standards should be no different" under either statute.[48] Reading a requirement of proof that the defendant's conduct creates a dangerous probability of monopolization as identical to a requirement of proof that the defendant's conduct may have the effect of substantially lessening competition wreaks havoc on the English language. In addition, it ignores the origin of the latter phrase, which Congress specifically added because it thought that the judiciary was misinterpreting the Sherman Act. The dissonance between the standards imposed by the Sherman and Robinson–Patman Acts is particularly stark in light of the fact that another portion of the FTC's opinion adopts a strict and narrow view of

43. 103 F.T.C. 204 (1984).

44. Id. at 367.

45. Id. at 368–69 (Pertschuk, C.).

46. Id. at 367 (emphasis added).

47. Id. In so doing, the majority completely ignored *Utah Pie*. As noted above, that decision may not deserve a great deal of reverence, but one would think that an administrative agency would at least discuss the leading Supreme Court decision in the area.

48. Id. (citing William Inglis & Sons Baking Co. v. ITT Continental Baking Co., 668 F.2d 1014, 1042 (9th Cir. 1981), cert. denied, 459 U.S. 825 (1982)).

attempted monopolization, requiring proof that the market was capable of being monopolized before any further inquiry can proceed.[49]

In a concurring opinion, Commissioner Patricia Bailey offered a sensible distinction between the Sherman Act's ban on attempted monopolization and the Robinson–Patman Act's prohibition of price discrimination that may have the effect of substantially lessening competition. Complaint counsel (the FTC staff) could prevail on a § 2(a) claim, she reasoned, by showing that the price was set below cost (although Bailey did not define the term), "severely weakened" the victims, and "augmented the predator's market power, albeit not to the very high levels which may be needed" to prove attempted monopolization.[50] Requiring proof of augmented market power is a useful way to determine whether the effect of primary line price discrimination may be to substantially lessen competition.

Nevertheless, like the majority's standard, Bailey's test ignores the other type of price discrimination prohibited by the Robinson–Patman Act—that which "injures competition with" the defendant. As is clear from the Robinson–Patman Act's background, selective predation that significantly injures or destroys the ability of even a single rival to compete violates the Act. To be sure, the law must distinguish price cuts that injure *competition with* the defendant from those that simply injure *competitors of* the defendant. The injury must affect the victim's ability to fairly compete on the merits. As is true in cases analyzing predation claims brought under the Sherman Act, evidence of both the defendant's profits (the price/cost ratio) and its intent are relevant to making this distinction, and the defendant's lack of market power, both generally and vis-a-vis the victim, may be a pertinent factor as well. But interpreting the law to require proof that the defendant possessed market power is contrary to the clear congressional judgment to impose a prophylactic standard to prevent predation.

Taking the reaction to *Utah Pie* one step further, the Fifth Circuit's decision in *International Air Industries, Inc. v. American Excelsior Co.*[51] renders the Robinson–Patman Act null and void as applied to primary line discrimination. Distinguishing *Utah Pie* in name only, the court sustained a jury verdict for the defendant, a powerful, entrenched firm that reacted to new entry in El Paso, Texas by selectively cutting prices in that city. The result reached by the Fifth Circuit was correct: the defendant should

---

49. Id. at 346–47.

50. Id. at 372.

51. 517 F.2d 714 (5th Cir. 1975), cert. denied, 424 U.S. 943 (1976).

have prevailed because the plaintiff matched each of the defendant's price cuts with its own, the dollar volume of the plaintiff's sales continued to increase during the period of discrimination, and the defendant's market share continued to decline. Thus, a jury could have concluded that there was neither a lessening of competition nor an injury to competition between the plaintiff and the defendant. However, in sustaining the verdict, the court held that, regardless of competitive effect, a discriminatory price charged by an entrenched firm does not violate the Robinson–Patman Act unless the lower price is below average variable cost. Thus, the court essentially adopted the predatory pricing test Areeda–Turner developed for monopolization and attempted monopolization cases,[52] and applied it to price discrimination.[53]

Like the Commission's decision in *General Foods*, the Fifth Circuit's ruling in *International Air* erroneously jumped from the proposition that "the basic substantive issues raised by the two statutes ... are identical"[54] to the conclusion that the standards for liability are also the same. In so doing, they were guided by Professors Areeda and Turner, who make the remarkable claim that their bright-line rule for predatory pricing (any price above variable cost is legal, any price below variable cost is illegal) can accurately determine whether or not a given pricing scheme has a tendency to lessen competition.[55] On the contrary, Areeda and Turner cannot extricate their test for monopolization from their premise that predation can rarely be employed successfully to monopolize, and thus a legal standard should err on the side of underinclusion by prohibiting only the clearest forms of misconduct. Congress' fear that the courts would be attracted to antitrust theories—like Areeda and Turner's—that are sanguine about the market's ability to remain competitive and skeptical about the likelihood of predatory conduct is precisely what motivated the adoption of a prophylactic standard in § 2(a).[56]

---

52. This test is discussed in Chapter 3, section D(3).

53. To be precise, the court said that a plaintiff can prevail on proof that the defendant's price is "below its short-run, profit-maximizing price" and barriers to entry are "extremely high." Id. at 724–5 & n.31. In a statement remarkable for its disdain for the policies underlying the Robinson–Patman Act, the court concluded that "we see no social utility in insuring the survival of inefficient firms where a new entry is possible." Id. at 725 n.31. Although the text of the opinion suggested that plaintiffs must satisfy the Areeda–Turner test only in order to

prevail "as a matter of law" (recall that the jury had ruled for the defendant in *International Air*), a footnote made it clear that this test applied to the "requisite elements of a prima facie Robinson–Patman case." Id. at 724 n.30.

54. Id. at 720 n.10.

55. Id. (citing Phillip Areeda & Donald Turner, Predatory Practices Under Section 2 of the Sherman Act, 88 Harv. L. Rev. 697, 727 (1975)).

56. Areeda and Turner argue that Congress intended the Robinson–Patman Act's prophylaxis to apply only to secondary-line discrimination cases. 88 Harv. L. Rev. at 727. While it is true

In limiting its inquiry into primary line injury to predation, and then defining that term narrowly, *International Air* revealed its hostility to the language and purpose of the Robinson–Patman Act. "By 'predatory' we mean that [the defendant] must have at least sacrificed present revenues for the purpose of driving [the plaintiff] out of the market" with hopes of later recoupment, the court said.[57] Although this definition may be suitable in Sherman Act litigation, the problem with applying it in this context is that the Robinson–Patman Act specifically bars pricing that has the effect not only of "destroying" competition with the discriminator, but also of "injuring" competition with the discriminator.[58] Thus, *International Air* used judicial fiat to exempt a discriminatory pricing strategy designed to significantly weaken the victim's ability to compete on the merits, even if the scheme fell within the literal scope of the Act's prohibitions. Moreover, the court's focus on the costs incurred by the defendant, rather than by the plaintiff, illustrates again how the court conflated the Act's lessening of competition standard with its injury to competition standard.[59] Although the court correctly found that the plaintiff was not injured, this conclusion was based on the *plaintiff's* ability to match the defendant's discount and the *plaintiff's* increased sales: an inquiry into the defendant's price was unnecessary. In adopting the Areeda–Turner test, the court strayed far from Congress' goal of ensuring that a discriminatory price would not have a disciplinary effect and totally ignored the Robinson–Patman Act's heightened concern that individual competitors might be eliminated one at a time.

that this was the primary focus of the entire statute, they provide no support for their suggestion that it was the exclusive purpose of the legislation. Nor is there any indication in the legislative history that Congress' concerns about a hostile judiciary and the need for a prophylactic statute did not apply to primary line discrimination. As the Supreme Court noted in FTC v. Anheuser-Busch, Inc., 363 U.S. 536, 549 (1960), the Robinson–Patman Act was intended to extend the price discrimination provisions of the Clayton Act, not solely to focus on secondary line discrimination.

In rejecting the argument that the prohibition on competition-lessening price discrimination contained in the original Clayton Act imposes a stricter standard than that applied under the Sherman Act, Areeda and Turner ironically dismiss the intent of the Clayton Act's authors, "given that no one knew what the Sherman Act rule on predatory pricing was or would come to be and that Congress may well have been operating on pessimistic assumptions." 88 Harv. L. Rev. at 727. It is difficult to imagine that even the most pessimistic legislator could have feared a judicial interpretation more damaging to aggressive antitrust enforcement than the Areeda–Turner test.

57. 517 F.2d at 723.

58. Section 2(a) makes it unlawful "to discriminate in price between purchasers of commodities of like grade and quality ... where the effect of such discrimination may be ... to injure, destroy, or prevent competition with" the person who grants the discrimination.

59. Id. at 724–25.

As noted in section A, one of the reasons for the controversy surrounding the Robinson–Patman Act is that banning selective price cutting tends to facilitate oligopoly pricing. This aspect of the Act may well justify its repeal. But merging the standards imposed by § 2 of the Sherman Act with those applied under § 2(a) of the Robinson–Patman Act represents an effort by some judges, impatient for Congress to act, to rectify this problem on their own. This is impatience well illustrated by *Pacific Engineering & Production Co. v. Kerr–McGee Corp.*[60] As discussed in Chapter 3, the Tenth Circuit properly concluded that the defendant's aggressive pricing practices did not violate the Sherman Act because prices were set above variable costs and the industry was plagued by excess capacity and declining demand. The court likewise found no violation of the Robinson–Patman Act, reasoning that the Sherman and Robinson–Patman Acts should be interpreted identically, even though the trial judge had found that charging high prices to some buyers gave the defendant an advantage that enabled it to undercut the plaintiff's prices. The appeals court recognized that its interpretation led "to the somewhat untoward result that the larger of two competitors will survive while the smaller may expire," and also acknowledged that the "Robinson–Patman Act was intended to provide small businesses with protection from abuses by large, powerful business". Nevertheless, the court held that "legitimate price competition" is not such an abuse; moreover, the "fact that [the defendant] was charging higher prices in another submarket does not change its legitimate competition into an injury to competition." [61] Here the court simply misreads § 2(a). Congress could not have more clearly expressed its belief that selective price differences do *not* constitute "legitimate price competition" where their effect is to injure or destroy a rival's competitive ability.[62] *Pacific Engineer-*

60. 551 F.2d 790 (10th Cir. 1977). The Sherman Act aspects of the case are detailed in Chapter 3, section D(3).

61. Id. at 798–99.

62. See William Stevens, Unfair Competition, 29 Pol. Sci. Q. 282 (1914). This article was cited extensively in the 1914 debates on the Clayton Act. Louis Schwartz, John Flynn & Harry First, Antitrust 130 n.144 (6th ed. 1983). In supporting the original price discrimination provisions contained in the Clayton Act, Stevens condemned the trusts' use of price cutting as a means for lessening competition. The specific behavior he wanted to ban was pricing "to a point below the cost of production in one or more of the localities where competition exists." Stevens recognized that the Act would prohibit a large trust from cutting prices even where it was losing business in a particular locale to an efficient smaller rival and where the price cuts were not necessarily below cost. Nevertheless, Stevens argued, if a price decrease is "allowed under extenuating circumstances like those supposed above, there is not and cannot be any guarantee that it will not be employed for other purposes, among which is chief would be to destroy all competition. In the above illustration the only method by which the trust should be permitted to regain the business lost to [its smaller rival] is by a general instead of a local price-cut." Stevens, supra, at 284–86.

ing may reflect sound policy, but it is bad law.[63]

(6) A possible synthesis.

As the Ninth Circuit explained in *William Inglis & Sons Baking Co. v. ITT Continental Baking Co*, "the distinction between vigorous, but honest, price competition and predatory assaults on the competitive process is just as important" in price discrimination litigation as in suits brought under the Sherman Act.[64] As discussed in Chapter 3, section D(2), the case involved allegations that Inglis had been driven from the private-label bread market by Continental's low prices, which were allegedly predatory (in violation of § 2 of the Sherman Act) and discriminatory (in violation of § 2(a) of the Robinson–Patman Act). If the standard for monopolization under the Sherman Act attempted to precisely differentiate between honest competition and efforts to injure a rival's continued ability to compete, the need for different tests is less crucial than if the Sherman Act standard is, per Areeda and Turner, a deliberately underinclusive one reflecting a prediction about the rarity of predation. But in establishing that similar principles applied to both Acts, *Inglis* did not adopt broad presumptions in favor of defendants' conduct, such as requiring proof of significant barriers to entry or prices above average variable cost. Indeed, the Ninth Circuit reversed the district court's grant of judgment n.o.v. to the defendant on both the monopolization and price discrimination counts, finding error in the trial judge's refusal to permit the plaintiff to present evidence of injury because the defendant's lower price was still above average variable cost. Although, in explaining its decision, the court rejected "a complete substantive synchronization of the Sherman and Robinson–Patman Acts," [65] it did not identify the remaining differences between the two standards.

---

63. In light of the Supreme Court's holding in *Utah Pie*, it is also an inappropriate decision coming from an inferior court. As Judge Frank Easterbrook wrote in A.A. Poultry Farms, Inc. v. Rose Acre Farms, Inc., 881 F.2d 1396, 1404–06 (7th Cir. 1989), "[s]cholars have cogently argued that *Utah Pie* employed the Robinson–Patman Act to condemn the process by which competition creeps into oligopolistic markets and undercuts excessive prices," and "[n]ary a voice has been heard in support of *Utah Pie* in years," but the Supreme Court has yet to revisit the case. "No case since *Utah Pie* questions its *holding*, as opposed to its outlook," Easterbrook noted, and therefore the lower courts, "in order to provide equal justice under law, must apply the holdings of cases still on the books." In short, "a belief that the Court would not reach the same decision today if the question were open anew is not a basis for disregarding the law on the books." Judge Easterbrook concluded that under the Robinson–Patman Act, unlike the Sherman Act, proof of pricing below average total cost combined with an intent to injure a competitor suffices to show injury. (Nonetheless, *Rose Acre* found no § 2(a) violation because the eggs sold at allegedly discriminatory prices were not of "like grade and quality." See section A(4), above.)

64. 668 F.2d 1014, 1042 (9th Cir. 1981), cert. denied, 459 U.S. 825 (1982).

65. Id.

While *Inglis* made a serious effort to synthesize a coherent standard for primary line violations of § 2(a), one portion of the Ninth Circuit's standard is particularly opaque. The court acknowledged that the competitive injury proscribed under § 2 of the Sherman Act is quite different from that prohibited by § 2(a) of Robinson–Patman because the latter requires only a showing of "an impermissible effect on competition by others with the defendant." Despite this recognition, the court wrote two paragraphs earlier that "the mere fact that Inglis suffered losses and eventually ceased operations is not sufficient to establish a section 2(a) Robinson–Patman Act violation."[66] Without elaboration, the court suggested that the plaintiff had failed to present evidence sufficient to sustain the jury's verdict on the Robinson–Patman claim, thus necessitating a new trial.[67] And when, on retrial, the jury again found Continental liable to Inglis on both the attempted monopolization and price discrimination counts, the Ninth Circuit reversed and directed judgment n.o.v. for the defendants.[68] The court held that Inglis' had failed to meet its burden of proof under § 2(a). The court wrote that:

> Inglis needed to prove that Continental "discriminate[d] in price between different purchasers of [bread] of like grade and quality" and that this difference may have tended "to lessen competition ..." 15 U.S.C. § 13(a) ... [69]

Significantly, the court's quotation omits a key portion of § 2(a), which prohibits price discrimination where the effect may be to "injure, destroy, or prevent competition with any person who ... grants ... such discrimination." In order to establish primary line injury, a plaintiff should not have to show more than the existence of discrimination and evidence that the discrimination caused an injury to the plaintiff's ability to compete with the defendant, because of either a financial crippling of the plaintiff, increased concentration of business among larger sellers, or a significant reduction in the number of sellers in the market.[70]

Perhaps the court was merely saying that Inglis did not present sufficient evidence of a causal link between the discrimination and its injury.[71] Evidence of causation would, of course,

---

66. Id.

67. Id.

68. 942 F.2d 1332 (9th Cir.1991), rehearing granted in part on other grounds, 970 F.2d 639 (9th Cir.1992). The court sustained, with slight modification, the jury's verdict for Inglis on a pendent claim for violating the California Unfair Practices Act, Cal. Bus. & Prof. Code §§ 17000–01.

69. Id. at 1337 (ellipses and brackets in original).

70. Cf. Dean Milk Co., 68 F.T.C. at 750, discussed in subsection (3) above.

71. The court noted that the only pieces of evidence supporting the federal antitrust claims were a price/cost study and some evidence of malice. The court found the study to be methodologically flawed, and the intent evi-

have to establish not only that Inglis was hurt by Continental's low prices, but also that Continental's sales elsewhere at higher prices facilitated Inglis' demise. Alternatively, the court may have incorrectly believed that proof that price discrimination caused the elimination of particular rivals is insufficient to establish a primary line violation under § 2(a).[72]

Meanwhile, the FTC and other circuits have adopted this erroneous interpretation of § 2(a). In doing so, they seem concerned primarily with avoiding rules that might possibly chill some legitimate conduct, even at the expense of permitting some predatory conduct. The propriety of applying such a standard under the Sherman Act is debatable, but it is a perversion of the Robinson–Patman Act to apply it to that statute.

(7) Causation.

Although the courts are divided as to what effect must be shown in a primary line case, it is clear that the defendant's differential pricing must cause the lessening of, or injury to, competition. This point was demonstrated by the Fifth Circuit's sensible analysis in *Borden Co. v. FTC*.[73] In that case, seven midwestern canners sold private label milk on a local basis without advertising. Borden, which sold its well-known branded milk at higher prices, took advantage of the location of its plants in Tennessee and South Carolina to sell private label milk at lower prices in those areas. The FTC found this price discrimination illegal, but the Fifth Circuit reversed.[74] First, the court explained,

---

dence insufficient to establish either attempted monopolization or an effect proscribed under the Robinson–Patman Act. 942 F.2d at 1336–37.

In a parallel proceeding before the FTC challenging Continental's pricing practices, the Commission cited *Inglis* with approval and noted that "there is little evidence to the effect that these exits [by victims of discrimination like Inglis] were occasioned by Continental's behavior, rather than by poor management, inefficiency, an overall reduction in the demand for white bread, or other unfortunate but nevertheless perfectly competitive explanations." *International Telephone & Telegraph Corp. (Continental Baking)*, 104 F.T.C. 280, 424 (1984).

72. The FTC reached this precise, albeit erroneous, conclusion in *IT&T (Continental Baking)*. Consistent with *International Air* and *General Foods*, the Commission wrote:

Moreover, even if the exit of one or more of these bakers could be attributed to the conduct of Continental, that would not be sufficient to establish the requisite injury to competition unless Continental's behavior could be characterized as predatory or otherwise anticompetitive. Vigorous, legitimate competition forces less efficient firms to exit constantly; that in fact is a frequent consequence of vigorous competition.

Id. This conclusion completely ignores the congressional determination that selective, discriminatory price reductions *are* anticompetitive where they injure the ability of victims to compete with the defendant, and that this type of discrimination is *not* "legitimate."

73. 381 F.2d 175 (5th Cir. 1967).

74. In a prior opinion, the Supreme Court held that Borden's branded and private label milk was of "like grade

Borden's rivals in the two areas "experienced an increase in absolute sales volume and have bettered their market position in approximately the same proportion as has Borden." [75] This fact certainly would make one wonder how Borden's price discrimination could have either lessened competition or injured competition between Borden and its rivals.[76] Second, the court noted that any injury was caused by the price difference between Borden's private label milk and its rivals' private label milk. The price differential between the branded milk and the private label milk sold by Borden was immaterial to the case because, as the court concluded, it simply reflected consumer perception that the former was a superior product. Therefore, this was simply not a case where the defendant's selective price cutting injured its rivals.[77]

Hopefully, readers of this treatise will agree that it is not a polemic, and that it often gives praise to sensible decisions, like *Borden*. With that exception, though, can we say that the primary line cases are really that egregious? Yes.

Section C: Secondary Line Injury

The principal evil Congress sought to remedy by passing the Robinson–Patman Act was the perceived victimization of small firms that paid more for identical goods than their larger, chain store rivals. This phenomenon is known as "secondary line" injury—when a seller's price differential reduces the ability of "disfavored" buyers to compete with "favored" rivals who received discounts.

(1) *Morton Salt*: virtual per se illegality.

FTC v. Morton Salt Co.[1] is the landmark case setting out the requirements for establishing a prima facie secondary line case. Morton sold its finest brand of table salt under a "standard quantity discount system." All purchasers paid a delivered price

and quality." 383 U.S. 637 (1966). See section A(4).

75. 381 F.2d at 179 (footnotes omitted).

76. Persuasive indicia that, absent the price discrimination, Borden would not have kept pace with its "victims" might provide a basis for inferring causation, but there was no suggestion that Borden's rivals were more efficient, offered a superior product, or gave any other plausible reason why they should have gained market share at Borden's expense during the relevant time period.

77. Id. at 180–81.

1. 334 U.S. 37 (1948).

(i.e., Morton paid for transportation) [2] based on the quantity purchased: orders that did not fill one railroad car were sold for $1.60 per case, and the price then gradually decreased for larger quantities, and purchases of 50,000 cases within a 12–month period priced at $1.35 per case. Only five companies bought sufficient amounts to get this lowest discount. The FTC held that Morton's system illegally discriminated between large grocery store purchasers and smaller retailers.

Initially, the Court rejected Morton's contention that the scheme was lawful because the quantity discount was available to all. While "[t]heoretically, these discounts are equally available to all," the Court reasoned, "functionally they are not." [3] This conclusion is compelled by a review of the statute's history. As the Court noted, this history "makes it abundantly clear that Congress considered it to be an evil that a large buyer could secure a competitive advantage over a small buyer solely because of the large buyer's quantity purchasing ability." [4] Given the cost justification defense provided in the statute (discussed below in section E), Congress clearly believed that a large buyer's increased "purchasing ability" reflected market power, not real cost savings. Moreover, the Robinson–Patman Act repealed the provision in the original version of § 2 of the Clayton Act that allowed quantity discounts. This legislative intent would have been eviscerated had Morton's contention been accepted.

Relying on the statute's background and structure, the Court also rejected two other arguments that would have allowed Morton to evade the Act's prohibition on price discrimination. First, Morton argued that purchases of carload lots provided such an obvious savings that these orders should not be compared to smaller ones. The Court noted that the statute provides a specific defense for cost-based differentials; savings were therefore irrelevant to the question whether the prima facie case was established. [5] A cost-justified price differential affects rivals in the same way—loss of business, inability to compete, etc.—as one that is not based on costs, even though the former may be lawful and economically desirable for society as a whole. Second, citing the Congress' clear intent that the Act serve as a prophylactic, the

2. An economist would say that the delivered price system itself was discriminatory. A buyer located within 10 miles of Morton's factory paid the same price as a buyer 1000 miles away, even though Morton paid far less to deliver to the first buyer. Thus, Morton was engaged in price discrimination from an economic point of view because its price/cost ratio differed between the two buyers. But because the Robinson–Patman Act prohibits only price *differences*, this sort of pricing does not violate the Act. See section A(6).

3. Id. at 42.

4. Id. at 43.

5. Id. at 48.

Court rejected the argument that salt is such a small item in grocery stores that Morton's particular discrimination could not really have any significant effect on the competitiveness of smaller grocers.

The Court reached this conclusion even though there was no evidence that Morton's scheme posed any serious threat to rivalry in the highly competitive retail grocery industry. Thus, the scheme could not have had "the effect of substantially lessening competition." However, § 2(a) also proscribes discrimination where the effect may be to "injure, destroy, or prevent competition with any person who ... knowingly receives the benefit of such discrimination." The precedential value of *Morton Salt* lies in the Court's interpretation of this key phrase.

The Court held that the "injury to competition" standard could be met simply by showing that disfavored buyers had to pay more than their rivals. The opinion declared: "Here the Commission found what would appear to be obvious, that the competitive opportunities of certain merchants were injured when they had to pay respondent substantially more for their goods than their competitors had to pay." [6] The Court added that the purpose of the Robinson–Patman Act is to permit "a finding of injury to competition by a showing of 'injury to the competitor victimized by the discrimination.' " [7]

By allowing plaintiffs to prove an "injury to competition with" the favored buyer simply by showing that they paid more, *Morton Salt* read *any* competitive effect test out of the Act and suggested that price differentials are per se illegal under § 2(a). Although the underlying goals of the Act were clearly Jeffersonian, its purpose was not simply to protect small business for its own sake, but to promote an equal opportunity for large and small firms to compete. Were protection of small business the sole purpose of the Act, Congress would not have included a cost justification defense, and it would have required a showing of "injury to a competitor" rather than "injury to competition with" the favored buyer. A more sensible interpretation of the injury to competition

---

6. 334 U.S. at 46–47.

The Court assumed that retail grocers that bought salt in less-than-carload lots were in competition with large supermarket chains buying in excess of 50,000 cases annually. Today, that assumption would be more questionable; mark-ups are consistently higher at smaller stores that continue to thrive because consumers are willing to pay higher prices for the convenience of purchasing a limited number of items at their neighborhood store. Thus, it is certainly not "obvious," even as a prophylactic matter, that the inability of high-priced convenience stores to obtain quantity discounts injures their ability to compete in the marketplace. See the discussion of United States v. Von's Grocery Co., 384 U.S. 270 (1966) in Chapter 6, section A(8).

7. 334 U.S. at 49 (quoting S. Rep. No. 1502, 74th Cong., 2d Sess. 4 (1936)).

standard in § 2(a) would be to require some showing that the discrimination, unless "nipped in the bud," would actually impair the victim's ability to *fairly* compete.

(2) Shifting away from *Morton Salt.*

The Court's broad language was not necessary to prohibit the defendant's pricing scheme. It *was* fair to infer that smaller buyers could not fairly compete with their larger rivals in *Morton Salt* for several reasons. First, the price discrimination was persistent, rather than a temporary reduction. Second, the profit margins in the grocery business are so small that virtually any significant increase in cost will hurt a disfavored buyer's ability to compete. Although the Court's language does not suggest that these facts were critical to its decision, the breadth of *Morton Salt* has been eroded by lower court opinions. These opinions have limited the *Morton Salt*'s inference of injury from the mere payment of a higher price to pricing practices that resemble the scheme at issue in *Morton Salt.*

For example, in *American Oil Co. v. FTC,*[8] the petitioner granted special discounts to its dealers in Smyrna, Georgia, a suburb of Atlanta, in response to a price war in that town, but did not grant similar discounts to dealers in neighboring Marietta. Because the FTC concluded that local motorists had ready access to gas stations in both towns, it found a violation of § 2(a). The Seventh Circuit reversed. Even after *Morton Salt*, the court held, the injury to competition test required "something more than an essentially temporary minimal impact on competition." Instead, "probative analysis must reveal a causal relation" between the price differential and the victim's injury.[9]

This causation requirement is easily met in highly competitive industries, like the gas station and grocery businesses, because increasing the wholesale price to some retailers will necessarily be reflected in differentials in the retail price. This is not true, of course, for all industries. *Minneapolis–Honeywell Regulator Co. v. FTC*[10] illustrates the point. The petitioner there had engaged in price discrimination in selling its temperature controls to oil burner manufacturers. However, there was no evidence to suggest that the higher price the disfavored buyer paid for this component increased the price of oil burners. Indeed, the record

---

8. 325 F.2d 101 (7th Cir. 1963), cert. denied, 377 U.S. 954 (1964).

9. Id. at 106. The FTC unsuccessfully sought certiorari, arguing that *Morton Salt* did not require the Commission to consider whether there had even been any diversion of business away from the disfavored dealers. Milton Handler, Harlan Blake, Robert Pitofsky & Harvey Goldschmid, Trade Regulation 1193 (3d ed. 1990).

10. 191 F.2d 786 (7th Cir. 1951), appeal dism'd, 344 U.S. 206 (1952).

showed that the least expensive oil burner was sold by a relatively disfavored buyer, while the most favored buyer sold its burners at the highest mark-up. These facts suggest that oil burner manufacturers had some significant pricing discretion, thus, there was no strong causal link between the price of temperature controls and an ability to compete in the oil burner market.

These cases elaborating on *Morton Salt* have improved the law by suggesting that injury to competition cannot be inferred when price discrimination is temporary or sporadic, when the victim does not simply resell the commodity in question but uses it as an input in making a finished product, or when the secondary line market is not competitive and the favored and disfavored buyers each exercise discretion in pricing their products.[11] Put more positively, injury to competition can properly be inferred when price discrimination is persistent, the commodity is resold in similar form, and the secondary line market is highly competitive—i.e., in cases like *Morton Salt*.[12]

(3) *Boise Cascade*: refuting or eviscerating *Morton Salt*?

In *Boise Cascade Corp. v. FTC*,[13] one of the nation's leading wholesalers in the office products industry received discounts of 5–33% from the manufacturers of those products. Although the discounts were ostensibly given in return for wholesaling services

---

11. The causal nexus between discrimination and secondary line injury is also broken by evidence that the disfavored buyer could have purchased the goods at a lower rate, but failed to take advantage of its opportunity to do so. For example, in Tri–Valley Packing Ass'n v. FTC, 329 F.2d 694, 703–04 (9th Cir. 1964), the court remanded an FTC finding of competitive injury for further consideration, because anyone could have obtained Tri–Valley's lowest prices at a marketplace in San Francisco. The court noted that a Denver wholesaler/retailer who appeared to be a disfavored buyer in at least one instance, had, on other occasions, bought at the lower San Francisco price.

12. The permissibility of this inference was reaffirmed by the Supreme Court in Falls City Industries, Inc. v. Vanco Beverage, Inc., 460 U.S. 428, 436–37 (1983). Falls City, found liable for selling its beer at higher prices in southern Indiana than in neighboring northern Kentucky, argued that *Morton Salt* should apply only in cases where

large buyers were preferred or where the seller engaged in predatory behavior. The Court rejected the argument, noting that the Act, although motivated by concerns about the power of large buyers, is of general applicability and that the *Morton Salt* inference made economic sense. In *Falls City*, the beer was sold at higher prices in Indiana for a substantial period of time, it was resold in identical form by wholesalers to retail liquor stores that faced significant competition, and thus it was appropriate to infer that the Indiana retailers' loss in sales was due to the price differential. *Falls City* reversed judgment for the plaintiff, however, because the defendant satisfied the meeting competition defense. This aspect of the case is discussed in section F(4), below.

Applying the *Morton Salt* inference to price differences between buyers at one level of distribution (e.g., wholesalers) and buyers at another level (e.g. retailers) is considered below in section D's discussion at functional discounts.

13. 837 F.2d 1127 (D.C. Cir. 1988).

Boise performed for the manufacturers, the FTC found a Robin-son–Patman violation because, unlike many other wholesalers, Boise often by-passed intermediate dealers and sold directly to retailers as well, and the discounts applied both to the products Boise resold as a wholesaler and to the items it sold directly to retailers. Relying on *Morton Salt*, the FTC inferred that persistent price differentials of this magnitude injured competition between Boise and non-integrated dealers. The inference was based on the ALJ's finding that the office products industry was intensely competitive (like supermarkets), that the disfavored dealers sold on a low margin (like small grocery stores), and that this margin (3–4%) was much less than the discount received by Boise.

The D.C. Circuit reversed the FTC's order, however, finding that the Commission had inadequately responded to Boise's claim that its discrimination caused no injury. The opinion's discussion of the legality of functional discounts—discounts given to wholesalers in return for performing the wholesaling function—is analyzed below in section D; *Boise Cascade*'s significance extends beyond the question of functional discounts for integrated wholesaler/dealers, however, because of the court's criticism of the FTC's traditional reliance on the *Morton Salt* inference.

Each judge on the appellate panel wrote separately, with Judges Kenneth Starr and Stephen Williams agreeing to remand the case back to the FTC. Boise defended its discount before the Commission by introducing evidence showing that its dealer rivals' sales had increased, that these alleged "victims" of price discrimination had realized a 22% profit margin, that Boise had taken certain customers from the victims but had lost others to them, and that the discount had existed for a long period of time without any noticeable affect on competition in the industry as a whole or on the ability of small, non-integrated firms to compete. Although the evidence did not conclusively prove innocence, Judge Starr thought that the FTC had the burden of explaining a theory of competitive harm in light of these facts.[14]

Dissenting, Judge Abner Mikva argued that evidence of sustained rivalry in an industry is insufficient to rebut *Morton Salt*'s inference,[15] and that § 2(a) reflects Congress' determination that "price discrimination between competing buyers tended by its very nature to injure competition."[16] Taken literally, these comments might suggest that Mikva, like the majority in *Utah Pie*, read the effects clause out of the statute. Why would Congress require a showing of injury to competition among rivals if injury is inherent

14. Id. at 1146 n.16.   16. Id. at 1153.
15. 837 F.2d at 1152.

in discrimination? Read in context, though, Mikva may simply have been responding to his colleagues' emphasis on continued vigor in the marketplace, for in the next sentence of his opinion he wrote that the Act should not be read to require "every court to establish the likelihood of marketplace injury," as opposed to injury to disfavored buyers' competitive ability of unlawful price discrimination.[17]

In a way, both judges were correct. Judge Mikva is surely right that continued vigor of the industry does not immunize price discrimination from illegality under § 2(a). Even the majority seemed to agree with the Commission that *Morton Salt* "could be overcome by a showing that market conditions unrelated to the price discrimination explained the lost accounts or shifted sales" or the disfavored rivals' lost profits or market share.[18] But language in the majority opinion suggested not only that the *Morton Salt* inference could be overcome by evidence explaining the lack of a causal connection between the price differential and injury,[19] but also that "[s]pecific, substantial evidence of absence of competitive injury [is] sufficient to rebut what is, after all, only an inference."[20] However, one of *Morton Salt*'s key holdings was that the defendant's price discrimination had injured competition between large supermarket chains and their smaller rivals even though there was *no* evidence of competitive harm to the smaller grocery stores. Nevertheless, Judge Starr may be correct that the FTC needed to explain why small non-integrated firms had not been affected notwithstanding the long-standing discriminatory pricing. It may well be that a § 2(a) challenge to the discounts would have been successful at their inception, given the prophylactic purposes of § 2(a), but that we can more safely say that prophylaxis is unnecessary when long-standing price differentials have not resulted in unequal treatment of smaller retailers.

Reading its instructions on remand quite narrowly, the Commission issued an opinion that responded to some of the D.C. Circuit's concerns and then adopted a four-part standard more faithful to *Morton Salt* than to the law of the case.[21] The FTC held that a § 2(a) violation could be found based on evidence of substantial, sustained price discrimination that led Boise *either* (1)

17. Judge Stephen Williams joined Judge Starr's opinion but added a concurrence, explaining why the nature of the functional discount offered by office furniture makers to Boise was probably lawful. This opinion is discussed below in section D(3).

18. Id. at 1137.

19. For two excellent examples of this analysis, see Commissioner Elman's dissent and the Seventh Circuit's opinion in *Dean Milk Co.*, 69 F.T.C. 710, 795, (1965), rev'd in pertinent part, 395 F.2d 696, 708–14 (7th Cir. 1968). *Dean Milk* is discussed in section A(6).

20. 837 F.2d at 1144 (italics deleted).

21. 5 Trade Reg. Rep. (CCH) ¶ 22,902 (1990).

to charge lower prices; (2) to provide more services; or (3) to enjoy higher profit margins than its retail rivals. The Commission reasoned that higher profit margins injured competition between Boise and its retail rivals because they gave Boise a superior ability to make capital expenditures and to weather business cycles.[22] If, for example, Boise could have shown that, even as to goods it sold directly to retailers, the cost of performing the wholesale function equaled the discount, this would rebut a claim that the discount caused lower prices, more services, or higher profits. Similarly, evidence to support Judge Williams' arbitrage theory (discussed below in section D(3)) would mean that Boise's rivals could match Boise's prices, services, and profits.

Writing for a two-member majority (with two members not participating), Commissioner Terry Calvani explained why none of the concerns raised by the D.C. Circuit altered the inference of competitive injury. Evidence that the disfavored buyers gained comfortable gross profits was irrelevant because of the numerous products they sold; such data said nothing about their ability to compete with Boise Cascade in the furniture market in question.[23] The mere fact that Boise Cascade lost some accounts to the disfavored buyers, while taking other buyers from them, was also insufficient, absent specific evidence explaining to why Boise's customers shifted to the disfavored buyers.[24] Finally, although "the longer a price difference prevails without visible manifestation of competitive injury, the less likely such injury is to occur in the future," in this case the disfavored buyers experienced "dragging down" in that they in earned lower net profits than Boise.[25] Unfortunately, in light of the controversial and divided nature of the opinions in this case, the litigation was settled prior to further review by the D.C. Circuit.[26]

Perhaps the best analytical approach to *Boise Cascade* was ignored by both the D.C. Circuit majority and the FTC. In light of

22. Id. at 22,585 & n.32.

23. Id. at 22,588–89.

24. Id. at 22,591–93. The D.C. Circuit noted the testimony of one witness that shifts of patronage were due to the identity of salespeople, not the amount of a discount. If true, this evidence would seem to rebut *Morton Salt*'s inference. See 837 F.2d at 1136.

25. 5 Trade Reg. Rep. at 22,596. Commissioner Mary Azcuenaga concurred separately, finding that the evidence Boise Cascade relied on did not actually support its contentions. Unfortunately, her opinion cannot be analyzed because, in a virtually unprecedented procedure for a major case, significant and critical parts of it were redacted. See id. at 22,601–03. Normally, government agencies keep sensitive business information confidential *unless* its use is necessary for an enforcement investigation. There is no explanation for redacting a 1991 discussion concerning the growth in Boise's direct sales during 1977–79 other than as an effort to discredit the concurrence or to avoid public embarrassment for Boise's position.

26. 5 Trade Reg. Rep. (CCH) ¶ 23,013 (1991).

evidence that Boise's discount was persistent and exceeded the victims' profit margin, how could the discrimination *not* have caused injury? *Morton Salt* clearly holds that the defendant cannot simply refuse to answer this question and instead insist that somehow rivalry remains vigorous in the marketplace. Absent a satisfactory answer, the FTC was entitled to infer injury.

Judge Stephen Williams, who concurred in *Boise Cascade*, may have given one possible answer to this question. As explained in more detail in section D(3) below, Judge Williams suggested that the market may have bid down the wholesale price to such a level that Boise's dealer rivals were able to obtain goods at the same effective cost as that paid by Boise. The FTC should have been required to reject plausible explanations, like Williams', explaining how persistent discrimination could continue without injury. Absent some explanation like that offered by Judge Williams, though, the courts impose an undue burden on Robinson–Patman enforcement if they ask the FTC or private plaintiffs to show more than *Morton Salt* requires.

(4) More remote effects.[27]

The Robinson–Patman Act applies to price discrimination that unfairly injures not only the seller's rivals (primary line) and the seller's disfavored purchasers (secondary line) but also others down the distribution chain (victims at the next level would suffer "tertiary line" discrimination). In *Perkins v. Standard Oil Co. of California*,[28] the defendant unsuccessfully sought to limit the scope of the Act. The defendant (known as Chevron) sold oil directly to Perkins. Chevron sold at a lower price to Signal, which in turn sold to Western Highway, which in turn sold to Regal; Regal competed against Perkins. Chevron argued that the statute did not apply, because § 2(a)'s language concerns only injury to competition "with any person who either grants or knowingly receives the benefit of such discrimination, or with customers of either of them." Thus, Chevron reasoned, the statute applied to itself, Signal, or Western Highway, but not to Regal, with whom Perkins competed.

The Court rejected this argument.[29] Because the injury was the same regardless of the level of distribution, the Court declined

---

27. Technically, this subsection does not belong with a discussion of secondary line effects. Analysis of tertiary and quadriary effects are included here, however, because of the brevity of the discussion.

28. 395 U.S. 642 (1969).

29. Although Justices Marshall and Stewart rejected the majority's reasoning, they concurred based on their conclusion that a secondary line violation occurred because Signal owned a majority of Western Highway stock and Western Highway owned a majority of Regal stock. Id. at 650–51.

to place an "artificial limitation" [30] on the scope of the Act. This holding is sensible. A contrary result would have made it easy to evade the statute simply by creating additional levels of distribution. Moreover, the statutory language is consistent with a finding of liability. Western Highway and Regal both "knowingly receive[d] the benefit of such discrimination" even though they did not directly purchase from Chevron. The requirement of knowing receipt only effectively preclude suits in cases where, unlike *Perkins*, purchasers further down the chain are truly independent of the initial favored buyer. Moreover, the *Morton Salt* inference of injury would probably not apply in remote effects cases involving independent buyers.[31]

Section D: Functional Discounts

Functional discounts are lower prices a producer offers to certain buyers that assume the burdens of distributing the producer's goods to the marketplace. Distribution functions include warehousing, delivery, and processing orders from small accounts, and identifying and selling to prospective buyers. Where firms are neatly categorized as either manufacturers, wholesalers, or retailers, Robinson–Patman Act problems rarely arise even when a manufacturer charges a wholesaler a lower price than a retailer. In such situations, wholesalers do not compete with retailers, so the discount cannot possibly have the proscribed statutory effect of lessening competition in a "line of commerce" or injuring competition between the recipient of the discount and its rivals. Legal problems frequently arise, however, in "scrambled" distribution systems where some firms operate at both the wholesale and retail level.

Where a wholesaler receives a discount that approximates the cost *savings* to the manufacturer from being spared the expense of getting the product to retailers, the manufacturer may raise the statutory defense for price "differentials which make only due allowance for differences in the cost" of distribution (the so-called "cost justification defense," discussed in section E). By contrast, functional discounts are best conceptualized as discounts that approximate the cost *burden* to wholesalers for the additional expenses they incur it in the distribution process or the *value* of these services to the supplier.[1]

---

30. Id. at 648.

31. See Panel Discussion, 53 Antitrust L.J. 967, 98 (1984) (remarks of James Rill): "I do not know of any cases other than *Perkins*, where there were ties of ownership, where that type of pricing structure has been considered unlawful."

1. When wholesale markets are not competitive, suppliers will be willing to pay (via a larger discount) a sum greater than the wholesaler's cost to get the

(1) *Doubleday* versus *Mueller.*

As soon as some wholesalers began competing against their retail buyers for the patronage of the ultimate consumers, and some retailers found it advantageous to perform the wholesaling function, the FTC began to challenge functional discounts as illegal price discrimination. In *Doubleday & Co.*,[2] the FTC staff presented a straightforward case for illegality: (1) the respondent sold books for ultimate resale to consumers at different prices (reflecting the functional discount to the wholesaler); (2) the favored wholesaler buyer also sold at retail and thus competed with the disfavored retailer buyer; (3) under *Morton Salt*, injury to competition can be inferred when the favored buyer receives a significant and persistent discount;[3] and (4) the respondent could not justify the discount as limited to a "due allowance" reflecting its own costs savings. The Commission rejected this argument, however, because it would "proclaim as a matter of law that the integrated wholesaler cannot possibly perform the wholesaling function.... Where a businessman performs various wholesale functions ... the law should not forbid his supplier from compensating him for service," the FTC reasoned. (Indeed, if an integrated firm incurs expenses for performing wholesaling functions and does *not* receive some discount, *it* is the victim of economic price discrimination.) Borrowing language from the 1955 Attorney General's report, the FTC cautioned, however, that it would "tolerate no subterfuge": "[t]he amount of the discount should be reasonably related to the expenses assumed by the *buyer*," and "should not exceed the cost of that part of the function [the buyer] actually performs...."[4]

The issue arose again in *Mueller Co.*[5] That case involved the sale of waterworks systems, which Mueller sold through "limit" and "regular" jobbers. The former were required to maintain an inventory on various items, while regular jobbers simply acted as intermediaries between Mueller and consumers. Limit jobbers were entitled to an additional 10% discount, which was challenged as discriminatory by the FTC staff. The administrative law judge found that the discount was no greater than necessary to reim-

---

services they desire. A small firm, for example, may find that operating its own warehouse would be prohibitively expensive and therefore would put a higher value on wholesaling services than the costs the wholesaler would incur in providing those services.

2. 52 F.T.C. 169 (1955).

3. See FTC v. Morton Salt Co., 334 U.S. 37 (1948), discussed above in section C(1).

4. 52 F.T.C. at 209 (emphasis added). Cf. Report of the Attorney General's Nat'l Comm. to Study the Antitrust Laws 208 (1955).

5. 60 F.T.C. 120 (1962), aff'd, 323 F.2d 44 (7th Cir. 1963), cert. denied, 377 U.S. 923 (1964).

burse the limit jobbers for the expense of inventory maintenance which otherwise would have been borne by Mueller. Relying on *Doubleday*, he dismissed the complaint.

On appeal by the FTC staff, the Commission rejected *Doubleday* and found that Mueller had priced unlawfully. The FTC decided that the Robinson–Patman Act recognized no defense for functional discounts. If a discount was aimed solely at reimbursing to limit jobbers for functions they otherwise would not have performed, then the regular jobbers were not victimized by the discrimination. A problem arises only when distributional services useful to the seller also redound to the benefit of the limit jobbers. A jobber "who has products of this type on hand is in a more favorable position than the jobber who does not," the FTC reasoned.[6] Rejecting *Doubleday*, a concurring commissioner wrote that it would be impossible to "divide a common service which may benefit both the buyer and the seller."[7]

The key to *Mueller*, noted by the FTC and emphasized by the Seventh Circuit in affirming the FTC order,[8] was not the unfairness of giving limit jobbers a 10% discount relative to regular jobbers, but Mueller's arbitrary determination as to who was allowed to become a limit jobber. Not only did Mueller fail to establish any objective standards in making this decision, but there was evidence that it was influenced by a desire to "protect 'old established jobbers.'"[9] Favoring certain buyers through price discounts not available to others, in a manner that injures the ability of disfavored buyers to compete, falls within the scope of the evil Congress sought to remedy in enacting the Robinson–Patman Act.

(2) Reconciling the precedents.

Doubleday and *Mueller* can be reconciled in a manner consistent with the publicly expressed rationale for the Robinson–Patman Act—rival buyers should have an equal opportunity to compete against each other on the merits. Thus, where (1) the seller grants favored functional status based on objective factors and (2) the functional discount reflects a reasonable reimbursement for expenses, the fact that the favored buyer also benefits from performing the function should not make the discount illegal. On the other hand, where the seller has unfairly singled out certain buyers and bestowed favored treatment upon them, the defendant should then have the burden of showing that this status does not

6. Id. at 129.

7. Id. at 211 (Secrest, C.).

8. See id. at 129–30; 323 F.2d at 46.

9. 323 F.2d at 46.

give the favored buyers a competitive advantage over rivals that
do not perform the same function.

This effort to reconcile the cases would not be consistent,
however, with the separate views expressed in *Mueller* by Commissioner James Mead. He found functional discounts inherently
anticompetitive because they "pave[ ] the way for the ultimate
annihilation of small retail dealers who are unable, by reason of
their inability to perform the same marketing functions as their
larger dual-functioning competitors, to successfully compete with
them." [10] This classic Jeffersonian preference for preserving small
businesses is not necessary to achieve equality of economic opportunity and conflicts with the goals of economic efficiency and
lower prices for consumers. Such arguments have generally been
rejected in interpreting other antitrust laws; because, as noted in
section A, supporters of the Robinson–Patman Act emphasized
benefits to the competitive process and fairness, rather than
protectionism, they should be rejected in this context as well.[11]

The Second Circuit adopted the approach suggested here for
reconciling *Doubleday* and *Mueller* in *FLM Collision Parts, Inc. v.
Ford Motor Co.*[12] At issue there was Ford's policy of offering a
special discount to its franchisees when they acted as wholesalers
in reselling automobile crash parts to independent repair shops,
but not when they sold parts to other wholesalers, such as FLM.
Distinguishing *Morton Salt*, the court found that the lower price
was "available to all purchasers, not only in theory but in fact." [13]
Distinguishing *Mueller*, the court observed that the "gravamen of
the discrimination" in that case was not the 10% differential
between limit and regular jobbers but "rather the fact that eligibility to enter this favored class was only selectively recognized
and not made equally available to all jobbers." [14] Thus, Ford was
not selling goods to different purchasers at different prices.

The Third Circuit followed the Second Circuit's lead in *Ed-*

---

10. 52 F.T.C. at 212 (concurring
opinion).

11. In fact, a broad reading of *Mueller* to condemn functional discounts as
inherently anticompetitive has harmed
many small businesses that have tried
to compete with larger rivals by forming buyers' cooperatives that can perform the wholesale function more efficiently than independent wholesalers.
The FTC has generally invalidated discounts given to these cooperatives,
which seems contrary to Commissioner
Mead's desire to protect small businesses. See Terry Calvani, Functional Dis-

counts and the Robinson–Patman Act,
17 B.C. Ind. & Comm. L. Rev. 543, 554–
55 (1976).

12. 543 F.2d 1019 (2d Cir. 1976),
cert. denied, 429 U.S. 1097 (1977).

13. Id. at 1025. In *Morton Salt*, the
Court struck down a quantity discount
scheme that was formally available to
all but, in reality, allowed huge discounts to only five large buyers. 337
U.S. at 42.

14. 543 F.2d at 1028.

ward J. Sweeney & Sons, Inc. v. Texaco, Inc.[15] In that case, Texaco's price to wholesalers and distributors included the cost of delivering gasoline to the buyer's plant. Distributors like Sweeney that picked up the fuel at Texaco's plant received a discount equal to the lowest amount it would have cost Texaco to deliver the fuel (either by hiring a trucking company or by using its own fleet). The wrinkle in this system, for price discrimination purposes, was that Sweeney could make extra money (i.e., lower its effective price) by picking up gasoline from Texaco and then delivering the gas immediately to service stations located between the Texaco plant and its own (since Texaco would reimbursed Sweeney for the full cost of shipping all the way back to the Sweeney plant).

Sweeney's complaint arose when Texaco exercised its contract right to change the source of supply from a New Jersey plant to one in Pennsylvania. The location of the new plant was such that Sweeney could no longer pocket excessive reimbursements for hauling; Sweeney therefore challenged Texaco's pricing system under § 2(a). The complaint correctly alleged that Texaco effective charged a different net price to different wholesalers: a wholesaler with many service stations located between the Texaco plant and its own effectively paid less than a wholesaler that could not take advantage of this subsidy.

The Third Circuit rejected the complaint, holding as a matter of law that a uniform pricing formula applicable to all customers does not constitute price discrimination under the Act.[16] The court declined to "elevate" an "isolated passage" in the Supreme Court's opinion in *Anheuser–Busch*[17]—which held that "price discrimination" as used in § 2(a) "is merely a price difference"—to an "all-inclusive definition."[18] *Sweeney* followed the Second Circuit's reasoning in *FLM Collision Parts* that the Act "'requires equality of treatment among purchasers, but it does not require a seller to adopt a single uniform price under all circumstances.'"[19] The court emphasized that each dealer had an equal opportunity to obtain the discounts, and that the "record also fails to show that small buyers, whom the act was primarily intended to protect, are disadvantaged by the formula."[20]

The key focus in these cases is on whether the defendants' uniform pricing formula implicate the underlying policy of the

15. 637 F.2d 105 (3d Cir. 1980), cert. denied, 451 U.S. 911 (1981).

16. Id. at 112.

17. FTC v. Anheuser–Busch, Inc., 363 U.S. 536 (1960), discussed in section A(4), above.

18. 637 F.2d at 120.

19. Id. (quoting *FLM Collision Parts*, 543 F.2d at 1026).

20. Id. at 121.

Robinson–Patman Act—to ensure an equal opportunity to compete. Unlike *Morton Salt*'s formally equal (but effectively unequal) pricing scheme, it was clear that neither Ford's functional pricing formula nor Texaco's hauling allowance formula favored large buyers (or any particular buyer, for that matter). When a plaintiff seeks an antitrust result that is inefficient, does not benefit consumers, and has no tendency to help smaller firms compete with their large rivals, the court is well justified in seeking a way to exonerate the challenged practice, even if, as one commentary suggested, the "result appears to be determined first and the legal rationale developed later." [21]

(3) *Boise Cascade*: refuting the inference of injury.

In *Boise Cascade Corp. v. FTC*,[22] the D.C. Circuit reversed the Commission's finding that one of the nation's leading office products wholesalers received an illegal functional discount from the manufacturers of those products. Unlike many other wholesalers who dealt only with intermediate dealers, Boise actively sold directly to retailers as well, and the FTC found that these discounts injured competition between Boise and non-integrated dealers. Boise received these substantial discounts on products it resold directly to retailers as well as on items sold to dealers. It therefore paid 5–33% less than non-integrated dealers for some goods, even though, as the court noted, "in its capacity as a dealer Boise performs essentially the same marketing functions for manufacturers as do other dealers." [23] Moreover, unlike *FLM Collision Parts* or *Sweeney*, the administrative law judge had found that the discounts were not practically available to disfavored dealers.[24] As noted in section C, the Judge Kenneth Starr's majority opinion finessed the *Doubleday/Mueller* issue by concluding that the Commission had failed to fully consider Boise's arguments that its dealer rivals had suffered no injury.

In his concurring opinion, Judge Stephen Williams concluded that no such injury likely occurred. If, on the one hand, the functional discount simply covered the actual costs incurred by Boise in performing the distributional function, Williams argued that it was lawful because it gave Boise no advantage over other dealer.[25] If, on the other hand, the amount of the discount exceeded Boise's wholesaling costs, any advantage gained by Boise and corresponding injury suffered by its dealer rivals would have

21. II ABA Antitrust Section, Monograph No. 4, The Robinson–Patman Act: Policy and Law 19 (1983).

22. 837 F.2d 1127 (D.C. Cir. 1988). The case is also discussed in detail in section C(3), above.

23. 837 F.2d at 1134.

24. Id. at 1137.

25. Id. at 1148.

been nullified by arbitrage. Whenever integrated wholesaler/dealers compete against non-integrated firms on both levels, Williams explained, any excessive discount given to wholesalers will be bid away through competition at the wholesale level, forcing the wholesale price lower and lower. The resulting price paid by non-integrated dealers will be so low that they will be able to compete on equal terms with integrated firms like Boise. Indeed, because Boise needed to sell at least 20% of its purchases to other dealers, Williams suggested that Boise itself would have had to lower its wholesale price down to a level that covered only its costs, lest it lose all patronage to other wholesalers.

Judge Williams' faith that the marketplace would work according to economic theory,[26] as well as his assumption that competition at the wholesale level would benefit retailers, may be questionable given that five firms controlled 60% of the wholesale market. Moreover, Judge Abner Mikva correctly noted in dissent that Williams' line of reasoning incorrectly presumes "noninjury" whenever economic theory suggests that arbitrage will occur.[27] Consistent with *Morton Salt*, however, it is the favored *buyer's* obligation to prove that arbitrage really does exist in order to break the causal nexus between discrimination and injury. Indeed, the facts of *Morton Salt* suggest that Williams' arbitrage theory would have been applicable there, as well—an arbitrageur could have bought Morton's salt in bulk for $1.35 (the largest quantity discount available in that case) and resold it to smaller retailers for $1.55 (saving the smaller retailers five cents per case).[28] Nevertheless, Judge Williams correctly faulted the FTC for failing to discuss the arbitrage issue at all in *Boise Cascade*, even if the Commission's ultimate response would have been to find the arbitrage theory unsupported by the actual facts.[29]

Much of the D.C. Circuit's majority opinion reflects the frustration of two judges (who are generally hostile to government

26. See id. at 1149 ("it is black letter economics that price discrimination cannot occur if the favored customers can resell to the disfavored").

To be sure, Williams' analysis reflects an economic outlook not shared by the 74th Congress. Certainly, Congress did not share his view that real markets operate consistent with the economic theory that price discrimination will not occur unless there are some significant barriers to arbitrage in the industry, id. at 1150, or it would never have bothered to pass a price discrimination law. In addition, Judge Williams noted that economic theory teaches that price discrimination cannot exist without market power, id. at 1151; yet the clear purpose of the Robinson–Patman Act was to eliminate the need to establish market power or similar Sherman or Clayton Act type of economic harm in order to prove a violation.

27. Id. at 1161.

28. See E. Thomas Sullivan & Herbert Hovenkamp, Antitrust Law, Policy and Procedure 819–20 (2d ed. 1989).

29. Indeed, Judge Mikva's explanations why arbitrage might not have been possible, 837 F.2d at 1162–63, are more detailed than any of the FTC's analysis.

intervention in the economy) with an intrusive pricing order issued by the FTC absent any indication that the marketplace was not functioning properly. The judges correctly raised an important question about functional discounts: does it make sense to infer that a disfavored dealer in a competitive market who resells a product without changing its form (so far, the *Morton Salt* inference) is injured when the favored wholesaler/dealer performs additional functions for the manufacturer? Unfortunately, *Boise Cascade* was not the best case in which to raise that issue because the record clearly showed that Boise also received the discount on goods for which it performed no functions not also performed by disfavored buyers. Thus, the judges in the majority were forced to vent their frustration by seeking to rewrite the entire law of secondary line injury (as discussed in the previous section).

(4) *Hasbrouck* : the latest word.

In *Texaco Inc. v. Hasbrouck*,[30] the Supreme Court attempted to clarify the issue of functional discounts. Certain language in the opinion suggests that such discounts do not violate the Robinson–Patman Act so long as they are limited to reimbursing for the wholesaler/retailer for performing of wholesaling functions. Other language continues to muddy the waters, however, and thus the law remains somewhat unclear.

Texaco sold directly to Hasbrouck, a licensed Texaco dealer in the Spokane, Washington area. Texaco also sold to Gull Oil Company, a firm that distributed oil to other retailers and operated several service stations itself. Gull's discount was so large that its retail prices, as well as those of the independent retailers who purchased gasoline from Gull, were barely above the price Hasbrouck paid Texaco. Hasbrouck filed suit under § 2(a). The district court rejected Texaco's cost justification defense as a matter of law; the jury rejected Texaco's meeting competition defense as well as its claim that the price differential was a reasonable functional discount. On appeal, Texaco argued that it was entitled to judgment n.o.v. because the price differential constituted a lawful functional discount.

First, Texaco argued that functional discounts were not discriminatory, as a matter of law, drawing on some legislative history that suggested price discrimination occurs only when goods of like grade and quality are sold at different prices to rivals at the same level of distribution. The Court rejected this argument, based on both *Anheuser–Busch* 's holding that § 2(a) applies to any price differences and the Court's reading of the statutory text. Section 2(a)'s reference to injury to competition between the

30.   496 U.S. 543 (1990).

victim and beneficiary of discrimination, "or with customers of either of them," demonstrates a concern with sales other than those to rivals at the same distribution level the Court said.[31]

Second, Texaco was joined by the federal government in adopting the strategy used by the D.C. Circuit in *Boise Cascade*: where the discrimination represents a functional discount, the disfavored buyer should not be able to use *Morton Salt* to infer injury simply because the defendant charged substantially different prices, the products were resold in similar form, and the retail market was a competitive one. The Court agreed, holding the *Morton Salt* inference does not apply where the defendant can show a legitimate functional discount—one limited to reasonably reimbursing the wholesaler for performing marketing functions. The probability of competitive injury is much less likely, the Court found, when the substantial price differences simply reimburse the favored buyer for assuming increased costs.[32] However, because the evidence clearly showed that Gull's discount did not reasonably relate to its marketing function, the Court considered the *Morton Salt* inference fully applicable and upheld Hasbrouck's verdict.

Under *Mueller*, the question whether Texaco's discount reasonably related to Gull's marketing function is irrelevant if the ability to engage wholesaling functions benefited Gull as well as Texaco. The Court's failure to discuss this issue, and its focus on the reasonable relationship between the discount the functional tasks performed by the favored buyer, suggests that *Hasbrouck* effectively rejected *Mueller* and instead adopted an approach similar to *Doubleday*. But the Court expressly refused to formally resolve the dispute between the two precedents.[33]

As Justice Antonin Scalia correctly observed in his concurring opinion, a functional discount is reasonable if it "is commensurate with the wholesaler's costs *incurred* in performing services for the supplier." This type of discount does not injure competition between the favored and disfavored buyers, Scalia explained, "since if it constitutes only reimbursement for the wholesaler one would not expect him to pass it on."[34] What is confusing about the majority's holding is that, rather than looking at the wholesaler's costs, it focused on whether the discount "constituted a

31. Id. at 557–59 (citing FTC v. Anheuser–Busch, Inc., 363 U.S. 536, 547–51 (1960)).

32. Id. at 561–62 & n.18 (citing James Rill, Availability and Functional Discounts Justifying Discriminatory Pricing, 53 Antitrust L.J. 929, 935 (1985)).

33. Id. at 564–65 n.21. Not only is *Hasbrouck* inconsistent with *Mueller*, but the Court expressly went further than *Doubleday* by rejecting that decision's requirement that functional discounts not exceed the favored buyer's costs. Id.

34. Id. at 580 (emphasis in original).

reimbursement for the *value to Texaco* of [the wholesaler's] actual marketing functions." [35]

By adding a cost justification defense to the Robinson–Patman Act, Congress explicitly dealt with discounts offered when the favored buyer saves money for the seller. As is explored in the next section, this defense may be excessively hard to prove, but that does not justify immunizing non-cost justified sales from Robinson–Patman scrutiny under the rubric of the functional discount. If the value Texaco gained from Gull's wholesaling activity—and thus Gull's discount—exceeded the cost Gull incurred performing that function, the discount might cause an injury to Hasbrouck's ability to complete. Nevertheless, the majority seemed persuaded by arguments made by Texaco and the federal government that § 2(a) should not proscribe functional discounts because they are desirable economic practices that really are cost-based, even if Texaco could not so prove under the unduly rigorous cost justification test. As Justice Scalia correctly reasoned, "[t]he short answer to this argument is that it should be addressed to Congress." [36]

A more persuasive reason to consider the value to Texaco, rather than focusing solely on the cost to Gull, is that the *Morton Salt* inference is simply a method of determining injury, not an end in itself. The prohibited effect—injury to competition between the favored and disfavored buyers—should be construed to mean an injury to the disfavored buyer's ability to compete. This interpretation best effectuates the Act's stated public policy of prohibiting discrimination that reflects favoritism or buyer power, while permitting price differences that reflect efficiencies. Thus, where a functional discount reflects the value to the seller, *and* is practically available to all on an equal basis, there is no secondary line injury. [37] Moreover, although a large, integrated manufacturer may be able to accurately assess the costs it saves by having someone else perform a particular wholesaling or distribution function, it would be nonsensical for a smaller manufacturer to set its discount based on that calculation because it couldn't possibly consider performing these functions itself. *Hasbrouck* should therefore be read consistently with the lower court cases that have reconciled *Doubleday* and *Mueller*. Texaco violated § 2(a) because its discount appeared to exceed the value Texaco received from the function involved, but also, and perhaps more significantly, be-

---

35. Id. at 562 (emphasis added).

36. Id. at 579.

37. A functional discount would not be lawful if the disfavored buyer also provided valuable services for the seller but received no discount.

cause Texaco refused to allow the plaintiffs to perform the same function and receive the same discount.[38]

Although it may be inappropriate to *infer* injury to non-integrated retailers where functional discounts are reasonable and equally available, such discounts may still violate § 2(a) if additional evidence provides *proof* of such injury. Evidence that a functional discount exceeds the costs incurred by the favored buyer in performing the function, that as a practical matter the disfavored buyer cannot realistically obtain the discount,[39] and that the disfavored buyer has suffered from a clear pattern of diverted sales and lower profits that are not explained by other factors should lead to the conclusion that the functional discount is unlawful unless cost justified.

———

The *Boise Cascade* and *Hasbrouck* majorities went out of their way to exonerate the functional discount as a practice that seems to make economic sense and that typically will usually not reflect the buyer power Congress sought to condemn in the Robinson–Patman Act. Functional discounts will usually be offered because the seller saves money when a wholesaler or distributor performs a distributional function. A novice reading the statute might conclude that a separate doctrine for functional discounts is unnecessary, given that § 2(a) specifically authorizes price differentials reflect the seller's cost savings. But the court's overly restrictive judicial interpretation of this cost justification defense, to which we turn in the next section, explains the willingness to stretch so as to interpret the statute to accommodate functional discounts.[40]

38. Texaco rejected requests by two retailers to obtain Gull's discount by hauling their own fuel, using their own tankwagons. Id. at 570. Special thanks to Irving Scher, whose insights persuaded me of this approach.

39. In *Boise Cascade II*, the FTC restated its view that "discounts are not practically available where a buyer must alter his purchasing status (e.g,. from a retailer as to a dual distributor) before receiving them." 5 Trade Reg. Rep. ¶ 22,902 at 22,598 (citing Dayton Rubber Co., 66 F.T.C. 423, 470–71 (1964), rev'd on other grounds sub nom. Dayco Corp. v. FTC, 362 F.2d 180 (6th Cir. 1966)). But see Panel Discussion, 53 Antitrust L.J. 967, 982 (1984) (remarks of James Rill) ("*Dayco* is bad law"). According to Rill, the courts are

taking a broader view than the FTC, finding that discounts are practically available to all so long as they are offered on minimum levels of purchase within the reach of the average buyer. In fact, he suggested that this approach would be appropriate in order to avoid interpreting the Robinson–Patman Act so as to lead to a price rigidity that conflicts with the policies of other antitrust laws. Availability and Functional Discounts Justifying Discriminatory Pricing, 53 Antitrust L.J. 929, 933–34 (1984).

40. It is true that there is some analytical difference between a discount based on money the seller saves in making a sale to a particular buyer, and a functional discount based on money the

Section E: Cost Justification

(1) The theoretical importance of this defense.

By its terms, § 2(a) of the Robinson–Patman Act does not apply to price differentials "which make only due allowance for differences in the cost of manufacture, sale, or delivery resulting from the differing methods or quantities in which such commodities are to such purchasers sold or delivered." [1] Section 2(b) gives the seller the burden of proving cost justification as a defense. The scope of this defense is the most important doctrine affecting the effective implementation of a price discrimination law.

Economic theory suggests that sellers typically have three motives for changing different prices to different buyers: (1) they are attempting to exploit those consumers who place a higher value on the product or who cannot turn to alternative suppliers; (2) they are acquiescing to the demands of powerful buyers,[2] who can command lower prices due solely to their size; and (3) they are charging lower (and thus different) prices to reflect the cost savings involved in manufacturing or distributing the product to some buyers. Without a cost justification defense, a price discrimination law would clearly stifle a seller's incentive to develop innovative or cheaper means of making and delivering products. Recognizing such a defense furthers the stated goal of the Robinson–Patman Act's sponsors: to distinguish between legitimate price differences, which are based on cost savings or the need to meet competition,[3] and illegitimate price differences, which Congress presumed to include any differences not so justified. Because of the role cost justification plays in weeding out legitimate differences, the scope of the defense is critical to all price discrimination law. An overly broad defense would allow firms to justify discriminatory pricing that reflects consumer exploitation, buyer power, or other unjustified favoritism. A crabbed defense, however, would prevent firms from considering economic realities in their pricing. The latter course, which is the one followed by the courts and the FTC, not only stifles incentives to innovate, but also creates more "economic" price discrimination—buyers are

---

seller saves because the buyer performs valuable services on the seller's behalf. See Panel Discussion, 53 Antitrust L.J. 967, 968 (1984) (remarks of veteran Robinson–Patman practitioner Bernat Rosner). The two inquiries share a fundamental similarity, however, in that they both seek to determine whether a discount reflects legitimate efficiencies or illegitimate favoritism or buyer power.

1. 15 U.S.C. § 13(a).

2. Contrary to economic theory, experience teaches that sellers will also acquiesce in giving lower prices to certain buyers because of favoritism or other arbitrary reasons.

3. The latter defense is considered in section F.

often charged the same price despite differences in the cost of making products for each of them.

The prevailing interpretation of the cost justification defense has had profound doctrinal effects as well. Because the defense is so difficult to establish under current law, many judges respond to Robinson–Patman cases that appear to involve legitimate behavior by finding other ways of exonerating the defendant. The Supreme Court's recent *Hasbrouck* decision, for example, establishes special protection for functional discounts, based in large part on the Court's recognition that charging different prices to wholesalers and retailers may well be legitimate but that many firms will be unable to defend that practice given the rigors of the cost justification defense.[4] The D.C. Circuit's recent decision in *Boise Cascade*[5] may have revised the way courts determine when injury to competition has occurred, again motivated by the majority's view that the price differences at issue there reflected neither consumer exploitation nor buyer power and therefore must have been cost justified, even though the difficulty of establishing the defense prevented Boise from so proving. These cases are two of many where the courts have felt obligated to engage in a guerilla attack on other provisions of the Robinson–Patman Act in order to preserve apparently legitimate price differences. Reconsidering the scope of the cost justification defense may therefore help serve the legislative purposes underlying the Act as well as permit a more coherent application of its other terms.

(2) *Goodyear*: back to the future of reasonableness.

The principal way to prove that price differences are cost justified is to introduce cost studies demonstrating that the differentials "make only due allowance for differences in the cost" involved. How precise these cost studies must be is of immense importance in interpreting the defense. Indeed, the principal source of the crabbed judicial interpretation of the defense lies in the requirement that these studies be unnecessarily precise.

Today's judges and commissioners could do worse than to return to the standard articulated in *Goodyear Tire & Rubber Co.*,[6] one of the earliest decisions to discuss the cost justification defense. Goodyear sold tires of like grade and quality to Sears at a substantial discount from the prices it charged independent tire dealers. Proceeding under § 2 of the original Clayton Act, prior

---

4. Texaco, Inc. v. Hasbrouck, 496 U.S. 543, 561 n.18 (1990). The case is discussed in section D(3).

5. Boise Cascade Corp. v. FTC, 837 F.2d 1127 (D.C. Cir. 1988). The case is discussed in sections C(3) and D(2).

6. 22 F.T.C. 232 (1936), rev'd, 101 F.2d 620 (6th Cir. 1939).

to enactment of the Robinson–Patman Act, the FTC determined that the quantity discount extended to Sears exceeded any reasonable approximation of costs that Goodyear saved in the transaction. Goodyear's records showed that it had sold approximately 19 million tires to Sears and a similar number to independents, yet showed a profit of only $7.7 million on sales to Sears compared to $20.4 million on sales to independents. Goodyear argued that, by purchasing in such massive quantities, Sears removed the hazard and instability of profit fluctuations inevitable in other sales.[7] But this type of buyer power—available only to large purchasers—was the precise evil at which the Robinson–Patman Act was later directed.

In rejecting Goodyear's cost defense, the Commission took a reasonable and sensible approach. Although price differentials cannot be justified based on "remote and unsubstantial differences in cost," the FTC was quite clear that "a discount is not to be condemned merely because it does not mathematically accord with cost differences." The Commission emphasized that the "problem is a practical one and must depend on the effect and intent of the scheme as a whole"; the pricing scheme should therefore be evaluated with an eye towards ensuring "equality to purchasers" and requiring that price differences "be reasonably related to the difference in cost and not a covert means of favoritism."[8]

Inexplicably, however, the FTC abandoned this approach of distinguishing between reasonable differences and favoritism shortly after passage of the Robinson–Patman Act—without even discussing *Goodyear*. As Chairman Edward Howrey lamented, these subsequent decisions "put respondents to strict cost accounting proof. While there were some lingering protestations that mathematical precision would not be required, the cost proviso was applied so as to require detailed showings of individual distribution costs."[9]

Nothing in the text or history of the Robinson–Patman Act suggests that *Goodyear*'s interpretation of the cost justification

---

7. 101 F.2d at 622. Goodyear suggested that its cost-plus contract with Sears legitimately reflected a lower rate of profit because, by agreeing to cover Goodyear's costs, Sears assumed the risk of any change in the cost of raw materials. It is not clear, however, why this shifting of the risk necessarily benefitted Goodyear, especially enough to justify taking less than 50% of its normal mark-up. After all, if the cost of raw materials were to decline, Goodyear would be worse off under a cost-plus contract than under a fixed-price agreement.

8. 22 F.T.C. at 329–30.

9. Sylvania Electric Products, Inc., 51 F.T.C. 282, 290 (1954) (concurring op.).

Because the FTC's practice in the period shortly after passage of the Robinson–Patman Act was not to issue opinions explaining its legal reasoning, the rationale for its failure to follow *Goodyear* is not apparent.

proviso in § 2 of the original Clayton Act is not fully applicable to the parallel provision in the Robinson–Patman Act. The court of appeals reversed the FTC's order in *Goodyear* based on its interpretation of language in the Clayton Act that was removed by the Robinson–Patman Act; that language had provided that § 2 did not prevent price discrimination "on account of differences in the grade, quality, *or quantity* of the commodity sold." In *Goodyear*, the FTC held that this section still required quantity discounts to be cost justified, whereas the appeals court thought that the statute provided a blanket defense for quantity discounts. In so ruling, the court was influenced by Congress' enactment of the Robinson–Patman Act, subsequent to the issuance of the complaint but prior to its own decision, and the specific amendment to § 2 to eliminate the quantity discount defense.[10]

Despite this history, the FTC has not returned to the reasonableness approach articulated in *Goodyear*. In fact, in *Automatic Canteen Co. of America v. FTC*,[11] the Supreme Court remarked on the "intricacies inherent in the attempt to show costs" as part of a § 2(b) defense. The FTC's practice of requiring data that cannot be obtained from ordinary business records "make[s] us aware of how difficult these problems are," the Court stated. Since the Commission started on the path away from *Goodyear*, the Court observed that the FTC had rejected accounting estimates of costs, insisting instead on stop-watch studies of time the seller spent performing specific functions and evidence from individual items on invoices to demonstrate precise cost savings. The FTC's refusal to develop workable criteria for establishing the defense and defendants' poor track record in cases raising this critically important defense led the Attorney General's study committee to conclude in 1955 that the defense "has proved largely illusory in practice."[12]

10. 101 F.2d at 623–24.

As Chairman Howrey observed, the Robinson–Patman Act's revision of the cost justification proviso was believed at the time to be "little more than a legislative restatement of the Commission's interpretation of the old proviso, namely, that price differentials should be 'reasonably related' to cost differences." *Sylvania*, 51 F.T.C. at 290. The Robinson–Patman Act amended § 2 of the Clayton Act by adding to the first sentence of subsection (a) the prohibition on discrimination "in price between purchasers of commodities *of like grade and quality*," and deleting the Clayton Act's language exempting price differentials the were due to "differences in

the grade, quality, or quantity of the commodity sold." Compare 49 Stat. 1526 (1936) with 38 Stat. 730 (1914). Thus, the Robinson–Patman Act continued the limitation on the section's scope to goods of like grade and quality, and repealed the quantity discount defense, but did not change the cost justification defense.

11. 346 U.S. 61, 68 (1953). The principal issue in the case, the imposition of liability on buyers for inducing a discriminatory price in violation of § 2(h), is discussed below in section H(1).

12. Report of the Attorney General's National Comm. to Study the Antitrust Laws 171 (1955). The FTC still has not issued guidelines on this issue. II

(3) Today's restrictive standard.

In *United States v. Borden Co.*,[13] the Court continued along the path away from *Goodyear* and endorsed an overly restrictive view of the defense. In that case, two Chicagoland dairies, Borden and Bowman, each sold milk to the A&P and Jewel supermarket chains at prices significantly lower than those charged to other customers. Both dairies introduced cost studies that placed milk buyers in two categories: (1) A&P/Jewel and (2) everyone else. Borden's study showed that the discount accurately reflected the lower average cost of selling to the large chains. Bowman's cost study carefully divided the costs of delivering milk according to the various functions performed by its employees. It found that substantial costs were associated with certain tasks that were never performed for the large chains (collecting cash, placing contents in a refrigerator, etc.). Bowman's study showed that the price differences resulted from the simple fact that Bowman did not have to include these costs in the price of milk sold to A&P and Jewel. The trial court concluded that these studies demonstrated that the differences were cost justified, but the Supreme Court reversed.

At the outset, the Court wisely rejected a literalist reading of the Act that would require any discrepancy in price to be individually justified. If defendants could not categorize buyers and allocate costs according to some classification system, the result "would be to eliminate in practical effect the cost justification proviso as to sellers having a large number of purchasers, thereby preventing such sellers from passing on economies to their customers." [14] Such an interpretation, the Court recognized, would frustrate Congress' clear intent to permit customers to receive the benefit of cost-justified discounts.

On the other hand, the Court correctly observed that price differentials should not be justified based on arbitrary classifications. "At some point," the Court observed, "practical considerations shade into a circumvention of the proviso." [15] If defendants were allowed to gerrymander categories of customers, they could immunize price differences primarily designed to exploit consumers or reflect buyer power.

The Court then proceeded to set out a standard for evaluating a seller's categorization of buyers for cost justification purposes. Each category must be limited to buyers "of such selfsameness as

American Bar Ass'n, Monograph No. 4, The Robinson–Patman Act: Policy and Law 100 (1983).

13. 370 U.S. 460 (1962).

14. Id. at 468.

15. Id.

454   *PRICE DISCRIMINATION*   Ch. 7

to make the averaging of the cost of dealing with the group a valid and reasonable indicium of the cost of dealing with any specific group member," the Court held. Moreover, there must be a "close resemblance of the individual members of each group on the essential point or points which determine the costs considered." [16] Although the Court properly rejected the two cost studies offered by the dairies, this test went much farther than necessary to balance the goal of allowing sellers to pass on efficient cost savings against the need to prevent circumvention of the Act.

The result was correct because the dairies' two categories, large chains and everyone else, did not come close to a reasonable classification scheme. As the Court noted, firms within the catch-all group "were substantially unlike [each other] in the cost saving aspects considered." [17] The costs of selling milk to the larger independent stores were closer to those incurred in selling to the chains than they were to the costs of selling to smaller independents. Similarly, many of the disfavored buyers of Bowman's milk did not use some or all of the costly services that allegedly formed the basis of the price differential. Of particular importance was the Court's finding that "classifications based on services received by independents were apparently frozen—making it impossible for them to obtain larger discounts by electing not to receive the cost-determinative services—with no justifiable business reason offered in support of the practice." [18] Moreover, as Justice William O. Douglas observed in his concurring opinion, the total costs of dealing with a chain as a whole are relevant only in cases involving centralized purchasing and delivery. Where, as apparently was true in *Borden*, purchase and delivery are decentralized, "the store-by-store costs are the only criteria relevant to the § 2(a) problem." [19] This point lends credence to the government's argument that the differentials were not wholly cost-justified but reflected, at least in part, either the dairies' exploitation of disfavored buyers (perhaps Jewel and A&P had alternative sources of supply not available to smaller stores) or, in Justice Douglas' words, a situation where "those with the most prestige get the largest discounts and the independent merchants are more and more forced to the wall." [20]

Borden went too far, however, in requiring that a seller's classifications be so precise that the cost to each and every buyer within a given category must "closely resemble" the cost to each and every other buyer. The unnecessary rigidity of that require-

16. Id. at 469.
17. Id.
18. Id. at 471 n.13.
19. Id. at 475.
20. Id.

ment was exacerbated by *National Dairy Products Corp. v. FTC*,[21]
another case where milk was sold to large supermarket chains at a
discount. In defending this pricing policy, National computed the
total cost of distributing its milk to all stores operated by each of
its purchasers, and then divided that total cost by the total dollar
amount of discounted milk bought by the purchaser. The favored
Kroger supermarket chain received a 12% discount, and National's computations showed that the average cost savings of delivering to *all* Kroger stores was at least 12%. The FTC and the
Seventh Circuit rejected the cost justification defense, relying on
Borden's requirement that discounts be given only on a store-by-
store basis. This result makes little sense. To be sure, the cost of
delivery to some smaller Kroger stores was higher and those
stores, standing alone, might perhaps have been entitled only to
the 6% discount received by some of Kroger's disfavored rivals.
Assuming, however, that National's study accurately calculated
the costs of distribution and the amounts of milk purchased, and
that those calculations justified giving Kroger an overall 12%
discount, the cost savings of delivery to Kroger's larger stores
must have exceeded 12%. *National Dairy Products* is therefore
quite different from *Borden*, where the Court correctly rejected a
cost study that averaged the relevant figures for *separate* chains.[22]

A superior approach to that taken by the FTC (as detailed in
Automatic Canteen) and the courts in *Borden* and *National Dairy
Products* would focus on achieving a balance that, as a matter of
practical business reality, allows sellers to pass on genuine cost
savings while barring the type of gerrymandering evidenced in
Borden. At the very least, as the Second Circuit recognized in
FTC v. Standard Motor Products, Inc.,[23] where the FTC (or presumably a private plaintiff) rejects a cost study, it should be
required to suggest an alternative system of classification that
would be practically administrable. (Obviously, the Commission
or the plaintiff need not actually conduct the study.)

In determining whether a classification is reasonable, the
courts should focus on the policy of ensuring equal economic
opportunity that underlies the Act. Unlike *Borden*, the classifica-

21. 395 F.2d 517 (7th Cir. 1968), aff'g, 70 F.T.C. 79 (1966).

22. Perhaps the FTC and the court of appeals thought the smaller firms were disadvantaged because the 12% discount given to Kroger and other large chains was the largest percentage discount offered by National. If the discounts had been offered on a store-by-store basis, Kroger's smaller stores would have paid more, but its larger stores would not have paid any less. How National structures its discount system, though, should be of no concern to antitrust officials as long as all discounts are cost justified. No useful purpose is served by requiring National to alter its system to achieve the identical result.

23. 371 F.2d 613 (2d Cir.1967), rev'g, 68 F.T.C. 1248 (1957).

tions in *Standard Motor Products* were functional, rather than arbitrary. They divided sales according to whether they were made by catalog, warehouse, or direct delivery, and thus buyers were not frozen into one category. Allowing sellers reasonable flexibility in classifying their buyers is particularly important in functional discount cases because the discounts are often given to wholesalers or jobbers that save small manufacturers money by providing services the manufacturers cannot feasibly provide.

Seeking a more balanced approach, the 1955 Attorney General's Committee advocated a standard of proof for the cost-justification defense that seems sound. They recommended that cost justification should be sustained whenever the seller demonstrates "in good faith through any authoritative and sound accounting principles" reasonably approximate actual cost variances.[24]

(4) Inherent problems with requiring proof of cost justification.

A more reasonable approach than that articulated in *Borden* would decrease the number of cases where the Robinson–Patman Act condemns efficient and cost-saving price differentials that reflect neither consumer exploitation nor buyer power. Giving defendants more flexibility in categorizing buyers is the interpretation most consistent with the stated policy goals of the statute's framers. Since 1936, though, there has been a significant shift in public values toward competition policy; interpretations of the Sherman, Clayton, and FTC Acts have reflected the view that the goals of economic efficiency and consumer protection should be given greater precedence. If either or both of these goals are given more weight, then even a reasonable statutory interpretation of the cost justification defense will overdeter efficient conduct and overprotect equality of opportunity, for several reasons.

First, the threat of treble damage litigation deters sellers from passing on cost savings to their buyers. There are no bright-line rules that can accurately establish whether a given categorization of buyers represents a genuine allocation of costs or unfair discrimination. Therefore, any study that purports to support a cost justification defense will necessarily be somewhat vague and subject to potential attack in litigation. Perhaps, like the law governing monopolization, the price discrimination law should condemn price differences only where the seller cannot raise a plausible cost justification defense, leaving it to the FTC to find, upon closer examination, that an arguable cost justification is really unreason-

24. Report of the Attorney General's National Comm. to Study the Antitrust Law 175 (1955).

able and thus an unfair method of competition in violation of § 5 of the FTC Act.[25] This approach would minimize the deterrent effect because § 5 does not provide a private right of action or multiple damages.[26]

Second, courts enforcing the Robinson–Patman Act quite properly require sellers to allocate fixed costs among all buyers. To illustrate, suppose that Borden was operating at 70% capacity and sold its milk at 30¢ per gallon, which allowed it to make a reasonable profit. Suppose that Jewel then offered to buy enough milk to bring Borden to full capacity, at a price of 26¢ per gallon—which would cover only Borden's variable costs (milk, delivery costs, and the minimal additional wear and tear on machinery) and a 1¢ profit. If Borden agreed to Jewel's offer, the resulting price differential would be a classic exercise of buyer power that could not be achieved by smaller buyers. A price discrimination law aimed primarily at preserving equal opportunity would condemn it. However, those interested solely in allocative efficiency would want to encourage this pricing scheme; those concerned solely with consumer protection would likewise have no objection unless the discount would likely lead to Jewel's acquisition of market power.

Similarly, a buyer whose additional purchases permit the seller to purchase new machinery or use new techniques for selling all its products may not receive the entire savings; rather, the savings must be spread among all consumers. This rule inhibits some cost-saving innovations.[27] But, as the legislative history of the Robinson–Patman Act makes clear,[28] permitting

25. See Chapter 3, section A(5).

26. A handful of states apply their "Baby FTC Acts" to cover the broad range of unfair methods of competition proscribed by § 5 of the FTC Act. See, e.g., Conn. Gen. Stat. § 42–110b; Fla. Stat. Ann. 501.204; Haw. Rev. Stat. § 480–2; Mass. Gen. L. ch. 93A, § 2; S.C. Code Ann. § 39–5–20. These statutes are enforceable by private parties: Hawaiian plaintiffs can receive treble damages, Haw. Rev. Stat. § 480–13; plaintiffs can recover up to treble damages for willful violations in two other states, see Mass. Gen. L. ch. 93A, § 11, and S.C. Code.Ann. § 39–5–140; the limit is actual damages in two other states, see Conn. Gen. Stat. § 42–110g and Fla. Stat. Ann. § 501.211. There do not appear to be any reported cases where plaintiffs have used these provisions to obtain treble damages for price

discrimination that would go beyond the Robinson–Patman Act.

27. As one economist has observed, in other contexts the government has even required price discrimination in the interest of efficiency—for example, by making regulated telephone and electric rates high during regular business hours and low in the evenings in order to encourage those with greater flexibility to avoid peak time usage. Corwin Edwards, The Price Discrimination Law 626 (1959).

28. See H.R. Rep. No. 2287, 7th Cong., 2d Sess. 10 (1936) (cost justification defense "precludes differentials based on the imputation of overhead to particular customers, or the exemption of others from it"). Accord, S. Rep. No. 1502, 74th Cng., 2d Sess. 6 (1936). See also 80 Cong. Rec. 9417 (1936) (remarks of Rep. Utterback, chair of the House

such pricing practices would require congressional amendment of § 2(a).

Perhaps, even more so than in other areas of antitrust law, the resolution of price discrimination issues depends both on one's antitrust values and on one's estimate of the prevalence of illegitimate discrimination in the marketplace. The process of calculating costs for any multi-product seller is inherently indeterminate, for it always involves a somewhat arbitrary allocation of overhead costs. Thus, there can never be a completely reliable finding as to whether a discriminatory price reflects true efficiencies or favoritism. Those who believe that few price differentials reflect consumer exploitation or buyer power should demand significant legislative revisions in § 2(a). In fact, under that view, fear of Robinson–Patman Act liability currently leads to a good deal of price discrimination in the economic sense because sellers charge the same price even when the cost of different sales varies. On the other hand, those who are more skeptical about the efficiency of the marketplace will feel more comfortable with a statute that requires sellers to justify price differentials. Using a more accurate standard than that adopted in *Borden*, the proponents of this view believe, will enable the law to satisfactorily reconcile the goals of economic efficiency, consumer protection, and equality of opportunity.

Section F: Meeting Competition

(1) Legislative background.

The original version of the Clayton Act proposed by the House Judiciary Committee would have imposed criminal penalties for price discrimination and would not have afforded a defense for those who engaged in price discrimination in order to meet competition. The proposal sparked an angry dissent from a minority of the Committee. The dissenters argued that it would force national firms either to "sit supinely by and see [their] trade taken away" or, to reduce prices everywhere and "meet with a great and destructive loss." [1] The House proposal would also have barred regional firms from expanding into new geographic markets where the competitive price level was lower.

Because the main purpose of the price discrimination provision in the original Clayton Act was to prevent large firms from

conferees) (if favored buyer's purchases make possible across-the-board reduction in seller's costs, "other customers are entitled to share also in the benefit of that reduction").

1. H.R. Rep. No. 627, 63d Cong., 2d Sess., pt. 2, 2–3 (1914).

targeting their smaller rivals for predatory pricing, the Senate added a proviso to § 2 that excepted price "discrimination made in good faith to meet competition." [2] The framers of the Clayton Act believed that this provision would differentiate between unfair predators and honest competitors. The proviso was amended by the Robinson–Patman Act. Focusing on the need to ensure that powerful buyers would not obtain unfair discounts, § 2(b) of the Robinson–Patman Act now provides a defense to firms that reduce prices "in good faith to meet an equally low price of a competitor." [3] The Act therefore makes it clear that a discount that exceeds those necessary to meet competition—i.e., a discount that is intended to beat, rather than meet, a rival's price—is unlawful.

The purposes of the meeting competition defense were articulated by the Supreme Court in *Standard Oil Co. v. FTC.*[4] Standard sold gasoline to jobbers at a 1½¢ discount below the price charged to retail stations. With this discount (which apparently exceeded the costs Standard saved by selling to jobbers), the jobbers themselves, and their retail customers, were able to gain a competitive advantage over retailers that bought directly from Standard. Standard's argument that it offered the discounts in order to meet a rival's equally low price was accepted by the hearing examiner. The Commission concluded, however, that the defense was not absolute, and indeed was irrelevant, where secondary line injury was present; in such cases the FTC held that the injurious effect of the discrimination outweighed any benefits of allowing Standard to compete against its own primary rivals.

The Supreme Court rejected the FTC's position. Recognizing that the Robinson–Patman Act might be based on somewhat different economic theories than the Sherman and Clayton Acts, the Court nevertheless concluded that "Congress did not seek by the Robinson–Patman Act either to abolish competition or so radically to curtail it" that a seller would be unable to honestly and fairly compete.[5] The language of § 2(b) also supports the Court's conclusion that the meeting competition defense is absolute. Although ungrammatically worded, the section provides that "*nothing herein contained* shall prevent a seller rebutting the prima-facie case thus made by showing that his lower price ... was made in good faith to meet an equally low price of a competitor." [6] Construing that language to exonerate a seller that charges a lower price to meet competition seems sounder than the FTC's interpretation—that evidence of meeting competition is

2. Frederick Rowe, Price Discrimination Under the Robinson–Patman Act 209 (1962).

3. 15 U.S.C. § 13(b).

4. 340 U.S. 231 (1951).

5. Id. at 249.

6. 15 U.S.C. § 13(b), (emphasis added).

simply a factor for the Commission to consider. Moreover, the
form of § 2(b)'s meeting competition proviso is identical to the
form of § 2(a)'s cost justification proviso, and the latter is universally considered an absolute defense.[7] Finally, the FTC's interpretation would erase the defense from the statute; if secondary line
injury trumps the defense, but secondary line injury is a necessary
element in a § 2(a) case, the defense is obviously eviscerated.[8]

On balance, the allowing an unqualified defense for meeting
competition represents sound policy. A national firm required to
establish uniform prices will usually set them high; rarely will it
be willing to lose business nationwide in order to meet competition
in a few areas.[9] A provision like the original House version would

---

7. 340 U.S. at 241. The cost justification proviso also begins with the
words "nothing herein contained." 15
U.S.C. § 13(a).

8. The Court's textual analysis and
its preference for preserving fair and
legitimate competition led it to find the
defense absolute notwithstanding some
strong indications to the contrary in the
legislative history. The Conference Report discussion of this issue seems to
support the FTC's more limited view of
the defense:

> The Senate bill contained a further
> proviso—
>
> That nothing herein contained shall
> prevent discrimination in price in the
> same or different communities made
> in good faith to meet competition.
>
> This language is found in existing law
> [§ 2 of the Clayton Act], and in the
> opinion of the conferees is one of the
> obstacles to enforcement of the pres-
> ent Clayton Act. The Senate reced-
> ed, and the language is stricken. A
> provision relating to the question of
> meeting competition, *intended to op-
> erate only as a rule of evidence in a
> proceeding before the Federal Trade
> Commission*, is included in subsection
> (b) in the conference text . . .

H.R. Rep. No. 2951, 74th Cong., 2d Sess.
6–7 (1936) (emphasis added). Moreover,
the chairman of the House conferees,
Representative Utterback, explained
that "this does not set up the meeting
of competition as an absolute bar to a
charge of discrimination under the bill.
It merely permits it to be shown in
evidence." 80 Cong. Rec. 9418 (1936).
See also id. at 9903 (statement of Sen.
Van Nuys) (proviso "is simply a rule of

evidence rather than a part of the substantive law").

The *Standard Oil* majority characterized the legislative history as "inconclu-
sive" and rejected Utterback's statement, arguing that it did not justify
"disregarding the proviso." 340 U.S. at
247 n.14. The Court noted that the text
of what is now § 2(b) appeared, in virtually identical form, as § 2(e) of the original House bill. Although the House
Committee Report, also authored by
Chairman Utterback, made it clear that
the defense was being narrowed from
the Clayton Act standard by limiting it
only to meeting an "equally low price"
of a competitor, the Judiciary Committee explained that under the proposed
legislation "the proviso permits the seller to meet the price actually previously
offered by a local competitor." H.R.
Rep. 2287, 74th Cong., 2d Sess. 16
(1936). The *Standard Oil* majority also
emphasized that its holding was consistent with post-enactment decisions and
statements made by FTC members and
staff, as well as by senior Justice Department officials. Id. at 246–47 & nn.
12–13. See also III Earl Kintner &
Joseph Bauer, Federal Antitrust Law
379 & n.31 (1983) (citing cases) (both the
FTC and the courts initially took the
view that meeting competition was a
complete defense).

9. Cf. Falls City Industries, Inc. v.
Vanco Beverage, Inc., 460 U.S. 428, 443
(1983) (Indiana law requiring liquor
wholesalers to maintain uniform prices
across the state led wholesaler to maintain high prices and forego business
along Kentucky border rather than lowering prices in Indianapolis and else-

therefore have deprived consumers of the benefit of fair and legitimate competition. On the other hand, one of the principal reasons for enacting the Robinson–Patman Act was to prevent sellers from offering favorable prices to powerful buyers. If such a buyer is able to induce one seller to give it a discount, then the defense allows all other sellers to match the discount, despite the significant injury to less powerful buyers. Nevertheless, absent systematic, industry-wide price discrimination (discussed below in subsection (4)), proper application of the meeting competition defense is tailored to serve the Act's goals. If Standard Oil sells at a discriminatory low price to favored jobbers only because they received an equally low offer elsewhere, these jobbers will have a marketplace advantage over Standard's disfavored buyers regardless of what Standard does, and nothing is gained by forbidding Standard from keeping the business itself.[10]

(2) The problem of overlapping markets.

FTC v. Sun Oil Co.[11] raises one of the knotty problems involved in the continuing struggle to distinguish between good and bad price differentials. McLean operated a Sunoco station on the same street corner in Jacksonville, Florida as a station operated by the independent Super Test company. After Super Test began a price war, McLean complained that he would be driven out of business unless Sun lowered its wholesale price to allow him to compete. When Sun acquiesced, McLean not only held his own against Super Test but attracted significant business from other Jacksonville Sunoco dealers as well The FTC challenged the differential between Sun's general wholesale price and its wholesale price to McLean, and rejected the meeting competition defense "because Sun was not meeting its own competition." The Fifth Circuit reversed on the grounds that "Sun, as a practical matter, was really competing with Super Test."[12] The Supreme Court reversed again, refusing to apply the meeting competition defense.

The Court adopted a narrow construction of the meeting competition defense, allowing the defense to be invoked only when the seller found it necessary to price discriminate in order to meet the price of one of its own competitors. The Court also noted that, as a matter of statutory interpretation, "it makes but little sense to talk, for example, of a wholesaler's meeting of the 'equally low'

where in order to meet competition in the southern part of the state).

10. See Hugh Hansen, Robinson–Patman Law: A Review and Analysis, 51 Fordham L. Rev. 1113, 1151–52 n.204 (1983).

11. 371 U.S. 505 (1963).

12. Id. at 510–11.

price of one of his purchaser's retail competitors." [13] The Court also reasoned that the thrust of Sun's argument—that all firms in a chain of distribution—are in competition with all firms in a rival chain of distribution would eviscerate the Act.[14] For example, if Giant Retail Stores claimed that it needed a discount in order to compete against Humongous Retail Stores, a broad interpretation of the defense would allow every one of Giant's suppliers to offer it a discount, giving Giant a tremendous advantage over small stores. Quite obviously, this result is contrary to the purposes of the Robinson–Patman Act.

In addition, the Court assumed that Super Test was able to undercut McLean's prices because of its own efficiencies (or willingness to operate on a lower profit margin), not because its own wholesale price was lower.[15] If so, allowing Sun to prop up its inefficient retailer by charging a discriminatory price that presumably was lower than Super Test's wholesale price would discourage retailers from aggressive interbrand competition, contrary to the general purposes of the antitrust laws.

Sun Oil is a complex case because it involved of overlapping markets. The discrimination arose because McLean competed both with Super Test (for price-sensitive patrons interested in the convenience of the particular location) and with other Sunoco dealers (for those customers with Sunoco brand loyalty), but the disfavored Sunoco dealers did not compete with Super Test. If all the firms had been in the same market, Sun would presumably have given the discount to all of them. Given the overlapping markets, however, Sun was given the Hobson's choice [16] of either cutting prices throughout a large region in order to meet competition on one street corner or allowing McLean to go out of business. Paradoxically, one other option Sun had was to acquire McLean's station itself through a vertical merger. Although this may have Sun's only attractive alternative, it is hardly consistent with the Jeffersonian ideal of maintaining individually owned and operated companies.[17]

13. Id. at 515.
14. Id. at 525.
15. Id. at 522.
16. The choices were undesirable only from Sun's perspective. Justice Arthur Goldberg's majority opinion makes clear that it would have preferred for Sun to respond to Super Test's price skirmish by launching a full scale price war, cutting wholesale prices throughout Jacksonville. See id. at 527 n.18. The opinion does not indi-cate, however, whether Sun's pre-"war" prices included supra-competitive profits. If not, there is no valid reason to force Sun into a price war.

17. Indeed, the Court seemed hostile to Sun because it operated via independent retail firms. See id. at 529 ("Having consciously chosen not to effect direct distribution through wholly owned and operated stations, Sun cannot now claim for itself the benefits of such a system.").

Following *Sun Oil*, the FTC seems to have effected a satisfactory resolution of the policy issues involved in cases involving overlapping markets. The Commission issued a policy statement, opining that Sun could have given McLean a discriminatory discount if it had shown either that Super Test was a vertically integrated supplier-retailer (i.e., Super Test competed at wholesale with Sun as well as at retail with McLean) or, if Super Test was not integrated, that Sun "had reason to believe that it was meeting only a reduction in its competitor's wholesale price and not a reduction in the retail price initiated by a dealer without the assistance of a supplier." [18]

(3) What is good faith?

The black letter definition of good faith for purposes of the meeting competition defense comes from *Continental Baking Co.*, where the FTC held that the standard should be "flexible and pragmatic." Thus, in pre-feminist terms, a seller acts in good faith if its pricing policies are in line with what would be expected from "the prudent businessman responding fairly to what he reasonably believes is a situation of competitive necessity." [19] The Commission rejected rigid rules or abstract theories, noting the ad hoc nature of each particular case. On the facts of that case, the FTC found that Continental had commenced a program of discriminatory discounts only after losing significant market share to rivals that were granting similar discounts, and had followed a corporate policy authorizing discounts "only where an equal or larger discount had been given by a competitor of [Continental] on a competing product line and [where it] would not be able to continue selling to the customer in question without granting such a discount." [20]

An early case rejecting a claim of good faith was *FTC v. A.E. Staley Manufacturing Co.* [21] Apparently following the standard practice among manufacturers of glucose and corn syrup, Staley maintained a discriminatory base point pricing scheme. Goods

---

18. 4 Trade Reg. Rep. (CCH) ¶ 10,-473, at 17,840 (1988).

19. 63 F.T.C. 2071, 2163 (1963). The Supreme Court quoted this standard with approval in United States v. United States Gypsum Co., 438 U.S. 422, 454 (1978).

20. 63 F.T.C. at 2164.

Cf. William Inglis & Sons Baking Co. v. ITT Continental Baking Co., 668 F.2d 1014, 1046–47 (9th Cir. 1981), cert. denied, 459 U.S. 825 (1982), where Continental was again accused of price discrimination, and the court upheld the jury's rejection of a meeting competition defense. That case involved price discrimination between Continental's Wonder Bread brand and its private label bread; the record showed that Continental used a costly and rigorous method of verifying that any discount on Wonder Bread was in response to a competitor's price, but used no similar procedure in offering widespread discounts on its private label.

21. 324 U.S. 746 (1945).

were sold at delivered prices, and all firms used Chicago as the base point (i.e., sales included the cost of transportation from Chicago).[22] Staley, located in Decatur, Illinois (about three hours south of Chicago), sold its goods at a lower price in Chicago than in Decatur itself, even though the cost of delivering goods to Chicago was obviously higher. Staley's claim that its pricing system was a good faith response to competition was rejected.

In a companion case decided simultaneously with *Staley*, the Supreme Court held that base point pricing violates § 2(a) where it causes secondary line injury.[23] In rejecting the meeting competition defense in *Staley*, the Court characterized the defendant's argument as an attempt to "justify a basing point delivered price system, which is otherwise outlawed by § 2, because other competitors are in part violating the law by maintaining a like system." [24] The Court noted that the Robinson–Patman Act's legislative history showed that the meeting competition defense was not intended to excuse conduct that was otherwise illegal.[25] Moreover, the Court explained, the defense focuses on individual competitive situations, not general price schedules. Although Staley might have lawfully lowered its prices in Chicago to meet competition from rivals located in that city, the defense did not permit it to use a pricing system that charged discriminatorily high prices in Decatur. Thus, the Court held, the defense only protects discounts from where competition forces a seller to depart from "normal, non-discriminatory pricing methods." Because Staley never attempted to establish its own lawful pricing scheme, and then reduce prices where necessary to meet competition, it could not avail itself of the defense.[26]

As an apparently separate ground for rejecting the meeting competition defense, the Court endorsed the FTC's criticism of Staley for offering discounts based on information received from sales representatives, brokers, or purchasers without any effort "to investigate or verify" their claims. The FTC found, moreover, "circumstances that strongly suggested that the buyers' claims were without merit." [27]

22. For a discussion of base point pricing, see Chapter 4, section F(5).

23. Corn Products Refining Co. v. FTC, 324 U.S. 726 (1945).

24. 324 U.S. at 753.

25. Id. at 754 (citing 80 Cong. Rec. 9418 (1936)).

26. Id. at 754–55. As the Court was to explain later in Falls City Industries, Inc. v. Vanco Beverage, Inc., 460 U.S. 428, 439, 441 (1983) (emphasis in origi-

nal), "the defense requires that the seller offer the lower price in good faith *for the purpose* of meeting competition," whereas Staley engaged in price discrimination for the purpose of maintaining a discriminatory and collusive pricing system. *Falls City* is discussed in detail below in subsection (4).

27. 324 U.S. at 758–59. The FTC found evidence of a pattern of discriminatory discounts following general price increases; Staley's sales agents

Given this second holding, the defendants in *United States v. United States Gypsum Co.*[28] tried to justify an agreement among oligopolists in an industry with a history of collusion to share detailed information about the prices they each offered individual customers—an agreement that would otherwise be illegal under § 1 of the Sherman Act[29]—as necessary to allow them to take advantage of § 2(b)'s meeting competition defense. The Court correctly rejected this justification for several reasons.

First, the Court observed, § 2(b) is a defense to liability and "not an affirmative right under the Act." Sellers can take advantage of the meeting competition proviso to escape Robinson-Patman liability for discriminatory pricing, but not if it proves necessary to violate other laws, such as the Sherman Act, in the process.[30]

Second, the Court held, evidence that a seller has done all that it reasonably can to support a good faith belief that lower prices are necessary to meet competition (short of violating the Sherman Act) satisfies the meeting competition defense. The Court listed a host of alternative ways to obtain information necessary to meet competition other than by talking to rivals; these alternatives included reports of similar discounts from other customers, a buyer's credible threat to cease purchases, documentary evidence available from the buyer, or publicly available market data.[31]

(4) Meeting persistently discriminatory competition.

In *Falls City Industries, Inc. v. Vanco Beverage, Inc.*,[32] the court sustained a scheme of persistent geographic price discrimination under the meeting competition test. Falls City charged Indiana wholesalers higher prices for its beer than it charged Kentucky wholesalers. As a result, Indiana residents living near the Ohio River crossed the border to purchase the beer in Kentucky, thereby injuring Vanco, Falls City's Indiana distributor.

Vanco claimed that the meeting competition defense was unavailable because the price differential did not result from Falls City's decision to lower prices in Kentucky, but rather from its

---

"booked" fictitious orders from favored buyers at lower prices, even though the buyers had not agreed to the purchases, because the agents assumed that in the future the buyers would prefer to purchase Staley products at the old, lower price. 34 F.T.C. 1362, 1371 (1942).

28. 438 U.S. 422 (1978).

29. See Chapter 4, section G(2).

30. 438 U.S. at 459 n.32. See also Exxon Corp. v. Governor of Maryland, 437 U.S. 117, 132–33 (1978) (meeting competition proviso of § 2(b) does not preempt state law that forbids price discrimination even where necessary to meet rivals' prices).

31. 438 U.S. at 455.

32. 460 U.S. 428 (1983).

desire to maintain prices there while raising them in Indiana. The plaintiff reasoned that the meeting competition defense was intended to extricate sellers from the dilemma choosing between of absorbing ruinous discounts in all their markets or foregoing competition in a lower priced area. Here, in contrast, Falls City opted to follow other brewers in raising prices in Indiana, when it could have chosen instead to increase its market share thereby maintaining the same prices in both states. The Court rejected this argument, observing that in inflationary periods, "vigorous price competition ... may take the form of smaller price increases rather than price cuts." [33]

The Court was likewise unpersuaded by Vanco's attempt to analogize Falls City's conduct to that condemned in *Staley.* Writing for a unanimous Court, Justice Harry Blackmun cogently distinguished *Staley* on the grounds that Staley, unlike Falls City, had participated in a collusive pricing scheme.[34] Although it is true that "[p]ersistent, industrywide price discrimination within a geographic market should certainly alert a court to a substantial possibility of collusion," *Falls City* involved the "unusual circumstance" where Indiana law required brewers to sell at uniform prices throughout the state. Thus, rather than cutting prices below competitive levels in Indianapolis, Gary, and Ft. Wayne, Falls City may well have made the sensible decision to keep Indiana prices high and hope that loyal patrons in the southern part of the state would cross the river for discounts.[35]

The Court also properly rejected two other arguments that would have unduly narrowed the meeting competition defense. First, Vanco argued that the defense should be available only to allow sellers to maintain existing customers, and not to obtain new patrons by lowering prices. As the Court noted, however, the Act "does not distinguish between one who meets a competitor's lower price to retain an old customer and one who meets a competitor's lower price in an attempt to gain new customers." [36] The Court endorsed a Seventh Circuit opinion vindicating a dissent written by FTC Commissioner Phillip Elman, who noted that such a distinction was unworkable and would inhibit new entrants from seeking to attract customers of entrenched firms.[37]

Second, Vanco cited the language in *Staley*'s requiring that price discrimination justified by the need to meet competition must be based on individual competitive situations, rather than

33. Id. at 444.
34. Id. at 441.
35. Id. at 443.
36. Id. at 446.

37. Id. at 446–47 (citing Sunshine Biscuits, Inc. v. FTC, 306 F.2d 48, 51–52 (7th Cir. 1962)). See also Sunshine Biscuits, Inc., 59 F.T.C. 674, 682–86 (Elman, C., dissenting).

general price schedules. Vanco's argument, which the court of appeals had accepted, was that this language meant that the defendant's decision to reduce prices throughout Kentucky, rather than on a customer-by-customer basis, did not qualify for the defense. In rejecting this argument, the Supreme Court clarified the language in *Staley*, holding that "reasonable pricing responses on an area-specific basis [are allowed] where competitive circumstances warrant them." The Court explained that a discriminatorily low price "may be extended to numerous purchasers if the seller has a reasonable basis for believing that the competitor's lower price is available to them." In addition, the Court noted, the contrary rule would have a perverse effect on a small brewery like Falls City because it might not be able to ascertain competitors' prices to each individual customer; such a rule might therefore preclude Falls City from engaging in meaningful price competition with larger national breweries.[38] The Court cautioned, however, that low prices must be "reasonably tailored to the competitive situation," must be based on adequate verification, and must continue only so long as the competitive circumstances justify.[39]

Although *Falls City* adopts a reading of the meeting competition defense that seems necessary to allow sellers to compete meaningfully with their rivals, it effectively sanctions the precise evil targeted by the Robinson–Patman Act—significant discounts based on buyer power. Permitting "a seller to treat different competitive situations differently" undermines the Act's fundamental precept.[40] The difficulties of reconciling the desire to allow sellers to meet competition with the goal of eliminating persistent price discrimination are demonstrated by *Callaway Mills Co. v. FTC*,[41] where carpet mills gave quantity discounts to major buyers. The existence of buyer power seemed clear in that case from the awarding of substantial rebates based on the cumulative total of separate sales, made without regard to the quantity of individual items of sale or to the costs of manufacture and delivery.[42] Callaway, which had introduced a new carpet-making process, had initially resisted the large buyers' demands for unjustified discounts, but, faced with an industry-wide practice of accommodating these buyers, it eventually went along. The FTC held that Callaway's response was not a good faith effort to meet competition. If each seller could defend discriminatory pricing practices by pointing to an industry-wide practice, the Commission

---

38. Id. at 448–49.

39. Id. at 450.

40. Herbert Hovenkamp, Economics and Federal Antitrust Law 354 (1984).

41. 362 F.2d 435 (5th Cir. 1966), rev'g, 64 F.T.C. 732 (1964).

42. 64 F.T.C. at 744 (Elman, C., dissenting).

reasoned, persistent price discrimination could never be challenged. In reversing, the Fifth Circuit read the statute correctly: Callaway's lower price was literally a good faith effort to meet competition. Unlike Staley, Callaway was not a participant in an illegal price scheme. Requiring the seller to prove that the price it was in fact meeting was lawful would significantly narrow the defense, with the result that many sellers would refuse to meet sporadic competition and would instead tend to engage in oligopoly pricing.[43]

Dissenting from the FTC opinion, Commission Philip Elman agreed with Callaway that it should not be held liable under the Robinson–Patman Act; instead Elman proposed that the Commission should conduct an independent proceeding to condemn the industry-wide price discrimination as an unfair method of competition in violation of § 5 of the FTC Act. Once the pricing was clearly held to be illegal, then *Staley* would bar reliance on the meeting competition defense.[44]

Both § 2(b)'s language and basic principles of fairness compel the conclusion that the competition defense should be available to firms that merely engage in "self-defense," and it is therefore

43. The FTC had also rejected Callaway's meeting competition defense because Callaway's product was arguably superior to those of its rivals and thus it was not of like grade and quality. Therefore, the FTC reasoned, meeting rivals' prices in this case really amounted to undercutting them, and undercutting rivals' prices is not protected by the defense. The Fifth Circuit reversed on this point as well: "[s]o long as [Callaway] conclusively show[s] that [its] products at various price levels generate public demand (or 'salability') substantially equivalent to that of competitors' carpeting at the same price levels, considerations of 'grade and quality' become unnecessary and indeed superfluous." 362 F.2d at 441.

44. 64 F.T.C. at 755.

An aggressive FTC enforcement program in the carpet industry ultimately produced the result Elman desired, notwithstanding the Commission's defeat in *Callaway Mills*. In addition to bringing the case against Callaway, the FTC had also sued 11 of Callaway's rivals on charges of illegal price discrimination. As a result, it obtained consent to cease and desist orders barring further discrimination in eight

cases and enforced similar orders in three adjudicated proceedings. See id. at 736 n.1. Two of the contesting respondents appealed the Commission's orders: the FTC prevailed in Philadelphia Carpet Co. v. FTC, 342 F.2d 994 (3d Cir. 1965), aff'g, 64 F.T.C. 762 (1964), where the meeting competition defense was not raised; and its order in Cabin Crafts, Inc., 64 F.T.C. 799 (1964), was vacated by the Fifth Circuit in a decision consolidated with *Callaway Mills*. Presumably, however, neither Callaway nor Cabin Crafts could justify further discrimination because the challenged discounts would not be necessary to meet competition from rivals that were under orders not to discriminate.

The willingness of the rival carpet manufacturers to agree to FTC orders prohibiting volume discounts is not surprising in light of their historic desire to avoid granting such discounts. See United States v. Institute of Carpet Mfrs. of America, 1 F.R.D. 636 (S.D.N.Y. 1941) (enjoining agreement not to give quantity discounts). A separate § 5 proceeding, like that advocated by Commission Elman, would be necessary, however, where the major firms were unwilling to agree to end discriminatory discount.

unfortunate that the Commission never acted on Elman's proposal. It offers the only realistic solution to persistent price discrimination caused by large buyer power—the principal evil targeted by the Robinson–Patman Act. As a result, when the meeting competition defense is combined with an unduly rigorous cost justification defense that disallows many nondiscriminatory price differentials, the result is that many legitimate and fair price differences are condemned or inhibited while some illegitimate exercises of buyer power are fully protected.

Section G: Brokerage and Promotional Allowances

In enacting the Robinson–Patman Act, Congress was concerned that powerful buyers might be able to use their economic power to evade the ban on unfair price discrimination contained in § 2(a). In an effort to minimize opportunities for evasion, subsections (c), (d) and (e), respectively, prohibit the use of undeserved brokerage allowances, discriminatory promotional payments, and discriminatory promotional services. Although these provisions have created a broad prophylactic to guard against circumvention of § 2(a), often they have proven ineffective in distinguishing between genuine competition and unfair exploitation of buyer power. As interpreted, they have hampered efficient and innovative business techniques and perversely handicapped the ability of small firms, especially those that act together in cooperatives, to compete with larger, national concerns.

(1) Illegal discounts in lieu of brokerage.

The traditional distribution system at issue in antitrust cases involves a manufacturer that sells its goods to a wholesaler, which then resells either directly to a retailer for ultimate sale to consumers or indirectly to the retailer via a distributor. A variant of this scheme involves the use of brokers. As a general rule, brokers do not actually purchase goods themselves, but instead arrange for the sale and shipment of goods from a manufacturer to a distributor or retailer. Section 2(c) of the Act prohibits a seller from giving "anything of value as a commission, brokerage, or other compensation, or any allowance or discount in lieu thereof, except for services rendered in connection with the sale ... either to the other party to such transaction or to an agent [of the other party]." [1]

FTC v. Henry Broch & Co. [2] illustrates what Congress had in mind in enacting this provision. In that case, Broch successfully

---

1. 15 U.S.C. § 13(c).   2. 363 U.S. 166 (1960).

brokered a sale from the manufacturer, Canada Foods, to J.M. Smucker Co., a large buyer. Smucker indicated that it would purchase a large amount of apple concentrate, but only if Canada Foods dropped its price from $1.30 per gallon to $1.25. Canada Foods was willing to agree to this discriminatory discount, but only if Broch agreed to drop its normal brokerage fee from 5% to 3% (so that Canada Foods and Broch would roughly split the lost revenue). The deal proceeded on this basis. The Supreme Court affirmed the FTC's holding that the sale unlawfully gave Smucker a discount in lieu of a brokerage fee in violation of § 2(c).

In reducing its price by 5¢ per gallon, Canada Foods was clearly engaging in price discrimination. The FTC could have avoided the thicket of interpreting § 2(c) simply by proceeding under § 2(a), but if it had done so, it would have had to prove injury to competition with either Canada Foods' or Smucker's rivals. In addition, Canada Foods might have tried to establish a cost justification defense. Therefore, the FTC chose to bring the case under § 2(c); conduct proscribed by that section is per se illegal.

In finding a violation of § 2(c), the Court noted that Smucker rendered no services in exchange for the discount. This unjustified favoritism is exactly what the Robinson–Patman Act was designed to prevent, and § 2(c) was intended to bar "all other means by which brokerage could be used to effect price discrimination."[3] The fact that Smucker gained an advantage over its rivals due to a discount financed in part by the broker, rather than by Canada Foods, was irrelevant.[4] The fact that Canada Foods' costs were reduced because of the lower brokerage fee was likewise irrelevant because § 2(c) contains no cost justification proviso. Because the favoritism toward a large buyer was so clear, and the discount seemed to fall within the literal meaning of a "discount in lieu of brokerage," the Court felt comfortable applying § 2(c) even though the price was openly discriminatory and therefore did not implicate the subsection's specific purpose, which was to force price differentials out into the open where they could be evaluated under § 2(a).[5]

The dissent incorrectly maintained that the majority's rule would destroy brokerage competition by freezing legitimate commission rates.[6] All the majority did was to proscribe one form of competition—selectively lowering a brokerage fee with the understanding that the reduction would be passed on as a discount to a

---

3. Id. at 169.

4. Id. at 174.

5. FTC v. Simplicity Pattern Co., 360 U.S. 55, 68 (1959).

6. Id. at 180 (Whittaker, J., dissenting).

favored buyer. To be sure, the Court's holding has some tendency to tamper with or stabilize pricing, but no more so than would any significant restriction on price discrimination.

The Court emphasized that it did not mean "to say that every reduction in price, coupled with a reduction in brokerage, automatically compels the conclusion that an allowance 'in lieu' of brokerage has been granted." [7] The only example the Court gave to illustrate its point, however, was a case where a manufacturer eliminated all brokers and lowered its price across the board.[8] But presumably any across-the-board reduction in commissions or brokerage fees, whether or not made in connection with generalized price discounts, would also pass muster under the Act. Significantly, the Court declared that a "price reduction based upon alleged savings [in brokerage fees] is an 'allowance in lieu of brokerage' when given only to favored customers," suggesting that such a reduction would not violate § 2(c) if it were made available to all buyers.[9]

(2) The perverse treatment of effective competition by small businesses.

Although some price discrimination statute may be necessary, despite the inevitable complexity it creates, in order to prevent abuses of economic power by large buyers, the marketplace does provide a significant ameliorative mechanism of its own—cooperative buying groups. These cooperatives are partnerships or corporations formed by smaller retailers so that they can take advantage of economies of scale in distribution and exercise the same clout as large single buyers. The congressional goals reflected in the Robinson–Patman Act—to preserve small, personally run enterprises and to ensure competition unfettered by abuses of economic power—are ideally served by a market consisting of many smaller retailers that can compete vigorously with larger concerns because of their cooperative buying power. Yet historically the FTC interpreted the brokerage provisions of § 2(c) to disadvantage cooperative arrangements; after a number of years, however, the FTC and the courts began to move toward eliminating this impediment to small businesses.

7. Id. at 175.

8. Id. at 176 (citing Robinson v. Stanley Home Products, Inc., 272 F.2d 601 (1st Cir. 1959). The Court also cited Main Fish Co., 55 F.T.C. 88 (1956), which held that discounts given to a large buyer were not in lieu of brokerage and therefore did not violate § 2(c) because the discounts varied in amount and thus could not be regarded as commensurate with the 5% brokerage fee Main Fish paid on sales to smaller buyers.

9. 363 U.S. at 176.

The key question in evaluating the permissibility of these coop arrangements is whether § 2(c) permits a buyer to perform brokerage services for itself. Unfortunately, answering this question through a coherent interpretation of § 2(c) is difficult, because the language and purposes of § 2(c), as well as the general goals of the Robinson–Patman Act, are directly contradicted by authoritative legislative history. Initially, the FTC concluded that § 2(c) forbade sellers from compensating buyers for any services rendered; under this interpretation, § 2(c) prohibited small business cooperatives from receiving the equivalent of a broker's discount in exchange for arranging orders and payments for their members. In *Henry Broch*, the Court noted that both the Commission and the courts had traditionally rejected "the contention that such a price reduction was lawful because the buyer's purchasing organization had saved the seller the amount of his ordinary brokerage expense." [10] Although the Court recognized that this interpretation had been criticized, it expressly refused to rule on the issue. There was no evidence in *Henry Broch* that Smucker (the buyer) rendered any services to Canada Foods (the seller) or to Broch (the broker), "nor that anything in [Smucker's] method of dealing justified its getting a discriminatory price by means of a reduced brokerage charge. We would have quite a different case if there were such evidence and we need not explore the applicability of § 2(c) to such circumstances." [11]

One of the lower court cases cited in *Henry Broch* was *Southgate Brokerage Co. v. FTC.*[12] In addition to performing traditional brokerage services in the food industry, Southgate purchased goods on its own account, assumed full title and risk, and then resold these products to wholesalers. Packers and canners gave Southgate a commission on these purchases. In its defense, Southgate emphasized the variety of services it performed for the packers and canners, and relied on the text of § 2(c), which makes it "unlawful for any person ... to pay ... anything of value as a ... brokerage, ... *except for services rendered in connection with the sale* ... either to the other party to the transaction or to an agent [of the other party]." [13] This language seems to contemplate

---

10. Id. at 172–73 & nn.10–14.

11. Id. at 163.

12. 150 F.2d 607 (9th Cir. 1945).

13. 15 U.S.C. § 13(c) (emphasis added). Southgate's case thus presented the issues more clearly than two other cases the Court cited in *Henry Broch* as examples of opinions narrowing the "services rendered" exception. In Biddle Purchasing Co. v. FTC, 96 F.2d 687 (2d Cir.), cert. denied, 305 U.S. 634 (1938), a divided panel concluded that Biddle received an illegal discount from the sellers because it really provided services as the agent of the buyers. In Great Atlantic & Pacific Tea Co. v. FTC, 106 F.2d 667 (3d Cir. 1939), cert. denied, 308 U.S. 625 (1940), the court upheld the FTC's finding that a price discount given to A&P was illegal because the discount had obviously replaced a pre-Robinson-Patman brokerage payment from the sellers to A&P's

that a seller may pay a brokerage fee to the buyer for services the buyer performed. Moreover, a buyer that receives a discount in return for performing costly services is not advantaged over another buyer that must pay slightly more for the goods but is spared the cost of the services (presumably provided, in the latter case, by a broker).[14] Nonetheless, the Fourth Circuit sustained the FTC's view that these commissions violated § 2(c).

Southgate explained that it was "not impressed with the argument that the company renders services to those from whom it purchases" because the "crucial fact is that all of the services upon which it relies are services rendered in connection with its own purchase."[15] It "is perfectly clear," the court declared, that "this provision forbids the payment of brokerage on a sale or purchase of goods to the other party to the transaction."[16] In so holding, the court relied on a key passage from the Conference Report supporting its view.[17]

Among *Southgate*'s critics was the 1955 Attorney General's study committee, which concluded that cases like *Southgate* had read the "services rendered" exception to § 2(c) out of the statute, or at a minimum had rewritten the Act to confine the exception to independent brokers.[18] Not only did *Southgate* rewrite the text of § 2(c), but the court's interpretation frustrated the Robinson-Patman Act's general purpose of promoting equal of economic opportunity for small firms while protecting consumers by preserving genuine efficiencies. Small businesses "have conspicuously suffered from rigid 'brokerage' clause enforcement," the study committee noted, because § 2(c) had been interpreted to prevent sellers from giving cooperatives a discount in lieu of brokerage for providing services to the sellers in connection with sales to coop

agents, and any services these agents provided to the sellers were "purely incidental" to services rendered to A&P.

14. It is possible that a large, efficient buyer could provide these services at a lower cost than brokers, thus giving the buyer a cost advantage over smaller rivals that are forced to deal through intermediaries. This situation is no different, though, from a straight discount in price offered to a large buyer because the seller spends less getting the product to the buyer, a discount that would be cost justified and thus lawful under § 2(a).

15. 150 F.2d at 610.

16. Id. at 609.

17. Id. The court cited H.R. Rep. 2951, 74th Cong., 2d Sess. 7 (1936) (emphasis added):

[T]his subsection permits the payment of compensation by a seller to his broker or agent for services actually rendered in his behalf ... but it prohibits the direct or indirect payment of brokerage except for such services rendered. It prohibits its allowance by the buyer direct to the seller, *or by the seller direct to the buyer*; and it prohibits its payment by either to an agent ... acting ... in behalf ... of the other.

18. Report of the Attorney General's National Comm. to Study the Antitrust Laws 188 (1955) [hereafter "Attorney General's Committee"]. Accord, III Earl Kintner & Joseph Bauer, Federal Antitrust Law 503–04 (1983).

members. Moreover, "the virtual legal monopoly conferred by section 2(c) on one type of middlemen clogs competition in the channels of distribution, and exacts tribute from the consumers for the benefit of a special business class."[19]

Notwithstanding the apparent meaning of the text of § 2(c) and the general purposes of the Robinson–Patman Act, *Southgate*'s interpretation would have merit if Congress had enacted the provision in order to protect brokers. In *Henry Broch*, though, the Court found legislative history to suggest that § 2(c) was instead designed to prohibit fictitious brokerage payments that did not compensate for services rendered to the seller, or other "'abuse[s] of the brokerage function for purposes of oppressive discrimination.'"[20] On balance, therefore, the language and specific purpose of § 2(c), as well as the Act's general purposes, all suggest that the one sentence in the Conference Report relied on by *Southgate* should be disregarded.

The FTC began to move away from *Southgate* in *Hruby Distributing Co.*[21] The facts of that case were virtually identical to *Southgate*: Hruby bought goods from food producers and resold them to food wholesalers. The administrative law judge found that the discounts Hruby received violated § 2(c) because they were labeled as "brokerage" and corresponded to the going rate for brokers.[22] The Commission dismissed the complaint, finding that "these discounts have no resemblance whatever to the practices at which section 2(c) was directed."[23]

In *Central Retailer–Owned Grocers, Inc. v. FTC*,[24] the Seventh Circuit likewise rejected *Southgate*'s interpretation. The Court

---

19. Attorney General's Committee, supra note 18, at 191.

20. 363 U.S. at 169 n.6 (quoting H.R. Rep. No. 2287, 74th Cong., 2d Sess. 14 (1936)).

21. 61 F.T.C. 1437 (1962).

22. In an earlier case, the Commission had held that a § 2(c) violation is presumed whenever the amount of a discount is mathematically equal to the customary brokerage fee. Venus Foods, 57 F.T.C. 1025, 1031 (1960).

23. 61 F.T.C. at 1447.

Hruby represented a major policy shift for the Federal Trade Commission, caused by an unexplained change of heart by Chairman Paul Rand Dixon. Just seven months earlier, in National Retailer–Owned Grocers, Inc., 60 F.T.C. 1208 (1962), rev'd sub nom. Central Retailer–Owned Grocers, Inc. v. FTC, 319 F.2d 410 (7th Cir. 1963), the FTC voted 4–1, over a dissent by Commissioner Philip Elman, to prohibit a cooperative from receiving a discount in lieu of brokerage notwithstanding services provided to sellers in arranging sales to its members. *Hruby* was decided by only three commissioners—Commissioner Sigurd Anderson was recused and Commissioner Leon Higginbotham had just been appointed to succeed Commissioner William Kern. Commissioner Everette MacIntyre, a proponent of aggressive Robinson–Patman enforcement, strongly dissented in *Hruby*, arguing that the majority's holding was "completely contrary to overwhelming precedent," particularly *Southgate*. Id. at 1455. Chairman Dixon joined Commissioner Elman's decision, which ignored these precedents.

24. 319 F.2d 410 (7th Cir. 1963).

held that a cooperatively owned corporation, which purchased goods for its own account, properly received cost-justified discounts for arranging direct delivery to its individual members and for coordinating payments, even if there was a "mathematic correlation" between the discount and the industry's normal brokerage commission. Contrary to earlier cases, the Court concluded that the fact that the coop rendered services to its own members did not convert any discounts it received into illegal allowances in lieu of brokerage. The court noted that language in *Henry Broch* seemed to limit § 2(c) to allowances in lieu of brokerage " 'given only to favored customers,' " and emphasized that the cooperative was "a worthy effort" designed to "reduce the ultimate sales price to the consumer" and to make the coop members "stronger in their competition with large chain stores." [25]

The Second Circuit was even more forceful in rejecting the FTC's policy toward a related practice in the garment industry. In *Empire Rayon Yarn Co. v. American Viscose Corp.*,[26] the court upheld a distribution system where two "appointed jobbers" bought yarn from American Viscose at a price below that available to the plaintiff, stored the yarn, and then sold it to smaller fabric manufacturers at prices fixed by American Viscose. The en banc court expressly adopted Judge Leonard Moore's earlier opinion, dissenting from the panel's judgment in favor of the plaintiff.[27] Reinvigorating the services rendered exception, Moore declared that the evil targeted by § 2(c) was " 'unearned brokerage, per se, not discrimination,' "[28] and endorsed the FTC's approach in *Hruby*. Whenever a challenged allowance is based on considerations other than a saved commission or fee, § 2(c) does not apply.[29] Moore thus rejected the approach taken in *Southgate*, declaring that "[r]ecognition of the vital economic function performed by distributors reselling to small wholesalers by the courts and the FTC is long overdue." [30]

These judicial decisions restore § 2(c) to the more limited role of accomplishing the purpose Congress intended the section to serve—to prohibit attempts to evade § 2(a) by disguising discounts as brokerage fees. They correct a line of FTC decisions that seemed to benefit entrenched brokers at the expense of small

25. Id. at 415 (quoting *Henry Broch*, 363 U.S. at 176).

26. 364 F.2d 491 (2d Cir. 1965) (en banc), cert. denied, 385 U.S. 1002 (1967).

27. Id. at 492 (citing 354 F.2d 182, 188–92 (2d Cir. 1965)).

28. Id. at 189 (quoting Robinson v. Stanley Home Products, Inc., 272 F.2d 601, 604 (1st Cir. 1959)).

29. Id. at 190 (citing Frederick Rowe, Price Discrimination Under the Robinson–Patman Act 341 (1962)).

30. Id.

firms that actually purchase and resell merchandise.[31]

(3) Advertising allowances.

In proposing price discrimination legislation, the House Judiciary Committee expressed concern that large buyers might exercise clout by receiving not only discriminatory price concessions but also special promotional or advertising allowances not available to smaller concerns. Thus, the Committee added §§ 2(d) and (e), which require that sellers make any such allowances available "on proportionately equal terms to all other customers competing in the distribution" of their products. Subsection (d) applies to cash allowances; subsection (e) applies to free services provided to buyers, such as handbills and displays at retail stores.

These provisions do not require proof of competitive injury in order to make out a violation, and they provide no cost justification defense. Thus, as *FTC v. Simplicity Pattern Co.*[32] made clear, these subsections absolutely prohibit unequal allowances. The respondent in that case sold tissue patterns used in sewing homemade clothing to two types of retailers. Department and variety stores, which tended to be larger and accounted for most of Simplicity's sales, resold the patterns at a profit. Fabric stores also purchased patterns at wholesale from the respondent, but sold them at no profit in order to stimulate fabric sales. The FTC found that Simplicity violated § 2(e) because department and variety stores received free catalogues and display cabinets, while fabric stores were not given such promotional allowances.[33]

Simplicity sought to "justify" its practices by demonstrating that the disparate treatment did not injure competition and was cost justified. The Court rejected these arguments, holding that "the only escape Congress has provided for discriminations in

31. See, e.g., Independent Grocers Alliance Distributing Co., 48 F.T.C. 894, 936 (1952) (Mason, C., dissenting):

[W]e are here enforcing a law which in effect decrees that a certain cut of the housewife's grocery dollar must go as a broker's gabelle or else be pocketed by the manufacturer himself rather than have it seep down to aid either grocer or consumer.

An astute student of mine noted the considerable irony in the FTC's practice of enforcing laws to entrench brokers, in light of the original English statutes that prohibited forestalling in order to eliminate brokers who interfered with traditional patterns of business. See Chapter 2.

32. 360 U.S. 55 (1959).

33. Simplicity did provide the fabric stores with a variety of other services, including demonstrations by its traveling staff, posters, and brochures that were more suited to their needs. Simplicity did not argue before the FTC that "this tailoring of services and facilities to meet the different needs of two classes of customers in fact constituted 'proportionately equal terms.'" The Court noted, however, that "the Commission has indicated a willingness to give a relatively broad scope to the standard of proportional equality under §§ 2(d) and (e)." Id. at 61 n.4.

services or facilities is the permission to meet competition as found in the § 2(b) proviso." [34]   In sharp contrast with the provisions in § 2(a), § 2(d) does not qualify its prohibition by requiring a competition-lessening effect.   One of the principal purposes of § 2(d) was to force price discrimination into the open.   Thus, if a seller wishes to favor certain buyers and believes that its favoritism will not injure competition, it can provide open and direct price discounts, which can then be tested under § 2(a)'s injury to competition standard.

As is true with many areas of antitrust doctrine, one's view of these provisions depends on one's values and one's perception of how firms behave.   Those who see promotional allowances as concealed discounts will interpret these subsections differently from those who see them as an efficient means of sharing the costs of legitimate, competitive advertising.   Among the latter group, those dedicated to Jeffersonian goals may still want all firms to have an equal opportunity to receive the allowances, even if not dictated by the economies of the marketplace.   Those viewing antitrust through a purely economic lens, however, will decry a broad interpretation of §§ 2(d) and (e) that forces a seller to pay for promotional activities that it does not desire.

The emphasis on equality of opportunity and the corresponding disregard for concerns that sellers might be forced to pay for unwanted promotion are exemplified by the FTC's decision in *House of Lord's, Inc.*[35]   The respondent there distributed women's dresses in the United States for a British manufacturer.   One of House of Lords' responsibilities was to allocate a sum of money made available by the manufacturer to subsidize a cooperative advertising campaign.   The FTC found that Lords' allocation system violated § 2(d) because its offer to pay half of retailers' advertising costs was limited to newspaper and magazine advertisements.   In the context of the retail garment industry, the FTC noted, offering to share the advertising costs of a small retailer that cannot afford newspaper advertising is "no offer at all." Thus, if a manufacturer or wholesaler "elects to give promotional money to one of its customers in a community, it has the duty, we believe, to devise and communicate to each of its other competing customers in that community a promotion plan *with at least one feature than can be used by each of them.*" [36]

This holding may push the prophylactic concerns about using of promotional allowances to give unjustified favors to powerful buyers too far.   Many sellers may have narrow promotional goals and may legitimately prefer a limited promotion available on a

34. Id. at 67.

35. 69 F.T.C. 44 (1966).

36. Id. at 83.

non-discriminatory basis; it is not clear why they should be forced to pay for more. In these cases, a seller may decide to offer only specific types of promotional allowances because of its own marketing plan, and not as the result of undue economic pressure from powerful buyers.[37] Once again, the FTC's decision is perverse. It disadvantages smaller manufacturers, which must rely on cooperative advertising, and favors large firms capable of performing their own advertising, which is not subject to §§ 2(d) and (e). By favoring firms capable of engaging in large national advertising campaigns, the case frustrates the Jeffersonian desire to preserve smaller, locally based firms.[38] Moreover, requiring a seller to provide allowances for advertising it does not consider cost effective results in an inefficient allocation of resources (either sums are spent on unnecessary advertising or expenditures are foregone because the seller chooses to avoid the whole § 2(d) problem) and harms consumers (either prices increase because of unnecessary advertising expenses or consumers are denied the benefit of useful advertising because the seller forgoes a cooperative advertising program).

Another complicated issue concerning §§ 2(d) and (e) involves the interpretation of the statutory requirement that promotional allowances be "available on proportionally equal terms" and that promotional services and facilities be "accorded to all purchasers on proportionally equal terms." In *Vanity Fair Paper Mills, Inc. v. FTC*,[39] for example, the seller's promotional program consisted of agreeing to consider any buyer's request that Vanity Fair participate in a one-time special promotion, such as an anniversary sale. Weingarten, a large retailer in southeast Texas and southwest Louisiana, asked Vanity Fair to participate in such a

---

37. In dissent, Commissioner Philip Elman argued that

> Congress did not require a seller to subsidize all customer 'promotional activity,' regardless of its value to him. Congress was aware that not all advertising would be of equal value to the seller, and section 2(d) did not require him to pay for all advertising. He need only pay for advertising which benefitted his business, and his payments had to be in proportion to the benefit he received.

Id. at 93. In support of his argument, Elman cited portions of the legislative history, including comments by the Senate floor manager indicating that § 2(d) was intended to "prevent services allowances when the use of them results in *unfair* discrimination," 80 Cong. Rec. 3116 (1936) (statement of Sen. Logan) (emphasis added), and the Senate Committee Report's explanation that § 2(d)'s requirement of proportionality meant that a smaller buyer had the right to a similar allowance to that afforded its larger rival when it could furnish promotional services or facilities "in less quality, *but of the same relative value.*" S. Rep. No. 1502, 74th Cong., 2d Sess. 8 (1936) (emphasis added).

38. Cf. Brown Shoe Co. v. United States, 370 U.S. 294 (1962) and United States v. Pabst Brewing Co., 384 U.S. 546 (1966), discussed above in Chapter 6, section A(3), which blocked mergers out of concern that the acquisitions would allow national advertising firms to dominate an industry.

39. 311 F.2d 480 (2d Cir. 1962).

sale, and received $215 for advertising in a local newspaper. Another rival received an allowance of $152, and none of the other 26 firms in the market requested any such allowance. In finding a violation of § 2(d), the Second Circuit noted that allowances are clearly not "available" if the seller has denied them to disfavored buyers or has affirmatively acted to conceal them from certain buyers. Applying this standard to the facts before it, the court sustained the FTC's conclusion that Vanity Fair's failure to direct its sales representatives to inform buyers about its policies violated § 2(d).[40] As an alternative basis for funding a § 2(d) violation, the court sustained the FTC's conclusion that Vanity Fair's vague and discretionary policy ensured, at most, that allowances *might* be available on equal terms, not that they *would* be available on such terms.[41] Unlike the *House of Lord's* requirement that at least some part of a sellers' promotion plans be usable by all buyers, *Vanity Fair*'s requirements—that promotional assistance plans be objectively verifiable and that all buyers be informed of them—make some sense in preventing evasion of the Act's mandate, even if they are somewhat burdensome.

(4) The pendulum swings back.

Recognizing that its prior interpretation of §§ 2(d) and (e) unduly protected certain firms without truly promoting the public interest in a fair and vigorous competitive process, the FTC has recently narrowed the scope of liability for unequal promotional allowances. Although this development is a positive one, some signs suggest that the pendulum may swing too far in the other direction if the commissioners exalt economic efficiency and a general faith in the markets over the policies underlying the Robinson–Patman Act.

In *General Motors Corp.*,[42] the FTC staff challenged GM's discriminatory practice of making substantial advertising allowances available only to the largest rental and leasing companies. The Commission found no violation of § 2(d) because that section applies only to allowances in connection with resale, not leasing. (Recall that § 2(a) is likewise limited to price discrimination involving sales, not leases.)

More questionable was the FTC's outright rejection of another count in the complaint, which alleged that GM's conduct was an unfair method of competition in violation of § 5 of the FTC Act. One of § 5's main purposes is to permit the FTC to proscribe

---

40. Id. at 485.

41. Id. at 487. *Vanity Fair* also held that, despite the linguistic differences between subsections (d) and (e), this re-quirement applied to both provisions. Id. at 484–85.

42. 103 F.T.C. 641 (1984).

anticompetitive conduct that conflicts with the values underlying the antitrust laws but that, for some technical reason, does not literally run afoul of the Sherman or Clayton Acts.[43] Arguing that the Robinson–Patman Act is "protectionist," rather than aimed at promoting competition, *General Motors* refused to similarly apply § 5 to proscribe conduct contrary to the values but not the letter of the Robinson–Patman Act, absent proof of "an anticompetitive impact." [44]

Just as the FTC indicated that "great caution" must be used in relying on § 5 to prohibit conduct that is inconsistent with the spirit of the Robinson–Patman Act,[45] care must be exercised in applying *General Motors* because its holding paints with too broad a brush. If, for example, GM's allowances to rental car companies were to be used only for national advertising, because GM believed that was the only cost-effective type of advertising, then requiring GM to partially fund the efforts of some small firm to distribute handbills at the local mall really is protectionist. At the other extreme, giving Hertz and Avis allowances based solely on their exercise of buyer power might enhance their brand loyalty and allow them to engage in oligopoly pricing because they would not need to fear serious competition from smaller companies. Such a scenario would probably suffice to demonstrate anticompetitive harm under the *General Motors* test. But suppose that Hertz, Avis, Budget, National, and Alamo all received allowances, thus making proof of oligopoly pricing more difficult; today's FTC might find no "anticompetitive impact" there. If the evidence showed that these allowances were allocated in a discriminatory fashion based on buyer power rather than efficiency concerns, § 5 ought to condemn them, even if they may not have the effect of substantial lessening competition, as a means of accommodating the efficiency and equal opportunity goals of the antitrust laws.

An example of an unwarranted swing toward underenforcement of equal opportunity concerns is shown by the dissents in *Max Factor & Co.*,[46] where a sharply divided Commission accepted a straightforward consent order requiring the respondent to make future promotional allowances available on proportionately equal terms to all customers and to make alternatives available to those customers that found Max Factor's basic promotional plans unusable or economically infeasible. Chairman Daniel Oliver and Commissioner Andrew Strenio objected because, in their view, promotional allowances paid by a small company like Max Factor

43. See FTC v. Brown Shoe Co., 384 U.S. 316, 321 (1966); Fashion Originators' Guild of America v. FTC, 312 U.S. 457, 463 (1941).

44. 103 F.T.C. at 701 (emphasis omitted).

45. Id.

46. 108 F.T.C. 135 (1986)

could not possibly injure competition in the highly competitive cosmetics industry.[47]

Strenio acknowledged that his view directly contradicts *Simplicity Pattern*'s holding that subsections (d) and (e) are per se prohibitions, designed to force discrimination out in the open. He avoided this problem by suggesting that *Simplicity Pattern* may no longer be good law. But his support for that suggestion was not a superior reading of § 2(d)'s language, or a compelling critique of the Court's method of implementing Congress' desire to prevent the use of promotional allowances to conceal price discrimination. Rather, he simply alluded to Supreme Court cases decided after *Simplicity Pattern* interpreted the broad language of § 1 of the Sherman Act to require the courts to consider the effect the challenged conduct will have on competition before imposing antitrust liability.[48] But these Sherman Act cases are totally inapposite in interpreting the detailed, specific terms of the Robinson–Patman Act. Strenio admitted that his views were tentative;[49] they should not be followed by his successors on the Commission.[50]

What may have been most objectionable about *Max Factor* was its fidelity to the *House of Lord's* requirement that the seller specially design alternative promotions for those who could not make use of its standard allowance programs. If the FTC wishes to make reforms in the § 2(d) area, it would do well to reconsider *House of Lord's*. Section 2(d)'s instruction that sellers must make allowances available on "proportionately equal terms" has some flexibility, and need not necessarily require this intrusive mandate.

(5) Allowances to indirect purchasers.

In interpreting the broad language of the Sherman Act, judges necessarily rely on their own views concerning the competing goals of antitrust and the efficacy of using antitrust enforcement to facilitate the competitive process. On the other hand, the courts have generally applied the detailed prophylactic provisions of §§ 2(c), (d), and (e) literally, even if the result does not effectuate their own view of optimal competition policy. This literal approach is particularly appropriate in light of the broader standards governing price discrimination under § 2(a), and agency or

47. Id. at 141 (Oliver, C., dissenting); id. at 144 (Strenio, C., dissenting).

48. Id. at 144 n.1 (citing Continental T.V., Inc., v. GTE Sylvania, Inc., 433 U.S. 36 (1977) (overturning per se illegality of non-price vertical restraints under § 1)).

49. Id.

50. Chairman Oliver based his dissent on the inherent discretion the FTC possesses to decline to prosecute law violates when enforcement is not in the public interest. Id. at 140.

judicial *expansion* of the tough provisions on brokerage and promotional allowances is totally unwarranted.

Nevertheless, this is exactly what happened in *FTC v. Fred Meyer, Inc.*[51] The respondent there was a large supermarket chain in Portland, Oregon. As part of an annual promotional campaign, it put together a 72–page coupon book offering savings on the products sold in its stores. These books were financed, for the most part, by a $350 fee paid by the sellers whose products were featured in the book. The Commission held that this program violated § 2(d) because the sellers had not given similar allowances to Meyer's competitors.[52]

Fred Meyer argued that § 2(d) was inapplicable because it was the only supermarket in Oregon that purchased goods directly from food manufacturers; the others bought through wholesalers. Thus, according to Meyer, neither the wholesalers nor Meyer's retail rivals were "other customers competing in the distribution of such products or commodities," and therefore they were not protected by the language of § 2(d). The Supreme Court rejected this literal interpretation, holding instead that the term "customers" includes indirect buyers that purchase the seller's goods through an intermediary. Thus, sellers would be required to deal either directly with these retailers, or indirectly through the wholesalers, in providing comparable promotional allowances.[53]

Justice John Harlan wrote a forceful dissent. Notwithstanding his candid disdain for the Robinson–Patman Act,[54] he properly noted that the "broad purpose of the Act was to protect small sellers from the advantages their largest competitors can obtain through greater buying power." In his view, the Court had no business departing from the terms of the statute in order to implement the majority's "own notions of how best to protect 'little people' from 'big people.'" Harlan convincingly scolded the majority for construing the word "customers" to mean "non-customers who the Court thinks need protection." Finally, he correctly pointed out that considerable administrative problems

51. 390 U.S. 341 (1968).

52. The FTC charged that Fred Meyer engaged in an unfair method of competition in violation of § 5 of the FTC Act by inducing a disproportionate allowance in violation of § 2(d). Id. at 346. The reason for using the FTC Act in this manner is discussed below, see note 62 infra and accompanying text.

53. 390 U.S. at 348–49.

54. See id. at 359–60 ("the statute imposes a hodgepodge of confusing, inconsistent, and frequently misdirected restrictions"). Although Harlan's candor may be commendable, it detracts from the persuasive force of his criticism for those who may disagree with his general hostility towards the Act as a matter of either competition policy or statutory interpretation. This is particularly unfortunate here because Harlan's harsh overall criticism of the Act was not necessary to make the fundamental points raised in the dissent.

would arise if suppliers were compelled to make promotional allowances available to retailers with whom they do not deal.[55]

The majority felt that it was effectuating Congress' goals by closing a loophole that would otherwise be available only to the large and powerful buyers whose behavior was the direct concern of the Robinson–Patman Act.[56] Creating a burdensome obligation to deal indirectly with retailers was unnecessary, however. The majority's error lay in its acceptance of the FTC's conclusion that under the respondent's narrow interpretation of § 2(d), "a retailer buying from a wholesaler and having no direct dealings with his supplier would receive no protection against discriminatory promotional allowances given his competitor who purchased directly from the supplier."[57] The Court did not need to misconstrue § 2(d) to avoid this loophole because providing discriminatory sale allowances can also be considered unlawful price discrimination in violation of § 2(a), as well as § 5 of the FTC Act.

It is noteworthy that § 2(a), unlike § 2(d), expressly covers not only those who compete with direct buyers, but customers of direct buyers as well.[58] Section § 2(a) can thus be used to protect small retailers that deal through wholesalers (although proceeding under that provision does require that the FTC show competitive injury and does allow the cost justification and meeting competition defenses). The court of appeals' opinion in *Fred Meyer* suggested that discriminatory promotional allowances might be actionable under § 2(a), but the Supreme Court declined to rule on that issue.[59]

In private litigation, some courts have suggested that §§ 2(a) and (d) are mutually exclusive, so that § 2(a) would not be available to bar discriminatory allowances in a situation like *Fred Meyer*.[60] That view is inconsistent with early FTC precedents that

---

55. Id. at 360–62.

56. Id. at 352.

57. Id. at 347.

58. See 15 U.S.C. § 13(a) (barring price discrimination that causes injury to competition with "any person who grants or knowingly receives the benefit of such discrimination, *or with customers of either of them*" (emphasis added).

59. See 359 F.2d 351, 362 (9th Cir. 1966). The Court's grant of certiorari was limited to the question raised by the FTC as to whether it could properly apply § 2(d) to ban disproportionate allowances given to Fred Meyer when the sellers dealt with Meyer's rivals only indirectly through wholesalers. 390 U.S. at 344 n.3.

60. See, e.g., Kirby v. P.R. Mallory & Co., 489 F.2d 904, 910–11 (7th Cir. 1973), cert. denied, 417 U.S. 911 (1974).

In making this suggestion, *Kirby* relied on two passages from the Robinson–Patman Act's legislative history. The first was the Senate floor manager's statement that subsections (d) and (e) covered a " 'second scheme' " designed to evade the price discrimination outlawed in the original Clayton Act. Id. at 910 (quoting 80 Cong. Rec. 6282 (1936) (statement of Sen. Logan)). *Kirby* read this comment to suggest that price discrimination and allowance discrimination are separate, exclusive types of "schemes." As the Supreme Court explained in FTC v. Simplicity Pattern Co., 360 U.S. 55, 68 (1959), how-

deemed discriminatory advertising allowances to be indirect price discrimination in violation of § 2(a).[61] Beginning in 1960, however, the Commission changed its mind, relying on an ambiguous portion of the legislative history to hold that § 2(a) did not apply to such allowances.[62] This holding should not be given too much

ever, subsections (d) and (e) serve the salutary purpose of forcing sellers "to confine their discriminatory practices to price differentials, where they could be more readily detected and where it would be much easier to make accurate comparisons with any alleged costs savings." The Court noted there that the practices outlawed by subsections (d) and (e) were often referred to as "secret" discriminations. Id. at 68 n.12 (citing 80 Cong. Rec. 8126, 8127, 8132, 8137, 8226 (1936)). Viewed in this light, the floor manager's reference to secret discriminations as a "second scheme" does not suggest that, where promotional allowances *are* detected, they do not constitute indirect price discrimination subject to § 2(a).

Kirby relied, second, on language in the House Judiciary Committee's report explaining that the Act's purpose was to proscribe discriminations " 'sometimes effected directly in prices . . . and sometimes by separate allowances to favored customers.' " Id. (quoting H.R. Rep. No. 2287, 74th Cong., 2d Sess. 7 (1936)). That Report, however, discusses the version of the legislation that existed before it was amended on the House floor to delete a narrow statutory definition of price. The Conference Report, which is more authoritative, refers to the adopted language of § 2(a) in broader terms, covering both direct and indirect price discrimination, H.R. Rep. No. 2951, 74th Cong., 2d Sess. 5 (1936), and discriminatory allowances would seem to fall within the definition of "indirect discrimination."

Kirby also suggested that subsections (d) and (e) would be surplusage if discrimination in promotional benefits constituted indirect price discrimination. This argument is incorrect. Not only do the per se prohibitions contained in those subsections serve the purpose of publicizing discrimination, as recognized in *Simplicity Pattern*, but their requirement of proportionality mandates a greater degree of equal treatment for promotional allowances

and services than is generally imposed on sellers by § 2(a).

61. Rowe, supra note 29, at 429–30 & n.39 (citing National Tea Co., 46 F.T.C. 829, 835 (1950); Atlantic City Wholesale Drug Co., 38 F.T.C. 631, 636 (1944); Miami Wholesale Drug Co., 28 F.T.C. 485, 491–92 (1939)). In each of these cases, the FTC was forced to use § 2(a)'s ban on price discrimination to prohibit a discriminatory advertising allowance because the respondents were buyers, and § 2(f), which imposes liability on buyers, applies only when they induce an unlawful discrimination in *price*. This issue is discussed further in section H(2).

62. Grand Union Co., 57 F.T.C. 382 (1960), modified on other grounds, 300 F.2d 92 (2d Cir. 1962).

The FTC relied on a statement made by Representative Utterback, who chaired the House Conferees. In describing § 2(f)'s prohibition of buyer inducement of illegal discriminations in price, Utterback commented:

That [provision] applies both to direct and indirect discrimination; and where, for example, there is discrimination in terms of sale, *or in allowances connected or related to the contract of sale*, of such character as to constitute or effect an indirect discrimination in price. . . .

80 Cong. Rec. 9419 (1936) (emphasis added). This statement could be read as distinguishing between allowances made in order to facilitate the original sale to the favored buyer, and allowances made in order to facilitate resale of the product by the favored buyer. The italicized phrase could therefore be read as limiting § 2(f), and thus § 2(a), to allowances facilitating the original sale, whereas subsections (d) and (e) apply only to allowances facilitating the *resale* of goods. But it makes no difference whether a promotional allowance is ultimately aimed at facilitating the seller's sale of the product or the buyer's resale of that product; in both cases, the seller may be willing to offer

weight, however, because it was not all that significant to the Commission given that the FTC can also challenge discriminatory allowances under § 5 of the FTC Act. As in *Fred Meyer*, for example, the Commission can use § 5 to condemn discriminatory promotional allowances as an unfair method of competition if it believes the allowances reflect the exercise of buyer power or will tend to reduce price competition among retailers. Thus, the FTC had the power to fully protect the legitimate interests of small retailers—the focus of congressional concern—without needing to expand the scope of § 2(d) to cover disproportionate allowances to direct and indirect purchasers.

Interpreting both §§ 2(a) and (d) to ban discriminatory promotional allowances would ensure that liability is imposed on all sellers that give unjustified allowances harmful to competition. Moreover, applying § 2(a) in a case like *Fred Meyer* would expose buyers to liability under § 2(f) for inducing a discriminatory price. Instead, *Fred Meyer* expanded the per se prohibitions of § 2(d) and created administrative havoc by requiring sellers to ensure that retail promotional allowances are made available to wholesalers (to be passed on to their customers) as well as to retailers with whom the sellers deal directly. This decision results in far greater intrusion than is required by the public interests underlying the Robinson–Patman Act, which by its terms seeks to harmonize the goals of ensuring that consumers benefit from an open and vigorous competitive process and preserving small businesses whose continued ability to compete is threatened by the unjustified exercise of buyer power. The end result of *Fred Meyer* is to afford undue protection to some specially situated firms and to perpetuate the general disdain for the Robinson–Patman Act that corrodes the ability of fair-minded judges and trade commissioners to reach a coherent balance of the conflicting goals of antitrust.

Section H: Buyer Liability

Section 2(f) of the Robinson–Patman Act imposes liability on buyers that "knowingly[ ] induce or receive a discrimination in

additional promotional allowances to favored buyers to encourage them to purchase greater quantities of its product. Especially in light of the breadth of the words "connected" and "related," discriminatory allowances made for resale seem to be covered by this passage as well.

Grand Union opined that "Congress intended to include knowing inducement or receipt of a disproportionate allowance within the purview of section 2(f) and its failure to do so was the result of an oversight." 57 F.T.C. at 422. Given its own precedents and one plausible reading of an ambiguous passage, however, the FTC did not explain why it was necessary to interpret the statute as a case of congressional negligence. See Rowe, supra note 29, at 436 (suggesting that FTC precedents finding that discriminatory promotional benefits constitute price discrimination were "perhaps caused because of *its* long oversight of the ostensible Congressional 'oversight' ") (emphasis in original).

price which is prohibited by this section." Although the main purpose of the Act was to prevent large buyers from abusing their economic power, these buyers are liable under § 2(f) only if their conduct was (1) knowing, (2) induced a discrimination in *price*, and (3) induced a sale that is illegal under the Act's other provisions.

The cases discussing buyer liability provide an appropriate closure for this discussion of price discrimination laws. These cases explicitly recognize the tension between the in Sherman Act's policy of encouraging free markets and aggressive competition and the Robinson–Patman Act's goal of avoiding unfair exercises of economic power.

(1) **What does the favored buyer have to know?**

Automatic Canteen Co. v. FTC[1] provided the Supreme Court with its first opportunity to construe § 2(f) in line with its declared policy of harmonizing the conflicting goals of the Sherman and Robinson–Patman Acts. The case seemed to represent the consummate evil Congress envisioned when enacting the price discrimination statute. Automatic Canteen was the dominant vending machine operator in the nation, and thus a substantial purchaser of candies and similar products. The FTC found the company guilty of violating § 2(f), based on evidence that it had received a 33% discount and had made no effort to ascertain whether that discount was cost justified.

Cost justification considerations are relevant, the FTC and the Court agreed, because § 2(f) applies only to price discrimination "prohibited by this section [i.e. § 2]." Because a cost-justified price differential is not barred by the Act, § 2(f) does not prevent a buyer from inducing such a differential. The key issue in the case was whether § 2(f)'s requirement that the inducement be "knowing" required proof the buyer knew that the sale was not cost justified. The FTC said no, and the Supreme Court reversed.

Although Justice Felix Frankfurter's majority opinion purported to be based on a straightforward reading of the statute, it was clearly influenced by two major policy considerations. First, the Court expressed an aversion to any interpretation that would chill vigorous bargaining over prices.[2] Such an interpretation would "readily extend beyond the prohibitions of the Act and, in doing so, help give rise to a price uniformity and rigidity in open conflict with the purposes of other antitrust legislation."[3] Thus, the Court made an effort to interpret the Robinson–Patman Act so as to cut a narrow path that effectuated the policies underlying

1. 346 U.S. 61 (1953).
2. Id. at 73–74.
3. Id. at 63.

that statute without encroaching on of the Sherman Act's goal of vigorous price rivalry. Second, the Court recognized that precedents had already made the cost justification defense extraordinarily difficult to establish.[4] Thus, requiring the *buyer* to prove that the *seller's* cost structure justified the discount seemed particularly burdensome.

The Court held that the language in § 2(f) requiring that the buyer's inducement of an illegal price discrimination be "knowing" obligated the FTC to prove that Automatic Canteen knew both that its price was different and that it was illegal—i.e., that it was not cost justified. The majority's attempt to base its holding entirely on the plain language of the statute runs into difficulty, however, when one considers the affirmative defense provisions of § 2(b). That section provides that the FTC can establish a prima facie case by showing "discrimination in price or services or facilities furnished"; once this showing has been made, "the burden of rebutting the prima-facie case thus made by showing justification shall be upon the person charged with a violation of this section ..."[5] This language suggests that the FTC correctly imposed the burden of justifying the price differential on Automatic Canteen. The Supreme Court held, however, that § 2(b) applies only to the element of a § 2(f) charge that requires proof of a discriminatory price, and not to the element that requires proof of "knowing inducement."[6]

Although Frankfurter provided only modest historical support for this conclusion,[7] he listed a host of policy arguments explaining why buyers should not bear the burden of proving that their

---

4. Id. at 68–69. See generally section E above.

5. 15 U.S.C. § 13(b).

6. 346 U.S. at 76.

7. The Court took note of remarks made by Representative Hubert Utterback, chair of the House conferees, in presenting the Conference Report to the House. Utterback explained that § 2(f)

affords valuable support to the manufacturer in his efforts to abide by the intent and purpose of the bill. It makes it easier for him to resist the demand for sacrificial price cuts coming from mass-buyer customers, since it enables him to charge them with knowledge of the illegality of the discount, and equal liability for it, by informing them that it is in excess of any differential which his difference in cost would justify as compared with him other customers.

80 Cong. Rec. 9419 (1936).

The Court therefore concluded that the House "contemplated [that] *only* the buyer who knew that the price was not justified by costs" would be liable under § 2(f). 346 U.S. at 73 n.15 (emphasis added). In so doing, the Court made a dramatic leap from Utterback's description of *a* benefit created by the section to the conclusion that that benefit was *the sole* purpose of § 2(f). Moreover, this interpretation is inconsistent with the Act's overall goals. The statute was designed to protect victims of discrimination, not sellers forced to discriminate, and there is no support for the notion that discrimination was somehow more tolerable if the seller did not fend off the buyer by mentioning the possibility of antitrust liability.

discriminatory sale was cost justified. Frankfurter argued that the purpose of § 2(b) was to shift the burden to the party with easiest access to the evidence; although this reasoning applies in § 2(a) litigation against sellers the court observed, it is not applicable in § 2(f) suits against buyers, who are in no better position than the government or a private plaintiff to learn the seller's costs.[8] Second, the Court opined that requiring buyers to obtain this information would discourage buyer pressure for discounts, a dynamic that is an integral part of the competitive process.[9] Third, acquiring evidence to justify a differential based on costs would be unfairly burdensome to buyers. Finally, such a requirement would encourage buyers and sellers to share sensitive price information, a practice often frowned upon by the Sherman Act precedents.[10]

Although the majority predicted that continued enforcement of § 2(f) against powerful buyers "should not be difficult," [11] *Automatic Canteen* brought FTC actions against larger buyers to a halt for years.[12] Nonetheless, the opinion did provide some examples of evidence that suffice to permit the inference that the buyer knew its discriminatory price was illegal. If the buyer knew that the seller used the same methods of sale and delivery for itself and the disfavored buyers, the courts would infer knowledge that the price difference was not cost justified. More typically, sales to a large buyer will involve different methods of sale and delivery than sales to its smaller rivals. Even in those cases, if it was well-known that the savings attributable to these different methods were smaller than the price difference, liability could be imposed on the buyer.[13]

The real issue in *Automatic Canteen* concerned the policies underlying the cost justification defense, not the buyer liability. Justice William O. Douglas argued in dissent that Canteen's "persistent and continuous efforts" in "wheedling and coercing suppliers into granting it discriminatory prices" was typical of the

8. 346 U.S. at 79.

9. Id. at 73–74.

10. Id. at 69.

11. Id. at 79.

12. See II American Bar Ass'n Section of Antitrust Law, Monograph No. 4, The Robinson–Patman Act: Policy and Law 75 (1983): "The impact of [*Automatic Canteen*] on enforcement of section 2(f) was seismic; the processing of section 2(f) cases at the Commission came to a dead stop."

Unfortunately, in its bureaucratic zeal to win some cases under § 2(f), the Commission staff turned its attention to small firms that had formed buying cooperatives. See, e.g., American Motor Specialties Co. v. FTC, 278 F.2d 225 (2d Cir.1960), cert. denied, 364 U.S. 884 (1960) (because coop members received discounts from the price they charged prior to formation of cooperative, they knew that discounts were not cost justified).

13. 346 U.S. at 80.

advantages large buyers enjoy over their smaller rivals.[14] Under this view, larger buyers should be discouraged from exacting pressure for lower prices and therefore sellers should be allowed to engage in discriminatory pricing only if they have ascertained beforehand that the sale is lawful (because it is cost justified, meets competition, etc.), and it does not seem extremely burdensome to require a buyer to take reasonable steps to ensure that the seller has made that determination before the sale is made. On the other hand, if cost justified discounts are typical and reflect an efficient market, sellers should be encouraged to discount whenever they find it advantageous to do so, and *post hoc* cost justification studies should be perfectly acceptable. Under this view, the burden the FTC sought to impose on Canteen really does interfere with sound policy.

(2) Buyer liability for discriminatory promotional benefits.

Section 2(f) applies to buyer inducements of discriminatory prices that violate § 2(a), and the receipt of illegal brokerage allowances is expressly prohibited by § 2(c). There are no provisions, however, that explicitly proscribe the inducement of discriminatory promotional allowances illegal under §§ 2(d) or (e).

Nevertheless, § 5 of the FTC Act authorizes the Commission to prohibit unfair methods of competition. One of the principal purposes of this provision was to allow the FTC to condemn anticompetitive acts that might violate the spirit, but not the letter, of the other antitrust laws.[15] Over the years, the FTC has grappled with the idea of using this power to attack price discrimination that does not fall within the literal scope of the Robinson–Patman Act. This question has arisen principally in cases where buyers induced discriminatory promotional allowances.[16]

Originally, both the FTC and the lower courts took the view that these allowances constituted indirect price discrimination under § 2(a), thus providing a basis for imposing liability on buyers under § 2(f).[17] Although the lower courts remain divided on that issue today,[18] the FTC eventually decided to pursue anoth-

14. Id. at 83–84.

15. FTC v. Brown Shoe Co., 384 U.S. 316, 321 (1966); Fashion Originators' Guild of America v. FTC, 312 U.S. 457, 463 (1941).

16. This issue is also discussed above in section G(5).

17. See Frederick Rowe, Price Discrimination Under the Robinson–Pat-

man Act 428–30 (1962) (listing FTC cases).

18. Compare Viviano Macaroni Co. v. FTC, 411 F.2d 255, 258 (3d Cir. 1968) (discriminatory payment of advertising allowances constitutes both price discrimination in violation of § 2(a) and disproportionate allowances in violation of § 2(d)), with Kirby v. P.R. Mallory & Co., Inc., 489 F.2d 904, 910–11 (7th Cir. 1973), cert. denied, 417 U.S. 911 (1974)

er course in attacking this type of buyer behavior. In *Grand Union Co. v. FTC*,[19] the Commission challenged a powerful buyer's inducement of discriminatory advertising allowances as an unfair method of competition in violation of § 5. Grand Union, a large New York supermarket chain, arranged with suppliers and an advertising firm to display a "spectacular" advertising sign in Times Square promoting the suppliers' products as well as Grand Union markets. One of the suppliers was Swanee, whose payment to help finance the sign was found to be an unlawful promotional allowance in violation of § 2(d).[20] Buyers are not liable under § 2(d), however. Moreover, because § 2(f) only proscribes inducement of an unlawful "discrimination in price," the FTC could not use Swanee's violation of § 2(d) as a basis for finding Grand Union liable under § 2(f). Rather than find that Swanee's allowance was also indirect price discrimination or let Grand Union escape liability on a technicality, the FTC held that § 5 gave it the power to bolster other antitrust statutes by outlawing acts which violate their "spirit," if not their letter.[21] A divided Second Circuit panel sustained this holding.

Judge Charles Clark's majority opinion noted that the Robinson–Patman Act's legislative history did not explain why Congress omitted buyers from the scope of § 2(d), while providing for liability for inducing brokerage (in § 2(c)) and price discrimination (in § 2(f)). In fact, the court observed, powerful buyers were the villains who had created most of the economic evils the Act was designed to remedy. Moreover, the FTC's action did not significantly expand the scope of the antitrust laws—after all, the very conduct at issue had already been proscribed by a cease and desist order directed against participating suppliers.[22] This reasoning appears consistent with Supreme Court precedents that give the FTC authority to "hit at every trade practice, then existing or thereafter contrived, which restrained competition."[23]

More controversial was the court's holding that an FTC proceeding against a buyer for inducing a discriminatory allowance, like a § 2(d) suit against the seller, does not require proof of competitive injury and does not afford a justification defense.[24] If the FTC has proceeded under § 2(f), based on its earlier precedent

(buyer that induced discriminatory payments in connection with the resale of a commodity, rather than the original sale, is not liable for inducing price discrimination under § 2(f)).

19. 300 F.2d 92 (2d Cir. 1962).

20. Swanee Paper Corp. v. FTC, 291 F.2d 833 (2d Cir. 1961), cert. denied, 368 U.S. 987 (1962).

21. *Grand Union*, 57 F.T.C. 382, 423 (1960).

22. 300 F.2d at 98.

23. FTC v. Cement Institute, 333 U.S. 683, 693 (1948).

24. Id. at 99–100.

indicating that Grand Union's inducement of the discriminatory advertising allowance constituted indirect price discrimination, it would have had to demonstrate competitive injury and Grand Union could have defended the inducement as cost justified. This may explain why the FTC chose to proceed under § 5, instead of § 2(f). But § 5 prohibits only "unfair methods of competition," and it is hard to see the unfairness in a discriminatory allowance that causes no competitive injury or is cost justified.

Because Grand Union was found liable under § 5, the court found it unnecessary to determine whether the payments also constituted "a discrimination in price" within the meaning of § 2(f).[25] The Supreme Court has likewise ducked this issue on two occasions.[26] As noted in section G(5), the Court's refusal to clearly hold that discriminatory allowances fall within the broad scope of § 2(a)'s ban on direct and indirect price discrimination is unfortunate. As a result, private parties, who cannot invoke § 5, face a significant hurdle in challenging discriminatory allowances, and large buyers have been immunized from treble damage liability for exercising their power to obtain such allowances. Moreover, although the purpose of the stricter standards contained in subsections (d) and (e) is to force price discrimination into the open, where it can be analyzed under § 2(a), *Grand Union* actually creates the opposite incentive: powerful buyers seeking illegal discounts or even discounts of questionable legality will prefer to receive favoritism via a promotional allowance (which does not subject them to private damage liability) rather than as an above-board price discrimination. At the same time, extending § 2(d)'s per se condemnation to buyers gives the FTC the authority, if it chooses to follow a bureaucratic imperative, to score meaningless victories by challenging cost justified or competitively insignificant inducements by buyers.

(3) *A&P*: the pendulum swings toward big buyers.

Borden and Bowman were two major dairies in Chicago for much of the post-World War II period. In 1951, they began giving special discounts to the large A&P supermarket chain; these discounts were struck down by the Supreme Court in 1962.[27] Continuing to request favored treatment, A&P sought a major contract for private label milk (sold under an A&P label) from the dairies in 1965. Borden offered to provide the milk to A&P at an annual cost savings of $410,000; Bowman countered with a lower

---

25. Id. at 95.

26. See FTC v. Fred Meyer, Inc., 390 U.S. 341, 344 n.3 (1968); Automatic Canteen Co. v. FTC, 346 U.S. 61, 73 n.14 (1953).

27. United States v. Borden Co., 370 U.S. 460 (1962), which is discussed in section E(3) above.

offer. A&P's Chicago buyer then contacted Borden's sales manager and said, "I have a bid in my pocket. You people are so far out of line it is not even funny. You are not even in the ball park." The A&P representative suggested that an additional $50,000 reduction in Borden's price "would not be a drop in the bucket." Borden had just invested more than $5 million in a new Illinois dairy, and losing a major account like A&P would create significant excess capacity. Faced with this prospect, Borden submitted a new bid offering A&P annual savings of $820,000, substantially underbidding Bowman.[28]

Based on these facts, the FTC staff charged that A&P had unlawfully induced a discriminatory price by failing to inform Borden that its new offer was significantly below Bowman's offer, and thus was greater than necessary to meet competition. In an unusual opinion, the Commission rejected the staff's claim that A&P's conduct constituted an unfair method of competition in violation of § 5, because the commissioners felt that imposing such a disclosure requirement was contrary to the public interest. Nonetheless, the FTC held that the identical conduct violated § 2(f) of the Robinson–Patman Act. The Commission rejected A&P's argument that, because Borden, if sued, would be able to show that its sale was a good faith effort to meet competition under § 2(b), it did not "knowingly induce or receive a discrimination in price which is prohibited" by the Act.

Borden's sale to A&P represents the classic evil that the Robinson–Patman Act was designed to prevent. A&P's ability to contribute so significantly to a dairy's output gave it leverage its rivals did not have. Nevertheless, in *Great Atlantic & Pacific Tea Co. v. FTC ("A&P")*, the Supreme Court reversed the FTC and found no liability under § 2(f).[29] Although the Court claimed that its decision was mandated by the plain meaning of the Act, parsing the statutory text reveals an alternative interpretation that would have permitted the imposition of liability on A&P. Especially in light of the numerous policy arguments the Court advanced in support of its holding, it is clear that these policies, rather than linguistics, best explain the Court's decision.

The Court's statutory interpretation began with the language in § 2(f) that imposes liability on buyers only for knowing inducement of violations "prohibited by this section."[30] The Court concluded that Borden did not violate § 2(a) in selling at a lower price to A&P because the facts suggested a good faith effort to

28. Id. at 72–73.

29. 440 U.S. 69 (1979).

30. Id. at 76.

meet competition.[31] Thus, the Court read the Act to excuse A&P from liability because Borden had an affirmative defense.[32]

There are at least two other ways to interpret the statute. Section 2(b)'s meeting competition proviso states that "nothing herein shall prevent a *seller* from rebutting the prima-facie case [of price discrimination] thus made by showing that his lower price ... was made in good faith to meet an equally low price of a competitor."[33] Section 2(b) makes no reference to buyers whatsoever. One possibility, then, is that buyers simply cannot take advantage of this proviso. There is actually some support for this interpretation because the first portion of § 2(b), which allocates the burden of proof generally for Robinson–Patman Act cases, places the burden "upon the person charged with a violation of this section," while the meeting competition proviso applies only to a "seller." Nevertheless, this interpretation makes little sense, for it would impose liability whenever a buyer who received a discount gave other sellers a good faith opportunity to match that discount.

Because Congress could not reasonably have intended to deprive buyers of the meeting competition defense, a better way to interpret § 2(b) is to read "seller" to mean "person charged with a violation of this section." Under this reading, advocated by Justice Thurgood Marshall's dissent,[34] *A&P*'s good faith, not Borden's, would be at issue. This approach would be consistent with the proviso's purpose of permitting sellers to deviate from the principle of non-discrimination "in self-defense against a price raid by a competitor."[35] It would also further the Act's purpose of promoting equal economic opportunity by allowing a buyer that will be favored in any event to permit several sellers to bid. Finally, it would serve the Act's purpose of preventing buyers' abuses of economic power because the holding in *A&P*—that a buyer cannot "knowingly" violate the Act if it believes that the seller could successfully invoke the meeting competition defense in litigation—exculpates the archetypal Robinson–Patman villain. Indeed, although the Court ducked the issue, its reasoning would also exonerate the super-evil buyer that deliberately defrauds the

31. Id. at 83. The Court held that Borden had met the standard adopted in United States v. United States Gypsum Co., 438 U.S. 422, 454 (1978), discussed in section F(3) above, having done everything it could to find out how low it had to bid to meet Bowman's offer, short of violating § 1 of the Sherman Act by contacting Bowman directly.

32. 440 U.S. at 76.

33. 15 U.S.C. § 13(b).

34. 440 U.S. at 87–88.

35. Standard Oil Co. v. FTC, 340 U.S. 231, 249 (1951).

seller into making a discriminatory discount by manufacturing the existence of another bid.[36]

The Court's choice among two plausible textual interpretations, however, was aided by the FTC's curious reasoning in the opinion under review. In declining to exercise its statutory authority to condemn A&P's conduct as an unfair method of competition under § 5, the Commission concluded that sound policy reasons counseled against holding A&P liable. Requiring a buyer to inform a seller of the precise amount of a competing offer would lead to an undue amount of price uniformity and rigidity, the Commission reasoned.[37] As the Court noted, the effect of reading § 2(f) to impose liability on A&P "is to impose the same duty of affirmative disclosure which the Commission condemned as anticompetitive, 'contrary to the public interest,' and 'contrary to normal business practice,' in dismissing the charge under § 5." [38]

Any statute like the Robinson–Patman Act that proscribes injury-threatening price discrimination, unless it is cost justified or the seller is forced to lower its price to meet a competitor's price, will obviously lead to increased rigidity and uniformity in prices. Certainly, modern economic theory teaches that powerful buyers are most likely to be the ones that can disrupt stable pricing and induce aggressive rivalry. The framers of the Robinson–Patman Act recognized that large buyers whose size permits genuine cost savings should receive (and hopefully pass on to consumers) the benefits of their efficient operations. But they also believed that unjustified discounts should not be permitted; and if forced to choose between a somewhat stable market and one where all the benefits of aggressive competition inured to large buyers and their consumers, it seems clear that they preferred the former.

Today, our principal focus is on promoting economic efficiency and benefitting the public as consumers, rather than on ensuring equality of economic opportunity and benefitting the public as a whole community by preserving independent entrepreneurs. *A&P* provides an appropriate closure to this Chapter, for it further erodes the extent to which the Robinson–Patman Act can be employed as a coherent scheme—albeit one premised on values no longer in vogue—to limit unjustified buyer power. Instead, it helps the Act transform an incoherent nuisance that hinders

---

36. Compare 440 U.S. at 81 n.15 (distinguishing Kroger Co. v. FTC, 438 F.2d 1372 (6th Cir. 1971), as a "lying buyer" case), with id. at 88, 91 (Marshall, J., dissenting) (suggesting that the majority opinion's logic would reject liability in *Kroger*).

37. Great Atlantic & Pacific Tea Co., 87 F.T.C. 962, 1050–51 (1976).

38. 440 U.S. at 81.

many legitimate transactions without furthering the societal goals
that it was designed to serve.

CHAPTER 8: ANTICOMPETITIVE HARM THROUGH GOVERNMENTAL ACTION

This Chapter examines the circumstances in which the courts permit state and local governmental entities to determine that competition is inappropriate and that society would be better served by using some other means to determine prices, output, and entry. A decision to displace the antitrust laws with some alternative involves not only economic theory but also empirical estimates about the effect of that decision on society, and, most important, value choices about the importance of free markets and the desirability of helping certain segments of society. Antitrust precedents consider judges unfit to make these kinds of social determinations.[1] In creating the state action doctrine, however, the Supreme Court held that state governmental officials are competent to make them. The Sherman Act therefore does not apply when state officials have decided to replace competition, provided they replace it with some form of regulation acceptable to the federal courts interpreting the Sherman Act. Section A discusses the complexities of this doctrine. Section B discusses a necessary corollary of the principles discussed here: if the courts will not entertain arguments that competition is poor social policy, they must allow those who seek to deviate from competition to make their case somewhere else. Accordingly, this petitioning activity is protected from antitrust liability, even if it results in a lessening of competition, under the so-called "*Noerr*" doctrine.

Section A: State Action

(1) Underlying principles.

Long-settled antitrust tradition rejects the notion that anticompetitive conduct can be justified, in the context of antitrust litigation, by arguments that the conduct is socially desirable. The courts have routinely held that the Sherman Act establishes that competition in the provision of goods and services is our national policy. Of course, competition does not always represent

---

1. See, e.g., United States v. Addyston Pipe & Steel Co., 85 Fed. 271, 284 (6th Cir. 1898), aff'd, 175 U.S. 211 (1899), where Judge William Howard Taft condemned judges who "set sail on a sea of doubt, and ... assume the power to say ... how much restraint of competition is in the public interest, and how much is not."

sound policy, but the courts have wisely determined that federal judges should not be the ones to decide whether or not a deviation from our general policy of competition is appropriate in a specific context.

Congress clearly has the power, which it has occasionally exercised, to expressly exempt certain conduct or even whole industries from the policies of competition underlying in the antitrust laws.[2] Likewise, in *Parker v. Brown*,[3] the Supreme Court held that the Sherman Act was not meant to proscribe state legislative judgments that regulation was superior to competition. The case involved a California statute designed to "prevent economic waste in the marketing of agricultural products" and to "conserve the agricultural wealth of the state" by creating a commission authorized to develop a marketing plan that would "prevent agricultural waste ... without permitting unreasonable profits to producers." If approved by a super-majority of the affected growers, the commission's plan could restrict or allocate the production of agricultural products. In *Parker*, a raisin grower challenged a plan that required raisin growers to dispose of approximately 20% of their crop as by-products, to sell 30% in the open market, and to place the rest in a "stabilization pool" to be sold by a committee "in such manner as to obtain stability in the market." [4]

The Court "assumed" (correctly) that the plan would violate the Sherman Act if organized and put into effect solely by private agreement.[5] Federal judges would not have allowed the raisin growers to show that competition had led to economic waste in marketing raisins, and the courts certainly would not have considered exonerating a private plan that required a determination of "unreasonable profits to producers." The Court also correctly assumed that Congress could constitutionally prohibit a state from maintaining this sort of program, as an undue interference with interstate commerce. After all, the raisin plan primarily benefit-

---

2. Another issue, beyond the scope of this treatise, concerns the extent to which the creation of federal regulatory regimes implicitly exempts the regulated industries from antitrust liability or modifies their liability in some respect. This issue is really one of statutory interpretation, necessitating the reconciliation of two federal statutes (the Sherman Act and the other regulatory legislation), and thus requires a case-by-case inquiry into the specific statutory schemes involved. See, e.g., Carnation Co. v. Pacific Westbound Conference, 383 U.S. 213 (1966) (antitrust liability for ocean carriers regulated by the Fed-

eral Maritime Commission); California v. FPC, 369 U.S. 482 (1962) (antitrust liability for natural gas companies regulated by the Federal Power Commission); United States v. American Telephone & Telegraph Co., 461 F.Supp. 1314 (D.D.C. 1978) (antitrust liability for telecommunications company regulated by the Federal Communications Commission).

3.   317 U.S. 341 (1943).

4.   Id. at 346–48.

5.   Id. at 350.

ed California farmers, while raising the price of raisins for consumers throughout the nation.[6] Nonetheless, in light of general principles of federalism, and the absence of any mention of state action in the Sherman Act's text or legislative history, the Court held that the Sherman Act was not meant to restrain a state, its officers or its agents from "activities directed by its legislature." Thus, because the raisin plan "derived its authority and its efficacy from the legislative command of the state and was not intended to operate or become effective without that command," it did not violate the Sherman Act.[7]

In dicta, the Court added a very important caveat to its holding. A state cannot, the Court wrote, "give immunity to those who violate the Sherman Act by authorizing them to violate it, or by declaring that their action is lawful."[8] For example, California could not simply authorize the raisin growers to fix prices, even if it did so in order to maximize profits for farmers whose economic health was deemed essential to the state's well-being. Thus, the state action doctrine allows states to make the judgment that the national policy favoring competition should be displaced by state regulation, but it does not allow them to determine that the public interest would best be served by displacing competition

6. Indeed, these facts suggest that the California statute might have been deemed an interference with interstate commerce because of its discriminatory impact on interstate raisin buyers. The Court held otherwise, however, noting that similar programs explicitly authorized by the federal Agricultural Marketing Act suggested that Congress approved this sort of state regulation. Id. at 368. Moreover, where a state seeks to resolve a legitimate problem of local concern (here, the overproduction of raisins, possibly bankrupting farmers), and does not discriminate against out-of-state producers, the courts will generally find that the state law does not unconstitutionally interfere with interstate commerce. Even though the California raisin plan may be seen as discriminatory because it disproportionately benefited California farmers at the expense of out-of-state buyers, the courts have usually found this sort of disparate impact is usually insufficient to invalidate state regulatory schemes as unconstitutionally discriminatory. See 1 Ronald Rotunda, John Nowak & J. Nelson Young, Constitutional Law: Substance and Procedure 609 (1986).

In any event, even if the California raisin regulation were entirely non-discriminatory, its effect on interstate commerce in raisins and products using raisins would be sufficient to permit congressional regulation. Wickard v. Filburn, 317 U.S. 111 (1942).

7. 317 U.S. at 350–51. The Court's presumption of legislative intent from congressional silence was necessarily a fiction, for Congress could not possibly have envisioned the state action doctrine when it enacted the Sherman Act in 1890. Under the then prevailing Commerce Clause jurisprudence, business activities were classified according to a strict dichotomy dividing intrastate and interstate commerce; the Sherman Act could not constitutionally be applied to the former, and state legislation could not constitutionally affect the latter. Only after New Deal-era decisions expanded the scope of Congress' Commerce Clause power did questions about state action and antitrust arise. See E.T. Sullivan & Herbert Hovenkamp, Antitrust Law, Policy and Procedure 923 (2d ed. 1989).

8. 317 U.S. at 351.

with private cartels, no matter how much private cartelization might further state economic policies.

There are several justifications for tolerating competition-displacing state regulation but not competition-displacing state authorization of private cartelization. First, given the Sherman Act's preference for competition, a requirement that carteleers secure official governmental approval for their specific anticompetitive activities makes it less likely that competition will be displaced, and more likely that the anticompetitive conduct really does serve the larger public interest. Second, the Sherman Act is grounded in Congress' belief that those who profit from restrained competition usually do so to the public detriment.[9] Thus, even if the Sherman Act the permits states to make a policy judgment that government regulation is superior to competition, it does not permit them to make an empirical judgment that particular private parties will exercise their state authorization to restrain trade in the public interest.[10]

The major analytical difficulty with the state action doctrine stems from the problems that arise when anyone other than Congress is entrusted with the power to "sail on the sea of doubt" and engage in the difficult judgment about when competition is or is not appropriate policy. The federal courts are not considered the proper fora for these decisions. The nature of the legislative process does give state legislatures greater competence in weighing competing values and making empirical predictions in areas where the evidence cannot possibly be conclusive. Nonetheless, delegating this decision-making authority to the states may not be appropriate either, because the legislative process is subject to bias and abuse. Consider the facts of *Parker*: how likely was it that the California Raisin Board adequately weighed the interests of consumers across the entire country against the interests of California farmers in setting raisin prices and output? Nor does it require a scholar familiar with the exploding literature on "public choice theory"[11] to realize that state and local politicians will often be subject to "regulatory capture"—that is, they will enact laws displacing competition not because regulation is in the public interest, but because it can benefit a special interest group that has successfully lobbied for the statute. Even if most of the nation's raisin-eaters were Californians, how likely was it that the California Raisin Board would have adequately considered the interests of in-state consumers compared to the well-organized

9. Einer Elhauge, The Scope of Antitrust Process, 104 Harv. L. Rev. 667, 712 (1991).

10. Id. at 708.

11. See generally Daniel Farber & Philip Frickey, Law and Public Choice (1991).

interests of a raisin growers' association and its political action committee?

Still, state and local governments must have some authority to enact legislation that lessens competition—not because of the need to balance the antitrust apple against the federalism orange, but rather because the Sherman Act itself does not reflect the policy that competition is *always* in the public interest. Rather, the Act reflects the policy that self-interested parties may not judge for themselves "how much competition is in the public interest, and how much is not" [12]—even if they can get a federal judge to agree that their judgment is correct. Like almost all other antitrust issues, resolution of the state action issue turns on conflicting views about the goals of antitrust, about the effectiveness of federal court litigation in achieving those goals, and about the degree to which state and local government decisions and the result of bias and abuse.

Several preliminary considerations should be kept in mind when evaluating the state action doctrine. First, the doctrine is a "default rule." Congress is always free to preempt specific instances or general categories of anticompetitive state regulation. Alternatively, if the Court were to significantly modify the doctrine to weaken immunity, Congress would be free to amend the Sherman Act by exempting specific types or general categories of anticompetitive state regulation from liability. Second, although *Parker* suggested that the doctrine may be a necessary ingredient in a "dual system of government in which ... states are sovereign," [13] the European Community has found that it can adequately protect the prerogatives of its member States, who have far greater sovereignty than state governments in this country, without the blanket immunity afforded by the state action doctrine.[14]

(2) The elements of state action immunity.

Parker left to subsequent cases the task of spelling out the limits on a state's ability to supplant the Sherman Act's policy of competition with its own views of economic/regulatory policy. To secure protection from Sherman Act liability, these cases generally hold that the state's regulatory scheme must have two essential elements: it must clearly reflect the legislature's policy to displace competition with regulation; and decisions about the key features of the restraint of trade (reduced output, higher prices, etc.) must be made by the state, through adequate supervision of decisions made by private parties.

---

12. *Addyston Pipe*, 85 Fed. at 284.

13. 317 U.S. at 351.

14. See Diane Wood, Lessons from the EEC: Why *Parker v. Brown* Is Not Inevitable (forthcoming).

In *Schwegmann Brothers v. Calvert Distillers Corp.*,[15] for example, the Court held that the Sherman Act was not displaced by a Louisiana statutory scheme whereby prices were set by liquor distillers rather than a state commission. The state authorized Calvert, a distiller, to fix resale prices for its liquor and Louisiana law declared that sales by retailers at prices below those set by the distiller constituted "unfair competition," thus enabling Calvert to obtain an injunction against Schwegmann's discounting.[16] Unlike *Parker*, however, consumers were forced to pay higher prices set not by a state regulatory commission but by Calvert. *Schwegmann* thus illustrates the effect of *Parker*'s caveat that the state action doctrine does not permit states simply to authorize its citizens to violate the Sherman Act.

Louisiana's law reflected the state legislature's policy judgment that fierce price competition among liquor retailers was "unfair competition." Moreover, the anticompetitive effect of the legislation—higher prices—was borne almost entirely by in-state consumers. Some critics have thus questioned why Congress, in enacting the Sherman Act, should care if Louisiana voters, most of whom are consumers, wanted to exploit themselves.[17] The effect of the statute was not felt only in Louisiana, however. If Calvert's liquor was priced above competitive levels, less liquor was sold. While Calvert might have preferred the higher prices to greater output, those who supplied Calvert with raw materials did not benefit from the higher prices and their output suffered as well. Although this effect may have been incidental, it explains why the

---

15. 341 U.S. 384 (1951).

16. As discussed in Chapter 5, section A(2), retailers that wished to avoid vigorous price competition made various attempts to preserve the benefits of resale price maintenance after the Supreme Court's decision in Dr. Miles Medical Co. v. John D. Park & Sons Co., 220 U.S. 373 (1911), declared the practice to be a violation of the Sherman Act. After their efforts to amend § 1 proved unsuccessful, these retailers persuaded a number of states to adopt "fair trade" laws that permitted resale price agreements between manufacturers and retailers, and then persuaded Congress to enact the Miller–Tydings Act exempting these fair trade agreements from Sherman Act liability. Proponents of fair trade laws believed that vigorous competition by discount retailers "unquestionably ... had a disastrous effect upon the small independent retailers," and "tend[ed] to create mo-

nopoly." S. Rep. No. 257, 75th Cong., 1st Sess. 2 (1937).

The conduct in *Schwegmann* was not protected by Miller–Tydings, however, because Schwegmann had not agreed to adhere to Calvert's prices. But Congress responded to *Schwegmann* in 1952 by enacting the McGuire Act, which extended the fair trade exemption to "non-signer" statutes like Louisiana's that barred any retailer from discounting below the "fair trade" price. Pub. L. No. 542, 66 Stat. 631 (1952). Finally, in 1975, Congress came full circle. Recognizing that vigorous competition by discount retailers actually helped competition and reduced prices, Congress repealed the entire fair trade exemption. See Consumer Goods Pricing Act, Pub. L. No. 94–145, 89 Stat. 801 (1975).

17. See, e.g., Frank Easterbrook, Antitrust and the Economics of Federalism, 26 J.L. & Econ. 23, 47–48 (1983).

Sherman Act covers all trade "affecting commerce." [18]   Moreover, the Court's decision to preempt Louisiana's authorization of resale price maintenance was consistent with both (a) Congress' policy judgment that resale price competition is generally in the public interest and (b) its empirical prediction that Calvert was unlikely to exercise its state-authorized prerogative to serve the greater public good.   Finally, if Louisiana's unfair competition law was the result of regulatory capture (by liquor distillers, full-price retailers, or both), an interpretation of the Sherman Act designed to protect consumers would preempt the state law regardless of its predominant intrastate effect.

Schwegmann was also significant in defining the preemptive role the Sherman Act often plays in evaluating anticompetitive state regulation.   In *Parker*, the challenged state law authorized agreements among competing raisin growers, and the state action doctrine operated to immunize agreements that literally restrained trade.   In *Schwegmann*, it was difficult to see who was violating the Sherman Act, as Calvert and Schwegmann had not agreed on resale prices.[19]   In effect, therefore, the Court held that where the state action doctrine is inapplicable, the antitrust laws preempt state regulatory legislation that requires one private firm to follow the dictates of another.

If a state cannot simply authorize private parties to violate the Sherman Act, what must it do to "clearly articulate" a policy of displacing competition with regulation?   The relevant Supreme Court opinions give a confusing answer.   In *Goldfarb v. Virginia State Bar*,[20] the Court found that the State Bar (a state agency) violated § 1 when it declared that attorneys behaved unethically by charging fees that consistently deviated from schedules adopted by county bar associations (which are private groups).   The Court noted that the Virginia Supreme Court had explicitly directed that "no lawyer should permit himself to be controlled [by a schedule] or to follow it as his sole guide." [21]   In framing its analysis, the Court wrote that the "threshold inquiry in determining if an anticompetitive activity is state action . . . is whether the activity *is required by the State acting as sovereign*."   The State Bar's invocation of the state action doctrine was quickly rejected "because it cannot fairly be said that the State of Virginia through its Supreme Court Rules required the anticompetitive activities" at issue.[22]

---

18.   15 U.S.C. § 1.

19.   Indeed, the absence of any agreement between the parties was the basis for the Court's determination that the Miller–Tydings antitrust exemption for fair trade "contracts or agreements" did not apply.   341 U.S. at 388.

20.   421 U.S. 773 (1975).

21.   Id. at 789 & n.19.

22.   Id. at 790 (emphasis added).

Cantor v. Detroit Edison Co.,[23] held that even where state law literally requires private parties to engage in anticompetitive conduct, antitrust liability may be imposed if the state has not established a clear competition-lessening policy. The defendant public utility in that case distributed light bulbs to residential customers as part of its electrical service. Cantor, a light bulb retailer, claimed that this behavior violated the Sherman Act by foreclosing competition in light bulbs. The utility argued that the practice had been approved by Michigan's public utilities commission and thus constituted state action. The Court rejected this defense, even though technically Michigan law "required the anticompetitive activities" of the defendant—Detroit Edison was obligated to implement its program once the commission had approved it. The Court noted however, that the program had been instigated by the utility and routinely approved by the commission. This background was important, for the Court recognized that it would be unjust to find Detroit Edison liable under the antitrust laws for doing nothing more than obeying Michigan's commands.[24]

Nonetheless, as Justice Harry Blackmun observed in a concurring opinion, the mere fact that the restraint was initiated by private actors cannot be dispositive, for the raisin marketing restraints immunized in *Parker* were likewise initiated by private parties pursuant to a general statutory scheme.[25] *Parker* and *Cantor* can be reconciled, however, because in the latter case the Court concluded that Michigan had not clearly articulated a state policy to displace competition in the light bulb market. The Court noted that there was no mechanism for regulating light bulb sellers, and that other electric utilities in Michigan did not, and were not required to, use the program. The commission did allow Detroit Edison to charge its retail customers $2.8 million for the costs of light-bulb distribution, but this was deemed insufficient to rise to the level of state action.[26]

23. 428 U.S. 579 (1976).

24. Id. at 592.

25. Id. at 609.

26. Although a 6–3 majority agreed that Detroit Edison's light bulb program did not constitute state action, there was no consensus as to the appropriate standard to be applied in determining when state-sanctioned private conduct is immune. Justice Stevens (joined by Justices Brennan, White, and Marshall) opined that *Parker* and its progeny were not applicable to challenges to private acts, and favored further development of the state action issue on remand. Id. at 591–92, 603. Chief Justice Burger concurred in the portions of Stevens' opinion that rejected Detroit Edison's state action defense because there was no evidence that the private conduct reflected state policy. Id. at 604–05. Justice Blackmun created a special rule of reason to govern the application of the Sherman Act to state-sanctioned anticompetitive private activity. Id. at 610–11. Finally, Justice Stewart (joined by Justices Powell and Rehnquist) dissented. In their view, private conduct that is required by operation of state law is immune, whether or not the conduct furthers state poli-

The Court clarified the law somewhat in *California Retail Liquor Dealers Ass'n v. Midcal Aluminum, Inc.*[27] That case involved a challenge to a California statute that required all wine producers and wholesalers to file price schedules with the state and barred licensed wine retailers from deviating from the price schedule. Although the statute seems indistinguishable from *Schwegmann*, Justice Lewis Powell's unanimous[28] majority opinion used the case as a vehicle to reformulate the standards for state action. To be considered state action, Powell said, the challenged restraint must be (1) " 'clearly articulated and affirmatively expressed as state policy,' " and (2) " 'actively supervised' by the State itself."[29] The Court concluded that the statute met the first standard: retailer adherence to fixed prices was clearly state policy. However, there was no supervision, much less active supervision, of the actual prices set by producers and wholesalers. As in *Schwegmann*, the state had simply authorized its citizens to violate the Sherman Act, and *Parker* expressly held that the states had no such power. Even though there was extensive cooperation among raisin growers in *Parker*, ultimately the state officials were responsible for any increase in prices there. In *Midcal*, by contrast, no official was accountable for the higher prices resulting from resale price maintenance on California wine. This is a key distinction, for the theory underlying the state action doctrine is that the preeminent federal policy of competition will give way only where accountable state or federal officials (and not judges) determine that some form of *regulation* is preferable.[30]

Following *Midcal*, the contours of the state action doctrine were somewhat clearer. *Midcal*'s two-pronged synthesis of the prior case law seems to overrule the suggestion in *Goldfarb* that private parties could invoke the state action doctrine only if their conduct was compelled by the state. But compulsion had never been a requirement of the doctrine. Indeed, the California raisin regulation upheld in *Parker* did not compel the growers to restrict output: the concurrence of both a state commission and a majority of the growers was necessary to implement any output reduction

---

cies or was initiated by the state as opposed to the regulated party. Id. at 624.

27. 445 U.S. 97 (1980).

28. The Court's unanimity concerning the appropriate standard to be used in applying the state action doctrine to acts of private parties was particularly remarkable in light of how fractured the Court had been when it previously considered the issue in *Cantor*. See note 26 supra.

29. Id. at 105 (quoting City of Lafayette v. Louisiana Power & Light Co., 435 U.S. 389, 410 (1978) (opinion of Brennan, J.)).

30. This distinction is not a purely abstract legal issue. After *Midcal*, wine and liquor prices declined by approximately 20% in several states. See Eleanor Fox & Lawrence Sullivan, Antitrust 539 (1989).

plan. On the other hand, *Midcal* demonstrated that the Court was serious when it said in *Parker* that the states may not simply authorize the illegal schemes of private parties. Instead, the state must clearly express a policy of displacing competition with regulation. Thus, where, as in *Cantor*, the restraint was instigated by a private party "with only the acquiescence of the state regulatory commission," [31] this prong of *Midcal* was not met.

(3) Applying of *Midcal* to private parties.

If strict state compulsion of the challenged conduct is not required, how much leeway may private parties exercise before the courts will conclude that the state's policy does not clearly express an intent to displace the Sherman Act's policy of competition? As applied, the *Midcal* test requires an ad hoc and fact-specific determination by the federal courts.

(3a) Clearly expressing a state policy to displace competition with regulation.

In *Southern Motor Carriers Rate Conference, Inc. v. United States*,[32] five southern states authorized rival trucking companies to agree on joint rates for intrastate trucking and then to file those rates for approval with the state regulatory commissions. Because the commissions reviewed the rates, the government conceded that *Midcal*'s active supervision requirement was clearly satisfied.[33] Nevertheless, the court of appeals held that the practice of joint rate filings was not state action because state law authorized but did not compel the truckers to file jointly. The Supreme Court reversed and upheld the challenged regulatory schemes.

The government did not challenge the states' regulation, but the defendants' collective decision to file their rates jointly. The Court had previously recognized that, because regulators often approve a range of rates within a zone of reasonableness, agreements among rivals as to precisely where their rates should fall within that zone constitute price fixing.[34] Thus, absent state action immunity, the truckers could not agree to submit a joint rate filing. The government argued that the states' policy of neutrality toward collective rate filing meant that the states were

31. This description of *Cantor* is taken from Bates v. State Bar of Arizona, 433 U.S. 350, 362 (1977).

32. 471 U.S. 48 (1985). **Caveat lector:** while an attorney in the Justice Department's Antitrust Division, I argued the appeal of a parallel state action case that advocated the same position taken by the United States in *Southern Motor Carriers*. United States v. Title Ins. Rating Bureau of Arizona, Inc., 700 F.2d 1247 (9th Cir. 1983), cert. denied, 467 U.S. 1240 (1984).

33. 471 U.S. at 62.

34. Georgia v. Pennsylvania Railroad Co., 324 U.S. 439 (1945).

either authorizing private parties to violate the law (contrary to *Parker*) or acquiescing in a private choice to jointly agree on rates (contrary to *Cantor*).

Writing for the majority, Justice Lewis Powell reasoned instead that the states had actually devised a creative scheme to balance the efficiencies caused by collective ratemaking (state agencies would be swamped if each trucker filed individually) and the competition fostered by individual submissions. The states anticipated that most truckers would file collectively, Powell explained, but if the rates were too high, others eager to increase their market share would file lower rates.[35] Moreover, given the sensibility of the state policy,[36] limiting the state action doctrine to cases where a state compelled joint filings might reduce competition by encouraging states to require collective ratemaking.[37] Thus, the states had clearly articulated a policy to supplant competition, even if they did not compel a particular form of private conduct.[38] Justice Powell's ability to articulate a sound reason for the states to chose their approach for reasons other than a desire to accommodate local businesses explains why state action was found in *Southern Motor Carriers* and not in *Cantor*.

(3b) The active supervision requirement.

Midcal's active supervision requirement was explained and applied in *Patrick v. Burget*.[39] Patrick, a surgeon in Astoria, Oregon, alleged that the revocation of his staff privileges at Astoria's only hospital was the result of a conspiracy among the members of the hospital's peer review committee, several of whom operated a clinic that competed with Patrick. Patrick alleged that the clinic's partners had initiated and participated in the hospital peer-review process in order to eliminate him as a competitor, rather than to improve competition by maintaining high standards. A jury ruled in Patrick's favor. Despite evidence suggesting bad faith, the court of appeals found that the defendants had

35. 471 U.S. at 59. Because the Court cited no authority in advancing this explanation of the states' motives, it is unclear whether it was creatively devised by Justice Powell, was offered by defendants' counsel as a post hoc rationalization, or reflected the actual intent of the legislatures.

36. The Court noted that Congress had established a similar scheme under the Interstate Commerce Act, which exempted from the antitrust laws collective rate filings submitted to the ICC. Id. at 60 n.22 (citing 49 U.S.C. §§ 10706(b)(2) and (d)(2)(C)).

37. In filing suit, the government presumably believed that, faced with a choice between requiring all truckers to be bound by a collective filing and barring any cooperation in filing rates, the states would select the latter.

38. The Court conceded that *Goldfarb* "did employ language of compulsion," but then noted, somewhat disingenuously, that "the language in *Goldfarb* is not without ambiguity." 471 U.S. at 61.

39. 486 U.S. 94 (1988).

complied with Oregon's statutory procedure for physician peer review and thus were protected from antitrust liability under the state action doctrine. A unanimous Supreme Court [40] reversed, concluding that the revocation of Patrick's hospital privileges was a private decision that was not actively supervised by the state.

The Court explained that the active supervision requirement is "designed to ensure that the state action doctrine will shelter only *the particular anticompetitive acts* of private parties that, in the judgment of the State, actually further state regulatory policies." Public officials must "have and exercise power to review particular anticompetitive acts of private parties and disapprove those that fail to accord with state policy." Otherwise, "there is no realistic assurance that a private party's anticompetitive conduct promotes state policy, rather than merely the party's individual interests." [41]

Having set forth this rigorous standard, the Court had no difficulty finding that it was not met on the facts in *Patrick*. Oregon's Health Division established procedures for terminating hospital privileges, but did not review the actual decisions made by peer review committees. The state's Board of Medical Examiners received notice of any termination of privileges (apparently so that it could consider instituting further proceedings, such as revocation of the physician's license), but likewise could not reverse a hospital's termination decision. Finally, the Court held that the availability of judicial review was inadequate to meet the active supervision requirement. Without deciding whether such review could ever suffice, the Court noted that Oregon case law had held that judicial review was limited to correcting procedural errors, not to considering the substance of whether a privilege termination was consistent with state regulatory policy.[42]

Not surprisingly, the defendants and various amici argued that effective peer review is essential in order to provide quality medical care and that the threat of antitrust liability will prevent physicians from participating in the per review process. The wisdom of the antitrust law's traditional refusal to consider such arguments was confirmed in these proceedings. The Court rejected the arguments, noting that challenges to the propriety of applying the antitrust laws to the sphere of medical care must be directed to the legislature.[43] Indeed, Congress responded to the Court's decision by granting limited antitrust immunity to peer review decisions undertaken in the "reasonable belief" that they

40. Justice Blackmun recused himself.

41. Id. at 100–01 (emphasis is added).

42. Id. at 102–05.

43. Id. at 105.

furthered quality health care.[44] This legislation would appear to satisfy legitimate concerns about protecting the peer review process while imposing liability on defendants like the conspirators in *Patrick*.

In *Patrick*, there was *no* state supervision of the challenged anticompetitive conduct, and the Court therefore had no reason to discuss how much supervision is necessary to satisfy *Midcal*. Recently, however, in *FTC v. Ticor Title Insurance Co.*,[45] the Court did address that issue, while reaffirming that the active supervision requirement plays a critical role in determining whether a state can displaced the national policy of competition. *Ticor* held that the existence of state laws permitting state regulators to review private rate-setting arrangements was insufficient to immunize the arrangements in that case because the evidence showed that the regulators had simply rubber-stamped the private agreements. The specific agreements at issue were entered into by rival title insurance companies and submitted, pursuant to state law, to regulators in Wisconsin and Montana. These states regulate by the so-called "negative option" method, whereby rates take effect within a specified number of days unless challenged by the state regulator. The FTC found, for example, that although the Wisconsin Insurance Commissioner is required to regularly examine the activities of the ratings bureau (the organization of private firms that set the joint rates in *Ticor*) and is authorized to hold hearings and reject rates, neither had been done in this case. In addition, a major rate filing had been approved in 1971 despite the fact that the title insurance companies had not supplied supporting justification until 1978.[46]

As Justice Anthony Kennedy's majority opinion explained, the state action doctrine immunizes certain private conduct "out of respect for ongoing regulation by the State, not out of respect for the economics of price restraint."[47] *Ticor* thus reaffirms that only a state's judgment to supplant competition with *regulation* warrants deference; federalism does not require the Sherman Act to give way to a state's decision to "confer antitrust immunity on private persons by fiat."[48]

In a somewhat opaque passage, the Court denied that its decision would deprive states of regulatory flexibility. Indeed, the Court expressly adopted the argument made in an *amicus* brief filed by 36 state attorneys general that states might be hampered

---

44. Health Quality Improvements Acts, of 1986, Pub. L. No. 99–660, 100 Stat. 37–84, 42 U.S.C. §§ 11111(a)(1), 11112(a).

45. 112 S.Ct. 2169 (1992).

46. Id. at 2175.

47. Id. at 2177.

48. Id. at 2176.

in their ability to regulate if any degree of regulation conferred antitrust immunity on the regulated entities.[49] This argument seems incorrect. If the states did not believe that price fixing among title insurers was in the public interest, why did they authorize it? And why did they tolerate such shoddy regulation by state administrators? Moreover, simply inserting a provision into state law declaring that it was *not* the state's policy to replace the competition mandated by the federal antitrust laws would surely have ensured that any state action defense would flunk *Midcal*'s first prong. Although *Ticor* does result in somewhat less flexibility for states, this constraint on state policy making is inherent in a doctrine that does not give states the flexibility to authorize private cartels.

Significantly, the Court articulated another function underlying state action jurisprudence: forcing states to accept full political accountability for actions that reduce competition. The Court wrote that

> [s]tates must accept political responsibility for actions they intend to undertake. . . . Federalism serves to assign political responsibility, not to obscure it. Neither federalism nor political responsibility is well served by a rule that essential national policies are displaced by state regulations intended to achieve more limited ends. . . . [O]ur insistence on real compliance with both parts of the Midcal test will serve to make clear that the State is responsible for the price fixing it has sanctioned and undertaken to control.[50]

As we explore below in subsection (5), the Court has apparently rejected similar concerns in cases involving state delegation to municipalities.[51]

Unfortunately, *Ticor* was also somewhat vague in defining precisely what was flawed in the states' exercise of regulatory oversight. At one point, the Court suggested that imprecise tort concepts of causation would be relevant, perhaps implying that the lower courts should determine antitrust liability based on whether state supervision was some sort of supervening cause of the challenged behavior.[52] At most, the Court noted, rate filings

---

49. Id. at 2178.

50. Id.

51. In City of Columbia v. Omni Outdoor Advertising, Inc., 111 S.Ct. 1344 (1991), which is discussed below, the Court found that South Carolina's grant of blanket authority to cities to regulate the location of structures in order to promote health, safety, and welfare was sufficient to make it clear that the State was responsible for a local ordinance that blocked any significant new entry into the local billboard market in order to protect the politically influential incumbent firm.

52. See id. at 2177: "Much as in causation inquiries, the analysis asks whether the State has played a substantial role in determining the specifics of the economic policy."

in Wisconsin were checked for mathematical accuracy, and some were not checked at all; moreover, in both Wisconsin and Montana, rate filings became effective despite the insurance companies' failure to file additional requested information. These facts, the Court held, were "fatal" to a successful state action claim.[53] As the dissenters argued, however, subjecting regulated entities to potential treble damage liability for jointly filing rates in states that use the "negative option" method of regulation, without providing any real guidance as to the applicable antitrust standards, will probably put an end to joint rate filings, thus substantially interfering with a state's flexibility in determining the appropriate level of regulation.[54]

The real point of the Court's holding in *Ticor* was not to increase the state's political accountability or its regulatory flexibility. Rather, it was to reaffirm *Parker v. Brown*'s significant limitation on state regulatory flexibility: no matter how accountable the state's lawmakers wish to be, the Sherman Act does not permit them to adopt a regulatory scheme that effectively allows private parties to violate the antitrust laws by imposing prices set by themselves.

(4) Application of *Midcal* to municipalities.

Special issues arise when competition is replaced by municipal, rather than state, action. It was not until 45 years after *Parker*, in *City of Lafayette v. Louisiana Power & Light Co.*,[55] that the Supreme Court first addressed the applicability of the state action doctrine to cities. Louisiana law authorizes cities to own and operate electric utility systems, both within and beyond city limits. Outside the city of Plaquemine (a co-petitioner), competition emerged between that city's utility system and one operated by Louisiana Power & Light, a private utility. Litigation ensued, with both sides alleging that the other had violated the antitrust laws.

The Court held that a municipally owned power company is not automatically protected from antitrust liability. Justice William Brennan's plurality opinion explained that, unlike states,

---

53. Id. at 2179.

54. Id. at 2182 (Rehnquist, C.J., dissenting); id. at 2183 (O'Connor, J., dissenting). Justice Clarence Thomas joined both dissents. Justice Antonin Scalia joined the majority opinion but filed a separate concurrence, noting his agreement with Rehnquist and O'Connor that many private parties would decline to take advantage of state authorized joint rate filings because of the ambiguities in the majority opinion.

Scalia nevertheless expressed his willingness "to accept these consequences because I see no alternative within the constraints of our 'active supervision' doctrine, which has not been challenged here; and because I am skeptical about the Parker v. Brown exemption for state-programmed private collusion in the first place." Id. at 2180–81.

55. 435 U.S. 389 (1978).

cities are not sovereigns and historically they have been historically required to comply with the substantive standards in other federal laws applicable to "persons." [56]   Brennan characterized the cities' claim that their goal was public service, rather than private profit, as "only partly correct."   Because a city might opt to replace competition for parochial reasons that conflict with state policies, local decisions "are not inherently more likely to comport with the broader interests of national economic well-being than are those of private corporations acting in furtherance of [private] interests."   In this case, for example, the private utility's counterclaim alleged that Plaquemine had illegally required non-residents who wanted to obtain water and natural gas to purchase its electricity as well, and that both cities had unlawfully participated in sham litigation before various courts and agencies in order to prevent construction of a nuclear generating plant that would have enabled Louisiana Power & Light to compete more effectively.   This alleged anticompetitive conduct benefited the cities' residents while imposing significant costs on others.[57]   Finally, the Court concluded that the antitrust laws would be unduly subverted if 62,437 units of local government, in addition to 50 states, could supplant the Sherman Act's policy of competition.[58]

In distinguishing the acts of a city from those of a state and concluding that the former are not automatically entitled to protection under the state action doctrine, the Court overturned the district court's dismissal of Louisiana Power's antitrust counterclaim against the cities.   The Court then remanded the case for further consideration of the question whether the cities' conduct was the kind of activity contemplated by the Louisiana legislature and therefore was entitled to state action immunity on that ground.[59]

In the next municipal antitrust case to reach the Supreme Court, *Community Communications Co. v. City of Boulder*,[60] the city argued that Colorado's constitutional scheme delegating all local power to "home rule" localities constituted a state policy allowing cities to displace competition with regulation.   The Court rejected this argument.   Instead, the Court held, the restraint challenged in the case—Boulder's moratorium on new cable franchises—did not constitute state action unless it "constitute[d] the act of the State of Colorado itself in its sovereign capacity" or met

---

56. Id. at 400–01, 412.

57. Id. at 403–05.

58. Id. at 407–08.

59. Id. at 393–94 (quoting with approval from the court of appeals opinion, 532 F.2d 431, 434–35 (5th Cir. 1976)).

60. 455 U.S. 40 (1982).

Midcal's requirement that the challenged action further a "clearly articulated and affirmatively expressed state policy."[61] The majority then concluded that the general authority delegated to home rule municipalities under the state constitution did not constitute the "clear articulation and affirmative expression" of state policy to displace competition necessary under *Midcal*.[62]

City of Boulder's straightforward application of *Midcal* to municipal regulation ignored the distinction drawn by Chief Justice Warren Burger in *City of Lafayette*[63] between the conduct of municipally owned businesses, like utility companies, and the exercise of traditional government regulatory power.[64] As Burger observed in *City of Lafayette*, there is no reason why the federal antitrust law should distinguish between companies engaged in profit-making activities simply because one happens to be municipally owned, unless the municipally owned company acts anticompetitively at the direction of the state.

Nevertheless, there are distinct policy reasons to apply the federal competition policy to municipal regulatory decisions. The best rationale, suggested by the plurality opinion in *City of Lafayette*, is that cities are too likely to restrict competition in a manner that benefits the parochial interests of their citizens and harms non-resident consumers. Moreover, local government entities are more easily subject to capture by special interests, even if resident consumers are the principal victims of the city's anticompetitive regulation.

61. Id. at 52.

62. Id. at 54–56. See also Wall v. City of Athens, 663 F.Supp. 747, 758 (M.D. Ga. 1987) (state statute declaring that all powers properly exercised by home rule municipalities constitute state policy and that Georgia's official policy is that home rule cities should be immune from antitrust liability is insufficient to qualify all local decisions as state action).

63. Burger provided the fifth vote needed to reject a wholesale exemption for municipalities, but he concurred separately. According to Burger, the key to *City of Lafayette* was that the cities were engaged in a business activity that realized a profit, and therefore ought be treated like any other business. 435 U.S. at 418, 424.

64. See *City of Boulder*, 455 U.S. at 55 n.18 (noting, and then ignoring, Boulder's contention that its challenged ordinance qualified for antitrust immunity because the activity is a traditional government function rather than a proprietary enterprise). The majority opinion in *City of Boulder* was authored by Justice Brennan, who wrote the plurality opinion in *City of Lafayette* that likewise failed to adopt Burger's distinction. Justice Blackmun, who dissented in *City of Lafayette*, switched to provide the fifth vote for the majority in *Boulder*. Blackmun's dissent in *City of Lafayette* distinguished the unilateral conduct of the city challenged there from a situation where a city conspires with private parties to restrain trade. *City of Lafayette*, 435 U.S. at 441. In *City of Boulder*, the plaintiff alleged that the city had indeed conspired with a rival cable company to prevent competition. 455 U.S. at 47 n.9. Chief Justice Burger joined the dissent in *City of Boulder*, which makes sense in light of the majority's implicit rejection of his view that cities are liable only when acting in a proprietary capacity.

Assuming for the moment that these concerns warrant antitrust scrutiny of municipal decisions, however, *Midcal* is a questionable means of addressing them. Cities may well be more
likely to act parochially than larger subdivisions. But in applying
Midcal to cities, Justice Brennan implicitly made the empirical
assumption that local ordinances that go beyond merely implementing a state policy to displace competition are likely to exploit
consumers and harm non-residents. Alternatively, however, it is
possible local ordinances might result in (1) increased competition
(presumably, the cities would ultimately prevail in these cases, but
only after a significant expenditure of costs by the cities and the
courts); (2) a better means of allocating resources, because the
regulation corrects market defects (i.e., competition really does not
work and regulation makes consumers better off); or (3) the
furtherance of non-efficiency values deemed more important to
the public interest than competition. In *City of Boulder*, for
example, the district court enjoined a local ordinance imposing a
three-month moratorium on the plaintiff's ability to expand cable
services. It would appear that the effect of the ordinance would
be felt almost entirely within Boulder's city limits, and the ordinance appeared to be in the public interest—to prevent the plaintiff, the sole provider of cable services in a portion of the city, from
extending its monopoly to other parts of the city before potential
rivals could enter.[65] Making an empirical assumption that these
alternative results are more likely than those feared by Brennan
suggests that municipal government should be trusted with the
power to displace competition with regulation, regardless of the
existence of a clearly articulated state policy.[66]

Although Boulder's regulation appeared to be pro-consumer,
Brennan's empirical assumptions may be more realistic given that

65. Part of the difficulty that arises
in analyzing *City of Boulder* is that the
plaintiff's theory as to why the ordinance was an antitrust violation was so
dubious. In a highly questionable decision, the district judge granted the
plaintiff's motion for a preliminary injunction against Boulder's cable moratorium ordinance. 485 F.Supp. 1035 (D.
Colo. 1980). In doing so, however, the
judge did not explain precisely what the
antitrust violation was. He noted that
"to influence competition Boulder unilaterally prevented further expansion
of the geographical area of the plaintiff's business," although he conceded
that the purpose of the ordinance might
have been a competitive one—to promote new competition by others—or an
anticompetitive one—to supplant the

plaintiff with another monopolist. Id.
at 1038.

Even if the purpose was to supplant
one monopolist with another, it is hard
to see how this would be anticompetitive. In any event, the three-month
moratorium's immediate effect was to
give the city the opportunity to decide
on how to proceed further. This decision seems clearly in the public interest. The fact that private interest of
other cable companies might coincide
with this public interest does not mean
that the ordinance was the result of
"regulatory capture" as that term is
generally used in antitrust.

66. See John Lopatka, State Action
and Municipal Antitrust Immunity: An
Economic Approach, 53 Fordham L.
Rev. 23 (1984).

cable viewers in other localities have not been so fortunate. For example, a Houston ordinance divided the city into numerous exclusive cable territories in a behind-closed-doors proceeding that was highly suggestive of regulatory capture.[67] Requiring cities to receive specific state authorization before regulating cable or other services may prevent some of these abuses, simply because it is costly for special interests to secure state approval. Some argue, however, that *Midcal* permits special interests to displace competition for their own purposes by "capturing" state officials.[68] If this is a widespread problem, requiring the state to comply with *Midcal* even when it delegates authority to a municipality may be better than relying on the state political process or the ability of citizens to change residences if they are unduly exploited.[69] One's resolution of these issues may depend in part on how specific the state authorization has to be under *Midcal*, and whether there are other feasible means of preventing capture. The first of these subjects is considered below, and the second is discussed in the following subsection.

In finding that municipal conduct constituted state action in *Town of Hallie v. City of Eau Claire*,[70] the Court significantly eased the obstacles *Midcal* imposes on municipalities that wish to dispace competition in the public interest. The Court held that *Midcal*'s requirement that the state actively supervise private conduct did not apply to decisions the state delegated to municipalities. The decision also illustrates what type of state law suffices to demonstrate a clearly articulated *state* policy to replace competition with municipal decisionmaking.

The litigation involved challenges by neighboring municipalities to Eau Claire's insistence that property owners residing outside city limits who wanted to use the city's sewage treatment facilities agree to annex their property to bring it within city limits. In a somewhat strange complaint, the plaintiff cities alleged that Eau Claire illegally used its "monopoly" in sewage treatment to control the "market" for certain municipal services.

In finding Eau Claire's actions protected by the state action doctrine the Court held, first, that the city's conduct was clearly authorized by the state. Wisconsin law specifically allowed cities operating public utilities to "delineate the area within which service will be provided and the municipal utility shall have no

67. Affiliated Capital Corp. v. City of Houston, 735 F.2d 1555 (5th Cir. 1984) (en banc), cert. denied, 474 U.S. 1053 (1986).

68. See John Wiley, A Capture Theory of Antitrust Federalism, 99 Harv. L. Rev. 713, 739 (1986).

69. For a discussion of the latter argument, see Easterbrook, supra note 17, at 43–45.

70. 471 U.S. 34 (1985).

obligation to serve beyond the area so delineated." [71]   Indeed, another provision of Wisconsin law demonstrated that the legislature had foreseen the precise problem arising in *Town of Hallie*: it authorized a state agency to order a municipal utility to serve additional territory, but only if the territory agreed to annexation.[72]   Moreover, the Wisconsin Supreme Court had rejected a challenge to similar practices brought under the state antitrust laws, on the ground that these annexation statutes reflected the legislature's intent to permit a city to demand annexation as a quid pro quo for providing sewer services.[73]

Second, the Court expressly held that *Midcal*'s requirement of active state supervision is inapplicable to cities.   Recognizing that language in *City of Lafayette*'s plurality opinion suggested the contrary result, the Court explained that municipal acts taken pursuant to clear state policy do not implicate the concerns expressed in *Parker* that a state might simply be authorizing private parties to violate the antitrust laws.   Moreover, while private parties acting pursuant to state authorization may decide to further their own interests rather than state policy, the Court suggested that cities are unlikely to become involved in a "*private* price fixing arrangement," and the "only real danger"—that a city "will seek to further purely parochial public interests at the expense of more overriding state goals"—is "minimal." [74]   This explanation goes too far.   If cities are unlikely to act contrary to the state's interest, why should they ever be subject to the antitrust laws?   Rather, a better justification for waiving the active supervision requirement for municipalities is *Town of Hallie*'s implicit conclusion that the state's political process operates better than federal antitrust litigation in determining whether a municipality is furthering purely parochial local interests at the expense of state goals.

71.   Id. at 41 (quoting Wis. Stat. Ann. § 66.069(2)(c)).

72.   Id. (citing Wis. Stat. Ann. § 144.-07(1)(m)).

73.   Id. at 44 n.8 (citing Town of Hallie v. City of Chippewa Falls, 105 Wis.2d 533, 314 N.W.2d 321 (1982)).

The Court went on to hint that the evidence in *Town of Hallie* far exceeded the minimum necessary to prove a clearly articulated state policy.   Rejecting a weak argument that Wisconsin had not clearly expressed a policy because there was no evidence of a specific intent to displace the antitrust laws, the Court held it sufficient to find that "anticompetitive effects logically would result from this broad authority to regulate."   Id. at 42.   This language is unduly loose.   *Town of Hallie* expressly distinguished Wisconsin's clear statutory scheme from Colorado's broad delegation of home rule, which was found insufficient to confer state action immunity in *City of Boulder*, yet it was certainly foreseeable that anticompetitive effects "logically would result" from Colorado's broad delegation of local control in Colorado's state constitution.   This language was critical to the Court's decision in City of Columbia v. Omni Outdoor Advertising, Inc., 111 S.Ct. 1344 (1991), which is considered in the following subsection.

74.   471 U.S. at 47 (emphasis in original).

(5) Confronting the problem of special interest capture.

The antitrust law's consistent refusal to consider a defendant's assertion that its restrictions on competition served the public interest is not based solely on the concern that judges should not "set sail on the sea of doubt" by trying to determine when competition should give way to other concerns.[75] When judges tell conspiring railroad owners, oil companies, medical associations or professional engineers that they simply will not consider their public interest arguments, they are implying that these organizations are not to be trusted when they argue that a restraint that is clearly in their own financial interest is somehow also in the public interest. The courts are far more trusting of local governments, however. As a result, they find it quite troublesome when private parties seeking to maximize their own financial gain try to use the Sherman Act to challenge local governmental regulations that unquestionably restrain trade but that appear to do so because the locality believes the public interest is better served. For example, environmental and health regulations frequently involve restrictions on output, and often favor existing firms over newcomers. When and how should the antitrust laws apply?

Language in the plurality's opinion in *City of Lafayette* suggested that local regulations are not protected state action simply because the state recognized that anticompetitive effects *could* result from its broad delegation of authority to municipalities. Rather, the opinion indicated, a city must demonstrate that the state legislature contemplated and authorized the specific type of activity challenged in the antitrust complaint.[76] Likewise, *City of Boulder* made clear that the antitrust laws are fully applicable to municipal regulations when state policy is neutral concerning the pros and cons of competition versus regulation. Although the opinion in *Town of Hallie* contains broad language, the holding of the case was fully consistent with these two opinions, finding state action based on state statutes that specifically authorized the city to engage in the precise conduct challenged and demonstrated a legislative awareness and approval of the specific behavior that was alleged to be anticompetitive.

Recently, however, in *City of Columbia v. Omni Outdoor Advertising, Inc.*,[77] the Supreme Court gave back to cities about 80% of what *Boulder* had taken away in terms of state action immunity. *Omni* also seems to reject special interest capture as a problem that the antitrust laws can meaningfully address. In

75. See note 1 supra.

76. 435 U.S. at 394 (citing lower court opinion with approval).

77. 111 S.Ct. 1344 (1991).

that case, Omni challenged a 1982 ordinance restricting the size, location, and spacing of billboards in Columbia, South Carolina. The ordinance was supported by numerous citizens who were concerned about the recent explosion in the number of local billboards, as well as by the regulation's chief economic beneficiary—co-defendant Columbia Outdoor Advertising, which had controlled 95% of the billboard market prior to Omni's entry in 1981. Omni claimed that the ordinance violated the Sherman Act because it was the result of a conspiracy between local officials and the politically influential dominant firm. The Court rejected the complaint on state action grounds.

The Justices unanimously rejected the Fourth Circuit's opinion that the ordinance was not entitled to immunity because it fell under a so-called "conspiracy" exception to *Parker v. Brown*. As Justice Antonin Scalia noted for the Court, the language in *Parker* distinguishing the restraints imposed there by the California Raisin Board from cases where a state or municipality became "a participant in a private agreement or combination by others for restraint of trade" [78] was intended to refer to situations "where the State acts not in a regulatory capacity but as a commercial participant in a given market." [79]

The Court then divided 6–3 on the question whether the state's authorization was sufficient to bring Columbia's restriction within the state action doctrine. The city's authority derived from a broad South Carolina statute permitting cities to "regulate and restrict the height, number of stores and size of buildings *and other structures*" for the purpose of "promoting health, safety, morals, or the general welfare of the community." [80] To be sure, this statute was somewhat more specific than the total grant of local home rule authority held insufficient in *Boulder*. However, in adopting as a holding *Town of Hallie*'s dictum that "[i]t is enough ... if suppression of competition is the 'foreseeable result' of what the statute authorizes," [81] *Omni* cannot be squared with *City of Boulder*. Some suppression of competition was, of course, the foreseeable result of the delegation of home rule authority in *Boulder*. This dictum was not decisive in *Town of Hallie* itself, because the Court correctly found that the legislature had explicit-

---

78. *Parker*, 313 U.S. at 351–52.

79. 111 S.Ct. at 1351. In drawing this distinction, Scalia noted, *Parker* cited Union Pacific R. Co. v. United States, 313 U.S. 450 (1941), which applied another federal statute to condemn certain rebates made by the City of Kansas City, Kansas, in its capacity as the owner of a produce market.

The dissent agreed that "the Court correctly applies principles of federalism in refusing to find a 'conspiracy exception' to the *Parker* state action doctrine when a State acts in a nonproprietary capacity." 111 S.Ct. at 1363.

80. S.C. Code § 5–23–10.

81. 111 S.Ct. at 1350 (quoting *Town of Hallie*, 471 U.S. at 42).

ly sanctioned the alleged anticompetitive acts—conditioning sewer hook-ups on annexation. In *Omni*, however, there was no indication that South Carolina explicitly sanctioned the restriction of billboard competition in order to preserve the economic power of a local monopolist, and thus the ordinance could only be considered state action by relying on a "forseeability" test inconsistent with earlier precedents. When we consider why cities are subject to the Sherman Act at all—because of the risk that they will act to harm non-residents while benefiting residents and because of the danger of regulatory capture—Columbia's billboard ordinance posed a far greater threat to competition than Boulder's cable moratorium.

The key to *Omni* is that the majority rejected the idea of predicating local antitrust liability on the risk of regulatory capture. Justice John Paul Stevens' dissenting opinion did not find the state's authorization insufficient simply because it was so broad. Rather, the dissent argued that the billboard ordinance violated § 1 because of regulatory capture. South Carolina's statute, Stevens noted, authorized local billboard restrictions only to promote non-economic concerns like health, safety, and welfare, and not economic concerns like protecting local businesses from competition. He expressed confidence in the ability of juries to identify cases, like *Omni*, where "the official action is the product of an agreement intended to elevate particular private interests over the general good." [82]

Stevens finessed the difficulties associated with capture-based tests, however, by advocating liability only when "the ordinance was enacted for the *sole purpose of interfering with access to the market*." [83] In response, Justice Scalia pointed out that such cases were an unusual "polar extreme[ ], which like the geographic poles will rarely be seen by jurors of the vicinage." The typical case involves mixed motives, Scalia noted, and he questioned whether it was possible to distinguish between lawful and unlawful municipal action that was only partly based on agreements with private parties. The dissent "does not tell us how to put this question coherently, much less how to answer it intelligently," the Court complained.[84] Stevens acknowledged that the persuasiveness of his approach turned on one's confidence in the ability of the judicial system to correctly assess the motivations of public officials.[85] In *Omni*, for example, the billboard ordinance, like most anti-growth local regulations, was supported by public-spirited,

82. Id. at 1361–62.

83. Id. at 1362 n.9 (emphasis added).

84. Id. at 1351 n.5.

85. Id. at 1357–58, 1362.

environmentally oriented citizens as well as by private-spirited, competition-fearing, entrenched, politically influential firms.

Given Scalia's criticisms and Stevens' concessions, the real alternative to Scalia's holding in *Omni* is not Stevens' narrow "sole purpose" test, but one offered by Professor John Wiley. Wiley would impose liability even where a city could raise a plausible public interest justification for its competition-lessening ordinance, if (1)(a) the ordinance arose as a consequence of support by the producers of goods or services who would benefit financially from it, and (b) this support was "decisive and preponderant" in securing passage of the ordinance, or (2) on its face, the ordinance appears to be attributable primarily to special interest capture, and the plaintiff demonstrates that the alleged public interest justifications are pretextual.[86] Wiley would resolve all close questions in favor of the city, so as to limit antitrust intervention to cases where the court is confident that competition has not been replaced by other public interest considerations.[87] Thus, it appears a plaintiff would probably be unable to show—in light of the environmentalist support for the legislation, that Columbia Outdoor's support was "preponderant," and therefore the Columbia's ordinance would pass muster even under his anti-capture test.

Omni appears to reject the capture approach. A capture-based test is based on the normative theory that "producers' use of anticompetitive state policies to enrich themselves at the consumers' expense is indeed illegitimate."[88] By contrast, the *Omni* majority argued that "it is both inevitable and desirable that public officials often agree to do what one or another group of private citizens urges upon them."[89] Because the dissent focused only on ordinances motivated solely by capture, the majority did not specifically address the workability of Wiley's proposal. However, others have seriously questioned whether the courts can determine with any confidence when capture was the decisive factor leading to a certain ordinance; even if judges are up to the task, Wiley's critics have argued that it is inappropriate for the federal courts to inquire into the motivation underlying official acts.[90]

Some critics of capture theory defend the *Midcal* test as the appropriate standard for municipal liability. They point out that the risk of capture is minimized when special interests must

---

86. John Wiley, A Capture Theory of Antitrust Federalism: Reply to Professors Page and Spitzer, 61 S. Cal. L. Rev. 1327, 1341 (1988)[hereinafter "Wiley Reply"]; Wiley, supra note 68, at 770–72.

87. Wiley, supra note 68, at 772.

88. Wiley Reply, supra note 86, at 1337.

89. 111 S.Ct. at 1351.

90. See, e.g., Elhauge, supra note 9, at 723.

persuade a state legislature, rather than simply a local council, to clearly articulate a policy favoring municipal regulation over competition. This argument loses force, however when statutes as broad as South Carolina's satisfy *Midcal*'s requirement of state authorization.

Although *City of Lafayette* suggested that municipalities could face substantial liability for antitrust violations, the risk of municipal liability is substantially reduced today. *Town of Hallie* permits the courts to confer state action immunity on municipal actions without requiring specific state supervision, and *Omni* seems to prevent plaintiffs from showing that municipal decisions that purport to supplant competition in the public interest are in reality the product of an agreement between city officials and special interests to elevate the latter's interests over the public good. Perhaps most significant, Congress enacted the Local Government Antitrust Act of 1984, which allows only injunctive relief in antitrust suits against localities or public officials acting in an official capacity.[91]

(6) When *Midcal* need not be satisfied.

In the two significant Supreme Court state action cases that have yet to be discussed, the Court ruled in favor of the defendants, even though they could not show that they acted pursuant to a clearly articulated state policy to supplant competition with regulation. The two cases are sufficiently unusual, however, that the Court's holdings may be limited to their special factual situations.

First, in *Hoover v. Ronwin*,[92] an unsuccessful applicant for the Arizona bar alleged that his failure to pass the bar exam was the result of a conspiracy among members of the Arizona Supreme Court's Committee on Examinations and Admissions—all attorneys—to reduce artificially the number of competing attorneys in the state. The gist of the plaintiff's complaint was that, although the Arizona Supreme Court delegated authority to the Committee to test applicants for competence and to recommend for admission those who were fit to practice, in reality the Committee members had established a grading scale that corresponded to the number of new attorneys they thought desirable, and they recommended only that number for admission.

In an obvious effort to dismiss a complaint it found meritless and dangerous,[93] the majority concluded that the Arizona Supreme

91. 15 U.S.C. §§ 35–36.

92. 466 U.S. 558 (1984).

93. Writing for the majority, Justice Lewis Powell (a former president of the American Bar Association) expressed concern that "lawyers of recognized

Court had delegated an advisory role to the defendants, but retained the final authority to grant or deny admission to the bar and to review the Committee's grading formula. Accordingly, the Court reasoned, Ronwin was injured not by the Committee, but by the Supreme Court, acting as sovereign. Indeed, Ronwin's injury was no more the product of a non-exempt antitrust violation than if a California Raisin Board marketing restraint were challenged because raisin growers had conspired to propose that the Board set unreasonable restrictions on output and to conceal the fact that these restrictions would increase prices.

In contrast, Justice Stevens' dissenting opinion read the complaint as alleging that a committee who had been delegated the responsibility of establishing competence standards for bar applicants had instead transformed the process, without any official direction or ratification, to one limiting entry. Recognizing the long history of entry limitations erected by tradespeople and professionals, Stevens found the majority's conclusion that the challenged action was that of the Arizona Supreme Court to be "plainly wrong." [94]

As the majority viewed the case, the Supreme Court of Arizona, acting as a sovereign, made a final determination on the admission of lawyers. It correctly concluded that such a determination would be state action, regardless of what nefarious acts a judicially appointed committee may have performed in recommending applicants for admission. As the dissent viewed the case, by contrast, the state court directed that the only criterion for admission was competence, but that instruction was then frustrated by the defendants' unlawful conspiracy. It correctly concluded that if the defendants, rather than the Arizona court, had restricted Ronwin's ability to practice law, the state court's general delegation of authority to the Committee was not a clearly articulated and affirmatively expressed policy to displace competition. The case appears to have limited doctrinal value because it was decided on a motion to dismiss for failure to state a claim and the Justices' differing views seem to resolve primarily around precisely what was alleged in the pleadings.[95]

standing and integrity" who serve on state bar committees "as a public duty and with little or no compensation" would be subjected to suits that were "likely to be frivolous." Powell observed that if the Court did not conclude that the entire process of bar admission was state action, complaints like Ronwin's that alleged improper motive would survive a motion to dismiss. As a result, these committees would face numerous suits brought by those

who had failed bar exams, and the litigation would require substantial discovery concerning the committee members' subjective motives. Id. at 580 n.34.

94. Id. at 588.

95. Compare id. at 563–64 (emphasizing that Arizona rules permit a rejected bar applicant to seek individualized review by filing a petition directly with the Arizona Supreme Court, that Ronwin submitted such a petition to

Hoover v. Ronwin may have broader implications, however, in those unusual situations where specific economic results are dictated by a state's legislature, governor, or supreme court. Whenever those who exercise the state's sovereign power perform the "active supervision" required by *Midcal*, it could be said that the "state" has acted and that the result cannot be challenged even if *Midcal*'s "clear articulation" requirement has not been met. To illustrate, suppose that in *Patrick v. Burget*,[96] the Oregon Supreme Court had determined *de novo* that Dr. Patrick was an unfit surgeon; *Hoover v. Ronwin* suggests that Patrick could not challenge the decision on the ground that his antagonists were really trying to prevent competition. Subsequently, however, the Court suggested that even this effort to read some slightly broader implications into *Hoover v. Ronwin* may be erroneous.[97]

The second case is *Fisher v. City of Berkeley*.[98] The plaintiff in that case alleged that Berkeley's rent control ordinance effectively required landlords to engage in maximum price fixing, and was therefore preempted by the Sherman Act. The Court held that a consumer-protection ordinance passed by the voters in order to protect renters did not constitute a conspiracy for purposes of § 1. Because there was no conspiracy, there was no antitrust violation and thus the *Midcal* test was irrelevant.

Traditional analysis fails to support the Court's holding. The Court correctly observed that even in the absence of a conspiracy, the Sherman Act preempts state laws that mandate, authorize, or place irresistible pressure on a private party to violate the antitrust laws in order to comply with state directives.[99] Although the Court sought to distinguish *Schwegmann* and *Midcal*, Justice William Brennan correctly observed in dissent that the effect of the statutes challenged in all three cases was to stabilize prices and eliminate the force of competition, contrary to the policies of the Sherman Act. According to the majority, the distinguishing feature of the two precedents was that there the prices were determined by private parties, whereas in *Fisher* they were set by

that court, alleging procedural and substantive irregularities with the bar committee's process, and that the court denied that petition, along with two rehearing petitions), with id. at 588–89 & n.12 (Stevens, J., dissenting) (finding "plainly wrong" the majority's conclusion that the Arizona Supreme Court made "any independent decision to admit or reject *any* individual applicant for admission to the Bar," and noting that the defendants did not make the argument relied on by the majority that the examination process' function was purely to advise the state court).

96. 486 U.S. 94 (1988), which is discussed above in subsection (3).

97. See *Patrick*, 486 U.S. at 104 (refusing to decide "the broad question whether judicial review of private conduct ever can constitute active supervision").

98. 475 U.S. 260 (1986).

99. Id. at 265 (citing Rice v. Norman Williams Co., 458 U.S. 654, 661 (1982)).

the publicly elected Rent Stabilization Board. As Brennan observed, though, this distinction is relevant to the question whether the challenged ordinance is state action immunized from § 1 liability under *Parker v. Brown*, but not to the question whether a § 1 violation exists at all.[100] Indeed, under the majority's reasoning *Parker* itself was not a conspiracy because the output restrictions were ultimately determined by a state agency there, too, not unsupervised private parties.

Concurring, Justice Powell tried to avoid the "difficult preemption question" raised by the majority by concluding that the Berkeley ordinance was state action.[101] The problem with Powell's approach is that the ordinance in question had not been ratified by the state legislature, and state statutes were expressly neutral about the authority of local governments to impose rent control.[102]

There are two alternative explanations for *Fisher*'s holding that appear more coherent than those offered by either the majority or concurring opinions. First, if, as many have argued, the principal purpose of § 1 is to protect consumers from exploitation, then a "conspiracy" by voters, who tend to be either renters or those with no economic stake in the rental market, to enact an ordinance limiting landlords' ability to exploit whatever market power they may have does not "restrain trade" and is therefore not subject to § 1. The fact that the rent control ordinance appeared to be unequivocally pro-consumer seems to be the only distinction between *Fisher* and *City of Boulder*. Although Boulder was also acting on behalf of cable consumers in delaying the expansion of one cable firm in order to study the possibilities of multiple entry into the cable market, the complaint in that case alleged a conspiracy between the city and an arguably favored rival cable firm. By contrast, the *only* favored private parties in *Fisher* were consumers.[103] Second, the *Midcal* test may be viewed as a rough proxy reflecting the concern that private parties may

100. Id. at 275–77 & n.2.

101. Id. at 273.

102. Powell relied on the fact that the California legislature had ratified an earlier Berkeley rent control ordinance in 1972. Id. at 272. At the time, however, California's constitution required legislative ratification of amendments to city charters. (The earlier ordinance was struck down on procedural grounds by the California Supreme Court. Birkenfeld v. City of Berkeley, 17 Cal.3d 129, 130 Cal.Rptr. 465, 550 P.2d 1001, 1008 (1976)). When the challenged ordinance was enacted by Berkeley voters in 1980, California no longer required legislative ratification of charter amendments, and no such ratification occurred. 475 U.S. at 280 n.3 (Brennan, J., dissenting). Moreover, California law expressly provided that the state code could not be construed as either a grant or repeal of any local rent control authority—i.e., state neutrality. Cal. Govt. Code § 65589(b).

103. John Wiley, The Berkeley Rent Control Case: Treating Victims as Villains, 1986 Sup. Ct. Rev. 157, 166.

have "captured" state agencies (including local governments) and influenced them to immunize private cartel behavior. Because Berkeley's anti-landlord ordinance could not possibly be the result of capture, it is not preempted by the Sherman Act and *Midcal*'s two-pronged analysis need not be applied.[104] Unfortunately, however, *Omni* seemed to reject capture as an appropriate basis for antitrust adjudication.

———

The state action doctrine is another manifestation of one of the few consistent threads running through antitrust jurisprudence—the distrust of claims that conduct that is hostile to competition is nonetheless in the public interest. The doctrine allows state governments to find that competition is not in the public interest, despite the fact that the antitrust laws do not give similar leeway to either federal judges or private parties. This special latitude is due to both the role that states play in our federal system and a concern that many state laws that promote health, safety, the environment, or other non-economic values might be improperly jeopardized by an "antitrust *uber alles*" approach. The Supreme Court has held that conduct can be immunized as state action only if the state legislature makes two explicit, politically accountable, and potentially controversial decisions: to declare a clear state policy to displace competition with some form of state regulation; and to assign a state official the task of actually making the output-reducing or price-fixing determination that would otherwise be illegal under the antitrust laws.

One category of potential Sherman Act violators—municipal corporations—have a special role under the state action doctrine. Although originally treated just like private firms because of concerns that local government officials were too likely to act contrary to the public interest of the state or the nation, recent Supreme Court decisions now afford local governments extremely lenient treatment. Although these decisions may deviate in theory from state action jurisprudence, their results were dictated, rightly or wrongly, by the Court's answer to the question that underlies this entire area: Whom do you trust?

Section B: Influencing Governmental Restraints on Trade

If federalism concerns justify immunizing state actions from antitrust liability, even if they restrict competition, democratic

---

104. Id. at 166–73.

concerns dictate that immunity likewise be extended to private parties when they petition the government to enact anticompetitive legislation. As the Court recently explained, it would be "obviously peculiar in a democracy, and perhaps in derogation of the constitutional right 'to petition the government for a redress of grievances,' to establish a category of lawful state action that citizens are not permitted to urge." [1] The doctrine that protects such petitioning activity is heavily influenced by First Amendment concerns, but antitrust immunity is an analytically distinct issue. In fact, some conduct that is not constitutionally protected is nonetheless exempt from antitrust scrutiny as petitioning activity. The key focus for antitrust purposes is on whether competition has been lessened directly by the defendant's misconduct, or indirectly by the defendant's political success in persuading the government to displace competition with regulation.

(1) Establishing the "*Noerr*" doctrine.

The first case to establish that the Sherman Act did not apply to joint efforts to obtain anticompetitive governmental restrictions was *Eastern Railroad Presidents Conference v. Noerr Motor Freight, Inc.*[2] Noerr, a bevy of other trucking companies, and the Pennsylvania Motor Truck Association alleged that a host of railroads, their trade association, and a public relations firm had conspired to restrain trade by waging a publicity campaign against the truckers that was "designed to foster the adoption and retention of laws and law enforcement practices destructive of the trucking business." The plaintiffs claimed that the campaign was "vicious, corrupt, and fraudulent" in that its sole motivation was not to serve the public welfare but to injure and eventually destroy competition between railroads and truckers. Its techniques allegedly included sponsoring publicity that appeared to be a spontaneous expression of support by neutral parties when the material had actually been prepared by the railroads. The only tangible damages for which relief was sought under § 4 of the Clayton Act were occasioned by the truckers' loss of business when Pennsylvania's Governor vetoed a "Fair Truck Bill" that would have permitted truckers to carry heavier loads within the state in direct competition with the railroads.[3]

The Supreme Court held that the Sherman Act does not prohibit efforts to influence the legislature or the governor to approve anticompetitive legislation or to defeat pro-competitive measures. The truckers' injury was due solely to the Governor's

1. City of Columbia v. Omni Outdoor Advertising, Inc., 111 S.Ct. 1344, 1353 (1991) (quoting U.S. Const. amend. I).

2. 365 U.S. 127 (1961).

3. Id. at 129–30.

veto; if the Governor had signed the bill, rivalry between truckers and railroads would not have been restrained, despite the railroads' publicity campaign. Recall the rationale underlying the state action doctrine: the Commonwealth of Pennsylvania has the authority to determine that competition between railroads and truckers within its borders is not in the public interest, notwithstanding the general antitrust policy favoring competition. Awarding antitrust damages to the truckers would require a judgment that the state's decision was incorrect, a judgment that the state action doctrine prevents the federal courts from making.

In support of this conclusion, the Court also pointed out that conspiracies to influence government action are not analogous to the types of conspiracies that were the principal concern of the framers of the Sherman Act. Moreover, the Court acknowledged that imposing antitrust liability would raise significant First Amendment problems.[4] Neither of these arguments suffice, however, to explain the holding in *Noerr*. The broad language of the Sherman Act condemns all unreasonable restraints of trade, not only those anticompetitive techniques familiar to Senator Sherman and his colleagues. Although many activities immunized by *Noerr* are also protected by the First Amendment's right to petition, the Constitution does not protect various sorts of sleazy, misleading misconduct that *Noerr* covers.[5]

The Court rejected two arguments raised by the truckers to justify an award of antitrust damages notwithstanding these general principles. First, the defendants' specific intent to monopolize did not require antitrust liability. Endorsing pluralist political theory, the Court suggested that modern government depends on the beneficiaries of legislation to provide information necessary to the legislative process. The Court explained:

> A construction of the Sherman Act that would disqualify people from taking a public position on matters in which they are financially interested would thus deprive the government of a valuable source of information and, at the same time, deprive the people of their right to petition in the very instances in which that right may be of most importance to them.[6]

Second, the fact that the defendants may have engaged in unethical or even illegal practices in obtaining what they wanted

---

4. Id. at 136, 138.

5. The railroads' undisclosed support for public statements made by third parties in support of the railroads' lobbying efforts would violate federal law, if directed toward Congress. 2 U.S.C. §§ 261–270. This statute has withstood First Amendment challenge. United States v. Harriss, 347 U.S. 612 (1954).

6. 365 U.S. at 139.

from the government did not forfeit antitrust immunity. Political misconduct should be regulated directly, the Court held; the Sherman Act's proscriptions, "tailored as they are for the business world, are not at all appropriate for application in the political arena."[7] This argument is supported by another consideration—the difficulties of proving causation in an antitrust challenge of this nature. The truckers assumed that the railroads' sleazy publicity campaign caused the Governor to veto pro-competitive legislation. Perhaps this was true; but the Governor may have been a long-time supporter of railroads who would have tried to protect them from competition anyway. The courts have traditionally been wary of testing the validity of a law based on the means used by private parties' to secure its passage.[8] This reluctance is particularly appropriate when the consequences are treble damages, which may well have a chilling effect on legitimate petitioning.[9]

In an important caveat, the Court recognized that conspirators, under the pretense of seeking to influence governmental action, might in reality be involved in "a mere sham to cover what is actually nothing more than an attempt to interfere directly with the business relationships of a competitor." In such cases, the Sherman Act would apply.[10] But to qualify under this exception, the plaintiff must show that the defendants were not making a genuine effort to influence legislation. Thus, any business lost by the truckers in *Noerr* because the railroads' publicity campaign may have led some shippers to patronize railroads would still not be compensable in antitrust litigation because the injury would be the "incidental effect" of lobbying.[11]

---

7. Id. at 141.

8. See I Philip Areeda & Donald Turner, Antitrust Law 49–50 (1978). In Fletcher v. Peck, 10 U.S. (6 Cranch) 87, 130 (1810), for example, the Supreme Court declined to invalidate a Georgia law allegedly enacted as a result of widespread bribery, on the theory that it was improper for the federal courts to inquire into the motives of Georgia legislators.

9. Because of these special concerns about chilling legitimate petitioning, this is one area where the state action and *Noerr* doctrines diverge. Just as the Court asks whether local producers were mainly responsible for securing passage of a protectionist state law challenged under the Commerce Clause, see Hunt v. Washington State Apple Advertising Comm'n, 432 U.S. 333, 352 (1977), it may be appropriate to consid-

er political influence in determining whether anticompetitive local legislation is preempted by the Sherman Act or protected under the state action doctrine. See John Wiley, The Berkeley Rent Control Case: Treating Victims as Villains, 1986 Sup. Ct. Rev. 157, 170, discussed above in section A(6). But imposing treble damages if such a post-enactment inquiry discloses that the legislation was unduly influenced by special interests would impermissibly deter political speech.

10. 365 U.S. at 144.

11. Id. at 143. In United Mine Workers of America v. Pennington, 381 U.S. 657 (1965), the Court held that union efforts to influence the Secretary of Labor to establish a minimum wage for coal miners were protected by *Noerr*. (Some therefore refer to this doctrine as the "*Noerr–Pennington*" doctrine.) Al-

(2) The sham exception.

California Motor Transport Co. v. Trucking Unlimited[12] gave
the Court an opportunity to expand on *Noerr*'s caveat that the
Sherman Act remained applicable to restraints on competition
that, albeit nominally aimed at petitioning the government, were
in fact intended to directly harm rivals. Prior to deregulation of
the trucking industry, federal law required motor carriers desiring
to transport goods across state lines to obtain prior approval from
the Interstate Commerce Commission. In *California Motor Transport*, one group of highway truckers sued a rival group under the
Sherman Act, alleging that the defendants had agreed to routinely
object to the plaintiffs' filings before the ICC in an effort to delay
or defeat the plaintiffs' operating authority. Although the trial
judge dismissed the complaint for failure to state a claim, the
Supreme Court remanded for trial because the defendants were
not seeking to influence public officials, but rather "to bar their
competitors from meaningful access to adjudicatory tribunals and
to usurp that decisionmaking process."[13] As the Court recently
explained, "[t]he 'sham' exception to *Noerr* encompasses situations
in which persons use the governmental *process*—as opposed to the
outcome of that process—as an anticompetitive weapon."[14]

To prevail under the sham exception, plaintiffs must show
that the challenged conduct is independently wrongful and is not a
genuine effort to influence policymakers. The requirement of
independent wrongfulness ensures that the Sherman Act does not
chill constitutionally protected petitioning activity. Because the
government already imposes sanctions for filing groundless complaints, abusing process, suborning perjured testimony, commit-
ting fraud on the patent office, and similar misdeeds, defendants
who commit such acts can hardly complain about constitutional
rights when they must pay damages because their misconduct
injured competition. The requirement that the nominal petitioning activity be disingenuous is particularly consistent with the
theory underlying the doctrine—unlike *Noerr*, the harm in *California Motor Transport* was not caused by a governmental decision, but by private actors' abuse of process. A key element of the
plaintiffs' antitrust claim was that the defendants had agreed to
routinely file objections with the ICC, without regard to the merits
of the plaintiffs' regulatory filing. Why would the defendants

though the Court rejected the plaintiff's
claim that the union violated the Sherman Act because its intent was anticompetitive, it held that evidence of petitioning activity would still be admissible, if not unduly prejudicial, in order
to show that the union intended to en-

gage in related non-petitioning conduct.
Id. at 670 n.3.

12.   404 U.S. 508 (1972).

13.   Id. at 512.

14.   *Omni*, 111 S.Ct. at 1354.

spend time and money filing meritless objections? Because they
gained a competitive advantage by delaying approval of the plaintiffs' entry into their markets. If conspirators are not really
seeking any official act, the need for protection under *Noerr* as a
corollary to the state action doctrine is not applicable.

Moreover, causation concerns that argued against liability in
Noerr point the other way in cases like *California Motor Transport.* Because the plaintiffs claimed injury resulting from the
delay in securing regulatory approval of their filings, there was
little doubt that the defendants' conspiracy caused this injury.
Unlike *Noerr*, then, the case did not require the courts to find a
factual nexus between a defendant's conduct and a public official's
political decision.[15]

In re Burlington Northern, Inc.[16] illustrates and somewhat
broadens the sham exception. The plaintiff in that case, a company that had unsuccessfully sought to build a coal slurry pipeline
between Wyoming and Arkansas, sued several railroads that were
in the business of transporting coal. The plaintiff claimed that
the defendants had conspired to prevent construction of the pipeline. The conspiratorial acts alleged in the complaint included the
railroads' participation in two lawsuits involving the plaintiff; the
defendants sought to block discovery of documents relating to this
litigation, arguing that their involvement in the suits was protected under *Noerr*. The Fifth Circuit first held that the trial judge
had erred in ordering discovery without determining whether the
railroads' litigation activities were protected,[17] but ultimately concluded that the plaintiff had made out a prima facie case that the
railroads' conduct was an unprotected sham.

In one non-controversial part of the opinion, the court found
that the defendants had engaged in obvious sham conduct. The
plaintiff's proposed pipeline needed to cross certain railroad
tracks; when the defendants would not grant a right-of-way, the
plaintiff found areas of the tracks where the pipeline could cross
over land the railroads did not own outright (but as to which they
merely had an easement). The plaintiff also obtained an ease-

---

15. Because the sham behavior in
California Motor Transport involved denial of the plaintiffs' meaningful access
to ICC regulators, some have argued
that *Noerr* does not protect any effort to
exclude a rival from participation in
the political process. The Court rejected this argument in *Omni*, reasoning
that "[a]ny lobbyist or applicant, in addition to getting himself heard, seeks by
procedural and other means to get his
opponent ignored." Thus, as long as
the defendant's efforts are part of a

genuine attempt to secure an official
act from the government, *Noerr* applies.
111 S.Ct. at 1355.

16. 822 F.2d 518 (5th Cir. 1987), cert.
denied, 484 U.S. 1007 (1988).

17. The court held that allowing discovery to go forward without such a
preliminary determination would chill
petitioning activities that *Noerr* considered desirable. Id. at 525.

ment, but the railroads took the position that their rights under their own easement did not permit construction of a pipeline crossing under the railroad tracks. They continued to assert this position even though they knew it was not defensible and despite its repeated rejection in court. Because the evidence suggested that the railroads' decision to file defensive pleadings and demands for discovery in these cases was not "significantly motivated by an honest and reasonable desire to influence the court's decision," the conduct was not protected by *Noerr*.[18]

More controversial was the court's refusal to extend protection to the involvement of two railroads in complex multi-party litigation seeking to block the pipeline's use of water from a federal reservoir. Unlike the railroads' total lack of success in the easement litigation, the courts actually ruled in favor of the plaintiffs (who included several states and organizations representing farmers and environmentalists as well as the Kansas City Southern Railroad) in the reservoir lawsuits. But the Fifth Circuit refused to hold that the railroads' success automatically protected them. The court acknowledged that prevailing in litigation is "persuasive evidence that the litigant in fact wanted the relief" sought because parties with meritorious claims are usually motivated by a desire to obtain relief. Nevertheless, in this case, the pipeline presented evidence that the railroads decided to participate in the reservoir litigation without considering the possible merit of the suit.[19]

Moreover, in a significant holding, the Fifth Circuit found that one of the two railroads participating in the reservoir litigation was not eligible for *Noerr* protection because it lacked standing to sue, and the other was unprotected because it was not actually a party to the suit but merely assisted in the legal efforts of one of the states that challenged the use of reservoir water.[20] The finding that the Kansas City Southern Railroad lacked standing meant that it had no right to petition the court for relief, the Fifth Circuit reasoned; accordingly, *Noerr* did not protect any petitioning activity related to the lawsuit. The court also held that *Noerr* did not cover the Union Pacific's role as a non-party in assisting Nebraska with its efforts to block the pipeline's use of federal water. Relying on language in *Noerr* that justified antitrust immunity in part because the government relies on interested parties to furnish information useful to governmental decision-making, the Fifth Circuit declared that applying the Sherman Act

18. Id. at 532–33.

19. Id. at 528.

20. The court did not address the question whether aiding a state attorney general's legitimate prosecution of litigation on behalf of the state was itself petitioning activity that might be protected.

to a non-party that offers legal assistance to the parties in anti-competitive litigation "subjects to antitrust scrutiny only those persons whose interests are such that Congress or the courts have independently determined not to be the proper parties to assert the claim in court." [21]

Although *Burlington Northern*'s refusal to immunize the railroads' conduct unless it was both honestly and reasonably intended to secure relief is consistent with *Noerr* and *California Motor Transport*, the opinion's view of the role of non-parties is too crabbed. Contrary to the court's reasoning, a statute or precedent denying a party standing to raise a claim does not mean that the party has no right to petition the court for relief. For example, *Burlington Northern*'s logic would expose those who participate in the now prevalent practice of filing *amicus curiae* briefs to antitrust liability. In many cases, the cost of litigation is such that those who are victimized by illegal conduct cannot afford to redress their legitimate grievances. If the state of Nebraska had standing to challenge an environmentally destructive (albeit pro-competitive) use of federal water, but could not afford to match the pipeline's legal resources, the fact that the Union Pacific Railroad had selfish motivations for helping the state's cause should not lead to denial of protection under *Noerr*.

(3) Improperly influencing ministerial or commercial government decisions.

In *Woods Exploration & Producing Co. v. Aluminum Co. of America*,[22] the Fifth Circuit held that filing false statements with a state agency to frustrate the implementation of state policy violates the antitrust laws where the effect is to restrain trade or monopolize. The parties in that case were rivals in the business of natural gas extraction, an industry heavily regulated under state law by the Texas Railroad Commission. Under state regulations, the Railroad Commission carefully limited the amount of gas that could be extracted. The Commission's allocation process began by determining the market demand for gas, and then applied a formula that dictated the prorated amount of this gas each firm could extract. Especially when demand was high, the Commission's formula tended to favor smaller companies like Woods over larger interests like Alcoa and the other defendants. In determining demand, the Commission relied upon "nominations" filed by the operators, stating the amount of gas they expected to be able to market each month. Woods' complaint alleged that the defen-

21. Id. at 531.   22. 438 F.2d 1286 (5th Cir. 1971).

dants had conspired to falsely underestimate demand, thus artificially reducing the amount of gas that could be extracted.

In finding *Noerr* inapplicable, the court reasoned that the "policies of the Sherman Act should not be sacrificed simply because defendants employ governmental processes to accomplish anticompetitive purposes." [23] The court emphasized that the defendants' false filings were not part of an effort "to influence the *policies* of the Railroad Commission," but rather to subvert the "subsequent implementation" of those policies.[24]

Woods' distinction between influencing government policy and influencing administrative implementation of policy is consistent with the view that *Noerr* is a corollary of the state action doctrine. Suppose that the defendants in *Woods*, like the railroads in *Noerr*, had used sleazy campaign tactics to persuade Texas officials to adopt an allocation formula favoring large producers. Finding this conduct illegal would implicitly require a determination that Texas ought not favor large producers, and the state action doctrine does not permit the federal courts to make such a determination. Thus, *Noerr* would have protected this type of campaign. In contrast, to condemn the filing of false statements in administrative proceedings does not require federal courts to second-guess any state policy determination. Moreover, filing false statements serves no legitimate purpose, and thus no First Amendment rights are chilled. Finally, causation is easy to establish; in the context of this apolitical administrative proceeding, there was a clear causal link between the defendants' false statements, the Railroad Commission's decision to reduce overall demand, and the resulting formulaic reduction in Woods' allowance.

(4) Indirect lobbying through standard setting organizations.

Special problems arise when government agencies rely on private organizations to establish standards that are then incorporated into regulatory decrees. The antitrust laws have long wrestled with the competitive problems that arise when rivals agree privately on standards and certification requirements for their industries. The law is fairly clear that agreements among competitors on seals of approval or other certification measures are judged under the rule of reason and are upheld unless a rejected plaintiff can make a strong case that the standards are unfair and improper; on the other hand, agreements among competitors to exclude rivals by refusing to deal with uncertified firms is per se

23. Id. at 1296.   **24.** Id. at 1297 (emphasis added).

illegal.[25] When firms convince their own private organization to deny a seal of approval, knowing that the decision will result in their rival's exclusion from the market because the private standard will be adopted as law by many government regulatory agencies, is this indirect lobbying protected by *Noerr* or is it direct, private harm to competitors subject to antitrust liability?

Those seeking to enforce the antitrust laws against indirect lobbying could not have asked for a better factual record than that presented by *Allied Tube & Conduit Co. v. Indian Head, Inc.*[26] The case involved an important private standard-setting procedure—the adoption by the National Fire Protection Association of the National Electrical Code. Many state and local governments routinely adopt the Code into law with little or no change; highly influential private certifiers, such as Underwriters Laboratories, normally will not approve a product that does not meet Code standards; and many underwriters will not insure structures unless they are built according to the Code.

Indian Head developed a plastic conduit (a hollow tubing used to carry electrical wires through walls and floors) and wanted the product listed as an approved type of electrical conduit in the 1981 Code. Indian Head alleged that its product was more flexible, cheaper, and less likely to short circuit than the traditional steel conduit. Some genuine scientific concerns were raised, however, that the plastic might burn during fires in high-rise buildings and emit toxic fumes. The association rejected Indian Head's efforts to obtain Code approval for the plastic conduit.

What made the litigation so attractive for Indian Head was the role that Allied Tube, the nation's largest steel conduit producer, played in the association's decision. Allied and several other steel conduit makers agreed to pack the association's annual meeting in order to overturn a professional panel's recommendation that the plastic conduit be approved. The steel interests recruited 230 people to join the association and attend the annual meeting, including Allied Tube's employees, sales agents, employees from non-electrical divisions, and the non-professional wife of a sales director. At the annual meeting, these voters were told where to sit and how to vote by group leaders using walkie-talkies; even so, they were able to prevail by only the barest of majorities, rejecting the panel's recommendation by a vote of 394 to 390.

A jury found that the anticompetitive effects of this conduct outweighed any pro-competitive benefits of setting standards, that although Allied genuinely believed plastic conduit was unsafe, it

---

25. See the discussion in Chapter 4, section H(4).

26. 486 U.S. 492 (1988).

had subverted the association's processes, and that Allied's conduct had unreasonably restrained trade. Still, consistent with *Noerr*, no damages were awarded for the losses Indian Head suffered as a result of the Code's adoption by governmental entities; but it did receive compensation for $3.8 million in lost profits that were the direct effect of the product's exclusion from the Code (presumably, lost sales where conduit purchasers could lawfully have used plastic but insurance, testing, or other factors caused them to choose Code products). The defendants maintained that subjecting them to even this more limited antitrust liability would interfere with their ability to indirectly petition the government, and thus that they should be immune under *Noerr*. The Supreme Court rejected the defendants' arguments and upheld the jury's verdict.

The Court emphasized that significant competitive risks exist whenever rivals participate in standard setting. Unlike the government, which is presumed to act in the public interest, private parties are presumed to act on their own behalf. Just as the state action doctrine does not permit a state simply to authorize private anticompetitive conduct, *Noerr* does not protect efforts to control private decision-making.[27] The Court stressed that it was refusing to extend *Noerr* only in cases where an "economically interested party exercises decisionmaking authority in formulating a product standard for a private association that comprises market participants."[28]

In reaching this conclusion, the majority reasoned that immunizing all conduct genuinely intended to exert an indirect influence on government action would enable competitors to fix prices as long as they wished to suggest those prices as the appropriate level for the government to set rates. Extending *Noerr*'s reach this far would protect unsanctioned agreements to obtain regulatory approval of specific rates, and boycotts designed to gain economic advantages from the government, two types of conspiracies heretofore considered Sherman Act violations.[29]

Two additional considerations, one explicit and the other implied, led the majority to distinguish *Noerr* and uphold the jury's verdict in *Allied Tube*. Whereas imposing antitrust liability in *Noerr* would have required the courts to regulate political conduct, the Court recognized that "the context and nature of petitioner's [standard setting] activity make it the type of commercial activity that has traditionally had its validity determined by

---

27. 486 U.S. at 501–02.

28. Id. at 510 n.13.

29. Id. at 503–04 (citing Georgia v. Pennsylvania Railroad Co., 324 U.S. 439, 456–63 (1945); Georgia v. Evans, 316 U.S. 159 (1942)).

the antitrust laws themselves." [30]   Consider, again, *Noerr*'s role as
a corollary to the state action doctrine.   If Congress had modified
the latter doctrine and preempted Pennsylvania's authority to
restrict truckers, Noerr Motor Freight would have suffered no
damages.   By contrast, if Congress had preempted anticompetitive
state or local electrical code regulations, Indian Head would still
have lost $3.8 million.   Indian Head's injury was the same as that
any non-approved seller suffers when buyers jointly refuse to
purchase a non-approved product.[31]

Justices Byron White and Sandra Day O'Connor dissented,
arguing that *Noerr* either applies when conduct "is part of a larger
design to influence the passage and enforcement of laws, or it does
not." [32]   In their view, the defendants' genuine aim was to influence local governments to disapprove of plastic conduit, and therefore the entire enterprise was protected.   Any private harm Indian Head suffered, like the harm to reputation endured by Noerr,
was "incidental" to the defendants' petitioning activities.

Implicit in the Court's refusal to accept this argument, and
the reason that *Allied Tube* can be reconciled with *Noerr*, is the
concern that public agencies are more easily defrauded by nonpartisan panels, upon whose expertise they rely, than by direct
lobbying.[33]   Moreover, rivals are typically allowed to combine in
order to set standards because society benefits from fair and
technically expert decisions;   when this process is abused, the
raison d'etre of the antitrust law's tolerance of the combination
evaporates.[34]

(5) Influencing government via anticompetitive means.[35]

In *Noerr*, the actionable harm to competition came from the
results of the defendants' efforts (the Governor's veto of pro-

---

30. Id. at 505.

31. See Radiant Burners, Inc. v. Peoples Gas Light & Coke Co., 364 U.S. 656
(1961) (illegal per se for members of the
American Gas Association to jointly refuse to buy plaintiff's non-approved gas
burner). This case is discussed above in
Chapter 4, section H(4).

32. 486 U.S. at 513.

33. See id. at 510: ("To the extent
state and local governments are more
difficult to persuade through [direct lobbying and traditional political expres-
sion], that no doubts reflects their preference for and confidence in the nonpartisan consensus process that petitioner has undermined.").

34. See id. at 506–07 (antitrust standards for the private standard-setting
process are more rigorous than those
applied to political decisionmaking because "private standard-setting by an
association comprising firms with horizontal and vertical business relations is
permitted at all under the antitrust
laws only on the understanding that it
will be conducted in a nonpartisan manner offering pro-competitive benefits").

35. Caveat lector: The analysis of
the issues set out above is consistent
with, and was influenced by, my *pro
bono* representation of two health care
professional organizations appearing as
amici curiae in National Org. for Wom-

trucker legislation), not from the means they used (a sleazy lobbying and publicity campaign). The Court dismissed any possible direct harm the defendants may have caused to the truckers' business reputation was "incidental" to the political lobbying. But suppose that defendants jointly reduce competition in order to influence government activity? In *FTC v. Superior Court Trial Lawyers Ass'n*,[36] the Supreme Court held that a joint refusal by lawyers to accept appointments to represent indigent criminal defendants violated § 1 of the Sherman Act, even though the boycott was intended to influence the D.C. government to increase their compensation.

As Justice John Paul Stevens explained for the majority, "the alleged restraint of trade [in *Noerr*] was the intended *consequence* of public action; in this case the boycott was the *means* by which respondents sought to obtain favorable legislation." [37] This distinction is sound. One of antitrust's main goals is to limit the use of economic power to confer political advantage. While the indirect use of power (power creates wealth, which permits lobbying and publicity campaigns) is beyond the reach of the Sherman Act and may be constitutionally protected, the direct use of such power is within the scope of the antitrust laws. There is a substantial difference between the railroads' use of whatever political power they might have possessed to secure the veto of competition-enhancing legislation in *Noerr*, and the harm that would have been caused if the railroads had threatened to shut down rail service in the entire state unless the legislation were vetoed.

More troublesome was Stevens' effort to distinguish another precedent, *NAACP v. Claiborne Hardware Co.*[38] In that case, the Court held that the First Amendment protected the NAACP from state law liability for losses suffered by white merchants in a Mississippi county who were the targets of a boycott organized to secure basic civil rights from the dominant white power structure. Unlike *Noerr*, and like *Trial Lawyers*, the issue in *Claiborne Hardware* was the *means* by which the NAACP sought to obtain favorable results from the government (a boycott), rather than the *ends* (civil rights). Stevens wrote that the NAACP's boycott "differ[ed] in a decisive respect" from that of the trial lawyers because those who joined the NAACP's boycott "sought no special advantage for themselves," but rather "only the equal respect and

en, Inc. v. Scheidler, 968 F.2d 612 (7th Cir.1992). The relevant issue in that case is whether otherwise illegal acts (such as trespass, trade harassment, and kidnapping) by anti-abortion protesters constitute a conspiracy to restrain the provision of abortion services. The court rejected arguments by plaintiffs and *amici* that this conduct violated the Sherman Act.

36. 493 U.S. 411 (1990).

37. Id. at 424–25 (emphasis in original).

38. 458 U.S. 886 (1982).

equal treatment to which they were constitutionally entitled." [39] The NAACP had no intent to destroy 'legitimate competition,' " [40] Stevens noted, and *Claiborne Hardware* emphasized that "the boycotters were consumers who did not stand to profit financially from a lessening of competition in the boycotted market." [41]

Stevens' efforts to distinguish the two cases is only partially successful. Consider a modest variation on *Claiborne Hardware*'s facts: faced with a history of racist employment practices and the difficulties of litigating under federal employment laws, suppose that the NAACP launched a boycott of merchants in order to influence a city council to adopt a regulation requiring municipal contractors to aggressively hire minority workers and executives. Would such a boycott violate the Sherman Act if the boycotters included a significant number of local African–Americans who would benefit from the regulation? Assuming that the regulation was intended to remedy purely private instances of racial discrimination (thus, the wrongs being redressed were not constitutional violations), would the boycotters be liable because the economic rights they were seeking to vindicate were not ones to which they were constitutionally entitled? If this hypothetical boycott would still be constitutionally protected (it probably would), then the only other justification for applying the antitrust laws to the trial lawyers, but not applying state business tort law to the NAACP, was that the end result of the NAACP's hypothetical boycott was not to harm competition, while the end result of the boycott in *Trial Lawyers* was allegedly to secure an anticompetitive increase in fees. *Noerr*, however, precludes basing Sherman Act liability on whether the government's response to petitioning activity lessens competition.[42]

The better way to distinguish *Trial Lawyers* from *Claiborne Hardware* is that the participants in the NAACP's boycott were consumers, whereas the trial lawyers' boycott involved providers of services. Because the antitrust laws are intended to protect consumers, an agreement among consumers to refuse to deal with certain sellers may be considered beyond the scope of § 1.[43] Put-

39. 493 U.S. at 426.

40. Id. at 427 (quoting *Claiborne Hardware*, 458 U.S. at 914).

41. Id. at 427 n.10 (citing *Claiborne Hardware*, 458 U.S. at 914–15).

42. See United Mine Workers of America v. Pennington, 381 U.S. 657, 670 (1965) ("*Noerr* shields from the Sherman Act a concerted effort to influence public officials regardless of intent or purpose").

43. Cf. Fisher v. City of Berkeley, 475 U.S. 260 (1986), which is discussed in section A(6). Without deciding whether a Berkeley rent control ordinance was state action, the Court concluded in that case that a "conspiracy" by voters to adopt such an ordinance by initiative was not within the scope of § 1. See John Wiley, The Berkeley Rent Control Case: Treating Victims as Villains, 1986 Sup. Ct. Rev. 157, at 163–66.

ting aside illegal conduct by NAACP members that was independent of the boycott (such as trespassing, vandalism, and efforts to physically intimidate or otherwise prevent consumers from patronizing the boycotted merchants), the NAACP's boycott did not harm consumers.[44] In contrast, the trial lawyers' boycott hurt consumers—both indigent defendants, who were denied legal services, and taxpayers, who were forced to pay more for subsidized legal representation.

Alternatively, the Court might have concluded that both the NAACP and the trial lawyers' boycott were actionable under § 1, but that the First Amendment prohibits applying the Sherman Act to peaceful consumer boycotts, while boycotts by sellers of goods or services are not constitutionally protected.[45] Indeed, the distinction between these two types of boycotts seems to underlie the disagreement between the *Trial Lawyers'* majority and the partial dissent written by Justice William Brennan and joined by Justice Thurgood Marshall [46]—although neither opinion so acknowledged. Justice Stevens' majority opinion simply ignored the dissent's forceful argument that, because of the rich history boycotts have played in our political life and the expressive component characterizing all boycotts, the First Amendment does not tolerate normal operation of the per se rule's presumption that boycotts injure competition. Justice Brennan's dissent, on the other hand, ignored the majority's forceful argument that all seller boycotts have some expressive component, but that their economic harm nonetheless justifies antitrust regulation. In eloquently pointing out that "boycotts have been a principal means of political communication since the birth of the Republic" [47] and that they are "irreplaceable as a means of communications" for

44. The Court made it clear that those who engaged in violence or other independently unlawful activities not protected by the First Amendment could be sued for damages proximately caused by their behavior. *Claiborne Hardware*, 458 U.S. at 916–18.

45. Although *Claiborne Hardware* was a business tort case brought under state law, it is clear that the result would have been the same had the NAACP been sued under the Sherman Act. However, the decision obviously does not explain whether the NAACP would have prevailed in antitrust litigation because its boycott fell outside the scope of § 1, or because it was nonetheless protected by the First Amendment.

46. Justice Harry Blackmun dissented separately. Blackmun noted that

the District of Columbia had the special power to require the defendants to represent indigent defendants without fee. Thus, he argued that the trial lawyers' boycott was not, as it might appear on its face, an exercise of economic power. Rather, the boycott required D.C. officials to make a political choice between exercising their authority to break the boycott or agreeing to a rate increase. "[I]n this unique market where the government buys services that it could readily compel the sellers to provide," a boycott could succeed only because of its political, rather than its economic effect, Blackmun noted. He therefore concluded that the First Amendment precluded a finding of antitrust liability. 493 U.S. at 453–54.

47. Id. at 447.

the politically powerless who may lack "established organizational techniques to advance their political interests," [48] Brennan failed to recognize that every boycott he cited, from the colonists' refusal to pay the stamp tax, through the Montgomery bus boycott, to a host of products targeted today, was a *consumer* boycott.

Basing distinctions in the application of a consumer-oriented statute on the effect the challenged conduct has on consumers seems preferable to eroding *Noerr* and determining antitrust liability based on the Court's view of the desirability of a given boycott's objective. The shortcomings of the rationale used in *Trial Lawyers* are illustrated by the facts of *Missouri v. National Organization for Women, Inc.*[49] In that case, the state of Missouri sued N.O.W. for its role in organizing a national consumer boycott of Missouri (targeting conventions and tourism) because the state had failed to ratify the Equal Rights Amendment. A divided Eighth Circuit panel held that *Noerr* protected the N.O.W. boycott from antitrust liability.

The court relied on two major arguments to support its conclusion that the Sherman Act did not prohibit N.O.W.'s boycott. First, the court found that the boycott was "aimed directly at the legislative process" by the symbolic gesture of declining to patronize non-ratifying states, leading Missouri businesses injured by the boycott to influence their legislators to support ratification. Second, the court noted that the boycott took place "in what is essentially a political context," that the "goal and sole purpose" of N.O.W.'s economic boycott campaign was ratification, and that N.O.W. was neither "motivated by any type of anticompetitive purpose" nor "in a competitive relationship with Missouri." [50]

The fact that the boycott was "aimed directly at the legislative process" (or some other arm of government) may be necessary to invoke *Noerr*, but it should not be sufficient to protect N.O.W. As Missouri argued, *Noerr* protected "a combination to get legislation harmful to others," whereas N.O.W. formed a "combination to harm others to get legislation." [51] Thus, N.O.W.'s boycott seemed more analogous to that at issue in *Trial Lawyers*, which held that conspirators could be subjected to Sherman Act liability for using anticompetitive means to achieve desirable ends.

Nor should the fact that N.O.W.'s motives were political, rather than anticompetitive, be dispositive. The notion that sell-

48. Id. at 451.

49. 620 F.2d 1301 (8th Cir.), cert. denied, 449 U.S. 842 (1980). The *Trial Lawyers* majority did not cite, much less attempt to distinguish, this case, although *Claiborne Hardware* cited it with approval.

50. Id. at 1302–03.

51. See id. at 1323 (Gibson, J., dissenting).

ers of goods or services can collectively use their economic (as opposed to political) power to achieve political ends goes far beyond *Noerr* and is contrary to the antitrust law's "Madisonian" goal of decentralizing power. As Justice Stevens noted in *Trial Lawyers*,[52] the risk that people will be harmed by speeding cars or stunt flying in congested areas warrants the prohibition of such conduct, even if the drivers/pilots hope to influence legislation by attaching streamers with political messages to their vehicles, and even if their dangerous activities help draw attention to those messages. Similarly, conspiracies formed by the sellers of goods or services to restrain free trade harm consumers, regardless of their underlying political motives and they should likewise be prohibited.

The purpose of the Sherman Act's ban on restraints of trade is to give consumers the option of selecting goods and services they desire and the benefits that occur when sellers compete to offer the highest quality at the lowest price. Thus, the better way to analyze *Missouri v. N.O.W.* would have been to hold that consumer boycotts are not subject to antitrust liability, either as a matter of statutory interpretation or because N.O.W.'s conduct was constitutionally protected.

———

Applying the significant penalties of antitrust liability to conduct involving the government raises difficult questions about the use of economic and political power and the need to avoid interfering with the constitutional right to petition. It is easier to avoid complicated doctrinal entanglements, however, by adopting a doctrine that protects conspiracies to influence the government as a corollary to the state action doctrine. Imposing liability for petitioning activity is inappropriate where a court must determine whether the government's response to private lobbying efforts deserved the public interest. Such conduct should also be protected from antitrust scrutiny if liability would chill communication that government officials need.

Some decisions in this area of the law have added unnecessary doctrinal confusion in an effort to protect those who seek to influence government through consumer boycotts. The antitrust law's treatment of these cases can be understood under two complementary analyses. One recognizes that *Noerr* and the First Amendment are not co-extensive. Illegal political misconduct that is not constitutionally protected might still be protected by *Noerr*; boycotts might be prohibited by the Sherman Act but still protected by the First Amendment. The better view is that so

---

52. 493 U.S. at 434.

long as these boycotts do not deprive consumers of the opportunity to patronize boycotted sellers, they do not restrain trade and simply are not subject to § 1. This view would allow the antitrust laws to unambiguously condemn exercises of economic power, even if politically motivated, while protecting consumers from harm. It therefore interprets of the Sherman Act so as to benefit and protect consumers—on whose behalf Congress acted to create the first federal antitrust law in 1890.

Statutory Appendix [1]
PRINCIPAL ANTITRUST STATUTES

SHERMAN ACT [2]

AN ACT To protect trade and commerce against unlawful restraints and monopolies.

That this Act may be cited as the "Sherman Act".

Sec. 1. Every contract, combination in the form of trust or otherwise, or conspiracy, in restraint of trade or commerce among the several States, or with foreign nations, is declared to be illegal. Every person who shall make any contract or engage in any combination or conspiracy hereby declared to be illegal shall be deemed guilty of a felony and, on conviction thereof, shall be punished by fine not exceeding one million dollars if a corporation, or, if any other person, one hundred thousand dollars, or by imprisonment not exceeding three years, or by both said punishments, in the discretion of the court.[3]

Sec. 2. Every person who shall monopolize, or attempt to monopolize, or combine or conspire with any other person or persons, to monopolize any part of the trade or commerce among the several States, or with foreign nations, shall be deemed guilty of a felony, and, on conviction thereof, shall be punished by fine not exceeding one million dollars if a corporation, or, if any other person, one hundred thousand dollars, or by imprisonment not exceeding three years, or by both said punishments, in the discretion of the court.

Sec. 3. Every contract, combination in form of trust or otherwise, or conspiracy, in restraint of trade or commerce in any

---

1. Only the principal statutes are reprinted in this Appendix. The CCH Trade Regulation Reporter includes these statutes in full. See 4 Trade Reg. Rep. (CCH) ¶ 25,000–25,282 (1982).

2. The Sherman Act was the Act of July 2, 1890, c. 647, 26 Stat. 209; 15 U.S.C.A. §§ 1–7.

3. The fine for a violation was increased from $5,000 to $50,000 by Act of July 7, 1955, c. 281, 69 Stat. 282. It was raised again to $1,000,000 for corporations and $100,000 for individuals by Act of December 21, 1974, Pub.L. 93–528, 88 Stat. 1708. The latter Act also redesignated violations as felonies instead of misdemeanors, and increased the maximum prison term by two years, for a total of three years.

Territory of the United States or of the District of Columbia, or in restraint of trade or commerce between any such Territory and another, or between any such Territory or Territories and any State or States or the District of Columbia, or with foreign nations, or between the District of Columbia and any State or States or foreign nations, is declared illegal. Every person who shall make any such contract or engage in any such combination or conspiracy, shall be deemed guilty of a felony, and, on conviction thereof, shall be punished by fine not exceeding one million dollars if a corporation, or, if any other person, one hundred thousand dollars, or by imprisonment not exceeding three years, or by both said punishments, in the discretion of the court.

Sec. 4. The several circuit courts of the United States are invested with jurisdiction to prevent and restrain violations of this Act; and it shall be the duty of the several United States attorneys, in their respective districts, under the direction of the Attorney–General, to institute proceedings in equity to prevent and restrain such violations. Such proceedings may be by way of petition setting forth the case and praying that such violation shall be enjoined or otherwise prohibited. When the parties complained of shall have been duly notified of such petition the court shall proceed, as soon as may be, to the hearing and determination of the case; and pending such petition and before final decree, the court may at any time make such temporary restraining order or prohibition as shall be deemed just in the premises.

Sec. 7. This Act shall not apply to conduct involving trade or commerce (other than import trade or import commerce) with foreign nations unless—

(1) such conduct has a direct, substantial, and reasonably foreseeable effect—

(A) on trade or commerce which is not trade or commerce with foreign nations, or on import trade or import commerce with foreign nations; or

(B) on export trade or export commerce with foreign nations, of a person engaged in such trade or commerce in the United States; and

(2) such effect gives rise to a claim under the provisions of this Act, other than this section.

If this Act applies to such conduct only because of the operation of paragraph (1)(B), then this Act shall apply to such conduct only for injury to export business in the United States.

Sec. 8. That the word "person," or "persons," wherever used in this Act shall be deemed to include corporations and associations existing under or authorized by the laws of either the United States, the laws of any of the Territories, the laws of any State, or the laws of any foreign country.

CLAYTON ACT [4]

AN ACT To supplement existing laws against unlawful restraints and monopolies, and for other purposes.

Sec. 1. That (a) "antitrust laws," as used herein, includes the Act entitled "An Act to protect trade and commerce against unlawful restraints and monopolies," approved July second, eighteen hundred and ninety; sections seventy-three to seventy-seven, inclusive, of an Act entitled "An Act to reduce taxation, to provide revenue for the Government, and for other purposes," of August twenty-seventh, eighteen hundred and ninety-four; an Act entitled "An Act to amend sections seventy-three and seventy-six of the Act of August twenty-seventh, eighteen hundred and ninety-four, entitled 'An Act to reduce taxation, to provide revenue for the Government, and for other purposes,'" approved February twelfth, nineteen hundred and thirteen; and also this Act.

"Commerce," as used herein, means trade or commerce among the several States and with foreign nations, or between the District of Columbia or any Territory of the United States and any State, Territory, or foreign nation, or between any insular possessions or other places under the jurisdiction of the United States, or between any such possession or place and any State or Territory of the United States or the District of Columbia or any foreign nation, or within the District of Columbia or any Territory or any insular possession or other place under the jurisdiction of the United States: *Provided,* That nothing in this Act contained shall apply to the Philippine Islands.

The word "person" or "persons" wherever used in this Act shall be deemed to include corporations and associations existing under or authorized by the laws of either the United States, the laws of any of the Territories, the laws of any State, or the laws of any foreign country.

(b) This Act may be cited as the "Clayton Act".

Sec. 2. (a) That it shall be unlawful for any person engaged in commerce, in the course of such commerce, either directly or indirectly, to discriminate in price between different purchasers of

4. The Clayton Act was the Act of October 15, 1914, c. 323, 38 Stat. 730; 15 U.S.C.A. §§ 12–27.

commodities of like grade and quality, where either or any of the purchases involved in such discrimination are in commerce, where such commodities are sold for use, consumption, or resale within the United States or any Territory thereof or the District of Columbia or any insular possession or other place under the jurisdiction of the United States, and where the effect of such discrimination may be substantially to lessen competition or tend to create a monopoly in any line of commerce, or to injure, destroy, or prevent competition with any person who either grants or knowingly receives the benefit of such discrimination, or with customers of either of them: *Provided,* That nothing herein contained shall prevent differentials which make only due allowance for differences in the cost of manufacture, sale, or delivery resulting from the differing methods or quantities in which such commodities are to such purchasers sold or delivered: *Provided, however,* That the Federal Trade Commission may, after due investigation and hearing to all interested parties, fix and establish quantity limits, and revise the same as it finds necessary, as to particular commodities or classes of commodities, where it finds that available purchasers in greater quantities are so few as to render differentials on account thereof unjustly discriminatory or promotive of monopoly in any line of commerce; and the foregoing shall then not be construed to permit differentials based on differences in quantities greater than those so fixed and established: *And provided further,* That nothing herein contained shall prevent persons engaged in selling goods, wares, or merchandise in commerce from selecting their own customers in bona fide transactions and not in restraint of trade: *And, provided further,* That nothing herein contained shall prevent price changes from time to time where in response to changing conditions affecting the market for or the marketability of the goods concerned, such as but not limited to actual or imminent deterioration of perishable goods, obsolescence of seasonal goods, distress sales under court process, or sales in good faith in discontinuance of business in the goods concerned.

(b) Upon proof being made, at any hearing on a complaint under this section, that there has been discrimination in price or services or facilities furnished, the burden of rebutting the prima facie case thus made by showing justification shall be upon the person charged with a violation of this section, and unless justification shall be affirmatively shown, the Commission is authorized to issue an order terminating the discrimination: *Provided, however,* That nothing herein contained shall prevent a seller rebutting the prima facie case thus made by showing that his lower price or the furnishing of services or facilities to any purchaser or purchasers was made in good faith to meet an equally low price of a competitor, or the services or facilities furnished by a competitor.

(c) That it shall be unlawful for any person engaged in commerce, in the course of such commerce, to pay or grant, or to receive or accept, anything of value as a commission, brokerage, or other compensation, or any allowance or discount in lieu thereof, except for services rendered in connection with the sale or purchase of goods, wares, or merchandise, either to the other party to such transaction or to an agent, representative, or other intermediary therein where such intermediary is acting in fact for or in behalf, or is subject to the direct or indirect control, of any party to such transaction other than the person by whom such compensation is so granted or paid.

(d) That it shall be unlawful for any person engaged in commerce to pay or contract for the payment of anything of value to or for the benefit of a customer of such person in the course of such commerce as compensation or in consideration for any services or facilities furnished by or through such customer in connection with the processing, handling, sale, or offering for sale of any products or commodities manufactured, sold, or offered for sale by such person, unless such payment or consideration is available on proportionally equal terms to all other customers competing in the distribution of such products or commodities.

(e) That it shall be unlawful for any person to discriminate in favor of one purchaser against another purchaser or purchasers of a commodity bought for resale, with or without processing, by contracting to furnish or furnishing, or by contributing to the furnishing of, any services or facilities connected with the processing, handling, sale, or offering for sale of such commodity so purchased upon terms not accorded to all purchasers on proportionally equal terms.

(f) That it shall be unlawful for any person engaged in commerce, in the course of such commerce, knowingly to induce or receive a discrimination in price which is prohibited by this section.

Sec. 3. That it shall be unlawful for any person engaged in commerce, in the course of such commerce, to lease or make a sale or contract for sale of goods, wares, merchandise, machinery, supplies or other commodities, whether patented or unpatented, for use, consumption or resale within the United States or any Territory thereof or the District of Columbia or any insular possession or other place under the jurisdiction of the United States, or fix a price charged therefor, or discount from, or rebate upon, such price, on the condition, agreement or understanding that the lessee or purchaser thereof shall not use or deal in the goods, wares, merchandise, machinery, supplies or other commodities of a competitor or competitors of the lessor or seller, where the effect of such lease, sale, or contract for sale or such condition, agreement or understanding may be to substantially lessen competition or tend to create a monopoly in any line of commerce.

Sec. 4. That any person who shall be injured in his business or property by reason of anything forbidden in the antitrust laws may sue therefor in any district court of the United States in the district in which the defendant resides or is found or has an agent, without respect to the amount in controversy, and shall recover threefold the damages by him sustained, and the cost of suit, including a reasonable attorney's fee. The court may award under this section, pursuant to a motion by such person promptly made, simple interest on actual damages for the period beginning on the date of service of such person's pleading setting forth a claim under the antitrust laws and ending on the date of judgment, or for any shorter period therein, if the court finds that the award of such interest for such period is just in the circumstances. In determining whether an award of interest under this section for any period is just in the circumstances, the court shall consider only—

(1) whether such person or the opposing party, or either party's representative, made motions or asserted claims or defenses so lacking in merit as to show that such party or representative acted intentionally for delay, or otherwise acted in bad faith;

(2) whether, in the course of the action involved, such person or the opposing party, or either party's representative, violated any applicable rule, statute, or court order providing for sanctions for dilatory behavior or otherwise providing for expeditious proceedings; and

(3) whether such person or the opposing party, or either party's representative, engaged in conduct primarily for the purpose of delaying the litigation or increasing the cost thereof.

Sec. 4A. Whenever the United States is hereafter injured in its business or property by reason of anything forbidden in the antitrust laws it may sue therefor in the United States district court for the district in which the defendant resides or is found or has an agent, without respect to the amount in controversy, and shall recover actual damages by it sustained and the cost of suit. The court may award under this section, pursuant to a motion by the United States promptly made, simple interest on actual damages for the period beginning on the date of service of the pleading of the United States setting forth a claim under the antitrust laws and ending on the date of judgment, or for any shorter period therein, if the court finds that the award of such interest for such period is just in the circumstances. In determining whether an award of interest under this section for any period is just in the circumstances, the court shall consider only—.... [5]

Sec. 4B. Any action to enforce any cause of action under section 4, 4A, or 4C shall be forever barred unless commenced within four years after the cause of action accrued. No cause of action barred under existing law on the effective date of this Act shall be revived by this Act.

Sec. 4C. (a)(1) Any attorney general of a State may bring a civil action in the name of such State, as parens patriae on behalf of natural persons residing in such State, in any district court of the United States having jurisdiction of the defendant, to secure monetary relief as provided in this section for injury sustained by such natural persons to their property by reason of any violation of the Sherman Act. The court shall exclude from the amount of monetary relief awarded in such action any amount of monetary relief (A) which duplicates amounts which have been awarded for the same injury, or (B) which is properly allocable to (i) natural persons who have excluded their claims pursuant to subsection (b)(2) of this section, and (ii) any business entity.

(2) The court shall award the State as monetary relief three-fold the total damage sustained as described in paragraph (1) of this subsection, and the cost of suit, including a reasonable attorney's fee. The court may award under this paragraph, pursuant to a motion by such State promptly made, simple interest on the total damage for the period beginning on the date of service of such State's pleading setting forth a claim under the antitrust laws and ending on the date of judgment, or for any shorter period therein, if the court finds that the award of such interest for such period is just in the circumstances. In determining whether an award of interest under this paragraph for any period is just in the circumstances, the court shall consider only—....

(b)(1) In any action brought under subsection (a)(1) of this section, the State attorney general shall, at such times, in such manner, and with such content as the court may direct, cause notice thereof to be given by publication. If the court finds that notice given solely by publication would deny due process of law to any person or persons, the court may direct further notice to such person or persons according to the circumstances of the case.

(2) Any person on whose behalf an action is brought under subsection (a)(1) may elect to exclude from adjudication the por-

5. Antitrust Reciprocity Amendment, Pub.L. 97–393, 96 Stat. 1964 (1982), the Clayton Act, 15 U.S.C.A § 15(b) allows foreign governments to recover in treble damage actions under certain circumstances.

tion of the State claim for monetary relief attributable to him by filing notice of such election with the court within such time as specified in the notice given pursuant to paragraph (1) of this subsection.

(3) The final judgment in an action under subsection (a)(1) shall be res judicata as to any claim under section 4 of this Act by any person on behalf of whom such action was brought and who fails to give such notice within the period specified in the notice given pursuant to paragraph (1) of this subsection.

(c) An action under subsection (a)(1) shall not be dismissed or compromised without the approval of the court, and notice of any proposed dismissal or compromise shall be given in such manner as the court directs.

(d) In any action under subsection (a)—

(1) the amount of the plaintiffs' attorney's fee, if any, shall be determined by the court; and

(2) the court may, in its discretion, award a reasonable attorney's fee to a prevailing defendant upon a finding that the State attorney general has acted in bad faith, vexatiously, wantonly, or for oppressive reasons.

Sec. 4D. In any action under section 4C(a)(1), in which there has been a determination that a defendant agreed to fix prices in violation of the Sherman Act, damages may be proved and assessed in the aggregate by statistical or sampling methods, by the computation of illegal overcharges, or by such other reasonable system of estimating aggregate damages as the court in its discretion may permit without the necessity of separately proving the individual claim of, or amount of damage to, persons on whose behalf the suit was brought.

Sec. 4E. Monetary relief recovered in an action under section 4C(a)(1) shall—

(1) be distributed in such manner as the district court in its discretion may authorize; or

(2) be deemed a civil penalty by the court and deposited with the State as general revenues;

subject in either case to the requirement that any distribution procedure adopted afford each person a reasonable opportunity to secure his appropriate portion of the net monetary relief.

Sec. 4F. (a) Whenever the Attorney General of the United States has brought an action under the antitrust laws, and he has reason to believe that any State attorney general would be entitled to bring an action under this Act based substantially on the same alleged violation of the antitrust laws, he shall promptly give written notification thereof to such State attorney general.

(b) To assist a State attorney general in evaluating the notice or in bringing any action under this Act, the Attorney General of the United States shall, upon request by such State attorney general, make available to him, to the extent permitted by law, any investigative files or other materials which are or may be relevant or material to the actual or potential cause of action under this Act.

Sec. 4G.   For the purposes of sections 4C, 4D, 4E, and 4F of this Act:

(1) The term "State attorney general" means the chief legal officer of a State, or any other person authorized by State law to bring actions under section 4C of this Act, and includes the Corporation Counsel of the District of Columbia, except that such term does not include any person employed or retained on—

(A) a contingency fee based on a percentage of the monetary relief awarded under this section; or

(B) any other contingency fee basis, unless the amount of the award of a reasonable attorney's fee to a prevailing plaintiff is determined by the court under section 4C(d)(1).

(2) The term "State" means a State, the District of Columbia, the Commonwealth of Puerto Rico, and any other territory or possession of the United States.

(3) The term "natural persons" does not include proprietorships or partnerships.

Sec. 4H.   Sections 4C, 4D, 4E, 4F, and 4G shall apply in any State, unless such State provides by law for its nonapplicability in such State.[6]

Sec. 5.   (a) A final judgment or decree heretofore or hereafter rendered in any civil or criminal proceeding brought by or on behalf of the United States under the antitrust laws to the effect that a defendant has violated said laws shall be prima facie evidence against such defendant in any action or proceeding brought by any other party against such defendant under said laws as to all matters respecting which said judgment or decree would be an estoppel as between the parties thereto: *Provided,* That this section shall not apply to consent judgments or decrees entered before any testimony has been taken.   Nothing contained

6.   Sections 4A and 4B were added by Act of July 7, 1955, c. 283, 69 Stat. 282–83. Sections 4C through 4H were added by Act of September 30, 1976, Pub.L. 94–435, 90 Stat. 1394. Sections 4, 4A, and 4C were amended to allow an award of interest to a plaintiff when equitable, by Act of September 12, 1980, Pub.L. 96–349, 94 Stat. 1156.

in this section shall be construed to impose any limitation on the application of collateral estoppel, except that, in any action or proceeding brought under the antitrust laws, collateral estoppel effect shall not be given to any finding made by the Federal Trade Commission under the antitrust laws or under section 5 of the Federal Trade Commission Act which could give rise to a claim for relief under the antitrust laws.

(b) Any proposal for a consent judgment submitted by the United States for entry in any civil proceeding brought by or on behalf of the United States under the antitrust laws shall be filed with the district court before which such proceeding is pending and published by the United States in the Federal Register at least 60 days prior to the effective date of such judgment. Any written comments relating to such proposal and any responses by the United States thereto, shall also be filed with such district court and published by the United States in the Federal Register within such sixty-day period. Copies of such proposal and any other materials and documents which the United States considered determinative in formulating such proposal, shall also be made available to the public at the district court and in such other districts as the court may subsequently direct. Simultaneously with the filing of such proposal, unless otherwise instructed by the court, the United States shall file with the district court, publish in the Federal Register, and thereafter furnish to any person upon request, a competitive impact statement which shall recite—

(1) the nature and purpose of the proceeding;

(2) a description of the practices or events giving rise to the alleged violation of the antitrust laws;

(3) an explanation of the proposal for a consent judgment, including an explanation of any unusual circumstances giving rise to such proposal or any provision contained therein, relief to be obtained thereby, and the anticipated effects on competition of such relief;

(4) the remedies available to potential private plaintiffs damaged by the alleged violation in the event that such proposal for the consent judgment is entered in such proceeding;

(5) a description of the procedures available for modification of such proposal; and

(6) a description and evaluation of alternatives to such proposal actually considered by the United States.

(c) The United States shall also cause to be published....

(d) During the 60–day period as specified in subsection (b) of this section, and such additional time as the United States may request and the court may grant, the United States shall receive and consider any written comments relating to the proposal for the consent judgment submitted under subsection (b). The Attorney General or his designee shall establish procedures to carry out the provisions of this subsection, but such 60–day time period shall not be shortened except by order of the district court upon a showing that (1) extraordinary circumstances require such shortening and (2) such shortening is not adverse to the public interest. At the close of the period during which such comments may be received, the United States shall file with the district court and cause to be published in the Federal Register a response to such comments.

(e) Before entering any consent judgment proposed by the United States under this section, the court shall determine that the entry of such judgment is in the public interest. For the purpose of such determination, the court may consider—

(1) the competitive impact of such judgment, including termination of alleged violations, provisions for enforcement and modification, duration or relief sought, anticipated effects of alternative remedies actually considered, and any other considerations bearing upon the adequacy of such judgment;

(2) the impact of entry of such judgment upon the public generally and individuals alleging specific injury from the violations set forth in the complaint including consideration of the public benefit, if any, to be derived from a determination of the issues at trial.

(f) In making its determination under subsection (e), the court may—

(1) take testimony of Government officials or experts or such other expert witnesses, upon motion of any party or participant or upon its own motion, as the court may deem appropriate;

(2) appoint a special master and such outside consultants or expert witnesses as the court may deem appropriate; and request and obtain the views, evaluations, or advice of any individual, group or agency of government with respect to any aspects of the proposed judgment or the effect of such judgment, in such manner as the court deems appropriate;

(3) authorize full or limited participation in proceedings before the court by interested persons or agencies, including appearance amicus curiae, intervention as a party pursuant to the Federal Rules of Civil Procedure, examination of witnesses or documentary materials, or participation in any other manner and extent which serves the public interest as the court may deem appropriate;

(4) review any comments including any objections filed with the United States under subsection (d) concerning the proposed judgment and the responses of the United States to such comments and objections; and

(5) take such other action in the public interest as the court may deem appropriate.

(g) Not later than 10 days following the date for the filing of any proposal for a consent judgment under subsection (b), each defendant shall file with the district court a description of any and all written or oral communications by or on behalf of such defendant, including any and all written or oral communications on behalf of such defendant, or other person, with any officer or employee of the United States concerning or relevant to such proposal, except that any such communications made by counsel of record alone with the Attorney General or the employees of the Department of Justice alone shall be excluded from the requirements of this subsection. Prior to the entry of any consent judgment pursuant to the antitrust laws, each defendant shall certify to the district court that the requirements of this subsection have been complied with and that such filing is a true and complete description of such communications known to the defendant or which the defendant reasonably should have known.

(h) Proceedings before the district court under subsections (e) and (f) of this section, and the competitive impact statement filed under subsection (b) of this section, shall not be admissible against any defendant in any action or proceeding brought by any other party against such defendant under the antitrust laws or by the United States under section 4A of this Act nor constitute a basis for the introduction of the consent judgment as prima facie evidence against such defendant in any such action or proceeding.

(i) Whenever any civil or criminal proceeding is instituted by the United States to prevent, restrain, or punish violations of any of the antitrust laws, but not including an action under section 4A, the running of the statute of limitations in respect of every private or State right of action arising under said laws and based in whole or in part on any matter complained of in said proceeding shall be suspended during the pendency thereof and for one year thereafter: *Provided, however,* That whenever the running of the statute of limitations in respect of a cause of action arising under section 4 or 4C is suspended hereunder, any action to enforce such cause of action shall be forever barred unless commenced either within the period of suspension or within four years after the cause of action accrued.[7]

7. The Clayton Act was amended by Act of July 7, 1955, c. 283, 69 Stat. 283, to provide for damage suits brought by the United States under Section 4A and to establish a statute of limitations.

Sec. 6. That the labor of a human being is not a commodity or article of commerce. Nothing contained in the antitrust laws shall be construed to forbid the existence and operation of labor, agricultural, or horticultural organizations, instituted for the purposes of mutual help, and not having capital stock or conducted for profit, or to forbid or restrain individual members of such organizations from lawfully carrying out the legitimate objects thereof; nor shall such organizations, or the members thereof, be held or construed to be illegal combinations or conspiracies in restraint of trade, under the antitrust laws.

Sec. 7. That no person engaged in commerce or in any activity affecting commerce shall acquire, directly or indirectly, the whole or any part of the stock or other share capital and no person subject to the jurisdiction of the Federal Trade Commission shall acquire the whole or any part of the assets of another person engaged also in commerce or in any activity affecting commerce, where in any line of commerce or in any activity affecting commerce in any section of the country, the effect of such acquisition may be substantially to lessen competition, or to tend to create a monopoly.

No person shall acquire, directly or indirectly, the whole or any part of the stock or other share capital and no person subject to the jurisdiction of the Federal Trade Commission shall acquire the whole or any part of the assets of one or more persons engaged in commerce or in any activity affecting commerce, where in any line of commerce or in any activity affecting commerce in any section of the country, the effect of such acquisition, of such stocks or assets, or of the use of such stock by the voting or granting of proxies or otherwise, may be substantially to lessen competition, or to tend to create a monopoly.

This section shall not apply to persons purchasing such stock solely for investment and not using the same by voting or otherwise to bring about, or in attempting to bring about, the substantial lessening of competition. Nor shall anything contained in this section prevent a corporation engaged in commerce or in any activity affecting commerce from causing the formation of subsidiary corporations for the actual carrying on of their immediate lawful business, or the natural and legitimate branches or exten-

Subsections (b) through (h) were added by Antitrust Procedures and Penalties Act, Act of December 21, 1974, Pub.L. 93–528, 88 Stat. 1706 and former subsection (b) was redesignated as subsection (i). Subsection (a) was amended by Act of September 12, 1980, Pub.L. 96–349, 94 Stat. 1157, to restrict the use of collateral estoppel as to findings made by the FTC. Also amended was subsection (i) to expand the tolling of the statute of limitations to include state actions.

sions thereof, or from owning and holding all or a part of the stock of such subsidiary corporations, when the effect of such formation is not to substantially lessen competition....

Nothing contained in this section shall be held to affect or impair any right heretofore legally acquired: *Provided,* That nothing in this section shall be held or construed to authorize or make lawful anything heretofore prohibited or made illegal by the antitrust laws, nor to exempt any person from the penal provisions thereof or the civil remedies therein provided.

Nothing contained in this section shall apply to transactions duly consummated pursuant to authority given by the Secretary of Transportation, Federal Communications Commission, Federal Power Commission, Interstate Commerce Commission, the Securities and Exchange Commission in the exercise of its jurisdiction under section 79j of this Act, the United States Maritime Commission, or the Secretary of Agriculture under any statutory provision vesting such power in such Commission or Secretary.[8]

Sec. 7A. (a) Except as exempted pursuant to subsection (c), no person shall acquire, directly or indirectly, any voting securities or assets of any other person, unless both persons (or in the case of a tender offer, the acquiring person) file notification pursuant to rules under subsection (d)(1) and the waiting period described in subsection (b)(1) has expired, if—

(1) the acquiring person, or the person whose voting securities or assets are being acquired, is engaged in commerce or in any activity affecting commerce;

(2)(A) any voting securities or assets of a person engaged in manufacturing which has annual net sales or total assets of $10,000,000 or more are being acquired by any person which has total assets or annual net sales of $100,000,000 or more;

(B) any voting securities or assets of a person not engaged in manufacturing which has total assets of $10,000,000 or more are being acquired by any person which has total assets or annual net sales of $100,000,000 or more; or

(C) any voting securities or assets of a person with annual net sales or total assets of $100,000,000 or more are being acquired by any person with total assets or annual net sales of $10,000,000 or more; and

(3) as a result of such acquisition, the acquiring person would hold—

8. Section 7 was amended by Act of September 12, 1980, Pub.L. 96–349, 94 Stat. 1157, to cover all persons, instead of just corporations, and to reach activities affecting commerce as opposed to just in commerce.

(A) 15 per centum or more of the voting securities or assets of the acquired person, or

(B) an aggregate total amount of the voting securities and assets of the acquired person in excess of $15,000,000.

In the case of a tender offer, the person whose voting securities are sought to be acquired by a person required to file notification under this subsection shall file notification pursuant to rules under subsection (d).

(b)(1) The waiting period required under subsection (a) shall—

(A) begin on the date of the receipt by the Federal Trade Commission and the Assistant Attorney General in charge of the Antitrust Division of the Department of Justice (hereinafter referred to in this section as the "Assistant Attorney General") of—

(i) the completed notification required under subsection (a), or

(ii) if such notification is not completed, the notification to the extent completed and a statement of the reasons for such noncompliance, from both persons, or, in the case of a tender offer, the acquiring person; and

(B) end on the thirtieth day after the date of such receipt (or in the case of a cash tender offer, the fifteenth day), or on such later date as may be set under subsection (e)(2) or (g)(2).

(2) The Federal Trade Commission and the Assistant Attorney General may, in individual cases, terminate the waiting period specified in paragraph (1) and allow any person to proceed with any acquisition subject to this section, and promptly shall cause to be published in the Federal Register a notice that neither intends to take any action within such period with respect to such acquisition. . . .

(c) The following classes of transactions are exempt from the requirements of this section—. . . .

(9) acquisitions, solely for the purpose of investment, or voting securities, if, as a result of such acquisition, the securities acquired or held do not exceed 10 per centum of the outstanding voting securities of the issuer; . . . .

(d) The Federal Trade Commission, with the concurrence of the Assistant Attorney General and by rule in accordance with section 553 of title 5, United States Code, consistent with the purposes of this section—

(1) shall require that the notification required under subsection (a) be in such form and contain such documentary material and information relevant to a proposed acquisition as is necessary and appropriate to enable the Federal Trade Commission and the

Assistant Attorney General to determine whether such acquisition may, if consummated, violate the antitrust laws; and

(2) may—

(A) define the terms used in this section;

(B) exempt, from the requirements of this section, classes of persons, acquisitions, transfers, or transactions which are not likely to violate the antitrust laws; and

(C) prescribe such other rules as may be necessary and appropriate to carry out the purposes of this section.

(e)(1) The Federal Trade Commission or the Assistant Attorney General may, prior to the expiration of the 30–day waiting period (or in the case of a cash tender offer, the 15–day waiting period) specified in subsection (b)(1) of this section, require the submission of additional information or documentary material relevant to the proposed acquisition, from a person required to file notification with respect to such acquisition under subsection (a) of this section prior to the expiration of the waiting period specified in subsection (b)(1) of this section, or from any officer, director, partner, agent, or employee of such person.

(2) The Federal Trade Commission or the Assistant Attorney General, in its or his discretion, may extend the 30–day waiting period (or in the case of a cash tender offer, the 15–day waiting period) specified in subsection (b)(1) of this section for an additional period of not more than 20 days (or in the case of a cash tender offer, 10 days) after the date on which the Federal Trade Commission or the Assistant Attorney General, as the case may be, receives from any person to whom a request is made under paragraph (1), or in the case of tender offers, the acquiring person, (A) all the information and documentary material required to be submitted pursuant to such a request, or (B) if such request is not fully complied with, the information and documentary material submitted and a statement of the reasons for such noncompliance. Such additional period may be further extended only by the United States district court, upon an application by the Federal Trade Commission or the Assistant Attorney General pursuant to subsection (g)(2)....

(g)(1) Any person, or any officer, director, or partner thereof, who fails to comply with any provision of this section shall be liable to the United States for a civil penalty of not more than $10,000 for each day during which such person is in violation of this section. Such penalty may be recovered in a civil action brought by the United States.

(2) If any person, or any officer, director, partner, agent, or employee thereof, fails substantially to comply with the notifica-

tion requirement under subsection (a) or any request for the submission of additional information or documentary material under subsection (e)(1) of this section within the waiting period specified in subsection (b)(1) and as may be extended under subsection (e)(2), the United States district court—

(A) may order compliance;

(B) shall extend the waiting period specified in subsection (b)(1) and as may have been extended under subsection (e)(2) until there has been substantial compliance, except that, in the case of a tender offer, the court may not extend such waiting period on the basis of a failure, by the person whose stock is sought to be acquired, to comply substantially with such notification requirement or any such request; and

(C) may grant such other equitable relief as the court in its discretion determines necessary or appropriate, upon application of the Federal Trade Commission or the Assistant Attorney General.[9] . . .

Sec. 8. . . .

No person at the same time shall be a director in any two or more corporations, any one of which has capital, surplus, and undivided profits aggregating more than $1,000,000, engaged in whole or in part in commerce, other than banks, banking associations, trust companies, and common carriers subject to Subtitle IV of Title 49, to regulate commerce, if such corporations are or shall have been theretofore, by virtue of their business and location of operation, competitors, so that the elimination of competition by agreement between them would constitute a violation of any of the provisions of any of the anti-trust laws. The eligibility of a director under the foregoing provision shall be determined by the aggregate amount of the capital, surplus, and undivided profits, exclusive of dividends declared but not paid to stockholders, at the end of the fiscal year of said corporation next preceding the election of directors, and when a director has been elected in accordance with the provisions of this Act it shall be lawful for him to continue as such for one year thereafter.

When any person elected or chosen as a director or officer or selected as an employee of any bank or other corporation subject to the provisions of this Act is eligible at the time of his election or selection to act for such bank or other corporation in such capacity his eligibility to act in such capacity shall not be affected and he shall not become or be deemed amenable to any of the provisions

---

9. Section 7A was added by Act of September 30, 1976, Pub.L. 94–435, 90 Stat. 1390.

hereof by reason of any change in the affairs of such bank or other corporation from whatsoever cause, whether specifically excepted by any of the provisions hereof or not, until the expiration of one year from the date of his election or employment.

Sec. 11. ...

(b) Whenever the Commission, Board, or Secretary vested with jurisdiction thereof shall have reason to believe that any person is violating or has violated any of the provisions of sections 2, 3, 7, and 8 of this Act, it shall issue and serve upon such person and the Attorney General a complaint stating its charges in that respect, and containing a notice of a hearing upon a day and at a place therein fixed at least thirty days after the service of said complaint. The person so complained of shall have the right to appear at the place and time so fixed and show cause why an order should not be entered by the Commission, Board, or Secretary requiring such person to cease and desist from the violation of the law so charged in said complaint. The Attorney General shall have the right to intervene and appear in said proceeding and any person may make application, and upon good cause shown may be allowed by the Commission, Board, or Secretary to intervene and appear in said proceeding by counsel or in person. The testimony in any such proceeding shall be reduced to writing and filed in the office of the Commission, Board, or Secretary. If upon such hearing the Commission, Board, or Secretary, as the case may be, shall be of the opinion that any of the provisions of said sections have been or are being violated, it shall make a report in writing, in which it shall state its findings as to the facts, and shall issue and cause to be served on such person an order requiring such person to cease and desist from such violations, and divest itself of the stock, or other share capital, or assets, held or rid itself of the directors chosen contrary to the provisions of sections 7 and 8 of this Act, if any there be, in the manner and within the time fixed by said order. Until the expiration of the time allowed for filing a petition for review, if no such petition has been duly filed within such time, or, if a petition for review has been filed within such time then until the record in the proceeding has been filed in a court of appeals of the United States, as hereinafter provided, the Commission, Board, or Secretary may at any time, upon such notice and in such manner as it shall deem proper, modify or set aside, in whole or in part, any report or any order made or issued by it under this section. After the expiration of the time allowed for filing a petition for review, if no such petition has been duly filed within such time, the Commission, Board, or Secretary may at any time, after notice and opportunity for hearing, reopen and alter, modify, or set aside, in whole or in part, any report or order made or issued by it under this section, whenever in the opinion of the Commission, Board, or Secretary conditions of fact or of law have so changed as to require such action or if the public interest shall so require: *Provided, however,* That the said person may, within sixty days after service upon him or it of said report or order entered after such a reopening, obtain a review thereof in the appropriate court of appeals of the United States, in the manner provided in subsection (c) of this section.

(c) Any person required by such order of the Commission, Board, or Secretary to cease and desist from any such violation may obtain a review of such order in the court of appeals of the United States for any circuit within which such violation occurred or within which such person resides or carries on business, by filing in the court, within sixty days after the date of the service of such order, a written petition praying that the order of the Commission, Board, or Secretary be set aside. A copy of such petition shall be forthwith transmitted by the clerk of the court to the Commission, Board, or Secretary, and thereupon the Commission, Board, or Secretary shall file in the court the record in the proceeding, as provided in section 2112 of title 28, United States Code. Upon such filing of the petition the court shall have jurisdiction of the proceeding and of the question determined therein concurrently with the Commission, Board, or Secretary until the filing of the record, and shall have power to make and enter a decree affirming, modifying, or setting aside the order of the Commission, Board, or Secretary, and enforcing the same to the extent that such order is affirmed, and to issue such writs as are ancillary to its jurisdiction or are necessary in its judgment to prevent injury to the public or to competitors pendente lite. The findings of the Commission, Board, or Secretary as to the facts, if supported by substantial evidence, shall be conclusive. To the extent that the order of the Commission, Board, or Secretary is affirmed, the court shall issue its own order commanding obedience to the terms of such order of the Commission, Board, or Secretary. If either party shall apply to the court for leave to adduce additional evidence, and shall show to the satisfaction of the court that such additional evidence is material and that there were reasonable grounds for the failure to adduce such evidence in the proceeding before the Commission, Board, or Secretary, the court may order such additional evidence to be taken before the Commission, Board, or Secretary, and to be adduced upon the hearing in such manner and upon such terms and conditions as to the court may seem proper. The Commission, Board, or Secretary may modify its findings as to the facts, or make new findings, by reason of the additional evidence so taken, and shall file such modified or new findings, which, if supported by substantial evidence, shall be conclusive, and its recommendation, if any, for the modification or setting aside of its original order, with the return of such additional evidence. The judgment and decree of the court shall be final, except that the same shall be subject to review by the Supreme Court upon certiorari, as provided in section 1254 of title 28 of the United States Code.

(d) Upon the filing of the record with it the jurisdiction of the court of appeals to affirm, enforce, modify, or set aside orders of the Commission, Board, or Secretary shall be exclusive.

(e) No order of the Commission, Board, or Secretary or judgment of the court to enforce the same shall in anywise relieve or absolve any person from any liability under the antitrust laws....

(*l*) Any person who violates any order issued by the Commission, Board, or Secretary under subsection (b) after such order has become final, and while such order is in effect, shall forfeit and pay to the United States a civil penalty of not more than $5,000 for each violation, which shall accrue to the United States and may be recovered in a civil action brought by the United States. Each separate violation of any such order shall be a separate offense, except that in the case of a violation through continuing failure or neglect to obey a final order of the Commission, Board, or Secretary each day of continuance of such failure or neglect shall be deemed a separate offense.

Sec. 12. That any suit, action, or proceeding under the antitrust laws against a corporation may be brought not only in the judicial district whereof it is an inhabitant, but also in any district wherein it may be found or transacts business; and all process in such cases may be served in the district of which it is an inhabitant, or wherever it may be found.

Sec. 13. That in any suit, action, or proceeding brought by or on behalf of the United States subpoenas for witnesses who are required to attend a court of the United States in any judicial district in any case, civil or criminal, arising under the antitrust laws may run into any other district: *Provided,* That in civil cases no writ of subpoena shall issue for witnesses living out of the district in which the court is held at a greater distance than one hundred miles from the place of holding the same without the permission of the trial court being first had upon proper application and cause shown.

Sec. 14. That whenever a corporation shall violate any of the penal provisions of the antitrust laws, such violation shall be deemed to be also that of the individual directors, officers, or agents of such corporation who shall have authorized, ordered, or done any of the acts constituting in whole or in part such violation, and such violation shall be deemed a misdemeanor, and upon conviction therefor of any such director, officer, or agent he shall be punished by a fine of not exceeding $5,000 or by imprisonment for not exceeding one year, or by both, in the discretion of the court.

Sec. 15. That the several district courts of the United States are invested with jurisdiction to prevent and restrain violations of this Act, and it shall be the duty of the United States attorneys, in their respective districts, under the direction of the Attorney General, to institute proceedings in equity to prevent and restrain such violations. Such proceedings may be by way of petition setting forth the case and praying that such violation shall be enjoined or otherwise prohibited. When the parties complained of shall have been duly notified of such petition, the court shall proceed, as soon as may be, to the hearing and determination of the case; and pending such petition, and before final decree, the court may at any time make such temporary restraining order or prohibition as shall be deemed just in the premises. Whenever it shall appear to the court before which any such proceeding may be pending that the ends of justice require that other parties should be brought before the court, the court may cause them to be summoned, whether they reside in the district in which the court is held or not, and subpoenas to that end may be served in any district by the marshal thereof.

Sec. 16. That any person, firm, corporation, or association shall be entitled to sue for and have injunctive relief, in any court of the United States having jurisdiction over the parties, against threatened loss or damage by a violation of the antitrust laws, including sections two, three, seven and eight of this Act, when and under the same conditions and principles as injunctive relief against threatened conduct that will cause loss or damage is granted by courts of equity, under the rules governing such proceedings, and upon the execution of proper bond against damages for an injunction improvidently granted and a showing that the danger of irreparable loss or damage is immediate, a preliminary injunction may issue: *Provided,* That nothing herein contained shall be construed to entitle any person, firm, corporation, or association, except the United States, to bring suit in equity for injunctive relief against any common carrier subject to the provisions of Subtitle IV of Title 49 in respect of any matter subject to the regulation, supervision, or other jurisdiction of the Interstate Commerce Commission. In any action under this section in which the plaintiff substantially prevails, the court shall award the cost of suit, including a reasonable attorney's fee, to such plaintiff.[10]

10. Section 16 was amended by Act of September 30, 1976, Pub.L. 94–435, 90 Stat. 1396, to provide for an award of costs to a successful plaintiff.

Sec. 20. That no restraining order or injunction shall be granted by any court of the United States, or a judge or the judges thereof, in any case between an employer and employees, or between employers and employees, or between employees or between persons employed and persons seeking employment, involving, or growing out of, a dispute concerning terms or conditions of employment, unless necessary to prevent irreparable injury to property, or to a property right, of the party making the application; for which injury there is no adequate remedy at law, and such property or property right must be described with particularity in the application, which must be in writing and sworn to by the applicant or by his agent or attorney.

And no such restraining order or injunction shall prohibit any person or persons, whether singly or in concert, from terminating any relation of employment, or from ceasing to perform any work or labor, or from recommending, advising or persuading others by peaceful means so to do; or from attending at any place where any such person or persons may lawfully be, for the purpose of peacefully obtaining or communicating information, or from peacefully persuading any person to work or to abstain from working; or from ceasing to patronize or to employ any party to such dispute, or from recommending, advising, or persuading others by peaceful and lawful means so to do; or from paying or giving to, or withholding from, any person engaged in such dispute, any strike benefits or other moneys or things of value; or from peaceably assembling in a lawful manner, and for lawful purposes; or from doing any act or thing which might lawfully be done in the absence of such dispute by any party thereto; nor shall any of the acts specified in this paragraph be considered or held to be violations of any law of the United States.

FEDERAL TRADE COMMISSION ACT [11]

AN ACT To create a Federal Trade Commission, to define its powers and duties, and for other purposes.

Sec. 1. That a commission is hereby created and established, to be known as the Federal Trade Commission (hereinafter referred to as the Commission), which shall be composed of five commissioners, who shall be appointed by the President, by and with the advice and consent of the Senate. Not more than three

11. Act of September 26, 1914, c. 311, 38 Stat. 717; 15 U.S.C.A. §§ 41–51. Certain less important amendments are omitted. Most of these were made by the Wheeler–Lea Act, Act of March 21, 1938, c. 49, 52 Stat. 111.

of the commissioners shall be members of the same political party. The first commissioners appointed shall continue in office for terms of three, four, five, six, and seven years, respectively, from the date of the taking effect of this Act, the term of each to be designated by the President, but their successors shall be appointed for terms of seven years, except that any person chosen to fill a vacancy shall be appointed only for the unexpired term of the commissioner whom he shall succeed: *Provided, however,* That upon the expiration of his term of office a Commissioner shall continue to serve until his successor shall have been appointed and shall have qualified. The President shall choose a chairman from the Commission's membership. No Commissioner shall engage in any other business, vocation, or employment. Any Commissioner may be removed by the President for inefficiency, neglect of duty, or malfeasance in office. A vacancy in the Commission shall not impair the right of the remaining Commissioners to exercise all the powers of the Commission.

The Commission shall have an official seal, which shall be judicially noticed.

Sec. 4. The words defined in this section shall have the following meaning when found in this Act, to wit:

"Commerce" means commerce among the several States or with foreign nations, or in any Territory of the United States or in the District of Columbia, or between any such Territory and another, or between any such Territory and any State or foreign nation, or between the District of Columbia and any State or Territory or foreign nation.

"Corporation" shall be deemed to include any company, trust, so-called Massachusetts trust, or association, incorporated or unincorporated, which is organized to carry on business for its own profit or that of its members, and has shares of capital or capital stock or certificates of interest, and any company, trust, so-called Massachusetts trust, or association, incorporated or unincorporated, without shares of capital or capital stock or certificates of interest, except partnerships, which is organized to carry on business for its own profit or that of its members.

"Documentary evidence" includes all documents, papers, correspondence, books of account, and financial and corporate records.

"Acts to regulate commerce" means Subtitle IV of Title 49, the Communications Act of 1934 [47 U.S.C.A. § 151 et seq.] and all Acts amendatory thereof and supplementary thereto.

"Antitrust Acts," means the Act entitled "An Act to protect trade and commerce against unlawful restraints and monopolies," approved July 2, 1890; also sections 73 to 77, inclusive, of an Act entitled "An Act to reduce taxation, to provide revenue for the Government, and for other purposes," approved August 27, 1894; also the Act entitled "An Act to amend sections 73 and 76 of the Act of August 27, 1894, entitled 'An Act to reduce taxation, to provide revenue for the Government, and for other purposes,'" approved February 12, 1913; and also the Act entitled "An Act to supplement existing laws against unlawful restraints and monopolies, and for other purposes," approved October 15, 1914.

Sec. 5. (a)(1) Unfair methods of competition in or affecting commerce, and unfair or deceptive acts or practices in or affecting commerce, are hereby declared unlawful.[12]

(2) The Commission is empowered and directed to prevent persons, partnerships, or corporations, except banks, savings and loan institutions described in section 18(f)(3), common carriers subject to the Acts to regulate commerce, air carriers and foreign air carriers subject to the Federal Aviation Act of 1958, and persons, partnerships, or corporations insofar as they are subject to the Packers and Stockyards Act, 1921, as amended [17 U.S.C.A. § 181 et seq.], except as provided in section 406(b) of said Act, [17 U.S.C.A. § 227(a)] from using unfair methods of competition in or affecting commerce and unfair or deceptive acts or practices in or affecting commerce.[13]

(3) This subsection shall not apply to unfair methods of competition involving commerce with foreign nations (other than import commerce) unless—

(A) such methods of competition have a direct, substantial, and reasonably foreseeable effect—

(i) on commerce which is not commerce with foreign nations, or on import commerce with foreign nations; or

(ii) on export commerce with foreign nations, of a person engaged in such commerce in the United States; and

(B) such effect gives rise to a claim under the provisions of this subsection, other than this paragraph.

12. The phrase, "and unfair or deceptive acts or practices in commerce," was added by the Wheeler–Lea Act, 52 Stat. 111 (1938).

13. The phrase "in or affecting commerce" was added by Act of January 4, 1975, Pub.L. 93–637, 88 Stat. 2193, to Sections 5 and 6.

Former subsections (a)(2) through (a)(5), added by the McGuire Fair Trade Act, Act of July 14, 1952, c. 745, 66 Stat. 631, were repealed by Act of December 12, 1975, Pub.L. 94–145, 89 Stat. 801. The phrase "savings and loan institutions described in section 18(f)(3)," was added by Act of July 23, 1979, Pub.L. 96–37, 93 Stat. 95, to Sections 5 and 6.

If this subsection applies to such methods of competition only because of the operation of subparagraph (A)(ii), this subsection shall apply to such conduct only for injury to export business in the United States.".

(b) Whenever the Commission shall have reason to believe that any such person, partnership, or corporation has been or is using any unfair method of competition or unfair or deceptive act or practice in or affecting commerce, and if it shall appear to the Commission that a proceeding by it in respect thereof would be to the interest of the public, it shall issue and serve upon such person, partnership, or corporation a complaint stating its charges in that respect and containing a notice of a hearing upon a day and at a place therein fixed at least thirty days after the service of said complaint. The person, partnership, or corporation so complained of shall have the right to appear at the place and time so fixed and show cause why an order should not be entered by the Commission requiring such person, partnership, or corporation to cease and desist from the violation of the law so charged in said complaint. Any person, partnership, or corporation may make application, and upon good cause shown may be allowed by the Commission to intervene and appear in said proceeding by counsel or in person. The testimony in any such proceeding shall be reduced to writing and filed in the office of the Commission. If upon such hearing the Commission shall be of the opinion that the method of competition or the act or practice in question is prohibited by this Act, it shall make a report in writing in which it shall state its findings as to the facts and shall issue and cause to be served on such person, partnership, or corporation an order requiring such person, partnership, or corporation to cease and desist from using such method of competition or such act or practice. Until the expiration of the time allowed for filing a petition for review, if no such petition has been duly filed within such time, or, if a petition for review has been filed within such time then until the record in the proceeding has been filed in a court of appeals of the United States, as hereinafter provided, the Commission may at any time, upon such notice and in such manner as it shall deem proper, modify or set aside, in whole or in part, any report or any order made or issued by it under this section. After the expiration of the time allowed for filing a petition for review, if no such petition has been duly filed within such time, the Commission may at any time, after notice and opportunity for hearing, reopen and alter, modify, or set aside, in whole or in part, any report or order made or issued by it under this section, whenever in the opinion of the Commission conditions of fact or of law have so changed as to require such action or if the public interest shall so require, except that (1) the said person, partnership, or corporation may, within sixty days after service upon him or it of said report or order entered after such a reopening, obtain a review thereof in the appropriate court of appeals of the United States, in the manner provided in subsection (c) of this section; and (2) in the case of an order, the Commission shall reopen any such order to consider whether such order (including any affirmative relief provision contained in such order) should be altered, modified, or set aside, in whole or in part, if the person, partnership, or corporation involved files a request with the Commission which makes a satisfactory showing that changed conditions of law or fact require such order to be altered, modified, or set aside, in whole or in part. The Commission shall determine whether to alter, modify, or set aside any order of the Commission in response to a request made by a person, partnership, or corporation under paragraph (2) not later than 120 days after the date of the filing of such request.[14]

(c) Any person, partnership, or corporation required by an order of the Commission to cease and desist from using any method of competition or act or practice may obtain a review of such order in the court of appeals of the United States, within any circuit where the method of competition or the act or practice in question was used or where such person, partnership, or corporation resides or carries on business, by filing in the court, within sixty days from the date of the service of such order, a written petition praying that the order of the Commission be set aside.... The findings of the Commission as to the facts, if supported by evidence, shall be conclusive. To the extent that the order of the Commission is affirmed, the court shall thereupon issue its own order commanding obedience to the terms of such order of the Commission. If either party shall apply to the court for leave to adduce additional evidence, and shall show to the satisfaction of the court that such additional evidence is material and that there were reasonable grounds for the failure to adduce such evidence in the proceeding before the Commission, the court may order such additional evidence to be taken before the Commission and to be adduced upon the hearing in such manner and upon such terms and conditions as to the court may seem proper. The Commission may modify its findings as to the facts, or make new findings, by reason of the additional evidence so taken, and it shall file such modified or new findings, which, if supported by evidence, shall be conclusive, and its recommendation, if any, for the modification or setting aside of its original order, with the return of such additional evidence. The judgment and decree of the court shall be final, except that the same shall be subject to review by the Supreme

14. Subsection (b)(2) was added by Act of May 28, 1980, Pub.L. 96–252, 94 Stat. 374.

Court upon certiorari, as provided in section 347 of Title 28 of the Judicial Code.[15]

(d) Upon the filing of the record with it the jurisdiction of the court of appeals of the United States to affirm, enforce, modify, or set aside orders of the Commission shall be exclusive.

(e) No order of the Commission or judgment of court to enforce the same shall in anywise relieve or absolve any person, partnership, or corporation from any liability under the Antitrust Acts....

(*l*) Any person, partnership, or corporation who violates an order of the Commission after it has become final, and while such order is in effect, shall forfeit and pay to the United States a civil penalty of not more than $10,000 for each violation, which shall accrue to the United States and may be recovered in a civil action brought by the Attorney General of the United States. Each separate violation of such an order shall be a separate offense, except that in the case of a violation through continuing failure to obey or neglect to obey a final order of the Commission, each day of continuance of such failure or neglect shall be deemed a separate offense. In such actions, the United States district courts are empowered to grant mandatory injunctions and such other and further equitable relief as they deem appropriate in the enforcement of such final orders of the Commission.[16]

(m)(1)(A) The Commission may commence a civil action to recover a civil penalty in a district court of the United States against any person, partnership, or corporation which violates any rule under this Act respecting unfair or deceptive acts or practices (other than an interpretive rule or a rule violation of which the Commission has provided is not an unfair or deceptive act or practice in violation of subsection (a)(1)) with actual knowledge or knowledge fairly implied on the basis of objective circumstances that such act is unfair or deceptive and is prohibited by such rule. In such action, such person, partnership, or corporation shall be liable for a civil penalty of not more than $10,000 for each violation.

(B) If the Commission determines in a proceeding under subsection (b) that any act or practice is unfair or deceptive, and issues a final cease and desist order with respect to such act or

---

15. Subsection (c) was first amended by the Wheeler–Lea Act, 52 Stat. 111 (1938). Subsections (c) and (d) were amended by Act of August 28, 1958, 72 Stat. 942–43. The substance of Section 240 of the Judicial Code, which has been repealed, may be found in 28 U.S.C.A. § 1254.

16. Subsection (*l*) was generally amended by Act of November 16, 1973, Pub.L. 93–153, 87 Stat. 591, to raise the maximum penalty to $10,000 from $5,000, and to empower the district courts to grant mandatory injunctions.

practice, then the Commission may commence a civil action to obtain a civil penalty in a district court of the United States against any person, partnership, or corporation which engages in such act or practice—

(1) after such cease and desist order becomes final (whether or not such person, partnership, or corporation was subject to such cease and desist order), and

(2) with actual knowledge that such act or practice is unfair or deceptive and is unlawful under subsection (a)(1) of this section.

In such action, such person, partnership, or corporation shall be liable for a civil penalty of not more than $10,000 for each violation.

(C) In the case of a violation through continuing failure to comply with a rule or with section 5(a)(1), each day of continuance of such failure shall be treated as a separate violation, for purposes of subparagraphs (A) and (B). In determining the amount of such a civil penalty, the court shall take into account the degree of culpability, any history of such prior conduct, ability to pay, effect on ability to continue to do business, and such other matters as justice may require.

Sec. 6. The Commission shall also have power—

(a) To gather and compile information concerning, and to investigate from time to time the organization, business, conduct, practices and management of any person, partnership, or corporation engaged in or whose business affects commerce, excepting banks, savings and loan institutions described in section 18(f)(3), and common carriers subject to the Act to regulate commerce, and its relation to other persons, partnerships, and corporations.

(b) To require, by general or special orders, persons, partnerships, and corporations engaged in or whose business affects commerce, excepting banks, savings and loan institutions described in section 18(f)(3), Federal credit unions described in section 18(f)(4), and common carriers subject to the Act to regulate commerce, or any class of them, or any of them, respectively, to file with the Commission in such form as the Commission may prescribe annual or special, or both annual and special, reports or answers in writing to specific questions, furnishing to the Commission such information as it may require as to the organization, business, conduct, practices, management, and relation to other corporations, partnerships, and individuals of the respective persons, partnerships, and corporations filing such reports or answers in writing. Such reports and answers shall be made under oath, or otherwise, as the Commission may prescribe, and shall be filed with the Commission within such reasonable period as the Commission may prescribe, unless additional time be granted in any case by the Commission.

(c) Whenever a final decree has been entered against any defendant corporation in any suit brought by the United States to prevent and restrain any violation of the antitrust Acts, to make investigation, upon its own initiative, of the manner in which the decree has been or is being carried out, and upon the application of the Attorney General it shall be its duty to make such investigation. It shall transmit to the Attorney General a report embodying its findings and recommendations as a result of any such investigation, and the report shall be made public in the discretion of the Commission.

(d) Upon the direction of the President or either House of Congress to investigate and report the facts relating to any alleged violations of the antitrust Acts by any corporation.

(e) Upon the application of the Attorney General to investigate and make recommendations for the readjustment of the business of any corporation alleged to be violating the antitrust Acts in order that the corporation may thereafter maintain its organization, management, and conduct of business in accordance with law.

(f) To make public from time to time such portions of the information obtained by it hereunder as are in the public interest; and to make annual and special reports to the Congress and to submit therewith recommendations for additional legislation; and to provide for the publication of its reports and decisions in such form and manner as may be best adapted for public information and use: *Provided,* That the Commission shall not have any authority to make public any trade secret or any commercial or financial information which is obtained from any person and which is privileged or confidential, except that the Commission may disclose such information to officers and employees of appropriate Federal law enforcement agencies or to any officer or employee of any State law enforcement agency upon the prior certification of an officer of any such Federal or State law enforcement agency that such information will be maintained in confidence and will be used only for official law enforcement purposes.

(g) From time to time to classify corporations and (except as provided in section 18(a)(2) of this Act) to make rules and regulations for the purpose of carrying out the provisions of this Act.

(h) To investigate, from time to time, trade conditions in and with foreign countries where associations, combinations, or practices of manufacturers, merchants or traders, or other conditions, may affect the foreign trade of the United States, and to report to

Congress thereon, with such recommendations as it deems advisable.

Provided, That the exception of "banks, savings and loan institutions described in section 18(f)(3), Federal credit unions described in section 18(f)(3) of this Act, and common carriers subject to the Act to regulate commerce" from the Commission's powers defined in clauses (a) and (b) of this section, shall not be construed to limit the Commission's authority to gather and compile information, to investigate, or to require reports or answers from, any person, partnership, or corporation to the extent that such action is necessary to the investigation of any person, partnership, or corporation, group of persons, partnerships, or corporations, or industry which is not engaged or is engaged only incidentally in banking, in business as a savings and loan institution, in business as a Federal credit union, or in business as a common carrier subject to the Act to regulate commerce.

The Commission shall establish a plan designed to substantially reduce burdens imposed upon small businesses as a result of requirements established by the Commission under clause (b) relating to the filing of quarterly financial reports....

No officer or employee of the Commission or any Commissioner may publish or disclose information to the public, or to any Federal agency, whereby any line-of-business data furnished by a particular establishment or individual can be identified. No one other than designated sworn officers and employees of the Commission may examine the line-of-business reports from individual firms, and information provided in the line-of-business program administered by the Commission shall be used only for statistical purposes. Information for carrying out specific law enforcement responsibilities of the Commission shall be obtained under practices and procedures in effect on May 28, 1980, or as changed by law.

Nothing in this section (other than the provisions of clause (c) and clause (d)) shall apply to the business of insurance, except that the Commission shall have authority to conduct studies and prepare reports relating to the business of insurance. The Commission may exercise such authority only upon receiving a request which is agreed to by a majority of the members of the Committee on Commerce, Science, and Transportation of the Senate or the Committee on Energy and Commerce of the House of Representatives. The authority to conduct any such study shall expire at the end of the Congress during which the request for such study was made.[17]

17. The proviso was added by Act of November 16, 1973, Pub.L. 93–153, 87 Stat. 592. The Act of January 4, 1975, Pub.L. 93–637, 88 Stat. 2193, amended

Sec. 7. In any suit in equity brought by or under the direction of the Attorney General as provided in the antitrust Acts, the court may, upon the conclusion of the testimony therein, if it shall be then of the opinion that the complainant is entitled to relief, refer said suit to the Commission, as a master in chancery, to ascertain and report an appropriate form of decree therein. The Commission shall proceed upon such notice to the parties and under such rules of procedure as the court may prescribe, and upon the coming in of such report such exceptions may be filed and such proceedings had in relation thereto as upon the report of a master in other equity causes, but the court may adopt or reject such report, in whole or in part, and enter such decree as the nature of the case may in its judgment require.

Sec. 8. The several departments and bureaus of the government when directed by the President shall furnish the Commission upon its request, all records, papers and information in their possession relating to any corporation subject to any of the provisions of this Act, and shall detail from time to time such officials and employees to the Commission as he may direct.

Sec. 9. For the purposes of this Act the Commission, or its duly authorized agent or agents, shall at all reasonable times have access to, for the purpose of examination, and the right to copy any documentary evidence of any person, partnership, or corporation being investigated or proceeded against; and the Commission shall have power to require by subpoena the attendance and testimony of witnesses and the production of all such documentary evidence relating to any matter under investigation. Any member of the Commission may sign subpoenas, and members and examiners of the Commission may administer oaths and affirmations, examine witnesses and receive evidence.

Such attendance of witnesses, and the production of such documentary evidence, may be required from any place in the United States, at any designated place of hearing. And in case of disobedience to a subpoena the Commission may invoke the aid of any court of the United States in requiring the attendance and testimony of witnesses and the production of documentary evidence.

Any of the district courts of the United States within the jurisdiction of which such inquiry is carried on may, in case of contumacy or refusal to obey a subpoena issued to any person, partnership or corporation, issue an order requiring such person,

the section by substituting "person, partnership, or corporation," for "corporation." The Act of May 28, 1980, Pub.L. 96–252, 94 Stat. 374, amended the section by adding the proviso to subsection (f), and by adding the last three undesignated paragraphs.

partnership or corporation to appear before the Commission, or to produce documentary evidence if so ordered, or to give evidence touching the matter in question; and any failure to obey such order of the court may be punished by such court as a contempt thereof.

Upon the application of the Attorney General of the United States, at the request of the Commission, the district courts of the United States shall have jurisdiction to issue writs of mandamus commanding any person, partnership, or corporation to comply with the provisions of this Act or any order of the Commission made in pursuance thereof.

The Commission may order testimony to be taken by deposition in any proceeding or investigation pending under this Act at any stage of such proceeding or investigation. Such depositions may be taken before any person designated by the Commission and having power to administer oaths. Such testimony shall be reduced to writing by the person taking the deposition, or under his direction, and shall then be subscribed by the deponent. Any person may be compelled to appear and depose and to produce documentary evidence in the same manner as witnesses may be compelled to appear and testify and produce documentary evidence before the Commission as hereinbefore provided.

Witnesses summoned before the Commission shall be paid the same fees and mileage that are paid witnesses in the courts of the United States, and witnesses whose depositions are taken and the persons taking the same shall severally be entitled to the same fees as are paid for like services in the courts of the United States.[18]

Sec. 10. Any person who shall neglect or refuse to attend and testify, or to answer any lawful inquiry, or to produce any documentary evidence, if in his power to do so, in obedience to an order of a district court of the United States directing compliance with the subpoena or lawful requirement of the Commission, shall be guilty of an offense and upon conviction thereof by a court of competent jurisdiction shall be punished by a fine of not less than $1,000 nor more than $5,000, or by imprisonment for not more than one year, or by both such fine and imprisonment.

Any person who shall wilfully make, or cause to be made, any false entry or statement of fact in any report required to be made under this Act, or who shall wilfully make, or cause to be made, any false entry in any account, record, or memorandum kept by any person, partnership, or corporation subject to this Act, or who

---

18. Sections 9 and 10 were expanded to reach persons and partnerships as well as corporations by Act of January 4, 1975, Pub.L. 93–637, 88 Stat. 2198.

shall wilfully neglect or fail to make, or to cause to be made, full, true and correct entries in such accounts, records, or memoranda of all facts and transactions appertaining to the business of such person, partnership, or corporation, or who shall wilfully remove out of the jurisdiction of the United States, or wilfully mutilate, alter, or by any other means falsify any documentary evidence of such person, partnership, or corporation, or who shall wilfully refuse to submit to the Commission or to any of its authorized agents, for the purpose of inspection and taking copies, any documentary evidence of such person, partnership, or corporation in his possession or within his control, shall be deemed guilty of an offense against the United States, and shall be subject, upon conviction in any court of the United States of competent jurisdiction, to a fine of not less than $1,000 nor more than $5,000, or to imprisonment for a term of not more than three years, or to both such fine and imprisonment.

If any persons, partnership, or corporation required by this Act to file any annual or special report shall fail so to do within the time fixed by the Commission for filing the same, and such failure shall continue for thirty days after notice of such default, the corporation shall forfeit to the United States the sum of $100 for each and every day of the continuance of such failure, which forfeiture shall be payable into the treasury of the United States, and shall be recoverable in a civil suit in the name of the United States brought in the case of a corporation or partnership in the district where the corporation or partnership has its principal office or in any district in which it shall do business, and in the case of any person in the district where such person resides or has his principal place of business. It shall be the duty of the various United States attorneys, under the direction of the Attorney-General of the United States, to prosecute for the recovery of forfeitures. The costs and expenses of such prosecution shall be paid out of the appropriation for the expenses of the courts of the United States.

Any officer or employee of the Commission who shall make public any information obtained by the Commission without its authority, unless directed by a court, shall be deemed guilty of a misdemeanor, and, upon conviction thereof, shall be punished by a fine not exceeding $5,000, or by imprisonment not exceeding one year, or by fine and imprisonment, in the discretion of the court.

Sec. 11. Nothing contained in this Act shall be construed to prevent or interfere with the enforcement of the provisions of the antitrust Acts or the Acts to regulate commerce, nor shall anything contained in the Act be construed to alter, modify, or repeal the said antitrust Acts or the Acts to regulate commerce or any part or parts thereof.

Sec. 12. (a) It shall be unlawful for any person, partnership, or corporation to disseminate, or cause to be disseminated, any false advertisement—

(1) By United States mails, or in or having an effect upon commerce by any means, for the purpose of inducing, or which is likely to induce, directly or indirectly, the purchase of food, drugs, devices, or cosmetics; or

(2) By any means, for the purpose of inducing, or which is likely to induce, directly or indirectly, the purchase in or having an effect upon commerce of food, drugs, devices, or cosmetics.

(b) The dissemination or the causing to be disseminated of any false advertisement within the provisions of subsection (a) of this section shall be an unfair or deceptive act or practice in or affecting commerce within the meaning of section 5.[19]

Sec. 13....

(b) Whenever the Commission has reason to believe—

(1) that any person, partnership, or corporation is violating, or is about to violate, any provision of law enforced by the Federal Trade Commission, and

(2) that the enjoining thereof pending the issuance of a complaint by the Commission and until such complaint is dismissed by the Commission or set aside by the court on review, or until the order of the Commission made thereon has become final, would be in the interest of the public—the Commission by any of its attorneys designated by it for such purpose may bring suit in a district court of the United States to enjoin any such act or practice. Upon a proper showing that, weighing the equities and considering the Commission's likelihood of ultimate success, such action would be in the public interest, and after notice to the defendant, a temporary restraining order or a preliminary injunction may be granted without bond: *Provided, however,* That if a complaint is not filed within such period (not exceeding 20 days) as may be specified by the court after issuance of the temporary restraining order or preliminary injunction, the order or injunction shall be dissolved by the court and be of no further force and effect: *Provided further,* That in proper cases the Commission may seek, and after proper proof, the court may issue, a permanent

---

19. Sections 12 through 18 were added by the Wheeler–Lea Act, 52 Stat. 111 (1938).

Section 12 was amended to reach activities having an effect on commerce, as well as in commerce, by Act of January 4, 1975, Pub.L. 93–637, 88 Stat. 2193.

injunction. Any such suit shall be brought in the district in which such person, partnership, or corporation resides or transacts business....[20]

Sec. 18. (a)(1) Except as provided in subsection (i), the Commission may prescribe—

(A) interpretive rules and general statements of policy with respect to unfair or deceptive acts or practices in or affecting commerce (within the meaning of section 5(a)(1) of this Act), and

(B) rules which define with specificity acts or practices which are unfair or deceptive acts or practices in or affecting commerce (within the meaning of such section 5(a)(1), except that the Commission shall not develop or promulgate any trade rule or regulation with regard to the regulation of the development and utilization of the standards and certification activities pursuant to this section. Rules under this subparagraph may include requirements prescribed for the purpose of preventing such acts or practices.

(2) The Commission shall have no authority under this Act, other than its authority under this section, to prescribe any rule with respect to unfair or deceptive acts or practices in or affecting commerce (within the meaning of section 5(a)(1)). The preceding sentence shall not affect any authority of the Commission to prescribe rules (including interpretive rules), and general statements of policy, with respect to unfair methods of competition in or affecting commerce.[21]

(b)(1) When prescribing a rule under subsection (a)(1)(B) of this section, the Commission shall proceed in accordance with section 553 of title 5, United States Code (without regard to any reference in such section to sections 556 and 557 of such title), and shall also (A) publish a notice of proposed rulemaking stating with particularity the text of the rule, including any alternatives, which the Commission proposes to promulgate, and the reason for the proposed rule; (B) allow interested persons to submit written data, views, and arguments, and make all such submissions publicly available; (C) provide an opportunity for an informal hearing in accordance with subsection (c); and (D) promulgate, if appropriate, a final rule based on the matter in the rulemaking record (as

---

20. Subsection (b) was added by Act of November 16, 1973, Pub.L. 93–153, 87 Stat. 592.

21. Subsections (a) and (b) were added by Act of January 4, 1975, Pub.L. 93–637, 88 Stat. 2193.

Subsection (a) was amended by Act of May 28, 1980, Pub.L. 96–252, 94 Stat. 376, to restrict the FTC's power to develop rules concerning "the regulation of the development and utilization of the standards and certification activities pursuant to this section."

defined in subsection (e)(1)(B)), together with a statement of basis and purpose.

(2)(A) Prior to the publication of any notice of proposed rulemaking pursuant to paragraph (1)(A), the Commission shall publish an advance notice of proposed rulemaking in the Federal Register. Such advance notice shall—

(i) contain a brief description of the area of inquiry under consideration, the objectives which the Commission seeks to achieve, and possible regulatory alternatives under consideration by the Commission; and

(ii) invite the response of interested parties with respect to such proposed rulemaking, including any suggestions or alternative methods for achieving such objectives.... [22]

Sec. 19. (a)(1) If any person, partnership, or corporation violates any rule under this Act respecting unfair or deceptive acts or practices (other than an interpretive rule, or a rule violation of which the Commission has provided is not an unfair or deceptive act or practice in violation of section 5(a)), then the Commission may commence a civil action against such person, partnership, or corporation for relief under subsection (b) in a United States district court or in any court of competent jurisdiction of a State.

(2) If any person, partnership, or corporation engages in any unfair or deceptive act or practice (within the meaning of section 5(a)(1)) with respect to which the Commission has issued a final cease and desist order which is applicable to such person, partnership, or corporation, then the Commission may commence a civil action against such person, partnership, or corporation in a United States district court or in any court of competent jurisdiction of a State. If the Commission satisfies the court that the act or practice to which the cease and desist order relates is one which a reasonable man would have known under the circumstances was dishonest or fraudulent, the court may grant relief under subsection (b).

(b) The court in an action under subsection (a) shall have jurisdiction to grant such relief as the court finds necessary to redress injury to consumers or other persons, partnerships, and corporations resulting from the rule violation or the unfair or deceptive act or practice, as the case may be. Such relief may include, but shall not be limited to, rescission or reformation of contracts, the refund of money or return of property, the payment of damages, and public notification respecting the rule violation or

22. Subsection (b)(2) was added by Act of May 28, 1980, Pub.L. 96–252, 94 Stat. 376.

the unfair or deceptive act or practice, as the case may be; except that nothing in this subsection is intended to authorize the imposition of any exemplary or punitive damages.

(c)(1) If (A) a cease and desist order issued under section 5(b) has become final under section 5(g) with respect to any person's, partnership's, or corporation's rule violation or unfair or deceptive act or practice, and (B) an action under this section is brought with respect to such person's, partnership's, or corporation's rule violation or act or practice, then the findings of the Commission as to the material facts in the proceeding under section 5(b) with respect to such person's, partnership's, or corporation's rule violation or act or practice, shall be conclusive unless (i) the terms of such cease and desist order expressly provide that the Commission's findings shall not be conclusive, or (ii) the order became final by reason of section 5(g)(1), in which case such finding shall be conclusive if supported by evidence.

(2) The court shall cause notice of an action under this section to be given in a manner which is reasonably calculated under all of the circumstances, to apprise the persons, partnerships, and corporations allegedly injured by the defendant's rule violation or act or practice of the pendency of such action. Such notice may, in the discretion of the court, be given by publication.

(d) No action may be brought by the Commission under this section more than 3 years after the rule violation to which an action under subsection (a)(1) relates, or the unfair or deceptive act or practice to which an action under subsection (a)(2) relates; except that if a cease and desist order with respect to any person's, partnership's, or corporation's rule violation or unfair or deceptive act or practice has become final and such order was issued in proceeding under section (5)(b) which was commenced not later than 3 years after the rule violation or act or practice occurred, a civil action may be commenced under this section against such person, partnership, or corporation at any time before the expiration of one year after such order becomes final.

(e) Remedies provided in this section are in addition to, and not in lieu of, any other remedy or right of action provided by State or Federal law. Nothing in this section shall be construed to affect any authority of the Commission under any other provision of law.[23]

23. Section 19 was added by Act of January 4, 1975, Pub.L. 93–637, 88 Stat. 2201.

Sec. 20. ...

(b) For the purpose of investigations performed pursuant to this section with respect to unfair or deceptive acts or practices in or affecting commerce (within the meaning of section 5(a)(1)), all actions of the Commission taken under section 6 and section 9 shall be conducted pursuant to subsection (c).

(c)(1) Whenever the Commission has reason to believe that any person may be in possession, custody, or control of any documentary material, or may have any information, relevant to unfair or deceptive acts or practices in or affecting commerce (within the meaning of section 5(a)(1)), the Commission may, before the institution of any proceedings under this Act, issue in writing, and cause to be served upon such person, a civil investigative demand requiring such person to produce such documentary material for inspection and copying or reproduction, to file written reports or answers to questions, to give oral testimony concerning documentary material or other information, or to furnish any combination of such material, answers, or testimony. ... [24]

Sec. 25. This Act may be cited as the "Federal Trade Commission Act."

ANTITRUST CIVIL PROCESS ACT [25]

AN ACT To authorize the Attorney General to compel the production of documentary evidence required in civil investigations for the enforcement of the antitrust laws, and for other purposes.

Sec. 1. That this Act may be cited as the "Antitrust Civil Process Act".

Sec. 2. For the purposes of this Act—

(a) The term "antitrust law" includes:

(1) Each provision of law defined as one of the antitrust laws by section 1 of the Act entitled "An Act to supplement existing laws against unlawful restraints and monopolies, and for other purposes", approved October 15, 1914 (38 Stat. 730, as amended; 15 U.S.C. 12), commonly known as the Clayton Act; and

(2) Any statute hereafter enacted by the Congress which prohibits, or makes available to the United States in any court of the United States any civil remedy with respect to any restraint upon or monopolization of interstate or foreign trade or commerce;

24. Section 20 was added by Act of May 28, 1980, Pub.L. 96–252, 94 Stat. 380.

25. 76 Stat. 548 (1962), 15 U.S.C.A. §§ 1311–14.

(b) The term "antitrust order" means any final order, decree, or judgment of any court of the United States, duly entered in any case or proceeding arising under any antitrust law;

(c) The term "antitrust investigation" means any inquiry conducted by any antitrust investigator for the purpose of ascertaining whether any person is or has been engaged in any antitrust violation or in any activities in preparation for a merger, acquisition, joint venture, or similar transaction, which, if consummated, may result in an antitrust violation;

(d) The term "antitrust violation" means any act or omission in violation of any antitrust law or any antitrust order;

(e) The term "antitrust investigator" means any attorney or investigator employed by the Department of Justice who is charged with the duty of enforcing or carrying into effect any antitrust law;

(f) The term "person" means any natural person, partnership, corporation, association, or other legal entity, including any person acting under color or authority of State law;

(g) The term "documentary material" includes the original or any copy of any book, record, report, memorandum, paper, communication, tabulation, chart, or other document, and any product of discovery; ....[26]

Sec. 3. (a) Whenever the Attorney General, or the Assistant Attorney General in charge of the Antitrust Division of the Department of Justice, has reason to believe that any person may be in possession, custody, or control of any documentary material, or may have any information, relevant to a civil antitrust investigation, he may, prior to the institution of a civil or criminal proceeding thereon, issue in writing, and cause to be served upon such person, a civil investigative demand requiring such person to produce such documentary material for inspection and copying or reproduction, to answer in writing written interrogatories, to give oral testimony concerning documentary material or information, or to furnish any combination of such material, answers, or testimony. Whenever a civil investigative demand is an express demand for any product of discovery, the Attorney General or the Assistant Attorney General in charge of the Antitrust Division shall cause to be served, in any manner authorized by this section, a copy of such demand upon the person from whom the discovery was obtained and notify the person to whom such demand is issued of the date on which such copy was served....

26. Sections 2 through 6 of the Act were generally amended first by Act of September 30, 1976, Pub.L. 94–435, 90 Stat. 1389, and then by Act of September 12, 1980, Pub.L. 96–349, 94 Stat. 1154.

Sec. 4. (a) The Assistant Attorney General in charge of the Antitrust Division of the Department of Justice shall designate an antitrust investigator to serve as custodian of documentary material, answers to interrogatories, and transcripts of oral testimony received under this Act, and such additional antitrust investigators as he shall determine from time to time to be necessary to serve as deputies to such officer....

Sec. 5. (a) Whenever any person fails to comply with any civil investigative demand duly served upon him under section 3 or whenever satisfactory copying or reproduction of any such material cannot be done and such person refuses to surrender such material, the Attorney General, through such officers or attorneys as he may designate, may file, in the district court of the United States for any judicial district in which such person resides, is found, or transacts business, and serve upon such person a petition for an order of such court for the enforcement of this Act....

Sec. 6. (a) Section 1505, title 18, United States Code, is amended to read as follows:

"§ 1505. Obstruction of proceedings before departments, agencies, and committees

. . .

"Whoever, with intent to avoid, evade, prevent, or obstruct compliance, in whole or in part, with any civil investigative demand duly and properly made under the Antitrust Civil Process Act, willfully withholds, misrepresents, removes from any place, conceals, covers up, destroys, mutilates, alters, or by other means falsifies any documentary material, answers to written interrogatories, or oral testimony, which is the subject of such demand; or attempts to do so or solicits another to do so; ....

"Shall be fined not more than $5,000 or imprisoned not more than five years, or both."

(b) The analysis of chapter 73 of title 18 of United States Code is amended so that the title of section 1505 shall read therein as follows:

"1505. Obstruction of proceedings before departments, agencies, and committees."

*

TABLE OF CASES

References are to Pages.

INDEX

References are to Chapter, section (subsection)

591

†